PUBLIC POLICIES
TOWARD BUSINESS

The Irwin Series in Economics

Consulting Editor
LLOYD G. REYNOLDS *Yale University*

PUBLIC POLICIES
TOWARD BUSINESS

CLAIR WILCOX
Late Professor of Political Economy
Swarthmore College

WILLIAM G. SHEPHERD
Professor of Economics
University of Michigan

Fifth Edition   1975

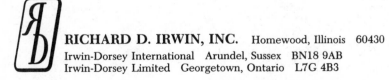

RICHARD D. IRWIN, INC.   Homewood, Illinois   60430
Irwin-Dorsey International   Arundel, Sussex   BN18 9AB
Irwin-Dorsey Limited   Georgetown, Ontario   L7G 4B3

Fifth Edition

First Printing, May 1975
Second Printing, November 1975
Third Printing, February 1976
Fourth Printing, July 1976

ISBN 0-256-01660-7
Library of Congress Catalog Card No. 74–24442

Printed in the United States of America

*To those of our students
who have warmed our hearts by
becoming economists*

Preface

This fifth edition continues the form and content of earlier editions. The main types of American policies toward business are presented, both in breadth and in some detail. Attention is drawn primarily to the economic content of policies, as they evolve in parallel with market conditions. The causes and effects of policies are resolved into their parts.

The intent of the volume is to instill an ability to analyze: to see what the policies actually are and to compare them with alternatives. This requires some degree of factual detail about policies and sectors. There are also comparisons with policies in other countries, to broaden perspective. These concepts and facts are animated by a concern for "good" economic performance and a candid awareness of political realities. The reader is invited to learn the nuts and bolts and to form independent judgments. But these are only applications of the main skill, which is to evaluate policies rationally.

The format and coverage are much the same as before. They are designed to fit the order of coverage which is now customary in teaching the subject. They also reflect the lessons from past and current research. For this edition, new parts have been added and the passages on some older issues have been condensed. The materials on industrial relationships and the concepts for policy analysis have been gathered in the opening chapters. Coverage of the financial sector has been augmented and located earlier, in Part III, since it is of increasing importance. The "special" cases at the end now include chapters on policies toward health care, arts and sports, and weapons buying.

Although no book can be "comprehensive" in this complex and shifting field, a balanced coverage must include a lot of parts and details. The present edition has a slightly more concise text than before, and a good deal of the detail is now grouped in tables. Since the bulk of the book has remained large, an effort has been made to lighten the tone (as many readers have urged). This edition returns to the more readable—even lively—ambience achieved by the original author, Clair Wilcox, in editions one and two.

The book is designed to fit a one-semester or two-quarter treatment of industrial policy at the upper college level. It also adapts to longer sequences. It is also intended to be useful in law and business courses that deal with competitive issues and the economic content of antitrust and regulatory law. Although the book's format gives a natural sequence, it can be used flexibly. Parts II through V, in particular, can be taken in different order.

A companion book of *Readings and Cases* gives added depth on many points, putting the student more directly into the literature. It adds flexibility, too, by providing a selection of landmark legal cases and of leading economic writings. It also includes numerous review questions for each topic.

The analysis presented in these pages is an outgrowth of many years of teaching at Swarthmore College and the University of Michigan. It also reflects extensive service by both authors in various public agencies. The content of the book further reflects research by both authors on a variety of issues in industrial economics and policy effects. We are aware that policies often have defects but also that they can on occasion be highly effective. The concepts we present here for analyzing policies are meant to reflect such distilled wisdom as the field has evolved.

In the years since 1960, the usual healthy rethinking of policies and emergence of new industrial problems appear to have quickened. The older policies now appear to be under unusual strain, so that the present period may be a watershed for new industrial policies. Still, old policies have remarkable inertia, and so the conditions in 1985 or 2000 may be little changed from now. These are, in any case, exciting times in this field, and this book is meant to convey that excitement as well as to encourage clear thinking. It is meant also to display the sheer zest of the subject, where tricks and absurdities abound and all acts are only too human.

April 1975   WILLIAM G. SHEPHERD

Contents

PUBLIC POLICIES
TOWARD BUSINESS

The issues are all around you—

Are you reading this page by electric light?
   It's probably lit by a "regulated utility" (Chapters 13 and 15)
Were you born in a hospital?
   Probably a public or nonprofit enterprise (Chapters 22 and 27)
Where did you learn to read?   Probably in public schools (Chapter 22)
Are you well fed and clothed?
   Mostly from competitive markets (Chapter 2, also Chapter 25)
Is your school tax-supported?   A public enterprise (Chapter 22)
Have you ever used a computer?   (Chapters 2 and 7)
Do you travel to campus by
      car?   see automobile industry (Chapters 2 and 7)
      bus?   see transport (Chapters 17 and 21)
      subway?   see urban public enterprises (Chapter 22)
      train?   see Amtrak (Chapter 21)
      airplane?   see regulated airlines (Chapter 17)
Do you use the telephone?
   The world's biggest private monopoly (Chapters 2, 7, and 16)
Have you ever gotten sick?
   see health care (Chapter 27) and drugs (Chapters 7 and 9)
Do you have money in the bank?   (Chapter 11) *Stock market?*   (Chapter 12)
Are you a union member?   (Chapter 24)
How about military service, handling weapons?   (Chapter 29)
Have you had a letter recently?   U.S. Postal Service (Chapter 21)
Do you have relatives over 65?   Medicare (Chapter 27)
Does this book make you weary?   Try a fresh-air walk (Chapter 26),
   television (Chapter 16), sports, or the opera (Chapter 28)

Part I

THE SETTING FOR POLICIES

CHAPTER ONE

Public Control:
The Basic Issues

Public policies toward business are of three main kinds: antitrust, regulation, and public enterprise. This book will train you to analyze their design, effects and fitness.

Policies are what "policy-makers" do. They are not chiselled in stone nor decreed from on high. They evolve in thousands of offices in Washington, D.C., in state capitols, in city halls, and in foreign cities. Problems come to a head, staffs recommend action, lawyers and their clients come in to persuade those currently managing the agencies.

Then policy choices are made, fudged, or postponed "for more study." The action is announced, kept secret, or leaked to the press and public, and the crisis abates or shifts to another set of offices or hearing chambers. As the stars twinkle in the night, so the work in these myriad offices brightens and fades in intensity. A few locations seem, at any one time, to be critically important. But the scene shifts, now to antitrust, next to an energy czar, perhaps to the Pentagon or the Postal Service, and back to antitrust. In other offices, meanwhile, other large issues are quietly settled or held aside.

Again, policies are what policymakers do. Done well, they are effective treatments, like successful medication or surgery. The main condition they treat is market power. The laws and agencies can have nearly any effect; creating, preventing, reshaping, or ignoring market power. Society's objective is to develop an optimum set of these treatments and to keep them attuned to the changing economy.

The problems are ancient and tantalizing, going back into the mists of time. In these modern times we speak scientifically about optimizing the levels and designs of policies. Yet the problems existed in prehistoric tribes, in ancient Sumer, and under the Pharaohs, centuries before the ancient Greeks named it *monopoly.* It flourished in Medieval Europe, in the Tudors' and Sun King's monopoly grants and under the Shogunate, well before Adam Smith prepared *The Wealth of Nations* to strike off the fetters of Mercantilism.[1] To gain control over a market—perhaps using public agencies or perhaps in spite of the laws—is the golden way to found a family fortune. And to seek wealth and security for one's family and posterity is only good sense.

Every day, a market economy is the arena for moves in countless real games of *Monopoly*. All of them are played in earnest, and some of them are for the very largest stakes, with every weapon put to use. In some markets, this striving for wealth results in a perpetual stand-off, with no final winner taking all the cards and cash. That is what competition means: the game goes on, fairly, among equals. Such competition prevails in large areas of the modern economy, in the United States, Western Europe, Japan, and others. But instead monopoly may be dictated by technology, or it may be created by strategy or by using the political process to gain the upper hand. Adam Smith and Karl Marx made it quite clear: the structure of the economy and how the society treats monopoly define much of its whole quality. Monopoly is closed, exclusive, unequal, rigid. Competition is—usually—open, inclusive, fair, flexible: efficient and equitable.

Yet such truths do not translate into simple policy rules, such as *Always Favor Competition*. Technology sometimes makes a degree of monopoly advisable: the great riddle is, *what* degree? And always it pays aspiring and actual monopolists to persuade us that their monopoly is beneficial, even if it really is not. Talk is cheap, and words are weapons, both for private interests and, yes, for public officials. Policies often *do* the opposite of what they *say*. Actions labelled as competitive policies often breed monopoly. Regulation often is just a ritual or even a cloak for utility monopolies. Some public enterprises merely line the purses of the well-to-do. Both private and public officials often have axes to grind. As Emerson said, when guests speak of their honor, we must count our spoons.

Your task is to treat the issues and claims skeptically. They will recur hundreds of times during this course and thousands of times during the rest of your life. The objective is to learn to weigh them with logic and good sense. Logic alone will not do, for one must weigh up complex matters of degree: how much monopoly, economies of scale, inequality, and changing at what rates, etc.? One must be wise, not doctrinaire. Logic—and clarity of language—is necessary but not sufficient.

The basic questions are simple: What is to be done about monopoly? What treatments have been used, or could be tried anew? What have the results been? To answer, one must cut beneath the veneer of rhetoric and formalities, to see what really happens. One looks carefully for the historical and social roots of policies, and also compares them with what is done abroad. One learns details *and* how to compare the results with the standards for good results. That is, *positive* knowledge is used to make *normative* appraisals.

Behind these dry concepts lurk great social interests. How monopoly was treated in 1870–1920 has shaped the corporate structure and family

---

[1] Try finding an earlier society free of market power and policies toward it. Start with the *Journal of Economic History* and the appropriate section in the library shelves. File your candidates away and recheck them at Chapter 30.

wealth of today. How it is treated now will do the same for many more decades. And how other countries treat *theirs* (Japan, Sweden, Britain, China, etc.) explains much of their distinctive economic performance and social structure.

Indeed, the stakes are even more fateful. Shall the State control markets, or shall private monopolists, or competition? The answer defines much of a civilization: compare Athens and Sparta, or Soviet Russia and the United States and China. How deeply should one member be permitted to exploit the others? The answer reflects the ethics of the people. These values shape the policies, and the policies shape the economy and the social structure. The subject is in the warp and weft of society.

Because the topic also has a certain byzantine complexity, one must start simply, with clear concepts and a good grasp of the basic processes at work. We build from the standard economic analysis of costs, competition, market power, and efficient allocation—of microeconomics—which you have either acquired already or can find in other texts. We extend it on several fronts, in Part I and later too. This equips us to study what policies *ought* to do—apart from what they *claim* to do or *really* do.

BASIC CONCEPTS: (1) PUBLIC (2) POLICIES (3) TOWARD (4) BUSINESS

We begin with basic concepts, which underlie all parts of the subject.

PUBLIC Policies toward Business: The Public Interest

The public is, of course, the whole community; individuals sharing citizenship and responsibilities. The economy can do us much good, by providing abundant goods and services, fair shares, interesting work, a minimum of pollution and ugliness, etc. These economic benefits are not all that we want: most of us also look for a rich culture, social cohesion, and fairness, and perhaps some spice and goodness in life. Yet the economic goals are important, as a few weeks of being broke can persuade anyone. It is easier to praise poverty than bear it.

These goals divide into two main categories—efficiency and equity—plus various others. The goals recur throughout the book, and they are the main purposes of public policies.[2] A short summary follows. More detail is given in an Appendix at the end of this chapter.

Efficiency. This means, basically, that there is no waste or avoidable destruction: the use of resources cannot be improved.

There are three categories of *static* efficiency:

1. Efficient management within the firm, so that no slackness or mistakes occur.[3]

---

[2] The proper goals are a matter of rich and endless debate. Here we touch only on the economic ones which industrial policies might affect. Yet even these go deeply into the character of society. See J. A. Schumpeter, *History of Economic Analysis* (Oxford: Oxford University Press, 1954) for some of the classic issues.

[3] Harvey Leibenstein called this "X-efficiency" in his intriguing landmark article, "Allocative Efficiency versus 'X-efficiency'," *American Economic Review,* 1966, pp. 392–415. The name has caught on among economists.

2. Allocative efficiency—this is the standard Pareto condition, with price in line with marginal cost for each good and each firm (see the Appendix to this chapter).
3. Avoidance of wasteful advertising, which attempts merely to persuade rather than inform.

Dynamic efficiency—or the optimum rate of technical change—is also a criterion. It occurs when the resources needed for invention and innovation are allocated efficiently and innovations are not retarded for private gain.

Equity.   Equitable means fair. Fair has many meanings, going straight to the heart of ethical standards of decency and a good society. Some citizens are very rich, while many are poor. Is the fair basis *to* each according to: (1) Effort? (2) Merit? (3) Luck? (4) Birth? (5) Marginal value product? (6) Equal shares? (7) Need? (8) Two or more of these? (9) Other? and *from* each according to: (1) Ability? (2) Equal effort? (3) Other? These riddles will test your wisdom for the rest of your life. (Try settling this yourself. List as many standards of fairness as you can (Might makes right?). Then ponder. Then set your top two criteria before the rest of the class and ask for unanimous approval.)

For now, note that economic fairness relates to three directions for sharing out the economic rewards:

1. *Wealth:* the assets we hold (cash, bonds, stocks, houses, land, gold coins, Rembrandts, etc.) *minus* our debts.
2. *Income:* the yearly flow of net purchasing power.
3. *Opportunity:* the chance to gain wealth, income, status, or other good things in life *in the future,* by dint of one's effort, talent, luck, or what-all.

Others.   These include security, cultural richness, the degree of freedom of choice, and many other broader social conditions. Perhaps the most important is the sense of identity and fulfillment in one's work. An efficient and monetarily fair society could still have everybody in jobs (and/or home chores) which they detest, within a barren culture.

These other goals may transcend the others in the end. Keep that in mind as you proceed, for competition is so economically fruitful that its social ambivalence is easy to forget.

Monopoly tends to distort market performance away from these goals. Those with market power usually restrain output and raise price, so that the value of their output exceeds cost at the margin. The excess profits sap the will to minimize costs, and they disequalize wealth and income. High degrees of market power usually retard innovation. And they reduce the freedom of choice for consumers and competitors alike. To be sure, a slight degree of market power can give security and continuity, which are part of the good society. But above that small degree, monopoly is usually an economic and social burden. Chapter 2 reviews these burdens in some detail.

Competition usually induces or compels firms to behave in line with all of these criteria. Consumers can choose among alternative sellers.

Efficient producers can undersell others, who must cut costs or be weeded out. The fittest survive. Competition drives price down and output up to the level at which social value (price) just equals social sacrifice (marginal cost). It also forces sellers to advertise their wares informatively. Competition fosters progress, by giving a free run to new blood and new ideas. It rewards the innovator and compels the others to imitate rapidly.

It also spreads income and wealth widely, by averting massive profits for the few, and by feeding further rewards to new operators and innovators. It also provides the widest opportunity for seeking success. Competition also enlarges freedom of choice for most citizens. And it may also give a certain cultural richness by catering to the full range of wants.

Yet competition can run to excess, and if the pre-existing distribution of wealth is unfair, competition can tend to worsen it, or at least not correct it. Competition can seem a grueling and heartless way of life, lacking in warmth and charity. Too, there may be economies of scale and external effects which justify abridging competition (though external effects usually call for competition *plus* some other treatment). Still, for the common run of conditions, competition is a remarkable all-round economic optimizer. Those who would abridge it bear the burden of proof.

The public interest is to see that the economy attains these standards as closely as possible. If there is waste or unfairness or other deviance, the public interest lies in removing it. This happy result is often difficult to reach, for three reasons.

1. The public policies themselves absorb resources, which can exceed the benefits they yield.
2. Waste and inequity are often fiendishly hard to measure, for lack of facts or because there are honest differences about what is efficient or fair.
3. Someone usually has an interest in averting an efficient policy, and there are many ways of doing so. "Someone" is frequently a powerful, skillful, and/or large group, or even many groups.

The public interest is therefore easier to define in theory than to apply in practice. Public policies—what public policymakers make—can and often do work *against* the public interest.

The public interest in good economic performance is an urgent one. Some economies do far better than others. Some have high GNP per head and stable prices, plus a fair distribution and healthy social conditions. Others are much inferior in one or all respects. The differences arise from natural resources, historical trends, national traits—*and* from policies toward industry.

Public POLICIES toward Business

The policies come in at least 57 varieties, but in the U.S. only several are prominent. Their basic position is shown in Figure 1–1. They are not free goods. Chapter 3 will show the kinds of costs they impose. They all

FIGURE 1–1

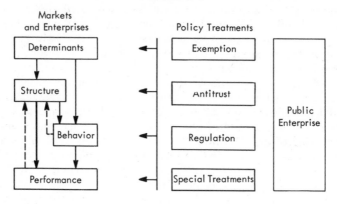

divide along two directions. One is the *degree of constraint* on the firm. This is measured by the effect on profits, either reducing them under tight regulation (to the right) or raising them via subsidy (to the left).

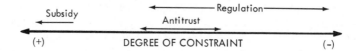

Antitrust lies in the middle. It overlaps with regulation; both have a range of effects from plus to minus (which Chapter 3 presents more fully). We will be asking, again and again in this book, what the effects of each policy have *really* been.

The second dimension is *ownership,* which ranges from totally private to totally public.

The two polar cases are easy to understand; for example, General Motors and the Government Printing Office. There is also a rich middle range, of joint or mixed ownership, which is more common abroad than in the U.S.

Figure 1–2 combines these two dimensions in a box diagram. Virtually any enterprise can be located in the box in line with its policy status. Figure 1–2 brings out the basic point that *public enterprise is a substitute for private enterprise, not for regulation or antitrust.* This point is often mistaken. It is orthodox instead to imagine that each of the main policies —antitrust, regulation, and public enterprise—is mutually exclusive with the others. And, so it goes, antitrust gets the mild cases, while the toughest ones are given the heavy-duty treatment—public enterprise—as

FIGURE 1–2

The Two Dimensions of Policy Choices

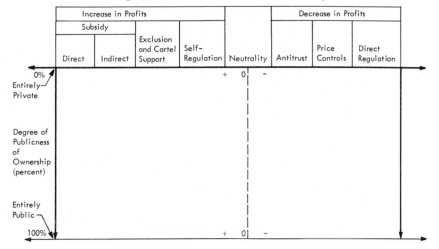

Degree of Enhancement of, or Constraint on, Profitability

	Increase in Profits					Decrease in Profits		
	Subsidy							
	Direct	Indirect	Exclusion and Cartel Support	Self–Regulation	Neutrality	Antitrust	Price Controls	Direct Regulation

a last resort. But in fact, these choices are along two different dimensions, which can and do overlap. Public enterprises can be, should be, and often are, under antitrust and/or regulation; example, the U.S. Postal Service. And a free economy—and an energetic and innovative one—can have a lot of public enterprise in it, as several European countries prove.

Though partly substitutable for each other, the policy treatments are *complementary* over wide ranges. Public firms routinely need a degree of antitrust and regulatory treatment. Regulated firms usually need—and often have—a degree of competition. And when one looks carefully, strictly private firms are often actually under close public constraints on much that they do.[4] Even further, many public firms behave as if they were private companies, as we will see in Part V.

Recent coverage of these policies in the U.S. is shown roughly in Tables 1–1 and 1–2 (Chapter 4 gives more detail). The present coverage seems traditional and even natural to most older observers. But: (1) It has evolved since 1900–1930 (with some major shifts since 1960); (2) It may not be working well; and (3) It will surely evolve and perhaps change markedly in the future. Moreover, it differs sharply from the policy packages in other countries.

The U.S. makes more use of antitrust and utility regulation, and less use of public enterprise. Therefore, it is an open question how well the special brands and packages of U.S. policies have worked, and how (if at all) they should change in the future. Is the U.S. aberrant, or the best

---

[4] The overlap can grow extreme and is often irrational. For example, Gulf Oil's president recently asserted that the company's fortunes were affected by some 61 different government agencies, of all sorts. *New York Times,* November 15, 1973. Much the same is true of other large firms and many smaller ones.

TABLE 1-1

Estimates of Policy Coverage by Sectors, U.S. Economy, 1974

Sector	Percent of National Income						Public Ownership (percent of national income)
	Total	Subsidy or Cartel Support	Public Purchases	Exempt	Antitrust	Regulation or Other Control Device	
Finance, etc.	11.4	6.5		4.2	.7	1.0	1.4
Manufacturing	26.5	1.0	3.5	11.5	9.5	2.2	.9
Utilities	4.2		.5	1.5		1.1	.7
Transport	3.8		.2	2.2	.3		.9
Government	16.0		16.0				16.0
Wholesale and retail	15.0			11.0	4.0		0
Services	13.1	3.0		9.1	1.0		2.0
Construction	4.6		.7	3.9			0
Mining	1.6			1.6			0
Agriculture, etc.	3.0	2.5		.5			0
Rest of world	.8						0
Totals	100.0	13.0	20.9	45.5	15.5	4.3	21.9

TABLE 1–2

Estimates of Policy Coverage by Sectors, U.S. Economy, 1924

		Percent of National Income					
Sector	Total	Subsidy or Cartel Support	Public Purchases	Exempt	Antitrust	Regulation or Other Control Device	Public Ownership (percent of national income)
Finance, etc.	15.1	2.0		13.1			0
Manufacturing	21.9			9.9	12.0		.4
Utilities	3.3			1.3		2.0	.5
Transport	7.5			3.0		4.5	.7
Government	9.6		9.6				9.6
Wholesale and retail	13.6			9.6	4.0		0
Services	11.6		.6	11.0			0
Construction	4.4		.4	4.0			0
Mining	2.5			2.5			0
Agriculture, etc.	10.5			10.5			0
Rest of world	0			0			0
Totals	100.0	2.0	10.6	64.9	16.0	6.5	11.2

archetype? In thinking about this, foreign experience will provide a useful perspective.

The basic American trait is to prefer open, arm's-length, formal dealings between policymakers and enterprises. Much transpires behind the scenes, but less so than in the western European economies and Japan. In these countries, informal controls and public enterprise are more routine, with little pretense at formal antitrust or regulation. Eastern command economies run to public enterprises and central controls, in great and changing variety. Less developed countries rely mainly on informal dealings and a growing range of public enterprises.

Public Policies TOWARD Business: How Policies Are Applied

The freshman image is that the legislature writes laws which (after testing, if necessary, in the courts) are *applied to*—or toward—private firms by executive agencies. The State stands outside the economy, acting—or interfering—to change it from its natural course.

This image is not quite false, but it needs much redrawing (more details are given in Chapters 3 and 4 and later). The policy setting has two basic elements: (1) a *political* process (democratic or otherwise) which carries out the evolving will of the people; this process is parallel to (2) the *economic* system. These two interact. The political process shapes the economic process, and vice versa. This leads to several cautions:

The political process is not perfect. It has pockets of monopoly, ignorance, and delay. It may be the best there is, but it also reflects the underlying power relationships, rather than strictly equal voter power.

The influence goes both ways between the economic and political processes. Policies toward firms A . . . F are shaped *by firms A . . . F* as well as firms G . . . Z and perhaps others.

Indeed,

Democracy moves slowly and openly, and so those affected can usually influence policy. And firms adversely affected by policy X will have strong incentives to shape policies their way. In doing this,

The rational firm will spend (on experts, lawsuits, lobbying, advertisements, and other persuasion) *up to the dollar amount that is at stake, in order to get its way.*

Therefore, in fact

Policies are evolved under pressure from all sides, rather than applied unilaterally. Policy actions usually strike reasonable balances, rather than push to doctrinaire extremes.

And policies usually lag behind events and needs.

Policy treatments are not usually done to or applied to firms, as an autocratic doctor might decide that a gall bladder must come out. Rather the policy move is usually by consent, including the reluctant consent (if not the virtual direction) of the firm itself. This reality differs from the high school civics view that a problem is solved by passing a law or taking a public action against it.

Public Policies toward BUSINESS

The businesses affected by public policies are, literally, of all kinds. Big business is of course squarely in center stage, just as it gets the lion's share of attention in the press. And—big or small—private companies are in business to make profits. Yet there are other angles to it.

a. There are conflicting interests *among* businesses. The business community is in fact a continent full of warring tribes: among firms, among industries, among sectors, big versus small, local versus international, etc. Competition itself is part of it, but not all. Firm A's gain is usually a loss to some firm B, C, or H. Good public policy recognizes these natural contraries, and indeed it often puts such opposed private interest to work. The deepest single contrast is between established firms and newcomers; between old-line, blue-chip, establishment firms, and outsiders.[5]

b. Industries differ gloriously in their ages and styles. Examples: steel and meat packing are old; cable TV and hand calculators are young. The styles are fascinating. Compare the patrician reserve of the investment banker with the fast talk of the car salesman; Wall Street with Main Street. Uniformity has not yet prevailed.

c. Enterprises include the conventional *private* firms and banks, *plus*

1. Public firms of many types and degrees (see Part V),
2. Partnerships (lawyers, doctors, small business),
3. Non-profit and charitable units (hospitals, universities, . . .)
4. Cooperatives, mutuals and other hybrid forms.

All of these produce and sell under some forms of constraint. All of them can monopolize, or conspire, or compete, and can innovate or stagnate. Public policies deal with them all, not just the standard private corporation.

d. Private firms often have deep public effects. Large firms each use the capital of thousands of investors, employ thousands of workers, buy from hundreds of suppliers, and sell to thousands or millions of customers. They affect jobs, prices, local prosperity, future resources, national security, and often the quality and meaning of life. The behavior of many private firms is properly a matter of public concern.

e. Firms should not be expected to be socially responsible on a conscious basis. Frequently it is argued otherwise; that large firms can and

---

[5] One's vantage point can be decisive. Consider these attitudes:

As seen by:	Established firms are:	Outsider firms are:
Established firms	Sound, efficient, far-sighted	Hucksters, irresponsible, raiders
Outsiders	Slow, narrow-minded, inefficient	Creative, forward looking

do serve as social stewards, doing good things that are not profitable. This may happen occasionally, but less so than is hoped or claimed. Such enlightened acts go against the grain of training, belief, and stockholder pressures in upper management. And the diverse social impacts of larger business choices often embrace so many elements and groups that Solomon himself could not find the best solution. Such impacts properly require a conscious social resolution, not amateur treatment by private officials trying to be charitable. Such special efforts are not immoral, as some purists say. But they are usually peripheral, fallible and no substitute for public policy.

f. Business is astonishingly resilient and inventive. Its managers and legal advisors can devise ways through—or around—almost any obstacle. This often frustrates public policies; if tactic A is prohibited, the firm can try tactics B through Z instead. But it also means that business can bounce back handsomely from almost any treatment, even radical ones. In fact, business routinely absorbs drastic shocks from all directions (as Chapter 2 will note); that is what good management and alert investing is all about. In short, business is not fragile; it can adapt well to almost any policy experiments (though of course it will try to persuade us otherwise).

PERSPECTIVE AND FORMAT

This book is about complex and lively issues, which inspire an extraordinary range of views and proposals. At one end are the champions of private property rights and laissez faire; at the other, the radicals wishing to replace the whole system with a better one. You already inhabit a place somewhere on this spectrum, and your position may shift a good deal as you learn more, grow older, and watch changing events.

This book aims to help you develop your views intelligently and independently, by thinking, not copying. It also seeks to help you develop a clear sense of priorities among parts of the economy, among problems, and among policy tools. Each of these items is numerous. You must learn which of them matter the most, and how they interrelate. These images will in turn shape your views about optimal policies.

Attitudes toward Policies. These divide roughly into four groups:

a. Believers. They think current policies are basically right, perhaps even to the last detail. Those who manage the policies are especially prone to this attitude, but many John Q. Publics also hold it.

b. Removers. These are skeptics (classical liberals), who think most policies have bad effects or are simply irrelevant. Since competition prevails, they believe, most public policies should be removed. Private power is slight, they hold, if the State is limited; then harmony will prevail.

c. Reformers. These critics want more and better policies, not less. Often called liberals, they want bigger staffs, tougher enforcement, higher quality officials, etc. The aim is to make capitalism work better, if necessary with some fairly strict treatments. They often give up their whole proposals in order to win a step in the right direction.

d. Replacers. These people think that patching will not suffice: the problems are at the core of the *system.* Private power is great and distorts both the economy and the political process. Rather than harmony prevailing, there are deep conflicts within society which must be resolved directly. This is *kontrardoctrine,* not *harmoniedoktrine,* as the old scholars used to say. Therefore the core—or even the whole—of the present system needs to be replaced.

Removers and Replacers are both radicals, and both distrust the present system of policies; but their solutions are largely direct opposites. Reformers are often said to be radicals, but in fact they are loyal to the heart of the status quo.

All writers on the subject—*everyone* mentioned and cited in this book, and of course the two people writing this book—have their personal views, which fit in or between these groups. Some strive to be strictly scientific in their research and debate, but others are simply out to convert. Indeed, many of them make their living by making a case (all lawyers, advertisers and public relations officials do). The facts are often so checkered, obscure, and rubbery that advocates can flourish, and even sincere scholars often exaggerate as they warm to the debate.

Therefore, the wise student is always on guard, treating each point skeptically. He (she) also takes his *own* acquired beliefs out of storage for a fresh review. How does he *know* if his prior image of the economy is sound? But he doesn't go too far into disbelief and assume that everyone is just peddling propaganda. There is much honesty and reliable facts on the subject, if one makes a good effort to sift them out. So the wise student is careful and good-humored, not cynical.

The cast of characters is fascinating: officials and scholars of all stripes, magnates, judges, plucky small businessmen, great inventors, the ever-present lawyers, etc. And the scene ranges from city offices, to State houses, hearing rooms and the marble halls of justice. We will get to know them too in this book. They—and we—all operate within a grand historical process which seems to move glacially but inexorably to the Left. Yesteryear's radical idea is often today's law, and in a few years it may be the rallying point for conservatives.

This Book Follows a Natural Format. First we lay out the economics of modern industry, defining its structure and performance, and pinpointing the most sensitive sectors. Then Chapter 3 sets forth the principles of rational policy choices. It also reviews the main policy tools which are—or could be—used.

Part II then presents policies to maintain or restore competition in the normal run of industries and trade. Part III treats the financial sector, important in itself and for the rest of the economy. Regulation of utilities is covered in Part IV. We then change planes in Part V to analyze public enterprise, in many forms and sectors. Together these four parts cover the core of the subject. By Chapter 23, you will be prepared to do it yourself: to analyze a market, compare policy tools, and choose.

Around this core turns a small galaxy of special cases, which Part VI explores. They range from arts and sports (Chapter 28), to subsidies (Chapter 25), to pollution (Chapter 26), and to life and death (Chapter 27).

They are the frosting on the cake. Also, in their eccentric way, they put the mainstream cases in perspective. Antitrust, regulation, and public enterprise are important, but happily they are not the whole of the subject.

<h2 style="text-align:center">APPENDIX TO CHAPTER 1:
THE CRITERIA OF OPTIMAL PERFORMANCE</h2>

The analysis is condensed in Figure 1–3. The basic contrast is between performance under pure competition and pure monopoly, but these are only polar cases. The same effects hold across the middle range, especially between two common states: (1) "effective" competition, with many sellers and potential entrants, and (2) dominance by one or two firms. The analysis here states the difference oversimply, but clearly and validly.

Take pure competition first. The firm is assumed to operate as one of an indefinite number of competitors selling in its market. Each firm has increasing costs at some moderate size, and so—where average costs are lowest—there is an optimum size. At that point (or possibly a range of sizes) its average costs reach a minimum and marginal costs equal average cost. Each of these firms has full knowledge of the main factors affecting it. Each can adjust quickly to whatever changes occur, as it

FIGURE 1–3

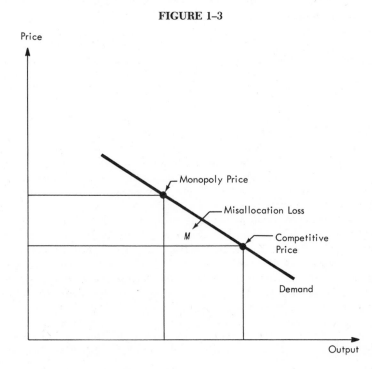

maximizes its own welfare. Each one is a price taker rather than a price maker. And, for simplicity, we presume that each makes only one product. Now its job is simply to decide how much to produce and sell.

On the demand side, there are also unnumbered buyers. Each operates independently, maximizing her or his own welfare. The summed individual demand curves are, in aggregate, the market demand curve. The market supply curve is the horizontal sum of the individual firm's marginal cost curves. The cost conditions arise from the basic technology within each firm. The shape of the cost curve is, of course, quite crucial to the economic outcome in the industry. The rising portion of the average cost curve reflects diseconomies of scale, which are caused either by (1) the increasing scarcity of a fixed factor, such as a talented manager, or natural resource, or by (2) the sheer loss of vitality and accurate control that often accompanies larger size.

Demand equals supply in market equilibrium. In the long run, this brings firms to or near their lowest average cost, so that their marginal cost is just equal to price. The profound lesson of this is that in a well-functioning competitive system, *marginal cost*—the social sacrifice necessary to produce another unit of input—*just equals price*—which measures how valuable that output is believed to be. Sacrifice is brought into line with value, and so a social optimum is reached. This is the familiar Pareto equimarginal efficiency condition, in which consumers, input suppliers, and producers share. Behind each of the individual demand and supply curves lies equilibria in individual choices, so that each of the economic actors is maximizing its own welfare.

This all adds up to the Smithian invisible hand, whereby the entire economy reaches an economic optimum. But there are limits. *First,* there may be external benefits in production or consumption. If these are large, they result in public goods, which will not be provided in sufficient volume, or perhaps in any amount at all, unless supported directly by the state. In more modest scope, these external costs involve *inter alia* smoke, water, and noise pollution. These also need special treatment. The *second* limit is that dynamic efficiency is not assured. Innovation and other forms of technical progress may lie outside the competitive equilibrium result. The *third* serious limit on competitive efficiency is that it does not address the problem of equity. The Pareto conditions can be consistent with the City of God or with preposterous or even vicious unfairness. One citizen may amass all the chips, or all may share equally, or one group may tyrannize over the rest: all alongside the efficient allocative conditions.

We now consider the simple introduction of monopoly into this competitive equilibrium. The new monopolist now faces the *industry* demand curve, and there is also a marginal revenue curve. This marginal revenue curve intersects the summed marginal cost of the monopolist's plants at an output level well below the competitive level. Price is now higher, and excess profits are probably earned. Since price now exceeds marginal cost, people are willing to pay more than the true cost of added output, *but the monopolist will not let them do it.* That is the crux of inefficient allocation.

Also, inputs are cut back, so that the values of their marginal products are well above their wages. To this degree they are exploited. Some of them are now out of work; they will have to try for other jobs at lower wages in other industries. The burden of misallocation is shown by the triangle *M* in Figure 1–3. It is, roughly speaking, the consumer surplus lost by the shift from competition to monopoly.

These effects of pure monopoly hold *pro rata* for partial monopoly: *e.g.* for market shares of 70, 50, or 30 percent. If there are several partial monopolists—*i.e.,* oligopolists—in a market, the resulting interdependence may give rise to a variety of outcomes, ranging from shared-monopoly cooperation to wild and woolly struggles.

FIGURE 1–4

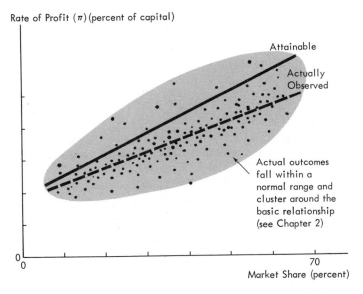

This can all be summed up by a simple diagram (Figure 1–4), showing that the rate of profit is related—more or less tightly—to the firm's market share. This yield to market share may stem from (1) market power *per se* (in causing pecuniary gains and price discrimination); (2) economies of scale; or (3) a string of good luck which yields both a high market share and a high profit rate; or some mix of all three. Chapter 2 will review these conditions in actual markets.

So far we have assumed that the firm operates with the utmost internal efficiency. But under market power, managers may not keep their shoulder firmly to the wheel. Their staff know that the excess profits give room to spare. Internal business efficiency—X-efficiency—may slacken. Actual profits may fall short of attainable profits, perhaps by a great deal. Pressure from stockholders and financial markets may limit the slack, but perhaps not tightly. This slackness effect may therefore shape the relation between market share and profits, as shown in Figure 1–4.

There is a *Schumpeterian proviso* to all this. Competition can be seen as a *process,* a series of moves rather than a state of rest. Its main yield would then be in progress over time rather than in efficient allocation at each point. The competitive process is perhaps a sequence of disequilibrium in which large firms contend for market control. Thus: firm X innovates and seizes most of the market. From this it draws extra profits, but these attract powerful rivals, who innovate yet again, vanquishing firm X for the time being. And so the process goes on. The result is anticlassical but is *competitive,* in a sense. No market power lasts, as market shares churn.

This is akin to a common *business* image of competition, as rivalry among established firms who compete by product as well as price competition. Here oligopoly is normal, and although price-cutting is mutually abhorred as a competitive tactic, there is much jockeying via changes in the product and via advertising. Such rivalry can be intense, but it differs from the Schumpeterian process in three ways. First, innovation is secondary or less. The rivalry may only cause a trifling with nonprice features. Second, market shares may change little, in contrast to the Schumpeterian shifts. And third, profits may be steady and high, rather than fluctuating sharply. In short, the business view of rivalry is far more subjective and closer to an apologia for market power. The Schumpeterian version—if it is valid—does contain powerful forces which cause visible changes and performance gains.

A more skeptical view is that all of these processes involve exploitation of those participants lacking market power. Nearly all workers and most petty businesses are in this category, while most firms in the great core of larger enterprises do have such power. Seen through these lenses, the process—whatever it is, equilibrium or disequilibrium—may be tolerably efficient, but it is thoroughly unfair. Contention among larger enterprises does not challenge their survival. Only occasionally do maverick entrepreneurs challenge the core of established firms.

Result: the main body of firms generate excess profits for owners, power and status for their managers, and varying degrees of exploitation for the rest. The plight of migrant workers, for example, is only one acute result of this hard face of capitalism. Other workers get lower wealth, income, and opportunity than a less exclusive, less power-ridden system would provide. Competition is part—perhaps the mainspring—of this unjust process. The modern capitalist economy merely continues, and may deepen, the social exclusion and privilege which it inherited.

Given these contrasting images, one proceeds with caution. Simple calls for maximizing competition are not in order. What form of competition? Couldn't extreme competition *worsen* matters? Who is to compete: All? Industrial firms? Financial units? On what terms: with unequal personal capital and social advantages?

Ultimately, the social worth of competition also must be held in question. Competition is stress; it is divisive, pitting man against man—and woman. It can glorify the ruthless operator, the Gradgrind and Babbitt, who gain by suppressing or exploiting humane motives. The tyranny of the bottom line can be immune to decency, kindness, forgiveness. Business life expresses the underlying culture, or lack of it: it also shapes that culture. Each people can choose its social standards, though many cultures simply submit to cults of religion or business "ethic." Usually competition is better than self-serving monopoly. But it must operate within a basically decent, fair, and rich culture. If not, it can become just another means of social oppression.

CHAPTER TWO

The Modern Economy

This chapter gives a compact summary of industrial structure and policy yields in the U.S. economy. The main parts of this economic system are shown in Figure 2–1. The objective is to learn the inner details and processes *and* to relate them as elements within the whole.

The first step is to review the nature of the firm, in its financial setting. Next we focus on the role of the largest firms and banks. Then we try to answer the basic three questions about the structure of individual markets: What *determines* structure? What *is* structure? and What are the *effects* of structure? The section before the chapter summary outlines five major industries with high market power, to give rounded examples.

THE FIRM

The firm is the building block of the economy. Started and maintained by human minds and wills, it has no life of its own, though there is usually continuity. It can be divided, reorganized, augmented, terminated, sold, or absorbed in another enterprise; such actions are the normal stuff of business life.

The firm produces and sells, covering its costs with revenues. Its choices are made primarily by managers, within the limits of the firm's opportunities. The constraints are set by the nature of the market and technology, the degree of competition, and by public policies. In private firms, the managers maximize long-run profits for the owners. In public and other hybrid firms (quasi-public, cooperatives, nonprofit entities, etc.), there may be different goals and net revenue targets. For all firms, the output itself is mainly a side-effect of pursuing the main financial goal.

Figure 2–2 shows the anatomy of a typical medium or large firm. Each group bears attention. MANAGERS are the pivotal group. They steer the firm, assessing prospects, studying alternatives, deciding both what the firm does and who gets promoted. The top ranks can take many forms, with real power held by the President, or the Chairman of the Board, or

FIGURE 2–1

Outline of Markets and Related Areas in an Industrialized Economy

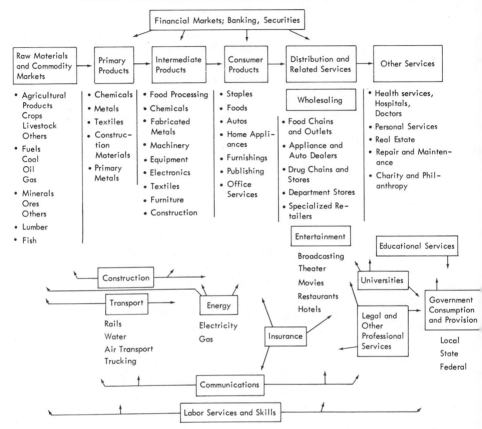

a three-person triumvirate, or some other package. Always it is a tiny cohort which actually manage, during the brief interval—three to five years is normal—while their turn at the top lasts. Usually they are promoted from within, on the basis of intense competition.[1] They usually take only one or two major actions during their spell at the top. What those actions are—a shake-up, a new product line, staving off a take-over, etc.—depends on the firm's condition, on their own ideas, and on outside forces. Apart from that, they keep things going, guided by data and ideas from those below them.

The constraints on them are usually many and tight, and the effects of action are often unpredictable, complex, and slow. Firms usually have a momentum and personality all their own, which the leaders can only

---

[1] The American convention of rugged individualism is not universal. For example, Japanese management operates by consensus, seniority, and mutual help. There is less force, fear, and tension. And it has seemed to perform well for at least 20 years.

FIGURE 2-2
The Firm and Its Setting

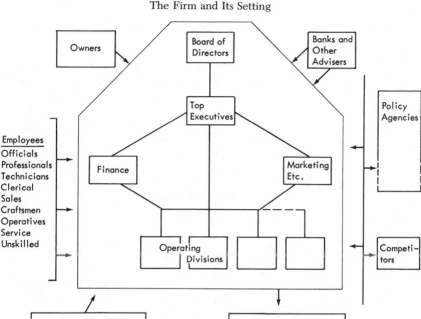

maintain or modify, not change sharply. Managers are the focus of many interest groups, often mediating as much as deciding. And they are supervised, formally by their Board and informally by their owners and financial backers.

OWNERS hold (1) voting shares of stock and/or (2) bonds.

Common shareholders are the titular "owners." Their votes elect the Directors and may also ratify proposals made by the managers. Shareholders receive dividends, which can vary as the firm's success—and net income—fluctuates. The Directors decide the dividend pay-out, which is usually about half of net income (the rest is reinvested). Shareholders hold for dividends and/or capital gains (which usually occur as the firm's prospective profits rise).

Bondholders get fixed money payments, set when the bonds are issued. Bondholders seek mainly income; capital gains occur mainly as general interest rates fall. They do not vote, as such. But if interest payments are not made or the bonds not redeemed on time, the firm is insolvent. Bondholders therefore often seek to influence management informally.

Both of the owner groups are numerous and mostly passive. But larger owners—both individuals and portfolio managers in institutions (banks, pension funds, insurance firms, etc.)—can exert pressure. In *public* firms, there are no voting shares, only bonds or nonvoting dividend shares. Ownership resides in the government (national, state, or local), and the degree of outside influence on the firm varies.

DIRECTORS supervise, in some degree. They usually include (1) several top managers, who dominate the proceedings, (2) several bank officials or others with large holdings, and (3) several "outside" directors from the top levels of other firms.[2] Boards are usually passive to management, requiring good management in general rather than directing in detail. Only when the firm gets into serious trouble do directors intervene, often belatedly.

Often more influential are the hidden and informal *banking relationships* of firms. In getting short- and long-term capital, the firm's managers are usually in an intimate and lasting relationship of mutual trust with their main backers. These usually involve one bank, an underwriter, and possibly an insurance firm (very large firms have more). These senior banking officials decide the terms of loans and stock offerings, often counselling and limiting the company's plans in detail. Often these close relationships are reflected in director's seats for bank and other officers. But the real financial setting lies beneath that surface, and it embeds most firms in close supervision.

THE MAIN OTHER GROUPS impinging on, or interacting with, the firms are: customers, employees, competitors, suppliers of inputs, and makers of public policies.[3] The firm's cost and demand conditions are vectors of all these influences. Managerial success is measured by the bottom line of the income statement, as in Table 2–1. This net income is the return on the firm's equity investment (net worth; the stockholders' share, as distinct from bondholders, who draw interest—compare with Chapters 13 and 14). A rate of return maintained above 15 percent is splendid, while 10 percent is scarcely above the norm for survival in competition. The cost of capital is normally 6–10 percent, and so returns below 6 percent for several years are not tolerable and usually provoke a shake-up in management. Public firms keep the same kind of accounts, in both western and eastern economies. Their managers' targets and objectives—and financial supervision—are often identical with private firms'.

The key decisions are about

1. Current production levels,
2. The prices to charge,
3. The levels and forms of investment, and
4. How to finance the investment (equity or bonds).

In large diversified firms, these choices are many and complex, but they are guided by the effort to maximize long-run profit. This translates into

---

[2] Recently among 327 large U.S. firms, 85 percent had senior executives of other firms on their boards, followed in frequency by retired company officers (56 percent), commercial bankers (55 percent), and lawyers (52 percent). Only 11 percent had women directors and only 9 percent had members of minority groups. Pay was usually in the range of $6,000–$10,000 per year. *Business Week,* November 10, 1973, page 201.

[3] Worker participation in management has developed in certain countries, especially China and Yugoslavia. But in the U.S., workers have no such role, except in a few special cases.

TABLE 2–1
Basic Financial Statements for Two Large Firms, 1972

GENERAL MOTORS CORPORATION
(in $billion)

Income Statement		Balance Sheet			
		Assets		*Liabilities*	
Revenues 30.6		Plant and property 15.5		Equity	
		Depreciation, etc. . . . . −9.3		Original shares 8	
Expenses				Reinvestment	
Operating 26.7		Net plant and property . . 6.2		earnings, etc. 10.9	
Depreciation,				Total equity 11.7	
etc. 1.8		Investment, etc. 1.4			
				Debt 8	
Net income 4.3		Current assets 10.5		Others 5.8	
				Total	
Taxes 2.1		Total assets 18.3		liabilities 18.3	
Net income after					
tax 2.2					

return on equity
capital = 18.9%

BRISTOL-MYERS COMPANY
(in $million)

Income Statement		Balance Sheet			
		Assets		*Liabilities*	
Revenues 1,219		Plant and property 349		Equity	
		Depreciation . . . . −130		Original shares 91	
		Net plant and property . 219		Retained earnings 390	
				Total equity 481	
Expenses					
Cost of sales 428					
Marketing, etc. . . . 624		Other 80		Debt 132	
Interest 15					
Total 1,067		Current assets 555		Current 240	
Net income 152		Total assets 854		Total liabilities . . . 854	
Taxes 68					
Net income after					
tax 84					

return on equity
capital = 17.5%

---

maximizing the discounted present value of the firm; this hypothetical figure is the summed value of the stream of profits the firm can expect in the future, discounted for time.[4] The stock market converts this quickly into a very real valuation, as the share prices rise and fall.

This "market value" of the company (current share price times the number of shares issued) reflects both (1) real factors, such as the firm's

---

[4] Thus,

$$\text{present value} = \frac{\text{profit}_1}{(1+r)} + \frac{\text{profit}_2}{(1+r)^2} + \frac{\text{profit}_3}{(1+r)^3} + \frac{\text{profit}_n}{(1+r)^n}$$

where n is the rate of time-discount and the right-hand terms are for successive years. For conventional values, an r of 10 percent and a time horizon of 20 years, present value is about 10 times the yearly profit level.

TABLE 2–2
The Power of Expectations to Make Values—and Change Them

	Number of Shares Outstanding (end of 1973) (million)	Price-earnings ratio, (end of 1973)	Market Value of Company Shares (end of 1972) ($billion)	Book Value of Stockholders' Equity (end of 1972) ($billion)	Ratio of Market Value to Book Value of Stockholders' Equity		Change in Market Value of Company Shares (end of 1972 to October 1974) ($billion)
					End of 1972	October 1974	
IBM	145	28	48.8	7.6	6.4	2.1	−23.0
AT&T	554	10	29.0	28.9	1.0	.8	− 4.6
Eastman Kodak	162	32	24.0	2.8	8.6	3.8	−12.2
General Motors	288	8	23.3	11.7	2.0	.8	−11.9
Exxon	224	9	19.8	12.3	1.6	1.1	− 5.0
Sears, Roebuck	157	27	18.2	4.5	4.1	1.5	−10.5
General Electric	182	20	13.5	3.1	4.4	2.0	− 9.7
Xerox	79	38	11.7	1.3	9.0	4.1	− 5.7
Procter & Gamble	82	28	9.1	1.6	5.7	3.6	− 2.8
Coca-Cola	60	41	8.9	.8	11.1	3.7	− 5.4
du Pont (E.I.) de Nemours	48	15	8.4	3.3	2.5	1.4	− 3.2
Avon Products	58	42	7.9	.4	19.7	3.4	− 6.4
IT&T	96	15	5.7	3.6	1.6	.4	− 4.3
Disney (Walt) Productions	29	49	3.4	.3	11.3	1.5	− 2.7
McDonald's	39	61	3.0	.2	15.0	3.5	− 1.9
U.S. Steel	54	5	1.5	3.6	.4	.6	+ .8

Source: *Fortune, Directory of the 500 Largest Industrial Corporations*, annual; Moody's *Handbook of Common Stocks*, quarterly; stock market reports.

market position, physical capacity, order backlog, product design, current profits, etc., and (2) expectations about the firm's future.

A rise in perceived prospects—on sound or fanciful grounds—causes increased buying of shares. The share price rises, capitalizing the expected gain. The force of expectations is great, as Table 2–2 shows.

The firm is now worth more; now it must deliver, or else the shares will *fall.* A sharp enough fall will stir efforts to get rid of the present managers. Lessons:

1. *Managers are on a treadmill,* to fulfill the expectations of investors.
2. *Excess profits are prediscounted,* so that the original owners cream off the excess in form of capital gains. Later investors can only get standard returns, even if the firm continues to earn high rates of profit on the book value of its real investment.

Managers of lucrative firms—from monopoly, innovation, or whatever —therefore have cross incentives. The excess profits provide a temptation for X-inefficiency, since the employees know that there is room for it. Yet the share price may fully discount the excess profits, so that any slacking off will cause capital losses. The firm's actual efficiency may vary widely.

FIGURE 2–3

Possible Rates of Return (percent on capital)

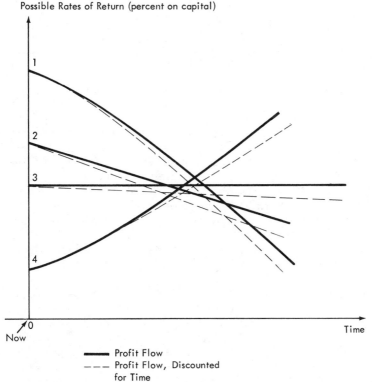

Now

Time

———— Profit Flow

– – – Profit Flow, Discounted for Time

Managers' motives and decision rules have developed interesting hybrids in large and complex firms. The basic long-run choice is straightforward, as illustrated in Figure 2–3. At each point, the managers can (1) go for maximum short-run profits but suffer a declining position, or (2) take a middle route, or (3) choose a steady long-run stream, or even (4) take losses now while building up (by loss leaders, an advertising campaign, etc.) to higher future profits. The choice reflects the firm's preferences, particularly the top managers' time preference (r) and personalities. Some are in a hurry, aggressive if need be; others take the long view. And managerial styles differ. Try to identify them in Table 2–3.

TABLE 2–3
Pick the Styles: Three per Industry

Industry		Descriptions of Managerial Styles (*add your own*)	
Movies	Investment bankers	Tycoons	Bureaucratic
Iron and steel	Real estate	Aggressive	Autocratic
Computers	Automobiles	Creative	Respectable
Hotels	Horse racing	Supercautious	Innovative
Used cars	Grain sales	Funereal	Affluent
Cattle ranching	Medical services	Flamboyant	Public spirited
Telephone utility	Postal services	Free wheeling	Honest
Advertising	Oil prospecting	Mired in the past	Anxious to please
Baseball team owners	Undertakers	Grizzled	Clubby
Cosmetics	Railroads	Grasping	Efficient

In short, corporate life is endlessly variable and inventive. Forms and styles differ and change as the whirligig of time spins round. Finance is the lifeblood, for it determines success and involves supervision from outside. Competition among firms arises from clashes in these corporate views and interests, but it is also an indirect battle between the financial backers of competing firms. To work well, any public policy must deal with these motives and controls.

Firms also vary in diversity, from one product up to thousands. The more diversified firms, or conglomerates, must decentralize management. As diversity increases, the top level becomes just a holding company, allocating funds and drawing profits. Some conglomerates are old and firmly set in the business establishment. Others are new, with an outsider's status and motives.

Conglomerates are a natural unit for merging with other firms. Mergers may be amicable or take-overs forced on the management.

Take-over occurs when a target firm A is performing below its potential, as appraised by an outside group B with access to funds. This may arise from clear mismanagement and/or because B's managers have a higher time preference—that is, are more aggressive—than A's. The acquiring firm usually must have financial sources big enough to overcome the present backing of firm A. Often working control requires only 20 or

30 percent of firm A's stock, so smallish firms can occasionally take over much larger ones.

Take-overs therefore reinforce or supervene in the direct supervision of a firm by its backers and Board. An active ginger group of conglomerate outsiders—of corporate raiders—is part of a healthy market system. As older conglomerates grow respectable, fresh ones usually spring up, and so the business establishment is kept alive by first resisting and then absorbing the flow of outsiders. (This is critical in understanding mergers: see Chapter 8.)

The firm's opportunities are influenced by the conditions of its industry. Each industry has a definite structure at each moment. But industries and their structures evolve. Many follow a predictable life cycle with several stages from birth to maturity. Some life-cycles are short, while others are long.

There are four standard phases:

Phase 1. Birth. A critical invention or other change makes production economic. There may be a crucial patent.

Phase 2. Growth. Demand rises rapidly and cost curves shift down and to the right. Demand grows even faster than optimum size.

Phase 3. Maturity. Technology standardizes on roughly a constant cost basis, while demand keeps growing. This phase is the longest one.

Phase 4. Decline. Demand shrinks and becomes more elastic, as substitutes emerge.

Structure also evolves. During the first growth phases, behavior may be highly monopolistic, while control is held by one or by a very few firms. As growth goes on, competition sets in so that both structure and the results of activity grow more competitive. New firms enter, and little ones grow especially rapidly. The industry continues onward toward a more normal growth rate, as the market becomes saturated. At length maturity is reached, in which there is some degree of competition between this product and others. Ultimately, the market comes under increasing stress from other newer products, so that eventually this market merges back into the competitive background. The broad trend, then, is from monopoly towards competition. If this cycle is not impeded, and if financial markets are open to new competitive firms and products, then this market's degree of monopoly cannot last long.

The sequence is not uniform; some industries avoid it or are reborn frequently. For most industries, though technology may prescribe large market shares in Phases 1 and 2, but not in the mature Phase 3. The likely evolution of the dominant firm is illustrated in Figure 2–4. The life cycle also changes the firm's prospects. In Phase 2 they are rich and wide: to monopolize a new growth industry is to strike it rich. But in Phase 4 the wise firm seeks to shift out into other markets. Again, managerial styles differ; and the transitions of growth shift talent from older to newer industries.

Most utilities, such as electricity, postal, telephones, and earlier railroads, trace out a clearer life cycle than do conventional industries. A key factor is often the political decision in Phase 2 to regulate it as a natural

FIGURE 2–4
Evolution of Market Shares

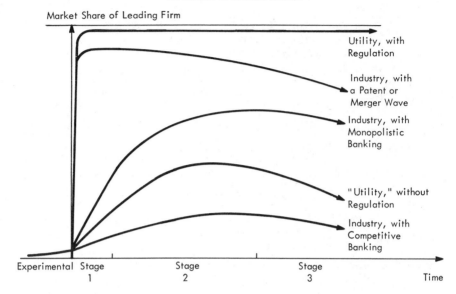

Market Share of Leading Firm

Utility, with
Regulation

Industry, with
a Patent or
Merger Wave

Industry, with
Monopolistic
Banking

"Utility," without
Regulation

Industry, with
Competitive
Banking

Experimental   Stage   Stage   Stage
               1   2   3   Time

monopoly. Like a key patent, regulation makes the monopoly bigger and longer lasting. How "utility" life cycles interact with regulation is analyzed in Chapter 13.

There are the basic concepts and processes. Now we turn to the real world, to see what the magnitudes and policy yields really are. Is big enterprise dominant? Does technology permit competition in most markets? Is market power rising? Are its effects large or merely trivial and fleeting? What, in short, is the economic content with which public policies deal?

A Word about Fact-finding. Research into industrial organization is incomplete and hampered by secrecy. The learning process interacts with—and is influenced by—the reality, as shown in Figure 2–5. Quantitative research only began in the 1930s and advanced slowly. Even now, only a handful of first-class objective researchers are at work on the more important issues. The main milestones are listed in Table 2–4. The student's sources of information are (1) scholarly research—monographs, journals, (2) reports by public agencies—Congressional committees, the Federal Trade Commission and other regulatory agencies, etc., (3) company data and reports, and (4) the business press, including specialized industry sources. Most of the critical facts—market shares, economies of scale, profit rates, degree of efficiency, and innovation—are kept secret and/or are difficult to measure.

THE LARGER SETTING

Each period has its giant firms, but size is relative. Large modern corporations have been present since the first main U.S. merger wave of

TABLE 2-4
Milestones in the Study of Industrial Organization

1776	Adam Smith, *The Wealth of Nations.*
1870–83	Karl Marx, *Capital.*
1901	J. B. Clark, *The Control of Trusts.*
1904	John Moody, *The Truth about the Trusts.*
1919	Alfred Marshall, *Industry and Trade.*
1922	J. M. Clark, *Studies in the Economics of Overhead Costs.*
1932	A. A. Berle and G. Means, *The Modern Corporation and Private Property;* Joan Robinson, *The Economics of Imperfect Competition;* Edward H. Chamberlin, *The Theory of Monopolistic Competition.*
1930s	First quantitative studies of industrial organization begin.
1939	Concentration ratios first published, by National Resources Commission.
1939–41	Hearings and reports by the Temporary National Economic Committee.
1942	J. A. Schumpeter, *Capitalism, Socialism and Democracy.*
1940s & 1950s	The "Mason group" at Harvard does a series of industry studies.
Late 1940s	G. W. Stocking and Myron W. Watkins, *Cartels or Competition?;* Corwin D. Edwards, *Maintaining Competition.*
1949	W. J. Fellner, *Competition among the Few.*
1952	J. K. Galbraith, *American Capitalism: The Theory of Countervailing Power.*
1956	J. S. Bain, *Barriers to New Competition.*
1959	C. Kaysen and D. F. Turner, *Antitrust Policy: An Economic and Legal Analysis.*
1960s	Econometric studies by L. W. Weiss, E. Mansfield, W. G. Shepherd, W. S. Comanor, F. M. Scherer, L. E. Preston, M. Gort, C. H. Berry and others.

FIGURE 2-5
The Interrelated World of Industrial Organization, Public Policy, and "Reality"

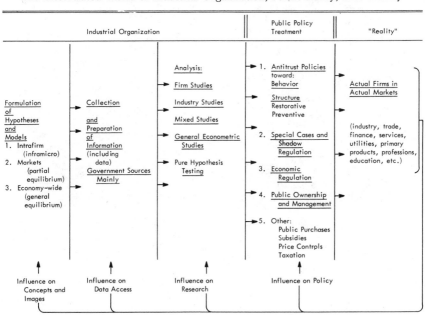

New problems arise (e.g., computer industry, conglomerate mergers, energy disequilibrium); old ones fade away.

Edward S. Mason (born 1899) founded at Harvard the modern study of industrial organization during 1938–55. His group included Joe S. Bain, Carl Kaysen, James W. McKie, Jesse Markham, Morris Adelman.

Joseph A. Schumpeter (1883–1950) described competition as a sequence of temporary monopolies in disequilibrium, in a process of creative destruction—the antithesis of neoclassical competitive equilibrium conditions.

Henry C. Simons (1901–47) a leader of the original "Chicago school," favored restructuring of industrial monopolies and public ownership of "natural" monopolies.

Joe S. Bain (born 1912) developed the structure-behavior-performance   format for analyzing industrial organization. He also stressed entry barriers as an element of structure.

1896–1904. They are now prominent in banking, minerals, manufacturing industry, utilities and retailing, but they coexist with great numbers of small and microscopic firms. When Galbraith speaks of the "technostructure" and "planning system" in large firms,—and others speak of "giant" megacorps—this extends to about 15 percent of national income.[5] Its role is augmented by (1) the special importance of banking, industry, and utilities, and (2) the loose network of financial and corporate ties surrounding large firms. The larger banks keep close ties with various of the larger firms (see Chapter 11).

The share of the largest firms in the entire economy is middling, rather than tiny or dominant. The largest 100 firms cover about 10–15 percent of economic activity (employees and value added). Yet in manufacturing alone, the largest 100 industrials have some 35 percent and their share of assets is just about 50 percent. Within finance, there is even greater dominance. There is thus a core of large firms which do have stability and large financial status.[6]

A small group of extra-large firms—about ten industrials, ten banks, five insurance firms, five retailers, and one telephone firm—do stand out as extra-large. But they are specialized, not an archetype for all markets.[7] Indeed, many large firms are unable to maintain efficiency. Despite much corporate rhetoric, the medium-size and small firm is the common form of enterprise.

Has the share of large firms in the economy been rising? Probably, though we cannot be sure. The rise is not fast, and other factors—financial ties and shares in individual markets—determine market power more closely. The rise was rapid during 1880–1904, 1920–29, and 1945–65, thanks to mergers and different growth rates in industries (see Figures 2–6 and 2–7).

Large firms are widely owned, but institutions (bank trust departments, insurance firms, pension funds, etc.) hold large blocks of their shares. Institutions now dominate securities trading, especially in the shares of the largest firms. This world of professional investing deals in advance information, gained from close study and from the network of financial ties and access which extends out from Wall Street (see also Chapters 11 and 12).

In many other countries, the share of large firms in the economy is higher. And in Britain, France, Japan, and West Germany the share has been rising more markedly in recent years. There are also closer ties between large firms and their banks, and there is even less shifting of these ties than in the U.S. A sizable minority of these firms and banks are publicly owned, in whole or part (see Chapter 19). Yet even the largest

---

[5] J. K. Galbraith, *The New Industrial State* (Boston: Houghton Mifflin, 1967) and *Economics and the Public Purpose* (Boston: Houghton Mifflin, 1973).

[6] See A. D. H. Kaplan, *Big Enterprise in a Competitive System,* rev. ed. (Washington, D.C.: Brookings Institution, 1965), and J. M. Blair, *Economic Concentration* (New York: Harcourt, Brace and Jovanovich, 1972).

[7] Almost all of the largest 25 industrial firms are either (1) in mature standardized product industries (automobiles, oil, and steel), or (2) holding companies. Medium size is the common form for producing firms.

FIGURE 2–6

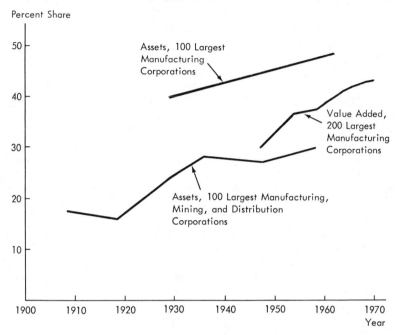

Percent Share

Assets, 100 Largest Manufacturing Corporations

Value Added, 200 Largest Manufacturing Corporations

Assets, 100 Largest Manufacturing, Mining, and Distribution Corporations

1900   1910   1920   1930   1940   1950   1960   1970

Year

FIGURE 2–7
Mergers in U.S. Mining and Manufacturing, 1895–1973

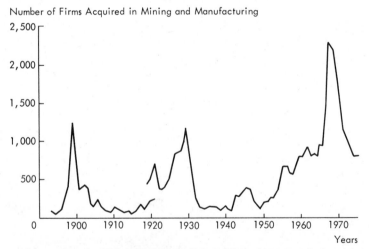

Number of Firms Acquired in Mining and Manufacturing

Years

Sources: Data for 1895–1920, Ralph L. Nelson, *Merger Movements in American Industry, 1895–1956* (Princeton: Princeton University Press, 1959), Table B-7; for 1919–1940, Willard L. Thorp, "The Merger Movement," in *The Structure of Industry*, Temporary National Economic Committee, Monograph No. 27 (Washington, D.C.: U.S. Government Printing Office, 1941), Part III, pp. 231–34; for 1940 to the present, U.S. Cabinet Committee on Price Stability, *Studies By the Staff* (Washington, D.C.: U.S. Government Printing Office, 1969); and recent trade sources.

foreign firms are usually half or less the size of their American counter-parts.

Many large firms receive large public subsidies for R & D and other work. These are mostly in aerospace and electronics, and the very largest firms are not heavily dependent. But the flows are important for an important set of firms (see also Chapters 25 and 29). Abroad, subsidies are also large, often intended to offset the American subsidies! Altogether, many large firms rely on large public subsidies and protections.

Multinational Firms. Many of the largest firms are heavily involved abroad, where their operations often earn profit rates higher than the firm draws in the U.S. This complicates our understanding of their American role and makes U.S. policy toward them more difficult. It also stirs anxieties abroad, where multinationals are accused of competing unfairly, of draining off resources and profits, and of eroding national sovereignty.

The issue comes and goes, and such firms have had a long history, from the East India Company on. They were already extensive by 1900 (see Table 2–5). They usually have a secure U.S. market position—examples are IBM, General Motors, Ford, Procter and Gamble, Eastman Kodak, Gillette and Coca-Cola—and are indeed able to direct large resources among countries and exert bargaining power. They often out-compete local firms by aggressiveness and modern techniques, as well as by drawing on their U.S. resources.

Though they are usually less unfair than charged, their global scope puts them beyond the reach of most national policies. Thus, they shift currency reserves to cope with exchange-rate crises, and thereby make the crises worse. And much of their activity transcends any antitrust control. Some of the largest multinationals are foreign. They stand even further above domestic controls in their home countries. American firms have entered deeply into foreign markets from the 1920s on. Only since about 1965 have foreign firms entered U.S. markets on any scale. The

TABLE 2–5

Number of Foreign Manufacturing Subsidiaries of 187 U.S.-controlled Multinational Enter-prises, by Area, Selected Years 1901–67

Area	1901	1913	1919	1929	1939	1950	1959	1967
Canada	6	30	61	137	169	225	330	443
Europe and								
United Kingdom 37		72	84	226	335	363	677	1,438
France 8		12	12	36	52	54	98	223
Germany 10		15	18	43	50	47	97	211
United Kingdom 13		23	28	78	128	146	221	356
Other Europe 6		22	26	69	105	116	261	648
Southern dominions 1		3	8	25	69	99	184	361
Latin America 3		10	20	56	114	259	572	950
Other 0		1	7	23	28	42	128	454
Total 47		116	180	467	715	988	1,891	3,646

Source: J. W. Vaupel and J. P. Curhan, *The Making of Multinational Enterprise* (Boston: Harvard Business School, 1969), chap. 3.

TABLE 2–6

The 20 Largest Industrial and Retailing Corporations, 1948: Assets in 1948 and Rank 1909–73

Rank								1948 Assets
1909	*1919*	*1929*	*1935*	*1948*	*1960*	*1973*	*Company*	*(million dollars*
2	2	2	1	1	1	1	Standard Oil Co. (New Jersey)...	$3,526
—	5	3	3	2	2	2	General Motors Corp.	2,958
1	1	1	2	3	3	14	United States Steel Corp.	2,535
—	30	4	5	4	9	13	Standard Oil Co. (Indiana)	1,500
—	9	7	4	5	7	7	Socony Mobil Oil Co., Inc.	1,443
95	16	9	11	6	6	3	Texaco, Inc.	1,322
30	18	12	9	7	8	19	E. I. du Pont de Nemours & Co.	1,304
—	36	15	12	8	5	10	Gulf Oil Corp.	1,191
16	11	11	13	9	11	12	General Electric Co.	1,177
—	7	6	6	10	4	4	Ford Motor Co.................	1,149
—	24	10	10	11	10	11	Standard Oil Co. of California ...	1,075
36	6	5	7	12	12	24	Bethlehem Steel Corp	1,029
46	29	30	27	13	14	8	Sears, Roebuck & Co.	789
—	20	25	22	14	16	23	Union Carbide Corp.	723
—	15	16	16	15	21	*	Sinclair Oil Corp.	710
25	28	29	33	16	20	21	Westinghouse Electric Corp.	694
3	19	28	23	17	42	52	American Tobacco Co.	687
6	13	17	14	18	22	35	International Harvester Co.	672
5	14	8	8	19	28	83	Anaconda Co...................	660
55	55	23	32	20	17	20	Western Electric Co.	650

* Merged with another firm.
Source: A. D. H. Kaplan, *Big Enterprise in a Competitive System*, rev. ed. (Washington, D.C.: Brooking Institution, 1965), p. 148, and *Fortune* magazine, *The Fortune 500 Directory* (New York: Time-Life, 1974).

scale is still small, and in most cases it is by imports rather than plants in the U.S.

A new wrinkle since 1972 is the increasing Arab power against oil firms and their spreading purchases of shares in western firms. This may become an acute issue as Arab oil revenues swell to a flood. Though the Arab interests were still moving gingerly as of 1975, they could in principle acquire control of a large share of western industrial capacity, at current market values for shares (see also Chapter 26).

Although there are dynamic elements in the economy, the whole array of large firms has become remarkably stable (see Table 2–6 and also section 4 below). Conglomerate mergers and changes in weapons purchases have caused certain shifts in recent years, and there is some movement as whole industries rise and wane.[8] But the top ranks in all

---

[8] And there has been much name-changing in recent years, to spruce up images or seek anonymity. Try matching up the names:

Old	New
Swift and Co., Standard Oil (New Jersey), U.S. Rubber, Sanitary Food Stores, General Aniline and Film, Montgomery Ward, National Dairy Products, Electric Storage Battery, Corn Products Co., National Cylinder Gas, United Fruit Co., Standard Railway Equipment.	Safeway, ESB Industries, GAF, United Brands, Uniroyal, Exxon, CPC International, Esmark, Stanray, Chemetron, Marcor, Kraftco.

Correct matchings are given in footnote 73, Chapter 9.

FIGURE 2-8

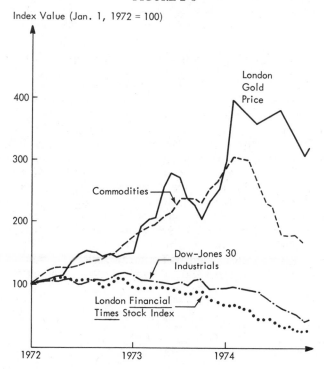

Index Value (Jan. 1, 1972 = 100)

London Gold Price

Commodities

Dow–Jones 30 Industrials

London Financial Times Stock Index

sectors now change relatively little.[9] Abroad, there is rather less stability, because mergers and the vagaries of international competition have had more effect than in the U.S. Even so, the leading firms and banks—and the ties among them—tend to be quite stable in all industrial economies.

Not all is static, and large risks and shocks do occur. In 1972–75 there were radical changes in many commodity prices and supplies. Many stock prices routinely ride the roller coaster. Shareholders are often rapidly enriched or pauperized. And the market as a whole gives and takes away massive amounts (see Figure 2-8 for examples). During 1969–70, for example, the decline on Wall Street wiped out $300 *billion* of stock values, nearly 40 percent of the whole. The 1973–74 bear market drop was more severe, with averages for the entire market plunging more than 50 percent. A 1972–74 slide in British stocks cut their total value from $158 billion to less than $50 billion. Foreign exchange rates also undergo large shifts. A portion of the labor force faces risks of lay-offs and loss of pension rights.

---

[9] This is partly because the dispersion of growth rates among industries has narrowed. The earlier surges of major new industries (autos, oil, chemicals, steel) are no longer so common. Anne O. Krueger, *Structural Change in the U.S. Economy* (Cambridge: Harvard University Press, 1969), and recent forecasting by economic models, make this clear.

In this rugged world, participants in the economy routinely accept risks and incur losses, even severe ones. Therefore, policy choices need not be hamstrung by trying to protect against all risks and impacts.

DETERMINANTS OF STRUCTURE

The rest of this chapter is about individual markets. We first ask what factors might shape market structure, how tight that influence is, and how much market power it necessitates.

Economies of scale in production are the most basic possible factor. They arise both within the *plant* and at the *firm*—i.e., multiplant—level. They reflect (1) the technology of the factory floor, (2) transport costs (if high, they inhibit centralizing in one big plant), and (3) problems in coordinating multiplant operations. Scale economies may be either technical or pecuniary. *Technical* economies are real, arising from actual organization in the firm. *Pecuniary* economies are strictly monetary, stemming merely from lower prices on inputs. Only technical economies count as a social justification for market power.

The present research consensus is that technical economies of scale are real but limited in most industries.[10] As illustrated in Figure 2–9,

FIGURE 2–9

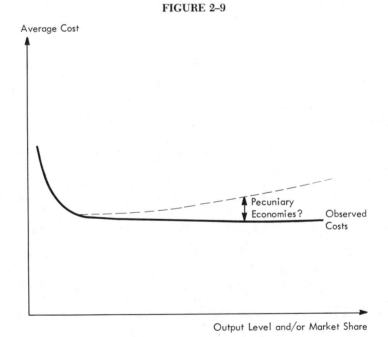

[10] The leading studies are Joe S. Bain, *Barriers to New Competition* (Cambridge: Harvard University Press, 1956), and F. M. Scherer, "The Determinants of Industrial Plant Sizes in Six Nations," *Review of Economics and Statistics,* May, 1973, pp. 135–45. See also W. G. Shepherd, *Market Power and Economic Welfare* (New York: Random House, 1970), Chapter 11; and John M. Blair, *Economic Concentration* (New York: Harcourt Brace Jovanovich, 1972).

minimum efficient scale is usually reached at a modest share in most markets. There is a long stretch of constant costs, above which diseconomies may set in.

Large firms now commonly expand not by enlarging old plants but by building new ones, and the newer plants are not built on an ever larger scale. Indeed, there is a trend toward smaller size; in 67 among 115 industries from 1947 to 1958, the share of output coming from the 8 largest plants actually declined. In many fields, new developments in technology appear to make for operation on a smaller scale. Transport by truck and the ability to transmit electricity over long distances permit decentralization.

New materials, such as the light metals, alloys, and plastics, and new processes, such as molding, welding, stamping, and die-casting, require less heavy machinery than did older ones. Light, multipurpose machines —independently operated, readily transferred from product to product and moved from place to place, run at varying speeds and turned on and off at will—displace the massive, rigid installations of an earlier day. The growth of technology, in the past, made for greater size. In many cases, now, it works the other way. In nearly all industries, plants with less than one or two percent of the market are quite as efficient as larger ones, and often they are more efficient.

At the level of the firm as a whole, the evidence is less one-sided. Both Bain and Scherer have found "multiplant economies"—the advantages of running plants as a group—to be slight or absent in most cases. And there are obvious bureaucratic problems in managing large firms, as layers of authority and coordination pile up above the basic plant operations. Top managers often bog down in complexity and the sheer mass of detail. Or they may lose touch with what is going on, adrift in tenth-hand information. Responsibility may dissipate and factions set in. Still, modern techniques and a computer may make close controls possible. And there may be economies in other company activities. Presently, proven multiplant economies are slight in most industries. But there may be exceptions.

Economies of innovation might favor high market shares. An intense debate in the 1950s suggested that large firms generally, and oligopoly in particular, are more innovative.[11] But research in the 1960s has reversed the burden of proof. Small scale and individual situations appear to be best for *invention*.[12] And though some *innovations* have required massive resources, many do not or can instead be financed from outside by small firms. Also, market shares above about 20 percent tend to retard innovation. Dominant firms commonly have incentives to follow and

---

[11] Recall Schumpeter's view from Chapter 1; and see J. K. Galbraith, *American Capitalism* (New York: Houghton Mifflin, 1956). The 1950s flowering of discussion was not the first; earlier versions were in vogue in the 1890s and 1920s.

[12] A theoretical basis for this is given in Kenneth J. Arrow, "Economic Welfare and the Allocation of Resources for Invention," in *The Rate and Direction of Inventive Activity,* National Bureau of Economic Research, Princeton University Press, 1962. A persuasive review of practical instances is in J. Jewkes, R. Sawers, and R. Stillerman, *The Sources of Invention,* rev. ed. (New York: St. Martin's Press, 1968).

imitate the innovations of others, not to lead.[13] And this is borne out in practice.[14] In any case, only a narrow set of industries have a high degree of innovation (aerospace, drugs, etc.), and so the issue is specialized. And public grants cover most of the R & D in most of those industries, so the underlying economic factors are not clear.

Advertising may also cause economies of scale, as national advertising is spread over high sales volume. Yet much advertising is merely *persuasive,* not *informative,* and so that part has little or no social value. And advertising is a large factor in only a small group of industries (toiletries, cereals, drugs, beer, cigarettes).

All of these factors provide little or no social justification for more than a scattering of market shares above 15 or 20 percent in industry, trade, banking and services. Nor do they justify high barriers to entry in most industries. The possible exceptions are: (1) utilities, during their early and middle life-cycle (see Chapter 13); (2) certain industries during their initial stages, and (3) a very few industries with extensive technical scale economies. In smaller economies abroad, a higher degree of market power may naturally occur, if the same basic technology prevails.[15] Research on these determinants is still in progress, but its findings persuasively place the burden of proof against market power even in utilities. The old cults of bigness and of R & D are now reduced to faith, for the facts do not sustain them.

STRUCTURE

How much market power is there, in fact? What is its trend? Does it last or fade away naturally?

Market power reaches high levels in a sizable minority of the economy. The firm's market share is the basic indicator. There is virtual monopoly in most utilities and market shares over 50 percent in a number of large industries and banking markets (see Table 2–7). These are known cases; secrecy hides many others, especially within diversified firms and at the regional and local levels. Concentration ratios (the total share of the largest four firms in each industry) roughly reflect the degree of oligopoly in manufacturing industries.[16] Properly adjusted to fit true market boundaries, they suggest that the typical industry is a moder-

---

[13] For a technical analysis, see F. M. Scherer, "Research and Development Resource Allocation Under Rivalry," *Quarterly Journal of Economies,* 1967, pp. 359–94.

[14] See Edwin Mansfield *et al, Industrial Research and Technological Innovation* (New York: Norton, 1973); and F. M. Scherer, *Industrial Market Structure and Economic Performance* (Chicago: Rand McNally, 1970).

[15] There has been good research on this. See Joe S. Bain, *International Differences in Industrial Structure* (New Haven: Yale University Press, 1965); C. F. Pratten, *Economies of Scale in Manufacturing Industries* (Cambridge: At the University Press, 1971); and F. M. Scherer, *op. cit.*

[16] They are available for 1935, 1947, 1954, 1958, 1963, 1966, 1967, and 1970. Data on less than four firms per industry are kept permanently secret by the U.S. Census. Other data on structure and financial ties are either not collected or are kept under strict secrecy.

2 / The Modern Economy

TABLE 2-7
Leading Cases of Substantial Market Power

| Utilities | Approximate Shares of the Largest | | Entry Barriers? |
	Firm	Four Firms	
Telephones	100	—	High
Electricity	100	—	High
Gas	100	—	High
Water and sewage	100	—	High
Urban transit	100	—	High
Industry			
Computers	70	85	High
Telephone equipment	95+	100	High
Automobiles	45	85	High
Heavy electrical equipment	50	100	High
Drugs	(50)*	(90)	High
Photographic film	70	100	High
Copying equipment	85	95	High
Industrial chemicals	45	80	Medium
Soaps and detergents	50	95	Medium
Aircraft and engines	50	100	High
Iron and steel	(35)	(70)	High
Petroleum refining	(35)	(70)	High
Cereals	45	95	High
Locomotives	75	100	High
Banking			
San Francisco	44	83	High
New York	19	58	High
Chicago	19	49	High
Los Angeles	32	77	High
Boston	37	75	High
Buffalo	51	96	High
100 smallest metropolitan areas	(50)	(96)	High

* Parentheses indicate an average of regional and product submarkets.

ately tight oligopoly.[17] There is a wide spread around the average degree of concentration at 60 percent (see Figure 2–10). But the normal condition is for every lasting firm to have some position—some identity and continuity—in its market. Accordingly, most markets have a concentration of at least 25 percent.

[17] Several studies confirm this, including Carl Kaysen and Donald F. Turner, *Antitrust Policy* (Cambridge: Harvard University Press, 1959); and W. G. Shepherd, *Market Power and Economic Welfare* (New York: Random House, 1970).

Official concentration ratios published by the Census Bureau are based on national totals. But many industries have distinct regional and local markets within them, where true concentration is higher. Also the industry definitions tend to be too broad. Imports also need to be adjusted for in a few industries. The net effect is that official ratios seriously understate true concentration, probably by over 20 percent on average. Examples: newspapers are listed at 14 percent concentration, but are really near 100 percent in most markets. Bread, milk, bricks, ready-mix cement, etc. are all similar. Figure 2–10 reflects one revision of the official ratios to reflect reality more closely. Other studies fit the same broad lesson.

FIGURE 2-10

Concentration Patterns in American Manufacturing Industries

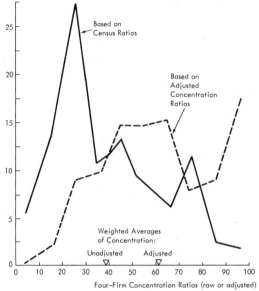

Value-Added in Industries in Each Concentration Bracket, as a Percent Share of All Value-Added in All Manufacturing

Four-Firm Concentration Ratios (raw or adjusted)

Source: W. G. Shepherd, *Market Power and Economic Welfare* (New York: Random House, 1970); and more recent data.

Barriers to entry also vary, from low to very high. They can only be estimated, often by guesswork covering a subjective mixture of barrier factors. But they appear to reinforce high market shares in a number of major industries. Many of them are created by *public* policies, as we will see later in the book.

Altogether, there is a core of major monopolies and tight oligopolies. Most of them probably go well beyond the levels needed for economies of scale. There is also much petty market power in small-scale local trades—petty, but it adds up to a lot. On the whole, the degree of monopoly in the U.S.—the core cases and the average for all industry—is at least as great as it is in other industrial economies.[18]

These formal market positions are often embedded in a web of informal agreements and ties which increase the actual degree of market power. Financial relationships often have such a restrictive role, with banks having interests in two or more competitors.[19] These ties are little known and hard to evaluate, but in some cases they are quite strong.

---

[18] They are quite visible to consumers and students. They include breakfast cereals, camera supplies (Eastman Kodak and Polaroid), razor blades (Gillette), Xeroxing, soda pop (Coca-Cola), soups (Campbell), newspapers, telephones, mail, medical services, computers, automobiles, drugs, toiletries, and even golf and tennis balls.

[19] These "interlocks" are often extensive, as massive Congressional reports have shown.

Abroad, such agreements are normally stronger than in the U.S., often taking elaborate and binding forms.

Is the trend of monopoly upward? It seemed so—and probably was—in industry during 1890–1904, in the 1930s, and in 1945–63. But the averages for manufacturing now seem steady. The rise of certain conglomerate firms in the 1960s scarcely affected the broad structural patterns. About the rest of the economy, one can only guess at a rough constancy.

A wave of banking mergers in 1950–63 raised shares in large-city banking markets, but there has been some reversion since then. Some utilities—electrical, railroads, telecommunications, postal—may have undergone slight competitive inroads since 1950. But there are countertendencies. The largely noncompetitive weapons sector has blossomed, as have the highly monopolized health, sports, and urban services sectors. Certain monopoly social enterprises (such as Medicare and schools) have had an expanding role. The net effect of these shifts cannot be neatly assessed.

FIGURE 2–11

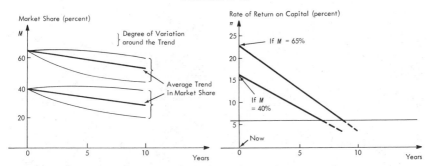

Does market power decay naturally? It could, either by free choice of the firm (discussed above) or by competitive pressure. If it did fade rapidly, policy treatments would not be needed. The point is crucial and defines one's whole outlook on the problem of market power.

In fact, a moderate decay process does appear to exist in industry. Market shares above 50 percent tend to fade about 1 point per year, while high profit rates probably go down somewhat faster (see Figure 2–11). Normally, a high and lucrative market share will last only a decade or two; the odds against keeping a very high share and profit rate more than ten years are very high.

Yet most of the core U.S. cases have somehow defied this tendency. Most of those in Table 2–8 have been in place for decades, some for nearly a century. The natural decline of such firms was much more rapid during 1910–35.[20] Possibly the rate of decay has slowed across all markets.

---

[20] See Kaplan, *op. cit.;* Blair, *op. cit.;* and W. G. Shepherd, *The Treatment of Market Power* (New York: Columbia University Press, 1975).

John D. Rockefeller (1839–1937) founded the Standard Oil monopoly during 1870–80 by a variety of pricing tactics, railroad rebates, and astute buying out of competitors. By 1900 he had retired from direct management and moved into other financial activities. These developed into parity with the Morgan group. (Shown about 1910.)

James B. Duke (1856–1925) created American Tobacco's monopoly during 1880–90 by a series of aggressive tactics. (Shown about 1900.)

J. Pierpont Morgan (1837–1913), the leading financier of his time, was instrumental in forming the U.S. Steel Corporation in 1901 and other major trusts. (Shown about 1900.)

George Eastman (1854–1932) founded Eastman Kodak Company in 1892, which dominated the industry by its celluloid film and convenient small cameras. Brilliant, urbane, solitary, and meticulous, he introduced profit-sharing and set high standards while establishing the firm's leading position. He is shown in 1890, already the leader in his industry.

Pierre S. du Pont (1870–1954), a pivotal figure in modern industrial organization. He developed du Pont's gunpowder monopoly and then negotiated a mild divestiture in 1911–13. During 1915–25 he guided General Motors' rise to dominance in the automobile industry. (Shown 1902.)

Thomas J. Watson (1874–1956) established International Business Machines as the dominant tabulating-machine firm by 1930. In the early 1950s, his sons overcame his opposition to IBM's shift into electronic computers. (Shown in 1951.)

TABLE 2–8
Leading Dominant Firms as of 1973, and Their Background

Sales Rank 1973	Firm	Markets	Estimated Average Market Share (percent)	Barriers	Average Rate of Return on Equity, 1960–73 (percent)	Present Position Dates Back to About
1	General Motors	Autos, locomotives, buses	55	High	20	1927
8	IBM	Computers, typewriters	70	High	18	1954
12	Western Electric	Telecommunication equipment	98	High	9	1880s
5	General Electric	Heavy electrical equipment	50	High	15	1900
25	Eastman Kodak	Photographic supplies	70	Medium	20	1900
41	Xerox	Copying equipment	85	High	24	1961
30	Procter & Gamble	Detergents, toiletries	50	Medium	17	1940s
59	United Aircraft	Aircraft engines	60	Medium	11	1950s
69	Coca-Cola	Flavoring syrups	50	Medium	19	1920s
139	Campbell Soup	Canned soups	85	Medium	13	1920s
235	Polaroid	Instant cameras	60	Medium	19	1950
158	Gillette	Razors, toiletries	70	Medium	28	1910
197	Kellogg	Dry cereals	45	Medium	20	1940s
229	*Times Mirror*	Newspaper	70	High	13	1960
394	*New York Times*	Newspaper	75	High	15	1966
	Various drug firms	Drugs	50–90	High	21	1950s

Source: *Fortune, Directory of the Largest 500 Industrial Corporations,* yearly; and various other references.

In any case it is now very low for the leading U.S. cases of market power. This is attested by comparison with Britain. There nearly half of the comparable leading cases of market power have undergone major changes in the 1960s. In several cases (automobiles, tobacco, and cement), dominant firms have chronically dwindled over time. Other cases are under direct government influence (steel, electrical equipment, computers). The contrast with the stability of American dominant firms is most marked in the largest industries (automobiles, computers, electrical equipment, telephone apparatus, and oil). And there has been in American industry nothing like the inroads of U.S. and other firms into many major U.K. industries. In all, market power in the U.S. is older, more stable, and less under public control.

On the whole, a good share of U.S. industry deviates from the degree of monopoly dictated by technology. The trend is not up, but there seems little tendency for the main deviations to be self-correcting. This stability probably arises from financial ties and various public policies, as well as defensive tactics by the firms.[21]

EFFECTS OF MARKET POWER

The effects of monopoly power were stated broadly in Chapter 1. Now they will be analyzed in some detail.[22] These effects define the yields for public policies; if market power had no effects, policies to treat it could have no positive social yields.

Financial markets tend to imprint their structure upon markets in other sectors (see also Chapter 11). They are usually tight oligopolies. This probably limits competition in many markets, for entrants and small firms often find the leading banks already committed to the established larger firms. Financial structure also increases insider problems, for timely information—the key to capital gains—is more confined to small circles of bankers and professional investors.

Prices are raised above costs in some degree. In most industrial cases, the rise is below 25 percent of costs, but instances of 100, 500, or even 1,000 percent are known. Price discrimination is also done systematically, especially at market shares of over 50 percent. Price-cost ratios for some customers may be as much as a multiple of those set for users with elastic demand (see Chapter 6). Such discrimination is often the means both for exploiting market power and for maintaining it.

Profitability is increased by market power. For each 10 points of market share (see Figure 2–12), the profit rate usually rises about 2.5 points. This reaches a rich harvest for market shares over 40 or 50 percent. At 70 percent of the market, profits may reach an average of 25 percent of

---

[21] Policies probably adding to monopoly include patents, bias in antitrust enforcement, R & D subsidies, tariffs, and utility franchises. Each is treated later in the book.

[22] For further detail on these patterns and how they are researched, see F. M. Scherer, *Industrial Market Structure and Economic Performance* (Chicago: Rand McNally, 1970); and Shepherd, "The Elements of Market Structure," *Review of Economics and Statistics,* February 1972, pp. 25–37.

equity, nearly triple the competitive rate. This *recorded* yield is lowered by X-inefficiency, so the total yield must be even higher (see below). Concentration is also related to profit rates, but of course more loosely (see Figure 2–12). Each 10 added points of concentration goes with about 1 extra point of profit rate. But the expected threshold at 50 percent

FIGURE 2–12

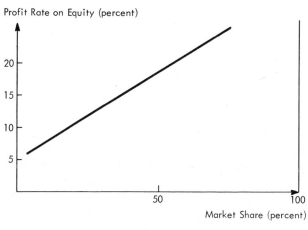

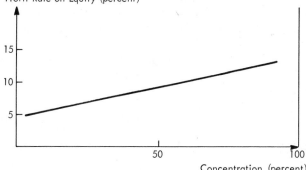

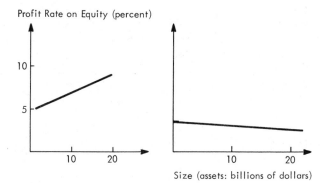

FIGURE 2–12 (continued)

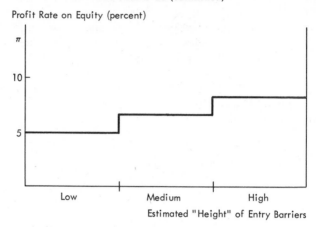

Profit Rate on Equity (percent)

concentration—the line roughly between loose and tight oligopoly—has not yet been solidly confirmed by research.[23]

Higher profits might be socially justified as a premium for greater risk. Capital theory and portfolio analysis have both suggested this for a long time.[24] Some industries *are* much riskier; that is one reason why managerial styles are so diverse (recall the first section).

The hypothesis of a positive general risk-return relationship has been tested in several ways, but so far with little success.[25] Risk is inevitably hard to measure, but several reasonably good indexes of it show little or no association with company rates of return. And in large stretches of industry—and on the over-the-counter stock market—returns are clearly *lower* where risk is *higher.* The risk-return hypothesis therefore does not dilute the observed link between market power and profit rates.

Bigness *per se* does not appear to add to the rate of return.[26] Many large firms are relatively low profit earners because of their size. This would contradict the likely advantages of bigness, as a source of leverage and power. Apparently, bigness incurs diseconomies of scale, so that the net gains to size are zero or slightly negative.

Intensive advertising, by contrast, does seem to yield relatively higher profitability, in those few advertising-intensive industries. Yet even there, advertising's punch is limited. Even at extreme levels of advertising intensity (20% of sales) the rate of return is not much higher than

[23] The importance of market share is affirmed in another thorough recent analysis; S. Schoefflei, R. D. Buzzell, and D. F. Heany, "Impact of Strategic Planning on Profit Performance," *Harvard Business Review* (March–April 1974), pp 137–45.

[24] See F. H. Knight's classic, *Risk, Uncertainty and Profit* (New York: Houghton Mifflin, 1921).

[25] These include I. N. Fisher and G. F. Hall, Jr., "Risk and Corporate Rates of Return," *Quarterly Journal of Economics,* 1969, pp. 79–92; and Shepherd, *The Treatment of Market Power, op. cit.,* Chapter 4.

[26] This surprising fact has been confirmed by nearly every recent study. See Shepherd, *op. cit.,* and sources cited there.

the competitive rate. Therefore advertising is a lesser influence on profits than is market share.[27]

More generally, entry barriers of various kinds (from size, advertising, R & D, or other sources) do not seem to be central elements of market structure. They matter somewhat, in cross-section evidence, but they are weaker than market share itself (see Figure 2–12). The policy implication is that treatments of market power should focus mainly on market share and only moderately on entry barriers. There will be exceptions to this, of course, where a specific barrier is clearly important, owing to a key patent or mineral right, for example. But these are departures from the rule.

These effects confirm the central role of market share. It is the key to excess profits, and so businessmen are sound in focusing their efforts on it (recall the motives in the first section). Wise public policy will deal primarily and precisely with market shares, rather than trying only to control concentration or entry barriers.

To some extent these profit yields might reflect economies of scale, as was discussed in the section just before. But as we have seen in the "Determinants of Structure" section above, these economies usually are relatively slight.

Market power also reduces *efficiency*. A degree of internal inefficiency usually emerges in secure firms, reaching perhaps 3–5 percent of costs on average when market shares reach 70 percent. Allocative inefficiency also occurs (the M triangle in Figure 1–3), but it is diffuse and has proven difficult to measure. These two types of loss, plus the share of advertising which is merely persuasive, probably total to about 3 percent of national income.

Technical progress is also probably retarded in dominant firms. Research suggests the form shown in Figure 2–13, with innovation fastest in firms with modest market shares. At high market shares, the firm slips more into an imitator's role (see Chapter 9). We do not know this precisely, for innovation eludes easy measurement. Also, federal policies have affected it artificially (recall the earlier discussion and see Chapter 25).

The effect on *equity* arises from the profit effects shown in Figure 2–12. The flows capitalize directly into wealth and can be realized immediately. The whole impact is large and has shaped wealth and social status, especially since 1890–1910.

These excess returns are, alas, no longer available direct to new investors nowadays. The market power was capitalized when it arose, often decades ago. In well-functioning capital markets, all returns are equalized. [Try to locate monopoly returns in the stock exchange pages of the *Wall Street Journal* or other paper. Work out your possible returns on stocks of the firms in Table 2–8, or other firms you know to be thriving.]

Who then reaps the gains, and how? Answer: he who hears first, has

---

[27] Also, only a few industries have intensive advertising. In recent years the highest advertising-sales ratios were: perfumes 15 percent, cereals 10 percent, drugs 10 percent, soaps 9 percent, beer 7 percent, pop 6 percent, clocks 6 percent, wines and cigarettes 5 percent. All others were less.

FIGURE 2–13
Real Effects of Market Power

Average Addition to Costs (percent of total costs)

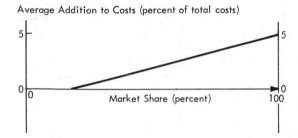

Difference in Rate of Technical Progress
(as a percent of yearly total costs)

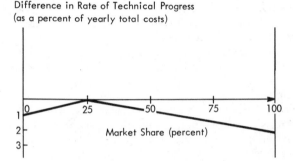

cash (or can buy on margin), and moves quickly. Otherwise, one can merely put one's money *early* on the monopolist in a new fast-growing industry—and hope. [Try, for practice, locating the firms which paid off best in the last ten years (look in Moody's *Investors Handbook* at the library). Can you list ten *future* such industries and the leading firm in each? Who would know this (professional investors? bankers? economists?)?]

And as structure has stabilized in recent decades, the structure of wealth also has hardened. This disparity has been only marginally affected by taxation or other public policies. Most of this family wealth has long since been detached from its original monopoly sources (recall that capital markets capitalize quickly). And many heirs have had favored access to positions in financial firms. Therefore, the older equity effects are deeply set and immune to action towards the markets themselves.

Fairness in employment has also been lessened. Most minority groups and women appear to face job discrimination at managerial levels in most firms holding market power.[28]

---

[28] This is increasingly clear both from research and from a series of major cases and settlements involving job discrimination in a very large number of the largest corporations. See also W. G. Shepherd and Sharon G. Levin, "Managerial Discrimination in Large Firms," *Review of Economics and Statistics,* November 1973, and W. G. Shepherd, "Market Power and Racial Discrimination in White-Collar Employment," *Antitrust* Bulletin, XIV (Spring 1969), pp. 141–161.

Altogether, the marginal social costs of market power are high. As a firm's market share goes above 20 percent, each added 10 points will normally add possibly 2 percent to social costs. And equity will also be appreciably reduced. There are exceptions to this rule, where scale economies, the conditions of innovation, or managerial skill depart from the norm. But the basic patterns hold.

Is It "Monopoly Capitalism"? Yes and no. Some perceptive observers have long regarded the U.S. economy as dominated by powerful firms under a financial plutocracy.[29] In these views, capitalists control power and wealth, while workers barely subsist because a reserve army of unemployed keeps wages down. Monopoly rises. Depressions grow more severe, and the disparity increases between the moneyed few and the propertyless many. The economy is driven toward militarism, and the nation attempts to dominate and exploit underdeveloped lands abroad. In short, there is Monopoly Capitalism and Imperialism.

In fact, market power is serious—much more serious than is commonly recognized—but it is not pervasive. There is a gentle trend toward greater aggregate concentration, but the economy is still in more than a few hands. High finance does exert some control. Wealth holdings are highly skewed and the disparities are not narrowing, on the whole. It is possible to go from poor to rich, but not easy or common. Fluctuations now are milder than Depressions, but they are not small. And there is now chronic underemployment, especially among a reserve army of unskilled minority groups (Western Europe also has its reserve army of foreign workers, *gastarbeiters,* now at about 25 percent of the labor force in many countries). The degree of reliance on military spending and exploitation of foreign resources may not be full-blown imperialism, but (especially in the 1960s) some element of it has existed. And the political process (the State) is swayed by financial and industrial interests, of the upper middle classes generally (see Chapter 4).

In these matters, one can select out facts for almost any viewpoint. But many conditions of monopoly capitalism are palpably present in some degree. Some of it can be abated by public policies; some of it feeds upon them. It has been much the same in the U.S. for a century or more, and it seems likely so to continue.

FIVE LEADING CASES

To show how these forms, causes and effects come together in real markets, this section reviews five prominent instances of market power.

Telephones. American Telephone and Telegraph Company (AT&T). Holding company for the Bell System (see Chapter 16), it has owned, supplied, and operated the main telephone system in the United States since the 1880s. It is the largest private firm in existence, with over 1

---

[29] Marx and Marxians are only one group among these critics. There have also been critiques by Schumpeter (a devout *anti*-Marxian: see his *Capitalism, Socialism and Democracy, op. cit.*), J. A. Hobson, and many other distinguished observers. See also Galbraith, *op. cit.,* and B. J. Cohen, *The Question of Imperialism* (Baltimore: John Hopkins University Press, 1973) for varying conclusions.

million employees and $67 billion in assets (next is Exxon with $25 billion). Formed soon after Bell patented the telephone in 1876, it adroitly used the Bell patent to eliminate others (see Chapter 9). By 1910 it covered most cities and all long-distance traffic in the U.S. Its Western Electric Co. subsidiary has supplied virtually all Bell System equipment since 1881. In 1913, it agreed to stay out of telegraph activities and interconnect with smaller systems, as part of an agreement letting it retain Western Electric as its exclusive supplier. In 1937 the Federal Communications Commission was created, with power to regulate interstate telephone operations. In 1948–50, the Bell System gained exclusive control of microwave transmission, which carries much intercity traffic.

Since 1950 Bell's share of telephones has tapered down to 80 percent, because some suburban growth has been in independent company areas. But the hold on large cities and trunk traffic remains. FCC rulings since 1968 are leading to a degree of competition in trunk traffic and customers' equipment.

The basic monopoly position in operations and supply of apparatus remains. The rate of return, regulated by the FCC and state commissions (see Part IV), is about 10–12 percent on equity. Rate structure has been only loosely regulated. Bell Laboratories has a notable research record. Certain research, construction, and operations are done for U.S. military agencies (at about $200–300 million yearly). The Bell System draws considerable political influence from its size and operations in nearly all locales. Also, its stock is held by nearly three million citizens and most large institutional investors.

Computers.   International Business Machines Corporation (IBM). Formed in the 1920s, it has sold 90 percent of tabulating equipment and, since 1953, about 70 percent of computers (plus 90 percent of electric typewriters). Its worldwide share is comparable and generates much of its profits. It also has large shares in electric typewriters and dictating machines. Now the eighth largest U.S. industrial firm in sales, it has assets of $12 billion and 274,000 employees. Its capitalized market value, however, has recently been over $40 billion, well ahead of the next firms (AT&T, Eastman Kodak, and General Motors). This reflects its steady profit rate of 18 percent on equity and its strong future prospects.

IBM has cultivated a high technical reputation, but it is said by many industry experts to be imitative. IBM has not been able to keep up with Control Data and others in the giant computer end of the market. Successive computer generations (the third IBM generation was the 360 line, introduced in 1965) have raised computing speed and capacity by orders of magnitude. Founded by T. J. Watson (his ubiquitous THINK motto and company pep songs were famous), it was run by his sons Thomas, Jr., and Arthur during 1954–72.

Competitors have been numerous, but many have failed. (General Electric and RCA have both recently exited, after incurring large losses). Presently the next largest firm has less than 7 percent of the market, and several of them are still unprofitable. IBM has been sued for monopolizing by the Department of Justice in 1932, 1952, and 1968 (the latter case is not yet to trial in 1975), and by many private firms since 1968. Its position, reinforced by a superb sales network and a thorough system of price discrimination, still appears secure.

Pharmaceutical Products. Numerous firms, including American Home Products, Warner-Lambert, Bristol-Myers, Pfizer, Merck, Eli Lilly, Sterling and Upjohn. The drug industry is a mosaic of submarkets, of varying competitiveness. Several major ones are virtual monopolies, based on patents. The industry has arisen since the 1930s, led by penicillin and then other "wonder" drugs, including antibiotics and contraceptives. There is much research and product development, aimed at finding patentable new drugs and modifications of old ones. Since 1960, the rate of actual discovery and innovation in the industry has declined. Patents are fully exploited, and the profit rate on equity is over 20 percent for most firms. Production cost is often one-tenth or less of the price of a drug. Price discrimination is extreme, and the sales forces are large. The industry's social impact is greater than its size alone suggests.

Automobiles. General Motors Corporation (GM). The leading U.S. automobile, bus, and locomotive producer for several decades. Sales are $36 billion, assets $20 billion, and employees 810,000. Formed in 1910–15 and under Pierre du Pont's leadership during 1918–24, it gained over half the U.S. car market by 1927 and has held it since.[30] It now has about 50 percent of new-car sales revenue in the U.S. (over 70 percent of luxury-class cars), 60–70 percent of bus sales, and over 80 percent of locomotives. During the 1920s, it established frequent model changes as the industry practice.

It has five car-producing divisions—Chevrolet (much the largest; itself equal to Ford Motor Company's car production), Pontiac, Buick, Oldsmobile, and Cadillac. It operates some 22 major plants in many states. Its traditional method of decentralizing management was partially reversed in 1969. It is much larger than most estimates of minimum efficient scale. It has extensive overseas operations. Its profit rates on equity have averaged 18–20 percent in recent years.

Copying Equipment. Xerox Corporation. Its dominant position in dry-paper copying equipment is based on the patented selenium drum technology and a marketing strategy much like IBM's. The basic technology, originated by Chester Carlson in the 1930s and 1940s, was finally applied by the small Haloid-Xerox company in the late 1940s and 1950s (see Chapters 7 and 9). Since 1961 Xerox has gained phenomenal growth and over 85 percent of the market, in the U.S. and abroad (*e.g.*, 95 percent in Britain). Sales are now $3 billion yearly, employees 94,000, and profit rates on equity have averaged 25 percent since 1961.

Xerox machines are only rented, not sold, as part of a brilliant strategy of promotion and price discrimination. Around the basic patent (which expires in 1978) the firm has accumulated nearly 2,000 interrelated patents to secure and extend its position. The whole strategy of pricing, patents, and product formation now seems impervious to erosion. Recent entry by IBM has gained only a foothold. Reflecting these past and pro-

---

[30] This is covered in the excellent volume by A. D. Chandler, Jr., and S. Salsbury, *Pierre S. du Pont and the Making of the Modern Corporation* (New York: Harper & Row, 1971).

spective results, Xerox stock rose during 1961–72 by a multiple of nearly 100.

SUMMARY

In this chapter we have analyzed the firm, its setting, and its motives. The common life-cycle of industries was described. Next we reviewed the role of large firms, as it has evolved and stabilized. The rest of the chapter was about individual markets.

The determinants of structure do not prescribe more than a scattering of high market shares in the economy. But high degrees of market power do exist in an important group of industries, utilities, and financial markets. The problem is chronic, if not increasing. The main cases now appear to be nearly immune from the normal decay of market shares. Such market power has no small social cost, in lost efficiency, innovation, and equity.

There is thus a serious problem for policy to grapple with, in many parts of the economy. To give a sense of priority, Table 2–9 assembles the sectors most likely to offer high policy yields. Market power's forms, causes, and effects are reasonably well understood. The problem is manageable rather than rampant, focused rather than universal.

TABLE 2–9
Probable High-Policy-Yield Sectors during 1975–80

1. *Financial*	3. *Utilities* (infrastructure)
Commercial banks and trusts	Communications, including cable TV
Underwriters	Power, especially ecological problems
Stock markets	Railroads and transit
2. *Industrial*	Water
Telephone equipment	Postal services
Computers	4. *Other special cases*
Automobiles	Old: Agriculture
Drugs	New: Health services (doctors, hospitals, blood, insurance), education, especially preschool and college, legal services, aging and death (nursing homes, funeral, etc.), arts, sports, weapons
Oil	
Steel	
Copying equipment	
Photographic supplies	
Heavy electrical equipment	
Soaps and detergents	
Cereals	

CHAPTER THREE

The Content of Policies

Policy is formalized in law; in legal prose, powers, and public agencies. Yet its essence is economic. Policies' costs and benefits are the thread which unifies the whole subject. Using careful cost-benefit analysis, one can evaluate policies, not just describe them.

Policy choices reach across a wide range of markets and policy tools. The custom has been to divide them into separate sectors and treatments—such as antitrust for industry, regulation for utilities—each with its own legal trappings. But this is not wise, for the content is really unified.

The cost-benefit concepts in this chapter provide the underlying unity of content. The method is actually just explicit common sense, such as we all use every day in guiding our own actions. Many policy choices are already made by using some rough version of it, to decide if the policy is "worth while." But the method is often used incorrectly or with biases, and many policy makers instead just follow rules by rote. The proper aim is to use it explicitly and completely, to make the quantities known, and to include the essential parts.

So this chapter presents cost-benefit analysis for industrial policies; an economic map for the whole continent of policy. General background is laid out in the "Background" section. Next, a simple model for evaluating policies will be set forth, fitted to the main conditions which are common in industrial cases. Discounting of benefits and costs is discussed, and this section also includes the cost-benefit choices which *private* firms make in trying to influence policies their way. The conditions of optimal choice are defined. Then specific biases in public-agency choices are identified. Biases in choices on the private side are also treated. Incentives and side-effects of policies are discussed next. Alternative criteria are noted, and the final section gives a summary.

BACKGROUND

Every public agency has certain *tools,* in the form of (1) resources and (2) legal powers, and *problems,* defined by its (3) jurisdiction and (4) the

57

severity of problems in it. For an agency to be effective, these four must be at least reasonably in balance. A large jurisdiction, embracing severe problems, requires abundant resources and/or powers. Resources and powers are often substitutable in some degree; with wider powers (e.g., to have final power of decision), an agency may need fewer resources (e.g., skilled lawyers to persuade an outside court). With larger problems, both the resources and the powers will usually need enlarging. An agency with large problems and small tools will usually be ineffective; indeed, it will also be a bar to other, really effective treatments. At the same time, however, resources and powers can be wasted if an agency is inefficiently operated (e.g., makes the wrong internal choices and develops internal bureaucratic slack).[1]

The basic resources used in public policies are of several main kinds:

Public supervision.   The most basic resource of all is the scarce ability of the political process to evaluate and to exert control in the *public* interest. At each point in time, the fund of public-control resources is finite (or, more precisely, it has rising marginal costs per unit of supervision). Information is costly, and the ability of citizens to acquire it, weigh it, and act upon it has high opportunity costs in time, energy, and attention (see Chapter 4 for more on this). Each task taken up for public action diminishes the accountability and control that can be applied in others.

Moreover, the control process itself is often biased, toward serving the interests of those with wealth and other strategic advantages. The social control process, such as it may be, is of course the only one we have. It must be used sparingly, and in ways which fit its strengths. Otherwise it will cause harm, not cure it (see Chapter 4).

Staff talent ranges from the highest orders of creative professional and strategic skills down to routine clerks and typists. Some of these people are entrepreneurs managing public enterprises, others are financiers, or civil servants, lawyers, engineers, theorists, economists, jurists,. and technicians. This pool of talent also is limited.

Public funds are also of several sorts. Most obvious are the budget levels of expenditure; $12 million for the Antitrust Division, $1.4 billion in postal subsidies, $12 billion in R&D grants, etc. Another cost is tax abatement to specific groups. Less obvious but equally real is the *public* absorption of *private* risks, such as loan guarantees to house-buyers, international firms, and farmers. These two costs are as real as the direct spending of public funds.

Certain other control devices do not entail costs in quite the same sense. Legal powers of compulsion—such as eminent domain to condemn land or simply the powers contained in the Sherman Antitrust Act—can simply be written into law, at relatively little direct cost. The Courts and, ultimately, the armed forces enforce these, though they usually are not required to act to do so. But even here the true opportunity costs are often larger than they seem. Getting a Congress, Parliament, or state legislature, or even a city council, to act effectively on one problem often causes

---

[1] See, for comparison, the fascinating treatment of legal processes by Richard A. Posner in *The Economic Analysis of Law* (Boston: Little, Brown, 1972). Posner does, however, treat questions of equity as peripheral.

less action, or possibly a counteraction, in other directions. And the enforcement of laws on the books often does take large flows of public resources.

These resources help to define the policies. There are also other surface dimensions of policy, which often are trivial. These include the supposed severity of the constraints as claimed in formal rules, and the asserted degree of public benefits. Instead of such formal items, one needs to dig beneath and analyze the real properties of policies. The supposed intent of a policy can be irrelevant to its nature and effects.

Now, policies presumably change things. The proper focus of analysis is the *net* change caused by any policy, compared with inaction or with specific other actions. Often the *status quo* would change radically if left alone, so that what looks like a drastic policy move will in fact yield only small real net effects.

Moreover, time flows only in one direction. Therefore, analysis must deal with the *future* effects of policies. This prepares us to judge which new policies to try and which old ones to change. The analysis can also be used to test choices that were made in the past. We wish to learn from the past so as to repeat its successes, not its errors. We wish especially to understand *preventive* treatments, which anticipate problems and often have higher yields than *restorative* actions.

This leads to five basic features of policies.

1. *Policies often do two or more things, rather than just one.* These components are often counterpoised and tilted in unexpected ways.

For example, a good antitrust policy in the U.S. has at least three main parts: preventing collusion, preventing certain mergers, and abating existing market power. The net effect of these parts—as they are in fact done, with checkered emphasis—may be to harden structure and to benefit dominant firms (see Chapter 10). This would be the opposite of the supposed effects. Or instead, they may limit market power and encourage innovation.

Regulation has two main elements: giving a franchise and constraining profit rates. The one raises profitability, the other reduces it; the net effect also is indeterminate (we shall try to understand it in Chapters 13–18).

Often the separate policy elements can be—and indeed are—managed independently. One must therefore know the elements, their actual and potential yields, and their side effects before one can understand and evaluate them.

2. *Sectors change over time, so that the effects—and appropriateness —of given policy tools also change.* There are few fixed points or boundaries, and the rate of change can exceed the rate at which policies are adjusted. Some changes are predictable and could be anticipated. But all require looking ahead and aiming at moving targets. Example: utilities go through phases which—unless obstructed—commonly end back in competitive status (Chapter 13). Further example: cities grow in size and complexity, so that new policy treatments (e.g., of transit systems) are needed.

The most basic instance of this is the natural rate of decay of market

FIGURE 3–1

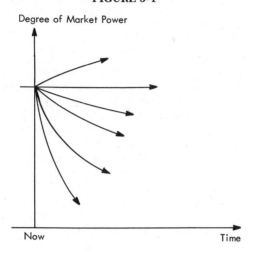

power (recall Chapter 2). Virtually all monopoly will eventually dwindle, unless fortified by extraneous devices. Eventually: but is the rate of decay fast or slow? Figure 3–1 illustrates the alternatives: a specific case of monopoly may be virtually permanent, or it may fade immediately. If it lasts, even slow treatments may have high yields. But if monopoly will disappear quickly, any but the speediest treatments will be superfluous. The rate of decay is therefore central to optimal policy choice, in antitrust, regulation and others (recall Table 2–8).

3. *Policies also evolve and cause adaptive responses in markets.* This evolution is, in some cases, contrary to the optimum direction (utility regulation is an example: see Chapter 13). In other cases, the adaptive response by private firms wholly anticipates and deflects the intent of the policy; the financial sector offers many examples of such flexibility and speed.

In any event, the policy choice must often be dynamic, or at least time-related. It must recognize the inner complexity and time-lags in actual policy tools.

4. *It is also intrinsic in policies that they apply incentives.* They either constrain or subsidize, or frequently they do both. The marginal incentives may be deep, even where their average effects are not. The firms affected (who have often also helped to design and enact the policy in the first place) then either have reduced, or increased, profit opportunities. There is probably no significant industry or firm that is not both constrained and subsidized by two or more public policies.

5. *Optimal policy treatments require both (1) information and (2) rational analysis.* Each is necessary but not sufficient. Most policy resources are used to gain information, by processing, hearings, investigations, etc. Information is not only critical but often costly. Also, the processes for gaining it may themselves contain biases. Even the wisest and most rational policy choosers will err if their information is incorrect.

Indeed, they will fail even to consider problems if they—and/or the political process which guides their activities—are kept unaware of them.

THE ANALYSIS OF CHOICE

The criteria by which one evaluates good performance—efficiency, equity, and others—were stated in Chapter 1. Now we will present a simple method for doing such evaluations.[2] The purpose is to define optimum public choices, in a system where private firms are—as is true in fact—also optimizing *their* choices.

As is usual in economics, there are two parts to the optimizing problem: (1) to get the right level of *total* policy resources, and (2) to maximize the net public benefits yielded by any given level of policy resources, across the detailed range of markets and policy types. Each policy is to be pursued quantitatively in each direction to the point where its marginal returns in net benefits are equal to the marginal returns on alternative actions. Each policy is also to be designed so that the benefits-cost gap is as large as possible for every given level of expenditure.[3]

Stated so simply, such rules are truisms, as economists have long been aware. But they can have great power. They are a consistent basis for thought, and they correctly require choices to be made among multiple alternatives, not just *for* or *against* a single policy tool. And the simple analysis will be enriched for the special features of industrial policies.

General Public Choice. We begin with a simple case. Consider a public decision-making agency whose tools and problems are in reasonable balance at the start. Suppose that setting a specific policy *j* at a level *l* will incur certain direct Costs$_a$ (*a* for agency) and probably yield certain benefits by changing efficiency and equity. These costs and benefits will occur over time *t*, from the present to some distant horizon *n*. The general expression for determining the economic returns to this policy level is the present-value expression:

$$(1) \quad \text{Net Benefits}_j = \sum_{t=1}^{n} \frac{\Delta \text{Efficiency} + \Delta \text{Equity}}{(1+i)^n} - \sum_{t=1}^{n} \frac{\Delta \text{Costs}_a + \Delta \text{Costs}_p}{(1+i)^n}$$

where *i* is a rate of time discount. Costs$_p$ are the private costs imposed by agency action. The agency has other policy tools to use its resources on, and it can also vary the levels of each tool. An optimum is reached

---

[2] Benefit-cost techniques and difficulties are surveyed in Alan R. Prest and Ralph Turvey, "Cost-Benefit Analysis: A Survey," *Economic Journal,* 1965, pp. 683–735; Peter O. Steiner, *Public Expenditure Budgeting* (Washington, D.C.: Brookings Institution, 1970); and E. J. Mishan, *Cost-Benefit Analysis* (New York: Praeger, 1971).

[3] Specific policy choices can be framed in two alternative ways. Where there is a straight choice between types of policies, then the one with the highest ratio of total benefits to costs is to be chosen. Alternatively, and more generally, one may regard policy resources as investments, and seek to optimize their allocation in terms of internal rates of return on the resources committed. In that case, each policy would be pursued to the point where the net internal rate of return on its resource investment just equals the marginal opportunity cost of public-sector funds. Normally these approaches will yield similar policy choices. In either case, the analysis must include *all* benefits and costs of each choice.

when all policies are adjusted so that their net marginal yields are equal to the true opportunity cost of the agency's resources, defined by some social rate of return (r_s). A necessary condition for efficiency is therefore that policy returns be in line with policy costs:

$$
(2) \qquad \frac{\partial\Delta\text{Benefits}}{\partial\Delta\text{Costs}_j} = b_j \geqq r_s
$$

Thus if policy j at level l yields a marginal return greater than r_s, then its level should be increased; and vice versa.[4]

One does not really expect precise figures to be available in evaluating most actual choices. These are only predictions, in a world full of blurs and guesses. Judgment will be needed; cost-benefit analysis faithfully carries out the mistakes of those using it. Yet it does clarify the elements of choice directly.

Figure 3–2 shows the basic results for a specific treatment. Its efficient level varies with r_s, the cost of public funds. There will be a surplus of average returns over r_s. If the *MR* function is flattish, the choice of r_s may strongly affect the levels of optimal treatment.

Treatments are assumed to have optimal *design*. Otherwise outcomes may be as at points 1 or 2, inside the *MR* and *AR* possibility frontiers. Here the design, not the level, is inefficient. Also, we assume—optimistically—that benefits and costs are included completely and measured without bias.

FIGURE 3–2

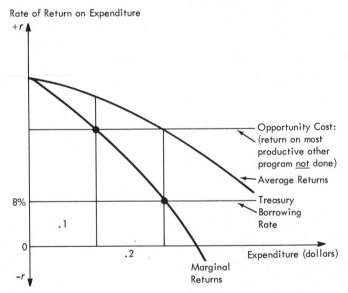

---

[4] There are various finer points to this. Thus, if there are certain time patterns of costs and benefits, it may matter in marginal cases whether one uses a present-value, internal-rate-of-return, or discounted-cash-flow method. But for this discussion, such questions are secondary.

Specific Discounts. The components in this simple model need discounting in three ways:

a. Time. The usual sequence is costs first, benefits later. To that extent, policy resources are investments. Where resistance by private interests lengthens this investment period, it reduces the present value of the benefits. This in turn normally reduces the efficient level of the policy. A correct choice will be free of any such time bias. *A neutral treatment also avoids putting time on the side of either the agency or the firm.* Otherwise, the ability to control the pace of action may decisively distort the outcome, by stalling or by railroading.

The correct discount rate is not easy to specify exactly, as an extensive literature attests.[5] Higher *i* values shrink the benefits from actions which take a long time to run their course. A higher *i* may reflect a true government-wide high rate of time preference on social expenditure, but short-run fluctuations in *i* (as urgency comes and goes) are assumed away.

[Try deciding what the correct time discount rate is, choosing among (1) the Treasury borrowing rate, (2) the private borrowing rate, (3) either of these plus a risk premium, (4) the average or marginal cost of capital in private markets, (5) the yield on other public policies, or (6) any others. Then Try to measure exactly what that rate actually is (presumably between 6 and 15 percent: or is it?).]

b. Probability. Future outcomes are always uncertain in some degree, and so the cost and benefit magnitudes need adjustment to reflect these probabilities. Two inherent causes of uncertainty are involved.

1. *Economic effects are not certain.* Research has established several broad relationships between elements of market structure and performance, as Chapter 2 noted. But (1) these are soft relationships, not clad in iron certainty, and (2) the specific case at hand may deviate from the general rule, for some special reason. In extreme cases, a predicted beneficial effect could turn out instead to be negative; most private arguments against public actions make precisely that claim.

Social science proceeds by hypothesis-testing, which can never be conclusive. In the absence of repetitive controlled experiments, statistical analysis of recent data can seek to confirm the patterns which theory suggests. But it can never finally prove or reject, never give tight answers. Worse, serious practical research problems are common. Crucial facts are hidden, the data for testing are usually inexact, the reality itself often changes. For example, profits and innovation are often extremely tricky to measure, and econometric patterns in the 1950s could be rejected as invalid for the 1970s.

In short, *any* policy choice contains a weighing of *probable* effects on both sides. *A correct weighing procedure will poise the burden of proof evenly.* This neutrality is often difficult to achieve. For example, courtroom standards of proof for criminal cases will be inappropriate for settling the optimum structure of an industry, since the courtroom burden of proof—beyond reasonable doubt—is one-sided. The law of private property ordinarily sets the burden of proof against changes in the *status*

---

[5] See the references in footnote 2 above.

quo; this is true also of much recent regulatory law. In principle, this will lead to incorrect decisions. Stated more generally: *policy choices not to make changes should have as robust empirical support as any other choice.*

2. *Even where economic effects are probable, their normative yield may be doubtful.* Choice A may make benefit X sure to happen, but X might come about even without A. This is the question of natural rates of decay (recall Chapter 2 and the first section above). And it is of course precisely the defense offered by most targets of policy actions: that the goals are, or will be, gained as well or better without the policy step.

The Schumpeterian amendment is that the market power arises from innovation, and can be powerfully beneficial while it lasts, by stimulating further innovation.[6] Yet the issues are more complex than that. Innovation *per se* shows nothing about policy yields, for an innovative industry (1) may have had unusually rich opportunities for innovation, and/or (2) may have innovated at *more* than the optimum rate.

Correct policy choices will therefore be prospective, time-discounted and probability-adjusted, and will *make comparisons with the results which could otherwise be reasonably expected to occur.* The performance criteria are partly conjectural and need to be set neutrally. The policy yields of any policy are the *net* changes from these alternative levels. Yet these alternative levels are themselves estimates, subject to probabilities.

These two uncertainty factors—about effects and normative standards—can be included by adjusting the *best estimate* values by probability factors. These will be set between 0 for impossibility to 1 for certainty. For simplicity, the notation here will include all such factors in a single summary multiplier p attached to each element of net benefits. Thus an estimated net benefit of $10 million at a p of .4 (a 40% chance) would have a value of $4 million. This is the simplest factoring scheme, and it omits quite a few subtleties about risk preferences and related elements.[7]

Obviously p is itself a matter for subjective estimate, and in most cases it cannot be known precisely. But large differences in the odds can usually be perceived, and at least there is value in making these factors explicit. That enables the arguable to be argued clearly.

c. Precedent. Each policy choice may set precedents which decide other cases. A single decision may therefore have an additional policy yield which, in landmark instances, can go very high. In such cases, an evaluation of the case's own yield is too narrow. Some sort of precedential multiplier m should be applied.

In routine infra-marginal cases, based on settled law; m will approach 1 (standard price-fixing cases are now of this sort). In marginal cases,

---

[6] Recall the discussion of the Schumpeterian process in Chapter 1.

[7] These include the classic questions about risk-return choices, discussed in M. Friedman and L. J. Savage, "The Utility Analysis of Choices Involving Risk," *Journal of Political Economy,* 1948, pp. 279–304; D. D. Hester and J. Tobin, eds., *Risk Aversion and Portfolio Choice* (New York: Wiley, 1967), and H. Markowitz, *Portfolio Selection: Efficient Diversification of Investments* (New York: Wiley, 1959).

which extend or retract the law, m may be more or less than 1. The latter holds if a case withdraws precedents which previously yielded net benefits or if extension of the law causes net costs in other cases. Such negative precedential effects—from economically mistaken decisions—are not rare at all; in some areas and periods, they are common. Positive multipliers are more frequent when the law is developing, by covering new ground or new practices. A special twist is what lawyers call *estoppel*. Bringing an action at one point often gives a period of grace during which the action cannot be brought again. For example, IBM was regarded as free from further antitrust action for at least a decade after the 1956 consent decree settling an earlier case. Therefore the estoppel effect amounts to an internal precedent factor which is less than one.

One must bear in mind, however, that precedents frequently arise from the structure of the law, which can be revised. For example, FCC decisions on cable TV can be superseded by new laws from Congress on the matter. In certain cases, m itself is subject to a probability factor, if revision of the law is in prospect!

With these three additions, the general model of agency choice now takes the form:

$$(3) \qquad \text{Net benefits} = m \sum_{t=1}^{n} \frac{(\Delta\text{Efficiency})p_e + (\Delta\text{Equity})p_d}{(1+i)^n}$$

$$- \sum_{t=1}^{n} \frac{(\Delta\text{Costs}_a)p_{ca} + (\Delta\text{Costs}_p)p_{cp}}{(1+i)^n}$$

which looks much more complex than it really is.

In terms of rates of return on policy resources, the efficiency condition at the margin now is

$$(4) \qquad b_j = m \frac{(\Delta\text{Benefits})p_b}{(\Delta\text{Costs}_p)\text{p}_{ca}} \geq r_s$$

The objective is still to reach an equimarginal set of optimizing conditions, of marginal yields among all policies. Roughly speaking, those whose benefits are definite and are landmark cases will be favored over others.

Typical flows of costs and benefits are illustrated in Figure 3–3: costs first, benefits later. Benefits easily exceed costs. But as the time discount rate (i) rises, the yield drops below the minimum. This is reinforced if benefits are less certain than costs. Yet, if this is a landmark case which will automatically gain benefits in 50 other cases without a cent of added costs ($m = 50$), its yield will be quite high enough.

The final evaluations will be made at any one of several levels: agency staff members and advisers, at the grassroots level; or agency head officers; or upper-administration officials; or the courts at various state and federal levels. The focus differs, in practice: agency staff members usually deal primarily with the benefits expression, while their head officers focus more on costs and precedents. In the judiciary, higher courts are

FIGURE 3–3

Costs, Benefits (dollars)

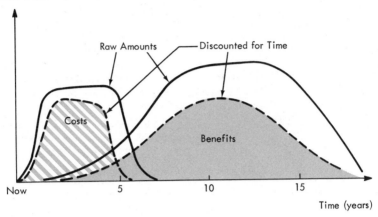

Time (years)

usually more concerned with precedential aspects than are the lower courts. Yet at each level, all elements in the evaluation should, in principle, be included.

Private-firm Choices. While agencies are choosing among possible constraints or subsidies to firms, the firms affected are also arranging their strategies. The result is commonly a sequence of choices and moves on both sides, with occasional resolutions but no real terminus. Issues are rarely settled. There are usually compromises and partial changes, and underlying conditions often change further. Therefore, an analysis of choices by private firms is complementary to the treatment of public agency choices.

We start with the conventional assumption that firms generally maximize profit for a given investment. For the entire firm, for period n, profits simply equal revenues minus costs:

(5) $$\text{Profit}_n = \text{Total Revenue}_n - \text{Total Cost}_n$$

For any specific project or direction of expenditures, the firm's expected yield (π) on investment must equal or exceed its opportunity cost of capital (r_c):

(6) $$\pi_n = \frac{\text{Revenue}_n - \text{Cost}_n}{\text{Investment}_n}$$

and

(7) $$\pi_n \geq r_c$$

One such direction of company expenditure is on efforts to anticipate, prevent and/or mitigate the constraints which public agencies choose to apply or to increase the subsidies obtained from the agencies.

Generally, any public policy which would reduce profits will be resisted *up to the point at which the marginal rate of return on resistance expenditures just equals the opportunity cost of capital.* At its simplest extreme, the excess profits at stake will all be used up by the firm in resisting the public agency, since otherwise they will be lost to the firm in any event.

Imagine a frictionless economy with no externalities, no equity problems, shared expectations about future events, and with a perfect political process. In such ideal conditions, both policy and resistance choices might turn out to be optimized, with the private and public opportunity costs of funds just equal at every margin;

(8) $\pi_n = r_c = r_s$

This optimum could occur even though the firms' evaluations are narrower than the agencies', as follows. A firm's concern with equity extends only to maximizing its own shareholders' wealth. The firm is oblivious to precedential effects which will impinge on other firms. And its efficiency concerns exclude any gains to other firms (especially actual and potential competitors) or any other external effects.

POSSIBLE BIASES IN PUBLIC-AGENCY CHOICES

Agencies operate within real constraints of their own. Their budgets and powers, the quality of their leaders, and the current range of politically acceptable actions, are usually controlled from outside. Agency managers must pursue actions within given legal systems and rules. Traditions and the technical nature of their treatments always limit what they can do and how fast they can do it.

It is possible to identify several resulting biases in public-agency choices, which often distort choices among industrial policies. These are familiar to skilled practitioners of private-firm resistance but not, in many cases, to public-agency officials and outside observers.

Information Bias. Public agencies need complete and timely information on sensitive variables (market shares, prices, costs, innovation choices, competitive tactics, and alternative treatments), both past and future. But they often lack it.

Such information is known intimately by firms, and when it influences profits, it will inevitably be secreted. Because firms also try to influence public fact-gathering policies, the data put out in the public realm are often scanty and peripheral. This causes bias in specific policy choices, as well as in the general evaluation of policy needs and urgency.

It affects both the degree of possible effects and the probability level at which we discount the effect. Until recently, market power could be measured mainly with concentration ratios, which are defective (recall Chapter 2). Therefore the supposed effects of market power were probably underestimated; that is, the regression coefficients and the goodness of fit were both biased downward because the data were incomplete and contained error. Until disclosure rules are liberalized and a greater range of company data are made public, this bias toward underestimating the general role of market power will probably continue. And yet, since industry largely controls disclosure policies, such an improvement in knowledge is unlikely to occur.

Meanwhile, the *costs* of treatment are more directly measurable and, in contested cases, are fully asserted by the target firms, often with a degree of exaggeration. Therefore, bias is likely to be present in specific cases as well as in the general setting of policy lines.

These biases have four effects. First, industrial policies are less firm and complete than they would otherwise be, because the problems and potential yields are underestimated. Second, whole problems, areas, and cases are ignored, because of ignorance. Third, agency resources have to be spent more lavishly on mere fact-gathering than a neutral information state would require. And fourth, actions are delayed and less complete. These biases may be cumulative.

Time Bias. Several time-biases are common. When one side can impose delay and gain benefits by doing so, then time is biased in its favor. This bias can be decisive, as we will see when we examine merger, restructuring, and regulatory actions. The bias often flows from specific procedures or rules, which can—in principle and in fact—be altered.

The time bias is strengthened by the brevity of most policymakers' tenure. New policies usually require at least 3 years to prepare and at least 10 years (often 20 years or more) for benefits to be fully harvested. Most antitrust and regulatory decisionmakers are in office less than 4 years (see Chapters 5 and 13). And their inexperience often neutralizes them for the first year or two. They commonly apply a high rate of time preference, and this myopia favors quick, visible and shallow steps, rather than basic ones. It also makes the advantage of having time on one's side particularly strong.

Probability Bias. Two important biases in the probability factors are recurrent. Procedures can be slanted in favor of inferior solutions. And the burden of proof can be tipped decisively.

The outcome may be procedurally uncertain. For example, an antitrust case to restructure an industry will require a court to find a firm guilty of monopolizing and to order a basic remedy; the odds on either or both actions may be low and imprecise because the procedures are slow and unsure. A price-fixing conviction and remedy may, by contrast, be nearly a sure bet (see Chapters 5 and 6). Regulatory and other outcomes are also often subject to such slanted uncertainties.

An aspect of procedural uncertainty is that the passage of time raises political uncertainty. As elections come and go and governments change, the direction of policy may be reversed from above, and then reversed again. Long-term actions are liable to be stopped in midstream, even though the conditions justifying them are unchanged.

An uneven burden of proof can bias the outcome sharply. Thus, western laws and traditions of private property rights normally set the burden of proof against changes in the *status quo*. Such a standard of proof often departs from an even choice among alternatives. An even burden of proof presumes, of course, that there is equal access to sensitive data. Without such equality of access, the actual burden of proof may be sharply tilted. The burden of proof is decisive in a remarkably wide range of cases.

As an illustration, Figure 3–4 compares hypothetical yields from two lines of antitrust treatments. The true basic yields are higher for restora-

FIGURE 3–4

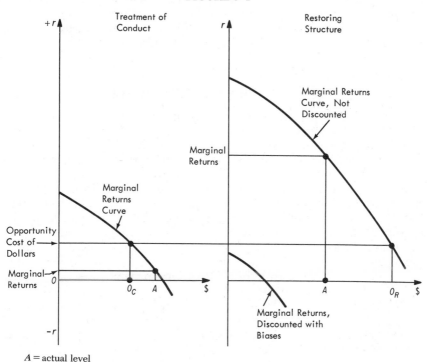

A = actual level

tive treatments than for conduct actions. But if restorative yields are discounted by the biases, the policy makers will regard them as too low throughout to qualify. The true optimal levels are O_R and O_C; but it appears that restorative treatments should be zero. Such conditions as these would lead to a marked imbalance in antitrust policy.

Private Costs. Public policies usually lead to private resistance costs, as when an antitrust suit evokes huge and costly defensive efforts. Should public agencies include these private resistance costs in appraising the real total costs of public actions? Perhaps yes: the costs are real and often predictable. Yet they are also often fully discretionary with the firm. Any knowledgeable firm would threaten large or unlimited resistance if doing so would slant the agency's choice toward weaker actions. (Indeed, its delaying tactics alone will cause such a slant.) To this extent, the firms themselves could control public policy. This is obviously unacceptable. Perhaps one could compromise by including only the nondiscretionary resistance costs in the public–agency evaluation. But is this a practical distinction? The best answer appears to be to leave private costs out on first-round evaluations and then put them in only if nondiscretionary costs are large, highly probable, and identifiable.

A final note: every policy action will help some and hurt others. In particular, any policy act or nonaction will redistribute income and capital in unforeseen ways. Therefore, that a policy will have a redistributive impact cannot validly serve as a conclusive argument against that policy (other than as a value for ΔEquity). Otherwise policy choices would be paralyzed. A requirement that policies be distributively neutral is inappropriate.

BIASES IN PRIVATE-FIRM CHOICES

The narrowness of the firm's evaluation will not necessarily cause it to be biased away from the social optimum, under ideal conditions. But lapses from these ideal conditions can be frequent and important. Bias can then arise because private firms are indifferent to precedential effects and external effects.

Private firms will often apply different rates of time discount than do the public decision makers; higher in some cases, lower in others. Often firms will rate the probability factors quite differently from the public agency. Bias may also occur when firms depart from strict profit-maximizing toward such other maximands as sales, risk-avoidance, market share, etc. The normative effect will vary from case to case, depending on the direction in which public policies are pressing.

Two other biases are quite systematic: taxes and speed of action.

Tax bias is embedded deeply in the system. Resistance costs ordinarily are tax-deductible, so that the firm's opportunity cost from resistance will usually be well below the true cost of the real resources absorbed. If the corporation income tax rate is T, then the profit-maximizing marginal condition of resistance costs and after-tax profits at stake is

$$(9) \qquad \qquad \text{Profit} \geqq \frac{\text{Cost}_p}{1 - T}$$

The present T of about .50 means that resistance costs would be extended until they are at *twice* the level of the marginal profits at stake. If, for example, the after-tax profits at stake (P) are $1 million per day (as they are in some cases: see Chapter 7), then the rational firm will spend up to about $2 million to achieve each *day* of delay. A significant T therefore enlarges the resistance to policy constraints, perhaps well beyond a neutral outcome, because it makes resistance dollars seem *cheaper* to the firm.

The general private-firm basis for a decision about resistance to policy j is therefore

$$(10) \qquad \qquad \pi_j = \frac{\text{Revenue}_j - (\text{Cost}_j/(1 - T))}{\text{Investment}_j}$$

Firms benefitting from the *status quo* (and its continuation in the future) will devote resources to retarding any change caused by public policy. If the time yield of delay is high, the stalling effect may be large, again possibly absorbing the whole sum of private and social benefits which are at stake.

Speed. As for the difference in speed of action, public choices are often made and applied at slower rates than are private ones. This reduces the range of public choice. The lags may cause the public actions, *when they take effect,* to stray far from the optimum levels. The classic instance of this is an antitrust restructuring case which, after many years of trial and appeal, is finally won *after* the industry has changed (again, recall Figure 3–1). Another is the stoppage of bank mergers *after* dominant banks have already been formed. Strict optimizing requires that public actions be as rapid as private ones, even if they are not immediate.

These two elements are critical to a preventive treatment. Unless they can be overcome, the choices will be confined to restorative actions, which tend to have higher costs and lower benefits.

In combination, these biases on the public and private sides can be strong. Occasionally they may offset each other, but that would be a fluke. Frequently they reinforce each other, causing divergences from the optimum. Such deviations are often not even recognized, because essential information is lacking. And there are ironic departures; for example, firms often achieve valuable delay by providing an agency with *too much* information, which its staff can assimilate only at a snail's pace (see "snowing," under antitrust in Chapters 5 and 7).

The reader can derive cases in which the biases would cause severe welfare loss, or nicely balance each other out. The essential fact is that the biases are numerous and can be powerful. Correct policies must allow for them explicitly.

OPTIMAL DESIGN

Treatment with optimal design will anticipate the biases in data, time, etc., and will apply incentives so that each party (firms *and* agencies) is induced to move toward the correct solutions. *Design* can be even more critical than policy *levels.* And optimizing it requires more than just making it bias-free, though that too is necessary.

First, it requires identifying which actors have the information and power to bring about the appropriate changes. These may be managers, shareholders, directors, workers, competitors, or a range of public officials. And their roles are not obvious. Thus, to induce managers to alter behavior or structure, it may be best to induce shareholders or directors to *make* the managers do it, not try to induce the managers directly.

Second, the efficient incentives need to be designed and applied. This requires knowledge of the motives of the actors, of the trade-offs among the costs and benefits, and of the ways to get treatments applied.

In general, treatment should make it so that market power pays the firm less, but without making efficiency and innovation less rewarding. Treatments will then fit the motives of the key actors, not run square against them. This will turn out in many cases to favor *therapy* (or behavior modification) over *surgery* (or enforced restructuring and penalties). It will also fit the general rule that preventive treatment is preferable to restorative actions. Incentives have their costs too, either in the form of cash compensation or in favoring one group over others; incentives for one party may mean penalties or exclusions for the rest. An incentive payment which exceeds the discounted social gains will rarely be optimal. Therefore incentives must often be combined with constraints.

In any event, policy choice must be preceded by searches for high-yield incentives, which maximize the inducement to comply for any given degree of loss to others. This principle is well known but rarely applied in utility regulation; it has scarcely even been perceived in the antitrust literature.

ALTERNATIVE CRITERIA

Benefit-cost analysis is evidently a sensible way to arrange rational choices. It is subject to abuse and biases, but it is also the proper analytical basis for identifying those biases and defining ways to correct them. Other policy criteria are often presented as alternatives to benefit-cost analysis. But on inspection, these turn out to reduce to nothing but benefit-cost statements in disguise.

Consider several such criteria.

1. Incipiency: monopoly should be stopped at the earliest possible point in its growth. This is an important criterion used in preventing certain horizontal mergers. It embodies the benefit-cost evaluation that the discounted benefits from preventive action against increasing market shares via merger exceed the discounted costs sufficiently to justify drawing the line at low market shares (see Chapter 8).

2. Competition is the objective pure and simple, even apart from its economic results. Actually, this just says that the total discounted benefits of competition are likely to be very large, so much that there is a rebuttable presumption against market power. That is: the burden of proof should strongly favor competition.

3. Laissez-faire. Let markets work freely to erode monopoly, and virtually all public efforts to restore or supplant it will be unnecessary and/or harmful. Translated into benefit-cost form: market power decays so rapidly that policy measures to reduce or constrain it have little or no net benefits.

Other criteria fit in the framework too. Some of them provide efficient rules of thumb or other consistent techniques. But their validity derives ultimately from a correct fit to the basic benefit-cost conditions. That is the context in which it can be assessed.

SUMMARY

We have now derived a way of defining optimum public policies toward business. Such optimum policies will neither over-expand nor under-provide public actions, nor *cause* deviations themselves. They will be well designed, with good use of incentives, as well as being set at the right levels. Cost-benefit analysis will not be exact in practice, but it underlies any rational way of thinking about policies.

Biases may occur. It is easy to omit important categories of costs and benefits, by mistake or because they are controversial or unknown. Probability factors are usually difficult to judge. *Special care is needed in:* (1) *setting the time discount rate,* (2) *avoiding letting time be on the side of one party,* (3) *posing the burden of proof evenly,* (4) *allowing for precedential effects, and* (5) *neutralizing the biases in private-firm choices (from taxes, better information, and speed of action).*

So one analyses policy yields and choices with care. The hope is to avoid large errors and omissions, rather than to reach perfect, comprehensive appraisals.

CHAPTER FOUR

Methods and Limits
of Control

Having learned how to define optimum policies, we now need to look closely at the processes shaping actual policies. They are rough and imperfect, like most human activities, and they may contain biases. But their broad effect might be to bring policy choices toward optimality, or at least to correct large deviations reasonably quickly.

"The Political Setting" section briefly reviews these processes. The next section analyzes the policy processes and institutions (courts, agencies, etc.). Then a bird's-eye view of the main industrial policies is given, with a brief history of them. An appendix sets out the legal foundations.

THE POLITICAL SETTING

A democratic process has great optimizing power, for it makes government officeholders subject to the preferences of the people. The analogy with a perfectly competitive economic system is close.[1] Politicians compete for official jobs by perceiving the most desired policies and promising them. Voters decide by strictly equal votes. Once in office, politicians must carry out the preferred policies, or they will lose office at the next election. Policies are just a by-product of the politicians' efforts to gain and hold office (though they also express personal beliefs in many cases).

But they are led toward optimality (as defined in Chapter 3) by individual maximizing choices, as if guided by a political Invisible Hand. There may be much muddling through, or instead a series of crystal-clear policies. There may also be a degree of leadership, or instead a lot of bland, small-scale compromises. The optimizing tendency is there, all

---

[1] For detailed analysis of democratic choice, see Anthony Downs, *An Economic Theory of Democracy* (New York: Harper & Row, 1957); K. J. Arrow, *Social Choice and Individual Values* (Chicago: University of Chicago Press, 1951); R. A. Dahl and C. E. Lindblom, *Politics, Economics and Democracy*, rev. ed. (New York: Harper and Row, 1968); and R. A. Dahl, *A Preface to Democratic Theory* (Chicago: University of Chicago Press, 1956).

FIGURE 4-1

Distribution of Voters by Their Preferences

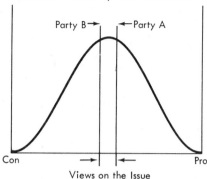

Views on the Issue

the same. And its tonic effects extend indirectly to the courts and the lower levels of the bureaucracy.

The process economizes on the decisions each voter has to make. Learning and deciding takes effort and time, so voters naturally focus on those few issues they care most about. Parties try to assemble the most popular set of positions ("Peace and prosperity," etc.) for easy choice by voters (the extreme case is pulling the party lever). Normally two political parties will compete for the central mass of voters with convergent sets of positions (see Figure 4–1). This is part of the tendency to suit policies to the Benthamite optimum: the most good for the most people.

This optimum has limits, some of them analogous to the economic optimum under perfect competition:

1. Preferences may differ in intensity, but the vote weights equally. Some voters may care acutely about one or all issues, while many others will be nearly indifferent. Intense concern can be exerted by working to influence others (precinct work, a campaign TV blitz, or lobbying) and, ultimately, by running for office. But these may not be sufficient. Democratic choices may therefore fail to fit true preferences.
2. Preferences may be sharply divided, rather than bunched in the middle (see Figure 4–2). The solution will then offend a large minority, perhaps even one with especially intense concern. No consensus may exist.
3. A party may gain and hold office with a package of policies, *some* of which are sharply nonoptimal.

These problems occur even if the process is otherwise *perfect.* If it is *imperfect,* more difficulties occur.

1. Preferences may be unclear or easily swayed.
2. Issues may be too technically complex for citizens to comprehend.
3. Information may not be fully available to all. It may be scarce, too costly for many citizens to bother to get. We have all faced lists of

FIGURE 4–2

Distribution of Voters by Their Preferences

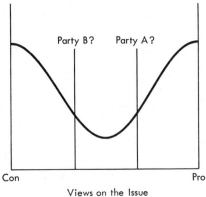

Views on the Issue

candidates we neither knew nor cared about. And access to information may be controlled by specialized interests.
4.   Resources for persuading voters may be unequally held.
5.   Policy actions may lag behind events.

All of these do occur in some degree, and their effects can reinforce each other. Therefore—from these causes alone, in addition to those in Chapter 3—policies may depart and remain far from the optimum.

Industrial policies are especially vulnerable to these imperfections. The issues are complex and abstruse. Most citizens have neither an understanding nor intense preferences about them. Access to key data is not even. Those who hold market power largely control the facts about it and its effects; subsidies are often hidden (see Chapter 25). These same groups have large resources for persuading voters not to intervene and for making hidden political deals. Industrial policies are not a central election issue, and so voters do not directly pronounce on it in party elections. Policy processes are slow, often because legal procedures can be used to cause delay.

These are a formidable set of defects. Perhaps the wonder is that industrial policies are not worse than they actually are. There is much merit in the classical liberal view that the political system is more likely to foster harmful policies than good ones, and that lasting monopolies arise more from manipulating the State than from economic causes.[2] The realist need not abhor all policies; indeed, that is not possible, for inaction is often a positive choice. Rather, one must understand how these economic and political defects relate. Between naïveté and nihilism there is much room—and need—for intelligent policy choice.

---

[2] This has been carried to its limits in 19th century Manchester School views (Nassau Senior, etc.) and neo-Chicago School views since the 1950s (George J. Stigler, J. F. Weston, etc.). The original Chicago mentors (Frank H. Knight and Henry S. Simons) were more moderate. Try answering this: Do the old Chicagoans see more or less monopoly, and more or less policy uses, than the new ones?

THE POLICY MAKERS AND POLITICAL ECONOMY

Policies evolve in three main governmental units, in the United States: executive, judicial, and legislative. Much of *the law* evolves as common law, from hosts of individual court decisions. This can be formalized or changed by explicit action in the Congress or lesser legislatures. This evolution is influenced by interest groups, by objective knowledge about the issues, and by sheer chance.[3] And, of course, changes in the economy force changes in the existing policies.

Laws are simply rules of the game. They (1) define actions or conditions, (2) attach rewards or penalties to them, and (3) specify the means for enforcement. All three branches often share in the origins of law, and all three are involved in applying every important law. The executive agencies choose how—and how extensively—to enforce it (total enforcement is commonly impossible or absurd). Legislatures control the funds for enforcement and modify the laws repeatedly. The courts interpret, and often reject, parts or all of a law.

Therefore the law is often a core of legal phrases embedded in a tissue of informal customs which really control what is done. The bigger the stakes, the more complex are the controversies about what the law *really is*. And the struggles shift freely among the governmental units, as the parties at interest seek their best chances one way and another, skirmish by skirmish.

So the formal divisions among the three branches of government often obscure the real interactions. And a large degree of overlap and clashes among official bodies is quite natural. Moreover, they are mostly managed by lawyers, trained to *advocate* one side and win, rather than to weigh social interests and create balanced solutions. They have learned to decide issues by rules and points of law, by rights rather than by optimality. This often slights economic analysis and a balanced evaluation. Or, in some cases, it leads to the opposite extreme, of accepting economists' opinions uncritically.[4]

Still the distinctive features of the branches of government need a brief review.

Executive Agencies. These administer, using resources and powers voted by the legislature. Their heads are usually political appointees, with only modest technical experience. They hold office only briefly, between two to three years on average. (Remember, it usually takes five years to start a new treatment, develop it, apply it, and carry it through, even within the existing laws. Major innovations often take 10 or 15 years.) Most decision makers are unable to understand or press basic actions, though many take office eager to do so. Their effect on policy can be shallow and disjointed, though some of them bring fresh viewpoints.[5]

---

[3] For more detail on these issues, see the Appendix to this chapter.

[4] This is preeminently evident in regulation, but it is also important in antitrust enforcement. See C. Donahue, Jr., "Lawyers, Economists, and the Regulatory Process," *Michigan Law Review,* 1971; R. A. Posner, "A Statistical Study of Antitrust Enforcement," *Journal of Law and Economies,* 1970, pp. 365–420.

[5] Still, many agency heads do a genuine sort of public service. Their salary is lower. They

The body of the agency is staffed by career experts, who provide continuity. Their salaries are modest, markedly lower than those of the private lawyers they contend with. Accordingly, agency lawyers are routinely outgunned as well as outnumbered. On occasion, agency staff are skilled, numerous, and tenacious. But often, too, career staff members grow passive.

Most agencies have cycles or waves of growth (e.g., antitrust during the 1937–44 era), which leave distinct cohorts of aging—if still dedicated—staff members. They have learned to survive rapid changes in their bosses, in industry and in the political climate.

Agency resources come from the legislature, which can exert control by the purse, by hearings, or by changing the law itself (perhaps even abolishing—or reorganizing—the agency). These resources are usually scarce, and so it is important to make optimal decisions. Yet most allocations evolve by muddling through from case to case, not by a clear analysis. This can optimize, but clear tests to verify it are lacking. Much effort goes to persuading the legislature and higher executive officials, as well as to making formal presentations in the courts—and simply to the minutiae of keeping the agency in being.[6]

Two semiexecutive agencies—independent regulatory commissions and public enterprises—share many of these features (see Chapters 13 and 19).

Legislatures. Legislators are politicians, whose trade is compromise. Many districts have a degree of political monopoly, which is reflected both in the membership and in the management of the federal and state legislatures. Committees shape actions toward industrial laws and agency budgets. Older members dominate the committees, commonly in sympathy with the older industrial interests. Committee hearings provide a forum for airing issues. But these are often timed and prepared to make a point or favor one side, and the Committees and legislatures are free to go their own way in actually framing new laws. Committee staffs prepare weighty reports, often of value but usually meant to support a pet position of the chairman or majority.

Legislators' formal actions (votes, bills, etc.) are always for public display, and so their real intent and effect are often beneath the surface. Bills or votes to do X are often done really *to prevent Y* (a bigger step) from being done. New laws are given honorific titles which frequently have little to do with the actual effect. And actions are often taken—or blocked—not for themselves but as part of some larger political or personal strategy. Moreover, action is piecemeal. At no time are industrial policies appraised and revised broadly. Finally, legislative rules provide many points for applying influence: at the committee stage, in one house, in the other house, in joint committee, at final votes; *and* then in authorizing funds; *and then* appropriating them, in both houses.

---

encounter stern, unexpected frustrations. Their positive actions are denounced in popular debate and, if they have come from private life, by their old colleagues. Either their zeal is sapped away, or they are cut short by a change of administration or by being moved out.

[6] Usually, small matters with deadlines force aside large issues which can be postponed. This Gresham's Law of Public Policy appears to be universal and will recur throughout this book.

FIGURE 4–3
The Federal Courts

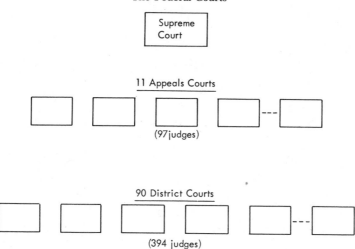

Legislatures therefore strongly *reflect* the established pattern of interests, especially in dealing with industrial policies. This can be a democratic virtue. But it leaves optimality—and indeed the meaning of each legislative action—quite in doubt, a matter for skeptical analysis.

Courts. The three tiers of the Federal courts (see Figure 4–3) handle most of the important industrial policy cases. Judges have small resources (their clerks do much research and drafting).[7] Their chief resource—courtroom time—is freely available for hearing and settling disputes.

An aggrieved party (plaintiff) files suit in the appropriate District Court. Major cases are usually tried in New York, Chicago, or Boston, where company headquarters are. Trial is held after all issues and facts needed in the case have been prepared. The basic rule is: no surprises at trial, only reasoned arguments and facts. Both sides fire lengthy lists of pretrial questions (interrogatories) at each other, both to get facts and often to confuse or delay. This pretrial activity often takes even more than the usual three-year delay on most federal court calendars. Either side can demand a trial by jury rather than by the judge alone. Complex cases usually are tried and decided by judges, but in damage cases (e.g., claims of unfair competition or monopoly damages) one side usually prefers appealing to a jury.

Trial may be lengthy, involving masses of documentation and ranks of expert witnesses on both sides. It is supposed to cover all issues of fact. Economists are frequently brought in to testify that the market is (or isn't) competitive, that scale economies are (or aren't) important, etc. For reasons we saw in Chapter 2, it is not hard to locate witnesses for either

---

[7] A clear introduction to the topic is given in C. Auerbach, L. Garrison, W. Hurst, and S. Mermin, *The Legal Process* (San Francisco: Chandler, 1961).

FIGURE 4–4

The Basic Policy Sequence

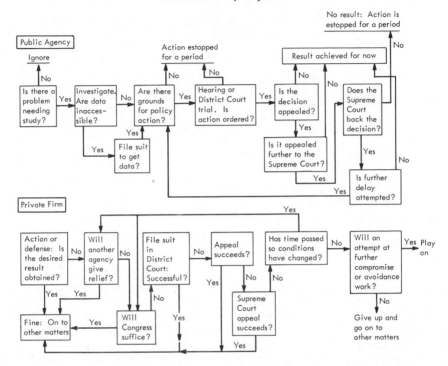

side.[8] In major cases, decision by the judge often takes another several months.

Either side may appeal. The Appellate court hears only a brief restatement by both sides; the original trial record (often running to thousands of pages) contains the facts. Further appeal to the Supreme Court is also possible. The delay is often a year before each appeal hearing, and half a year more before the decision is given out.

The upper courts can declare for either side, revise the issues, and/or send the case back down to the District Court for (1) retrial on some or all points, or (2) a practical remedy. The whole sequence can take 10 or 15 years in complex cases, as each side exhausts its chances to win or delay: see Figure 4–4. At any point, a compromise may be reached or relief be obtained from some other quarter (e.g., getting Congress—or a city council—to change the law directly).

Throughout, the emphasis is on attaining "perfect justice": ample time for preparation, for all sides to be heard fully, for avoiding mistakes

---

[8] The witnesses are usually sincere enough, and the facts are often arguable. Still, the work is rewarding, normally at $300 per day or more. Since the ranks of good objective researchers are so small, these consulting activities do affect the flow of research. For every day in court, the expert has usually consulted for many other days. And much consulting work is on other, nontrial matters. The lawyers, incidentally, log their time at from $250 to $1500 and more per day (see also Chapter 22).

of procedure at virtually any cost.[9] Courts are liberal in letting virtually all suits be heard and in letting both sides use all possible tactics.

Lower court judges are former lawyers, most of them ambitious to reach still higher judgeships. To be reversed on appeal is therefore a setback, and this insures that the lines laid down by the higher courts will soon be applied generally. Lower courts send up a wide range of *fact situations* and doctrines, from which the upper courts select some to change or establish precedents. The really critical, divisive ones are usually declined, in favor of a political resolution in Congress. Generally, lower-court judges are more conservative, drawn directly as they usually are from local commercial-legal life. Higher-court judges usually take broader views and often try new departures.

Decisions are guided by precedent and usually turn upon a crucial legal phrase or point of fact. The economic optimum is often never perceived or applied at all. Each party continually assesses the probability-adjusted value of its options and takes the best one. Virtually all law reduces to arguing: "My client's situation is *like* these others," or "My client's situation is *not* like these others." Every possible distinction can be wrung dry over and over, and every fact can be challenged.[10] The only limits on advocacy are (1) the English language, (2) rules of evidence and procedure, (3) fears of offending the courts' sense of fair play, and (4) money to cover legal fees.

This slow and unruffled process is superb for airing facts, probing issues, and resolving many disputes. But it is slow and often abused. There are many ways of stalling for tactical advantage.[11] The merits of the two sides often do not relate to their relative ability to finance a court fight: a deep pocket can win a weak case or crush a small opponent.

Even without these defects, *justice* may ignore optimal economic criteria. The process is legal, run by lawyers and reaching legal answers. As in other branches, the underlying social yields—efficiency, fairness, etc.—may be scarcely perceived during the strife.

The Political Economy.   The formulation of policies is influenced by pressure groups. The strongest pressures that beat upon the government are those that come from powerful producer groups. Consumers are interested in goods in general; their interest in the products of particular industries is likely to be weak. The interest of producers, on the contrary, is concentrated on the revenue to be obtained from a particular product. The members of producer groups are bound together by the fact that all of them derive their income from a common source. Their interest, accordingly, is compelling, and producers organize to make it felt.

Producer pressure groups maintain lobbies in the state and national capitals. Through such organizations, they keep constant watch on the processes of legislation, preparing bills for introduction and checking on

---

[9] M. Fleming, *The Price of Perfect Justice* (New York: Basic Books, 1973).

[10] Thus a lawyer does not see a white horse in a field. He sees only a horse that appears to be white *on this side*.

[11] Indeed, courts are congested by masses of trivial cases and private disputes which could be better heard by private arbitrators or specialized tribunals. Many of these cases are filed *because* the courts make stalling or other abuses possible. Chapter 22 discusses this further.

bills that are introduced by others, following bills through committee hearings and action to the floor of each house, estimating prospective votes, and rallying their forces to insure enactment or defeat. At the same time, they keep in contact with administrators, attempting to influence appointments, decisions as to policy, and the use of the veto power. To attain their ends, they employ the arts of persuasion, in public and in private. If need be, they resort to coercion, threatening withdrawal of political support. Here, their strength depends upon their ability to influence elections by contributing to campaign funds, by getting out the votes of their members, and by enlisting wider support through all of the devices of publicity. Their work is highly specialized, employing the skills of experts. It is carried on, as we have seen, with great effect.

Each group of enterprises in the United States—manufacturers, distributors, and servicemen; miners, lumbermen, and fishermen; builders, realtors, and mortgagors; bankers, brokers, and insurers; transport companies and public utilities; publishers, broadcasters, exhibitors, and the like—has its trade association, dedicated to the promotion of its interests. These bodies number in the thousands. Some of them are powerful; some are comparatively weak. All of them are on the job 12 months a year. The achievements of such bodies are evidenced by the success of the National Association of Retail Druggists in whipping resale price maintenance through the legislatures of 45 states and the Congress in Washington, by the success of the Committee of American Steamship Lines in obtaining shipping subsidies, and by the success of the associations of petroleum producers in getting percentage depletion, prorationing, import curbs, and the transfer of the offshore oil lands to the states.

There are organizations, too, that specialize in particular aspects of public policy, such as taxation and international trade. Thus, the Trade Relations Council (formerly the American Tariff League) and the Nationwide Committee on Import-Export Policy bring together manufacturers of china, pottery, glassware, watches, textiles, and other products who are interested in restricting imports. These groups have been highly effective, in past years, in curtailing the President's power to negotiate trade agreements and in opening escapes from agreements already made.

There are organizations, finally, that undertake to speak for business as a whole. Of these, the Chamber of Commerce is more comprehensive in its scope, the National Association of Manufacturers more limited. But both have a diverse membership with varying interests. They tend, therefore, to focus on broad issues where their members are agreed: on labor policy, for instance, and on public regulation and public enterprise. Here, their opinion carries weight.

In numbers, businessmen form a small fraction of the electorate. But they are keenly conscious of their common interests. They command substantial financial resources. They enjoy considerable prestige. They have ready access to officials in the legislative and executive branches of government. Their political influence, therefore, is disproportionately large.

Comparison Abroad.   Elsewhere, parliamentary democracy com-

FIGURE 4–5
Formal and Actual Policies Can Diverge

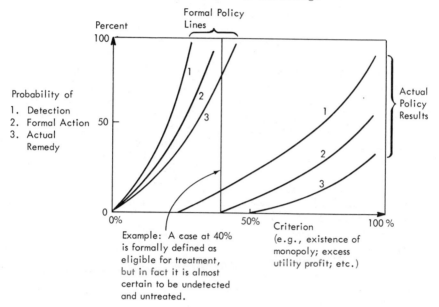

Percent

Formal Policy Lines

Probability of
1. Detection
2. Formal Action
3. Actual Remedy

Actual Policy Results

Example: A case at 40% is formally defined as eligible for treatment, but in fact it is almost certain to be undetected and untreated.

Criterion (e.g., existence of monopoly; excess utility profit; etc.)

monly combines the executive and legislature much more closely. The Premier and Cabinet members are closely and continuously involved in lawmaking and must appear regularly for debate. The government can be toppled and an election held at any time. Positions taken by the administration therefore move more briskly into law, and accountability is closer. Opposition parties criticize and modify the policies continuously and they develop *shadow cabinets* and coherent policies of their own, ready to apply quickly on taking office.

This directness and coherence is in contrast to the looseness and fragmenting apparent in the U.S. But the U.S. is a much larger and more diverse country; Britain or Denmark are comparable only to a region. Therefore, a parliamentary system might cope badly with the greater diversity and strains in the U.S. Moreover, the systems abroad do not yield perfect policies. Industrial policies are more unified and directly managed abroad. They may not be superior. But their differences arise in part from the difference in political systems.

There are thus numberless ways and places for pursuing the public interest and private interests. And a mastery of these intricacies is often critical to the outcome. The result is that formal policies diverge in some degree from their real roles. A genuine social need often causes a formal treatment to be put on the books. But enforcement is always less than total, and the true effect can be far less. Figure 4–5 portrays this. Small deviations will scarcely be detected, or dealt with, or even corrected. Large deviations may be treated, but the odds are lower than is formally declared.[12] The reader should keep this diagram in mind throughout the book, and for 45 years longer.

Finally, plain corruption may also occur. The stakes are large, the participants only human. This problem is more common at local and state levels, but various degrees and forms of it are endemic on the national scene.[13]

Beneath this complex surface of forums and strategies, the very substance of law evolves. Three points abʌut it are drawn briefly here: the Appendix to this chapter presents the legal foundations in some detail.

The Law Grows.   The economy evolves new business methods and new social interests. New ways are devised to get around old rules without actually breaking them. *The law* must grow, to deal with these and to reconcile new clashes of interests. This growth can occur by rewriting the laws or by new actions in enforcing the old ones. Agencies and courts usually have discretion in applying the laws. Their new interpretations, in response to changing issues, are a natural and proper source of growth and freshness in public policies.

Power Is Less than It Seems.   Many laws set absolute prohibitions on activities, results, or states of being. The laws will empower agencies to prohibit, and seek penalties for, infractions. But the process of legislation will have evolved the laws so that they inherently reflect the underlying social compromises. And the carrying out of the laws will usually involve more compromise.

The agency's powers will always be tested, if they challenge important private interests. The agency will need budget expertise, and standing at the political and judicial forums. It will therefore be seeking practical power from the legislature which assigned its large tasks, and legislatures often deny the resources to enforce fully.[14] Even with full resources, the agency will need support from above, and this often wavers. Even if it does enforce fully, the agency's tasks and mandates may have been highly diluted in the original passage of legislation. Therefore the ultimate *power* to carry out a balanced and optimal economic policy is problematical.

Due Process.   Due process is the phrase covering all those customs and explicit rules which try to give every side its say.

But due process is not a magic wand.

First, the hearing itself does not guarantee a fair result. A process which seems to air all interests may instead be simply a device for deflating social protest, or deceiving the parties into believing that they have been listened to.

Second, due process takes time. There often are time biases, favoring one side or the other. Therefore due process can inherently tip the out-

---

[12] Try placing ten examples in Figure 4–5. Begin with speed limits, shoplifting, auto theft, rules against billboards on turnpikes, and then insert laws you know that are tightly or loosely enforced.

[13] For a diverting view of one such seamy side, see Bill Veeck, *Thirty Tons a Day* (New York: Viking Press, 1972).

[14] Try to find five such cases—of disputes over incomplete enforcement—in a current issue of the *Wall Street Journal, Business Week* magazine or other national newspaper. You are almost sure to succeed.

come, or be deliberately abused. To study further, to look again, is to delay.

Third, due process is not free. It takes resources, including legal talent, research efforts, and simply the time and attention absorbed in mounting and winning one's fight. Moreover, one side or the other may be better able to bear these costs, or use them to have its way.

Fourth, due process does not inherently guarantee the optimal outcome. It does regularize and extend the process of fact-gathering which precedes a social decision. The end result can still be defective. Further, due process proceeds within the setting provided by existing law. If the need is to go outside current law and develop new treatments, due process in itself does not bring it about and can stand in the way.

Still, due process is an important guiding principle. Actually it is a rubric covering a variety of methods and solutions. Due process in one country may be mere ritual in another; and often a seemingly full airing of the issues will be regarded as a cover for just another backroom deal.

TOOLS AND POLICY SETS

Within these basic forms and processes, there are many policy devices which can be used, singly or together. We will set them out in a row and then describe the main American policy sets.

Methods

Common law is the evolving body of precedents set by decisions in private cases. With roots in early English law, this process defines contract rights, damages, and public interests. It underlays the formal growth of antitrust and regulatory laws. It is limited. Parties may be ignorant or lack legal resources. It is passive and often sporadic; there is no initiative to enforce the public interest.

Statutes and ordinances codify or extend common law. They may be forceful or subtle, penalizing directly or exerting supervision and pressure. Usually they are stated broadly and enforced in detail by executive agencies.

Franchises, certificates, and licenses are widely used to control entry. They grant a degree of monopoly, either complete for single firms (utilities) or partial for many competitors (licensed trades). They are often paired with regulatory controls, but often not. The range of markets is very wide; utilities, transport, broadcasting, and professions of all kinds. The grants may be permanent, temporary or indeterminate; in practice, they usually become perpetual. Licenses are often used also as a source of public revenue.

Regulation is by a specialized agency; a department, commission, board, etc. Powers vary, from complete to slight; resources also vary. So the degree of control varies. Often, regulators are dominated by the regulated firms in their own interests. At its best, regulation applies expert knowledge, continuous supervision, flexibility, and promptness, stressing inducement and prevention rather than penalties.

Taxes, expenditures, and subsidies can set controls, as well as feed funds through. Taxes can handicap a group of sellers (e.g., importers) or competitive products. Tax rules can induce changes in behavior (e.g., investment and oil discovery incentives). Public purchases can foster production; stockpiling can smooth price changes; and related controls can shape industries. Lending and credit guarantees induce growth in specific markets. And subsidies take many forms in rewarding and altering business behavior.

Industry self-regulation usually involves a public backing for private interests to control their own markets. Much public regulation actually is of this barefaced sort. It lacks means for identifying the public interest and supervising behavior. It usually tends to work against optimal results.

Investigations and publicity can apply pressure on behavior, by means of hearings and reports. But they are often empty or stir meaningless controversy. They are in any case a crude instrument. Wage-price guidelines—widely used as part of incomes policies—usually rely mainly on the uncertain power of publicity.

Emergency controls during wars and crises have been of many kinds. Strategic resources have been allocated directly, and entire businesses have been nominally taken over by the state.

Public ownership and operation are of endless degrees and varieties. They can provide direct control or any shade of isolation from political influence.

How Are These Tools Actually Used in the United States?

The conventional policy tools have become: *antitrust* for the "competitive" sector (which is primarily industry and trade), *regulation* for "utilities," and *public enterprise* for certain supposedly "intractable" cases and large parts of the social infrastructure. There have also been a wide range of special cases—weapons, farming, oil, shipping, health, sport, etc.—whose scope and variety have recently been growing.

Their main outlines now and 50 years ago were shown earlier in Tables 1–1 and 1–2. The patterns reflect both the formal domains and simple usage. Though many areas are debatable, the main outlines are clear enough.

Table 4–1 roughly summarizes the public funds used directly on policies. It understates, for some of the costs (such as for court hearings of antitrust cases) are indirect, though real. Table 4–1 also indicates some of the *private* resources employed in responding to, or anticipating, the public policies.

One draws three lessons from these tables. First, there have been changes in sectors and in the extension of policy coverage to some new sectors. Yet, second, the original coverage of the traditional policies has been little changed. Meanwhile, third, the range of exceptional, *ad hoc* cases has risen.

Antitrust is mainly a federal policy. It has three main parts. (1) It attempts to reduce *cooperation* among competitors. (2) It screens *mergers* between firms and stops some of them. And (3) it tries to abate *exist-*

TABLE 4–1

Policy Resources under Selected Programs, U.S., 1970–71

	Estimated Levels of Resources Used in 1970–71 (*$million*)	
	Public Agencies	Private Units
Antitrust[a]		
Antitrust Division	11 ⎫	
Federal Trade Commission...........	8 ⎬	150+
Regulation		
Federal Commissions[a]...............	108[d]	350
State Commissions[b].................	28[e]	150
Public Enterprises[a]		
Postal (deficit)......................	1,583	
Federal Courts.....................	40[c]	
Bureau of Reclamation..............	149	
Federal Prison Systems	79	
Veterans Administration		
Medical Care......................	1,633	
Public Purchases[a]		
Department of Defense..............	21,584	
NASA	3,367	
Atomic Energy Commission..........	2,501	
Subsidies[f]..........................	48,240	

[a] See U.S. Government Budget for 1970–71.

[b] See C. F. Phillips, Jr., *The Economics of Regulation*, rev. ed. (Homewood, Ill.: Richard D. Irwin, Inc., 1969), chap. 3; and various state commission annual reports.

[c] This represents a minority share of the costs of Federal Courts.

[d] The raw total is $270 million; 60 percent of it is assumed to be applied to functions other than economic regulation.

[e] The total is $80 million; 65 percent of it is assumed to be applied to functions other than economic regulation.

[f] See Chapter 25.

ing market power. Though its main focus is in industry and trade, it has been reaching recently into certain regulated sectors. Its tasks are vast; its resources are slight. (See Part II.)

Regulation involves ratifying one or several firms as a utility and, in return, putting it under some degree of constraint by a commission. Price changes—either up or down—must be approved by the commission. The criteria are (1) the profit rate is to be "fair," and (2) the price structure is to be "just and reasonable." Federal, state, and local commissions exist, overlap and fight each other in many sectors. (See Part III.)

Public enterprise exists in a variety of sectors, but it is relatively least evident in industry, finance, and utilities. The U.S. is unique in its reliance on regulation of private utilities in place of public ownership. Table 4–2 shows comparative patterns in other economies. The public corporation has become a standard form for public enterprises, but other varieties (joint ventures, holding companies, etc.) are being increasingly tried. (See Part IV.)

Pseudo-regulation. Many sectors are permitted to engage in self-regulation. They tend to raise industry profits, to limit competition among members, and to erect barriers against new entry. (See Chapter 24.)

Purchases by public agencies impinge strongly on many industries.

TABLE 4-2
Public Ownership Shares in Major Economic Sectors

Economic Sector	West Germany 1950	Japan 1960	Switzerland 1960	United States 1960	France 1954	Sweden 1960	United Kingdom 1962	Yugoslavia 1953	Poland 1960	Soviet Union 1963	East Germany 1964
Total	9%	10%	11%	18%	18%	20%	25%	30%	48%	58%	71%
Utilities (electricity, gas, water, sanitation)	43	20	60	28	83	71	} 70	100	100	100	100
Transport and communication	74	42	63	18	69	53		100	96	100	96
Services (public administration, defense, professional, other)	33	40	31	46	41	56	87	86	90	98	84
Construction	0	14	6	12	1	12	8	100	90	100	67
Manufacturing and mining	1	0	1	6	8	4	9	72	83	93	84
Commerce and finance	0	0	2	10	5	5	3	79	53	92	55
Agriculture, forestry, fisheries	2	1	3	1	2	5	2	3	8	14	17

Based on the share of employment in publicly-owned units. Some figures are estimates.
Source: Adapted from F. L. Pryor, *Property and Industrial Organization in Communist and Capitalist Nations* (Bloomington: University of Indiana Press, 1974).

One is weapons. Other programs are also important, in purchasing R&D activity, nuclear development, construction of schools and highways, and medical services. It is usually done in ways which permit —even foster—market power for the suppliers. (See Chapter 29.)

Subsidy programs are very large, extending into many recesses of the economy, and totalling at least $70 billion per year. Some of the subsidies are direct payments; others are by abating taxes; still others by guaranteeing risks. Most subsidies are managed by a friendly agency, which also crystallizes the plans and rationales for setting the levels and terms of the subsidies. (See Chapter 25.)

Trade barriers. Tariffs and quotas are high in a range of industries.

Patents. These grant a monopoly on new inventions for 17 years. They are critical in a few industries, significant for many, and largely irrelevant to most. (See Chapter 9.)

Taxation. Taxes have certain side effects on structure by influencing merger motives, etc. They have almost never been used clinically and in detail to abate market power or to gain public revenues from it.

A BRIEF HISTORY

Modern policies all have roots and antecedents in the past. The current versions often differ just in being more detailed, in covering bigger industries, and in some cases being *less* sophisticated. Tariffs, monopoly grants and limits, public ventures, most all have been tried before.

A look backward helps clarify (1) the nature of present treatments, and (2) where the trends in policies are heading. Is public control on the rise? Is antitrust—or regulation, or public enterprise—an experiment or a fixture?

One goes back beyond the Renaissance, to the origins both of the modern economy and of modern public policies. There are three early areas in which policy came to be important: usury, gilds, and food supply.

Usury was the practice of charging high interest rates on loaned capital. It often touched closely on royal power and finance, as well as on the wider use of capital throughout society. Therefore there was a chronic struggle—with religious and ethnic overtones—over the rate of interest and other terms of loans. From scripture were derived rules limiting the interest that could be charged.

Gilds were the cartels set up by master craftsmen to control their own behavior and the entrance of new talent. This too was important to the structure of power and wealth, for gild membership was widespread and the use of the gilds' products was virtually universal. As the middle ages blended into the preindustrial growth period, the power of the gilds to control competition abated.

The third policy area was agricultural supply to the towns. It was natural for the suppliers or middlemen to try to restrict supply and skim the cream, at the expense of the city dwellers. In various forms, this was called forestalling, engrossing, and regrating. It too involved basic social struggles, affecting the well-being and power of major social groupings.

By the 16th Century, early industrial development was stirring. There were monopolistic pockets, some stemming from powers of the nobility to exact tolls or other privileges. While the early economic growth was dissolving and bypassing many of these powers, monarchs were—on the contrary—resorting to grants of monopoly as devices to foster new industrial growth. The technique was much used and reached extensive scope under the Tudor monarchs of England and under Louis XIV in France. In addition, these royal promoters also used public enterprise of various sorts, to manage key parts of the economy and to start others. During this mercantilist period, kingship went with the deliberate restriction of competition in various directions, by what we would now call an infant-industry strategy. The restrictions affected not only production but also trade, imports, and other sectors.

It was against this that Adam Smith and other classical economists strove, to clear away barriers and controls, so that private interests could operate freely to maximize true national wealth (capacity, not gold). Tariffs, controls, and monopoly grants were the targets. This coincided with the main eruption of industrial growth in Britain during 1780–1840, which we now call the Industrial Revolution. Whether the reduction of controls caused the growth, or vice versa, or neither, is a matter of much debate. In any case, they both occurred, enough to mark the 19th Century distinctly off from the earlier two centuries. Even so, there was much state promotional activity. Late in the 19th Century, the common-law reliance on open competition had become crystallized. But it was not the only trait. In addition, there was a willingness to mark off some markets as "affected by the public interest." Also, public involvement in infrastructure was large, both in the U.S. and elsewhere.

The heyday of the Manchester School, the assertion of unfettered power of those with capital, was largely over by 1890 in England. But its legacy was strong: private enterprise had become the ruling form for most of the economy in both the U.S. and Britain by 1860. Other European countries remained more willing to create economic capital directly by the state.

From 1860 to 1900 the crest of social Darwinism occurred in the U.S. The survival of the fittest was said to happen in industry as well as in the population. Out of the ferment of this period grew those policies which now prevail. Modern markets were widening and deepening, so that the range of structures and constraints on them offered a wide area of choice. Turbulent events were creating not only industrial unrest but also massive changes in the structure of industry. Moreover, these industrial shifts and new monopolies were generating large fortunes, some of which still loom large in the structure of society.

In short, the period from 1860 to 1900 was a watershed for industrial policies throughout the modern world. The results of this came to the surface in the decades from 1900 to 1920. The U.S. made decisive choices about antitrust, regulation, and public enterprise. And in Europe too occurred major changes.

In the U.S. the decisive changes were in applying antitrust—under Roosevelt, Taft, and Wilson before 1916—with some strictness and in franchising private utilities under regulation rather than extending public enterprise. By contrast, in Europe there was a growth in the reliance on public enterprises, both at the municipal level and on a national basis in economic and social sectors.

The U.S. move towards antitrust and regulation was primarily a conservative shift. Antitrust enforcement was sharp in several directions, and the Federal Trade Commission was created in 1914. But with the onset of World War I, antitrust activity was virtually halted after 1915. Likewise, the creation of state commissions regulating utilities seemed to be a progressive move, but instead it was usually sought by the utilities themselves. The 1920s brought a growth of federal regulation in a few utility sectors, but a fading away of antitrust activity. In the 1930s, the Great Depression ushered in several varieties of policy activity. The basic American patterns of antitrust and regulation were hardened and extended during this decade. There was a massive cleaning up of holding-company and regulatory abuses. These extended into utilities and finance, in great detail. There was the experiment in industry cartels under the National Recovery Administration. TVA was begun, as a major symbol of public enterprise. Antitrust was reborn under Thurman Arnold during 1938–44.

The 1940s brought the rise of large new gray areas, in which the now-conventional policy controls were blurred and weak. Weapons were a prime case, but the oil industry, insurance, shipbuilding, and agriculture also posed new problems. Antitrust and regulation were ripe for reassessment but continued in the old patterns. In short, by 1952 policies were overdue for basic reappraisal.

Instead, there has been mainly a standstill. Since 1952, there has been nearly a moratorium on antitrust treatment of established market power.[15] Regulation continued in a passive stance until the 1960s, when there was an increase of quality and vigor in some federal commissions. Weapons and space expenditures were high, and remained largely outside efficient policy treatments. Other agencies had various impacts in the area of public ownership, but there was no marked refinement of public enterprise nor a clear understanding of the public enterprise that already existed.

In a longer perspective, the antitrust and regulatory experiments have now reached maturity or perhaps run their course. The 1970s appear to be a period of disequilibrium and turbulence in most sectors. From this ferment, perhaps, the main lessons about policy accomplishments and defects can be drawn and applied in new directions.

In Europe, more recent decades have brought some contrasts with American policy. British reliance on public enterprise shifted upwards during 1945–50 when a brace of new public enterprises were created, primarily in utility sectors. Since then, public enterprise has grown only marginally. Meanwhile, a distinct growth in British antitrust activity has occurred since 1955, so that its policies are now nearly as firm as are those in the United States. In a few antitrust areas, in fact, British policy is now stricter.

---

[15] Yet activity has begun to quicken during 1969–75 (see Chapter 7).

In other European countries, the development of public enterprise has been more fertile since the 1930s. Especially in Italy, public enterprise has gone beyond the older type of utility monopoly, into a more luxuriant growth of public holding companies, quasi-control, and industrial branching. The whole variety of these have become increasingly related to national economic planning in Italy, France, and Germany.

Both Germany and Japan underwent bouts of Allied antitrust restructuring after World War II. These had limited but real effects for perhaps a decade at the most.

Finally, the 1970s have brought experimentation with price controls in several countries, including the United States. Their effects have been marginal at best (see Chapter 24).

In this whole sequence, there appears to be no major trend towards increasing government interference. Rather, the main impression is of increasing variety, in a continuing process of trial and error. At any time, each country has a portfolio of current policies, some of which are major and some minor. Over time, this set evolves, as new treatments are tried and old ones are discarded. This shifting is also caused by the rise and fall of individual sectors, for which the suitable policy treatments differ.

There is also a mixing of motivations for actual policies. Not only do policies often follow strange paths, but frequently the reasons given for policies are quite different from the real ones. Drastic policy steps turn out instead to be conservative. And conservatives often impose drastic new policies. Countries regarded as reactionary often are radical.[16]

Altogether, the evolution of policies reflects (1) the past, (2) national culture, and (3) the political economy of struggles among various private interests. Whether this evolution fits or strays from an efficient set of policies is, of course, the core question around which this book turns.

APPENDIX: LEGAL FOUNDATIONS

This review gives more detail on the legal foundations of industrial policies.

The Structure and Powers of Government

In the government of the United States, four fundamental principles affect the application of controls: (1) Under the federal system, powers are distributed between the nation and the several states. The national government possesses the express powers that are delegated to it by the

---

[16] The true policies often belie the stereotypes. The Wilson administration of 1912-20 was essentially conservative on industry, despite the rhetoric. Franklin D. Roosevelt's aim and effect was to preserve capitalism. Public enterprise, and actions against established finance and the larger monopolies, were largely avoided.

And Richard Nixon proposed a number of seemingly efficient policies, favoring more competition in banking and satellite communications, a minimum of subsidy in agriculture and railroading, neutrality toward conglomerate take-overs (after 1970), deregulation of gas field prices, greatly increased equal employment enforcement, the volunteer army, and even home-city TV viewing of pro football games. Despite other lapses, these proposals and actions fit the true Nixon position as *outside* the core financial interests, not as serving *establishment* interests exclusively.

Constitution, the implied powers that may be inferred therefrom, the resulting powers—such as the power to issue paper money and make it legal tender—that are consequent upon a combination of express powers, and the inherent powers—relating primarily to international affairs— that are an attribute of national sovereignty. Under the Tenth Amendment, all other powers were reserved to the states. (2) Within both state and federal governments there is a separation of legislative, executive, and judicial powers. Protection against arbitrary action is thus afforded by a system of checks and balances. (3) These governments rest on written constitutions, containing guarantees of individual rights through which their powers are limited. (4) The acts of legislators and executives are subject to judicial review. The constitutions and the laws are interpreted, laws found to be unconstitutional are voided, and the acts of administrators are approved, modified, or reversed by the courts. This structure of government, and these limitations to its powers, determine whether a particular method of control may be employed and, if so, by whom, and how.

The Distribution of Powers. The economic powers delegated to the federal government by the states, as enumerated in Article I, Section 8 of the Constitution are these:

To lay and collect Taxes, Duties, Imposts and Excises, to pay the Debts and provide for the common Defence and the general Welfare. . . .
To borrow Money. . . .
To regulate Commerce with foreign Nations and among the several States . . . and with the Indian tribes;
To establish . . . uniform laws on the subject of Bankruptcies. . . .
To coin Money, regulate the value thereof . . . and fix the Standard of Weights and Measures. . . .
To establish Post Offices and post Roads;
To promote the progress of Science and useful Arts, by securing for limited Times to Authors and Inventors the exclusive Right to their respective Writings and Discoveries. . . .

The most important of these clauses, for public control of business in time of peace, is the one—generally referred to as the interstate commerce clause—that gives the Congress power "To regulate Commerce . . . among the several States. . . ." Of even greater importance, however, are the extensive powers, conferred by subsequent clauses, to declare and wage war. And also significant, in some cases, is the fact that the states are forbidden to enter into treaties by Article I, Section 10 of the Constitution, while the President and the Senate are authorized to do so by Article II, Section 2.

The enumerated powers of the federal government are those expressly set forth in the Constitution. The implied powers are those inferred from the final clause of Article I, Section 8 of that document which authorized the Congress "To make all laws which shall be necessary and proper for carrying into Execution the foregoing Powers, and all other Powers vested by this Constitution in the Government of the United States. . . ." This may not have been intended as a grant of further powers, but it was so interpreted by the Supreme Court in the famous case of *McCulloch* v. *Maryland* in 1819.[17] The state of Maryland had imposed a tax on notes issued by a bank established by the federal government. When sued, it advanced the defense that nothing in the Constitution had empowered the Congress to set up a bank. The Court admitted that this power was not explicit, but held that it could reasonably be deduced from those that were. Said Chief Justice John Marshall, "Let the end be legitimate, let it be within the scope of the Constitution, and all means which are appropriate . . . which are not prohibited, but consist with the letter and spirit of the Constitution, are constitutional. . . ." This decision, as must be obvious, was of paramount importance in extending the scope of federal powers. From this time on, the national government was permitted, not only to do things that the Constitution said, but also to do things that the Court was willing to infer.

All governmental powers, save those denied them by the Constitution, are retained by the several states. Laws affecting business have thus been enacted, in the interest of public safety, health, and morals, and the general welfare, under what has been known as the police power of the states. This power, though not mentioned in the Constitution, has long been recognized by the courts.[18] Without definite limits, it has afforded a basis for such activities as the licensing of automobile drivers to insure public safety, the inspection of dairies to protect public health, the censorship of motion pictures to safeguard public morals, and the payment of mothers' pensions to promote the general welfare.

When state and federal powers come into conflict, the latter must prevail. "This Constitution," says Article VI, "and the Laws of the United States which shall be made in Pursuance thereof . . . shall be the supreme Law of the Land." And this phrase was repeated by Justice Marshall in *McCulloch* v. *Maryland,* when he denied the states the right to tax a federal agency. "The government of the United States," he said, "though limited in its powers, is supreme; and its laws, when made in pursuance of the Constitution, form the supreme law of the land."

There has been a steady trend, over the years, toward increasing centralization of functions in the federal government. The reasons for this development are not hard to find. (1) Some regulatory activities require the establishment of uniform standards throughout the country if they are adequately to be performed. This is true, for instance, of the grading of commodities. (2) In other cases, the industries controlled extend beyond state borders, and controls must be given equal scope if they are to work at all. It was the failure of state regulation that led to the federal regulation of railway transport and interstate sales of gas and electricity. (3) Elsewhere, a state may fail to act because its producers, if compelled to incur higher costs, would be placed at a disadvantage in competing with producers in surrounding states. Here, if competitors are to be put upon an equal footing, federal action is required. The establishment of a system of unemployment insurance is a case in point. (4) Sometimes,

---

[17] 4 Wheaton 316.

[18] *Brown* v. *Maryland,* 12 Wheaton 419 (1827); *Charles River Bridge* v. *Warren Bridge,* 11 Peters 420 (1837); *Cooley* v. *Board of Wardens of Port of Philadelphia,* 12 Howard 299 (1852).

responsibility for a service is assumed by the federal government because it has not been met by the states. This is why Washington went into the business of conserving natural resources and providing social security. (5) The federal government can raise more money than the states. There is no constitutional limit on its power to borrow. And it can reach the larger incomes with progressive taxes, wherever their possessors may reside. As a result, it has been in a stronger position than the states to finance additional activities. (6) Each of these factors makes for centralization. But the great centralizers are war and depression.

In some cases, common programs have been undertaken in regions larger than the separate states without concentrating their management in Washington. Three means of doing this have been devised. (1) The federal government has made grants, when matched by state appropriations, laying down certain conditions, but leaving detailed administration to the states. This method has been used in building roads, in providing low-rent housing, and in giving assistance to dependent children and the aged. (2) The federal government has imposed a tax, but granted exemptions where states have levied a comparable tax to finance a specified activity. It was through the tax offset device that unemployment insurance systems were set up in the several states. (3) The Constitution, in Article I, Section 10, forbids the states to enter into compacts with one another without the consent of Congress. In certain cases, this consent has been obtained. Interstate compacts have governed the sharing of water rights on lakes and rivers and provided for curtailment of the production of petroleum. They might well have been used with greater frequency had not interpretation allowed so broad a scope to federal powers.

The Separation of Powers. Within the state and federal governments, distinct responsiblities are traditionally assigned to three separate branches: the enactment of laws to the legislature, their enforcement to the executive, and their interpretation to the judiciary. Under the constitutions, these branches are equal. None has authority over the others, but each of them can check the others. The executive can veto a bill passed by the legislature. The legislature can pass it over his veto. The courts can change its meaning by interpretation. The legislature can revise the law, restating its former purpose, and pass it again. The executive may change the complexion of the courts when he appoints new judges. But these appointments must be confirmed by the upper house of the legislature. Through such checks and balances, protection is afforded against precipitate and ill-considered action and against the arbitrary exercise of power.

Though the three branches of government are equal, the courts have succeeded in establishing their own supremacy in one respect. The state courts can find a local ordinance or a state law to be in violation of the state or federal constitutions; in interpreting a state constitution, the highest court in the state is the final authority. The federal courts can find state or federal laws to be in violation of the federal Constitution, and here the Supreme Court of the United States is the final authority. The power of the Supreme Court to invalidate state laws is clearly indicated in the provision of Article VI that the Constitution itself, and the enactments of the Congress, shall be the supreme law of the land. Its power to invalidate federal legislation was not mentioned in the Constitution but asserted by the Court in the historic case of *Marbury* v. *Madison* in 1803.[19] In the words of Justice Marshall, "an act of the legislature, repugnant to the Constitution, is void. . . ." The doctrine of judicial supremacy, thus established, now has behind it the prestige of tradition and the force of popular support.

The practice of government departs in another respect from the nominal pattern of three coequal branches, each with a distinctive duty to perform. The legislature has been forced, by the increasing complexity of the problems with which it must deal, to delegate authority to the executive. It may assert the broad outlines of a policy, but must leave it to administration to fill in the details. In doing so, it confers the power to legislate. Executive agencies—departments and commissions—may issue rules and regulations that come to have the force of law. They may perform judicial functions, too, hearing complaints and rendering decisions, subject to appeal, in much the manner of a lower court. They thus combine, in varying degrees, the work of the administrator, the legislator, and the judge.

The blueprint of governmental organization is further complicated by the independent status usually accorded the regulatory commission. It is located within the executive branch. Its members are appointed by the governor or the President. But usually they may not be removed except for serious misconduct. And their terms of office may be so arranged as to make it difficult for him readily to obtain a majority committed to his policies. The independent commission is dependent on the executive to initiate its appointments, on the legislature to provide its powers and appropriations, on the judiciary to interpret its statute and enforce its rules. Sometimes described as a fourth branch of government, it is still a creature of the other three.

Constitutional Safeguards for Individual Rights. In both state and federal constitutions, the rights of citizens are protected against invasion by the acts of governments. State constitutions limit state action, some of them setting forth restrictions in elaborate detail, all of them safeguarding the rights of person and property in general terms. The federal Constitution imposes limitations on both state and federal governments. The limitations on control of business by the federal government are found in the due process clause of the Fifth Amendment and in its protection against abuse of the right of eminent domain: "No person shall . . . be deprived of life, liberty, or property without due process of law; nor shall private property be taken for public use, without just compensation." This Amendment was adopted when the Constitution was ratified, as a part of the Bill of Rights. The limitations on the power of the states to exercise controls over business are contained in the contracts clause in Article I, Section 10 of the Constitution itself, "No State shall . . . pass any . . . Law impairing the Obligation of Contracts . . . ," and in the

---

[19] 1 Cranch 137.

clauses contained in the Fourteenth Amendment—adopted in connection with the abolition of slavery at the time of the Civil War—which relate (1) to the privileges and immunities of citizens, (2) to due process of law, and (3) to equal protection of the laws: "No State shall make or enforce any law which shall abridge the privileges or immunities of citizens of the United States; nor shall any State deprive any person of life, liberty, or property, without due process of law; nor deny to any person within its jurisdiction the equal protection of the laws." These provisions should be memorized, together with the enumeration of Congressional powers set forth above, for it is upon them that the system of law that governs the public control of business in the United States is based.

Judicial Review. The courts are at once powerful and impotent. They can invalidate or modify an act if it is brought before them. They cannot question it if it is not. They can veto legislation or, in effect, rewrite it. But they cannot initiate a law. They must wait for someone—a public prosecutor or a private plaintiff—to sue or to appeal a suit. It is only then they can speak.

The courts interpret the Constitution and the laws, determining whether laws shall stand, by giving the Constitution one meaning or another, and giving meanings to the laws themselves. In the process of interpretation, they follow precedents. But the precedents on both sides of an issue may be so numerous that judges are free to pick and choose. The Supreme Court of the United States, moreover, does not consider itself to be bound by earlier decisions. It may overrule them explicitly; it may do so silently; it may reverse them, in actuality, while arguing persuasively that it has made no change. The last word spoken by the last court, at any moment, is the law.

Interpretation has seemed to be narrow, ambiguous and inconsistent, shifting and even reversing its direction from time to time. This may be true, in part, because judges are influenced by their background, training, and social outlook, because the Supreme Court, as Mr. Dooley once remarked, "follows th' illiction returns," and because the composition of the Court has changed. With the replacement (or conversion) of a single judge, the minority in a 5 to 4 division may form a majority in the next 5 to 4 vote. It is true, too, because decisions are handed down in specific cases, where issues may differ in detail, because differences in skill of presentation may lead to different judgments on similar facts, and because the courts confine themselves to narrow issues, leaving the way open to arrive at different decisions on the basis of somewhat different facts. It is true, finally, because the problems brought to judgment are complex and confusing, because lawyers and judges—and economists— fail to understand them, and because the answers, at best, are far from clear. It is easy to berate the judiciary, more difficult to fulfill the duties of a judge.

Judicial Limitations on Control

When the validity of a law or an order regulating business is questioned, the courts may decide against it on any one of several grounds.

They may find that the government enacting it has exceeded its powers: that a state has attempted to control an industry that is in interstate commerce, that the federal government has attempted to control one that is not, that it has made improper use of its taxing power, or gone beyond its power to make treaties or its power to wage war. They may hold that the separation of governmental functions has been disregarded: that the executive branch has acted without legislative authority, or that the legislature has made an undue delegation of powers. They may conclude that the safeguards of individual rights have been violated: that property has been taken without just compensation, that contracts have been impaired, that persons have been denied equality of treatment, or deprived of liberty or property without due process, whether by the procedures employed in a law's administration or by the substance of the law itself. The courts thus have wide latitude in passing judgment on controls established and administered by other branches of the government, and they have used it, from time to time, with varying effects.

Interstate Commerce.   The Supreme Court first defined the word "commerce" in the case of *Gibbons* v. *Ogden*[20] in 1824. The scope it gave the term was broad. Commerce, said Justice Marshall, "is traffic, but it is something more. . . . It describes the commercial intercourse between nations and parts of nations, in all its branches. . . ." The concept was thus extended beyond the act of buying and selling across state lines to comprehend all of the processes through which trade is carried on. The Court applied it specifically to navigation in the Gibbons case, and to other forms of transport and communications in cases decided in 1872 and 1877.[21] But it has gone much farther. In 1871 it upheld federal regulation of a steamer carrying goods between two ports in Michigan on the ground that the out-of-state origin and destination of these goods made the vessel "an instrument" of interstate commerce.[22] In 1914 it permitted the federal government to fix railway rates between points within the borders of a state because this traffic bore "such a close and substantial relation to interstate traffic that the control is essential or appropriate."[23] And in 1922 it approved the regulation of grain elevators and stockyards, saying that such enterprises, though tied to one location, were situated in the "stream" or "flow" of commerce.[24]

The trend of opinion, in these decisions, favored the federal government. But federal controls, in other cases, were limited in scope or completely outlawed, for many years, through narrow interpretations of the commerce clause. Thus, in 1887 and 1895, the Court ruled that manufacturing was not commerce, excluding the entire area from the scope of federal power.[25] In 1918 it invalidated a law prohibiting interstate shipment of the products of child labor, on the ground that their production

---

[20] 9 Wheaton 1.

[21] *Railway* v. *Van Husen,* 95 U.S. 465 (1872); *Pensacola Tel. Co.* v. *Western Union,* 96 U.S. 1 (1877).

[22] *Steamer Daniel Bell* v. *U.S.,* 10 Wallace 557.

[23] *The Shreveport Rate Cases,* 234 U.S. 342.

[24] *Lemke* v. *Farmers Grain Co.,* 258 U.S. 50 (1922); *Stafford* v. *Wallace,* 258 U.S. 495 (1922).

[25] *Kidd* v. *Pearson,* 128 U.S. 1 (1887); *U.S.* v. *E. C. Knight Co.,* 156 U.S. 1 (1895).

was not interstate.[26] In 1935 it found the National Industrial Recovery Act to be unconstitutional, for one reason, because the relation between industries covered by NRA codes, on the one hand, and interstate commerce, on the other, was remote.[27] And in 1936, invalidating a law providing for wage and price fixing in the coal industry, the Court asserted that the federal government could not control an intrastate activity unless its effect on interstate commerce was not merely "close and substantial," but "direct."[28]

The restrictive effect of these decisions was sharply reversed in 1937, when the Court upheld the constitutionality of the National Labor Relations Act. This law, requiring collective bargaining and giving a federal board the power to deal with unfair labor practices, was challenged by companies manufacturing steel, trailers, and men's clothing. In each case the Court held that the law applied.[29] Congress cannot be held powerless to regulate, said Chief Justice Hughes, "when industries organize themselves on a national scale, making their relation to interstate commerce the dominant factor in their activities. . . ." In later decisions the law was also held to cover a cannery that shipped only a third of its output to other states[30] and a power company that sold an insignificant fraction of its current across state lines.[31] In 1941 the Court went on to approve the Fair Labor Standards Act, a law forbidding interstate shipment of goods made by persons paid less than legally determined wages or required to work for more than legally determined hours, thus reversing the position it had taken in 1918, when the same method was used to eliminate child labor[32] And in 1942, it upheld the Agricultural Adjustment Act of 1938, which enabled the federal government to control the quantity of a crop that a farmer could offer for sale.[33] In this decision, the Court explicitly rejected the rule it had laid down in the case of the coal industry in 1936: "Even if the appellee's activity be local and though it may not be regarded as commerce, it may still, whatever its nature, be reached by Congress if it exerts a substantial economic effect on interstate commerce, and this irrespective of whether such effect is what might at some earlier time have been defined as 'direct' or 'indirect.' "[34] In 1944 the Court upheld the application of a federal statute to the insurance business,[35] and in 1945 to retail trade.[36] It thus appears that the interpretation of the commerce clause is no longer likely to impose significant limits on federal power.

---

[26] *Hammer* v. *Dagenhart,* 247 U.S. 251.

[27] *Schechter* v. *U.S.,* 295 U.S. 495.

[28] *Carter* v. *Carter Coal Co.,* 298 U.S. 238.

[29] *NLRB* v. *Jones & Laughlin Steel Corp.,* 301 U.S. 1; *NLRB* v. *Fruehauf Trailer Co.,* 301 U.S. 49; *NLRB* v. *Friedman-Harry Marks Clothing Co.,* 301 U.S. 58.

[30] *Santa Cruz Packing Co.* v. *NLRB,* 303 U.S. 453 (1938).

[31] *Consolidated Edison Co.* v. *NLRB,* 305 U.S. 197 (1938).

[32] *U.S.* v. *Darby Lumber Co.,* 312 U.S. 100.

[33] *Wickard* v. *Filburn,* 317 U.S. 111.

[34] *Ibid.,* p. 125.

[35] *U.S.* v. *South-Eastern Underwriters,* 322 U.S. 533.

[36] *U.S.* v. *Frankfort Distilleries,* 324 U.S. 293.

The clause may still be used, however, to reject regulation by the states. Laws that incidentally affect interstate commerce are usually allowed to stand. But those that unduly burden or obstruct it may be found to trespass on federal authority. And where state and federal regulations overlap, those of the federal government are given precedence and those of the states must be made to conform.[37]

The General Welfare. The Supreme Court has shown no desire to restrict the activities of the federal government under its war or treaty powers. It has, however, rejected efforts by Congress, made under cover of its power to tax, to impose controls for which it had no other authority. The Constitution gives Congress the power "To lay and collect Taxes . . . and provide for the common Defence and general Welfare. . . ." But the Court long held that this reference to the general welfare conferred no power in itself, but merely described the purposes for which tax money would be used. It did not object to the imposition of taxes to check the sale of oleomargarine,[38] narcotics,[39] or firearms,[40] accepting the fiction that the levies were intended as a source of revenue. But in 1922 it branded as unconstitutional a second Congressional attempt to outlaw child labor, this time by taxing the profits of the children's employers.[41] In 1936 it nullified the Agricultural Adjustment Act of 1933 on the ground that collection of taxes from processors and payment of benefits to producers of agricultural commodities, in order to curtail their output, involved the use of taxation not for revenue but in the interest of a special group, in order to exercise control where power had not been delegated to Congress but reserved to the states.[42] And in the same year, in rejecting regulation of the coal industry, the Court denounced the effort to compel adherence to minimum wages and prices by taxing producers who did not cooperate in the program and exempting those who did.[43]

With the tax power, as with the commerce power, interpretation was reversed in 1937. In that year the Court was called upon to consider two programs of social insurance adopted under the Social Security Act of 1935. In the first, the federal government induced the states to enact unemployment insurance laws by taxing payrolls and allowing an offset where the states imposed such taxes to finance insurance benefits. In the second, it levied further taxes on wages and payrolls but obligated itself to pay annuities to wage earners upon their retirement from work. Each of these programs was held to be constitutional. Under the first, said Justice Cardozo, the tax was legitimate as a source of revenue, and the offset did not involve coercion of the states, in contravention of the Constitution, but merely afforded a temptation to cooperate.[44] Under the second, the taxes were again legitimate, and the decision of Congress to

---

[37] *The Shreveport Rate Cases,* 234 U.S. 342.
[38] *McCray* v. *U.S.,* 195 U.S. 27 (1904).
[39] *U.S.* v. *Doremus,* 249 U.S. 87 (1919).
[40] *Sonzinsky* v. *U.S.,* 300 U.S. 506.
[41] *Bailey* v. *Drexel Furniture Co.,* 259 U.S. 20.
[42] *U.S.* v. *Butler* (the Hoosac Mills case), 297 U.S. 1.
[43] *Carter* v. *Carter Coal Co.,* 298 U.S. 238.
[44] *Steward Machine Co.* v. *Davis,* 301 U.S. 548.

provide benefits for the aged lay within its power to spend for the general welfare. The concept of welfare, said Justice Cardozo, is not a static one; it changes with the times. Its content is for Congress to decide. The courts will not interfere "unless the choice is clearly wrong, a display of arbitrary power, not an exercise of judgment."[45] The power to control by taxing and spending, in consequence, is virtually unlimited.

The police power, as we have seen, was retained by the several states. Nowhere in the Constitution or in the decisions of the courts is this power given to the federal government. But Congress has none the less acted, under the authority of its other powers, to protect public safety, health, and morals, and to promote the general welfare. In addition to taxing oleo, narcotics, and firearms and providing insurance benefits, it has also excluded fraudulent and obscene materials from the mails and prohibited the interstate movement of lottery tickets, stolen automobiles, and women for immoral purposes. It has used its powers, too, to insure the purity of foods and drugs, to enforce grain standards and plant quarantines, to improve conditions of labor, and to prevent misrepresentation in the distribution of securities. As a result, reference is sometimes made to the police powers of the federal government. Strictly speaking, no such powers exist. But their absence, today, presents no handicap.

Powers of the Executive. Action may be reversed not only because it exceeds the powers conferred upon the government but also because it violates the separation of powers. It may be found that the executive branch has gone beyond its own authority, or that the legislative branch has gone too far in delegating authority to the executive.

In most cases where the delegation of power has been questioned, it has been upheld. Congress, in general, is permitted to delegate where it states its purposes and lays down rules to limit the exercise of delegated powers.[46]

The Obligation of Contracts. State laws impairing contracts may be invalidated under Article I, Section 10 of the Constitution. Federal laws having the same effect may be held to be in violation of the due process clause of the Fifth Amendment. The safeguards against impairment apply both to private contracts and to those to which a government is a party, such as charters and franchises. They do not apply to commitments that are lacking in consideration or to contracts involving commitments that are contrary to public policy. The safeguards are not absolute. Impairment is permitted when incidental to legislation enacted under the police powers of a state. The only condition laid down by the courts is that the end sought by a law must be legitimate and the means employed appropriate. This interpretation is inescapable, since, in its absence, a multitude of contracts would bar the enactment of legislation in the public interest.

---

[45] *Helvering* v. *Davis,* 301 U.S. 619.

[46] See *U.S.* v. *Shreveport Grain & Elevator Co.,* 287 U.S. 77 (1932), upholding the Food and Drug Act; *U.S.* v. *Rock Royal Cooperative,* 307 U.S. 533 (1939), upholding the Agricultural Marketing Agreements Act; *Yakus* v. *U.S.,* 321 U.S. 414 (1944), upholding the Emergency Price Control Act; *American Power & Light Co.* v. *SEC,* 329 U.S. 90 (1946), upholding the Public Utility Holding Company Act; and *Lichter* v. *U.S.,* 332 U.S. 742 (1948), upholding the renegotiation of war contracts.

One of the most serious issues that has arisen here relates to the constitutionality of laws giving relief to debtors in periods of business depression. Such laws do impair the obligation of contracts. But they may also preserve human values and social stability in times of stress and strain. Here the Supreme Court has applied the test of reasonableness, upholding laws that postponed payments for a limited period but compensated the creditor for his loss, and invalidating those that seemed to go too far in depriving the creditor of his rights.[47]

Any Person. The Fifth Amendment forbade the federal government to deprive any *person* of life, liberty, or property without due process of law; and the Fourteenth Amendment forbade the states (1) to abridge the privileges or immunities of *citizens,* (2) to deprive any *person* of life, liberty, or property without due process of law, and (3) to deny to any *person* the equal protection of the laws. The clause relating to privileges and immunities has never been employed to limit regulation of business, since business units have not been held to qualify as *citizens.* But the other clauses have been so employed, ever since the Supreme Court decreed, in 1886, that a corporation is a *person.* In 1873, when a corporation challenged a Louisiana law zoning slaughterhouse locations, the Court had rejected this interpretation, and Justice Miller had expressed the view that the Fourteenth Amendment would never be used for any purpose other than its obvious one of protecting the Negro against discrimination.[48] But 13 years later, in the case of *Santa Clara County* v. *Southern Pacific Railway,*[49] the Court extended the scope of the two amendments to cover corporate enterprise. This position was challenged, in 1938, by Justice Black, who stated flatly, in a dissenting opinion, "I do not believe that the word 'person' in the Fourteenth Amendment includes corporations."[50] But this was not the view of the majority; the rule of 1886 still stands.

When applied to corporations, the clause assuring equal protection has been used to invalidate laws that discriminate against one business in favor of another. But this clause has not been so interpreted as to prevent distinctions based on principles of classification that are not arbitrary or capricious. The Supreme Court has thus upheld a minimum wage law for women, in Arizona, that exempted railway restaurants;[51] a tax on retail stores, in Indiana, that was graduated in accordance with the number of stores in a chain;[52] and a federal tax on payrolls that did not apply to employers with fewer than eight employees.[53] The equal protection clause, moreover, adds little to the safeguards of the law. For where a measure is rejected as discriminatory, it can also be found to

---

[47] *Home Building & Loan Assn.* v. *Blaisdell,* 290 U.S. 398 (1933), upholding the Minnesota moratorium law; and *Louisville Joint Stock Land Bank* v. *Radford,* 295 U.S. 955 (1935), invalidating the Frazier-Lemke Act.

[48] *The Slaughter House Cases,* 16 Wallace 36.

[49] 118 U.S. 394.

[50] *Connecticut General Life Insurance Co.* v. *Johnson,* 303 U.S. 77, 85.

[51] *Dominion Hotel* v. *Arizona,* 249 U.S. 265 (1919).

[52] *Indiana* v. *Jackson,* 283 U.S. 527 (1937).

[53] *Steward Machine Co.* v. *Davis,* 301 U.S. 548 (1937).

violate due process. It is under the heading of due process that the most serious restrictions on public control have been imposed.

Liberty or Property. The liberty that is guaranteed by the due process clause has been held by the Supreme Court to include the freedom to enter into contracts. And the preservation of this freedom has been advanced by the Court, from time to time in the past, as its reason for rejecting laws that provided for the establishment of maximum hours and minimum wages. In 1905 the provisions of a New York law limiting the hours of bakers to 10 per day or 60 per week were denounced as "mere meddlesome interferences with the rights of the individual."[54] But in 1908 an Oregon law limiting the hours of women was upheld on the ground that the state, under its police powers, might safeguard the health of mothers in order to preserve the health of the community.[55] And in 1917 an Oregon law establishing a 10 hour daily limit for men as well as women, in factories, was also upheld as falling within the police powers of the state.[56] In 1923, however, the Court invalidated a law fixing minimum wages for women in the District of Columbia. The differences between the sexes, said Justice Sutherland, "have now come almost if not quite to the vanishing point." Consequently, "we cannot accept the doctrine that women of mature age *sui juris* require or may be subjected to restrictions upon their liberty of contract. . . ."[57] And again in 1936, in the Tipaldo case,[58] a New York law fixing minimum wages for women was overthrown, by a 5 to 4 decision, on the same ground.

To prevent persons (i.e., human beings) from being deprived of *liberty* without due process, it is no longer held that men and women must work for long hours at low pay. But to prevent persons (i.e., corporations) from being deprived of *property* without due process, it is still held that measures affecting the size of corporate incomes or the value of corporate assets, if questioned, must have the approval of the courts. And it is here that the due process clause has found its major use.

Affected with a Public Interest. Recognizing the necessity of approving regulation of the services rendered and the prices charged by natural monopolies, but unwilling to permit extension of such controls, under the due process clause, to industry in general, the Supreme Court, in 1877, hit upon the device of establishing a separate category of businesses affected with a public interest, and confining regulation to those that it might so define. In the famous case of *Munn* v. *Illinois,*[59] decided in that year, the Court approved a law, enacted by the state of Illinois, controlling the charges made by grain elevators and warehouses. In the words of its opinion: "Property does become clothed with a public interest when used in a manner to make it of public consequence, and affect the community at large. When, therefore, one devotes his property to a use in which the public has an interest, he, in effect, grants to the public an

---

[54] *Lochner* v. *New York,* 198 U.S. 45.
[55] *Muller* v. *Oregon,* 208 U.S. 412. ˙
[56] *Bunting* v. *Oregon,* 243 U.S. 426.
[57] *Adkins* v. *Children's Hospital,* 261 U.S. 525.
[58] *Morehead* v. *New York ex rel. Tipaldo,* 298 U.S. 587.
[59] 94 U.S. 113.

interest in that use, and must submit to be controlled by the public for the common good. . . ." The elevators along the Chicago waterfront were found to stand "in the very gateway of commerce, and take toll from all who pass." It was permissible, therefore, that they be regulated, so that they might "take but reasonable toll."

This concept was subsequently employed in approving public regulation of such industries as the railroads, and water, gas, electric, and telephone companies. It was called upon in 1914 in upholding a Kansas law providing for the regulation of fire insurance rates.[60] But it was used for a decade to invalidate laws extending public controls to other fields. In 1923 the Court rejected a Kansas law providing for compulsory arbitration of labor disputes in basic industries;[61] in 1927, a New York law fixing the markup of theater ticket agencies;[62] in 1928, a New Jersey law regulating the fees of employment agencies;[63] in the same year, a Tennessee law controlling the price of gasoline;[64] and in 1932, an Oklahoma law retricting entry into the ice business.[65] In each of these cases, the Court, usually speaking through Justice Sutherland, held that the business concerned was not affected with a public interest. But no standards of judgment were consistently applied. Whether an industry could be regulated depended on no objective criteria, but upon the undisclosed predispositions of the members of the Court.

The concept of a peculiar category of industries affected with a public interest was abandoned in 1934 when the Court handed down its decision in the Nebbia case.[66] The state of New York had set up a milk control board and empowered it to fix the retail price of milk. The board had fixed the price at 9 cents per quart. Nebbia, a grocer in Rochester, had sold two quarts for 18 cents and thrown in a loaf of bread. When sued for violating the law, he argued that the milk business was competitive rather than monopolistic, having none of the characteristics of a public utility, and that the state was therefore powerless to regulate the prices that it charged. The Court, in a 5 to 4 decision, rejected this defense.

Having thus broken with the past, the Court went on, in the next few years, to uphold a state law fixing the charges of tobacco warehouses,[67] federal laws requiring inspection of tobacco,[68] restricting the quantities of tobacco that could be marketed,[69] providing for the establishment of minimum prices for milk,[70] and providing—a second time—for minimum prices for bituminuous coal,[71] and a state law curtailing the output

[60] *German Alliance Insurance Co.* v. *Kansas,* 233 U.S. 389.
[61] *Wolff Packing Co.* v. *Court of Industrial Relations,* 262 U.S. 522.
[62] *Tyson* v. *Banton,* 273 U.S. 418.
[63] *Ribnik* v. *McBride,* 277 U.S. 350.
[64] *Williams* v. *Standard Oil Co.,* 278 U.S. 235.
[65] *New State Ice Co.* v. *Liebmann,* 282 U.S. 262.
[66] *Nebbia* v. *New York,* 291 U.S. 502.
[67] *Townsend* v. *Yeomans,* 301 U.S. 441 (1937).
[68] *Currin* v. *Wallace,* 306 U.S. 1 (1939).
[69] *Mulford* v. *Smith,* 307 U.S. 38 (1939).
[70] *U.S.* v. *Rock Royal Cooperative,* 307 U.S. 533 (1939).
[71] *Sunshine Anthracite Coal Co.* v. *Adkins,* 310 U.S. 381 (1940).

of petroleum.[72] This legislation, arising largely from conditions of business depression, carried state and federal governments into new regions of control. Its approval by the Court removed a major barrier to the further extension of regulatory activity.

Due Process: Procedural and Substantive. The concept of due process originally had to do with the criminal law. Its extension to administration was a later development. In recent times, however, the courts have evolved a set of rules to govern the procedures of administrative agencies. Such agencies must have jurisdiction over the matters with which they deal. They must give fair hearings to all persons affected by their rulings. They must give adequate notice of such hearings well in advance of the dates when they are held. Their officers must be impartial, with no personal interest in the questions upon which they are called to pass. Their decisions must be based upon substantial evidence. In the orders they issue, specific findings of law and fact must be set forth. The persons affected by such orders must be given an opportunity to appeal. This is due process, in the procedural sense of the term.

Such safeguards against arbitrary administrative action are clearly in the public interest. There is danger, however, that administrative agencies might come to be so bound by procedural requirements that it would be impossible for them to operate efficiently. This danger is illustrated by two decisions handed down by the Supreme Court. In the first,[73] where the Secretary of Agriculture had issued an order on the advice of a trial examiner, following extensive hearings, the Court complained that the Secretary had not himself read each of the 13,000 pages of testimony and 1,000 pages of exhibits in the transcript. In the second,[74] it invalidated one of the Secretary's orders on the grounds that the respondents had not received a copy of the trial examiner's intermediate report in time to use it in preparing their final brief. Whatever the merits of these two cases, it is clear that administration might well be put in a strait jacket if the courts were too meticulous in their insistence on form.

In the name of due process, the courts have gone on to interest themselves not only in form but also in substance. Instead of confining themselves to determining whether administrative orders were based upon sufficient evidence, they have arrived at independent judgments by going into the evidence themselves. From a review of questions of law they have slipped over into a review of questions of fact. When the Supreme Court upheld state regulation of public utility rates, in *Munn* v. *Illinois* in 1877, it did not attempt to pass upon the rates themselves. But in 1886 the Court issued a warning that the "power to regulate is not a power to destroy."[75] In 1890 it asserted that "the reasonableness of a rate . . . is eminently a question for judicial investigation."[76] And in 1898, in the

---

[72] *R. R. Commission* v. *Rowan & Nichols Oil Co.,* 310 U.S. 573 (1940).
[73] *Morgan* v. *U.S.,* 298 U.S. 468 (1936).
[74] *Morgan* v. *U.S.,* 304 U.S. 1 (1948).
[75] *Stone* v. *Farmers' Loan & Trust Co.,* 166 U.S. 307.
[76] *Chicago, Milwaukee & St. Paul Rwy.* v. *Minnesota,* 134 U.S. 418.

historic case of *Smyth* v. *Ames,*[77] it enumerated the matters of substance that commissions would be required to take into consideration in fixing rates in order to give assurance that due process had been observed. From then on for nearly half a century the Court undertook to pass judgment, not only on the procedures employed in rate making, but also on the legitimacy of the rates themselves.

This position was substantially modified by the decisions handed down in the Natural Gas Pipeline and Hope Natural Gas cases[78] in 1942 and 1944. Said the Court, in the first of these cases: "The Constitution does not bind rate-making bodies to the service of any single formula or combination of formulas. . . . Once a fair hearing has been given, proper findings made, and other statutory requirements satisfied, the courts cannot intervene in the absence of a clear showing that the limits of due process have been overstepped. If the Commission's order, as applied to the facts before it and viewed in its entirety, produces no arbitrary result, our inquiry is at an end."[79] The boundaries of court review were thus narrowed by judicial self-restraint. Concern with the end result was not abandoned, but the presumption was made to run in favor of the substantive determinations of administrative agencies.

Ownership and Operation. Although the courts have handicapped the federal, state, and local governments in their efforts to preserve the system of private enterprise through the maintenance of competition and the regulation of monopoly, they have interposed no obstacles to public ownership. If a government seeks to socialize an existing private business whose owners do not wish to sell, it may do so by exercising the sovereign right of eminent domain. Under federal and state constitutions, the usual limitations are that the property must be taken for public use, and that just compensation must be paid. The courts have shown little disposition to question legislative judgment as to public use, or to check acquisition of property by supporting an unconscionable price. If a government goes into business by obtaining the assets of a private company through voluntary sale, or by itself constructing new facilities, the constitutional limits are those upon its power to spend. And these require only that expenditures be made for a public purpose or to promote the general welfare. The projects challenged on this basis have invariably been upheld.[80] The courts for many years strained at the gnat of public regulation and swallowed the camel of public ownership.

The Changing Constitution. For the better part of a century the Supreme Court raised no serious barriers to the expansion of public authority. From the founding of the republic to the end of the Civil War it declared only two acts of the Congress to be unconstitutional. It approved the granger legislation of the seventies, including the regulation

---

[77] 169 U.S. 466.

[78] *FPC* v. *Natural Gas Pipeline Co.,* 315 U.S. 575; *FPC* v. *Hope Natural Gas Co.,* 320 U.S. 591.

[79] 315 U.S. 586.

[80] See *Jones* v. *City of Portland,* 246 U.S. 217 (1917); *Green* v. *Frazier,* 253 U.S. 233 (1920); *Standard Oil Co.* v. *City of Lincoln,* 275 U.S. 504 (1927); *Puget Sound Power & Light Co.* v. *Seattle,* 291 U.S. 619 (1934); *Ashwander* v. *TVA,* 297 U.S. 288 (1936); *Tennessee Electric Power Co.* v. *TVA,* 306 U.S. 118 (1939); *Oklahoma* v. *Atkinson Co.,* 313 U.S. 508 (1941).

of services and rates. But from the middle 80s until the middle 30s, a period of 50 years, the Court made of the Constitution an instrument with which to impose upon the country the philosophy of laissez faire. It restricted the regulatory powers of government, extended to corporate enterprise the guarantees of personal freedom, and transformed procedural safeguards into substantive restraints. The conservatism of the courts, during this period, led to repeated demands for judicial reform. It was Theodore Roosevelt who proposed, in 1912, that decisions declaring laws unconstitutional should be subject to reversal by popular vote.

In recent decades, the courts have shown but little resistance to the application of controls. The institution of judicial review has been preserved by the exercise of moderation in its use.

Part II

POLICIES TO PROMOTE COMPETITION

ANTITRUST

The powers of antitrust seem quite replete
To make great businessmen, and small, compete.

No miscreant's too slight to catch and charge,
But cuts go slow when market shares are large.

This corporal's guard with continents to rule
Strives valiantly but often seems the fool.

With meager means, yet lordly aims and bold,
Is antitrust controller or controlled?

CHAPTER FIVE

Antitrust Tasks and Tools

Antitrust is the generic name for laws, agencies, and actions to promote competition. The American experiment with it dates from 1890, and interesting hybrids have sprouted abroad since 1945. The economic aim is clear in concept: to optimize the degree and form of competition in the economy—everywhere, not just in "normal" industry and trade. How and whether this occurs is the question before us in the next six chapters.

There are many antitrust tools to choose among. American antitrust is just one special combination, though its age and broad reach have made it seem the norm. Actually it has changed and evolved. It is a thriving legal industry, with roots deep in American economic and social policy.[1]

But nobody really knows what effects it has. It treats, not solves, its problems, and the economy generates endless new situations for it to cope with. It is here to stay: like most social policies, it is always travelling (sometimes backwards) but never arriving.

This part of the book presents policies applied by such mainline antitrust agencies as the Antitrust Division and the Federal Trade Commission. Other public agencies affect competition too, as later sections will explore. Here we begin with the tasks and laws, and then analyse the agencies' inner processes.

THE ECONOMIC TASKS

As Chapter 3 showed, a correct or optimal policy will increase competition up to the margin at which the benefits of extra competition are just offset by the lost technical economies of scale. Perfect competition is not sought or expected. Rather, agencies operate in the great middle range, where a greater degree of healthy competition and rivalry is usually

---

[1] For a superb review of antitrust origins and scope, see Donald J. Dewey, *Monopoly in Economics and Law* (Chicago: Rand McNally, 1959). See also Hans Thorelli, *The Federal Antitrust Policy* (Baltimore: Johns Hopkins Press, 1954); and William Letwin, *Law and Economic Policy in America* (New York: Random House, 1965).

worth seeking. The rationale for antitrust is firmly grounded on research and experience in real markets (see Chapter 2), not just on the analysis of perfect competition.

Antitrust is to have optimal *design;* applying the right incentives, and operating leanly. And in each market, antitrust is to be applied just to the *extent* and intensity where marginal social benefits equal costs. The benefits are those above what the natural market processes would generate by themselves. In naturally competitive markets, little antitrust effort is needed, but where scale economies exist, antitrust will often need to be most active and sophisticated.

The two basic classes of industrial pathology are (recall the structure-behavior-performance triad in Figure 1–1:

1. Cooperation among firms (anticompetitive *behavior,* or *conduct*). This takes many forms, including direct collusion among competitors, informal ties, tacit collusion, etc.
2. Market dominance (*structure,* plus certain types of behavior). This occurs when a firm gets and holds a large share of a market, often helped by some other public policy (patent, utility franchise, public purchases, etc.). The dominant firm can then do internally what smaller firms could do only by collaboration. Treatment requires either reducing market share or keeping it from rising (such as by mergers).

An effective procompetitive policy will try to treat these conditions in all markets, including finance, utilities, weapons, professions, and services, as well as the main stream of industry and trade.

The practical tasks of antitrust are:

1. To set priorities, by identifying the markets where antitrust yields are relatively high.
2. To develop efficient policies and eliminate costly and obsolete ones.
3. To apply treatments to the optimum extent in each market *and* to strike the right total balance among the whole set of tools. Policy is to be efficient in the small *and* the large.

ANTITRUST LAW

The basic American laws are firmly set, after 85 years of use. Their language is wide: but precedents have limited their reach, and many sectors have been exempted out entirely. We consider first the laws, next their background, and then their coverage. (Table 5–6 at the chapter's end defines the terms commonly used in antitrust law.)

The Laws

The Sherman Act of 1890 is the first and basic law, outlawing monopoly and collaboration in very broad terms. In 1914 the Clayton Act made certain specific acts illegal: it was amended in 1936 on price discrimination and in 1950 toward mergers. In practice, the laws have become a well-knit body of rules and precedent.

The Sherman Act's two main sections are:

Section 1. Every contract, combination in the form of a trust or otherwise, or conspiracy, in restraint of trade or commerce among the several states, or with foreign nations, is hereby declared to be illegal. Every person who shall make any such contract or engage in any such combination or conspiracy, shall be deemed guilty of a misdemeanor. . . .

Section 2. Every person who shall monopolize, or attempt to monopolize, or combine or conspire with any other person or persons, to monopolize any part of the trade or commerce among the several states, or with foreign nations, shall be deemed guilty of a misdemeanor. . . .

Section 1 is against cooperation. The key words are "Every . . . conspiracy . . . in restraint of trade . . . is . . . a misdemeanor." The classic Section 1 target is price fixing. Section 2 makes market dominance illegal: "Every" monopolization or "attempt" is a misdemeanor. The classic Section 2 case is against a firm with 90, 80, or perhaps 70 percent of a market.

This seems to be a very tough law. In both clauses, the prohibition is quite absolute and broad, and injured parties could sue for triple damages. But the limits are also quite clear. Only *interstate* and foreign commerce is covered, not markets that are local or within state borders. The offense is only a misdemeanor, with moderate penalties. And industries could seek exemption by Congress from the law (see Table 5–2 below).

The Clayton Act outlawed four specific practices, and added a general rule against unfair methods of competition.

The particular devises that were outlawed by the Clayton Act were discrimination in prices, exclusive and tying contracts, intercorporate stockholdings, and interlocking directorates.

Section 2 of the Act forbade sellers "to discriminate in price between different purchasers of commodities," but permitted such discrimination where there were "differences in the grade, quality, or quantity of the commodity sold," where the lower prices made "only due allowance for differences in the cost of selling or transportation," and where they were offered "in good faith to meet competition."

Section 3 forbade sellers to "lease or make a sale or contract for sale of . . . commodities . . . on the condition that the lessee or purchaser thereof shall not use or deal in the . . . commodity . . . of a competitor. . . ."

Section 7 forbade any corporation engaged in commerce to acquire the shares of a competing corporation or to purchase the stocks of two or more corporations that were competitors.

None of these prohibitions was absolute; the three practices were forbidden only where their effect, in the words of the law, "may be to substantially lessen competition or tend to create a monopoly. . . ."

Section 8 prohibited interlocking directorates between corporations engaged in commerce where one of them had a capital and surplus of more than $1 million and where "the elimination of competition . . . between them would constitute a violation of any of the provisions of the antitrust laws."

The broader prohibition contained in Section 5 of the accompanying Federal Trade Commission Act provided, simply, "that unfair methods of competition in commerce are hereby declared unlawful."

In 1936 the Robinson-Patman Act amended Clayton Section 2 to limit price cutting in various ways (see below). In 1950, the Celler-Kefauver Act amended Section 7 to prevent anticompetitive mergers, no matter how they are done (see also below).

In short, the Sherman Act is the basic law, while the Clayton Act, as further amended, has refined it.

History

These laws derive from traditions and precedents rooted deep in the past. Monopoly has anciently been resisted as a social evil. In some societies and periods, those in power have deliberately granted monopolies for any number of purposes. In others, monopolies have been officially removed, or at least resisted. The ethics of monopoly have throughout been a basic social concern.

In earlier centuries, economic power was woven into the cultural fabric, especially where the economy was feudal and agrarian. The rise of mercantile trading eventually challenged this structure in the later middle ages as, indeed, new markets and merchants are ever the source of new competition against the established economic order. But the "industrial revolutions" in Britain (1780–1840) and then the United States (1850–1900) made it both a more separable and a more urgent problem. The policy treatment of it which took form during 1890–1920 reflected a long competitive tradition.

The Common Law.   In England, during the 17th century, the courts denounced as illegal grants of monopoly by the Crown.[2] Their disapproval did not extend to grants conferred by Parliament, to monopolies acquired through individual effort, or to those resulting from private agreement. In the 18th century, however, monopolistic agreements were also condemned. A single person could still monopolize, but not a group. The courts had also refused since the 15th century to enforce contracts which restrained trade. This refusal was narrow at first but gradually broadened.

During the 19th century, the doctrine of restraint of trade was extended to cover any arrangement whereby competitors sought to exclude outsiders from the market or otherwise to limit freedom to compete. From state to state, decisions differed in detail. But in most jurisdictions the courts came to reject all contracts that involved such practices as curtailment of output, division of territories, fixing of prices, and pooling of profits. And here no rule of reason was applied: these practices were held, by their very nature, to harm the public interest, and contracts that required them were not enforced.

The maintenance of competition was thus supported by the common

---

[2] On the extent of these monopolies, see W. H. Price, *The English Patents of Monopoly* (Cambridge: Harvard University Press, 1913). See also Dewey, *op. cit.*

law. But as an instrument of public policy the common law was limited in its effectiveness. Where all of the participants in an agreement voluntarily adhered to its terms, and where no one had the courage or the means to sue for damages, no case was brought and here monopoly continued undisturbed. If competition were to be restored in such cases, it was necessary to make provision, through legislative enactment, for public prosecution and the imposition of public penalties.

The Antitrust Movement. In the United States, during the years that followed the Civil War, the pattern of industrial organization was rapidly transformed. With the construction of a network of railways, local and regional markets broadened to national scope. With the boundaries of markets thus extended, the scale of industrial operations was increased, production was mechanized, and small shops were displaced by large factories. Large, capital-intensive corporations arose, able to sweep away or absorb small firms. Deflation and depression aggravated the tendency for larger firms to cut prices.

During the 1880s, efforts to contain "cutthroat" competition—and to gain monopoly profits—led to agreements or mergers in many industries, including petroleum, cottonseed oil, linseed oil, meat packing, cordage, sugar, lead, coal, whiskey, tobacco, matches, and gunpowder.

As this process continued, many groups in the community—farmers, producers of raw materials, small businessmen, and laborers—suffered injury. The farmers, in particular, experiencing a persistent decline in farm prices, complained of high freight rates charged by the railroads, high interest rates charged by the banks, and high prices charged by the makers of agricultural implements and other manufactured goods. Producers of raw materials, where manufacturing was monopolized, found themselves selling to a single buyer who manipulated the market to depress the prices they received. Independent businessmen, if they refused to be absorbed, were ruthlessly driven from the field. Workers were crowded into growing cities, made dependent on industrial employment, and faced with increasing competition for uncertain jobs.

These conditions gave rise to a strong political movement against monopoly, uniting Populists, Grangers, and many other groups. It arose among farmers in the West and South, and among the nascent labor unions and many small businessmen. The movement bred farmer-labor parties, ran an antimonopoly candidate for the presidency, elected a number of members to Congress, and came to control the legislatures of several states. As it grew in strength, the older parties sought to win the votes of its adherents by themselves professing opposition to monopoly. In this way, the movement soon achieved part of its purpose: toward the end of the decade, antitrust laws were enacted by state and federal governments.

Since the new monopolies were trusts (rather like holding companies), the actions and laws against them were called *antitrust.* The trust as a legal device was soon abandoned, but the name has stuck. (In Europe, one often hears it pronounced an-*ty*-trust.)

Led by Kansas in 1889, 18 states enacted antitrust laws by 1891 and most states now have them. They vary in detail, but most have proven feeble and unused, mainly because the major cases reach far beyond state boundaries.

In the national election campaign of 1888, both major parties sought the farmer vote by pledges against monopoly. The Democrats, then in office, denounced the tariff as the mother of the trust. The Republicans, proposing higher duties, replied that they could compel competition at home while preventing competition from abroad. Following the Republican victory, President Harrison sent a message to Congress, in 1889, asking that this pledge be redeemed. A number of antimonopoly bills were introduced, one of them by Senator Sherman of Ohio. There was little

Culver Pictures, Inc.

Senator John Sherman

popular interest in the legislation at the time. Attention was centered, rather, on the effort to grant business and labor further protection against competition by raising the tariff and on the effort to assure farmers higher prices by passing the Silver Purchase Act. The antitrust law was included in the legislative package to quiet the critics of these measures. No hearings were held; the bill that finally emerged from the Congressional committees was enacted, following a brief debate that raised no fundamental issues, with only one dissenting vote in the Senate and without a record vote in the House. It was signed by the President on July 2, 1890. Bearing little or no resemblance to the bill originally introduced by Senator Sherman (and later said by him to be of little consequence), the law was given his name.[3]

The Sherman Act. The act contained little new doctrine. Its real contribution was to turn restraint of trade and monopolization into offenses against the federal government, to require enforcement by federal

---

[3] The act was much diluted in passage and shorn of strict penalties. None of the powers and resources needed to reduce monopoly were provided for. See Walton Hamilton and Irene Till, *Antitrust in Action*, TNEC Monograph No. 16, U.S. Government Printing Office, 1941.

TABLE 5-1
Milestones of Antitrust

1870s	Agitation grows against railroad monopolies.
1890	Sherman Antitrust Act passed.
1897	*Addyston Pipe* decision against restraints of trade.
1902–4	*Northern Securities* case: the first "trust-busting" action.
1906–15	Major wave of investigations and cases against industrial monopolies.
1911	*Standard Oil, American Tobacco* and *du Pont* gunpowder; the three "great" restructuring actions. The "rule of reason" is read into Section 2.
1914	Clayton and Federal Trade Commission Acts passed.
1915	International Harvester convicted in District Court.
1920	U.S. Steel acquitted 4–3 by the Supreme Court.
1929	*Trenton Potteries* confirms that price fixing is illegal.
1933–35	The National Recovery Administration experiment: antitrust is suspended.
1936	Robinson-Patman Act passed.
1938–52	Antitrust revived by Thurman Arnold and then others.
1940	*Socony* reaffirms that price-fixing is illegal *per se*.
1945	*Alcoa* decision rejects the "rule of reason."
1945–48	Allied restructuring proceeds partially in Germany and Japan.
1948–49	Basing point systems declared illegal.
1949	Celler-Kefauver Act passed, closing the merger loophole.
1949–51	Two major Section 2 cases filed: Western Electric (1949) and IBM (1951).
1950	*American Can* settlement gives modest relief.
1955–56	Western Electric and IBM cases are settled by compromise.
1956–62	Explicit collusion is largely eliminated in Britain.
1958	*Bethlehem-Youngstown* decision begins tight merger policy.
1962	*Brown Shoe* tightens horizontal and vertical merger limits.
1963	*Philadelphia National Bank* applies merger limits to banks.
1966	*Von's Grocery* proscribes nearly all horizontal mergers.
1969	Section 2 suit against IBM is filed. Major conglomerates ITT and LTV are also sued.
1971–72	FTC initiates action toward cereals firms and Xerox. Conglomerate merger suits are settled before appeal.
1973	Antitrust limits on mergers and restraint are applied to electric utilities: *Otter Tail Power* and *American Electric Power*.
1974	Xerox seeks to settle FTC case. Major case filed against AT&T.
1975	Government's IBM case finally scheduled for trial.

officials, and to provide for the imposition of penalties. It has small penalties, and it was not applied with much force until 1904. But since 1911 it has been the fulcrum of all U.S. competitive policy. Senator Sherman is a ghostly board member of most large firms and many small ones.

The Clayton and Federal Trade Commission Acts. There was increasing dissatisfaction, in the years before 1914, with the operation of the Sherman Act. During the administrations of Cleveland and McKinley, the laws had scarcely been enforced. Powerful new combinations had been formed in steel, tin cans, corn products, farm machinery, and many other industries. During the administrations of Roosevelt and Taft, monopolistic abuses had been disclosed in hearings before committees of Congress, in the reports of public agencies, and in the evidence presented in cases brought before the courts. Though it was shown that competition had been eliminated by particular business practices, these practices had not been held to be in violation of the law. And in 1911 the Supreme Court had declared that combinations that were not unreasonable would be allowed to stand. Following these developments, the trusts again became an issue in the national campaign of 1912. Monopoly was denounced and further legislation promised by the Democrats, the Roosevelt Progressives, and the Republicans.

In 1913 the new Democratic Congress reduced the tariff, set up the Federal Reserve System, and inaugurated the income tax: in 1914 it turned to the problem of monopoly. Consideration of the problem was now more thorough than that accorded it a quarter-century before: the issues raised were subjected to exhaustive hearings and extended debate. The aim was to define anticompetitive acts clearly. But agreement could be reached only on four specific acts.[4] These were written into the Clayton Act, and a general clause against "unfair" competition was included in the Federal Trade Commission Act. Both were enacted in 1914. The FTC's powers were slight: it could only tell violators not to repeat.[5]

By 1936, small-grocer pressure against the new chain stores (especially the Great Atlantic and Pacific Tea Company: A&P) had grown strong enough to cause a protective change in the Clayton Act. The aims were (1) to eliminate advantages of the chain stores in buying their goods and (2) to restrain their ability to cut prices against their small rivals (see Chapter 6). The Robinson-Patman Act has had a checkered reputation, but it has regularized the treatment of price discrimination.

The original Section 7 of the Clayton Act was construed by the courts to permit mergers even by direct competitors.[6] From 1920 to the 1950s, this detour around the law was heavily travelled. Concentration was both induced and permitted to rise. Absurd though it clearly was, competitors who could not legally cooperate on prices were fully free to merge entirely. This loophole was finally closed in 1950 by amending Clayton Section 7 to cover all legal devices of merging. And the merger could not "substantially . . . lessen competition or . . . tend to create a monopoly in any line of commerce in any section of the country," very broad language indeed.

To summarize the laws, it is illegal:

1. To enter into a contract, combination, or conspiracy in restraint of trade (Sherman Act, Section 1);
2. To monopolize, attempt to monopolize, or combine or conspire to monopolize trade (Sherman Act, Section 2).

---

[4] Try to specify ten anticompetitive acts that could be made illegal. Are some of them often procompetitive?

[5] For an argument that the FTC was part of a reactionary effort, see Gabriel Kolko, *The Triumph of Conservatism* (Glencoe, Ill.: Free Press, 1963).

[6] *Thatcher Manufacturing Co.* v. *FTC; Swift & Co.* v. *FTC,* 272 U.S. 554, (1926); and *Arrow-Hart & Hegeman Electric Co.* v. *FTC,* 291 U.S. 587 (1934).

In cases where the effect may be substantially to lessen competition or tend to create a monopoly, it is illegal:

3. To acquire the stock or the assets of competing corporations (Clayton Act, Section 7 as amended by Celler-Kefauver Act);
4. To enter into exclusive and trying contracts (Clayton Act, Section 3);
5. To discriminate among purchasers to an extent that cannot be justified by a difference in cost or as an attempt made, in good faith, to meet the price of a competitor (Clayton Act, Section 2 as amended by Robinson-Patman Act, Section 2-a).

And, in general, it is also illegal:

6. To pay a broker's commission if an independent broker is not employed (Robinson-Patman Act, Section 2-c);
7. To provide supplementary services to a buyer or to make allowance for services rendered by a buyer unless such concessions are equally available to all buyers (Robinson-Patman Act, Sections 2-d and 2-e);
8. To give larger discounts than those given others buying the same goods in the same quantity, or to charge lower prices in one locality than in another (Robinson-Patman Act, Section 3);
9. Knowingly to induce or receive an illegal discrimination in price (Robinson-Patman Act, Section 2-a);
10. To serve as a director of competing corporations (Clayton Act, Section 8);
11. To use unfair methods of competition (Federal Trade Commission Act, Section 5);
12. To employ unfair or deceptive acts or practices (Federal Trade Commission Act, Section 5 as amended by Wheeler-Lea Act, Section 3).

Scope and Coverage

The antitrust laws do not reach everywhere, either by the letter or by usage. Large parts of the economy have been exempted. And a doctrine of moderation has been built in. Also the resources are scant, providing little more than a corporal's guard to wage a large and growing campaign.

Scope. The courts have usually tried to give antitrust wide scope.[7] Local industry has often been held to affect interstate trade. Foreign operations are also within reach, if they can be shown to affect domestic markets. A wide variety of sectors have been expressly included by the Court, such as railroads by an 1897 decision, ocean shipping companies in 1917, milk producers in 1939, and medical groups in 1943.[8] Others have

---

[7] After a wobbly start in the E. C. Knight case. This first major Section 2 case was against the American Sugar Refining Company, which controlled 98 percent of the market. The Supreme Court held that the business was exempt, being manufacturing rather than commerce (*U.S.* v. *E. C. Knight Co.*, 156 U.S. 1). This hairsplitting was never repeated, but it did deter antitrust efforts for a decade or more, until after the main trust wave was complete. Therefore it was a *crucial* decision.

[8] *NLRB* v. *Jones & Laughlin Steel Corp.*, 301 U.S. 1; *U.S.* v. *Trans-Missouri Freight Assn.*, 166 U.S. 290; *Thomsen* v. *Cayser*, 243 U.S. 66; *U.S.* v. *Borden Co.*, 308 U.S. 188; *U.S.* v. *American Medical Assn.*, 317 U.S. 519.

TABLE 5–2
The Main Antitrust Exemptions

As a Matter of Law	Discussed in Chapters
Agriculture and fishing organizations	24
Labor unions	24
Regulated industries	
Public utilities: electric, gas, postal, telephone, railroads	13–18
Others (partial or self-regulation): banks, stock exchanges, insurance,	11, 12
airlines, trucking, ocean shipping, pipelines,	17
broadcasting	16
Baseball, football	28
Newspaper mergers	8, 24
Export cartels	24

As a Matter of Usage	
Most local trades and services	24
Professions (law, medicine, scores of others)	24
Urban services (transit, sewage, water)	22
Health services	27
Education	22
Governmental services and enterprises	19–23
National defense suppliers	29
Patent-intensive industries: drugs, etc.	7, 9

included insurance in 1944, news services in 1945, real estate brokerage in 1950, newspapers in 1951, building construction in 1954, and all sports except baseball by decisions in 1955–57.[9] The court continues to draw the antitrust borders widely, when given a chance to do so.

But coverage has actually turned out to have more holes than Swiss cheese. The Court's doctrinal leads often lapse, because the agencies do not continue enforcing, especially in local trades and professions. And firms often get from Congress the exemption that the Courts have denied. That has occurred for many of those markets just listed: railroads, ocean shipping, milk producers, insurance, newspapers (in part), and football. A summary of literal and *de facto* exemptions is given in Table 5–2; Chapter 24 presents more details. One cannot measure antitrust coverage exactly, but it surely covers less than half of the economy, and this share is probably shrinking. Yet recently the courts have been willing to extend coverage back into certain regulated sectors (bulk electric power, bank mergers, etc.). The lines are often blurred and changing.

Rules of Reason. The Sherman Act is absolute: "every" monopoly

___
[9] *U.S.* v. *South-Eastern Underwriters Assn.,* 322 U.S. 533; *U.S. Alkali Export Assn.* v. *U.S.,* 325 U.S. 196; *U.S.* v. *Associated Press,* 326 U.S. 1; *U.S.* v. *National Assn. of Real Estate Boards,* 339 U.S. 485; *Lorain Journal Co.* v. *U.S.,* 342 U.S. 143; *U.S.* v. *Employing Plasters' Assn.,* 347 U.S. 186; *Federal Baseball Club of Baltimore* v. *National League,* 259 U.S. 200 (1922); *Toolson* v. *New York Yankees,* 346 U.S. 356 (1953). On the economic and legal issues involved here, see "Monopsony in Manpower: Organized Baseball Meets the Antitrust Laws," *Yale Law Journal,* Vol. LXII (1953), pp. 576–639; *U.S.* v. *Shubert,* 348 U.S. 222; *U.S.* v. *International Boxing Club,* 348 U.S. 236; *Washington Professional Basketball Corp.* v. *National Basketballers' Assn.,* 147 F. Supp. 154; *U.S.* v. *National Wrestling Alliance,* 1956 Trade Cases Par. 68, 507; *Radovich* v. *National Football League,* 352 U.S. 445.

and trade restraint. At first it seemed to go beyond the common law, which had allowed certain secondary (ancillary) restraints to stand.[10] But in 1911, Chief Justice White read a "rule of reason" into both sections of the law, finding Standard Oil and American Tobacco guilty for monopolizing, *unreasonably:* for being "bad" trusts, not just trusts.[11] This enervated antitrust for several decades, since agencies now had to prove both (1) that a monopoly or restraint existed, and (2) that it had "unreasonable" origins or effects. Further, the Court in 1920 held that later good behavior could exculpate a monopolist. The rule of reason held sway for several decades, stopping efforts to restructure the original trusts and to apply it to new monopolies and restraints. Despite a bold rejection of it by Judge Hand in the 1945 *Alcoa* decision, its spirit has continued to govern Section 2 (see Chapter 7).[12]

Some such reasonable evaluation must be made in any case, as Chapters 3 and 4 noted. The economy is full of degrees of monopoly and collusion, of probabilities of effect, and of trade-offs among goods and bads. Moreover, agency resources are scarce and cannot cover every slight deviation. Still the presence of a "rule" of reason as an effective legal doctrine does give genuine exemption to broad classes of firms with market power.

In short, antitrust laws have become a specialized tool for certain sectors. Courts will usually apply them broadly, but Congress grants many legal exemptions and large *de facto* exemptions also occur. Much depends on the agencies, in mounting broad-scale cases and in resisting exemptions.

THE AGENCIES

Recall that optimal treatment requires (1) that the agency's jurisdiction and tasks be in balance with its powers and resources, and (2) that policies be optimal in design as well as extent. In this light, the record of antitrust enforcement is broadly as follows: *Its jurisdiction is wide and its tasks are difficult, yet its powers are moderate and its resources slim. Therefore, it has become strict in some directions (price fixing, mergers) but gentle in others (especially toward dominance). Its design is often poorly suited to the needed incentives. It is enforced less widely than the letter of its laws. To some extent, its broad incidence accentuates market power, rather than abating it.*

---

[10] The common law distinguished between ancillary and nonancillary restraints. An ancillary restraint is incidental to a legal purpose; it may occur, for instance, when a person selling a business, a partner withdrawing from it, or an employee leaving it undertakes to preserve its value by refraining from competition with its purchaser, a remaining partner, or a former employer. Here the courts came to apply a rule of reason, enforcing such restrictions when they were limited in duration and extent, and refusing to do so when they were not.

[11] *Standard Oil Co. of N.J.* v *U.S.,* 221 U.S. 1; *U.S.* v. *American Tobacco Co.* 221 U.S. 106.

[12] More recently, antitrust chief Donald Turner in 1965–68 explicitly took over the "reasoning" function, by bringing only cases which were deemed to have a clear economic basis. This gave the Supreme Court a narrowed set of choices. And so indeed, they convicted on nearly all of them (thereby seeming tougher than they were!) and could not reach out to newer doctrines and areas.

The laws are absolute. But their application by the Antitrust Division and the FTC has been checkered and changeable. The variance arises —as in all of the treatments in this book—partly from choice, partly from the lack of resources.

Resources

The agencies have always been small, even microscopic, in comparison to their tasks (see Table 5–3). The total budgets and expert staffs are slender, and much of them are taken up by secondary chores. They contend with private resources which routinely dwarf them.

TABLE 5–3
Antitrust Resources

	Antitrust Division			FTC		
	Lawyers	*Economists*	*Budget ($ million)*	*Lawyers*	*Economists*	*Budget ($ million)*
1905.........	7	a	0.1	—	—	—
1915.........	18	a	.1	60	a	0.5
1925.........	25	a	.1	180	a	1.
1940.........	200	a	1.3	200	a	2
1949.........	300	15	3.4	280	20	3
1959.........	250	20	6.2	290	25	12
1969.........	275	25	8.4	290	40	20
1974.........	316	38	13.0	300	45	22

Some figures are estimates.
a. Not available.

Thus, the Division's yearly budget is less than one *week's* profit at stake—and therefore available for resistance efforts—in any one of several major industries (recall Chapter 2). Even if multiplied by five, as many experts now suggest, antitrust resources would be tiny compared to a $1.3 trillion economy of great and increasing complexity. No economic appraisal guides the setting of these agencies' budgets, even though the marginal yields on antitrust resources are probably well over 100 percent.[13]

The resources have to be thinly spread. On average, there is only the equivalent of two or three full-time lawyers working on each of the five or so largest industries. For the rest—and especially for new industries— there is little or no continuous attention, by lawyers assigned part-time to several industries. A big case—with perhaps four or five lawyers, two economists and supporting staff: and perhaps many more as trial approaches—can take a large slice of agency resources and attention.

---

[13] To these direct yields one must add the implicit yields from the prior presence of antitrust; without it, both structure and behavior would be very much more monopolistic.

Francis Miller, TIME-LIFE *Agency*

Officials of du Pont (seated) and their senior attorneys in the du Pont-General Motors case (November 1952).

Antitrust Division
attorneys on the
du Pont-General Motors case
(November 1952).

Francis Miller, TIME-LIFE *Agency*

The average quality of antitrust staff also tends—with many exceptions!—to be lower than their private adversaries. This reflects their far lower pay, plus frustrations which often leach away one's dedication to public service. Indeed, the agencies are partly a training ground for private lawyers. A year or more in the agencies gives a staff attorney valuable experience. Many of the present antitrust "superlawyers" owe their eminence (and astonishingly high fees) to such a start. Negotiations, trials, and appeals commonly pit former agency officials against present officials (some of whom will shortly join the private side too!).

There are some offsets to the imbalance of resources. The agencies can invoke broad powers, impose expensive litigation, and call on some outside resources (e.g., the FBI for simple investigations). On some matters the heads of the agencies need only a little willpower, rather than seek large new resources. But there are counter-offsets too, such as unequal access to data and private recourse to other public agencies (Congress, White House, the Defense Department, etc.) for relief.

The antitrust agencies are genuinely too small: in technical terms, their resource levels are below the optimum, at which discounted marginal benefits would equal costs.

The Setting

These resources and their uses are influenced by the setting of the agencies, shown in Figure 5-1. It has changed little since 1920.

Congress. Budgets are set by Congress, after hearings which usually are routine but do not entertain requests for large increases. Congress also acts on exemptions from antitrust; there are always a few in the mill. There is a heavy volume of inquiries and gentle persuasion—and sometimes a hard sell—from members of Congress on behalf of their constituents. From industry and the public come information, persuasion, and complaints—by customers, competitors, takeover targets, etc.

Executive Branch. Other parts of the Executive Branch often influence Antitrust Division moves, though this is usually done quietly and mainly in acute cases. The White House also sets implicit limits by its general tone toward business and by its appointments to both agencies.

Appointees to head the Antitrust Division are usually of high technical quality, thanks to long traditions set in part by the private Antitrust Bar. The FTC has suffered from many mediocre appointments: very junior and very senior politicians, obscure businessmen, loyal White House aides, etc.

The agencies have much independence, because they are not within a larger business-related department, such as Commerce. At the Justice Department, the concern of higher officials is mainly with legal consistency, rather than industrial politics.[14] This independence also keeps an-

---

[14] There are important exceptions: the IBM and AT&T consent decrees under Herbert Brownell in 1955–56 (chapter 7); Ramsey Clark's "losing" of the AT&T suit in 1967–68 (chapter 7); and action on the ITT mergers under Richard Kleindienst in 1970–71 (chapter 8). But the point holds, that such interference would be far greater within a business-oriented department.

FIGURE 5-1

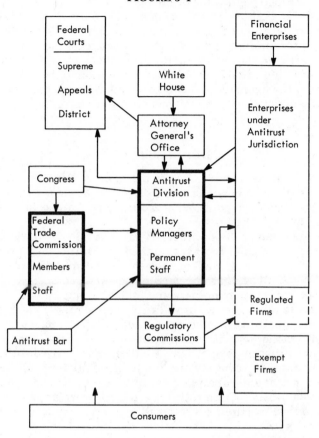

titrust free of adventurous actions, which political guidance could cause on occasion.

The private Antitrust Bar is the several thousand lawyers—in law firms and on corporate and banking staffs—who specialize in antitrust matters. Their pecking order runs from suave superlawyers whose mere presence commands respect, down to small town attorneys with small-scale clients.[15] Some litigate in court; others solely advise, prepare strategy, and negotiate. They are an influential and well-paid group, dedicated to the continuation of active antitrust. It is their livelihood, win or lose.

Large firms have their own legal staffs, some with scores working solely on antitrust. They advise and warn managers about risky courses of action, counsel on private and public suits, and negotiate with all parties. Outside counsel—from prestige law firms—are often brought in to handle delicate and critical matters. Fees are high, often $100 per *hour*

---

[15] See Martin Mayer, *The Lawyers* (New York: Harper & Row, 1967).

on up to over $1500 per day for leading lawyers. Fees for larger firms and cases routinely cumulate into millions of dollars. It is a fascinating world, blending diplomacy, a mandarin language, and poker-playing —and plain scrambling and grit—over stakes reaching into billions.

The federal courts process and decide those issues which become cases because they are not resolved by negotiation or preavoidance. And filtering into the agencies and courts are new research evidence about the parameters of the problem: economies of scale, monopoly effects, trends, etc.

Inner Conditions

In short, antitrust is embedded in a setting of influences, traditions, budget limits, and mechanisms which define what it can do—and is expected to do—at each point. What *is* done depends also, in part, on who is running the agencies.

The top decision positions are nearly always filled by lawyers: always at the Antitrust Division, mainly so at the FTC. During their brief tenure, they can set a new level of effort, start some new actions, and reach into the pipeline to pull ahead some pending cases.[16] But most basic changes take five years or more to prepare and follow through, and so the degree of toughness tends to veer within a fairly narrow range. The key permanent staff members are also lawyers. They usually mingle an inner hostility toward monopoly with—as they age—a bureaucratic resignation to the likelihood that no large changes will ever be carried through.

Lawyers excel at advocacy and the interpretation of rules. They are not trained in economic analysis, quantitative judgment, or, for that matter, basic social issues. Their training instills respect for private property and due process. And their efforts on all major cases must proceed slowly through the courts.

Therefore staff lawyers tend to go for the cases which (1) they can win and/or (2) which look active and tough. The courts—also staffed by lawyers—partly guide the flow of action. But the agencies have a great range of choice and often choose only a narrow set of cases to deal with. In short, the lawyerly control of antitrust yields long-run trends in emphasis, and short-run shifts in strictness, which may stray from the optimal patterns.

Since the agencies' resources are scarce, allocation choices are critical. One result is that large areas of enforcement are routinely neglected; that is, existing powers are not applied. Big cases that are brought are accused—often with some justice—of being too episodic and unexpected, of singling out a few victims rather than treating all offenders evenly.

Also, the agencies' capacity to absorb key information is limited, especially in the Antitrust Division. Because the Census Bureau secretes all data on individual companies, the agencies lack direct and timely information. Repeat: they do *not* have access to secret information in other

---

[16] They are also often amateurs in three key respects. (1) They usually know little about managing an agency. (2) They are not expert in economic analysis and (3) They are not skilled in the political pressures which surround them.

agencies. They must conduct their own research, such as it is, from scattered sources. Even the FTC's large economic staff is capable of doing this for, at the most, several large cases at a time.[17] The Antitrust Division's economists have been capable only of providing simple data required by the staff lawyers. There is little chance of mounting thorough complex research on major industries, on the scale which the Bureau of Corporations reached during 1906-14.

Therefore the Division's reach has automatically been limited to simpler cases.[18] It must rely on court trials to bring out full information. This means that in the broad range of major industries, antitrust choices are starved of thorough information. And the courts often lack means or procedures to carry out remedies, even when the need for change has been established.

Allocation

In the grip of these pressures, the agencies divide their resources mainly among

1. *Policing conduct,* to stop cooperation among firms to fix prices or restrain trade in other ways (Sherman Act, Section 1, and Clayton Act, various sections),
2. *Preventing new structural monopoly,* via mergers (Clayton Act, Section 7),
3. *Restoring competitive conditions in established monopoly* (Sherman Act, Section 2).

The two agencies have to discover these violations, proceed against them and get convictions in the courts, and then make sure the remedies are adequate. Figure 5-2 shows the broad trends in litigation activity.

Some of their tasks are hard, others quite easy. Restorative cases against existing monopoly are hard; the agencies usually must prove—against severe resistance by the firms—that some new structure would be better than the existing or evolving one. Price-fixing cases are much easier, for the agency lawyers need prove only that an attempt to fix prices was made, not that it was successful or that the industry's conditions need changing.

The bulk of antitrust resources go to *policing* conduct; price-fixing, patent restrictions, predatory pricing agreements, and so forth. A reasonable approximation for the Antitrust Division in recent years is 40 percent to conduct, 20 percent to mergers, 15 percent to restorative treatment

---

[17] Over 40 economists now labor both at the FTC and at the Antitrust Division. But most are specialized on a sector or a problem, and the level of training has been low. The complexities of researching a major Section 2 case, in the face of sophisticated company resistance and the lack of sound official data, are ample to deflect even the most highly trained specialist. Recently the status of economists at the Division has been formally improved, but the effects remain to be seen.

[18] This could conceivably be changing. Also, from 1965 to 1973 there was a yearly appointee as Special Economic Assistant to the Division head (including the present junior author during 1967-68). This provided for close contact and advice on all manner of cases, small and large.

FIGURE 5-2

Trends in Case Activity

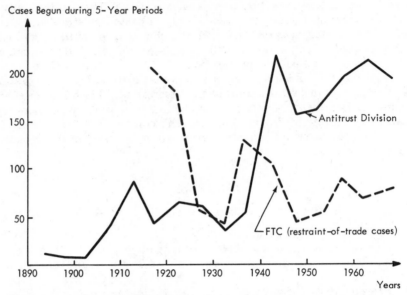

Source: R. A. Posner, "A Statistical Study of Antitrust Enforcement," xiii, *Journal of Law and Economics*, 365 (1970), Tables 1 and 2.

in regulated industries, 10 percent to restorative action in industry and trade, and the rest to miscellaneous others. Table 5-4 roughly indicates the various directions of activity. At the FTC, the shares are perhaps 60, 20, 5, and 15 respectively.[19] Many of these are extremely detailed and complex matters, but most are relatively simple. The number of investigations is high, but even these may be only a small sample of the actual incidents. Most of the cases are settled informally by consent decree or by a lower court decision. Most are of slight importance; worth doing, but small and not making new law (there is no precedential multiplier).

Certain acts are illegal *per se:* price fixing, market sharing. Conviction requires only a showing that the act occurred or was attempted, not that the result was harmful. Yet such strict rules are not as broad as they seem. Because of the many exemptions of sectors (see above and Chapter 24), the *per se* rules cover only a minority of activity in the economy. And they induce efforts to attain the same results by similar tactics.

Preventive actions are mainly towards mergers. These absorbed a rising share of resources in the 1960s as the merger wave rose and crested (recall Chapter 2). Only a few mergers, among thousands each year, are intensively studied and even fewer are eventually opposed. These are usually intended to set precedent in marginal areas. These cases tend also to be quickly dispatched. As the rules against horizontal and vertical

---

[19] This estimate is based on personal observation and discussion with officials. See also Kaysen and Turner, *op. cit.;* and Posner, *op. cit.*

TABLE 5-4

Types of Cases Brought: Antitrust Division

Period in Which Case Was Instituted

	1890 to 1894	1895 to 1899	1900 to 1904	1905 to 1909	1910 to 1914	1915 to 1919	1920 to 1924	1925 to 1929	1930 to 1934	1935 to 1939	1940 to 1944	1945 to 1949	1950 to 1954	1955 to 1959	1960 to 1964	1965 to 1969	Total
Horizontal conspiracy	3	7	28	62	29	50	36	19	5	34	179	114	122	122	104	75	989
Monopolizing	3	1	9	25	3	7	8	9		14	65	60	62	45	40	19	370
Acquisitions short of monopoly		1	2	2	3	1	1	5	1	3	2	5	3	26	61	80	194
Boycott		1	2	15	9	10	20	5	5	8	43	20	44	38	18	12	245
Resale price maintenance					2	4	2	1	1		1		4	4	8		27
Vertical integration			2	3	3		1	1	2	7	6	11	6	6	7	1	53
Tying arrangements				3	3	2	1	1		4	8	23	12	5	4	2	65
Exclusive dealing			1	9	9	1	3	1		4	16	24	29	23	22	6	140
Territorial and customer limitations	1					3		1	10					28	24	6	74
Violence	4	1	3	2	2	8	10	7	7	5	7	2	4	4		13	47
Price discrimination	1		3	6	2	1	4	4	5	29	20	16	15	14	6		123
Other predatory or unfair conduct	1		3	2	3	1	2	1	5	27	17	7	4	11	4		88
Interlocking directorates					2	2	1			5	4	2	2				16
Clayton Act, sec. 10										1		1	1				3
Labor cases	3		2		6		16	6	7	18	35	2	17	7	5	1	125
Patent and copyright cases				6	6	1	8	3	2	3	36	45	22	15	13	11	165
Total cases in period	9	6	39	91	43	66	69	30	57	223	157	159	195	215	195		1551

Table shows distribution of allegations, not of cases.

Source: Computed from the Bluebook, as reported in Posner, "A Statistical Study of Antitrust Enforcement," xiii, *The Journal of Law and Economics*, 365 (1970).

mergers have been extended (see Chapter 8), the more subtle issues of conglomerate mergers have come to the fore, especially since 1965. Here, the agencies are entering more marginal issues, different from those in horizontal mergers. Also the Antitrust Division is increasingly involved in screening mergers by regulated firms, such as airlines, electric utilities, banks, and railroads. This often requires arduous efforts to convince the regulatory commissions—and often the Courts, on appeal—to disallow or modify merger proposals.

Remedial (or restorative) activities toward existing market power deal with both regulated and unregulated sectors. Antitrust attempts to reduce monopoly and open up entry into regulated markets have grown recently, in such sectors as communications, transportation, and stock exchanges.

In the unregulated sectors, by contrast, restorative policies have dwindled since 1952 to a trickle (see Chapter 7). In a small revival since 1968, changes have been sought in the computer, copying equipment, cereals and telecommunications industries.[20] Restructuring can occur only by initiating action to prove that monopoly exists and to require remedies. This, we will see in Chapter 7, is usually a difficult and protracted procedure.

Yet the near-monopolies are often also *quasi-regulated,* informally by the antitrust agencies. Their market positions and profitability are reviewed indirectly, as possible triggers for restorative action or other penalties. So the firms may have—or believe they have—incentives to absorb some profits in costs, and to moderate their price discrimination. These are similar to conventional regulation (see Chapters 13 and 14).

Sanctions and Levers

The agencies' tools are narrow, but they pack various kinds of power. The agencies can inflict these costs:

1. *Investigation.* The study process can be large, long and costly to the firm, by choice either of the agencies *or* of the firms themselves.
2. *Suit.* A case inflicts
   a. Direct costs of litigation. These can run very high, as we have seen, and cases involve far more legal activity than lay observers realize.
   b. Diversion of executive attention. This indirect burden on management can be extensive.
   c. Bad publicity. This can affect a company's image and goodwill, though it usually has little direct effect on its market position and long-run yields.
3. *Stoppage of company action.* The contested action is often stopped as soon as it is challenged, even if it is eventually exonerated. In merger cases, a stay or preliminary injunction is often obtained to prevent the merger until the case is argued and decided.

---

[20] There are also lesser actions involving certain tire and oil firms, but these are more limited in reach and prospects.

4. *Conviction.* This is only a decision on the legal outcome. Its power lies solely in leading to these penalties:

   a. Fines and other civil or criminal penalties;
   b. Remedies, which are of two main sorts.
      1) Constraints on behavior ("injunctive relief"),
      2) Changes in company structure (the traditional 3D's: divestiture; divorcement and dissolution).
   c. Private damage suits. (But note that a consent decree or a *nolo contendere* plea, if accepted by the court and agency, does not give a basis for damages).

Fines have been unimportant for most large defendants, and so most experts now recommend raising their ceilings. The $5,000 limit set in the Sherman Act was raised to $50,000 in 1955, but this is a fly-speck for the largest several hundred firms. In December, 1974, the ceiling was raised again, to $500,000 for individuals and $1 million for firms.

Lawyers incessantly figure the odds and values of their clients' alternatives and advise them accordingly. The yield to be gotten *now* from violating often far exceeds the discounted present value of a small, distant—and perhaps avoidable—fine. The average fine on firms in 1955 to 1965 was only $12,778.[21] Though the impact can be great, for small firms, this is peanuts for large companies.

Criminal penalties have been rarely used, and before 1959 no significant industrialist had ever spent a day in jail for violating the Sherman Act. Then two cases brought some change. Four officers of hand-tool companies were sentenced to 90 days in jail. And the electrical equipment price-fixing case of 1960 put 7 officials in jail for 30 days (see Chapter 6). Jail is now possible. But the sentences are light, and the penalties are used only for occasional brazen cases. Though criminal penalties were stiffened in 1974 for Section 1 offenses, they are still likely to be applied sparingly.[22]

Remedy. Injunctive reliefs can stop specific actions, but without penalizing what has been done earlier. They are specific to the firm and action in question: other firms and tactics are not touched. They have recently become effective against certain mergers.

Affirmative remedies do change existing structure, but they have been sparingly used since 1913 (see Chapter 7).[23] District Courts have to settle on the remedies, in the end. These judges have been easily persuaded that "breaking" up companies is hazardous. In any event, they have no resources or expertise to carry out the changes. The courts only decide; the agencies and firms have to agree on remedies. Though it is quite

---

[21] James M. Clabault and John F. Burton, Jr., *Sherman Act Indictments, 1955–65* (New York: Federal Legal Publications, Inc., 1966), p. 104.

[22] Criminal violations were changed from a misdemeanor to a felony, and the maximum sentence was raised from one year to three.

[23] Dissolution breaks up a business unit into several parts. Divorcement separates the units in a combination. Divestiture requires defendants to dispose of particular assets: either physical properties or stockholdings in other concerns. Whatever the legal form of action, each of them involves disintegration of a common enterprise.

132   *Public Policies toward Business*

FIGURE 5–3
Trends in Antitrust "Wins" and Consent Decrees

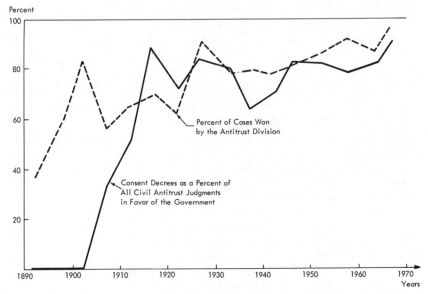

Source: R. A. Posner, "A Statistical Study of Antitrust Enforcement," xiii, *Journal of Law and Economics*, 365 (1970), Tables 5 and 11.

normal in private affairs, altering business structure has come to be treated by the courts as an exotic act, used only in the last resort.

Private damages can be levied at triple the amount of harm shown to have been caused to an injured party. Therefore a clear agency win can trigger scores of private suits by overcharged customers, excluded competitors, etc. This impact often dwarfs all the other penalties, and fear of it often is the real reason for a relentless defense.

Consent decrees require a special word. They are a compromise reached in a civil suit; in fact, about nine-tenths of the suits are settled in this way. It is possible at any point, as each side reckons its prospects, comparing one bird in the hand with two in the bush. The agreement is then filed with the court.

It is a flexible, cheap, and often sophisticated method, especially attractive to hard-pressed agencies. Often it achieves creative results. And it has been used increasingly, as hinted in Figure 5–3.

Yet there are drawbacks. The settlements are reached in private, with no records. Soft bargains are often struck, or outright retreats. Settlements prevent a clear legal answer, which could set precedent—recall the precedential multipler—and give a basis for compensating third parties. Economic aspects are regularly neglected as the lawyers bargain. And many decrees are quickly forgotten and unenforced.

Consent decrees were heavily used in the 1950s and extolled as a new approach. But their use is now more sparing and realistic.

Some of these tools are potent and can, in extreme cases, exert great power, especially on small firms. The normal steps in using them are shown in Figure 5–5 below. The trail can be a long one, but it can be cut off by a compromise at virtually any point. The agencies also supervise and monitor behavior in continuing ways; and firms can, and do, get agency advice on what to expect if doubtful actions are tried.

The antitrust tools are also narrow, relying on specific processes and penalties. The agencies can threaten and press, but they cannot give positive rewards. FTC actions involve certain additional mthods, but the basic process, and the ultimate appeals to the courts, are the same for both agencies.

THE ANTITRUST DIVISION

We now look at the two agencies separately. The Antitrust Division is centered in the third floor of the gray Justice Department building at 10th and Constitution Avenue in Washington, D.C. The head offices are grand, the lesser offices and halls rather bleak. Here exist both high industrial power and mind-numbing drudgery, a messianic spirit and plodding details.[24]

FIGURE 5–4
Structure of the Antitrust Division

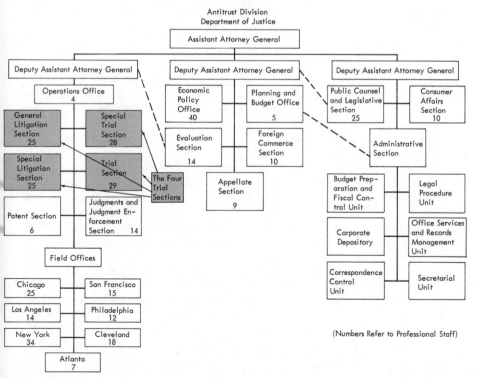

(Numbers Refer to Professional Staff)

[24] For a lively account of the inside details and color, see M. J. Green and others, *The Closed Enterprise System* (New York: Grossman, 1972).

Antitrust Division's bi-weekly meeting of top officials (February 1966). Donald F. Turner (back to camera), then heading the Division, expounds to permanent staff section chiefs.

In the structure of the Division, as shown in Figure 5–4, there are a variety of functional sections, all staffed by *career* lawyers. Their work is managed mainly under the Director of Operations. Above this are the current antitrust chief and his small appointed staff, which the permanent staff more or less fondly call the "front office," or on occasion, the "Gold Coast."

The four trial staffs develop possible cases which, if eventually approved, are "sent upstairs" to the Attorney General for signing and filing in court. Or instead, the suit may be returned for further work, or just delayed.

The four trial sections are the core, the dray horses of antitrust. Other sections handle specific tasks. The Appellate Section prepares appeals to higher courts. Public Counsel handles matters relating to other official agencies, such as railway mergers (Department of Transportation) and electric utility mergers (the Federal Power Commission). The Judgments Section polices the old court orders and consent decrees—more or less zealously, often less. The Foreign Section deals with international aspects (the State Department, etc.). And the Economic Policy Office services the lawyer's requests for data, on markets, market shares, and other routine matters (since 1973 it has also begun doing some substantial research).

The process by which antitrust decisions are posed and made is fascinating and important to understand.[25] The basic actor is the staff lawyer, specializing in one or several industries. He is like a small entrepreneur, seeking to maximize his record of successful cases—and to get to be a Section Chief. Large and old industries may have several lawyers, in each agency; small and new ones are often thinly covered or unassigned. The lawyer has latitude to ferret out possible violations; on his own, or on an assigned investigation, or solely in response to a private complaint or lead.

A case or investigation is usually triggered by a complaint or an important change reported in the press. Investigation may also involve staff economists and, on occasion, an outside consultant.[26]

The investigation looks mainly for *documents* and also for witnesses. Documents are of all sorts (letters, notes, reports, data, etc.), and the critical ones are usually buried in the target company's own files. The agencies must somehow learn or guess where they are, and ask for them. Then the firm's lawyers may produce them: (1) voluntarily if the firm is co-operating (to show it has nothing to hide), or (2) under a court order (a civil investigative demand: CID) if the firm is fighting the action.[27]

The agency must often fish a little, without giving the firm a good chance to criticize it or to snow the investigating lawyer with masses of irrelevant materials. The firm's lawyers must often sift out and hand over documents which they know to be damning to their client. Why do they do such a tantalizing thing? Because destroying evidence is a felony, leading also to disbarment. Also, the lawyer is only a hired advocate, out to make the best case but not desperate to win at any cost. In any event, the countertactic is popular and effective: to *snow,* swamping the investigator for months, often literally with carloads of paper.

Note that the lawyers learn to rely only on such documents for *proof.* Research findings are usually too soft for courtroom use, even though they would help to determine the optimum treatment.

The antitrust investigator or group does a research report (a fact memo) on whether a violation of antitrust law has occurred and a suit against the offender is justified. The criterion is, of course, legal: can a violation of the law be proven? If the attorney recommends suing, he also draws up a draft complaint. This pair of drafts—the grist of antitrust—then passes up in the mill for discussion, further work, and decision at higher levels.[28] In the Antitrust Division, the Assistant Attorney General for Antitrust decides, usually after more study, whether to approve suit. Then, *if* the Attorney General also approves, often after wider consul-

---

[25] This is essential to evaluating the results and the alternative approaches. It is little changed since Walton Hamilton's and Irene Till's superb description of it in their *Antitrust in Action,* Monograph No. 16 for the Temporary National Economic Committee, Washington D.C.: U.S. Government Printing Office, 1941), especially pp. 23–100.

[26] Consultants are often unavailable, especially for large and important cases. Firms have incentives and ample resources to co-opt leading experts as consultants.

[27] CID's have been available only since 1962. Previously, documents could only be required under subpoena, and subpoenas were available only after suit had been filed or an indictment obtained. So Catch-22: data needed to decide if suit were justified could be gotten only after filing suit. For 60 years this absurdity prevailed and affected antitrust choices.

[28] The firm under study is usually able to keep well-informed of matters as they progress, and commonly its lawyers come in to make frequent efforts to persuade against action.

FIGURE 5-5
The Process of Antitrust Decisions and Litigation

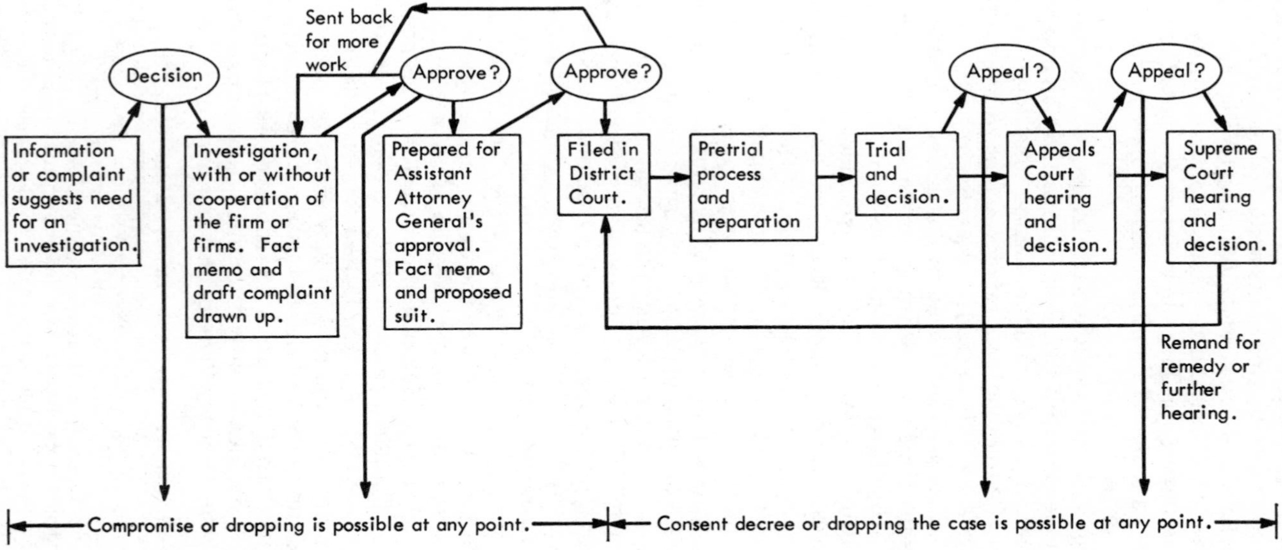

tation, the case is filed. Trial may take several years to begin (the 1969 suit against IBM is taking 6 years just to begin); after decision, appeals may take several more years.[29] And in big cases, the Supreme Court may send the case back down for practical remedies, which may take another several years. At the other extreme, actions against planned mergers may have effect in a matter of weeks or even hours. Here time favors the Division in resisting change, since judges commonly prevent full consummation of the merger until the basic issues are clarified.

The sides favored by the burden of proof and by having time in one's favor can be summarized roughly as follows:

Subject of Action	Burden of Proof Favors	Time Delay Favors
Price fixing	Neither	Neither
Mergers	Agency	Agency
Restorative	Firm	Firm

In any event, the natural roles are for staff attorneys to make out the best possible case for suit. They will naturally favor small, simple winnable cases which *they* can control. The policy managers then select from this portfolio those cases which look best in legal and, perhaps, economic terms. The courts then further select those cases which have merit, with the judicial procedure leaning toward conservative results. The Supreme Court, at the end, can also select the correct margins of policy treatment. In short, a rule of reason can be applied at all levels. But only if the agencies lean on balance toward strictness will the courts have a range for selection.

Most Division actions require at least a year or two to run their course, but the variation in times is extreme (see Figure 5–6). Some matters take but a few days: a merger folds when the Division announces it will investigate, price-fixers capitulate when caught. But others take years: e.g., about 1953 to 1972 for the El Paso Natural Gas case, and 1947 to 1969 for United Shoe Machinery. The average time for completing a litigated antitrust case has been about $5\frac{1}{2}$ years (see Figure 5–7).

The delays are partly inherent, since it takes time to investigate, prepare suit, carry out pretrial jockeying, try, appeal, and win a suit, and then apply remedy. But often the delay reflects sheer sluggishness or even bungling. Frequently the Division allows itself to be euchred into being snowed with irrelevant documents, which it must then plow patiently through, looking for needles in the haystack.

Where the stakes are high, private parties have managed to stall for years—and reap further monopoly gains—by astute procedural tactics. And justice delayed is justice denied; or rather, policy delayed is policy nullified. The Division can be endlessly patient, but it cannot usually muster large corps of lawyers for major cases. Treatment therefore tends to be labor-saving and time-using. And court resources are treated virtually as a free good.

---

[29] A trial, moreover, may drag on for many months. The trial of the Aluminum Company in the District Court ran from June 1, 1938, to August 14, 1940. The judge, when asked on a second occasion by the same attorney to grant a day's adjournment at the birth of a child, warned that such favors were not to be expected when grandchildren began to come along.

FIGURE 5–6
Some Cases Last Long; Others Longer

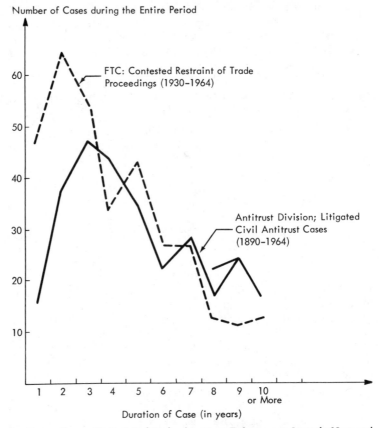

Number of Cases during the Entire Period

FTC: Contested Restraint of Trade
Proceedings (1930–1964)

Antitrust Division; Litigated
Civil Antitrust Cases
(1890–1964)

Duration of Case (in years)

Source: Posner, "A Statistical Study of Antitrust Enforcement, *Journal of Law and Economics*, 1970, Tables 8 and 10 (see note to Figure 5–2).

Litigation poses special problems. In a civil action guilt must be established by a preponderance of evidence. In a criminal suit it must be proven beyond a reasonable doubt. The evidence, however, may be largely circumstantial; documentary proof may be wanting and witnesses reluctant to testify. The complexities of business organization and practice may be difficult for the prosecution to explain and for the jury and the judge to understand. The defendants may be eminently respectable, members of the best clubs, active in charitable enterprises, and pillars of the church. The course of conduct of which they are accused may appear to be quite normal. The jury may hesitate to convict, the judge to provide appropriate remedies.

The matter at stake in a trial is the behavior of an industry in the *future*. The matter discussed is the evidence of its wrongdoing in the *past*. Whatever the issues, the prosecution must seek a conviction, the defense an acquittal. And the process often becomes a ritual game.

FIGURE 5–7

Average Length of Antitrust Division Cases in Months

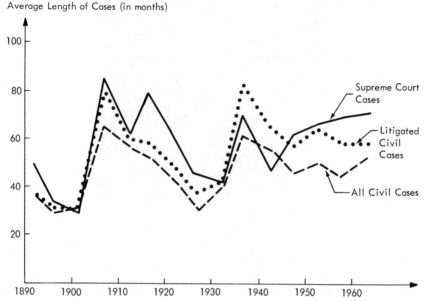

Source: Posner, "A Statistical Study of Antitrust Enforcement," *Journal of Law and Economics,* 1970, Table 7 (see Figure 5–2).

It brings to the settlement of questions of economic order the processes, hazards, confusions, evasions, circumlocutions, delays, of the legal folkways. . . . Persons competent in the habits of industry must give way to those skilled in the techniques of legal combat. . . . The opposing champions are well versed in demurrer, interlocutory motion, the tactics of seeking or avoiding a general engagement. . . . The staging of the question as an adversary proceeding sets lawyer against lawyer. . . . Every move, every witness, every fact, every document becomes a counter in a legal game. "The record" has come to do vicarious duty for an analysis of the industry in operation; and every item, favorable to one side, can win admission only against the heavy cross-fire of the other. Every procedural device which may arrest or speed action, flank or snipe the verbal minions of the enemy, color the conduct on parade with innocence or guilt is called into play. . . . Again and again the attorney and the witness raise their antiphonal voices; the counsel for the adverse party chants the approved formula "incompetent, irrelevant, and immaterial"; the judge from the loft above interjects a responsive "sustained" or "overruled"; and the loser, who intends to fight another day, comes in dramatically with "exception". . . . It takes the final summing up of the lawyers to bring the jury back to the dominant legal issue. And somehow antitrust as an instrument of public policy has gotten lost in the scuffle.[30]

The case presents peculiar difficulties to the judge:

He is expected to have a critical mastery of corporate finance, marketing practice, industrial structure; to have a sound grasp of physics, chemistry, electrodynamics,

---

[30] Walton Hamilton and Irene Till, *op. cit.,* pp. 59–62.

Leading Antitrust Chiefs

Culver Pictures

George Wickersham. Taft's Attorney General. A leading private lawyer. Conducted the Standard Oil, American Tobacco and other major cases brilliantly. Returned to private practice.

Culver Pictures

Thurman W. Arnold. Born 1891. In office 1938–43. Appointed after writing *The Folklore of Industry,* which said antitrust could do little. Revived antitrust and tried industry-wide studies. Developed or pressed on several Section 2 cases (Alcoa, American Tobacco). Became a federal judge, then returned to private practice.

Fortune Magazine

Donald F. Turner. Born 1922. In office 1965–68. Brilliant, trained both in law and economics, leading antitrust scholar, a Harvard law professor. Proposed deconcentrating major industries in *Antitrust Policy* (1959). Stressed economic content, raised economists' role. Extended activity to regulated sectors, patents, reviewing old decrees, issuing merger guidelines, prepared big monopoly cases. Did not launch deconcentration program. Returned to Harvard.

Leading Antitrust Chiefs

William Allen, Business Week

Wide World Photos

Richard W. McLaren. Born 1918. In office 1969–1971. A leading antitrust practitioner from Chicago. Filed major cases against ITT and LTV, the leading conglomerates. Settled both by consent decree before final decision. Moderate in other directions. Became a federal judge in Chicago. Survived the shadow of Nixon scandals.

Thomas E. Kauper. Born 1935. In office 1972– . Law professor at University of Michigan. Has pressed actions against conduct and expanded the role of economists. Also, he filed the big AT&T case in 1974, pressed the IBM case, and expanded other Section 2 activity.

in fact the fundamentals of all the mechanical arts. . . . In a word, he must be alike omnicompetent in law and industry—an expert in the multiplex of affairs and disciplines which converge upon the case. . . . In the face of his own ordeal, his tendency is to retire somewhat from the domain of industrial reality and to fortify his judicial performance with a meticulous observance of the technicalities. . . . Even the judge himself becomes an obstacle to bringing into sharp relief the pattern of the industry and its point of restraint.[31]

In preparing his opinion, the judge makes no investigation of his own, but chooses among the alternatives presented to him by counsel for the prosecution and counsel for the defense. The record that he (and his clerk) must study is often voluminous and mind-numbing.[32]

An appeal from the decision of a lower court is taken on the basis of error, and error is concerned exclusively with points of law. Here, again,

---

[31] Ibid., pp. 71–72. Few federal judges have had experience or background either in antitrust law or in economics.

[32] In the A & P case, the judge was confronted with 45,000 pages of testimony and 7,000 exhibits; in the Aluminum case with 58,000 pages of testimony and 15,000 pages of documents. From such a mass of materials, the judge must make his findings of fact and his application of the law to these facts. To.work his way through the complexities of the arrangements involved, he must take time. In the *Sugar Institute* case, the judge spent 14 months writing a 50-page finding of facts and a 178-page opinion. Mark S. Massel, *Competition and Monopoly* (Washington, D.C.: Brookings Institution, 1962), p. 145.

the arcane skills that are brought to bear on questions of economic policy are those, not of economic analysis, but of the law.

No simple measure can portray the importance of cases, nor the Division's batting average in the courts. One landmark merger case, for example, can stanch a flood of new mergers. Still, the Division's peak periods of activity were clearly 1901–15 and 1937–52, with a recent rise also visible. The major Section 2 cases were bunched in those periods, and new ground was broken by the courts. Since 1952 the pace of activity has been moderate, with a spreading of efforts in several new directions.

Before 1901, antitrust activity was minimal. Then Theodore Roosevelt seized the issue, becoming the "Trustbuster." Yet Taft outpaced him. Roosevelt started 44 suits in his two terms: Taft started 90 in one. Wilson also started 90; his beginning was interrupted by World War I. Under Harding, Coolidge, Hoover, and Roosevelt's first term, the Antitrust Division went into hibernation.

In 1938 Roosevelt switched from the NRA detour (see Chapter 24) to a highly publicized campaign against monopoly, under Thurman Arnold until 1943. This continued under Truman, with major cases coming along until 1952. The Eisenhower years of moderation brought a deliberate pullback in restorative actions, especially those toward IBM and AT&T. After several slow years, there was a modest revival after 1958.

The pace continued moderate in the 1960s. Under Donald F. Turner, a leading antitrust scholar, there was a rise in economic consistency during 1965–68. But the broad attack on tight oligopoly, which Turner had earlier advocated, did not occur.[33] Only a case against IBM was finally filed. And action against the rising tide of conglomerate mergers was studiously moderate.

Richard Nixon's appointee was Richard W. McLaren, an experienced private antitrust lawyer eager to demonstrate strictness. He launched a blitz on conglomerate mergers, but let IBM and other Section 2 matters slide. Since 1972 Thomas Kauper has promoted actions against conduct and raised the economists' role in decisions. He has also put large Division resources into the IBM case (see Chapter 7), and in 1974 he filed a major suit against AT&T (most of which had been prepared under Turner).

Antitrust has become bipartisan since 1936, on the whole, but there are distinct swings in emphasis among the three main lines of action. The Supreme Court has led the way, especially during the early 1960s in tightening merger policy. But on Section 2 it has been given little to work with since 1952.

THE FEDERAL TRADE COMMISSION

The FTC's basic tasks and tools have come to overlap with the Antitrust Division's. But such an independent administrative agency might avoid the evident defects of the Division, in trying to use the judicial process to reach an economic optimum. In practice, these possibilities

---

[33] Kaysen and Turner, *op. cit.*

FIGURE 5–8
Steps in FTC Actions

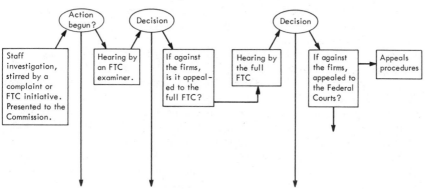

Resolution of the matter, by stopping action, compromise, or compliance.

have scarcely been realized. The FTC has mostly wallowed in trivia, rising only occasionally to serious treatments. Frequently being "revitalized," it is rarely vital.

Formally, the FTC can both raise issues and decide them, as shown in Figure 5–8. But in practice its important decisions usually are appealed to the courts, and so they share the same problems as the Division's actions. And half its modest resources are taken for small-scale consumerist questions: labelling, truth in advertising, cigarette warnings, etc.[34] This leaves its antimonopoly resources about on par with the Antitrust Division's.[35]

Commissioners have been of dubious quality and many have scarcely understood the FTC's economic task. There has commonly been no clear leadership by the Chairman nor a coherent set of economic priorities.

Investigations start with thousands of private complaints and—the more important cases—a relatively few FTC choices. If a formal complaint is lodged, the respondent can reply and settle (as most do), or the issue goes to an FTC examiner. A decision of guilty brings a "cease and desist" order (no penalty) against further acts. On appeal, the whole Commission hears and decides. On further appeal, the matter may reach the Supreme Court, which reverses the FTC only on issues of fact. In some actions—a merger, for example—a final FTC victory gets definite relief. But in many others, it is not followed up. There is much procedure and ritual, but little tight remedy and control.

The FTC's procedures can avoid much of the delay which inhibits Antitrust Division actions. But the results have been meager. The Com-

[34] In addition to its duties under the Clayton and Trade Commission Acts, the Commission administers the antitrust exemption granted to export trade associations under the Webb-Pomerene Act of 1918; polices the advertising of foods, drugs, and cosmetics under the Wheeler-Lea Act of 1938; and enforces the Wool Products Labeling Act of 1939, the Fur Products Labeling Act of 1951, the Flammable Fabrics Act of 1953, the Textile Fiber Products Identification Act of 1958, and the Fair Packaging and Labeling Act of 1966.

[35] The funding has been thin in the past. In one case, there were 102 law firms on the private side, against one principal FTC attorney and two part-time assistants.

mission is put under political pressure when it is active. Congress controls funds tightly and has reached out to forbid specific actions (such as a study of the largest 1,000 firms in the early 1960s). The FTC therefore has bent with political winds and tended toward passivity, despite its formally independent status.

Swings in FTC zeal have been even wider than those of the Antitrust Division. Its high point was roughly 1945 to 1951, when it attacked basing-point pricing, horizontal mergers, and several major oligopolies, on a shoestring budget. During the 1920s and 1930s, it did more to promote collusion than resist it. Under Paul Rand Dixon, it decayed in the 1960s so far that abolition was seriously suggested.[36] A revitalization was begun in 1969 under Miles Kirkpatrick, but it mainly consisted of a crackdown on deceptive advertising. Like the anticonglomerate moves by Richard McLaren at Antitrust at the same time, this seemed tough. But in fact it skirted the core problems of market power.

There were also FTC actions toward cereal firms and the Xerox Corporation begun during 1971–72, plus studies of the oil industry and other major industries. One can regard the recent degree of strictness as rising but moderate (see also Chapter 10).

During the 1920s, 1940s, and 1960s, the FTC's Bureau of Economics has played a strong role. Its studies are extensive, if often flawed and incomplete. With more than 30 economists on the staff, the FTC could now at long last tackle several major cases at once. And the findings have provided much of the impetus for later FTC actions.[37] This research capacity has been much greater than the Antitrust Division's resources. Moreover, FTC economic studies are published, often with great impact, while economic material at the Division is submerged in fact memos and the preparation of individual cases. The result is far less than the "pitiless publicity" that Woodrow Wilson promised. But it is not trivial.[38]

Dual Enforcement.   The two agencies have come to overlap widely in their coverage and basic actions. Mergers, restructuring, collusive and possible predatory devices, all these and more are treated by both agencies over nearly the whole range of industry. This could cause strife and

---

[36] American Bar Association, *Report on the Federal Trade Commission,* 1969; and E. F. Cox, R. C. Fellmeth, and J. E. Schultz, *The Nader Report on the Federal Trade Commission* (New York: R. W. Baron, 1969).

[37] The studies made by the FTC, throughout the years, have been uneven in quality. Some of them have been superficial and apologetic; others have been searching and significant. Studies of general economic interest have dealt with national wealth and income, industrial concentration, the merger movement, interlocking directorates, and international cartels. Studies of business practices have covered open price reporting, delivered pricing, resale price maintenance, and the marketing of gasoline. Studies of particular industries have included among others: copper, motor vehicles, petroleum, pipelines, and electrical utilities. They have also included, in response to agricultural interests, industries from whom the farmers buy or to whom they sell: farm machinery, fertilizer, flour milling, meat packing, and the distribution of milk and dairy products, and fruits and vegetables. The information provided by such investigations has led to the enactment of a number of important statutes, the outstanding example being that of the 78-volume report on the electrical utility industry which laid the foundation for the Public Utility Holding Company Act of 1935.

[38] However, the economists' role may be shrinking, with their removal from the FTC's main building in 1972 to an office many blocks away.

error, and every so often there are proposals to replace them with one superagency, to coordinate and fortify the treatments.

In fact, most experts praise the duality for enabling variety, experimentation, and—yes—competition in carrying out policy.[39] There are no serious disputes over jurisdiction. Budding cases are mostly divided along the heavy-light industry line, but with many sharp exceptions whenever an agency has a special interest. One agency can add its own treatment if it regards the others' as too weak; this has happened in several important cases. And a passive—or hyperactive—spell in one agency can be offset by the other. To force them into one meta-agency would invite *monopoly* behavior!

ALTERNATIVES

Private Suits. Private parties also use and—indirectly—enforce the antitrust laws. The stakes are often high, when a plaintiff (a customer, competitor, or other) can assert large losses from an anticompetitive act and claim triple that amount in damages. Few are the monopolists that don't face a steady drumfire of private cases; IBM is a classic instance (see Chapter 7). Private cases have mounted into the thousands in recent years, enough in some eyes to take the place of *public* agency work.[40] Yet, as we will see, private cases often fail to crop up where they are most needed and most expected. The agencies still carry the burden of setting mainstream policy.

Foreign Experiments. Abroad there has been a growth of antitrust in Britain, Canada, and Australia since 1948 and—even more mildly—in France, Germany and the Common Market. Of course, all countries take actions affecting competition, often abridging or excluding it. But the more formal policy ventures favoring competition deserve mention, for comparison with U.S. treatments.

Most of the activity is mere formality, studying but not deciding or enforcing. Only in Britain and Australia have there been real effects. Nearly all formal price-fixing has been ended in Britain since 1956–61, and resale price maintenance was stopped in 1965. The U.K. Monopolies Commission has deflected some mergers and required certain changes. But it has scarcely affected most dominant firms, though it has studied

---

[39] For two earlier studies commending the dual system, see the Hoover Commission report, Commission on Organization of the Executive Branch of the Government, *Task Force Report on Regulatory Commissions* (Washington, D.C.: Government Printing Office, 1949), p. 132; and *Report* of the Attorney General's National Committee to Study the Antitrust Laws (Washington D.C.: U.S. Government Printing Office, 1955), pp. 372–73.

[40] During the first 50 years of the Sherman Act, there were only three or four private suits per year. The plaintiffs succeeded, moreover, in less than a tenth of these. In later years, however, such suits came to be more important. In 1947, a Chicago movie exhibitor collected $360,000 in damages from a movie distributor who refused to lease him first-run films. Profiting by this example, a number of other exhibitors sued to collect similar damages. Attorneys for plaintiffs found such litigation to be lucrative. Business concerns and agencies of state and local governments brought increasing numbers of suits. From 1957 through 1961, there were 1,200; in 1962 and 1963, there were nearly 2,400. Plaintiffs, moreover, have been successful, winning two-fifths of their cases, with damages running into millions of dollars in a single case.

many of them thoroughly (see Chapter 7). Several industries have been treated more directly, by public enterprise, R&D grants, and forced reorganization: these include steel, aircraft, ship-building and computers. During 1965–70, mergers and price increases were also influenced directly.

SUMMARY

The economic tasks of antitrust are to stop cooperation and reduce dominant positions, to the margin where the benefits of competition are balanced by possible economies of scale. The basic laws, the Sherman and Clayton acts, appear to fit these tasks well in concept. They reflect long traditions but a checkered legislative history. There are many exemptions to them, and reasonable enforcement of them leaves further areas out.

The two antitrust agencies are bantams, slight and weak compared to their responsibilities. They are influenced by a variety of public and private groups. They are run by lawyers, concerned to apply rules and win cases. Access to the critical data is limited. Recently, most effort has gone toward conduct and mergers, rather than to remedial actions against dominant firms. The agencies usually penalize by onerous proceedings and by reinforcing private damage claims, more than by formal convictions and fines.

The process of study and treatment is often slow and confused by legalisms. Activity has fluctuated sharply, but the long trend is to bear down on medium firms while letting the largest dominant firms stand. The FTC has had a mediocre record. Dual enforcement tends to promote balance and variety. Private suits are not substitutes for public action. And antitrust abroad is often mere ritual, even more than in the U.S.

The U.S. experiments in antitrust have been narrow and increasingly limited by delay and form. Their effects are likely to be complex, perhaps with unknown side effects, too. Consider a broad hypothesis about its effects, which Chapters 6 through 10 will cast light on:

Hypothesis. Let us suppose that the early restorative actions did reduce market power in certain industries (oil, cigarettes, aluminum, tin cans: see Chapter 7). But as effort has shifted to policing conduct, the whole treatment has tended to constrain lesser firms relative to dominant ones. They can neither cooperate nor merge, and yet dominant firms are untouched. This twist of policy is natural, in light of the motives and constraints on agency managers as they briefly hold office. But it could fit optimal treatment only if there is a high rate of decline in dominant firms. If, instead, dominant firms tend to hold their positions, then the peculiar bias of antitrust is perverse—and may even help to preserve those positions and to *increase* the degree of structural monopoly. In any case, antitrust is seemingly inequitable, by ratifying dominant firms while restraining lesser ones from doing what dominant firms do internally.

Alternative Hypothesis. Antitrust has ensured that oligopoly, not monopoly, prevails. It prevents collusion among firms, and only permits monopoly when it is achieved by innovation and superior efficiency. Therefore, antitrust tends to foster competition and progress.

Which is it? Or both, or neither? Nobody has definitive answers. You must decide for youself. (Try to list now the key information you need in order to decide the question.) Ponder these and other possibilities as you proceed.

TABLE 5–6

Legal Terms Often Used in Antitrust

Appeal: request for a reversal of a lower court decision.

Big case: involves a long and vast trial record; need not involve a "big" company; may take 15 or more years.

CID: antitrust agency request for data, enforced by court order.

Citation: in the title of a case the plaintiff is named first, e.g., Victim *v.* Offender. Even on appeal, the final decisions are usually cited with the plaintiff named first.

Consent decree: a formal compromise, filed with a court.

Conspiracy: any joint action.

Damages: the alleged value of harm suffered by a party.

Expert witness: engaged by one side to present objective opinion which strengthens that side's claim. In antitrust, often an accountant, engineer, economist, or financial specialist.

Great victory: dramatic, complete win in court. May involve large sums or only a point of law; large effect or trivial change.

Injunction: a court order stopping a specified act, under possible penalty of contempt of court.

Interrogatories: questions exchanged by parties before trial on matters of fact or anything else germane to the trial. May be brief or extensive.

Per se: "as such," without further evidence. *E.g.,* price fixing is a *per se* violation if a mere showing that price fixing existed will always bring a conviction.

Precedent: a line drawn in one case which governs decisions in later similar cases. What the line *is* is often intensely debated.

Prosecutorial discretion: the latitude which agency managers have to choose specific cases and to interpret "the law."

Record: the printed account of all materials presented at trial and all proceedings of the trial. Appellate decisions cannot go beyond it.

Remedy (or relief): the corrective changes required after decision, in order to stop further violations.

Snow: vernacular for overwhelming an opponent's investigation with useless, undigested materials. Routinely successful in buying time.

CHAPTER SIX

Restrictive Practices: Collusion, Exclusion, and Discrimination

Restrictive practices are *actions* which move the market outcome toward the monopoly result. They are done by firms holding only part of the market (monopolists are treated in Chapters 7 and 13–19). Price fixing, exclusion and price discrimination are the main forms they take, among endless varieties. They lurk in oligopolies of all sorts, and often exert powerful effects. Some of them (like price fixing) are hard-core causes of social harm; others are more mixed or even procompetitive. Policies toward them also vary in severity, from flat prevention to softer treatments. And prohibitions on one practice often simply move the effort into other forms.

First, the basic problems are analyzed to show how these practices arise. Then the policies toward collusion, exclusion, and discrimination are taken up in that order.

ANALYSIS

We consider two basic practices: (1) restricting competition so as to raise the *level* of prices, and (2) price discrimination, which affects the *structure* of prices. Both, of course, tend to raise profit levels.

Raising Price Levels

The cardinal point is that cooperation is partial monopoly. By cooperating, a pair or group of competitors can get part of the gains which merging to form a monopoly would yield. Done secretly, this collusion gives real market power beneath an illusion of competition. It is endemic in markets ranging from loose oligopoly to virtual monopoly, roughly from concentration of 30 percent to 100 percent. In the upper ranges, of tight oligopoly, collusion can often be tacit, as if in a "shared monopoly." In the lower ranges of medium and loose oligopoly, it must be more explicit and binding if it is to work at all.

FIGURE 6–1

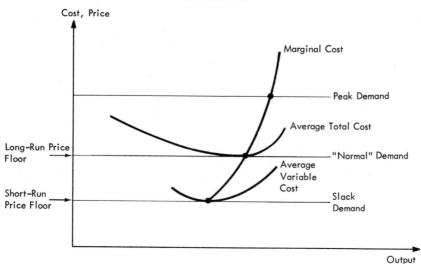

Oligopoly pricing proceeds within a range of likely outcomes.[1] The *floor* level for price is marginal cost (either short or long run, depending on the situation being analysed: short-run marginal cost varies more widely than long-run marginal cost). Where overhead costs are large, marginal costs may be far below average costs, as in Figure 6–1. Then fears of ruinous price cutting will be common, for indeed a slump in demand will make it rational to cut prices deeply.[2]

The ceiling on oligopoly pricing is the pure monopoly level, which is reached only if cooperation is perfect and complete. The actual price depends on how well cooperation succeeds. It can arise from soft or rigid arrangements, and it can come and go dramatically. Figure 6–2 illustrates the general conditions, with a scattering around the central relationships (recall Figure 2–12 in Chapter 2). The probable margin of price over costs varies with concentration and market share, plus other factors.

At any time, there may be incentives for each firm to cut price and gain business: toward average cost in normal times, toward marginal cost in slack periods. Price cutting is therefore endemic, and dynamic sequences of price cutting, once started, can go very deep. A successful cartel must fit the varying interests of its members, some of whom are newer, larger, and/or more efficient than the others. Some, in particular, may have greater overhead costs and lower marginal costs. And the lower concentration is, the more it must be made up by tight pacts and controls among the firms.

Collusion often pays its members well. Yet it is even better to be *out-*

---

[1] Landmark studies are E. H. Chamberlin, *The Theory of Monopolistic Competition*, 8th ed. (Cambridge: Harvard University Press, 1962); and W. J. Fellner, *Competition among the Few*, Norton, 1949).

[2] See J. M. Clark, *Studies in the Economics of Overhead Costs* (Chicago: University of Chicago Press, 1923); and Scherer, *op. cit.*, Chaps. 5–8.

FIGURE 6–2

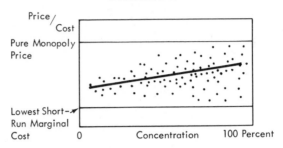

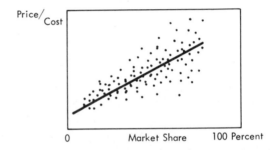

side a working cartel, shaving price and taking clientele from the others. This temptation eventually erodes many conspiracies, despite the members' outrage against "chiselling" by "renegades." The cartel attempts to bind members by quotas, penalties, policing or, best of all, pooling of profits. The conditions for a successful cartel have been worked out in some detail.[3] They require quick exposure of renegades and effective ways to threaten sharp penalties. Evidently, explicit price fixing occurs typically among many obscure firms in rather scrappy industries, rather than among the famous few in leading industries.

Customers also try to kill off collusion among their suppliers, by vertical tactics to encourage chiselling or by bringing in the law. (Some customers may be passive and let collusion go on. Regulated utilities, subsidized firms, and public agencies are said to be so, in their purchases (see Part IV and Chapter 29). Monopolies may also be so, as one form of X-inefficiency).

Oligopoly is best seen as an arena for constant strife, as the balance sways between collusion and independence. Because price is only one among many directions for collusion—others include product quality, advertising, investment, etc.—actual collusion is often as elusive as quicksilver.

---

[3] Donald J. Dewey, *op. cit.;* P. W. MacAvoy and Daniel Orr, "Price Strategies to Promote Cartel Stability," *Economica,* 1965, pp. 186–97; and George J. Stigler, "A Theory of Oligopoly," *Journal of Political Economy,* 1964, pp. 44–61.

Within the range of outcomes, there are also endless possibilities for mutual strategies: bluffing, misleading, etc. Game theory once promised great insight into these.[4] It has not, in fact, clarified the main problems; rather, it helps to illustrate some of the variety of outcomes, and to study the motives of the cooperator-competitors.

Generally, the leading firms will be best able to select the prices that will serve to maximize the joint profits and to see that it is actually adopted. The resulting price-leadership will influence the actual level of price, to some degree. But often price-leadership is erratic. And even a lock-step pattern of led prices may reflect merely a barometric role of the leader: *finding* the new price level, not *making* it. If so, it does not prove that cooperation exists.

Therefore, it is not easy to infer collusion from price behavior, especially—and paradoxically—in tight oligopolies where it is most likely and effective. Instead, one must usually rely on concrete evidence of collusion: notes, initialled agreements, etc. And these usually exist only in the lesser, more futile efforts to get loose oligopolists to coordinate.

Actual cooperative schemes are endlessly varied, reflecting both the complexity of actual market conditions and the sheer ingenuity of the human mind. The main types in the U.S. have been: (1) simple conspiracies and bidding rings, (2) trade associations, (3) intercorporate links (directorships, joint ventures, etc.), (4) resale price maintenance ("fair trade"), (5) delivered pricing systems, (6) intracompany conspiracy, and (7) tacit collusion (including price leadership). Their policy treatments will be evaluated in a later section.

These conditions promote collusion: (1) tightness of structure, with few sellers, (2) large overhead costs, as a share of total costs, (3) similarity of conditions among these firms; costs and homogeneity of products, (4) bias in information favoring sellers against buyers and exposing price cutting quickly, and (5) passive buyers. One can therefore single out the minority of markets that are ripe for collusion.

Collusion always causes social harm: lost efficiency, innovation, equity, etc. Its agents often claim social benefits, though the really convincing one—economics of scale—is simply absent. The others are as follows:

Avoiding Cut-throat Competition (Ruinous, Destructive, etc.). The claim—popular since before 1890—has little merit. Short-term fluctuations may induce price cutting below long-run average cost, but only temporarily. Capacity need not fall below long-run normal levels nor undergo a wasteful sequence of scrapping and replacement. Long-term declines in demand will induce chronic price cutting below profitable levels. But that is precisely what is needed, to ensure that excess capacity is drawn down to long-run efficient levels. Competition may seem to do this cruelly and too rapidly. But evaluating the net social effect is not easy, and better ways than price fixing can be used to ease the impact.

Reducing Risk. Price fixing may stabilize prices and output. But this is not necessarily a benefit, and Chapter 2 has noted that reducing

---

[4] von Neumann and Morgenstern, *op. cit.;* and M. Shubik, *Strategy and Market Structure* (New York: Wiley, 1959).

risk has not been shown to lower the needed profit rate. And price fixing may *not* reduce risk: prices may undergo sharper bumps as price fixing works, then collapses, then returns, etc. Flexible, sensitive pricing is in the very stuff of competition and efficiency.

Making Other Valuable Actions Possible. The excess profits might be devoted to greater service, innovation, or inventories. Colluders might also pool resources for large-scale projects (e.g., clean air technology for cars). Yet competition is as likely to induce the optimal levels of these as is collusion. And claimed needs for these have never withstood objective scrutiny.

These claims do not persuade, because they have no sound factual basis nor proof that collusion will give a specific result superior to competition. The assertions are usually vague, and the element of self-pleading is strong.

Exclusion

Exclusion is a class of activities which also attempt to raise price and profitability. They narrow the market, or segregate parts of it. No new analysis is needed, since their intent and effects—and claimed benefits —are on much the same footing as those of price fixing. The main types of exclusion have been: (1) vertical restraints imposed from one level to another, and (2) tie-ins between two products.

Price Discrimination

Price discrimination is a difference in the price-cost ratios in the selling of like goods to different customers.[5] It occurs when buyers have differing demand elasticities, can be charged differing prices, and cannot resell to each other. It is accentuated when overhead costs are large; then the marginal costs of each unit are low and there are large floating costs which can be assigned at the seller's will.

A perfect monopolist can discriminate with utmost precision, nicely extracting all consumer surplus and heading off any new competition. More often, customers can only be grouped broadly. Utilities and professionals are the classic discriminators, because of their control over supply (see Chapters 14 and 24).

But discrimination is nearly ubiquitous under market power, and in many industries it is epidemic. As Figure 6–3 shows, it can cause prices to differ sharply, sometimes by an order of magnitude. Drugs are only the most marked among many such instances; the weekly grocery ads in every hometown newspaper are full of discrimination. (Indeed, try to list ten items you have bought which involve it and ten which don't. Which ten are easier to find?).

Discrimination can be pro- or anticompetitive, depending on quite simple conditions, as follows.

---

[5] The *locus classicus* is Joan Robinson, *The Economics of Imperfect Competition,* (New York: Macmillan, 1933). See also J. M. Clark, *Studies in the Theory of Overhead Costs* (New York: Macmillan, 1922).

FIGURE 6–3

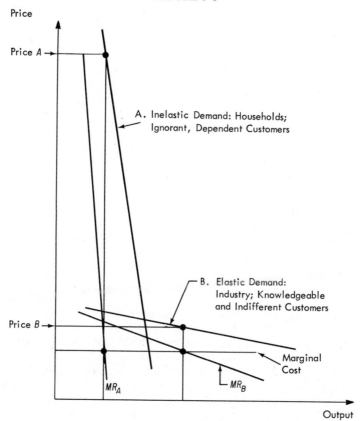

1. *Market share of the firm.* Done by a dominant firm, it impedes competition. Done by a small firm, it adds to competition.
2. *Systematic or sporadic.* Systematic discrimination may reduce competition and prevent entry, while sporadic discrimination usually promotes it and improves the allocative process.

This is summed up in Figure 6–4. The effect can be on two levels:

1. *First-level effects* are on the competitive status of the *discriminator* and his rivals. Example: Disc Inc. strengthens its market share and profitability by discriminating.
2. *Second-level effects* are on the relative status of the *buyers.* Example: The electric company discriminates, and so Acme Inc. get electricity cheaper than its competitor, cuts price, and gains more market share.

Discrimination by a dominant firm can improve allocation, *if* scale economies are important and cannot be achieved by single pric-

FIGURE 6–4
Price Discrimination May Increase or Reduce Competition

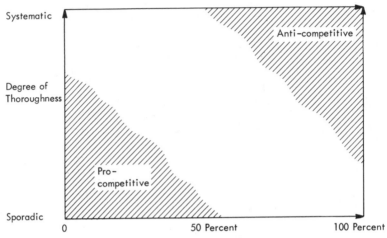

Market Share of the Firm Doing the Discrimination

ing.[6] This special case is analysed in Chapter 14. It is often claimed but rarely proven to exist, except in utilities. Indeed it is usually too good as an antitrust defense, because it makes a strong case *for regulation.* Unless there are heroic economies of scale—making for a natural monopoly—the efficiency gain from discrimination will be slight.

Price differences can and do arise because costs differ. This is a valid defense for price discrimination: that it is not discrimination at all. Indeed, if costs differ then *uniform* prices will be discriminatory: this occurs frequently.

Costs may differ because (1) the products differ (e.g., are bigger, better, shipped further, supplied at peak or off-peak), and (2) larger sales can be made at lower unit costs, justifying quantity discounts. Costs are often the very devil to measure, especially when large overhead or joint costs must be assigned arbitrarily. Sellers usually can allocate costs so as to justify a price structure which precisely accords with discrimination.

Hard-core discrimination by monopolists is treated in Chapters 7 and 13–18. In Section 4, we consider only its role in looser market structures, under antitrust.

PRICE FIXING

Recall the basic condition: the optimum treatment will draw the line of legality at the efficient margin, in light of benefits and costs of the practice and the practical nature of the treatment (its costs, burdens of

---

[6] The original analysis of this is by Joan Robinson, *op. cit.* It is standard fare in microeconomic texts. See also Fritz Machlup, *The Political Economy of Monopoly* (Baltimore: Johns Hopkins Press, 1952); and section 4 below.

proof, speed, etc.). A simple, definite and clear rule is better than a complex, uncertain one, if it approximates the efficient margin.

Simple Conspiracies

In fact, the legal lines are drawn sharply in U.S. antitrust. Simple conspiracies are illegal *per se,* without any further proof of intent or effect.

Simple conspiracies are usually covert, or clothed in honorific reasons (to stabilize markets, promote innovation, etc.). The core is an agreement on prices and market shares. Territories may be divided, and outsiders excluded from entry. In the tightest cartels, output is sold by a joint sales unit and profits are pooled.[7] Where cartels are illegal and secrecy is necessary, the methods are cruder, weaker, and more transient in effect.[8]

Agreements involve rancorous dispute among tough men who—in the U.S.—know that they are breaking the law. There may be furtive meetings in hotel rooms (trade association meetings are a common arena), memoranda, and secret codes. Usually the firm's lawyers must be kept in the dark, and the company's top officers are often insulated from direct knowledge. These awkward details shade into the more cosmopolitan tacit parallelism of major tight oligopolies, where there is no direct contact but a deeply ingrained familiarity and understanding among rivals.

This *per se* policy applies to control of output, market sharing, and the exclusion of competitors by boycotts or other coercive practices. All an Antitrust Division attorney (or private plaintiff) needs to show in court is that competitors actually tried to fix prices or otherwise rig the market. A scribbled memorandum, an annotated price list, tape recording, any evidence of a conspiracy is usually enough to convict. No evidence that prices actually rose, or rose above some "reasonable" level, is essential, although such evidence will encourage stiffer sentences and larger awards for damages.

This *per se* rule was first formed in 1899, was firmly set by the Supreme Court in 1927, and was reaffirmed in 1940.

The earliest cases involving restrictive agreements among competitors were those of the Trans-Missouri Freight Association in 1897,[9] the Joint Traffic Association in 1898,[10] and the Addyston Pipe & Steel Company in 1899.[11] In the *Trans-Missouri* and *Joint Traffic* cases, groups of railroads had fixed and enforced freight rates. In the *Addyston* case, six producers of cast iron pipe had assigned certain markets to each of their number and determined the allocation of contracts elsewhere by operat-

---

[7] For the flavor and variety of collusion, see G. W. Stocking and M. Watkins, *Cartels in Action* (New York: Twentieth Century Fund, 1946).

[8] On the seamy side of this are rackets of various kinds, which have occurred on occasion in construction, laundrymen, undertakers, truckers, distributors, and various dealers in commodities, as well as in what have been defined as "illicit" trades. Their methods are less polite; their aims and effects are the same as those of "gentlemen" conspirators.

[9] *U.S.* v. *Trans-Missouri Freight Assn.,* 166 U.S. 290.

[10] *U.S.* v. *Joint Traffic Assn.,* 171 U.S. 505.

[11] *Addyston Pipe & Steel Co.* v. *U.S.,* 175 U.S. 211.

ing a bidding ring. In all three cases the defendants argued that their restrictions were required to prevent ruinous competition and that the resulting rates and prices were reasonable. And, in each case, the Court rejected this defense, holding the arrangements to be illegal in themselves.

These precedents were followed faithfully for 20 years, decisions being rendered against collusive bidding by purchasers of livestock,[12] exclusion of competing railways from a terminal,[13] the use of patent licenses to fix the price of bathtubs,[14] and the operation of a boycott by retail lumber dealers.[15] In 1918, in a decision of limited significance, the Court refused to condemn a rule adopted by the Chicago Board of Trade requiring those buying and selling grain outside of trading hours to do so at the price at which the market closed.[16] In 1923, it upheld limits on the output of hand-blown window glass, but only to meet the peculiar problems of a declining trade in a dying industry.[17]

The leading decision on restrictive agreements came in 1927 in the Trenton Potteries case.[18] Firms producing four-fifths of the domestic output of vitreous enamel bathroom fixtures had agreed to fix prices and to sell exclusively through jobbers. The Court was emphatic in its refusal to accept the reasonableness of the prices fixed as a defense.

The purpose of the law, said the Court, is to protect the public by maintaining competition. Every agreement to fix prices, however reasonable, is therefore condemned.

Doubts concerning this position were raised by the Court's decision in the Appalachian Coals in 1933.[19] But in the Socony-Vacuum case[20] in 1940, the Court reaffirmed the rule of Trenton Potteries. This case involved an agreement, under which the major oil companies in ten midwestern states raised and maintained the price of gasoline by purchasing marginal supplies from independent refineries. The Court again rejected the defense that the price established was no more than fair. Said Justice Douglas:

Any combination which tampers with price structures is engaged in an unlawful activity. Even though the members of the price-fixing group were in no position to control the market, to the extent that they raised, lowered, or stabilized prices they would be directly interfering with the free play of market forces. The

---

[12] *U.S.* v. *Swift & Co.,* 196 U.S. 375 (1906).

[13] *U.S.* v. *Terminal R.R. Assn.,* 224 U.S. 383 (1912).

[14] *U.S.* v. *Standard Sanitary Mfg. Co.,* 226 U.S. 20 (1912).

[15] *U.S.* v. *Eastern States Retail Lumber Assn.,* 234 U.S. 600 (1914).

[16] *Chicago Board of Trade* v. *U.S.,* 246 U.S. 231.

[17] *National Assn. of Window Glass Mfrs.* v. *U.S.,* 263 U.S. 403.

[18] *U.S* v. *Trenton Potteries Co.,* 273 U.S. 392.

[19] *Appalachian Coals, Inc.* v. *U.S.,* 288 U.S. 344. In this case 137 companies, producing a tenth of the bituminous coal mined east of the Mississippi River and around two-thirds of that mined in the Appalachian territory, had set up a joint agency to handle all their sales. The Court recognized that this arrangement established common prices for the firms involved, but it went on to find that the industry was seriously depressed, that competition in the sale of coal had been subject to various abuses, and that the selling agency did not control enough of the supply to enable it to fix the market price. On this basis, the arrangement was allowed to stand.

[20] *U.S.* v. *Socony-Vacuum Oil Co.,* 310 U.S. 150.

Act places all such schemes beyond the pale. . . . . Under the Sherman Act, a combination formed for the purpose and with the effect of raising, depressing, fixing, pegging, or stabilizing the price of a commodity in interstate or foreign commerce is illegal *per se*. . . . Whatever economic justification particular price-fixing agreements may be thought to have, the law does not permit an inquiry into their reasonableness. They are banned because of their actual or potential threat to the central nervous system of the economy.[21]

The ruling of the Court could not have been more sweeping; any such agreement, even though affecting a minor portion of the market, was forbidden; any manipulation of prices, whatever its purpose, was against the law.

Bidding rings are one form of conspiracy. Many public purchases and construction projects are set by competitive bidding. Specifications are published, bids are invited and received by a fixed date, the sealed bids are then opened, and the lowest bidder wins. Yet often the bids are rigged beforehand, with the chosen winner low and the others high; the winners rotate among the group, and competition is avoided.

These rings too are illegal *per se*. The biggest one yet caught was the conspiracy among the makers of heavy electrical equipment, tried and convicted in 1960. For decades, collusion had been a way of life in selling transformers, switchgear and generators. Sometimes the collusion came unstuck, but often it put prices up by 20 percent or more and profits up by hundreds of millions of dollars.

The defendants had allocated contracts, selecting the low bidder by drawing names out of a hat, by rotating them in alphabetical order, and by making allotments according to a formula based upon the phases of the moon. The low bidder had then informed the others regarding his bid, and they had adjusted their bids accordingly. The conspirators had met under assumed names in luxury hotels in various cities, in motels, in mountain-top retreats, in cabins in the Canadian woods, and at a Milwaukee bar known as "Dirty Helen's." To maintain secrecy, they had used codes in referring to the companies and their executives, called one another from public telephones, sent letters to their homes rather than their offices, in plain envelopes without return addresses, and destroyed these communications when received.

Twenty-nine companies and 45 of their officers, including General Electric and Westinghouse and 16 of their officials, pleaded guilty or offered no defense in 20 criminal suits. Seven officers spent brief periods in jail. The total fines were only $1.9 million, but 1,900 treble damage suits were filed. One by Consolidated Edison of New York was for $100 million and another by Commonwealth Edison of Chicago was for $75 million. (Note: no private utility had earlier complained of overcharging or helped start the suit. And the damage claims were widely regarded in the trade as soft).[22]

In the first suit tried, Philadelphia Electric proved damages of $9.6

---

[21] *Ibid.*, pp. 221–226.

[22] See F. M. Westfield, "Regulation and Conspiracy," *American Economic Review*, 1965, pp. 424–43, and Chapter 14 below for the reasons for this softness. A lively account of the conspiracy is in R. A. Smith, *Corporations in Crisis* (New York: Doubleday, 1963), pp. 113–66.

It so happens, Gregory, that your Grandfather Sloan was detained by an agency of our government over an honest misunderstanding concerning certain antitrust matters! He was not "busted by the Feds"!

Drawing by W. Miller; © *1971* The New Yorker Magazine, *Inc.*

million and was awarded $28.8 million. The companies then settled the rest privately. The payments ultimately totalled some $600 million, though a special tax ruling—defining these payments as the "normal" costs of doing business and therefore tax-deductible!—reduced the impact to about $300 million.[23]

In 1969, 15 of the country's largest manufacturers of plumbing fixtures were found to have met in a hotel room in Chicago to set the prices of bathtubs, toilets, and sinks. And three of the leading pharmaceutical houses were found to have agreed upon the prices to be charged for antibiotic "wonder drugs." Agreements restricting competition in national markets have occurred in scores of other cases, ranging from eyeglasses to explosives and including such important products as soap, cheese, watches, electric lamps, typewriters, ball bearings, newsprint paper, stainless steel, fertilizers, and various chemicals.

The government has been highly successful in cases brought against restrictive agreements under the Sherman Act. Down to 1951, there were 437 instances (69 in litigated decrees and 368 in constant decrees) in which price fixing, market sharing, control of output, collusive bidding, and the use of a common buying or selling agent were enjoined.[24] Since

---

[23] *Business Week,* October 14, 1967, p. 130.

[24] Arthur T. Dietz, "An Analysis of Decrees under the Sherman Act," unpublished doctoral dissertation, (Princeton University, 1953), pp. 336–53, 365.

then there have been hundreds more, with 15 or 20 usually going at any time. The Division's batting average has been very high. With good reason, company lawyers spend much effort telling their executives *never* to discuss prices with competitors.

Such sleuthing is a major part of the antitrust effort, even though the *per se* rule makes conviction relatively easy. And yet it touches only certain activities in a relatively small range of middling-size industries.

The *per se* rule is probably quite efficient (recall Chapter 3). It treats most price-fixing cases correctly, for there is usually no social benefit at all to offset the monopoly effect created by rigging prices. In a few special cases (perhaps dying industries), some social benefit may result, and so a *per se* rule risks losing these benefits. But to evaluate this separately for all such cases would mire policy in long, byzantine confrontations among rival claims and witnesses. The cost of this would far exceed the possible benefits in the few special cases. And these benefits are usually obtainable by other routes. The alternative to a *per se* rule is paralysis.

In short, the *per se* rule is clean and efficient. Also, its scope is not universal, for many sectors have managed to get exempted from antitrust (recall Chapter 4). This fits the general pattern: a tight rule will have narrow coverage. Put the other way round, the rule can be strict *because* so many of the border cases (and some central ones!) have been taken out from it.

Comparison Abroad. In Britain, restrictive agreements are now outlawed nearly as strictly as in the U.S.[25] The 1955 Restrictive Practices Act required all such agreements to be registered and dropped, unless an affirmative case could be made for them before the new Restrictive Practices Court. By 1964 some 2,500 agreements had been filed, an astonishing array from the full range of industry and trade. By 1973 only 11 had been let stand, on special grounds. Although some of the collusion has simply shifted to informal means, Britain has—virtually at a stroke—erased the heritage of its 1930s cartel craze.

Elsewhere, cartels are only lightly constrained. In France and Germany, the burden of proof is the other way; price fixing must be shown to have net antisocial effects. The Common Market has strict formal rules against collusion, but enforcement has been slight. Japan has "Fair Trade" laws against price fixing, but they too are scarcely enforced. Indeed, "depression cartels" have been officially sponsored and approved during recessions. Though their effects may be limited and weak, they still contrast directly with U.S. policy.

Trade Associations

Every trade has its association; some are large and powerful (e.g., druggists, aerospace), others just a name, an officer, and a secretary. There are thousands of them, promoting their members' interests by economic and political means. Their activities are diverse, some of them neutral to competition, while others reduce it. In the 1930s and earlier,

---

[25] See annual *Reports of the Registrar,* Restrictive Practices, especially for 1960–66.

trade associations commonly had negative effects in the U.S. And elsewhere, especially in Britain, trade associations were the nucleus for tight new cartels in hundreds of industries.

Recently, trade associations have probably faded in economic importance, thanks partly to antitrust. And their effects tend to be relatively marginal and to occur in lesser industries. Yet they still have a variety of effects, particularly in more local trades. We consider several of their technical activities.

Typical association activities include industrial research, market surveys, the development of new uses for products, the operation of employment bureaus, collective bargaining with organized labor, mutual insurance, commercial arbitration, the publication of trade journals, joint advertising and publicity, and joint representation before legislative and administration agencies. These may serve a trade without disservice to its customers. But they also include the establishment of common cost accounting procedures, the operation of price reporting plans, the collection and dissemination of statistics, the standardization of products and terms of sale, the provision of credit information, the interchange of patent rights, the joint purchasing of supplies, and the promulgation of codes of business ethics. Each of these may operate to restrain competition in quality, service, price, or terms of sale.

Cost accounting may just standardize reports. But it often slips over into describing uniform mark-ups and circulating average-cost data, or even urging members to set prices at the average.

Price-reporting systems are operated by perhaps 15 percent of associations. Through these systems, association members make available to one another, and sometimes to outsiders, information concerning the prices at which products have been, are being, or are to be sold. It is argued that such systems, by increasing the amount of knowledge available to traders, must lessen the imperfection of markets and make for more effective competition. Whether they do so, in fact, depends upon the characteristics of the industries which use them and upon the characteristics of the plans themselves.

Price reporting may improve market functioning when the market (1) has low concentration and entry barriers, (2) homogeneous output, (3) elastic demand and (4) stable demand. This describes a textbook competitive market. In others, price reporting is likely to support agreement and quicken pressure against price cutters.

The reporting plan will need to: (1) be fully available to all sellers *and* buyers, (2) not identify traders, (3) cover only past sales, not present or planned ones, (4) avoid circulating average prices (focal points for new price agreements), and (5) be free of any controls or penalties on sellers.

If any one of these strict conditions—both of industry and plan—are not met, a reporting system is likely to reduce competition.

Other ambiguous activities may also be carried to the point where they restrain competition. Circulation of statistics on production, inventories, unfilled orders, idle capacity, sales, and shipments may serve merely to inform traders concerning the state of the market; it may also be used to facilitate a scheme for curtailment of output and sharing of sales. Standardization of products may contribute to convenience and lessen waste; it may also lessen competition in quality and restrict the consumer's range of choice. Standardization of terms of sale may benefit purchasers by saving time, preventing misunderstandings, and affording a common basis for price comparisons; it may also promote collusion by preventing indirect departures from an established price. Provision of information on credit risks may increase the safety with which credit may be granted; reporting on customers may also be employed as a means of boycotting those who deal with outsiders or fail to observe a recommended price.

The pooling of patents may afford a readier access to technology; it may be so administered that technology is monopolized. Joint purchasing may increase efficiency in buying; it may be used to establish prices that are unfair to suppliers and to exact concessions that are unfair to competitors. The promulgation of a code of ethics is avowedly designed to raise standards of conduct among the members of a trade, but such codes frequently contain provisions denouncing practices that are found to be offensive merely because they are competitive. Where an association lacks the power of enforcement, these prohibitions are merely persuasive. But where some measure of coercion is at hand, they may take on the force of law.

Cooperation or Conspiracy? As Adam Smith remarked in 1776: "People of the same trade seldom meet together, even for merriment and diversion, but the conversation ends in a conspiracy against the public or in some contrivance to raise prices."[26] Does this observation apply to the modern trade association? No one knows. There are thousands of trade association offices in the United States. In each of them a staff is working, presumably five days in every week and 52 weeks in every year, to administer activities in which competitors do not compete. Upon occasion the Federal Trade Commission or the Department of Justice makes an investigation and certain practices of an association are proscribed by the Commission or the courts. But no such sporadic action can be expected to disclose each of the cases in which competition is restrained.

The lines of policy have come to fit the economic criteria reasonably well. Four seminal cases in the 1920s involved lumber, linseed oil, maple flooring, and cement.[27] The Court held against pervasive reporting schemes which violated the first four conditions just above: access, anonymity, past sales, and no averages. Where an anticompetitive tendency could be seen, the system was rejected. In 1936, an even vaster scheme in the sugar industry was also enjoined from violating the five conditions.[28]

And in 1969 the treatment was confirmed in the major *Container Corp.* case.[29] Cardboard box sellers in one region had a system allowing each seller to learn instantly of any other seller's latest sale. This was

---

[26] *Wealth of Nations,* Book I, chap. x, Part II.

[27] *American Column and Lumber Co.* v. *U.S.,* 257 U.S. 377 (1921); *U.S.* v. *American Linseed Oil Co.,* 262 U.S. 371 (1923); *Maple Flooring Mfrs. Assn.* v. *U.S.,* 268 U.S. 563 (1925); *Cement Mfrs. Protective Assn.* v. *U.S.,* 268 U.S. 588 (1925).

[28] *U.S.* v. *Sugar Institute,* 15 F. Supp. 817 (1934); *Sugar Institute* v. *U.S.,* 297 U.S. 553 (1936) 601.

[29] *U.S.* v. *Container Corp. of America,* 393 U.S. 333, 1969.

struck down: (1) because it would discourage price cutting by making exposure quicker, and (2) because buyers did not have equal access.

Apart from marginal details, the main policy treatment is pretty clear. But it is not pressed hard.

About ten cases involving restrictive trade association activities are brought by the Antitrust Division each year. These are usually settled by consent decrees. In a few serious cases, they end in dissolution of the associations concerned. The Federal Trade Commission regularly gives advisory opinions on association activities. It may warn an association, for instance, not to agree on wages that are to be reflected in setting prices, not to recommend certain profit margins as being fair, or not to use a common rate book in pricing services. The Commission, however, now rarely makes a formal complaint against an association or issues an order to cease and desist.

The courts, in general, have refrained from passing on particular elements of a trade association program, directing attention rather toward the consequences of the program as a whole.

Intercorporate Links

The financial setting of corporations often connects them in links of varying firmness (recall Chapter 2). We consider three of these: interest groupings, interlocking directorates, and joint ventures.

Interest groupings exist quietly in many forms. Large blocks of shares in competing firms are owned by a family group, or a bank trust department, an investment bank, an insurance firm, or pension fund. Similarly accounting firms, security underwriters, law firms, engineering firms, and others deal intimately with competing firms. This tissue of interests is extensive and intricate in many major industries.[30] It softens independence and inculcates a degree of uniformity.

How deeply this abridges competition nobody can say precisely.[31] Though there is increasing evidence that it influences some industries, it is well short of being a super-web of controls. It is, in any case, beyond the current reach of antitrust policy, or indeed of any policy control now existing. Instead, antitrust deals with the more superficial versions, such as directorates.

Interlocking directorates were common before the Clayton Act, Section 8, made them illegal in 1914. Direct interlocks—one person on the Boards of two competing firms—have now mostly disappeared, but marginal cases still occur. In 1968, the Antitrust Division—after much delay and with no penalties—required direct interlocks to be ended between leading automobile firms and oil companies, who compete in selling batteries and other supplies to drivers. Moreover, there are direct inter-

---

[30] U.S. House Subcommittee on Antitrust, *Interlocks in Corporate Management* (Washington, D.C.: U.S. Government Printing Office, 1965); and U.S. House Subcommittee on Domestic Finance, *Commercial Banks and Their Trust Activities* (Washington, D.C.: U.S. Government Printing Office, 1968), 2 volumes.

[31] Only the Securities and Exchange Commission requires some reporting of certain stockholder conditions (holdings above 10 percent). This does not touch the main substance of the problem.

locks between firms and potential entrants, and interlocks between finance and industry which formalize the favored access to capital, materials, or markets which dominant firms often have.

There also remain a vast number of indirect interlocks where two officers of a bank, law firm, etc., sit on boards of competing firms. Some of these connect the largest banks and firms much more closely than a random selection among directorial talent could yield.

These too are virtually untouched by antitrust or other policies. Their effects may be slight, beyond formalizing the underlying closeness. Others are surely powerful. Still, they are immune.[32]

Joint ventures are of endless variety, for many purposes. They range from agreements over to new producing firms. Some produce ores, others explore new technology, and still others enter new foreign markets. When set up by competing firms, they obviously make for common interests and may reduce competition in all the firms' activities. The defense is usually that, instead, they make possible large benefits while leaving competition unabated. As in other antitrust issues, one compares the real benefits and costs. The benefits are often quite accessible without the joint venture.

The most pervasive joint ventures are in metal ores, especially steel and copper, where ore supply is vital to competitive strategy. The steel industry is actually three tight interest groups, not a medium-tight oligopoly, because control over ores is tightly shared.[33] Many of the largest copper deposits in the world have been owned and mined jointly by the largest copper firms. They are claimed to be so large that joint financing is needed to raise enough capital. Yet the companies are not so small, nor capital markets so imperfect, that they could not go it alone in most cases.

Generally, it is *large* companies that do joint ventures, not small ones. This goes against the claim that they make expensive projects possible. Yet this burden of probability is reversed in actual policy. The anticompetitive effects must be shown to exist and offset the benefits of cooperation; or restrictive behavior attending the joint venture is used to condemn it. Most joint ventures therefore are immune. And recently, even when a new joint venture reduced the likelihood of competition among two chemical firms—in this field or many others—a divided court let it stand.[34] Once again, the burden of proof is critical to the content of policy.

These links matter most in industries with middling degrees of concentration, say 30 to 80 percent. Above that, they are unnecessary; below it, they have little effect. Some are as elusive as quicksilver, but others have stood rock-like for many decades. Though some of the hard-core

---

[32] Abroad, the connections are commonly at least as close and even more fully accepted. Family and bank holdings often link firms directly, giving a degree of quasi-merger. Boardroom connections are often close. And in some cases, cooperation and joint control are encouraged by the government. In Britain, Canada, and Australia, direct connections are resisted as a restrictive practice. But indirect connections are untouched.

[33] Daniel R. Fusfeld, "Joint Subsidiaries in the Iron and Steel Industry," *American Economic Review*, May 1958, pp. 578–87.

[34] *Penn-Olin Chemicals Co.* v. *U.S.*, 378 U.S. 158 (1964); *U.S.* v. *Penn-Olin Chemicals Co.*, 389 U.S. 308 (1967). This is discussed further below in section 7, Chapter 8.

links have been stopped, the others have scarcely been touched by study and treatment.

Resale Price Maintenance

RPM (called Fair Trade by its friends) is usually said to have started first with manufacturers, who wished to foster loyal and professional-quality dealers.[35] Then it became a retailers' device for cooperation, imposed on the producers. The usual version is a price "recommended," or actually printed on the product, by the maker. RPM agreements are signed contracts, enforceable under state laws. A key question is whether *nonsigners* of RPM agreements can be deprived of supply or sued to keep them from discounting. The price-cost margins set are often high.

RPM has been declining in importance, partly from antitrust resistance, partly from the spread of discounting. It is now regarded as primarily a variety of horizontal collusion among retailers—that is, an attempt at exemption from Sherman Section I.

Its monopoly effect in raising price is clear, as readers of almost any book (including this one!) are likely to attest. (Try to list ten items you have bought recently which had "recommended" or printed prices. It should be easy. Start with books, records, and sporting goods). Social benefits are usually slight or nil. RPM might foster "full service" dealers, who advise, carry a large inventory, do honest repairs, and generally give good service (examples: bookstores, photography stores, hi-fi studios).

Yet RPM is neither necessary nor sufficient for this. RPM may give *private* benefits, preserving an image of product quality, encouraging dealers to plug a fair-traded brand, or just giving excess profits. But it almost always causes social harm. It raises price, eliminates flexible price adjustments, and prevents the growth of more efficient retailing.

Before the 1930s, RPM had lost every court battle, both under the Sherman and FTC acts. During the 1930s, the retail druggists led the way in getting fair trade legalized in most states, at breakneck speed and usually without hearings. These laws bound nonsigners to RPM. A federal law legalizing RPM was also euchred through, the Miller-Tydings Act in 1937. After 14 years, the Court finally freed nonsigners from RPM. Schwegmann, a nonsigner, had resold Calvert and Seagram whiskey in New Orleans at $3.35 rather than the $4.24 set by RPM. Exonerating Schwegmann, the Court condemned "a program whereby recalcitrants are dragged in by the heels and compelled to submit to price fixing."[36]

A bout of price cutting followed, from Macy's and Gimbels to 40 other cities. The retailers rebounded with intensive lobbying and got through the McGuire-Keogh Act in 1952. It yoked in nonsigners explicitly and was upheld by the Court in 1953 and later.

Yet fair trade has dwindled away. In 1958, it was dropped by appliance and other producers. Most of the state laws have been repealed or gutted

---

[35] See E. T. Grether, *Price Control under Fair Trade Legislation* (New York: Oxford University Press, 1939); and Basil Yamey, ed., *Resale Price Maintenance* (Chicago: Aldine, 1966).

[36] *Schwegmann Bros.* v. *Calvert Corp.* and *Schwegmann Bros.* v. *Seagram Distillers Corp.,* 341 U.S. 384 (1951).

by court decisions. Discounting has eaten deeply into the old ways. Fair trading is still strong in some states and many goods, but primarily by habit and tacit collusion. Price cutting may be infrequent in many trades, but the cutters cannot be so easily threatened or taken to court. Other ways of keeping prices up are used, of course, especially in retail drugs. And lobbying campaigns for new fair trade laws are mounted every so often. Yet in 1975, Congress seemed likely to outlaw all RPM.

Fair trade has been eroded by legal decisions and the spread of discounting (which it encouraged). But it lingers on, in pockets of legality and wide areas of tacit adherence. It was outlawed and dropped in Britain after 1965. In that antitrust area, Britain has been stricter than the U.S.

Delivered Pricing

Many goods are sold at delivered prices: the nominal factory price plus a shipping markup equals the actual price. The resulting configuration of prices is like a contour map. Competition may obviously be reduced by this, if: (1) the buyer has no option to buy at the factory instead and ship it himself, and (2) several or all firms adopt the same set of delivered prices. Moreover, the location of industry may be distorted.

Such schemes and effects were important before 1949, in the steel, cement, and several other industries. Since 1948 the practice has been diluted and now is of marginal concern. Yet some of its earlier effects live on, and the practice deserves a brief analysis.

Analysis. Delivered pricing matters when output is: (1) *uniform* (e.g., steel, cement, corn oil), (2) *bulky,* so that transport costs are large, and (3) *centralized* around special inputs (e.g., ores, farm products). Consider the simplest system, say a steel industry whose dominant firm is located at Pittsburgh. That firm (call it U.S. Steel) sets prices at $50 per ton at Pittsburgh plus freight (as shown in Figure 6–5) and publishes a detailed price book listing every city in the country. This is a "Pittsburgh-plus" system, with Pittsburgh as the "basing point." All other producers reprint

FIGURE 6–5
Basing-Point Economics

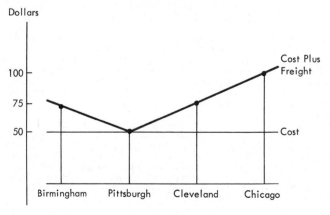

the price-book as *their* price lists. Result: buyers at each location face identical prices. A seller (1) whose full cost is below $50, or (2) who has idle capacity, or (3) who wishes to break in and get new clientele, does not cut price to do so. First effect: rigid, identical delivered-pricing schemes prevent competition. The identical prices reflect cooperation, not the free play of market forces.[37] This causes the usual losses in efficiency and equity.

Location of industry is soon affected in two ways. New steel *makers* may locate away from Pittsburgh, selling at "Pittsburgh-plus" and pocketing the plus as "phantom freight." But if they fear being made a basing point themselves, they will choose Pittsburgh instead. The net effect may go either way, toward overcentralizing or spreading the industry out thinner than the underlying costs prescribe. Only by a fluke will location happen to be efficient. Meanwhile, steel *users* are induced to locate at Pittsburgh more than is efficient. Second effect: the location of producers and users may be strongly distorted.

Also, buyers have no incentive to minimize transport costs by buying from a nearby producer. Third effect: transport resources are wasted.

There may soon be several basing points. The locational and transport-wasting effects will be less severe, but they will exist. Even if every plant is a basing point, new steel-plant choices may be affected. And even with universal basing points, the collusive role remains.

Actual Systems and Treatments. The practice began in steel in 1880, grew slowly until 1890, and by 1900 embraced nearly every steel firm and product. In 1901 the United States Steel Corporation was organized, and from then on the level of prices was effectively controlled, first through open agreements, then through the Gary dinners, and finally through price leadership. From 1901 to 1903 most steel was sold on a zone price

---

[37] The degree of identity in prices was often astonishing. During the 30s, when the purchasing agent for the Fort Peck Dam opened ten sealed bids for reinforcing bars, each of them was for $253,633.80. When the Navy Department opened 59 bids for steel pipe, each of them was for $6,001.83. And when the Army Engineers opened 11 bids for cement at Tucumcari, New Mexico, each of them was for $3.286854 a barrel, identity being carried to the sixth decimal place. Again in 1947, when the Illinois Department of Highways asked for bids on cement to be delivered in each of the 102 counties in the state, those submitted by eight companies were identical for each of the 102 deliveries. Such identities cannot be attributed to mere chance. The mathematical probability of accidentally arriving at those reported in Illinois has been computed as 1 in 8 followed by 214 zeros, a possibility that is even more remote than the random selection of a single electron from the entire universe. Identical prices may be a product of competition. They are more likely to reveal the presence of monopoly.

On the anticompetitive effects of delivered pricing, see F. A. Fetter, *The Masquerade of Monopoly* (New York: Harcourt, Brace & Co., 1931); "The New Plea for Basing Point Monopoly," *Journal of Political Economy,* Vol. XLV (1937), p. 577; "Exit Basing Point Pricing," *American Economic Review,* Vol. XXXVIII (1948), p. 815; Vernon A. Mund, *Open Markets* (New York: Harper & Bros., 1948); "The Freight Allowed Method of Price Quotation," *Quarterly Journal of Economics,* Vol. LIV (1940), p. 232; "Monopolistic Competition and Public Price Policy," *American Economic Review,* Vol. XXXII (1942), p. 727; Fritz Machlup, *The Basing Point System* (Philadelphia: Blakiston Co., 1949).

Arguments on behalf of delivered pricing include J. M. Clark, "Basing Point Methods of Price Quoting," *Canadian Journal of Economics and Political Science,* Vol. IV (1938), p. 477; "Imperfect Competition Theory and Basing Point Problems," *American Economic Review,* Vol. XXXIII (1943), p. 283; "The Law and Economics of Basing Points," *American Economic Review,* Vol. XXXIX (1949), p. 430; C. R. Daugherty, M. G. de Chazeau, and S. S. Stratton, *The Economics of the Iron and Steel Industry* (New York: McGraw-Hill Book Co., 1937), Vol. I, chap. xii; Vol. II, chap. xxii; Arthur Smithies, "Aspects of the Basing Point Problem," *American Economic Review,* Vol. XXXII (1942), p. 705.

basis. But thereafter all products but rails were priced at Pittsburgh-plus. In 1917, during World War I, the War Industries Board ordered the industry to establish a Chicago base. But the order was rescinded within a year at the suggestion of one of the members of the Board (none other than E. H. Gary, the former U.S. Steel Chairman).

The Antitrust Division had filed its great Section 2 suit against U.S. Steel in 1910. The firm was eventually acquitted in 1920 (see Chapter 7). But strangely, the case and pleadings ignored the basing-point system, the Division apparently being unaware of its anticompetitive role. Had that factor been used and tipped the 4–3 vote in 1920, the thrust of antitrust and the shape of industry could have been deeply altered.

In 1919, immediately after the war, fabricators in the West and the South began to organize and to carry complaints to the Federal Trade Commission concerning the prices they were forced to pay for steel. In 1920, when the government returned the railways to their owners, a 40 percent increase in freight rates pushed these prices even higher by adding to the plus in Pittsburgh-plus. Protests mounted, resolutions condemning the basing-point system were passed by the legislatures of 11 states, and 32 states joined in organizing the Associated States Opposing Pittsburgh-Plus. In response to this pressure, the Commission issued an order, in 1924, directing U.S. Steel to cease and desist "from quoting for sale or selling . . . rolled steel products upon any other basing point than that where the products are manufactured or from which they are shipped."[38] The Corporation then filed a statement promising to obey the order "insofar as it is practicable to do so" and proceeded to set up a multiple basing-point system in place of Pittsburgh-plus. The new system aided fabricators in the West and in the South by establishing bases at Chicago and Birmingham. But for many years, these gains were offset, in part, by making base prices higher at these centers than at Pittsburgh. Prices east of Pittsburgh were still Pittsburgh-plus; those west of Chicago were Chicago-plus. The Corporation plainly failed to obey the Commission's order. But the Commission made no attempt to have it enforced.

Under the NRA in 1933, an industry code further tightened the basing-point system, with U.S. Steel and Bethlehem in effective control. The code, in effect, gave to U.S. Steel and Bethlehem the legal right to fix the price of steel. And it provided that other firms, if they departed from this price, should be fined $10 per ton on the steel they produced. As a result, the industry could not obey the Federal Trade Commission's order without violating the NRA code. And it could not adhere to the code without disobeying the FTC.

This situation persisted until the NRA was found to be unconstitutional in May of 1935, and the FTC order again came into force. The industry, however, continued to employ the multiple basing-point system throughout the following decade. During the war, ironically enough, the mechanism afforded by the basing-point system was used by the Office of Price Administration in establishing, not minimum prices, but maximum prices for steel.

In the case of cement the story is much the same. Here, in 1902, a

[38] FTC, *Practices of the Steel Industry,* 73d Cong., 2d Sess., Senate Doc. 159, p. 61.

multiple basing-point system was established by the first of a series of trade associations, and in 1925, as we have seen, the activities of such an association were held by the Supreme Court to be within the law. From 1933 to 1935, as in the case of steel, the industry's system was legalized and enforced by a trade association acting as a code authority. Here, too, the system remained in force after the demise of NRA. In 1937, however, the Federal Trade Commission issued a complaint against the Cement Institute and 74 cement producers, following it in 1943 with an order to cease and desist from a long series of restrictive acts.

The system thus outlawed by FTC was then being used by OPA in fixing ceiling prices for cement. The industry appealed the Commission's order, and in 1946 the Court of Appeals upheld it in part and reversed it in part. The government then appealed, and the final decision of the Supreme Court was handed down in 1948, after price control had been abandoned.

The cement order was a major move in a general campaign against basing-point pricing in corn products, malt, milk cans, crepe paper, rigid steel conduits, and bottle caps. A complaint was also issued, in 1947, against the American Iron and Steel Institute and 101 steel companies. The corn products cases were the first to reach the courts.

The challenge could be based on Sherman Section 1 (conspiracy) or Section 2 (monopolizing by a dominant firm), or Clayton Section 5 (unfair competition), or even the Robinson-Patman amendment to Clayton Section 2 (geographic price discrimination). Both Sherman I and Clayton 2 eventually carried the day, in major cases decided in 1945, 1948, and 1949.

In *Corn Products,* the Court held collective, systematic discrimination to injure competition.[39] In *Cement Institute,* the Court repeated the holding.[40] And in *Triangle Conduit and Cable,* it broadened the prohibition; basing points as such were condemned, not just the associated acts of agreement.[41] After a Congressional exemption of basing-point systems was vetoed by President Truman in 1950, the practice faded.

Some universal basing-point systems remain, but they are not collusive or mandatory for buyers. Shipping choices are open, and the old phantom freight and locational influences are gone. The court victories scarcely led events; trucking was already destroying the rail-shipments basis of the systems. Indeed, the systems were in force for at least 40 years before policy caught up. There are longer delays to be seen in Chapter 7. But this was not nimble policy.

Conspiracy within a Firm

Odd though it may seem, conduct *within* a company may be held to reduce competition. Branches may be instructed to limit their purchases to other branches of the firm. And when the parent company only holds

---

[39] *Corn Products Refining Co.* v. *FTC,* 324 U.S. 726; *FTC* v. *A. E. Staley Manufacturing Co.,* 324 U.S. 746.

[40] *FTC* v. *Cement Institute,* 333 U.S. 683 (1948).

[41] *Triangle Conduit and Cable Co.* v. *FTC,* 168 F. 2d 157 (1949).

part of the shares, the working arrangements among them have an element of collusion.

The Courts have tended to go beyond clear economic lines. There is usually a vertical element in such conspiracies.[42] And where partial ownership is present, the ownership could be as easily attacked as the later agreement. The problem and the treatments are relatively peripheral and lack clear content.

Tacit Collusion

All of these collusive acts involve concrete agreements, which the lawyers can dig out and document in court before a skeptical, practical-minded judge. What about the great realm of tight oligopoly, which lies between Sherman Sections 1 and 2? Since the discovery of oligopoly in the 1930s, joint maximizing in a shared monopoly, without concrete agreements, has been an enigma. A brace of cases in the 1940s seemed to put it within reach of Section 1, but no solution followed and action faded away. Interest recurred in the 1960s, but the only practical action has been an experimental FTC case against cereals companies started in 1972. The hard core of tight oligopoly remains immune from treatment, as long as it is clean of explicit cooperation.

The main problems are (1) to define it and make it provable in court as a social evil, and (2) to design remedies. The joint maximizing often clearly approaches monopoly results, where everyone in a market shares decades of experience and common interests. But the patterns are economic, not legal, and usually too soft to convince a court that *illegal* behavior occurred. The root cause is structure, not behavior. But Section 2 only reaches down—in practice—to market shares of about 60 percent, and Section 1 only covers concrete acts. One must argue that tight oligopoly has probably given near-monopoly results, from lock-step pric-

---

[42] In 1941 General Motors and its subsidiary, the General Motors Acceptance Corporation, were held to have violated the Sherman Act when GM required its dealers to finance installment sales of automobiles through GMAC, thus excluding competitors from the financing business. (*General Motors Corp.* v. *U.S.,* 121 F. 2d 376, certiorari denied, 314 U.S. 618). In 1947 in the *Yellow Cab* case, a manufacturer of taxicabs had acquired control of companies operating cabs in several cities (including notably Chicago) and required them to purchase their cabs from him, excluding other manufacturers from the market and preventing the operating companies from buying where they chose. The Court rejected the defense that sales within a corporate family cannot involve conspiracy. An unreasonable restraint, it said, "may result as readily from a conspiracy among those who are affiliated or integrated under common ownership as from a conspiracy among those who are otherwise independent." *U.S.* v. *Yellow Cab Co.,* 332 U.S. 218, 227. The Supreme Court reversed the lower court on the point of law and remanded the case for trial on the facts. The lower court acquitted Yellow Cab, finding no intent to monopolize. The Supreme Court allowed this decision to stand (*U.S.* v. *Yellow Cab Co.,* 338 U.S. 338, 1949).

These precedents were followed in later cases. In 1948 in the *Griffith* case, a company operating a chain of movie houses was found to have conspired with its subsidiaries when it pooled their buying power to bargain for choice pictures, first runs, and long clearances in regions where it had competitors. *U.S.* v. *Griffith,* 334 U.S. 100. In 1951 the Seagram Company, which owned the controlling shares of its nominal competitor Calvert, was found to be conspiring with Calvert when it required Calvert to adopt Seagram's prices for whiskey. *Kiefer-Stewart Co.* v. *Joseph E. Seagram & Sons,* 340 U.S. 211. And in the same year, the Timken Roller Bearing Company was held to have conspired with the subsidiaries that it owned jointly with its British and French competitors to divide the roller-bearing markets of the world. *Timken Roller Bearing Co.* v. *U.S.,* 341 U.S. 593.

ing or high profits. But these can be explained away as super-fast competitive price-matching and the rewards of efficiency. The burden of *proof* therefore is against treatment of tight oligopoly; so too is *time*, for the cases are always easy to postpone and delay.

And remedy is even more difficult. The structure must be changed, for it is the cause. Yet often no firm has over 30 or 40 percent, and so a further reduction in share seems implausible and would be awkward in practice. Scale economies will also be sacrificed, it is argued. And several firms, not just one, must be touched. Against this, the possible gains may come to seem small and uncertain.

And yet shared-monopoly is a real problem. From 1888 to 1940, the largest meat-packers had virtually identical market shares, week in and week out, year after year. Market shares in the steel and automobile industries have been remarkably stable since World War II. Recently, oligopolists have learned to soften the appearance of control, and so price leadership rarely occurs now in the older rigid patterns.

Still, prices are often stable despite recessions, and change in virtually identical patterns, despite differences in costs and incentives. From shared expectations and experience often derives a shared monopoly. Though simple monopoly remains a higher-priority problem (see Chapter 7), tight oligopoly is also unsolved and untreated.

From 1939 to 1953, the Court was willing to define parallel behavior as a Section 1 "conspiracy." In the *Interstate Circuit* case in 1939 the operator of a chain of movie houses in Texas had entered into separate contracts with eight distributors of films, agreeing to show their pictures for an admission charge of 40 cents, on condition they not be rented later to be shown for less than 25 cents or run on a double bill. There was no evidence that the distributors had consulted one another or agreed among themselves. But such evidence said the Court, "was not a prerequisite to an unlawful conspiracy. It was enough that, knowing that concerted action was contemplated and invited, the distributors gave their adherence to the scheme and participated in it. . . . Acceptance by competitors, without previous agreement, is sufficient to establish an unlawful conspiracy under the Sherman Act."[43] A similar position was taken in the *Masonite* case in 1942. Here, a manufacturer of hardboard had signed an agency agreement with each of his competitors, authorizing them to distribute his product and fixing the prices at which they could sell. And here, again, there was no evidence of agreement among the other companies. But the Court found the plan to be illegal, holding that each of them must have been "aware of the fact that its contract was not an isolated transaction but a part of a larger arrangement.[44]

In these cases there was evidence that plans had been proposed by Interstate and Masonite; the inference of conspiracy among the other companies was drawn from their adherence to these plans. In the second *American Tobacco* case, a criminal suit against the three leading producers of cigarettes, decided in 1946, no such proposal was in evidence.

---

[43] *Interstate Circuit Co.* v. *U.S.,* 306 U.S. 208, 226–27.
[44] *U.S.* v. *Masonite Corp.,* 316 U.S. 265, 275.

Statistics of purchases, sales, and prices were relied upon for proof. In buying tobacco, it was shown, these companies had purchased fixed shares of the supply, each of them paying the same price on the same day. In selling cigarettes, they had adopted identical price lists, changing their prices simultaneously. In other practices, too, there was striking uniformity. But the case, says William Nicholls, "was probably unique in that there was not a whit of evidence that a common plan had even been contemplated or proposed. The government's evidence was admittedly wholly circumstantial. The fact of identity of behavior was offered as the basis for inferring both the existence and the elements of the alleged common plan and the defendants' knowledge of that plan. Each was alleged to have acted similarly with the knowledge that the others would so act, to their mutual self-interest."[45] But the character of the evidence did not deter the Court. Conspiracy, it said, "may be found in a course of dealings or other circumstances as well as in an exchange of words."[46] The companies were found, accordingly, to be in violation of the law. The decision, says Nicholls, "brought wholly tacit, nonaggressive oligopoly wholly within the reach of the conspiracy provisions of the Sherman Act."[47]

Conspiracy was also found by the Supreme Court in cases where firms had agreed to identical provisions in the licenses granted them by the owner of a patent[48] and in cases involving delivered pricing systems, as we have seen. The doctrine was carried furthest in the case of *Milgram* v. *Loew's* in 1950. Here, eight distributors of motion pictures had been sued by a drive-in movie for refusing to supply it with first-run films. A district court found the distributors guilty of conspiracy, holding that their common refusal to supply first runs could not have been due to independent business judgment but was sufficient, in itself, to establish violation of the law. A meeting of minds need not be proven; identity of behavior was all that was required.[49]

But there was a fatal flaw: conviction usually was not followed by basic remedies. Much of the structure and habits remained. And after 1952 the boldness in inferring conspiracy disappeared both from the FTC and the Court. In decisions involving investment banking (1953), movie distribution (1953), and meat-packing firms (1954), the Court turned about and rejected parallelism as proof of conspiracy.[50]

A landmark book by Kaysen and Turner in 1959 urged action again against shared monopoly under Section 2.[51] But Turner himself did not

[45] William H. Nicholls, "The Tobacco Case of 1946," *American Economic Review,* Vol. XXXIX, No. 3 (1949), pp. 284–96, esp. p. 285.

[46] *American Tobacco Co.* v. *U.S.,* 328 U.S. 781, 810.

[47] *Nicholls, op. cit.,* p. 285.

[48] *U.S.* v. *Line Material Co.,* 333 U.S. 282 (1948); *U.S.* v. *Gypsum Co.,* 333 U.S. 364 (1948).

[49] *Milgram* v. *Loew's,* Inc., 94 F. Supp. 416.

[50] *U.S.* v. *Morgan,* Civil No. 43–757, District Court of the U.S., Southern District of New York, October 14, 1953. *U.S.* v. *Armour & Co.,* Civil 48–C–1351, discontinued March, 1954. *Fanchon & Marco* v. *Paramount Pictures,* 100 F. Supp. 84, certiorari denied, 345 U.S. 964. *Theater Enterprises, Inc.* v. *Paramount Film Distributing Corp.,* 346 U.S. 537, 540.

[51] Carl Kaysen and Donald F. Turner, *Antitrust Policy* (Cambridge: Harvard University Press, 1959); see also Turner's rethinking of the problem in "The Scope of Antitrust and Other Regulatory Policies," *Harvard Law Review,* Vol. 82 (1969), pp. 1207–44.

mount cases during his tenure as Antitrust chief in 1965–68 (see Chapter 7). Posner argues for trying out Section 1 again.[52] In July 1972, Senator Hart put in an Industrial Reorganization Act, based on exhaustive hearings on concentration during 1964–69. While the issue remains so wide open, tight oligopoly is safe from proceedings and remedies.

EXCLUSION

The basic effect of exclusion is simple: by subdividing the market or keeping potential competitors out, one increases true market share and the degree of monopoly. Certain social benefits may also occur. The question always is: do these benefits exceed the monopoly loss? The policy answer has been, very broadly: exclusions by dominant firms are virtually illegal *per se,* while fringe firms have nearly a free hand.

Exclusions take many forms, some central and others peripheral to competition. Like agreements, exclusions tend to infest rather small markets and to have moderate effects. Being complex and concrete, they are a lawyer's delight, and the law on them has become luxuriant, litigious, and changing. The larger trend is toward strictness. Yet there are few clean *per se* rules and every precedent stirs ingenious new devices. We can look here only at the main policy lines: on territorial and exclusive agreement and tying.

Territorial and Exclusive Agreements

Producers often foster a network of franchised dealers, separate in degree but also partially controlled. Many industries and all towns have something of this. Automobiles are a prime example, with over 20,000 dealers. Others among the 750 franchisers and 450,000 franchisees include tires, gasoline, shoes, bicycles, hotels and, of course, hamburgers and fried chicken. The franchisee promotes, sells and services; for this he gets the franchise plus the backing of the franchising corporation. He is intermediate between an internal sales network (such as Xerox and IBM deploy) and anonymous distributors (which handle most ordinary products). He is also usually in a love-hate relationship with his franchisor, who often tolerates but also uses him. Thus auto dealers are usually in a state of partial mutiny toward the producers.

Why should a producer franchise separate dealers, or have dealers at all? Only a specific type of industry is involved. (1) The product is complex, and many users need reassurance about quality. (2) The product is important enough to be a major activity of a dealer (not, like pins, just one of hundreds of items to sell). (3) The producer is distinct from others, via a patent, trade name, or simple fewness of sellers, and dealers can both use and maintain this identity.

Such a branded product may fetch a larger margin through dealers than through discounting, and so the maker may go to great lengths to keep it out of discounters' hands. These conditions are variable, and so much strife arises when one side tries to overplay its advantages. Some

---

[52] R. A. Posner, "Oligopoly and the Antitrust Laws: A Suggested Approach," *Stanford Law Review,* Vol. 21 (1969), pp. 1562 *ff.*

franchised products soon sink back into anonymous retailing. And dealers are ever eager to add new products, which dilute the franchisors' identity.

These *vertical* problems recur in most exclusion issues. The central point is that the seller usually prefers that his product be retailed *competitively.* He extracts what monopoly profit he can in selling, and then wants the product sold as widely and as cheaply as possible. He will try to restrict dealer competition only: (1) during an initial growth and building-up stage, or (2) to foster dealer loyalty and excellence in repairs and service. He may try to keep dealers exclusive: selling neither competitors' goods nor anything else at all. Or he may—as with druggists—try merely to get dealers' favor and help. He may be coerced into helping dealers suppress competition among themselves (as with resale price maintenance: Fair Trade). Or he may dominate the dealers.

Geographic Monopoly. Frequently producers assign *geographic areas* to dealers. In fact, location is always a crucial issue. Policy has come to limit the tightness of these "territorial agreements."[53] Franchising is legal, but franchees must be free to seek and accept customers from each others' areas. They cannot conspire to stop direct sales to discount houses. Coercion or threats by either side to prevent competitive sales are illegal *per se.* Certain legal fine points arise: if the maker keeps legal title to his goods—the dealer then is only an "agent" selling on "consignment"—then more restrictions on dealers are permitted. During the 1960s, territorial restrictions approached *per se* status as violations, if done by a leading firm. They do, after all, flatly stop competition and confer a geographical monopoly.

By 1973 the strict line on territorial agreements had begun to soften, as a rash of cases explored special conditions. The Coors beer company claimed that territorials helped maintain high-quality dealers to offset its cost disadvantage. The American Automobile Association policy was to have only one approved affiliate in each area. The FTC tried in 1972 to place tighter restraints on large pop bottlers than on small ones.

By 1974 the treatment was close to a *per se* basis but not quite. A territorial agreement would probably be struck down in court. But there was room to fight, in special cases where some real need could be shown. The burden of proof against territorial agreements can be overcome, but it is clearly against them.

Exclusive Supply. Makers often require that dealers sell only their products. Thus, nearly all new-car agencies are tied to one company, formally until 1949 and implicitly since then. The problem is endemic in many industries, where dealers would prefer to offer a variety but the dominant producers are implacably opposed. If the largest producer imposes sole supply, then the lesser firms must defensively do the same. Sole supply offers few social benefits, if any. It has become virtually a *per se* violation when the producer has a large market share.

The leading cases involve gasoline, film, auto parts, salt, coal, and shoes. Early FTC cases involved gasoline franchises and GM dealers and

---

[53] The leading cases are: *White Motor Co.* v. *U.S.,* 372 U.S. 253 (1963); *U.S.* v. *General Motors Corp.,* 384 U.S. 127 (1963); and *U.S.* v. *Arnold, Schwinn and Co.,* 388 U.S. 365 (1967).

were treated liberally.[54] But the producer's market share has long been the key test. Before 1947, in all of the cases where the rule against exclusive contracts was enforced, the seller employing such contracts dominated the markets in which he sold.

In the Standard Fashion and Butterick cases in 1922 and 1925, firms making two-fifths of the dress patterns sold at retail excluded their competitors from the best stores in the cities and from the only outlets available in many smaller towns.[55] In the Eastman Kodak case in 1927, a firm producing more than nine-tenths of the motion picture film made in the United States entered into an agreement with its customers, through an association of laboratories making motion picture prints, forbidding them to purchase film imported from abroad.[56]

In the Carter Carburetor case in 1940, the principal manufacturer of carburetors gave discounts to dealers who bought exclusively from him and denied them to those who bought from his competitors.[57] In the case of the Fashion Originators' Guild in 1941, an association of dress manufacturers, whose 176 members made three-fifths of the dresses sold at retail for $10.75 and up, sought to prevent "design piracy" by signing contracts with 12,000 retailers forbidding them to buy from imitators.[58]

In all of these cases, exclusive dealing was enjoined on the ground that its use by a dominant seller had substantially lessened competition and tended toward monopoly. In later cases, a less rigid criterion was employed.

In the International Salt case, where a contract tying the sale of salt to the lease of a patented salt dispenser was found to be illegal in 1947, the Supreme Court went on to say that ". . . it is unreasonable *per se,* to foreclose competitors from any substantial market. . . ."[59] This reasoning was applied to exclusive dealerships in the Standard Oil of California case in 1949.[60] Standard Oil, producing 23 percent of the gasoline sold in seven western states, contracted with some 6,000 independent dealers, handling less than 7 percent of the gasoline sold in the area, to fill all of their requirements for petroleum products and, in some cases, for tires, tubes, batteries, and other accessories. The lower court held Standard's contracts to be illegal on the ground that competition is substantially lessened when competitors are excluded from "a substantial number of outlets."[61] Standard appealed and the Supreme Court, in a 5 to 4 decision, affirmed the lower court's decree. It is enough, said Justice Frankfurter, to prove "that competition has been foreclosed in a substantial share of the line of commerce affected." Standard's contracts created "a potential clog on competition."

---

[54] *FTC* v. *Sinclair Refining Co.,* 261 U.S. 463; and *Pike Mfg. Co.* v. *General Motors Corp.,* 299 U.S. 5 (1936).

[55] *Standard Fashion Co.* v. *Magrane-Houston Co.,* 258 U.S. 346; *Butterick Co.* v. *FTC,* 4 F. 2d 910, certiorari denied, 267 U.S. 602.

[56] *FTC* v. *Eastman Kodak Co.,* 247 U.S. 619.

[57] *FTC* v. *Carter Carburetor Corp.,* 112 F. 2d 722.

[58] *Fashion Originators' Guild* v. *FTC,* 312 U.S. 457.

[59] *International Salt Co.* v. *U.S.,* 332 U.S. 392, 396.

[60] *Standard Oil Co. of California* v. *U.S.,* 337 U.S. 293.

[61] *U.S.* v. *Standard Oil Co. of California,* 78 F. Supp. 850, 857.

This precedent was followed in the *Richfield Oil* case in 1951. Richfield's exclusive contracts with filling stations on the Pacific Coast accounted for but 3 percent of the gasoline sold in the area, but the rule of quantitative substantiality was applied and the contracts condemned.[62] In the light of these decisions it appeared that exclusive arrangements were to be outlawed *per se.* But later developments point the other way.

During the 50s, the Federal Trade Commission declined to proceed against exclusive arrangements that appeared to be harmless, confining its orders to cases in which the probability of actual injury to competition could be shown. Then, in 1961, in the case of *Tampa Electric Co.* v. *Nashville Coal Co.,*[63] the Supreme Court modified its earlier position. Tampa had contracted to purchase from Nashville, for 20 years, all of the coal required for one of its generating stations. Since this affected only 1 percent of the Nashville area coal market, and did give both partners a degree of security, it was let stand.

In 1963, joint GM-dealer efforts to stop discount houses in Los Angeles from getting deliveries were held illegal.[64] (Yet, auto dealerships remain thoroughly exclusive; legal action seems quite powerless to change it!) Brown Shoe's inclusive requirements—that its 650 stores sell only Brown's shoes—were struck down in 1966.[65]

Tying. The typical tie requires customers to buy a second product in order to get the one they want. Often the first product is patented, and so tying clearly extends the monopoly. Commonly, also, a machine producer requires that only its supplies be used with "its" machines (e.g., IBM cards with an IBM computer, "authorized" parts for automobiles under warranty). A seller may even require that its equipment be the only ones used in an installation.

Again, the problem is endemic and manifold, since such leverage is used under all manner of conditions. It can be resisted under Sherman 1 (a restraint), Sherman 2 (monopolization), or Clayton 3, which cites it specifically. During the 1950s, tying came to be virtually a *per se* offense where the seller has any significant market share in the first product. The likelihood of an appreciable effect on competition is enough to disqualify a tie.

That a patented good cannot be tied was decided early on, in cases involving movie projectors (1917), salt (1942), and salt machinery (1947).[66] Copyrighted materials were firmly included, in a 1962 decision on the use of motion pictures on television.[67]

By 1936, the *per se* rule against tying a monopolized good (e.g., with

---

[62] *U.S.* v. *Richfield Oil Corp.,* 99 F. Supp. 280 (1951), sustained per curiam 343 U.S. 922 (1952).

[63] 16/365 U.S. 320.

[64] *U.S.* v. *General Motors Corp.,* 384 U.S. 127.

[65] *FTC* v. *Brown Shoe Co.,* 384 U.S. 316 (1966). The issue was part of a crucial merger case; see Chapter 8.

[66] *Motion Picture Patents Co.* v. *Universal Film Manufacturing Co.,* 243 U.S. 502 (1917); *Morton Salt Co.* v. *G. S. Suppinger Co.,* 314 U.S. 488 (1942); and *International Salt Co.* v. *U.S.,* 332 U.S. 392 (1947).

[67] *U.S.* v. *Loew's, Inc.,* 371 U.S. 38 (1962).

a sizable market share) was clear.[68] It wobbled in 1953. The *Times-Picayune*—New Orleans' only morning newspaper—was owned jointly with the afternoon *States,* which competed with the afternoon *Item.* Under the unit plan, an advertiser could put an identical advertisement in both papers, but not in either one separately.

The Court said that the tie would be illegal *per se* if the *Times-Picayune* had a monopoly. But by labored reasoning, it decided that the share (of all advertising) was modest. The acquittal thus retained the rule but permitted a large market share (up to 40 percent) to slip by. In 1958, the rule was stretched to cover a very small market share, thus becoming virtually *per se.*[69]

The *Jerrold* decision in 1961 moved the border out to keep a supplier from refusing to let users mingle its product with others.[70] Jerrold created cable TV technology after 1948, and argued that chaos would ensue if users added non-Jerrold apparatus. By 1961 Jerrold dominated the business and so this effort to sell only full systems had shifted from pro to anticompetitive. The Court so held.

Many weaker attempts exist but do not reach the courts. Thus auto makers' repair warranties hold only if authorized parts (made by the auto firms) are used. This is a tie.

PRICE DISCRIMINATION

The logic of discrimination was given in Section 1. It increases profits and can protect dominant positions. Its competitive effect depends on how systematic it is, and how large the discriminator's *market share* is. It occurs in many forms and in a remarkable variety of markets. Often it is steep in the extreme and has deep effects. In special situations it may improve allocation by some degree.

Consider these varieties of discrimination.[71]

Personal Discrimination

Haggle-every-time.   Common in bazaars and private deals.

Give-in-if-you-must.   Shading off list prices.

Size-up-his-income.   Fit the price to the customers. Doctors, lawyers and other professions have long done this.

Measure-the-use.   Even if marginal costs are low, charge heavy users more. Xerox uses this strategy; IBM did.

Group Discrimination

Kill-the-rival.   Predatory price-cutting to drive out a competitor. Said to have been commonly done by American Tobacco and Standard Oil before 1900.

---

[68] *International Business Machines Corp.* v. *U.S.,* 298 U.S. 131; see also *United Shoe Machinery Corp.* v. *U.S.,* 258 U.S. 451 (1922).

[69] *Northern Pacific Railway Co.* v. *U.S.,* 356 U.S.1.

[70] *U.S.* v. *Jerrold Electronics Corp.,* 187 F. Supp. 545; 365 U.S. 567 (1961).

[71] See Fritz Machlup, *The Political Economy of Monopoly* (Baltimore: Johns Hopkins Press, 1952).

Dump-the-surplus. Selling at lower prices in foreign markets (where demand is more elastic) has occurred for drugs, steel, TV sets, and others. But complaints about dumping are often bogus.

Promote-new-customers. Common in magazine subscriptions, this lures in new customers.

Favor-the-big-ones. Volume discounts are steeper than cost differences. Endemic in many markets.

Divide-them-by-elasticity. The general result, common in utility services.

Product Discrimination

Pay-for-the-label. The fancy (premium) label gets a higher price, even if the good is the same as a common brand.

Clear-the-stock. "Sales" are used to stabilize inventory. Any college town has scores each year.

Peak–off-peak differences. Prices may differ by more or less than costs do, between peak-hour congested times and slack off-peak periods. Nearly universal in utilities (Chapters 14–17 and 21–22).

Policy toward it fits its competitive role reasonably well. Extreme, systematic discrimination by dominant firms is illegal, and the agencies have not ignored it (see Chapter 7 and, for utility regulation, Chapter 14). More mixed cases get into litigious detail, but the same principle holds: the lower the share and the briefer the discrimination, the less it is culpable. Sporadic discrimination ". . . like a high wind, seizes on small openings and crevices in an orderly price structure and tears it apart."[72] This is broadly incorporated in policy. However, this correct doctrine is usually applied only with weak *force* to actual dominant firms (see Chapters 7 and 14–17).

Markets are divided up in many different ways. Buyers at different locations are separated by transport costs and, in the case of international trade, by artificial barriers. Customers are segregated according to the use they make of goods or services: those who drink milk are segregated from those who make it into butter, those who burn electricity at home from those who burn it in factories, those who ride in Pullman cars from those who ride in coaches, and those who ship lumber from those who ship television sets. Purchasers are separated by the time of day, the day of the week, or the season of the year: movies cost less in the daytime and long-distance calls at night; golf courses have lower rates on weekdays than on weekends; resort hotels are cheaper out of season, coal in the summer, and furs at the August sales.

Buyers are separated by age, sex, and status: children are carried at half fare; students are given educational discounts when buying magazines. Consumers are segregated by ignorance and by variations in prestige, the same product being sold at different prices under different labels or in different shops. Distributors are classified according to the func-

---

[72] M. A. Adelman, "Effective Competition and the Antitrust Laws," *Harvard Law Review,* Vol. LXI, pp. 1289–1350, esp. pp. 1331–32.

tions they perform, and different discounts are given to those who sell at wholesale and at retail.

Recall that discrimination can affect competition among both (1) the *sellers* of the good (the primary line) and (2) the *buyers* of the good (the secondary line). The firm and its favored buyers will usually assert that its price differences or discounts reflect (1) true cost differences (a cost defense), or (2) merely meeting a competitor's price, in good faith. Large buyers always ask for quantity discounts and often get them. (Secret discrimination by utilities was a main root of many new U.S. monopolies during 1870–1910. Thus, Standard Oil drew great advantages from secret rebates from the railroads, some of which directly penalized its competitors. The users forced these on the railroads, using them to reduce secondary-level competition). Where this reflects real cost gains in supplying large batches, a classic dilemma between efficiency and preserving small business arises. The Robinson-Patman Act of 1936 was a small-business protective law, shifting the trade-off more toward the Jeffersonian yeoman tradition.

Actually, the social choice is often just about *how fast* small retailers will be done in by large chains and discounters. Some analysts have gloried in the carnage, wishing only to wipe out the inefficient small shopkeepers even faster. But that is narrow-minded and often socially destructive. There is merit in easing such shifts, for they do touch on deep social folkways in urban society and affect many thousands of older citizens. Above the convoluted details which follow in the Appendix, the broader questions are (1) the pace at which small shops are closed and (2) the prevalence of local versus national firms.

The legal provisions were given in Chapter 5. The early concern under the Clayton Act Section 2 was to preserve local firms from "predatory" price cutting by larger national firms. Though such temporary and selective price cutting is often less fruitful than its *victims* claim, it is often quite rational.[73] The agencies and courts have consistently resisted this. Until recently, a large multi-area firm could only set price in a market lower than it charged elsewhere if its share in that market were small.[74] In 1967, the Court held that three national food companies had reduced competition by setting pie prices lower in Utah than elsewhere, even though the local firm had the largest share.[75] Geographic discrimination is virtually illegal *per se.* Yet a degree of it is still common in many food markets (e.g., bread).

The cost and good faith defenses are now scarcely ever used, because the burden of proof is on the firm. The standards of proof have been too strict, in most cases, to save the defendant. And only sporadic discounts can be justified as good faith price-matching.

---

[73] John S. McGee has argued that it never is rational ("Predatory Price Cutting: The Standard Oil (N.J.) Case," *Journal of Law and Economics,* 1958, pp. 137–69). But this holds only for pure conditions; see Scherer, *op. cit.,* pp. 274–76.

[74] *L. L. Moore* v. *Mead's Fine Bread Co.,* 347 U.S. 1012 (1954). *Balian Ice Cream Co.* v. *Arden Farms Co.,* 104 F. Supp. 796, 231 F. 2d 356, certiorari denied, 351 U.S. 672.

[75] *Utah Pie Co.* v. *Continental Baking Co.,* 386 U.S. 685 (1967). The decision drew criticism from many economists. But in fact Utah Pie did not continue its dominance; instead, it went out of business two years later!

Quantity discounts have been consistently rejected when brought to court. Often the FTC's cost measures have been poorly done, allocating overhead costs too widely rather than recognizing true marginal costs (the problem recurs under regulation too: see Chapter 14). And the courts have weighted the anticompetitive effect heavily, compared to the possible efficiency gain.

But the policy balance may be about right on geographic and quantity discounts. The burden of proof is set on those who can best meet it. And enforcement is so incomplete that pricing is only moderately constrained. Much discrimination persists—perhaps the more beneficial kinds—while the most harmful types have been abated. An Appendix to this chapter gives more detail on enforcement of the Robinson-Patman Act.

There is much confusion and tedium in these issues and in policy itself. The core economic concepts are clear and compact, but the case law is a jungle of mind-numbing complexities. Broadly, policy does fit the economic criteria. Certain dubious details reside in Robinson-Patman rules, but their practical effect is probably must less harmful than the literal wording seems.

SUMMARY

The broad trend is toward clear and strict lines against price-fixing, territorial agreements, tying, exclusion, and price discrimination under certain conditions. Policies fit the main lines of economic criteria, distinguishing between what dominant firms do to tighten monopoly and lesser firms do to increase competition.

Yet enforcement is quite incomplete, leaving a great mass of moderate violations. And controversy and litigation still flourish at the edges. This reflects the development and waverings of court doctrines. It also arises from the ingenuity of business in trying out new ways to replace prohibited devices.

APPENDIX TO CHAPTER 6: A BRIEF TOUR THROUGH ROBINSON-PATMAN

Many orders have been issued by the Federal Trade Commission under the civil sections of the law. During the first 20 years after the law was enacted, nearly half of these orders were issued under the brokerage section, another fifth under the section dealing with advertising allowances and services. Where these orders have been appealed, the Commission has almost invariably been upheld. But it is in connection with the remaining third of the Commission's orders, issued under the section dealing with discrimination in general, that the most important issues of interpretation have occurred. Here the courts have been called upon to define the concept of injury to competition, to decide upon the legitimacy of regional, functional, and quantity discounts, and to determine the availability of the cost defense and the good faith defense.

Brokerage

Section 2-c of the Act, forbidding the payment of a broker's commission to anyone but an independent broker, has been so interpreted as to make such payments illegal *per se*. One of the first cases to come before the courts under this section involved the A&P. The company sought to justify its discounts, showing that its agents in the field not only served its purchasing department but also gave advice to sellers and aided them in disposing of their surpluses, and contending that sellers had been saved the cost of employing brokers' services. But the Court rejected this defense, finding the prohibition of such payments to be absolute.[76]

The law has been rigidly applied, not only where brokerage has been received by mass distributors, like the A&P, but also where it has been collected by independent intermediaries or cooperative buying groups and passed on to the benefit of many small concerns. In the *Biddle* case, an independent purchasing company sold market information and buying services to 2,400 clients, passing on to them in lower prices the commissions it obtained.[77] In the *Quality Bakers* case, brokerage was collected and transmitted by an agency set up by 70 bakers to make cooperative purchases of flour, equipment, and supplies.[78] In all such cases, payments that were helpful to small independent dealers have been prohibited. In its enforcement, the law that was supposedly enacted to protect the independent dealer has boomeranged.

Allowances and Services

Sections 2-d and 2-e of the Robinson-Patman Act forbid the seller to allow discounts to the buyer for merchandising services rendered him by the buyer, or himself to render merchandising services to the buyer, unless such allowances or services are made available to all buyers "on proportionally equal terms." This means that they cannot be given secretly; and they must be made available to all. If the form in which allowances or services are provided is such that some buyers cannot make use of them, sellers must offer genuine alternatives. Allowances, moreover, may be made only for services actually rendered, and they must not be substantially in excess of the cost of these services to the buyer or their value to the seller.

In court, proof of injury to competition has not been required. Nor is discrimination to be justified by showing differences in cost or by proving the need—in good faith—to meet the offers of competitors. If allowances and services are not given on proportionally equal terms, they are held to be illegal per se.

But proportional to what? There are various possibilities. One is proportionality to the dollar volume of purchases made by various customers. Another is proportionality to the cost to the buyer of the services rendered by him to the seller. Still another is proportionality to the value

---

[76] *A&P* v. *FTC,* 106 F. 2d 667 (1939), certiorari denied, 308 U.S. 625 (1940).

[77] *Biddle Purchasing Co.* v. *FTC,* 96 F. 2d 687 (1938), certiorari denied, 305 U.S. 634 (1938).

[78] *Quality Bakers* v. *FTC,* 114 F. 2d 393 (1940).

of such services to the seller. The Commission has employed proportionality to dollar volume as a rule of thumb.

The effect of enforcement of this section has apparently been to force some manufacturers to discontinue the use of demonstrators in larger sales outlets and to discourage them from experimenting, on a local basis, with new forms of sales promotion. In some cases, promotional allowances, instead of being made generally available, have been reduced or abandoned. Whether these changes have materially benefited the smaller retailer, it is impossible to say.

Injury to Competition

Other forms of discounts, covered in Section 2-a, are illegal only when their effect may be substantially to injure competition. The word "may" has come to be interpreted as denoting reasonable probability.

As for the injury to competition, the law provides two tests, a broader and a narrower one. The broader test is concerned with the vitality of competition in general. The narrower test is concerned with the impact of competition on particular classes of competitors. The Federal Trade Commission has emphasized the narrower test, seeking to defend firms harmed by discrimination.

These tests are applied in judging the effect of discrimination on competition on either side of the market: between the seller and his competitors and between the buyer and his competitors. On primary line competition, the Commission has held that a discriminating seller's competitors were injured whenever trade was diverted from them to him and has inferred diversion from the mere existence of a difference in price. The result has been in effect, to outlaw all price differences that are large enough to divert trade and thus to prohibit all price cuts save those extended to buyers as a whole.

On secondary line effects, the Commission has inferred, likewise, that competitors were injured whenever there has been a substantial difference in the prices they have paid. And it has held to this position in the face of evidence that the disfavored buyers have grown and prospered, and despite the buyers' testimony that they have not been hurt. In the view of the Commission, the only cases in which discrimination involves no injury to competition are those where a seller discriminates among noncompeting buyers or where his discrimination is minimal in amount.[79]

The Commission's use of the narrow test injury was upheld by the Supreme Court in the *Morton Salt* case in 1948. Here, quantity discounts had been given to chain stores on a product that represented an insignificant share of the grocery business. But the Commission found that independent grocers hade been injured, and the Court agreed. Morton's discounts, it said, had impaired "the competitive opportunities of certain merchants." Congress, in passing the Robinson-Patman Act, "was especially concerned with protecting small businesses." The law "was in-

---

[79] See Corwin D. Edwards, *The Price Discrimination Law* (Washington, D.C.: Brookings Institution, 1959), chap. xvi.

tended to justify a finding of injury to competition by a showing [in the words of a Senate report] of 'injury to the competitor victimized by the discrimination.' "[80]

Functional Discounts

Sellers have long followed the practice of classifying their customers, dividing them into noncompeting groups on the basis of the functions they perform—manufacturing, wholesaling, retailing—and giving a different discount to the members of each class. These discounts are usually graduated according to the buyer's position in the chain of distribution— larger discounts being given, for instance, to wholesalers and smaller discounts to retailers. They may thus be regarded as payment for different types of distributive services. The size of a buyer's discount does not depend upon the volume of his purchases or the costs incurred by the seller in serving him. It is governed solely by his status in the classification of the seller's customers.

Where buyers are not in competition with one another, discrimination between them is not in violation of the law. The Commission, accordingly, has never issued an order against a functional discount as such, but has explicitly held such discounts to be legitimate. The producers of spark plugs were thus permitted to charge lower prices to automobile manufacturers, who used them as original equipment, than to distributors of accessories, who sold them as replacement parts. Where different classes of buyers compete in reselling to the same customers, however, and where the members of one class compete with the customers of another, the law has been held to apply.

The degree of immunity afforded to functional discounts creates the possibility that sellers might evade the law relating to quantity discounts by establishing special customer classes for the purpose of granting discounts that could not be justified by differences in cost. The Commission has thus been forced to pass upon the methods by which customers are classified. In general, it has held that classifications may not be arbitrary, that they must conform strictly to the nature of the operations undertaken by different types of customers, and that buyers at the same level— such as independent retailers, mail order houses, and chain stores—must be put in the same class.

Volume and Quantity Discounts

Volume discounts are given on quantities purchased over periods of time, without regard to the size of individual orders or deliveries. They are designed to encourage customers to continue buying from a particular supplier. The Commission has forbidden such discounts, holding that cumulative purchases cannot be shown to cut the costs incurred in selling and delivering.

Quantity discounts are given on quantities purchased at a single time.

---

[80] *FTC* V. *Morton Salt Co.,* 334 U.S. 37, 46, 49.

These discounts, as such, were held by the Supreme Court, in the case of Bruce's Juices, not to be unlawful.[81] But quantity discounts have been prohibited, in many cases, by the FTC. The Commission, for instance, has forbidden larger discounts on orders placed by chains and cooperative buying agencies where deliveries are made to separate stores, finding no saving in costs. It is only discounts related to quantities delivered to one place at one time that have been found to be justified by differences in cost.

Even these discounts, in the circumstances of the Morton Salt case, were found in violation of the law. Morton's price per case of salt was $1.60 for less than carload lots and $1.50 for carloads of 1,035 cases each and was $1.50 for 5,000 cases and $1.35 for 50,000 cases when these were bought within a single year. Nominally the lower prices were equally available to all of the company's customers. But the only ones who bought enough salt in a year to get it for $1.35 were five large grocery chains. Independent retailers, competing with the chains, obtained supplies from wholesalers who had been required to pay $1.40 or $1.50. The Commission held these differences to be injurious to competition. It found the carload as well as the cumulative discounts to be unjustified by differences in cost. And it ordered the company to desist from selling to retailers at prices lower than those charged wholesalers whose customers compete with them. This order was sustained by the Supreme Court in a decision handed down in 1948.[82] The precedent still stands.[83]

Buyer's Liability

The prohibition contained in Section 2 applies also to buyers who "knowingly" induce or receive an unlawful discrimination in price. This provision came before the Supreme Court in the Automatic Canteen case in 1953.[84] The automatic Canteen Company leased candy dispensing machines to distributors and sold them candy for distribution, doing more than half of this business. It obtained discounts from 80 among 115 candy manufacturers, insisting on getting lower prices than those paid by its competitors. The FTC ordered the company to cease and desist from demanding these concessions. The company asserted that its lower prices were justified by the sellers' lower costs. The Commission asked for proof. The company replied that it could not reasonably be expected to prepare analyses of the costs of its suppliers. The Supreme Court agreed. The knowing receipt of a lower price, it held, did not in itself violate the Act. Knowledge that the lower price was unjustified would do so. But here, the burden of proof was on the Commission, not on the company.

Buyers can still be prosecuted, however, where they knew that their discounts could not be justified. This is true, for instance, where the price a buyer pays is one already found to be unlawful, where he makes his

[81] Bruce's Juices v. American Can Co., 330 U.S. 743 (1947).
[82] FTC v. Morton Salt Co., 334 U.S. 37.
[83] See also Mueller Co. v. FTC, 60 FTC 120 (1962) and 323 F. 2d 44 (1963).
[84] Automatic Canteen Co. v. FTC, 346 U.S. 61.

purchases in the same manner and in the same quantity as do his competitors, and where his experience in the trade should make it clear that a difference in price exceeds a difference in cost. And in this, the Commission has been upheld by the courts.[85]

A Summary

In principle, the Robinson-Patman Act relates differences in price to differences in cost. But in many respects, the law departs from this principle. It was designed to reduce the buying advantages of the chain stores and other mass distributors. It was thus intended, not to prevent discrimination in general, but to prevent discrimination in favor of larger buyers and to permit or require discrimination in favor of smaller ones. It was concerned less with the maintenance of competition than with the survival of small competitors. It thus embodies a policy that has been characterized as "soft competition" in contrast to the "hard competition" demanded by the Sherman Act.

From the point of view of the small retailer, the effects of the Robinson-Patman Act have been diverse. It has reduced the discriminatory advantages of mass distributors, virtually eliminating the payment of brokerage to any but independent brokers, making allowances and services more broadly available, and reducing the buyers' pressure for concessions of other types. But it has also worked against the interest of the small concern. It has encouraged the mass distributor to buy a plant's whole output or to manufacture a product for himself; here, his costs may be cut, but no discrimination is involved. The law has not stopped the growth of the supermarket or the discount house. It has even been turned against the small retailer in some cases, being used to check the advantages of agencies buying collectively for independent firms. Whether it has operated, on balance, to help or to harm the small distributor, it is impossible to say.

The law has made for some inefficiency, forcing the seller to use brokers when he does not need them, to buy services that he does not desire, and to provide services that have no use. It has moderated the vigor of competition. By requiring that discounts be justified by actual rather than potential differences in cost, it has discouraged price reductions that might profitably have been made. By outlawing the practice of setting lower prices, in some part of a market, to test the possibility of increasing sales, it may have prevented reductions that would soon have been generalized. Under conditions of oligopoly, it has limited one form of competition that operates to lessen price rigidity.

Certain changes in the law are probably needed. The law should permit sporadic price discrimination but forbid persistent cuts in one substantial market when they are not extended to others or when deeper cuts are made in one market than in others. The cost defense should be liberalized. Freedom to make discriminatory price cuts should not be limited, as is now the case, to reductions made to meet the prices of competitors

---

[85] *American Motors Specialties Co.* v. *FTC,* 298 F. 2d 225, certiorari denied, 364 U.S. 884 (1960).

but should be extended to reductions that are designed to undercut them. The law should permit discrimination to be used, not only as a means of retaining old customers, but also as a means of attracting new ones.

There is danger, finally, that competition will be injured when large distributors use their bargaining power to exact from suppliers prices lower than those charged their competitors. Here, however, the law should be directed not against the seller but against the buyer. And, the test of injury to competition should be the broader one. Buyers should be forbidden, in making purchases, to impose the condition that equally favorable terms are not to be granted to their competitors. Here, the buyer's defense will depend upon the willingness of the seller to cooperate in presenting an analysis of costs. For this purpose, too, the cost defense should be liberalized.[86]

---

[86] See also Carl Kaysen and Donald F. Turner, *Antitrust Policy* (Cambridge, Mass.: Harvard University Press, 1959), pp. 183–88.

CHAPTER SEVEN

Monopolization

T he social aim is to abate existing monopolies and prevent new ones, as industries evolve. Even if scale economies do justify a high degree of monopoly for a time, its negative effects are to be held to a minimum. These concepts are clear, Sherman 2 gives a firm legal base, past actions have been strict, and the candidates for action are relatively few. This seemingly manageable task is probably pivotal to competitive policy, as earlier chapters have noted.

Yet standard Section 2 treatment has receded recently to a trickle, touching only a few industries. Policy has heeded the advice of Finley Peter Dunne's old Mr. Dooley: " 'Th' trusts,' says he, 'are heejuous monsthers built up be th' enlightened intherprise iv th' men that have done so much to advance progress in our beloved country,' he says. 'On wan hand I wud stamp thim undher fut; on th' other hand not so fast.' "

American treatment is primarily the Section 2 case, alleging monopolization and seeking conviction and a remedy. Its essential parts are proofs that (1) monopoly exists (a market share of 60 percent or more) and (2) the firm sought monopoly deliberately (shown by acts of various kinds). There are many loopholes in practice—which we shall see—despite Section 2's flat prohibition of monopoly. So the Section 2 route is long, uncertain and now largely in disuse. Is Section 2 becoming a blue law, neither used nor usable?

We begin by defining monopoly and its abuses in some detail. Then we assess the remarkable series of Section 2 actions since 1890. Current prospects are reviewed in this chapter, and foreign experience is compared. The alternatives and complements to Section 2 are also passed in review.

THE PROBLEM

Questions: What is the market? When does the firm have "a monopoly" in it? We have already seen the forms, sources and effects of market power (Chapters 1 and 2) and the special features of policy choice

(Chapters 3, 4 and 5). Monopoly is defined by present and future market share, plus perhaps specific entry barriers. Several technical problems now need attention: defining the market, vertical aspects, monopolistic abuses, and then the main candidates for treatment.

The Relevant Market

A critical element is the market share of the firm, which in turn depends on the true extent of the market. Defining the market often determines the treatment.

A market is a grouping of buyers and sellers, communicating quickly and exchanging goods which are substitutable. Perfect markets carry these conditions to extremes: perfect substitution and instant adjustment within the market, but zero substitutability and adjustment across the market's edges. Substitutability in demand is the basic criterion, but substitutability in supply can also be a factor. Cross-elasticities of demand depend both on hard physical facts of the product and on mental images which advertising or other experience may instill. Geography also can enter in, if there are local submarkets within regional and national industries. To define a market, one must know (1) the nature of the product and its alternatives, (2) subjective images of the product, (3) geographic limits on interchanging the products (both on suppliers and users).

Many markets have shaded edges, layers of quality levels, and submarkets. Even if there were precise data on these conditions, one would still have elbow room in defining "the" market. And the cross-elasticities, images and distance factors are often hard—even impossible—to measure at all precisely. In research and in court, many markets can only be roughly estimated, and plausible estimates can differ as night and day. The leading firm will always define the market broadly: its competitors and public agencies often make it out to be narrow. The extremes are (1) that each product competes against everything else for the consumer's dollar, or (2) that each firm's products are unique.

Despite all this, most markets can be reasonably well defined when a decision must be made. Judgment, comparisons with previous decisions, and research on the main customers, suppliers and alternatives often suffice. Often, too, one needs only to decide if a *substantial* degree of market power, in a *significant* market, is involved. Ultra-precision is often unnecessary. Court decisions have defined markets with some sophistication, though there have been marked shifts and some plain lapses.

The main legal tests have been the *line of commerce* (roughly, defined by the degree of cross-elasticity of demand) and the geographic market. The court debates can be astonishingly long and involved, with scores of witnesses put under intense cross-examination, splitting hairs. The choice usually comes down in the end, as it must, to a reasonable but arbitrary guess. Leading recent court choices are shown in Table 7–1: note how strictness has waxed and waned. Details follow.

Line of Commerce   (*reasonable interchangeability of products*).

TABLE 7-1

Evolving Ways of Defining the Relevant Market

Case (year decided)	Relevant Market and the Resulting Share, According to the			Action Taken
	1. Defense (percent)	2. Agency (percent)	3. Court in Final Action (percent)	
Alcoa (1945)	All ingot and scrap (33)	Ingot sold (90)	Ingot sold (90)	Alcoa convicted
Times-Picayune (1953)	All local advertising (33)	Advertising in morning newspapers (100)	All newspaper advertising	Acquitted
du Pont cellophane (1953)	Flexible packaging (18)	Cellophane (75–100)	Flexible packaging materials (18)	Acquitted
du Pont–General Motors (1957)	Automotive finishes and fabrics (1 to 3)	GM purchases of these items (60 to 100)	GM purchases (60–100)	Convicted
Bethlehem-Youngstown merger (1958)	Structural metals and plastics (1 to 3)	Regional steel markets (25 plus)	Regional steel markets (25 plus)	Merger enjoined
Brown Shoe (1962)	All shoes (5)	Various types of shoes, in various cities (up to 50)	Specific markets (up to 50)	Merger enjoined
Philadelphia National Bank (1963)	National banking (trivial)	Philadelphia banking (36)	Philadelphia banking	Merger enjoined
Rome Cable (1964)	All conductor wire (3)	Bare aluminum conductor (33)	Bare aluminum conductor and others (33)	Merger enjoined
Continental Can and Hazel-Atlas (1964)	Glass and metal containers are separate markets	Containers (25)	Containers (25)	Merger enjoined
Pabst-Blatz (1966)	National beer market (5)	Wisconsin beer market (24)	Wisconsin beer market (24)	Merger enjoined
Von's Grocery (1966)	Los Angeles retail grocery (7.5)	Los Angeles retail grocery (7.5)	Los Angeles retail grocery (7.5)	Merger enjoined

Sources: Various cases, as discussed in the text and indexed at the end of the book.

Since the 1930s, the courts have increasingly tried to use cross-elasticity of demand in defining products. But other facts have swayed the judges, even when cross-elasticities are known precisely. Relative price levels and movements, technological factors, production facilities, and even common sense and folklore find their way in.

Early decisions often drew the market too narrowly. Thus, sea-green slate, linen rugs, red-cedar shingles produced in the state of Washington, parchment paper, and hydraulic oil well pumps were held to occupy distinct markets, though in each case substitutes were readily available.[1]

The *Alcoa* case (1945) poses with special clarity the problem of defining the product and the market. Judge Hand accepted the Division's view, *excluding* aluminum scrap and *including* not only the ingots Alcoa sold to others but also the ingots it consumed itself. In this way Alcoa's share of the market was found to stand at 90 percent. Scrap competes with ingots but was excluded on the ground that it had been derived from products made from ingots that Alcoa had once produced, though evidence was lacking that Alcoa controlled the scrap supply. Had scrap been included in measuring the market, Alcoa's share would have stood at 60–64 percent. And if Alcoa's consumption of its own ingots had been excluded, its share of the open market would have stood at 33 percent. By adopting the first of these definitions of the market, the Court was enabled to make a finding of monopoly. Judge Hand also added the dictum that 90 percent "is enough to constitute a monopoly; it is doubtful whether 60 or 64 percent would be enough; and certainly 33 percent is not."[2] This comment has become the rule of thumb for all Section 2 cases since then.

In *Times-Picayune,* the court leaned the other way (as Chapter 6 noted). It found that the *Times-Picayune* had no monopoly, having reached this conclusion by defining the market to include all three dailies instead of separating the morning and evening markets and recognizing the *Times-Picayune* monopoly in the morning field.[3]

A landmark decision involved du Pont, which was charged with monopolizing cellophane during 1924–50. If the market in question were that for cellophane alone, it was clear that the company had a monopoly, since it accounted for 75 percent of the output of the product and, together with its licensee Sylvania, for all of it. But if the market were all flexible packaging materials, including glassine, parchment papers, waxed papers, pliofilm, and aluminum foil, du Pont's share was only 18 percent. The first definition was urged by the government; the second by du Pont. Judge Leahy, in the district court, found for the defense, but cited du Pont's "creative" behavior as much as the definition of the market. The Supreme Court sustained the verdict by 4 to 3, viewing cello-

---

[1] *O'Halloran* v. *American Sea Green Slate Co.,* 207 Fed. 187 (1913); *U.S.* v. *Klearflax Linen Looms,* 63 F. Supp. 32 (1945); *Gibbs* v. *McNeeley,* 118 Fed. 120 (1902); *Story Parchment Co.* v. *Paterson Paper Parchment Co.,* 282 U.S. 555 (1931); *Kobe, Inc.* v. *Dempsey Pump Co.,* 198 F. 2d 416 (1952).

[2] *U.S.* v. *Aluminum Co. of America,* 148 F. 2d 416, 424.

[3] *Times-Picayune Publishing Co.* v. *U.S.,* 345 U.S. 594.

phane as "reasonably interchangeable by consumers for the same purposes." The relevant market, therefore, was that for flexible packaging materials.[4]

This was dubious. Cellophane's price had been from two to seven times that of the other materials during 1924 to 1950. And when it had been cut sharply, the price of others held steady or even rose. The Court's minority cited this: "We cannot believe that . . . practical businessmen would have bought cellophane in increasing amounts over a quarter of a century if close substitutes were available at from one-seventh to one-half cellophane's price. That they did so is testimony to cellophane's distinctiveness."[5] "Reasonable interchangeability" was now very broad.

It was drawn back next year in *du Pont–General Motors*.[6] The defense had urged that du Pont's sales of automobile finishes to GM were only 3.5 percent of all its sales of industrial finishes, and its sales of fabrics to GM only 1.6 percent of all its sales of fabrics. But the Court held that the characteristics of automotive finishes and fabrics were sufficiently peculiar to make them distinct, and that GM in itself constituted a substantial market for these products. The product was defined in terms, not of interchangeability, but of its peculiar characteristics.

In the Bethlehem Steel case in 1958 (see chapter 8), the defendants sought to have their product so defined as to include nonferrous and plastic substitutes, following the precedent established in cellophane.[7] Judge Weinfeld refused, holding that the line of commerce involved was a series of products having characteristics sufficiently peculiar to make them distinct, thus following the precedent established in *du Pont–GM*.

In the Brown Shoe case in 1962, the Supreme Court recognized three markets: those for men's, women's, and children's shoes. The defense sought recognition for infants' and babies' shoes, misses' and children's shoes, and youths' and boys' shoes and, within the sex and age groups, for medium-priced and low-priced shoes. The Court refused:

The outer boundaries of a product market are determined by the reasonable interchangeability of use or the cross-elasticity of demand between the product itself and substitutes for it. However, within this broad market, well-defined submarkets may exist which, in themselves, constitute product markets for antitrust purposes. The boundaries of such a submarket may be determined by examining such practical indicia as industry or public recognition of the submarket as a separate economic entity, the product's peculiar characteristics and uses, unique production facilities, distinct customers, distinct prices, sensitivity to price changes, and specialized vendors.[8]

This was nearly a hunting license to find any indicia which could show submarkets, regardless of cross-elasticities.

In the Rome Cable case in 1964, the District Court had defined the product as including both aluminum and copper conductors. The Supreme Court found that the two types of conductors had different uses,

---

[4] *U.S.* v. *du Pont*, 118 F. Supp. 41 (1953).

[5] *U.S.* v. *du Pont*, 351 U.S. 377.

[6] *U.S.* v. *du Pont*, 353 U.S. 586.

[7] *U.S.* v. *Bethlehem Steel Corp.*, 168 F. Supp. 576.

[8] *Brown Shoe Co.* v. *U.S.*, 370 U.S. 294, 324.

aluminum being used overhead and insulated copper underground. It found, too, that aluminum cable sold at half to two-thirds of the price of copper cable and that cross-elasticity of demand between them was low. It therefore reversed the District Court, defining the product as aluminum conductor alone.

The government won the Rome Cable case on a narrow definition of the product market. It won the Continental case, decided in the same month, on a broad definition. The metal containers made by Continental and the glass containers made by Hazel-Atlas were found to constitute a single product. "In our view," said the Court, "there is and has been a rather general confrontation between metal and glass containers and competition between them for the same end uses which is insistent, continuous, effective, and quantitywise very substantial.[9] The prices of the two containers differed and cross-elasticity of demand between them was low. But these facts, while recognized as relevant, were held to be inconclusive. For price is only one factor in the canner's choice. Consumer preference (the housewife's preference, for instance, for glass rather than metal in the packaging of baby foods) may lead him to use a container that costs him more. "This may not be price competition," concluded the Court, "but it is nevertheless meaningful competition between interchangeable containers."

In 1966, the Court decided that "accredited central station protective services" were a market, which Grinnell Corporation had monopolized.[10] This reflected distinct characteristics, compared to watchmen, local alarm systems, proprietary systems and unaccredited central systems. Justice Fortas could dissent that it was Procrustean, tailoring the market to the defendants and ignoring services which were in "realistic rivalry." Either choice was plausible.

Evidently, "the" market has come to be any product domain within which competition may be appreciably affected. Cross-elasticity is a main test, but other pointers are freely used.

The Section of the Country.   The courts have also been willing to regard small geographic areas as markets (or submarkets), even where much larger areas could be accepted. This leaning to the narrower definition became marked in the 1960s.

In a case involving two publishers of farm papers, decided in 1934, where a Court of Appeals had found for the defendant on the ground that it did not have a monopoly of the national market for farm advertising, the Supreme Court reversed the decision, holding that the relevant market was confined to the eight states in which the papers of the plaintiff and the defendant had their major circulation.[11] In the Paramount case in 1948, where the lower court had found that the five major producers of motion pictures did not have a monopoly of the business of exhibiting pictures, the Supreme Court held that they did have a monopoly of exhibition at the first-run theaters in the 92 largest cities of the country.[12]

---

[9] *Continental Can Co.* v. *U.S.,* 378 U.S. 441, 489

[10] *U.S.* v. *Grinnell Corp.,* 384 U.S. 563 (1966).

[11] *Indiana Farmer's Guide* v. *Prairie Farmer,* 293 U.S. 268.

[12] *U.S.* v. *Paramount Pictures,* 334 U.S. 141

Determination of the relevant geographic markets is equally important under the Celler-Kefauver Act. In defining these markets in the Bethlehem Steel case, Judge Weinfeld listed them as (*a*) the United States as a whole, (*b*) the northeast quadrant of the United States, (*c*) Michigan, Ohio, Pennsylvania, and New York, (*d*) Michigan and Ohio, (*e*) Michigan, and (*f*) Ohio. Such a definition makes little sense. If the market within which supply and demand operate to affect the price of steel-mill products is the United States, or its northeast quadrant, or a four-state or two-state area, it cannot be confined to Michigan or to Ohio alone. It is true, however, that the projected merger would have lessened competition in Michigan and along the border of Ohio and Pennsylvania, where Bethlehem and Youngstown had both made sales. On this basis, the merger was properly held to be in violation of the law.

In the Brown Shoe case, the Supreme Court found different markets to be relevant in considering the probable effects of horizontal combination and vertical integration. The combination of retail outlets, it held, would affect competition in "every city with a population exceeding 10,-000 and its immediate contiguous surrounding territory" in which both Brown and Kinney sold shoes at retail through stores they either owned or controlled.[13] The integration of manufacturing and distribution would affect competition in the United States as a whole.

A much broader view was taken in a major bank merger case, Continental Illinois National Bank in Chicago in 1962.[14] The bank's national activities were taken as crucial, rather than its new local market share of 40 percent. The merger (one of the last of the big bank mergers: see Chapters 8 and 11) was permitted.

But a year later the Court put local banking markets foremost, after all. In the Philadelphia-Girard case, the defendants argued that the combined bank would be in a stronger position to compete for business with banks in New York City and asked that the market be defined to include New York. The Court refused:

The proper question to be asked . . . is not where the parties to the merger do business or even where they compete, but where, within the area of competitive overlap, the effect of the merger on competition will be direct and immediate. . . . In banking . . . convenience of location is essential to effective competition. Individuals and corporations typically confer the bulk of their patronage on banks in their local community; they find it impractical to conduct their banking business at a distance.[15]

On this basis, the Court found the relevant market to consist of the four-county area of metropolitan Philadelphia.

Interpretation of the law regarding geographic market boundaries was given a curious twist by the Court in the Pabst Brewing Co. case[16] in 1966. Pabst had acquired the Blatz Brewing Co., giving it 24 percent of the market for beer in Wisconsin, 11.3 percent of the market in the

---

[13] *Brown Shoe* v. *U.S.* 370 U.S. 294, 336.

[14] The merger was eventually approved under the 1966 Merger Act Amendment.

[15] *U.S.* v. *Philadelphia National Bank,* 374 U.S. 321, 409–10.

[16] *U.S.* v. *Pabst Brewing Co.,* 384 U.S. 546.

three states of Wisconsin, Illinois, and Michigan, and 4.5 percent of the market in the United States as a whole. The government contended that Wisconsin and the three-state area were the markets involved. The district court dismissed the case, finding the relevant market to be the country as a whole. The Supreme Court reversed this action, ordering the combination dissolved. But Mr. Justice Black, in the opinion brushed aside the issue of market boundaries, holding that the law did not require these boundaries to be delimited but demanded only a showing that competition had been substantially impaired "anywhere in the United States." Mr. Justice Harlan disagreed, insisting that all of the statistics presented in a case relate, of necessity, to a particular geographic market, and that this market must therefore be defined.

The Court now freely recognizes local markets for closely defined products, but not in every case where it might. The 1960s may have been the peak of such strictness. There are many data to justify either narrow or broad market edges. Behind the specific reasons often lurks the judges' real interest in being stricter or more liberal toward monopoly in general.

The Market Share

How much market share makes a "monopoly"? There is no clear threshold. Monopoly effects occur for shares over 15 percent, and they are usually significant for shares of 25 percent and above (recall Figure 2–12 in Chapter 2). A share of 35 percent or more would normally deserve careful economic study and perhaps treatment, especially if serious entry barriers or other imperfections existed.

Actual policy has been vague and rubbery about the concepts, but it also has set quite definite thresholds in practice. It reflects both the Court's decisions and the agencies' choices about what cases to bring. The Court has been willing at times to convict "abusive" combinations with as little as 20 percent and yet to absolve "good" monopolists with as much as 90 percent. The present consensus is that an established market share below 60 percent is safe in the Court, and even 70 or 75 percent may escape (and 85 to 90 percent shares have existed unchallenged for decades).[17] This reflects Judge Hand's *Alcoa* dictum—it was not a true precedent—that 90 percent is monopoly, 60 percent may be, and 33 percent is not.

Yet mergers are usually prevented if their new share is above 10 percent (see Chapter 8). This yawning gap between 60 and 10 percent is caused both by various biases and by sound economic factors, which will be clear by Chapter 10. Still, it is a double standard, possible because no sound economic definition of "monopoly" has ever been adopted in policy.[18] Or, rather, it reflects a verbal oddity: the problem is dominance, but Sherman 2 only mentions "monopoly."

[17] In Britain, a "monopoly" position is now defined to include shares as low as 25 percent. In other European countries, there is little hesitation in recognizing that dominance is the real issue.

[18] In bank mergers, the limit on share is higher, at about 20 to 30 percent. But the safety level for established market shares is also higher, at virtually 100 percent; that is, there is

Vertical Integration and Size. Vertical integration is widespread and often a source of efficiency. A baker with ovens in the back and display cases in the front is vertically integrated, and it is often efficient to combine several stages of production. Risks may be reduced, costs saved, and planning improved.

Still, integration is an element in market structure. It takes intracompany sales off the open market, and so it may restrict competition. The net social effects may be positive, if the economies are great. But the exclusive effect still exists (and there may be abuses: see below).

Bigness *per se* has faded out of antitrust decisions about monopoly. This is correct, on the whole. Yet sheer size can give a degree of power and insulation, because capital markets are not perfect (recall Chapter 2 and see Chapters 11–12). Therefore, current doctrine ignoring size goes slightly too far.

Monopolistic Abuses

Apart from its basic economic ill-effects, monopoly may cause—and arise from—specific abuses. These include such practices as maliciously interfering with the production and sale of competitive goods, excluding competitors from access to supplies, obtaining unduly discriminatory prices in purchasing supplies, excluding competitors from access to markets, obtaining preferential markets for themselves, squeezing the margins of nonintegrated independents, and engaging in discriminatory and predatory pricing in an effort to drive competitors to the wall. Such abuses have shaped the present structure, and they continue in many markets.

Several of them need discussion.[19]

Exclusive and Discriminatory Buying. Firms dominant in a field have sometimes prevented the emergence or survival of competitors by excluding them from access to productive facilities, credit, equipment, and materials. They have made preemptive purchases, buying in quantities greater than those required to satisfy their needs. They have forced

---

no effort at restructuring banks whatever, or even a consideration of it (see Chapters 11 and 12).

[19] Grosser forms of abuse are fewer now than before, but the classic case of it—*National Cash Register Co.* at the turn of the century—deserves mention:

The company set out deliberately to destroy its competitors. It hired their employees away from them. It bribed their employees and the employees of railroads and telephone and telegraph companies to spy on them and disclose their business secrets. It spread false rumors concerning their solvency. It instructed its agents to misrepresent the quality of their goods, interfere with their sales, and damage the mechanism of their machines in establishments where they were in use. It publicly displayed their cash registers under labels which read, "Junk." It made, and sold at less than cost, inferior machines called "knockers," which it represented to be just as good as theirs. It threatened to bring suit against them and their customers for alleged infringements of patent rights. It induced their customers to cancel their orders and repudiate their contracts. It intimidated prospective investors in competing plants by publishing lists of defunct competitors and by exhibiting in a "grave yard" at its factory samples of the machines which they had formerly made. Such practices, carried on over a period of twenty years, gave the company control of 95 percent of the nation's production of cash registers.

Clair Wilcox, *Competition and Monopoly in American Industry,* T.N.E.C. Monograph No. 20, 1940.

suppliers to sign exclusive contracts, refusing to buy from those who sold to their competitors. They have also handicapped their rivals by demanding and obtaining from suppliers discriminatory concessions that could not be justified by differences in cost. Such practices were characteristic of the early trusts.

Thus, several of the trusts persuaded the railroads to grant them substantial rebates. Standard Oil not only recovered 40–50 percent of the sums which it paid the roads for carrying its own products but also collected a similar share of the rates paid by its rivals. The Aluminum Company of America, enjoying a patent monopoly in its early years, made preemptive purchases of deposits of bauxite and sites for the generation of hydroelectric power, and bought power elsewhere under contracts which forbade suppliers to sell to other producers of aluminum. To the same end, more recently, producers of the leading brands of cigarettes bought up the stocks of tobacco required for the production of 10-cent brands; and exhibitors of motion pictures prevented other houses from obtaining films by renting more features than they had time to display in their own theaters.

There is also reciprocal buying, where Company A refuses to buy product x from Company B unless Company B will buy product y from Company A. Thus, General Motors was charged, in 1963, with telling railroads that if they did not buy GM locomotives, GM would ship freight on other lines. Consolidated Foods was found, in 1965, to have forced its suppliers to buy dried onions and garlic from one of its subsidiaries, and U.S. Steel agreed, in 1969, to discontinue the practice of providing its purchasing agents with records of its sales so that they would buy from its customers. This "you-scratch-my-back-and-I'll-scratch-yours" practice is followed by thousands of companies in doing business with one another. When the firm involved controls a small share of the market for the goods it buys and when it invites reciprocal purchases rather than requiring them, the harm done its competitors will be small. But when it is a major buyer and when it uses coercion to force reciprocal purchases, its competitors may find their market opportunities substantially curtailed.

Exclusive Selling.   Large concerns have frequently attempted to exclude their smaller rivals from the market by imposing contracts upon their distributors which forbid them to handle goods produced by other firms. Contracts of this sort have been employed, in the past, in the sale of biscuits and crackers, cameras, dress patterns, canned syrups, petroleum products, and many other goods.

Products have been tied (recall Chapter 6), directly or subtlely. Shoe machinery, cans, computers, mimeograph machines, and many others have been sold only with ties to other goods.

There has been full-line forcing, requiring dealers to carry a whole line of products, thus keeping specialized producers off the markets. Farm equipment and movies have been among those involved, and it is present to a degree in many markets.

Vertical Integration.   Despite its benefits, integration can reduce competition and make abuses possible. Ownership of joint-venture pipelines by major oil firms has reduced competition in several ways. By owning both the making and leasing of sleeping cars, Pullman excluded competition on the manufacturing side. AT&T integration of Western Electric's production with telephone operations has excluded other producers from telephone equipment markets.[20]

The classic complaint against integrated firms is that they can and do "squeeze." Where an integrated firm is tapered—with a larger share in early stages than in later ones—it will sell to independent firms. To the integrated firm, the prices and margins at successive stages are a matter of convenience, of internal bookkeeping. To its nonintegrated competitors, they are a matter of life and death. Such an integrated concern is thus in a position to squeeze its rivals by raising prices in the markets where they buy and reducing prices in the markets where they sell.

Thus Alcoa, competing with independent companies in the fabrication of aluminum products, was for many years the only source from which these independents could obtain their supply of aluminum ingots and sheets. By raising the price of raw materials and lowering the price of finished products, the company has been said to have made it unprofitable for its rivals to remain in business. A similar squeeze has been experienced by independent refiners of petroleum.

Squeezes occur less often than their victims allege, but they are occasionally quite powerful. The squeeze is difficult for antitrust authorities to attack, since price changes may be adjudged competitive or monopolistic according to their motivation, and motives are difficult to prove.

Discriminatory and Predatory Pricing. We have seen that systematic discrimination by dominant firms is both (1) anticompetitive and (2) a main source of monopoly profits. It may arise impersonally, or it may be a series of specific predatory incidents. Sharp versions of it helped to build up and maintain the early trusts. Nowadays one finds mainly the impersonal types, with complex systems of discrimination persisting for years, even decades. It is defended as "only rational," "meeting competition" and as "necessary to build up the market," and to "get funds for innovation." But it is anticompetitive (recall Chapter 6), even if—or, perhaps, especially because—it is inherent in the monopoly situation.

These "abuses" surround many dominant positions, helping create, maintain, and exploit them. They have come to be the usual second leg of Section 2 cases—monopoly *plus* monopolizing behavior—in the U.S., as we shall shortly see. Yet they are often hard to discover and interpret, for their intent can often be made out as merely good "vigorous" competition. And they are superfluous in a sound economic appraisal: the degree of monopoly *exists,* apart from these acts.

The Candidates

The main firms eligible for study and treatment can be divided into two categories: near-monopolies and oligopolies. The groups shade into

---

[20] And du Pont's ownership of 23 percent of GM from 1918 to 1961 led to influence over GM's purchases of car finishes and fabrics. This probably excluded competition in those

TABLE 7-2

Changes in Market Position, Leading Dominant Firms, 1910–35

Asset Rank Among All Industrial Firms in 1910	Firm	Estimated Degree of Market Power 1910[a] (percent)	Estimated Assets, 1909–10[b] ($ million)	Estimated Degree of Market Power 1935[a] (percent)	Estimated Change in Market Power 1910–35 (percent)	Specific Policy Cause of Change?
1	United States Steel	22.0	1,804	17.0	− 5.0	(Informal antitrust effects?)
2	Standard Oil (New Jersey)	27.0	800	15.3	−11.7	1911 case
3	American Tobacco	27.0	286	13.3	−13.7	1911 case
6	International Harvester	25.5	166	15.0	−10.5	(Informal antitrust effects?)
7	Central Leather	21.0	138	6.0	−15.0	
8	Pullman	29.3	131	27.0	− 2.3	
10	American Sugar	21.0	124	14.7	− 6.3	
13	Singer Manufacturing	25.7	113	19.7	− 6.0	
16	General Electric	23.0	102	21.8	− 1.2	
19	Corn Products	21.0	97	17.3	− 3.7	
21	American Can	22.0	90	19.7	− 2.3	
25	Westinghouse Electric	20.5	84	19.3	− 1.2	
30	E. I. du Pont de Nemours	29.5	75	13.5	−16.0	
34	International Paper	18.5	71	11.0	− 7.5	
37	National Biscuit	18.5	65	11.0	− 7.5	
55	Western Electric	33.0	43	33.0	0	
59	United Fruit	27.0	41	27.0	0	Exemption in 1913
61	United Shoe Machinery	31.7	40	30.5	− 1.2	
72	Eastman Kodak	29.5	35	29.5	0	
c	Alcoa	32.9	35	29.5	− 3.4	

[a] Based on estimated market shares and entry barriers. It is the rate of profit which the firm's market position would normally be expected to yield. See Shepherd, "The Elements of Market Structure," *Review of Economics and Statistics*, 1972, pp. 25–38.

[b] Based on A. D. H. Kaplan, *Big Enterprise in a Competitive System*, rev. ed. (Washington, D.C.: Brookings Institution, 1965), chapter 7.

[c] Not available.

TABLE 7-3
Changes in Market Position, Leading Dominant Firms, 1948–73

Asset Rank Among All Industrial Firms in 1948	Firm	Degree of Market Power 1948[b] (est.) (percent)	Assets, 1948[a] (est.) ($ million)	Degree of Market Power 1973[b] (est.) (percent)	Change in Market Power 1948–73 (est.) (percent)	Specific Policy Cause of Change?
2	General Motors	22.0	2,958	21.8	− .2	
9	General Electric	20.5	1,177	20.5	0	
20	Western Electric	33.0	650	32.6	− .4	Exemption
29	Alcoa	28.0	504	17.0	− 1.1	Remedy of 1950
33	Eastman Kodak	27.0	412	27.0	0	
38	Procter & Gamble	19.5	356	19.5	0	
47	United Fruit	27.0	320	22.0	− 5.0	Remedy
60	American Can	20.0	276	14.8	− 5.2	Remedy of 1951
69	IBM	29.5	242	23.5	− 6.0	Consent decree?
76	Coca-Cola	22.0	222	19.5	− 2.5	
c	Campbell Soup	28.2	149	28.2	0	
c	Caterpillar Tractor	19.5	147	19.5	0	
c	Kellogg	19.5	41	18.3	− 1.2	
c	Gillette	24.5	78	24.5	0	
c	Babcock and Wilcox	22.0	79	19.5	− 2.5	
c	Hershey	25.8	62	23.5	− 2.3	
c	du Pont (cellophane)	30.5	(65)	22.0	− 8.5	Lapse of patent?
c	United Shoe Machinery	29.2	(104)	18.5	−10.7	Remedy

[a] Sources: A. D. H. Kaplan, op. cit.; Moody's Industrial Manual; and G. W. Stocking and W. F. Mueller, "The Cellophane Case and the New Competition," American Economic Review, 1955, pp. 29–63.
[b] See Table 7-1 for the meaning of this index.
[c] Not available.

each other, but their character and antitrust status are roughly distinct.

Near-monopolies. Leading firms which probably have high shares were noted in Table 2–8 in Chapter 2, so far as data permit. Their evolution is clarified by Tables 7–1 and 7–2.

In 1910 there was indeed a large core of dominant firms in major industries, including U.S. Steel, Standard Oil, American Tobacco, and others.[21] Most of these were created by the trust movement of 1890–1901. By 1948, as Table 7–3 shows, the cast of characters changed considerably. Automobile, electric, and other companies lead the list, but they are scattered further down among the ranks of all firms than the leaders were in 1910. By 1973, Table 2–8 shows that there had been still further changes. But many of the present leaders are familiar from 1948. These include General Motors, IBM, Western Electric, General Electric, Eastman Kodak, Procter & Gamble, and others. There are probably scores of other near-monopolies, most of them unknown for lack of data.

This core of market power is stable and important. The gains from abating much of it would probably be large. Yet the problem is not metastasizing the way it seemed to be in 1895–1925, and the whole economic loss does not appear to be calamitous or ballooning.

Tight Oligopoly. Some of the main tight oligopolies are listed in Table 7–4, roughly in decreasing order of aggregate market power. Some of these are industries in which antitrust treatments during 1905–20 or 1937–52 were *not* tried or carried out; steel, oil, copper, aluminum, glass, and rubber. Now often permeated with a degree of X-inefficiency and cooperative habits, they are probably intractable to structural treatment alone, and they do not engage in overt price fixing.

Therefore, the discounted policy yields seem lower than they are for dominant firms. The probabilities of net benefits are lower, especially for technical progress. Restructuring action would embrace several firms, not one, perhaps with higher transition costs. There are few clean cases: most tight oligopolies are now encumbered with special conditions, such as vertical integration, mineral rights, ingrained cooperative behavior, and indirect boardroom interlocks. Moreover, half-loaf antitrust treatments in the past have created estoppel problems for some of them.

These two groups—near-monopolies and tight oligopolies—are the core and periphery of the structural problem in U.S. industry. What treatments have there been, with what effects? And what is presently being done?

PAST TREATMENTS

Treatments were extensive during two earlier periods, 1906–20 and 1938–52. More recently, Section 2 has gone into cool storage. Its wording

---

products. And du Pont's control of U.S. Rubber (now Uniroyal) through stockholdings may have given du Pont a preferred market for tire fabrics and U.S. Rubber a preferred market—in the GM companies—for tires. *U.S.* v. *du Pont,* 353 U.S. 586.

[21] The rankings in these tables are based on estimates of the aggregate market power held by these firms. That arises from their market shares and barriers, and the extent of the markets they inhabit. These estimates are not precise, but they give a fair picture of the main antitrust problems. Whether or not the market power they hold has been great or moderate, their relative positions in the larger pattern are reasonably clear.

TABLE 7–4

Major Tight Oligopolies, U.S. Manufacturing, 1970

Industry Code Number	Industry	Value of Shipments ($ million)	Official 4-Firm Concentration Ratio (percent)	Actual Average Concentration (estimated) (percent)	Imports (percent)	Are There Major Geographic Submarkets?
2911	Petroleum refining	22,737	33	(65)	Slight	Yes
3312	Iron and steel	9,328[a]	47	(80)	~25	Yes
3211	Flat glass	670	92	92	Slight	No
3641	Electric lamps	892	92	92	Slight	No
3522	Farm machinery	4,367	40	70	Slight	No
3334	Primary aluminum	1,758	90+	90+	Slight	No
3331	Primary copper	673	75	75	Slight	No
2111	Cigarettes	3,503	84	84	Slight	No
2026	Fluid milk	8,253	20	(60)	Slight	Yes

[a] Value-added is given; value of shipments is not reported.

Source: U.S. Census Bureau, *Value-of-Shipment Concentration Ratios*, Annual Survey of Manufacturers, 1970, M70(AS)-9, U.S. Government Printing Office, 1972; and W. G. Shepherd, *Market Power and Economic Welfare* (New York: Random House, 1970), Appendix Table 8.

is unconditional and would touch even moderate degrees of monopoly: "Every person who shall monopolize, or attempt to monopolize, or combine or conspire with any other person or persons, to monopolize any part of the trade or commerce among the several states, or with foreign nations, shall be deemed guilty of a misdemeanor. . . ." *Every* monopoly or attempt to monopolize *any part* of the trade or commerce is illegal.[22] There are no provisos about scale economies, good behavior, or intent. Yet by now, and especially since 1952, application of Section 2 has become infrequent and unpredictable.

Two conditions have been informally added to the law. The courts will now require proof of monopoly position (1) *plus* some evidence of intent to monopolize and (2) *plus* evidence that the monopoly can be abated without giving up important economies of scale or capacity to innovate.[23] If the defense can show that the high share arises from (1) superior skill, foresight or industry, or (2) scale economies in any important direction, including innovations, then acquittal will usually follow.[24] To convict would be regarded as either (1) punitive against good performance, and/or (2) irrational, since no efficient remedy could ensue.

This judicial restraint has been further extended by the antitrust agencies. Potential cases against firms with high market shares are simply not prepared or brought, wherever scale economies are thought possibly to loom as significant. And by a perverse twist, the high market share itself often persuades agency staff members to hold off because large scale economies might be present or can, at least, be successfully alleged.

The upshot is that the true conditions are not investigated in depth, neither by the agencies nor by a process of exposure in a court trial. If Section 2 were applied as it reads, no such paralysis would occur. Monopolists would be simply defined as such. The proper remedies would still pose intricate problems, but the law would apply as it is written.

In this perspective, we can now assess the two major waves of Section 2 cases in the past, which were in 1906–20 and 1938–52. The main actions are outlined in Tables 7–5 and 7–6.

Scope.   The first set of cases started with Roosevelt's "trustbusting," flowered under Taft, and was stalled and then stopped by World War I and its aftermath.[25] Its coverage was extraordinarily complete. It touched virtually every major case of high market share at the time, including a majority of the largest ten industrial corporations. Although conviction and restructuring were obtained in only three cases, these led to major changes. Little direct relief was gained in most of the other

---

[22] For discussion of the dilution of the bill before its enactment, see Hamilton and Till, *Antitrust in Action, op. cit.;* also H. Thorelli, *The Federal Antitrust Policy,* Allen and Unwin, 1954); and W. Letwin, *Law and Economic Policy in America* (New York: Random House, 1965).

[23] Though not in the letter of the law, these conditions do apply.

[24] This was important in the du Pont cellophane case and United Shoe Machinery; a case against the General Motors near-monopoly in buses was withdrawn in 1965 on the second ground.

[25] Despite his reputation, Roosevelt's actions were moderate. Thurman Arnold later described him as the man "with his big stick that never hit anybody."

TABLE 7–5

Major Section 2 Cases, 1905 to 1920

Cases	Time between Monopolization and Remedy		Time between Action Begun and Finished[a]		Outcome
	Years	Interval (years)	Years	Interval (years)	
American Tobacco	1890–1916	26	1906–12	6	Dissolution into three main firms.
Standard Oil	1875–1918+	43+	1905–12	7	Dissolution into about a dozen regionally dominant firms.
du Pont (gunpowder)	1902–13	11	1906–12	6	Mild dissolution; reversed quickly by effects of World War I.
Corn Products	1897–1920	23	(1910)–19	(12)	Slight changes from a consent decree.
American Can	1901–	—	(1909)–20	(11)	No change.
U.S. Steel	1901–	—	(1907)–20	(13)	Acquittal. Informal limits on further mergers.
AT&T	1881–	—	(1909)–13	(4)	Compromise. AT&T retained its position; agreed to interconnect and avoid further mergers.
Meatpackers (Armour, Swift, Wilson, Cudahy)	1885	—	(1905)–1920	(12)	Compromise. Packers agreed to stay out of adjacent markets and to cease coordination.
American Sugar	1890–	—	1908–14	6	No action. American Sugar's position had slipped already.
United Shoe Machinery	1899–		(1908)–18	10	USM leasing restrictions were modified.
International Harvester	1902		1906–18	12	Compromise. Trivial divestiture.

[a] Based on estimates of the start of official investigation and the end of official action. Parentheses indicate estimates.

Sources: S. N. Whitney, *Antitrust Policies* (New York: Twentieth Century Fund, 1958), 2 vols.; and various other references.

TABLE 7-6
Major Section 2 Cases since 1937

Cases	Time between Monopolization and Remedy		Time between Action Begun and Finished[a]		Outcome
	Years	Interval (years)	Years	Interval (years)	
1938 to 1952					
Alcoa	1903–(1953)	(50)	1934–50	16	War plants sold to new entrants.
National Broadcasting Company	1926–43	17	1938–43	5	"Blue Network" divested (became American Broadcasting Corp.).
Pullman	1899–1947	(65)	(1937)–1947	(10)	Divestiture of sleeping car operation. Manufacturing monopoly was not directly changed.
Paramount Pictures	1914–48	34	(1935)–1948	(13)	Vertical integration removed.
American Can	1901–(1955)	(54)	(1945)–1950	(5)	Compromise: certain restrictive practices stopped, to foster entry.
du Pont (GM holdings)	1918–61	43	(1945)–1961	(16)	Divestiture.
United Shoe Machinery	1899–1970	71	(1945)–1969	(61)	Share reduced to 50 percent.
United Fruit	1899–1970	71	1948–70	22	Moderate divestiture.
American Tobacco	(1920)–	—	1938–46	8	Conviction but no significant remedy.
du Pont (cellophane)	1925–	—	(1945)–1956	(11)	Acquittal.
Western Electric	1881–	—	1946–56	10	Case effectively abandoned.
IBM	(1925)–	—	1947–56	9	Case effectively abandoned.
Since 1968					
IBM (1969 case)	(1925)–	—	1965–	—	Trial delayed until 1975.
Cereals (1972 case)	(1950)–	—	1970–	—	In process.
Xerox (1972 case)	1961–	—	1970–	—	In process.
AT&T (1974 case)	1881–	—	1965	—	In process.

[a] Based on estimates of start of official investigation and end of official action. Parentheses indicate estimates.

Sources: S. N. Whitney, *Antitrust Policies* (New York: Twentieth Century Fund, 1958). M. J. Green et al, *The Closed Enterprise System* (New York: Grossman, 1972), and various other sources.

actions, but implicit constraints were placed on such firms as U.S. Steel and International Harvester.[26]

The second wave during 1938–52 was confined to firms ranking much lower down in the national lists, but these firms still included nearly all of the major firms with market shares over 50 percent. Several of these cases were successful legally, but others were inconclusive, and the two most important ones—IBM and Western Electric—were abandoned in the 1950s.

Since 1968 a modest revival has occurred, with several sizeable actions started. These touch on IBM, cereals firms, Xerox, and AT&T. Their outcome remains to be seen.

The First Series

Railroads. In 1904, the Court ordered the dissolution of the Northern Securities Company, a holding company that controlled the Great Northern and Northern Pacific railroads, parallel competing roads that were in competition with other transcontinental lines.[27] In 1912, it found that joint ownership of the Terminal Railroad Association of St. Louis by a number of railroads entering that city was an illegal combination and ordered the Association to admit, on reasonable terms, any other road that might apply.[28] In the same year, the Union Pacific Railroad came before the Court. The Union Pacific's line had stopped at Ogden, Utah. The Company had sought to extend it to the coast by buying stock in the Southern Pacific, which controlled the Central Pacific which ran from Ogden to San Francisco. The Court held that this acquisition violated the law even though the two lines served different cities and operated between different termini.[29] In 1922, moreover, the Court held Southern's ownership of stock in Central to be illegal, though they were not competing lines.[30] Two other cases involved joint ownership of railroads and anthracite coal mines. In 1920, the Court ordered dissolution of the Reading Company, a holding company which controlled the Reading Railroad and mines producing a third of the country's supply of anthracite.[31] And it ordered the Lehigh Valley Railroad to divest itself of shares in mines producing another fifth of the supply.[32] In all of these cases, the Court held that the attainment of market power through combination was illegal even though that power was not abused.

Industry: The "Bad" Trusts. The first case of a manufacturing combination to come before the Court was the E. C. Knight case, involving the sugar trust which then held 95 percent of the market. Here, the Court held, in 1895, that the law did not apply because its scope was limited

[26] See Whitney, *Antitrust Policies, op. cit.*
[27] *Northern Securities Co.* v. *U.S.,* 193 U.S. 197
[28] *U.S.* v. *Terminal Railroad Assn.,* 224 U.S. 383
[29] *U.S.* v. *Union Pacific Railroad Co.,* 226 U.S. 61
[30] *U.S.* v. *Southern Pacific Co.,* 259 U.S. 214
[31] *U.S.* v. *Reading Co.,* 253 U.S. 26
[32] *U.S.* v. *Lehigh Valley Railroad Co.,* 254 U.S. 255

to business engaged in interstate commerce and thus did not cover manufacturing.[33] If this interpretation had stood, the law would have been gutted. In fact, it was ignored.

In 1911, in cases involving the Standard Oil trust[34] and the American Tobacco trust,[35] the Court applied the law to manufacturing. It was in these cases that it enunciated the rule of reason. But it ordered each of the combinations to be dissolved. Standard Oil controlled all of the important pipelines and nearly 90 percent of the country's refining capacity. It had attained its position by exacting rebates from the railroads on its own shipments and on those of its competitors, by cutting prices in one region at a time to drive its local rivals out of business, and by resorting to other predatory practices, the mere listing of which filled some 57 pages of the record. Yet Standard Oil's grip was already slipping and the monopoly had existed for about 40 years already.

American Tobacco controlled three-quarters of the country's output of smoking tobacco and around nine-tenths of its output of chewing tobacco, cigarettes, and little cigars. This company, too, had attained its position by unfair methods of competition: by excluding its rivals from sources of supply, by buying plants to shut them down, by local price cutting, and by the production of fighting brands which were sold at a loss to destroy competitors and abandoned when their purpose had been served. In its decisions in these cases, the Court placed its emphasis, not on the fact of combination or even on the attainment of monopoly, but on the monopolistic intent of the defendants and on their use of unfair tactics in eliminating competition and excluding new competitors. It dissolved the trusts, not because they possessed monopoly power, but because they had so flagrantly abused it.

The virtual monopoly of du Pont in gunpowder since the 1890s was also ended in 1913.[36] The firm had been less abusive, but its intent to monopolize was clear, its defense was inept, and dissolving it into its parts was relatively easy. Yet du Pont retained the greater and better parts, and World War I immediately nullified the effects and vastly enriched the firm. The du Pont family then took major holdings in General Motors, U.S. Rubber, and other firms.

The government also threatened action against AT&T for monopolizing both telephone and telegraph services, and for its internal monopoly with Western Electric (recall Chapter 2 and see Chapter 16 below). Moderate concessions were gained from AT&T in 1913, but it retained its monopoly in telephone production and operation.

Major cases against International Harvester, U.S. Steel, American Sugar, American Can, major meatpackers, and Corn Products Co. ad-

---

[33] *U.S.* v. *E. C. Knight Co.,* 156 U.S. 1. Also read Alfred Eichner, *The Origins of Oligopoly* (New York: Columbia University Press, 1971) for an exhaustive account of the Trust and its fate.

[34] *Standard Oil Co. of N.J.* v. *U.S.,* 221 U.S. 1.

[35] *U.S.* v. *American Tobacco Co.* 221 U.S. 106.

[36] See Alfred Chandler and Stephen Salsbury, *Pierre S. du Pont and the Making of the Modern Corporation* (New York: Harper & Row, 1971).

vanced in the courts, and by 1915 a broad restructuring of industry—reversing much of the trust movement—was in prospect. But then World War I intervened, the mood changed, the rule of reason began to tell, and the effort collapsed.

The "Good" Trusts. In 1916, a lower court refused to convict the American Can Company, controlling nine-tenths of the output of tin cans, because the defendant "had done nothing of which any competitor or consumer of cans complains or anything which strikes a disinterested outsider as unfair or unethical."[37] In its decision in the U.S. Steel case in 1920 the Supreme Court revealed a similar complacency. It was the doctrine contained in this decision that, for the next 25 years, granted virtual immunity to monopoly in manufacturing.

The United States Steel Corporation, created in 1901, was a combination of 12 concerns, themselves resulting from earlier combinations of 180 separate companies, with over 300 plants. It was the largest merger in the nation's history, extending vertically from mining to fabrication and horizontally to all the types of steel mill products, and controlling, at its inception, around two-thirds of the output of the industry. When this colossus came before the Court, it still controlled one-half of the supply of steel. But in a 4 to 3 decision, with two of its members abstaining, the Court found that the combination did not violate the law.[38]

The majority eked out its reasons as follows: (1) The organizers of the Corporation had intended to monopolize the industry, but they had not succeeded in doing so and, recognizing their failure, had abandoned the attempt. The law was directed, said Justice McKenna, not against an expectation of monopoly but against its realization. Its specific prohibition of attempts to monopolize was thus ignored. (2) Admittedly, the Corporation had conspired with other companies, in earlier years, to fix the price of steel. But this only served to prove its lack of monopoly. The practice, moreover, had been abandoned; the evidence showed that the industry was now competitive. The monopolistic character of the Pittsburgh-plus delivered pricing system was not explained or understood. (3) The decision was thus confined to a narrower issue: the legal status of a combination controlling half of an industry. Certainly the Corporation was big and powerful. But, said the Court, "the law does not make mere size an offense. It . . . requires overt acts and trusts to its prohibition of them and its power to repress and punish them." (4) The question, then, was whether the Corporation had abused its power. Had it acted, by itself, to fix monopolistic prices? Had it excluded others from the market? On the contrary, said the Court, its behavior was exemplary: "It resorted to none of the brutalities or tyrannies that the cases illustrate of other combinations. It did not secure freight rebates; it did not increase its profits by reducing the wages of its employees . . . , by lowering the quality of its products, nor by creating an artificial scarcity of them; . . . it did not undersell its competitors in some localities by reducing its prices there below those maintained elsewhere . . . ; there was no evi-

---

[37] *U.S.* v. *American Can Co.,* 230 F. 859, 861 (1961)
[38] *U.S.* v. *U.S. Steel Corp.,* 251 U.S. 417 (1920).

dence that it attempted to crush its competitors or drive them from the market." In short, though the Corporation was big, it was not bad. And, accordingly, it was not dissolved. The law was thus held by the majority of the Court, as Justice Day remarked in his dissent, to be "intended merely to suppress unfair practices."

When this decision was announced, the government withdrew its appeals in several pending cases, including the one against American Can. The issue of size was presented to the Court again in 1927, however, in a further case against the International Harvester Company. This concern, a combination of five producers of agricultural implements and machinery, controlled 85 percent of the output of such equipment when it was established in 1902, and 64 percent when it was brought before the Court. Its leadership in setting prices was followed by the other members of the industry. These facts, however, did not impress the justices. Six of them, with three abstaining, adhered to the precedent set in the case of U.S. Steel. The law, they said, "does not make the mere size of a corporation, however impressive, or the existence of unexerted power on its part, an offense, when unaccompanied by unlawful conduct in the exercise of its power."[39] Price leadership was rejected as offering evidence of monopoly. In the words of the opinion: "The fact that competitors may see proper, in the exercise of their own judgment, to follow the prices of another manufacturer, does not establish any suppression of competition or show any sinister domination."

The Court had turned about. It was evidently determined now not to touch dominant firms except in the most extreme cases. Market shares were safe virtually up to 100 percent. The other cases ended in defeat or peripheral consent decrees.[40]

The Second Series

Efforts languished until 1938, when Alcoa was brought to trial for the monopoly it had held since before 1900. Other cases followed thick and fast under Thurman Arnold and on until 1952. The decisions on Alcoa in 1945 and United Shoe Machinery in 1953 resurrected Section 2 to a degree; in doctrine, shares of 60 percent could be treated. But in practice, large gaps remained even in this moderate coverage. And after 1952 treatment lapsed once again.

Alcoa had dominated aluminum production under the original Hall and Bradley patents since 1903, realizing very high and steady profit rates. An early Section 2 suit in 1912 was settled with little effect.

The government brought suit against the Aluminum Company of America in 1937, charging that it had monopolized the manufacture of virgin aluminum and the sale of various aluminum products, in viola-

---

[39] *U.S.* v. *International Harvester Co.*, 274 U.S. 693, 708.

[40] The meatpackers decree of 1920 did prevent integration into adjacent markets. Though mild at the time, it came to be challenged vigorously by the firms in 1929 and the 1950s. Denied both times in the courts, the firms finally obtained an administrative release from the Division in 1975. The junior author helped design an efficient revision of the decree in 1968. It would have let the packers into eight industries which have high concentration. The change in 1975 roughly followed these lines.

Wide World Photo

Learned Hand (1872–1961), senior Judge in the
4th District (Southern New York). His Alcoa decision
of 1945 is the modern landmark for Section 2 actions.
(Shown 1942.)

tion of Section 2 of the Sherman Act, and asking that it be divided into several parts. The monopoly, originating in a basic patent now expired, had been extended and preserved, according to the government's complaint, by resorting to oppressive tactics, including the elimination of competing fabricators by squeezing the spread between the price charged them for crude aluminum and the prices offered customers for finished goods. After a trial that ran for more than two years the District Court found Alcoa not guilty and the government appealed.[41] When the justices who had previously been connected with the prosecution disqualified themselves, however, the Supreme Court could not muster a quorum of six to hear the case. The judicial code was then amended by Congress to enable a Court of Appeals to serve, in such circumstances, as a court of last resort. The case was certified to the Court in the second circuit, and the decision of this Court, having the effect of a Supreme Court ruling, was rendered by Judge Learned Hand in 1945.[42]

The Court found that Alcoa manufactured more than nine tenths of the virgin aluminum ingot used in the United States, the rest coming in from abroad, and concluded that this was "enough to constitute a monopoly."[43] It then considered the argument that the power conferred

---

[41] *U.S.* v. *Aluminum Co. of America,* 44 F. Supp. 97 (1942).
[42] *U.S.* v. *Aluminum Co. of America,* 148 F. 2d 416.
[43] *Ibid.,* p. 424.

by this monopoly, though it existed, had not been exercised. This distinction, said the Court, "is . . . purely formal; it would be valid only so long as the monopoly remained wholly inert; it would disappear as soon as the monopoly began to operate; for, when it did—that is, as soon as it began to sell at all—it must sell at some price and the only price at which it could sell is a price which it itself fixed. Thereafter the power and its exercise must needs coalesce."

The doctrine of the Steel and Harvester cases, that the mere existence of unexerted power is no offense, was thus explicitly reversed. Price fixing was found to be inherent in monopoly. The acquisition of market power became the test of illegality. The double standard of interpretation, which condoned the single-firm monopoly while holding agreements among competitors to be unlawful, was rejected as "absurd."

Alcoa had attained its position, however, not by combining with others, but by reinvesting its earnings and expanding its capacity as the market grew. Was this against the law? It did not follow from the company's position, said the Court, "that it 'monopolized' the ingot markets; it may not have achieved monopoly; monopoly may have been thrust upon it."

But Alcoa might have avoided this development:

It was not inevitable that it should always anticipate increases in the demand for ingots and be prepared to supply them. Nothing compelled it to keep doubling and redoubling its capacity before others entered the field. It insists that it has never excluded competitors; but we can think of no more effective exclusion than progressively to embrace each new opportunity as it opened, and to face every newcomer with new capacity already geared into a great organization, having the advantage of experience, trade connections, and the elite of personnel.

To retain monopolistic power merely by growing with the market was thus to violate the law. Nor could the fact of monopolization be excused by the absence of intent to monopolize. To read Section 2 of the Sherman Act "as demanding any 'specific' intent makes nonsense of it, for no monopolist monopolizes unconscious of what he is doing. So here, 'Alcoa' meant to keep, and did keep, that complete and exclusive hold upon the ingot market with which it started. That was to 'monopolize' that market, however innocently it otherwise proceeded." The defense of good behavior was likewise unavailing. The Court condemned the use of squeeze tactics in the past and enjoined their repetition in the future but made clear that it was holding Alcoa guilty of monopolization "regardless of such practices."

The firm was not found to be abusing its position at the time of the trial, but a verdict for the government was held not to require the proof of such abuse. Congress, said the Court, "did not condone 'good trusts' and condemn 'bad' ones; it forbade all." The antitrust laws were not intended merely to regulate business practices. It was one of their purposes "to perpetuate and preserve for its own sake and in spite of possible costs, an organization of industry into small units which can effectively compete with each other."

Judge Hand's decision is a landmark in the interpretation of the law. It made a clean break with the Steel and Harvester precedents. It resurrected Section 2 of the Sherman Act. But the great doctrinal victory ended in very modest relief.[44] Alcoa's structure was not touched. Instead government aluminum plants built during World War II (and operated by Alcoa) were reserved for new competitors, which turned out to be Reynolds and Kaiser. Alcoa still dominated the tight oligopoly, being required only to license its patents and cut its ties with Aluminium, Ltd., of Canada.[45]

The Alcoa doctrine was extended to the leading three cigarette firms (recall Chapter 6) and movie theatres.[46] By 1948 the Court was saying: "It is not always necessary to find a specific intent to restrain trade or build a monopoly.. . . It is sufficient that a restraint of trade or monopoly results as the consequence of a defendant's conduct or business arrangements . . . Monopoly power, whether lawfully or unlawfully acquired, may itself constitute an evil and stand condemned under Section 2 even though it remains unexercised."[47]

United Shoe Machinery. This Corporation, a combination of three concerns, controlling 95 percent of the output of shoe machinery, was brought before the Supreme Court in 1913 charged with violation of the Sherman Act. At that time, the Court found the combination to be innocent, holding that each of the companies had been given a legal monopoly by its patent rights, and that the machines they made were not competitive but complementary.[48] Forty years later, the company, still maintaining its dominant position (though only a smallish firm), was again tried on the same charge. But this time it was found to have violated Section 2 of the Sherman Act by monopolizing the industry.

The decision in the case was handed down by Judge Charles Wyzanski in 1953.[49] It followed the precedent established in the Aluminum case. But Judge Wyzanski's reasoning went beyond that of Judge Hand. Monopoly, he agreed, is lawful if it is "thrust upon" the monopolist. A concern's monopoly power is unlawful, however, if that power is to any substantial extent the result of barriers erected by its own business meth-

---

[44] The case had been remanded for relief to Judge Knox in Chicago. His action in 1950, after five years' wait, exemplifies the way conservative district judges can dilute or reverse a strict decision. He first swamped the competitive standard in other factors:

"In determining the extent of permissible power that is consistent with the antitrust laws in a particular industry, the following factors are relevant: the number and strength of the firms in the market; their effective size from the standpoint of technological development, and from the standpoint of competition with substitute materials and with foreign trade; national security interest in the maintenance of strong productive facilities, and maximum scientific research and development; together with public interest in lowered costs and uninterrupted production."

He then treated Alcoa as untouchable. Aluminum, said the Court, must compete with other materials made by large concerns. Dismemberment of Alcoa's research staff and its managerial personnel would lessen its ability to do so. Success in interproduct competition "can be achieved only by companies that are rich in resources, and which are capable of undertaking extensive scientific and market experimentations. At the present juncture, the weakening of any aluminum producer would lessen the buoyancy of the industry as a whole."

[45] See M. J. Peck, *Competition in the Aluminum Industry* (Cambridge: Harvard University Press, 1961).

[46] *American Tobacco Co.* v. *U.S.* 328 U.S. 781, 811; and *U.S.* v. *Griffith,* 334 U.S. 100, 105–7.

[47] *U.S.* v. *Griffith,* 334 U.S. 100, 105–7

[48] *U.S.* v. *Winslow,* 227 U.S. 202.

[49] *U.S.* v. *United Shoe Machinery Corp.,* 110 F. Supp. 295

ods (even though not predatory, immoral, or restraining trade in violation of Section 1 of the Sherman Act), unless the enterprise shows that the barriers are exclusively the result of superior skill, superior products, natural advantages, technological or economic efficiency, scientific research, low margins of profit maintained permanently and without discrimination, legal licenses, or the like.

Systematic price discrimination was the main behavior pattern which, taken with the high share, violated Section 2. United's business practices—such as price discrimination, leasing rather than selling its machines, and making long-term contracts on exclusive terms—were not *per se* immoral or illegal. But the company had not achieved and maintained its overwhelming strength solely by virtue of its "ability, economies of scale, research, and adaptation to inevitable economic laws." Instead, given its dominant position, its business practices, however legal in themselves, had operated to exclude competitors from the field. Judge Wyzanski, thus, did not find monopolization to be illegal as such. But he imposed on the monopolist a stricter standard of conduct than that applying to competitive concerns. The former, he said, must be denied the right to follow practices in which the latter may safely be permitted to engage. The decision was appealed by the company and was upheld in 1954 by the Supreme Court.

The government asked the court to split United into three competing firms. Judge Wyzanski refused to do so, ordering the company, instead, to sell as well as lease its machines, shorten its leases, modify their terms, and grant licenses under its patents to its competitors. During the next decade, United diversified its business, reducing shoe machinery to 10 percent of its sales and reducing its share of the shoe machinery market to 60 percent. The Antitrust Division asked that the case be reopened, holding that 60 percent was still too large a share. The judge refused, the government appealed, and his decision was overruled by a unanimous Supreme Court. In 1969, accordingly, the company was required to dispose of enough of its shoe machinery business to reduce its share of that market to a third.

The USM victory was largely doctrinal (USM's shoe machinery revenue was in 1968 less than *1/100* the size of IBM), and in fact the doctrine was weak. Conviction required evidence that the high market share did not represent superior performance. And no sharp remedy was granted. To lawyers the *Shoe Machinery* case is important; to economists it is trivial.[50]

There were other actions during 1937–52. In the A&P case, where the company was found in 1946 to be employing its wholesale produce subsidiary, the Atlantic Commission Company, to obtain discriminatory advantages over its competitors, a consent decree accepted in 1954 provided that ACCO be dissolved.[51] The *Paramount* decision severed links be-

---

[50] Judge Wyzanski did hold that dominance created a "rebuttable presumption" of illegality, which could be offset only by a showing of "superior skill, superior products, natural advantages, technological or economic efficiency." This gives a correct burden of proof. But it has not been taken up in later actions, and it would affect only conviction, not remedy.

[51] *U.S.* v. *Great A. & P. Tea Co.*, 67 F. Supp. 626 (1946); affirmed 173 F. 2d 79 (1949);

tween movie makers and theater chains and it stopped block booking of movies, which tied the best films to inferior ones.[52] The National Broadcasting Company was forced to divest its Blue network in 1943; this became the basis for the American Broadcasting Company. Pullman was required to separate its production and leasing of sleeping cars.[53] AT&T and Western Electric were sued in 1949, seeking divestiture and a division of Western Electric. It and the IBM case of 1951 were withdrawn later. But the whole Section 2 effort was large and—though far less central than the 1905–20 wave—did cause some marginal changes.

Retrospect on 1905–20 and 1937–52. Before considering actions since 1953, let us take stock on the first two series of Section 2 actions. Both waves touched fairly thoroughly on the near-monopolies then existing: in 1910 they were at the corporate pinnacle, in 1948 they were further down. But remedies were mild and cases had grown lengthier. In both periods, tight oligopoly was scarcely touched. Only the meatpackers decree of 1920 and the 1946 tobacco case are exceptions to this, and their effects were slight. Tight oligopoly remained virgin territory.

Severity of Remedies. The severity of remedies was moderate even in the big 1911 cases; it abated sharply after 1911; and it has dwindled further since the 1920s. Relief in the 1911 cases merely undid earlier mergers. Since 1913 there has been virtually no direct restructuring in manufacturing industry, and the conduct remedies have been moderate. Some current weak-performing firms in basic industry were defendants which escaped conviction or other strict remedies in the 1913–35 period: examples are steel, meat packing, and glass. Major wars have played a role in forestalling treatment. World Wars I and II and the Korean War all interrupted the thrust of enforcement waves and softened judicial attitudes toward major firms. In all, the end probability of achieving a full remedy under existing procedures has gone down, probably as far as .1 or .2 and even lower in the biggest cases.

Duration. The duration of actions—from initial study to remedy—has lengthened, from about 6 years to about 20 years. The average interval from the original monopolization to remedy, which was already over 20 years in 1911 (35–40 years for Standard Oil), has now grown even longer. In the two major 1911 cases, Standard Oil and American Tobacco, remedy was applied two or more decades after the monopoly was created, and only after the firm's market position was already weakening.

Indeed, restructuring has always lagged at least 20 years behind monopolizing, and the lag is rising. In no case has treatment been applied quickly enough to intercept a rising position of market power. The 1951 IBM case could have turned out to have that effect on the embryonic computer industry. But that opportunity was thrown away.

Original Offenders. In no case has the action removed much or most of the capitalized monopoly gain from the original monopolizers. Rockefeller, du Pont, Duke, and other major family wealth was virtually un-

---

Civil Action 52–139, District Court of the U.S. Southern District of N.Y., Consent Decree, January 19, 1954.

[52] *U.S.* v. *Paramount Pictures,* 334 U.S. 131 (1948)

[53] *U.S.* v. *Pullman Co.,* 50 F. Supp. 123.

touched by the early antitrust actions. And the second set of actions was even more remote from the original gains. In effect, a full amnesty for monopolizers has applied. Only the later shareholders have been exposed to antitrust risk.

Conditions for Success. The two pre-conditions for bringing suit were (1) a high market share, and (2) a high degree of profitability. There were virtually no suits against oligopolists or against firms with average or depressed rates of return. The elements of a legal victory in the two sets of cases were, in the main: (1) A well-conceived and thorough economic case for action, based on extensive research on the critical points. The old Bureau of Corporations supplied this in the first wave; it was often lacking during the second wave, partly because the Antitrust Division lacked adequate research powers and resources. (2) Grassroots support, both political and in the form of private and state suits against the target company. This was true of Standard Oil by 1911. (3) Brilliant antitrust strategy, particularly to prevent delay by snowing and procedural detours. This was helped when (4) The private side was caught by surprise, complacent, or inept, and if it had displayed abusive actions and markedly excess profits. (5) A specific, feasible basis for remedy had to be available, lest its absence chill the case from the start.

An effective remedy might be ordered, *if* (1) there were a technical basis for splitting, such as decentralization and an origin in recent mergers, (2) the product were relatively simple and standardized, so that innovation or national military involvement were not major questions, (3) a moderate weakening in the monopolists' total position were already in progress, so that potential competitors were active and expectations were not sharply reversed by divestiture (but not so severe a weakening as to make action superfluous), and (4) the stock were closely held, so that the expected or actual impact was not widespread.

Yields. The net yields of actions appear to have been high, especially for the earlier moves.[54] The results taper down in the more recent actions, mainly because major cases were dropped and relief was slow and slight. The best cases have (1) treated large near-monopolies, (2) moved quickly after the original monopolization, and (3) required major structural change.

A Third Series, Starting in 1969?

Since 1953. From 1953 to 1968, little Section 2 action occurred toward any of the leading candidates. United Fruit consented in 1958 to end its

---

[54] A recent estimate of the benefit-cost ratio for major cases gives a rough idea of the probable yields:

Standard Oil	67	Alcoa	19
American Tobacco	21	American Can	7
International Harvester	22	United Shoe Machinery	5
Corn Products	8		

For the estimating procedure, see W. G. Shepherd, *The Treatment of Market Power, op. cit.,* Chapter 7 and Appendix 3. In these and other cases, more thorough and timely treatments could have given larger yields. And the yields forgone from stopping treatment in other cases would presumably be comparable.

old pre-1900 banana monopoly, agreeing to create from its assets a firm capable of handling 35 percent of the market by 1970. But Castle & Cook and Del Monte intruded after 1964. By 1973, United Fruit (now United Brands) no longer led, and it had shifted mainly into other lines.[55] Bicks's "GM team" in the Division started suits against GM's bus and locomotive monopolies (over 85 percent each), but Turner dropped these by 1966 for lack of foreseeable relief. With only one plant in each case, could there be restructuring? Grinnell was convicted in 1966 for monopolizing the market in "accredited central station protective systems," but the market was small and the doctrine was not new.[56]

In 1966 the Division recommended suing AT&T once again to divide out Western Electric (now among the several leading industrial monopolies). But Ramsey Clark, then Attorney General, would not file the case and later professed not even to have known of it.

Since 1968, four significant cases have been started: IBM, cereals, Xerox and AT&T.[57] Major oil firms have also come in for minor actions. Turner's chance to treat tight oligopoly came to naught.[58] There has been much study and increasing grass-roots support for action. Also, new economic factors may be slowly eroding market power in automobiles, computers, and aircraft. But policy is still dormant, and the three recent cases now seem unlikely to end with timely and effective relief.

---

[55] By 1973, Castle & Cook had surged ahead with 40 percent, with United's "Chiquita" at 39 percent and Del Monte with 21 percent. The antitrust case had not created this new competition, but it had paved the way. Bananas were one-fourth of United Brands' revenues.

[56] The relief given in 1967 was easy to arrange and remarkably effective. Grinnell divested American District Telegraph Co. and the restrictive terms were stopped. Firms increased from 40 to 190 by 1969. ADT grew rapidly, became much more efficient, and was soon thriving (see *Forbes* magazine, November 15, 1973, p. 65). The economics of competition under Section 2 operated with high fidelity.

[57] Since 1960, the agencies have also studied several of the candidates, and in some cases specific actions have been prepared, but not started. These include automobiles, detergents, and the nuclear power equipment industry.

The automobile industry was studied several times, and action was recommended but never quite crystallized under Turner.

W. S. Comanor researched the role of advertising in the detergent markets for the Division in 1967–68. He established that the predicted relationship between advertising intensity, profitability and market share did exist. But no action was then taken or even prepared, primarily because no adequate remedy available *under conventional antitrust processes* seemed to exist. Doubts about relief therefore prevented a court evaluation of whether monopoly existed. Finally an expensive study of the nuclear power equipment industry was commissioned by the AEC during 1967–69. But the study was shallow and inconclusive, partly because no real effort was made to get the inside information on costs and pricing necessary for a thorough analysis.

[58] In 1967–68, Turner started a study at the Division to identify tight oligopolies which needed treatment under the Kaysen-Turner approach of 1959. The junior author helped organize this survey of priority candidates and the attempt to evaluate them toward legal actions. The 12 prime candidates (apart from automobiles, which was given separate analysis) appeared to be: electric lamps, tires, flat glass, steel ingots, metal containers, explosives, sulphur, primary batteries, carbon and graphite, cereals, auto rentals. "Marginal" cases were transformers, copper, trucks and gypsum (see Green, *op. cit.,* pp. 305–07).

But some of these candidates were old and now unprofitable. Others stemmed mainly from patents or advertising, and so remedy would clearly be difficult to bring about. Still others could be argued to face monopsony power; tires, for example. And several were relatively trivial cases. Finally, all of them were less promising legally and economically than such near-monopoly cases as Western Electric and automobiles, which at that time were not being brought. Therefore, there seemed little reason to put scarce resources on these marginal cases, since ones with much higher priority were blocked. Furthermore, the remedies for tight oligopoly require resources which are not available via Section 2 and the courts. That the Kaysen-Turner proposals were not applied therefore had strong practical reasons at the time.

IBM. The Division sued IBM under Section 2 in January 1969, after an investigation since 1966 in which IBM formally cooperated.[59] The filing was prompted by a brace of private suits against IBM, by the failure of several competitors, and by data showing IBM to have a market share of 70 percent and a thorough pattern of price discrimination. The suit charged that IBM held a monopoly, that the discrimination prevented effective competition by smaller specialized producers, and that the introduction of the major 360 line of computers in 1965 was done in ways which eliminated competition. This closely fits the precedents of United Shoe Machinery.

Discrimination has been both (1) vertical (among machine types, with higher profit rates on smaller machines, where competition was weaker), and (2) horizontal (among the various users of each computer model). Vertical patterns were known from IBM pricing memos about the 360 line of computers about to be introduced in 1964. Horizontal discrimination occurs widely, as IBM salesmen promise free programming and other help to swing the customers.[60] Discrimination is systematic and inherent in IBM's position.

The suit seeks a structural change, not yet determined: possibly a vertical separation between the producing and leasing functions, and possibly horizontally into two or three successor firms. Presently, Burroughs, Control Data, Sperry Rand, and Honeywell are surviving at less than one-seventh of IBM's size.

Five years later, trial had still not begun (see Figure 7-1). It is a fine instance of the "big case" plagued by delay, passive handling by the Division, and uncertainty about objectives.[61] IBM drew large benefits from delay, probably about $1 million per day.[62] Parties to the case listed nearly 600 witnesses, and the evidence was expected to run into *millions* of pages.

A private plaintiff, Telex, meanwhile won damages of over $200 million in 1973 (on appeal at this writing).[63] And Control Data settled its 1968 suit in 1973, gaining $101 million and IBM's Service Bureau Corpora-

[59] *U.S.* v. *International Business Machines Corp.,* 69 CIV 200, So. Dist. of N.Y.

[60] Though IBM unbundled these services in late 1968 in an effort to avert the Division's suit, the unbundling has not been complete.

[61] The junior author prepared parts of the economic content of the Division's case against IBM during 1967–68. The core of the case was highly compact and complete by mid-1968. The delay in bringing the case to trial has reflected extreme efforts and clever strategy by IBM counsel and, during 1969–72, a lapse in Antitrust Division handling and passive behavior by the court. The Division staff permitted such tactics as extensive tangential interrogatories and snowing by masses of irrelevant documents. The IBM defense was led by Bruce Bromley, a grand old man of the antitrust bar, who had once said, "Now I was born to be a protractor. I quickly realized in my early days at the bar that I could take the simplest antitrust case that Judge Hansen [Hansen was the antitrust head at the time] could think of and protract it for the defense almost to infinity." "Judicial Control of Antitrust Cases," 23 F.R.D. 417 (1959). Under Kauper, the case was given far greater resources and was handled more aggressively.

[62] Suppose that about one-fourth of IBM's profits (now running around $1.7 billion yearly) are at stake under Section 2. This is equivalent to $1 million per day; IBM's gain from delay. After adjusting for the tax factor (recall equation 7 in Chapter 3), the resources which IBM might rationally devote to delay are about double, or $2 million per day. This dwarfs the resources available to the public agencies and for objective outside study.

[63] *Telex Corp.* v. *IBM Corp.,* U.S. District Court, N. Dist. of Oklahoma, IPF35–F55 and C10–C14, Sept. 17, 1973. Telex had been nearly bankrupted by IBM's tactics in selling periph-

FIGURE 7–1
Legal Actions against IBM (including significant antitrust suits filed against the company prior to the Telex decision)

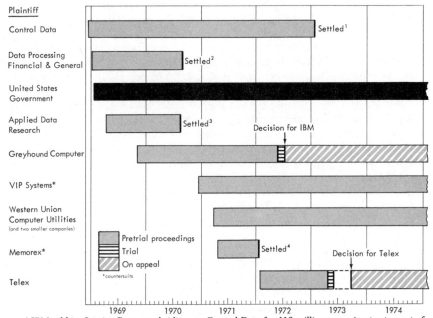

[1] IBM sold its Service Bureau subsidiary to Control Data for $16 million, agreeing to stay out of the data-services business for six years. It also agreed to give C.D.C. six months free rent on the computers in the Service Bureau (worth about $5 million), to buy at least $25 million worth of data services from C.D.C., and to pay $26 million toward Service Bureau employee benefits. IBM reimbursed C.D.C. $15 million for legal expenses, and will contribute $30 million to joint research efforts. The estimated value of the settlement is over $100 million.
[2] IBM refinanced $42 million that D.P.F. owed it and paid about $1 million toward legal fees.
[3] IBM paid A.D.R. $1.4 million to reimburse it for legal fees and its investment in computer programs; IBM also agreed to pay at least $600,000 over three years for royalties and services.
[4] Both sides abandoned their claims, and agreed not to undertake additional legal proceedings against each other for at least a year. No money changed hands.
Source: *Fortune*, November 1973, p. 152.

tion.[64] Private cases were now numerous, as IBM's aggressive tactics became legally vulnerable and treble damages loomed large. A Division victory would in fact trigger large damage claims and settlements, apart from any economic relief. That has assured IBM's relentless resistance.[65]

The case exemplifies the weaknesses in current Section 2 processes.

---

eral equipment. The issues were complex, but IBM was held to have deliberately used its dominant position to eliminate competition, without any saving grace of greater efficiency.

[64] Control Data also agreed to destroy a large filing system for trial documents which it had been preparing for use by itself and the Antitrust Division. This added at least a year's delay to the Division's case. Though cited as contempt of court and fined moderately, the package was evidently worth its cost to IBM in delay.

[65] In 1974, the Division was said to be devoting the equivalent of 12 full-time staff members to the case. IBM was probably using about 300, though it would not give direct estimates. Senior members of at least five of the country's leading law firms were also involved.

The firm can delay almost endlessly. The court can only hear, decide, and then mediate a remedy; it has no resources to investigate expertly and to bring about change directly. And any conviction will provoke damage claims so severe that the firm must resist tooth and nail against even a mere airing of the issues.

Cereals. The FTC charged major cereal producers—Kellogg, General Mills, General Foods, and Quaker Oats—with a shared monopoly in 1972. Since then there have been lengthy arguments before a hearing examiner. The case tries to break new doctrinal ground—citing Clayton Section 5: "unfair" practices—but it relies heavily on arguments that intensive advertising has artificially stifled competition. Even if it is shown that large and unfair advertising has blocked entry, the firms can point to much mutual competition via advertising and other tactics. The leaders have had very high profitability in cereals (around 15–20 percent). But the complexity of the issues and the lack of easy remedies suggest that the outcome will not give new precedent or major change. Note that cereals is a relatively low-priority and small candidate among tight oligopolies (recall Table 2–8).

Xerox. The FTC started action against Xerox in early 1973, alleging a market share of 95 percent in plain paper copiers and 86 percent in the whole office copier market (recall Chapter 2). A series of Xerox's pricing, leasing and patent acts were said to exclude competition. Many of the conditions and charges—price discrimination; leasing rather than sales; rapid growth; sales network—closely paralleled IBM and United Shoe Machinery. But the acts were not so clearly inherent. Xerox leases, not sells; IBM had been forced to sell some machines under its 1956 consent decree. Xerox's pricing strategies are deliberate and could be enjoined. And its web of 2,000 patents was deliberately assembled.

The relief envisioned by the FTC did not include restructuring. Instead, free patent licensing, selling of machines, and severing ties with Rank Xerox (the British affiliate) were the main proposed remedy. These would dent but not sharply alter Xerox's position. In late 1974, a preliminary settlement was reached, providing more access to Xerox's patents. But it would not touch the more basic pricing and innovation strategies which maintain Xerox's position.[66]

Oil Firms. As the "energy crisis" first broke in 1973, the FTC issued a complaint against eight major oil firms for squeezing out independent gasoline sellers. The case was paralleled by actions by many states; this was the first such grass-roots antitrust movement since the first Standard Oil suits in 1906–9. The actions did not seriously threaten the basic position of these and other leading oil firms in refining. At best, damages would be levied but little change in market structure seemed likely to occur.[67]

AT&T. In November 1974, the Division filed an ambitious suit

---

[66] Litton Industries in 1972 and SCM Corporation in 1973 also sued Xerox, seeking over $1 billion in damages and basic relief.

[67] A staff report underlying the suit did recommend separating out the pipelines and a portion of refining capacity. Bank interlocks among the oil firms are also cited as anticompetitive (*New York Times,* Feb. 25, 1974). But the case was aimed mainly at retail squeezes.

against AT&T. It included the traditional efforts to separate Western Electric from AT&T and divide it into several parts. This would open up markets for Bell System purchases and assure fairer competition in the peripheral equipment used by customers. The suit also contemplated separating out the Long Lines Department, "some or all" of the Bell operating companies, and Bell Laboratories from AT&T.

The whole challenge to the Bell monopoly was fundamental and sophisticated, and much comment in the business press was favorable. The Bell response was adamant, and the case seemed likely to be long and voluminous, if it were not settled by compromise. Chapter 16 considers the issues in more detail. Despite this remarkable suit and the others since 1968, Section 2 is still largely dormant toward the main array of candidates.

Meanwhile, *private suits* have made some inroads; 1,300 were filed in 1972, compared to 96 by the Division. Several have taken small bites out of IBM, and others are pending against IBM and Xerox. Eastman Kodak has been sued in 1973 by Bell & Howell, Berkey Photo, and GAF Corporation for monopolizing and various abuses. Divestiture into as many as 10 separate firms is asked, plus large treble damages. Kodak has modified some practices on new-product technology to meet these cases.[68] And in 1972 ITT persuaded a District judge in Hawaii to order GT&E to divest *all* of its equipment capacity and operating companies acquired since 1950. These were $3.7 billion of GT&E's total $9 billion in assets (see Chapter 16).

Taken altogether, restructuring by public policy has virtually ceased, despite the test-tube perfection of the Grinnell outcome and the actions begun since 1968. A Section 2 case may result in therapy, which changes practices and, perhaps, eventually structure. And certain shareholdings or other vertical ties may be cut, as in *du Pont-GM.* But unified, large dominant firms appear to be secure from horizontal restructuring.

The contrast between formal and actual policy is illustrated in Figure 7–2 (also recall Figure 4–5). For any given market share, a firm is much less likely to be investigated, sued, convicted or changed than is indicated by formal policy. Even formal policy lets moderate market shares alone. The lines for actual policy have shifted to the right after the two waves of cases. (Try (1) to locate the current position of the curves in Figure 7–2 according to *your* judgment; and then (2) to locate in Figure 7–2 the main dominant firms from Table 2–8. What are their chances for treatment?)

Despite the lack of formal action, the agencies exert a remarkable degree of regulatory constraint on many dominant firms, directly or by anticipation. Since profit rates can tip a Section 2 decision, they may be moderated by a variety of company actions. Price structures too are often monitored and modified. Companies must expect their price structures and strategies to be sifted by agency staff and possibly in court.[69] Product strategies also come under scrutiny.

---

[68] *Wall Street Journal,* April 30, 1973, p. 10.

[69] Precisely that occurred in the present IBM and Xerox cases and in United Shoe Machinery. It could be central for automobiles, film, telephone equipment, and drug firms, among

FIGURE 7-2
Formal and Actual Treatments of Established Monopoly: An Estimate

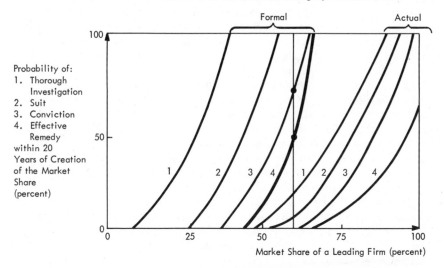

This informal regulation may yield benefits at very small costs. Yet it is incomplete and not done publicly. And it is often amateurish, because antitrust agencies lack resources and regulatory expertise.

CAN SECTION 2 BE EFFECTIVE?

In short, there is real question that Section 2 can deal effectively either with near-monopoly or oligopoly. The courts are likely to resist restructuring or even convicting, because of five conventional beliefs: efficiency gains are speculative, transitional costs would be high, innovation may be stopped, innocent new shareholders will unfairly suffer capital losses, and market power is fading away in any event.[70] These are actually prejudgments of the key decision variables: discounted costs and benefits. Though untested and perhaps wrong, they do govern action. And these images foster added resistance by defendants.

The net result comes close to being a *de facto* repeal of Section 2. In practice it has been milled away and encrusted with provisos, while the agencies have been left without sufficient resources to preresearch the cases and to carry out remedies. The very power to damage the defendant—via treble damages which a conviction triggers—ensures total resistance and delay. The agencies lack resources to frame and carry out remedies. And other possible constraints, via other kinds of agencies, are simply lacking. The U.S. now has only one main shot in its locker—Sec-

---

others. The degree of thoroughness can easily exceed that in much utility regulation (see Chapter 13–17).

[70] Example: General Motors was said to be declining sharply in 1961 because of imported small cars, in 1971 because of safety and ecology, and in 1974 because of fuel shortages and the shift to small cars. Try to determine if it has; look also at IBM, Xerox, and Eastman Kodak.

tion 2—and it does not suit its task. For this reason, and perhaps also because of corporate power, it is disused.

Actual restructuring has nearly all been along moderate and obvious lines; reversing mergers, selling war surplus plants (Alcoa), or detaching subsidiaries (Standard Oil). An aura of untouchability has arisen around more unified conditions, and some firms now centralize in order to immunize against divestiture.[71]

The causes of meager Section 2 action are primarily the biases identified in Chapter 3: (1) the scientific basis for estimating costs and benefits has been diluted by the lack of information for research about structure and performance; (2) the agencies have mandates which exceed their resources and powers, either to study, to prosecute, or to carry out remedies; (3) the candidates control most of the germane information, including the costs of remedy; (4) the court process sets the burden of proof and of time against the agencies, rather than evenly; (5) a lack of deadlines further biases the time-structure of decisions against action rather than leaving them neutral; and (6) taxes add to the firms' incentives to resist. The dual-agency system—for all its other merits—means that no one is responsible for a lack of effective restorative action.

The shortness of tenure of the agency heads accentuates this. Section 2 cases are believed in the agencies to have no precedential value. Though this is probably not true, it still influences current policy choices. Meanwhile, candidate firms do routinely resist up to the margin at which after-tax gains equal the tax adjusted costs of resistance. And changes or remedies are forced upon defendants: there are no tax or internal incentives for the owners or managers of the firms to comply either after conviction or in anticipation of suit.

Finally, the very infrequency of recent action has made it seem erratic. Defendants can plausibly assert that an action against them is (1) *unfair,* since like cases are escaping treatment, and (2) *injurious* to innocent third parties (e.g., shareholders), since action is so unpredictable that it creates intolerable risk. These are often persuasive points in court. A thorough and systematic program of treatment would resolve them.

To sum up, large instances of market power remain from the past, even though some instances have been abated, mostly in earlier decades. And apart from mergers by newcomers (see Chapter 8), new instances of monopoly—once established—need not seriously fear treatment by public policy for at least 15 years, if at all. This probably leads to large discounted economic losses in a range of reasonably identifiable cases. Conceivably, the discounted costs of applying structural remedies to these cases might be even larger: only that could justify the pause since 1952 on Section 2.

More likely, well-designed actions are justified by cost-benefit conditions. The further irrationality in present policy is that these matters are not getting studied thoroughly or even at all, and that alternative treatments are simply not being considered. The reasons for these biases are understandable. It is not clear that effective treatments can be designed and applied within the present system of laws, agencies and resources.

---

[71] In 1969 General Motors was reliably reported, without denial, to have markedly recentralized its operations in order to forestall antitrust action.

Foreign Experiments. Other countries face a smaller problem and have been more inventive.

Dominance is usually less extensive and durable abroad (recall Chapter 2). It tends to attract imports or new foreign subsidiaries, when profitability is high. American firms especially have added competitive elements in soaps, oil, automobiles, drugs, and tin cans, among many others, in western European countries.

The British Prices and Income Board assessed profits and, on occasion, management performances, while screening price increases during its brief 1966–71 life. Among the 160 industries it considered, it stopped or reduced price increases in many, and it also halted a number of restrictive arrangements. Public holding companies own part or all of certain leading firms in Italy and several other European countries. And public ownership—partial or complete—gives a degree of public influence in many industries, including steel and coal in Britain and automobiles and aircraft in France (see Chapters 19 and 20).

Public buyers exert monopsony power against leading firms in some other industries, especially via public enterprises and national health programs, as Chapter 2 noted. In Britain and other European countries, such major industries as electrical equipment, telephone apparatus, drugs, steel rails and rolling stock face such public monopsonies, some of which use their bargaining power actively.

Even antitrust strategies are being tried in interesting ways.[72] The new (1973) Office of Fair Trading in Britain is surveying the range of dominant firms carefully, looking toward further Monopolies Commission actions in industry and finance. Earlier the Monopolies Commission had issued thorough studies on important dominant positions in industry.[73] Usually, proposed changes were mild and the Board of Trade would not apply them in full.[74] The Office of Fair Trading is expected to have greater power and expertise.

The only important restructuring abroad occurred after World War

---

[72] Thus, in 1966 the two main U.K. detergent makers, Procter & Gamble and Lever Bros., were required to introduce new brands free of advertising and priced 20 percent below the standard advertised brands. These brands—Tide and Surf—started with about 20 percent of the market, slipped to about 18, and then rose to a steady 23–25 percent. Profitability has been significantly reduced, along with consumer prices. The firms are on notice that slippage below 20 percent will land them again in Monopolies Commission action, presumably more drastic.

See various reports of the U. K. Monopolies Commission; and C. K. Rowley, *The British Monopolies Commission* (London: Allen and Unwin 1966); and W. Pengilley, "Australian Experience of Antitrust Regulation," *Antitrust Bulletin,* Summer 1973, pp. 355–74. In 1973, long efforts to reduce drug prices in Britain finally resulted in a government order to Hoffman-La Roche to cut prices on its Librium and Valium tranquilizers by half. Roche's British unit was paying its Swiss parent $925 a kilogram for Librium ingredients and $2,300 a kilogram for the Valium ones, when these materials could be bought from Italy at $23 and $50. Hoffman, concerned that other countries might follow suit, fought the action even to the House of Lords and threatened to move research activity out of Britain (*Wall Street Journal,* April 30, 1973, p. 34). Hoffman has sold over $2 billion of the drugs and its prices are actually lower in Britain than in some other countries. Still the profits from British sales were computed at 70 percent of capital, pre-tax.

[73] These included light bulbs (1951), wires and cables (1952), tires (1955), gases (1957), electrical machinery (1957), fertilizers (1958), cigarettes (1961), gasoline (1965), color film (1966), flat glass (1968), beer (1969), tin cans (1970), cereals (1973), and shoe machinery (1973), among others. It also screened mergers (see Chapter 8).

[74] Yet Kodak Ltd. was required to cut the price of color film by 25 percent, and Hoffman-La Roche was made to reduce the price of Librium by 60 percent and Valium by 70 percent in 1974.

II, when the victorious Allies sought permanent preventatives against fascism in Germany and Japan.

It was widely believed that the Axis powers had waged war because of the link between powerful monopolists and fascist politics.[75] Nobody knew—or knows even now—whether economic power fostered absolutist regimes, or were used by them. But the combines did thrive during the War, and it seemed critical to fragment the war machines and create competitive conditions. This would also make a viable base for the democratic process in these countries.

Parallel programs were started in both Germany and Japan in 1945–46 to take apart the combines in heavy industry and finance. In Japan especially, heavy industry had come to be under the control of wide-ranging combines—Mitsui, Mitsubishi (remember the Zero?) and Sumitomo were the largest—which united a vast array of industrial activities, finance, utilities, primary products, and others.[76]

This restructuring contained mainly two elements. The first was directed towards the industrial combines themselves. It sought to dissolve the central control of these systems, to create variety and independence out of what had been tightly knit systems. The efforts focused on the best known and most prominent cases, but also reached down into some of the middle-range enterprises.

The second layer of activity dealt with the financial sources of the combines, especially the links between banks and producing enterprises. These connections have always been more important abroad than in the U.S., and it was recognized that lasting changes in these economies could only be reached by untying them.

Under John J. McCloy in Germany and General Douglas MacArthur in Japan, these efforts got quite far. But the programs were stopped in mid-course by political resistance from the U.S., where industrial interests believed that these strict steps might eventually become to be tried also in the U.S. if they worked well abroad. Therefore, by 1949 there were high-level missions and lobbying in order to arrest the restructuring efforts. They succeeded, in time to preserve banking from action.

As a result, both programs were truncated and partial. Within ten years, in fact, both countries had seen massive waves of reforming most of the original industrial patterns. By 1965, scarcely a trace remained of these remarkable programs. In Japan, perhaps, coordination within the combines has been looser.

Two lessons may be drawn from this experience. First, drastic industrial changes are likely to come only in unusual conditions, during which the economic and political status of large industry and finance has been jolted. Second, private enterprise can display enormous resilience in adjusting to and eventually absorbing the effects of major structural changes.

---

[75] T. A. Bisson, *Zaibatsu Dissolution in Japan* (Berkeley: University of California Press, 1954).

[76] See Eleanor T. Hadley, *Antitrust in Japan* (Princeton: Princeton University Press, 1971), for a masterly and favorable evaluation of the program, and for other references. Ms. Hadley was a leading participant in the restructuring program.

ALTERNATIVES

If Section 2 is in a cleft stick, what alternatives are there to supplement it or take its place? There are several conventional alternatives, which follow. Useful as they may be, they are specialized and have a narrower reach than is often thought. And they are difficult to apply.

Reductions in Trade Barriers. This has been a staple and attractive proposal since Adam Smith's time. Tariffs were integral with the trust issue between 1870 and 1900 in the U.S. And in such trading economies as Britain, Japan, and Germany, these levers could clearly be powerful; they already are powerful in many industries.

For the U.S. there are two main limits. One is that the tactic is extremely unlikely ever to be applied very far. The other is that even if it is tried, the effects will be limited and many problem cases will remain untouched.

Trade barriers go through periodic general shifts, as protectionism waxes and wanes. But it seems impossible to get deliberate, specific cuts in trade barriers in order to apply new competitive forces. The resistance to cuts is focused and effective; either the protected firms are profitable and have a large stake, or they are stagnant and so imports will cause extensive structural changes. There is also a natural unwillingness of any nation to reduce its own trade barriers unilaterally. The political economy, therefore, makes the prospects for using this strategy remote, as is indicated by long experience in the U.S. and abroad.

In any event, the possible scope of tariff cuts would indeed be highly selective, covering a limited range of industries and missing many of the main problem cases.[77] In some instances, the leading U.S. firms are also leading actual or potential importers, and so the effects of tariff-cutting would be diluted. Among the prime examples of this are computers, film, oil, automobiles, copying equipment, soaps, drugs, and toiletries.

Import competition has been powerful in certain cases, particularly steel and automobiles. Yet others—such as computers, copying equipment, soaps, electrical equipment, glass, and telephone equipment—appear to be virtually immune. The causes of immunity vary, ranging from high transport costs for glass, soap, and many other products, over to specific conventions or rules against buying imports (as in most telephone equipment, aircraft, drugs, and electrical equipment). Among the main tight oligopolies, only automobiles, steel, aluminum, and copper appear sensitive to this treatment. And in steel, for one, the recent direction has been toward more protection, not less.[78]

Patents. Patents and advertising are among the many possible causes

---

[77] They include primarily flour, liquor, cigarettes, various chemicals, certain nonferrous metals products, electrical equipment, batteries, ships, films and specialized instruments. On the measurement of trade barriers—a most difficult subject—see B. N. Vaccara, *Employment and Output in Protected Manufacturing Industries* (Washington, D.C.: Brookings Institution, 1960); and B. Balassa, "Tariff Protection in Industrial Countries: An Evaluation," *Journal of Political Economy*, 1965, pp. 573–94. See also Chapter 24.

[78] An informal international cartel arrangement to limit imports to the U.S. was created in 1968, with strong State Department efforts. These limits have not stopped import competition, but they have reduced it.

of entry barriers (recall Chapter 2). We will consider possible limits on them, taking patents first (see also Chapter 9 on patents).

Patents focus in certain industries. Presently they underlie market power especially in the drug and photocopy equipment industries. It appears from general analyses (see Chapter 9) that shorter patent lives would not sacrifice substantial degrees of inventive and innovative activity. The marginal benefit in induced innovation from additional years of patent life is of low probability, while the marginal restrictive effects are definite.

Yet even if this were definitively known, a general shortening of patent lives, even down to five years, would not soon touch the existing problems in these industries. The structure has now hardened sufficiently that, as in many consent decrees which open up patents, little would happen from altering old patents. For these industries, a specific measure to shorten existing patents and constrain their use might be mildly effective.

Only in drugs and copying equipment are restorative gains from altering existing patents likely to be significant. Yet this effect could well take decades. This suggests that: (1) patent changes can have only a slight effect on existing market power, and (2) it is especially important that the patent laws fit preventive goals; that is, they do not create lasting dominance.

Advertising may be an important barrier. Yet the problem is narrowly focused and difficult to treat.

The issue is complex, and it revolves around the ability of large advertisers to achieve increasing returns in nationwide selling activities.[79] Moreover, advertising is often a weapon for entering a market or establishing a new brand; in short, for *increasing* competition. Therefore, only if (1) advertising scale economies were not as genuine as other input economies, and if (2) its anticompetitive effects outweigh its procompetitive role, would restrictions on it be efficient.

Even then, designing optimal restrictions would be difficult. A blanket limit on advertising—restricting it, say, to 2 percent of sales—would penalize the *lesser* firms, since the leading firm already has a lower percent because of the scale economies of saturation advertising. Also, many firms would easily adapt by shifting selling expenditures into other forms, such as sales networks and promotional discounts. These problems defeated in 1968 the only direct antitrust attempt ever made to identify and constrain the role of advertising.[80] Advertising apparently did operate to limit competition and enhance the leading firm's profit. Yet no effective remedy appeared possible, even if conviction under a novel interpretation of the antitrust laws were possible. The current FTC case against leading cereals companies is also facing this dilemma.

This negative lesson actually has a limited scope, because only a handful of rather small industries are strongly influenced by advertising in any event (recall Chapter 2, footnote 25). Even if antitrust doctrine and

---

[79] See W. S. Comanor and T. A. Wilson, *Advertising and Competition* (Cambridge: Harvard University Press, 1974) and other sources cited there.

[80] Recall footnote 57 above.

strategic devices were favorable, abating advertising's effects would be a limited strategy.

Applying Monopsony Power.   Public agencies and firms purchase from a wide range of industries. Where they have monopsony power, it could be exercised to constrain market power and to induce a more competitive structure. In the U.S. this tactic would affect certain problem industries, but only a minority. Abroad, the coverage is more complete.

One candidate is the drug industry, which sells in bulk to large groups (public agencies, nonprofit hospitals, and regulated buyers) at prices far below those to small customers.[81] Unified monopsony purchasing may ultimately be the only practical way to abate market power in the drug industry. It works, to a degree and with some exceptions, under universal health programs in Western Europe. The present U.S. system of medical insurance—with passive regulated paying groups such as Blue Cross, fragmented among the states—operates almost as if it were designed to *minimize* the effectiveness of such monopsony behavior.[82] The possible gains from changed behavior, even with no changes in structure, could be large.

Other sectors are weapons supply and utility equipment. Past treatments have been erratic and often perverse. The tendencies toward passivity and mutual interests in these cases may be inherent in the given structure, so that other changes may be needed in order to improve performance (see Chapters 13 and 29). Similarly, stockpiling of materials as a constraint device has tended, instead, to be operated so as to minimize the impact on industry pricing.

In short, public monopsony is an unfulfilled possibility, which may need a different setting or incentive structure from what has yet been tried. And its potential reach in the U.S. is not broad.

Price Controls.   Direct controls on prices have been tried both in war and peace, and some form of control may be inevitable in modern economies. Moreover, controls are commonly focused on the core monopolistic industries. In principle, this constraint could replace all the other policy tools. But in fact, controls are likely to be cumbersome and have costly side effects. These will be treated in Chapters 13, 14 and 24.

A Reorganization Commission.   A more direct treatment may avoid the present traps for Section 2 action. A special Commission, proposed by Senator Hart in a bill in July, 1972, illustrates the strengths and weaknesses of such an approach. The bill is unlikely to pass, but there have been lengthy hearings and much public debate. It might eventually be enacted in modified form.

The Industrial Reorganization Act would create a Commission, with expert staffing and a large research capacity. Its powers parallel those of the Sherman Act: the Commission would simply determine whether high market power exists, and then remedy it directly or by referral to

---

[81] See Senate Committee on Small Business, *Hearings on Drug Industry Prices and Profits* (Washington, D.C.: U.S. Government Printing Office, 1968). In December, 1973, it was announced that drugs covered by Medicare and Medicaid would be paid for only at the lowest price for which the drugs are generally available. The effectiveness of such assertions remains to be seen. See also Chapter 27.

[82] See Irene Till, "High on Drug Profits," chapter in M. J. Green, ed., *The Monopoly Makers* (New York: Grossman, 1973).

other agencies. It would avoid judicial delay, and be able to carry out changes directly. The Commission would look primarily at seven industries, including most of those in Table 2-8. Once it had treated them—within 10 or 15 years—it would be disbanded.

Even were the Commission created, its effectiveness would probably be far less than its stated capacity. This is because the proposal grants a general amnesty for all prior behavior and profits. This would cut out at one stroke the treble damage provisions. The amnesty would make the Commission more politically acceptable, in some quarters, but the resistance of the major industries to treatment presumably would continue.

In action, the Commission would be prone to lengthy research and adversary proceedings. And it would *not* be likely to dispatch the major cases directly. Instead, because they are so large and complex, such cases would almost certainly be referred to Congress for special treatment, to cope with the broader political repercussions. This is recognized in the present bill, and it would in any case occur. Therefore the Commission would probably not solve these problems, but only—at best—expedite a more fundamental resolution in other forums.

Still the proposal has interesting possibilities. It could make more progress on the dominance problem than is presently occurring. And, at the least, it might bring out into the open, for the first time, something approaching the whole facts on these individual cases.

SUMMARY

The treatment of established market power has come to be slow and possibly ineffective. There exists a core of large industries with dominant firms or light oligopoly. Though markets are often difficult to define, the basic patterns are reasonably clear. Such cases often, but not always, are linked with abusive or systematic monopolizing behavior.

There have been two main series of Section 2 cases, in 1905–20 and 1937–52. These cases have grown ever longer to process, and they now usually occur long after the original monopoly was formed. They have increasingly focused on middling priority candidates, compared to the higher incidence of earlier efforts (the recent IBM and AT&T cases are exceptions).

Conviction now requires (1) a monopoly market share, plus (2) monopolizing acts of some kind, plus also (3) high profitability and (4) clear prospects for relief that will not imperil innovativeness. The burdens of proof and time are both set against Section 2 treatment, and court processes can be used to get long delays. The agencies must, in practice, establish that a change will be enough superior to the existing structure to justify conviction and the costs of transition.

Few good alternatives to Section 2 now seem available. Freer trade and patenting, abating of advertising, the use of public monopsonies, even a reorganization commission, seem to offer only narrow gains. Dominant firms are largely immune from treatment for the time being. They can continue to do what lesser firms cannot cooperate to do: to control pricing and behavior over a large share of their markets. This central riddle of antitrust is unsolved.

CHAPTER EIGHT

Mergers

M ergers are distinct events, visible, often dramatic and occasionally spectacular. The merger boom of the 1960s has subsided (recall Figure 2–7), but there are still over five thousand mergers each year and some experts predict another big wave soon. Most of these mergers are small and prosaic, and even many large mergers are neutral or have high social value. But others pose—or seem to pose—severe policy problems.

Merger policy is simple in some directions, complex in others. Merger policy also shows how the law grows, with a series of landmark cases marking out new areas. And merger policy tests one's ability to reach good appraisals in the midst of self-serving claims.

First, we consider the reasons why mergers occur and the effects they have. Then we look at the benefit-cost conditions they involve, and at the rhythm of actual merger activity in the past. Then U.S. policies toward horizontal, vertical and conglomerate mergers are reviewed. Policies abroad are also compared.

REASONS FOR MERGERS

A *horizontal* merger unites side-by-side competitors: see Figure 8–1. A *vertical* merger links suppliers and users in the chain of production. A *conglomerate* merger is—in the pure case—anything with no horizontal or vertical element. Conglomerate mergers may link geographic areas (e.g., bakeries in two distant towns); these are called market-extension mergers. Or they may fill out a product line; these are called product-extension mergers. Most mergers of any significance mix the three elements—horizontal, vertical, and/or conglomerate—but one is usually prominent.

Actual mergers are only the visible fruit of the endless process of horse-trading—of wheeling and dealing—which goes on under the surface in the market for corporate assets. Far more combinations are conceived, negotiated, rethought, and hammered out than ever see the light

FIGURE 8–1
Types of Mergers

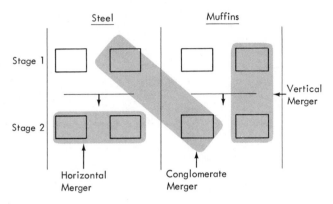

of day.[1] There is a small army of promoters at work in New York, London, and elsewhere, profiling candidates, seeking partners, and working out astonishingly complex terms of possible mergers. This functioning of the market for companies and control helps enforce good performance and accomplish needed change. But the cadre of promoters—most of them investment bankers—also helps to raise the volume of merger activity.

Among all possible mergers and quasi-mergers, why do those that occur actually occur? There are five main categories of reasons:

1. Pecuniary Economies. All three kinds of mergers may make it possible for the firm to buy its inputs more cheaply. These pecuniary gains (as was noted in Chapters 1 and 2) may affect any input used by the firm. Raw materials, advertising space, managerial talent, capital, and others may be bought more cheaply by the merged firms. Also, mergers often achieve tax benefits, in the pooling of loss-making and profit-making units. These gains are only pecuniary, but they may be powerful.

2. Technical Economies. Mergers may also permit genuine technical efficiencies (i.e., a lowering of the average cost curve). A larger firm may be able to use more efficient equipment. It may be able to borrow more efficiently. It may combine vertical processes into a more efficient operation. More broadly, the merger may reduce the risks of the firms, by pooling diverse operations. Such economies are routinely claimed for every merger. The policy question in each case is whether they do exist *and* whether they can be achieved by other routes, such as internal growth or long-term contracts between the firms.

3. Entry to a New Market. Entry is usually easier by merger than by starting afresh. Conglomerate mergers always involve entry of a new outside firm into the market. Such entry does not add new capacity, and so its net competitive benefits are always less than entry by internal growth. Moreover, the new entrant often had already cast a long shadow on the market as a potential entrant, before the merger.

4. Exit: The "Failing Firm" Case. Many mergers involve the absorp-

---

[1] One leading investment house (Lazard Frères) estimates that 70 percent of its work is on arrangements that do not come to pass.

FIGURE 8–2
Is This Firm Failing?

tion of a firm which is in straits, or even, in the extreme, failing. Failure, of course, simply means bankruptcy, which need not cause actual closure and dissipation of the company's activities. Often, indeed, bankruptcy simply leads to a merger. In any case, mergers can salvage failing companies. The difficult policy question often is: how much failure is required for *failure?* Is it a down-turn in sales, the beginning of financial losses, several months or a year or two of red ink, or actual imminence of bankruptcy? Often companies don sackcloth and ashes, claiming failure is imminent even though it is actually well in the future or quite unlikely.

5. Take-over. Among the many merger types, take-over is the most colorful and, perhaps, socially important. It involves a move by one firm to take over, or seize, another firm against its management's will. In the byzantine world of business strategy, one often has difficulty telling who is taking over whom; whether the event is amicable, hostile, or a mixture of the two (perhaps with some board members favoring take-over, and others against). The key element is that management in the target firm comes under a different control. The would-be new owners typically make a tender offer to buy a controlling amount of the stock at a price above the current market price.[2] This premium reflects their belief that they can manage the company so much better that the stock price will rise even beyond the take-over price.

A take-over often requires close finanical support for the taker, and the resisting management usually appeals for backing from *its* financial allies. So in fact, a genuine take-over is usually—at least in part—a struggle among members of the financial sector.[3] Take-overs are usually done

---

[2] The premium in recent years has been remarkably consistent at 20 percent over the market price; see P. O. Steiner, *Mergers: Motives, Effects, and Policies* (Ann Arbor: University of Michigan Press, 1974).

[3] An embattled management often ginns up a friendly alternative merger partner, to forestall the real threat. This complicates the bidding terms and legal footing, so that either time is gained to fight the take-over, or a preferred merger occurs, or the eventual take-over price for shares is enhanced. But few such defensive merger projects actually occur.

by certain kinds of corporate outsiders, aiming primarily at sluggish firms with substantial market positions, which have been sitting on unexploited resources and opportunities. In any event, take-overs differ in motives, tactics, and effects from the other kinds of routine market mergers.

Mergers often involve selling off parts of a firm to new owners, and so the reasons for disposing of assets also matter. Many firms carry marginal or even heavily-losing branches for decades, either from inertia or as part of larger strategies (e.g., to offer a full line of products). Disposal of them may reflect new financial stress, a promoter's efforts, or a change in managerial strategy.

In any event, mergers are often difficult to classify and fathom, for they may touch on the bedrock of corporate and financial power. The stakes are high, the action is swift, and the policy choices are often put under great stress.

EFFECTS OF MERGERS

The direct effects of mergers fit in three main categories: (1) they may affect competition, (2) they may affect performance, and (3) they increase global aggregate concentration.

Competition

Horizontal mergers obviously reduce competition. Part of the market process is made internal, under direct control. Power to raise price is increased. The larger the increase in combined share, the bigger will be the loss of competition, as Chapter 2 noted. Though small firms often claim that by merging they can compete better against dominant firms, this point has little merit unless scale economies are present.

Vertical mergers need not alter competition at either level.[4] Yet they will reduce competition if: (1) the merger raises entry barriers (by making new entrants join both levels at once, thereby raising the level of capital needed), and (2) the merger triggers a wave of parallel mergers, which sharply reduce the scope of open market sales. And if the possibility of price squeezes is increased, the mere threat of this may induce independent firms to behave more passively. *How much* competition is reduced depends on these conditions.

Conglomerate mergers are often—some economists say always—neutral to competition. But in certain conditions they can reduce or increase it. The new parent company may have better access to capital, advertising, or other resources for competitive strategies. If these are made available to a dominant firm, the effect will usually be to entrench it further. Such an increase in dominance may occur automatically, as lesser competitors adjust to their reduced possibilities. Or it may arise from direct

---

[4] Bork asserts that it *will* not, in "Vertical Integration and the Sherman Act: The Legal History of an Economic Misconception," *University of Chicago Law Review*, 1954, pp. 157–201. For a counter view, see W. Adams and J. B. Dirlam, "Steel Imports and Vertical Oligopoly Power," *American Economic Review*, 1964, pp. 626–55.

tactics by the dominant firm, using its new resources forcefully.[5] In the extreme, a web of conglomerate ties may induce behavior among conglomerates to be diplomatic. Each can retaliate elsewhere against moves in any one market. So competition may subside.[6]

Yet competition will probably be increased if the merger takes in a lesser firm. The new advantages will enlarge its opportunities to take market share away from the leading firms.

One further angle: if the acquirer had been a known, important potential entrant, then the merger may reduce competition by leaving one less among all actual plus potential competitors. The net effect on competition will often be slight and obscure, but still real.

Performance

The level of performance may, on balance, rise. (1) Economies of scale may be realized by horizontal mergers. (2) Economies of integration may arise from vertical mergers. (3) A failing firm may be restored. If these gains could be gotten by alternative ways (internal growth, contracts), then the merger yields no net benefit. One always asks why the change is not being made in ways which undergo market tests of efficiency.

Different from this is: (4) Efficiency induced by the threat of take-over. This gain can be large, both from the general threat and from specific take-over attempts (recall Chapter 2). To keep the threat credible, take-overs must actually be permitted. They harness private self-interest and skill to the task of discovering inefficiency and correcting it. X-inefficiency in a firm is often tolerated by a passive board of directors. The rules, customs, and power relations in large corporations often make it difficult to apply external pressure on lagging managers and directors. Take-over is the necessary device to apply such constraints, by threat or deed.

Other claimed economies of conglomerate mergers are dubious. "Synergism"—a "dynamic" process in which disparate managerial resources created new learning and skills: "2 plus 2 equals 5"—is mainly a 1960s catchword, with no scientific basis. Capital may be deployed efficiently, even creatively, within a diversified firm.[7] But the net benefit over allocation by the capital market may be small or zero.

Global Concentration

A series of giant-firm mergers may increase the aggregate concentration of the economy in a few hands. This can weaken the political and social fabric, increasing regimentation at the expense of individual freedoms and self-determination. Marked rises in global concentration have

[5] See Harlan M. Blake, "Conglomerate Mergers and the Antitrust Laws," *Columbia Law Review*, March 1973, pp. 555–92, for a thorough review of these factors.

[6] This is said to be true of Japanese combines and the interwoven conglomerates within the U.S. chemicals industries.

[7] For an abstract case that diversified firms are a distinct management form with special efficiency, see O. E. Williamson, *Corporate Organization and the Theory of the Firm*, (Englewood Cliffs, N.J.: Prentice-Hall, 1972).

occurred in the U.S. and abroad, with a range of negative effects. Even national sovereignty can be reduced by large international mergers; this may on balance cause social loss. These global effects are often diffuse and hard to plumb, but in the end they may easily transcend the specific economic ones.

COST-BENEFIT ASPECTS

To evaluate a merger, one first defines the market (recall Chapter 7) and then measures the increase in market share from the merger. For a conglomerate merger, one appraises the two firms' positions in their markets and any special advantages which they may pool.[8] From these structural facts, one can then roughly estimate the net social benefits and costs of the merger, adjusting the figures for time, probability, and precedent (recall Chapter 3). This is the heart of sound evaluation: simple in concept, possible to do only roughly in practice. Something like it is done in the antitrust agencies, in deciding whether to oppose individual mergers.

Since only *net* gains matter, the direct efficiency benefits from all three types of mergers will usually be quite small and of low probability. Vertical economies from merger will often be larger and more definite than those from horizontal mergers. Yet these too can usually be gotten by building new plants or long-term contracting.

Social costs from the loss of competition will usually be relatively large for horizontal mergers and some vertical ones. By comparison, the costs of stopping the merger are relatively small, and any private losses suffered by blocking the merger will be focused on deserving parties (not, as in some Section 2 cases, on third parties who can claim to be innocent). In practice, too, the burden of proof is generally against the merging firms. Time is also on the agencies' side, because the merger needs to go through on the agreed terms, before conditions change. By contrast to existing structure (recall Chapter 7), merger policy can operate quickly and strictly.

In short, cost-benefit analysis usually favors stopping of a wide range of horizontal and vertical mergers. And current antitrust arrangements make that rather easy and cheap to do. But they also make it easy to stop conglomerate mergers, which might offer net social benefits. Therefore the optimum social treatment of mergers involves not only a relatively strict line on horizontal and vertical mergers, but also a relatively open policy on conglomerates.

There is also an additional dimension to the problem in those many markets which have dominant firms. In those markets, a strict line against horizontal mergers, even by small firms, does tend indirectly to defend the dominant firms, by keeping their competitors smaller and more passive (recall Chapter 7). To ban mergers above 10 percent but let 60+ percent firms stand is unfair on its face. And it may mean that

---

[8] The effect on potential competition may also be appraised, but this is usually complex, difficult, and marginal (see the "Conglomerate Mergers" section, p. 248).

a strict merger policy is, on balance, firming up the market power of dominant firms.

PAST MERGER PATTERNS

There have been three major waves of mergers in the U.S. The first great wave was in 1897–1904, a period of great industrial turbulence and change.[9] The mergers primarily were horizontal, forming firms with 60 to 90 percent in scores of large and small industries. Much of the activity was strictly promotional, by Morgan, Rockefellers, and other financiers. It was widely believed that these groups would combine their interests on a new plane of financial superpower.[10] This merger wave climaxed in 1901 with the great blockbuster, U.S. Steel. The wave was stopped primarily by changing stock market and economic conditions, plus some effect of Roosevelt's new use of antitrust in 1902. Many of these mergers were overblown and ill-fated, declining almost as soon as they were formed. But others created dominant firms which remain to this day..

FIGURE 8–3
Mergers since 1951

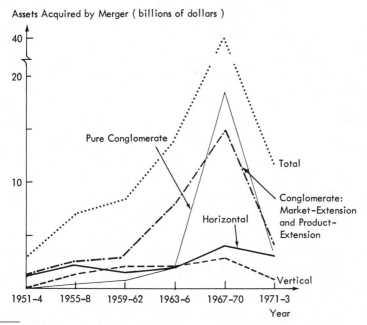

Assets Acquired by Merger (billions of dollars)

---

[9] See Ralph L. Nelson, *Merger Movements in American Industry, 1890–1956* (Princeton: Princeton University Press, 1962); and John Moody, *The Truth about the Trusts* (Moody, 1904).

[10] See John Moody, *The Truth About the Trusts* (New York: John Moody, 1904); F. L. Allen, *The Lords of Creation* (New York: Harper Brothers, 1935); and F. L. Allen, *The Great Pierpont Morgan* (New York: Harper and Row, 1949).

Credit: *University of Wisconsin*

Willard F. Mueller (born 1925), Director of Economics at the Federal Trade Commission 1961–68. A leading opponent of conglomerate mergers, he organized major FTC studies of their nature and effects. Now at the University of Wisconsin.

This early trust wave was parallel to direct monopolizing activity in a number of industries.

The second merger wave, in the 1920s, swarmed over both industrial firms and utilities. It formed oligopolies rather than dominant firms. The industrial mergers tended to form second and third-ranking firms, nearly as large as the existing dominant firms (examples: steel, tin cans, automobiles). This occurred partly because many dominant firms had been put on notice not to make further mergers (recall Chapter 7). In any case, by 1929 the main outlines of industry as we know it were firmly set.

The third merger wave in the 1960s—the great "go-go years"—mainly involved conglomerate mergers (see Figure 8–3). Yet there were also many horizontal and vertical mergers, and many conglomerate mergers had strong horizontal or vertical features. New conglomerates made a series of highly publicized mergers, some of them take-overs. But a wide range of older firms—both unified and diversified—made conglomerate mergers too. Table 8–1 gives a selection.

Despite some fears that the whole of industry was being transformed, actually structure and global concentration were only slightly altered.[11] The merger boom was punctured by the 1969–70 bear market drop of 40 percent (see Chapter 11), by the antitrust attack on conglomerate mergers during 1969–71 (see below), and by growing disenchantment with the wilder 1960s claims for merger magic. By 1972, indeed, many conglomer-

---

[11] FTC, *Report on Mergers,* Washington, D.C., 1971.

TABLE 8–1

A Selection of Large U.S. Industrial Mergers, 1952 to 1972

Year	Type	Acquiring Company	Acquired Company	Assets ($ million)
1952	PE	Mathieson Chemical	Squibb, E. R. and Sons	106
1953	H	Kaiser-Frazer (cars)	Willys Overland (cars)	120
1954	H	Nash Kelvinator Corp. (cars, etc.)	Hudson Motor Car Co.	108
	C	Mathieson Chemical	Olin Industries, Inc. (equipment)	232
	H	Studebaker Corp.	Packard Motor Car Co.	135
1955	H	Sunray Oil Co.	Mid-Continent Petroleum Corp.	186
	PE	Sperry Corp. (electrical)	Remington Rand, Inc. (office equip.)	207
1956	H	Gulf Oil Corp.	Warren Petroleum Corp.	163
1958	C	Socony Mobil Oil	Freeport Sulphur Co.	100
1959	V	General Telephone & Electronics (telephone systems)	Sylvania Electric Products, Inc.	264
1960	H	Standard Oil (N.J.)	Monterey Oil Co.	102
1961	C	Ling-Temco Electronics	Chance Vought Aircraft, Inc.	101
	PE, V	Ford Motor Co.	Philco Corp. (appliances, batteries)	242
	ME	Standard Oil Calif.	Standard Oil Co., Kentucky	141
1963	PE	Eaton Mfg. Co. (auto equipment)	Yale & Towne Mfg. (engineering products)	114
1964	ME	Interlake Iron	Acme Steel	134
1965	ME	Boise Cascade Corp. (wood and products)	Minnesota & Ontario Paper Co.	110
	C	Gulf & Western Ind. (conglomerate)	New Jersey Zinc Co.	143
	ME	Union Oil California	Pure Oil Co.	766
1966	PE	Continental Oil Co.	Consolidation Coal Co.	446
	H, ME	Atlantic Refining Co.	Richfield Oil Corp.	499
	C	American Tobacco Co.	Sunshine Biscuits, Inc.	109
	ME	Phillips Petroleum Co.	Tidewater Oil (western manufacturing & marketing properties)	372
1967	PE	Warner-Lambert Pharm. (drugs)	American Optical Co.	111

H = horizontal, V = vertical, ME = market extension, PE = product extension, and C = "pure" conglomerate.

TABLE 8–1 (continued)

Year	Type	Acquiring Company	Acquired Company	Assets ($ million)
	PE	Kerr-McGee Corp. (oil)	American Potash & Chemical Corp.	117
	PE, V	Glen Alden Corp. (textiles, etc.)	BVD Co., Inc. (clothes)	113
	V, PE	U.S. Plywood Corp.	Champion Papers, Inc.	359
	H	McDonnell Co. (aircraft)	Douglas Aircraft Co.	850
	C	Tenneco Corp. (gas, pipeline, etc.)	Kern County Land (land, construction equipment)	706
	C	Signal Oil & Gas Co.	Mack Trucks Inc.	303
	C	Hunt Foods & Industries	McCall Corp. (publishing)	149
	PE	North American Aviation	Rockwell-Standard Corp.	454
	C	Gulf & Western Ind. (conglomerate)	South Puerto Rico Sugar Co.	122
	C	Ling-Temco-Vought, Inc. (conglomerate)	Wilson & Co., Inc. (meat, sports, drugs)	196
	C	Studebaker Corp.	Worthington Corp. (engineering products)	296
1968	PE	Squibb, E. R. & Sons	Beech-Nut Life Savers	172
	C	Gulf & Western Ind.	Brown Co. (paper)	196
	PE	Hunt Foods & Ind.	Canada Dry Corp. (soft drinks)	105
	C	Gulf & Western Ind.	Consolidated Cigar Corp. (largest)	127
	C	Montgomery Ward & Co.	Container Corp. of America	397
	C	IT&T	Continental Baking Co. (largest)	186
	PE	Singer Co.	General Precision Equip. Corp.	322
	PE	Occidental Petroleum	Hooker Chemical Corp.	366
	PE	Occidental Petroleum	Island Creek Coal Co.	115
	C	Ling-Temco-Vought, Inc.	Jones & Laughlin Steel Corp.	1,092
	PE	Owens-Illinois, Inc. (bottles)	Lily-Tulip Cup Corp.	108
	C	Loew's Theatres, Inc.	Lorillard Corp. (cigarettes)	375
	C	Tenneco Corp. (gas pipelines and industrial)	Newport News Shipbuilding & Dry Dock Co.	139
	C	Kennecott Copper Corp.	Peabody Coal Co.	315
	ME	Northwest Industries	Philadelphia & Reading Corp. (R.R. etc.)	318

H = horizontal, V = vertical, ME = market extension, PE = product extension, and C = "pure" conglomerate.

TABLE 8–1 (concluded)

Year	Type	Acquiring Company	Acquired Company	Assets ($ million)
	H	Wheeling Steel Corp.	Pittsburgh Steel Co.	193
	C	IT&T	Rayonier, Inc. (fibers, fabrics)	296
	C	Glen Alden Corp. (textiles)	Schenley Industries, Inc. (liquor)	570
	ME	Sun Oil Co.	Sunray DX Oil Co.	749
1969	C	American Standard Inc. (plumbing equipment)	Westinghouse Air Brake Co.	302
	C	General Host Corp. (conglomerate)	Armour & Co. (meat)	560
	V	Crane Co. (construction equipment)	C.F. & I. Steel Corp	235
	C	IT&T	Grinnell Corp. (alarm systems)	184
	ME	Amerada Petroleum	Hess Oil & Chemical	491
	C	Norwich Pharmacal	Morton International (salt, etc.)	163
	PE	Xerox Corp. (copying equipment)	Scientific Data Systems (computers)	113
	H	Atlantic Richfield (oil)	Sinclair Oil Corp.	1,851
1970	C	Greyhound Corp. (buses, etc.)	Armour	607
	ME	Standard Oil of Ohio	British Petrol. Hold/BP Co. Ltd.	627
	V	Cleveland-Cliffs Iron (ore)	Detroit Steel Corp.	145
	H	Honeywell, Inc. (computers, office equipment)	General Electric Computer Components (from G.E. Co.)	547
	PE	American Motors Corp.	Kaiser Jeep Corp. (from Kaiser Industries)	168
	PE	Nestle Alimentana	Libby, McNeil & Libby (foods)	267
	H	Warner Lambert (drugs)	Parke Davis & Co. (drugs)	399
1971	H	National Steel Corp.	Granite City Steel Co.	312
1972	PE	Colgate-Palmolive Co. (toiletries)	Kendall Co. (health products, etc.)	194

H = horizontal, V = vertical, ME = market extension, PE = product extension, and C = "pure" conglomerate.
Source: Bureau of Economics, Federal Trade Commission.

ate mergers had come undone. Table 8–2 shows a few which came to grief: there were many others.

Elsewhere, there were also merger waves, primarily breeding horizontal mergers, some with very high market shares. In Britain, France, Germany, and Japan, major new dominant firms capable of facing the American grants were formed in several industries—autos, electrical

Richard Knapp, Business Week

Felix Rohatyn (of the New York investment banking firm, Lazard Freres & Co.), the most prolific merger arranger. Born 1929. Involved with at least 43 significant mergers during 1964–73, including such ITT mergers as Airport Parking, Levitt & Sons, Rayonier, Continental Baking, Canteen Corp., Grinnell, Hartford Fire and Casualty Co., and Eurofind. Also RCA's acquisitions of Random House, Hertz, Stamper Foods and Coronet Industries; and McDonnell-Douglas, Owens-Illinois—Lily Tulip, Loew's-Lorillard, Atlantic Richfield-Sinclair Oil, Kinney-Warner Brothers and AMP-Head Ski. A leader among hundreds of active merger arrangers working in major financial centers.

equipment, steel, computers, aircraft, and others. The worldwide bear market since 1971, plus growing doubts about the benefits of size, has reduced this boom.

The current status of U.S. merger activity and policy needs to be interpreted in this perspective. The basic industrial structure continues in parallel with a variety of merger events which might alter that structure. But mergers are no longer a major cause of industrial change in the U.S. The industrial structure (including many solid old conglomerates) is not likely to change by means of merger activity.

TABLE 8–2
Mergers by Mistake

	Value of Merger or Demerger	
Merger Partners	Acquisition ($ million)	Later Sale or Other Result ($ million)
Heublein		
Hamm's Beer	$62(1965)	~$10(1973)
Leasco (now Reliance)		
Pergamon Press (U.K.)	$60(1969)	~$4(1974)
ITT		
Levitt (the largest housing developer)	~$90(1967)	~$12(1975)
Pennsylvania R.R.		
New York Central R.R.	$2,400(1968)	Bankruptcy in 1971
Slater, Walker (U.K.)		
Franklin Stores (U.S.)	$15 (May, 1973)	$8 (May, 1974)

MERGER POLICIES

The formal evolution of merger policies came mainly during the 1950s and 60s. There was series of landmark decisions, which illustrate neatly how antitrust law can grow. The sequence also shows how objective research and new concepts filter into judicial thinking and take affect.

Even well before 1950, some mergers were constrained by antitrust agencies, on an informal basis.[12] Although events aborted the first series of Section 2 actions after 1914, an implicit limit on most dominant-firm mergers remained. Even in the Roaring Twenties, when antitrust was at a low ebb, the leading dominant firms in major markets were well aware that any substantial merger activity on their part would trigger an agency attack. By 1950, leading firms were established in many industries, and many of these firms were also conglomerates (such as General Electric, Westinghouse, chemicals firms, RCA). In the financial sector the two Banking Acts of 1933 and 1935 had neatly fenced off banking from other economic sectors. Accordingly, banks were free from takeover, as also were utilities (see Chapter 15). Various state and federal banking laws also made it difficult if not impossible for banking firms to change structure by branching or other competitive devices.

In short, the strict merger treatments since 1958 came upon a scene containing well-established industrial and financial positions of market power. Rather than prevent the growth of incipient market power in industry or finance, merger policies could only aspire to avert further rises in market power by secondary firms.

The 1950 amendment to Clayton Act Section 7 was critical in making

---

[12] See S. N. Whitney, *Antitrust Policies* (New York: Twentieth Century Fund, 1958, 2 vols), and recall Chapter 7 above.

possible, for the first time, a meaningful treatment of mergers. After a slow start, policy evolved quickly: by 1966 most significant horizontal mergers were effectively ruled out, as were most vertical and some conglomerate mergers. By 1973, the agencies had brought over 300 merger actions and had not ultimately lost a single important case or point in court.

Coverage. Coverage by the Division and FTC has grown. The older convention of exempting regulated industries has been eroded, after strenuous and resource-absorbing efforts especially by the Division under Turner. Among the sectors retrieved since 1960 are banking, insurance, shipping, airlines, railroads, broadcasting, electricity, gas, and telephones. The agencies must often take regulatory agencies to court in order to assert and maintain their jurisdiction over mergers. They have gotten no additional resources to handle these added tasks. And this new merger coverage does not enable them to go further and reduce existing dominance.

There are now few sectors wholly exempt from merger treatment. Yet many individual mergers which clearly reduce competition have recently been forced through as exceptions. In practice, the agencies' strict treatment does have loopholes. (This roughly parallels the exemptions from the *per se* treatment of price-fixing; recall chapter 6).

Procedure. Much policy is applied under the surface. Firms often come in ahead of time to urge officials not to oppose a planned merger.[13] Negotiations and threats may grow quite complex, and many times the Divisions' threat or decision to sue will cause a proposed merger to fold. Mergers are often modified to fit antitrust criteria. Take-over targets often rush in to demand of the agencies that they stop the merger, "to protect competition" (as well as their own skins). Actual court cases often merely signal that informal bargaining has broken down, or that a new policy line is being set.

The normal regimen is as follows:

1. Firms planning to merge may quietly sound out an agency beforehand, finding out what modifications might be necessary to make it acceptable.
2. A merger plan is announced by one or both firms, with shareholders to approve in a month or two and the merger to follow shortly after.
3. If the agency suspects or knows that the merger will reduce competition, it asks for delay—usually one to three months—while it studies and decides. During that time, negotiations and advance notice may occur. The agency's decision usually fits within the Guidelines given below.
4. If the agency opposes, it files suit and asks the judge for a temporary injunction against the merger until the issues have been aired in trial.
5. At trial, the agency need only show that competition is likely to be reduced (in line with precedent; see the Guidelines). The firm must

---

[13] Often the lawyers for a firm have warned it that the merger will be opposed. But the managers will try their luck, and frequently they succeed, to the lawyers' mingled annoyance and amusement.

TABLE 8–3
Justice Department Merger Guidelines: Mergers Which Will Probably Be Challenged

---

Market definition. There may be several appropriate "markets" in which to test the competitive effects of a merger. Both "product" and "geographic" dimensions are relevant.

Economies will not usually serve to prevent a challenge by the Department, because they are hard to evaluate and are often available by other routes.

---

1. *Horizontal Mergers.* Criteria are mainly market structure.
    a. In highly concentrated markets (over 75% in the four largest firms), these shares will normally not be challenged:

Acquiring firm	Acquired firm
4%	4%
10%	2%
15%	1%

    b. In medium concentrated markets, the limits are looser:

Acquiring firm	Acquired firm
5%	5%
10%	4%
15%	3%
20%	2%

    c. If market concentration has been increasing, all mergers involving over 2% will be challenged.
    d. Also, *any* acquisition of a competitor which is unusually competitive or has unusual competitive advantages.
    e. Failing firms are exempt if they would clearly fail and have tried to make other mergers which fit the guidelines.
2. *Vertical Mergers.* Mergers which foreclose competition and raise entry barriers are to be challenged. Normally,
    a. If a firm that is a customer for a product makes 6% of the purchases and a firm supplying the product makes 10% of the sales, unless their merger raises no significant barrier to entry, or
    b. If a firm that is a customer for a product has 10% of its own market, if the product is essential to its business, and if a firm supplying the product makes 20% of the sales, or
    c. If a customer or a supplier is acquired by a major firm in an industry with a significant trend toward vertical integration, if such a combination would raise barriers to entry, and if it does not promise to cut the costs of production, or
    d. If a customer or a supplier is acquired for the purpose of barring competitors from the market or otherwise putting them at a disadvantage, or
    e. If the acquired firm is not genuinely failing (see above),
    then the merger will be challenged.
3. *Conglomerate Mergers.* Since policy is still formative, at least these categories of merger will normally be challenged:
    a. If a firm that has a large share of a market seeks to acquire a firm that is the only potential entrant to the market or one of the only two potential entrants.
    b. If a merger creates the danger of substantial reciprocal buying.
    c. If the merger creates severe disparity in size between the acquired firm and its competitors, or gives advertising advantages, or otherwise gives leverage to the acquired firm.
    d. (Since 1969.) If any of the largest 200 industrial firms seeks to acquire any significant other firm (roughly, above $10 million in assets).
    e. If other anticompetitive effects appear to follow.

show the merger to be innocent. If the merger is held to violate Clayton 7, it is permanently enjoined.

6. At any time a consent decree may be reached, whose provisions can reach beyond this merger into other actions by the firms (e.g., prohibiting certain other mergers by the firms for a period of years). Or either side may withdraw.

Time and the burden of proof favor the agencies. Mergers can be delayed or stopped cold with minimal effort. And since 1950 the agencies have been upheld by the courts in every major action they brought and on every point of legal interpretation involving mergers.[14]

The main lines of U.S. merger policy were codified in 1968 in guidelines issued by the Division (see Table 8–3 for details).[15] The Division (and the FTC) is likely to challenge any significant horizontal merger, especially if the market's concentration is high or rising. Vertical mergers are not quite as strictly limited. Conglomerate mergers must not reduce potential competition or breed reciprocity; and they may give toeholds but not dominant positions. FTC rules are similar but slightly stricter on conglomerates.[16] The agencies will usually not be deterred by claims that the mergers will achieve economies. Rather, they require hard evidence, which would stand up in court, that there are net economies which can only be achieved by merger.

The margins and directions of treatment are still evolving, but the main lines set since 1960 look remarkably firm. They are much tighter than in other countries. We now consider how they took form since 1957.

HORIZONTAL MERGERS

Formal treatment began with the Bethlehem-Youngstown case of 1958, tightened with Brown Shoe in 1962, and Rome Cable and El Paso Natural Gas in 1964, and reached its present lines with Von's Grocery in 1966.

Bethlehem-Youngstown. The first case to be brought before the courts by the government under the new law involved a proposed merger between Bethlehem Steel and Youngstown Sheet & Tube. Bethlehem, the nation's second largest steel producer, had notified the Department of Justice in 1956 that it planned to acquire Youngstown, the sixth largest, thus raising its own share of the nation's output from 15 percent to 20 percent, and the share of U.S. Steel and Bethlehem together from 45 percent to 50 percent. The Department sued to enjoin the merger, and

---

[14] This may reflect phenomenally strict policy. Or it may show that the agencies were too far below the correct margin of policy, giving the Court no range of choice. Try to decide which it was; or both.

[15] Drafting the Guidelines, in which the junior author took part, involved codifying the court precedents and the economic analysis which underlies them. All leading law firms and companies were already fully aware of the precedents. The Guidelines simply make them more widely and consistently available to lesser firms.

[16] The FTC has issued guidelines only for specific industries, including dairy products, food chains, cement, and tires.

the case went to trial in 1958 under Judge Edward Weinfeld in a federal district court.[17]

The defense argued that the merger would make the industry more competitive, since it would enable Bethlehem to compete more effectively with U.S. Steel. It directed the court's attention, in particular, to the market near Chicago. Here, Bethlehem had no plant and shipped in less than 1 percent of its output. By acquiring and expanding Youngstown's Chicago facilities, it would provide more vigorous competition for U.S. Steel in this area. It declared that it would not otherwise enter the market.

These contentions were rejected by Judge Weinfeld, who was not persuaded that the merger afforded the only means by which the supply of steel in the Chicago area could be increased. In any case, he said, the argument was irrelevant, since Congress "made no distinction between good mergers and bad mergers. It condemned all which came within the reach of the prohibition of Section 7." The merger was enjoined.[18] Bethlehem did not appeal. In three years it *did* indeed enter the Chicago market by building a large plant at Burns Ditch!

Brown Shoe. The Supreme Court's first decision under the Celler-Kefauver Act was handed down by a unanimous court in the Brown Shoe case in 1962.[19] The Brown Shoe Company, which manufactured 4.0 percent of the nation's output of shoes, had acquired the Kinney Company, which manufactured 0.5 percent. Brown was the third largest distributor of shoes with 1,230 retail stores; Kinney the eighth with 350 stores. In certain local markets for particular types of shoes, the combined share of the two concerns amounted to 20 percent or more.

The Court put less emphasis on the existing structure of the market than on the historical trend toward increasing concentration in the shoe industry. "We cannot avoid the mandate of Congress," it said, "that tendencies toward concentration in industry are to be curbed in their incipiency, particularly when these tendencies are being accelerated through giant steps striding across a hundred cities at a time. In the light of the trends in this industry, we agree . . . that this is an appropriate place at which to call a halt."[20]

The Court observed that Congress did not intend to prevent a merger between two small companies that would enable them to compete better with larger ones or a merger between a corporation which is financially healthy and one that is failing and is thus unable effectively to compete. But *incipiency* was established as a criterion, where an important market is rising in concentration.

Alcoa-Rome. The Court went on, in 1964, to uphold the application

---

[17] At first Division officials regarded the merger as immune from suit. But one staff economist, Harrison F. Houghton, persisted in doing a massive study of the industry and these firms. He discovered enough overlaps in submarkets to justify a try in court, which resulted in a "great victory" (recall chapter 5).

[18] *U.S.* v. *Bethlehem Steel Corp.,* 168 F. Supp. 756.

[19] *Brown Shoe Co.* v. *U.S.,* 370 U.S. 294.

[20] *Ibid.,* p. 345.

of the law in cases where an acquired firm produced a tiny portion of total output and where the competition of such a firm was only potential. The Aluminum Company of America, producing 27.8 percent of aluminum conductor output, had purchased the Rome Cable Corporation, producing only 1.3 percent. But the Court found that Rome was "an aggressive competitor . . . a pioneer" with "special aptitude and skill . . . and an effective research and sales organization." It was "the prototype of the small independent that Congress aimed to preserve by Section 7."[21]

El Paso. The El Paso Natural Gas Company, the only firm bringing gas into California, had acquired the Pacific Coast Pipeline Company, which operated outside the state. Pacific had attempted to enter the California market without success. But its efforts, said the Court, "had a powerful influence on El Paso's business attitudes."[22] Its potential competition should be preserved. In both *Alcoa-Rome* and *El Paso,* the Court ordered divestiture.

Von's Grocery. This case set the seal on horizontal limits, in 1966. It involved the merger of two retail food chains in Los Angeles. Von's Grocery, the third largest food chain in the area, had acquired the Shopping Bag, the sixth largest, thus moving into second place. But Von's share of the market, after the merger, was only 7.5 percent. The share of all the market leaders was declining, and there was no barrier to the entry of new concerns. But the Court noted that the number of stores operated by individual owners had fallen. And it found the merger to be unlawful on the ground that it was the purpose of the law "to prevent concentration in the American economy by keeping a large number of small competitors in business."[23]

Yet this new strict policy on horizontal mergers in mainstream industrial cases has been perforated by a series of exceptions. These exceptions include the Atlantic-Richfield (now Arco) merger in 1966, the Penn-Central Merger in 1968, the merger between the McDonnell and Douglas aircraft companies in 1967, a series of newspaper mergers, the merger between the two professional football leagues in 1967, and the merger between the Warner-Lambert and Parke, Davis drug companies in 1970.[24] Some failing-firm mergers have also been permitted.[25] This par-

---

[21] *U.S.* v. *Aluminum Co. of America,* 377 U.S. 271, 280.

[22] *U.S.* v. *El Paso Natural Gas Co.,* 376 U.S. 651, 659. This remarkable case dragged on for some 16 years, with El Paso using every opportunity for delay.

[23] *U.S.* v. *Von's Grocery Co.,* 384 U.S. 280 (1966). There were sharp minority dissents in both Brown Shoe and Von's Grocery, arguing that the effect of the mergers would be trivial or procompetitive. The minorities were basically setting a higher burden of proof on the government.

[24] Also, the National Steel-Granite City Steel merger in 1971 involved 70 markets with overlaps exceeding the Guidelines. But it was permitted. This and Warner-Lambert may be freakish, since cases were blocked by the Attorney General's office in direct violation of the traditional independence of the Division.

[25] These are mostly in the beer industry, where smaller local brands have been dying. Yet "failing" is often deceptive. In the Rupert-Rheingold case in 1968, Rheingold gave accounting data to show that losses were already occurring, sales plummeting, and plants were obsolete. Making it divest Rupert's brand name would ensure bankruptcy. The case was withdrawn. Within 6 months Rheingold was booming; within a year its common stock doubled in value.

Also, the GE and RCA computer divisions were sold, after severe losses, to other computer firms in 1970 and 1972.

allels the general rule seen in Chapter 6 on conspiracy: as a policy line tightens up, more exceptions to it will be found.

Is strictness good economics? Most experts now say yes. In few cases will the policy stop genuine net economies from occurring (recall Bethlehem's going into the Chicago market after all). The treatment is clean and quick, sparing of public and private resources. Genuine net economies can still be proven by the firms, to the agencies or in court. Exceptions may be irrational in actual cases, but they are possible where justified.

VERTICAL MERGERS

Vertical merger policy has not had a steady evolution. Most cases present unique features, and claimed economies are often provable. The Yellow Cab decision in 1947, Paramount in 1948 and A&P in 1949 had established that vertical integration could not be used to foreclose competition at either level. But specific practices had been adduced in these cases: no general rule against vertical integration *per se* was applied. Since then the Court has drawn closer limits, nearly accepting that a large rise in vertical integration is *per se* likely to have the effect of foreclosing competition and raising entry barriers.

du Pont-General Motors.   The case was filed in 1949, alleging that du Pont's holding of GM stock gave it preference in the market for automobile fabrics and finishes (recall Chapter 7). The district court acquitted in 1954, saying that a loss of competition had not been proven. On appeal, the Supreme Court reversed by 4 to 2, citing the original Clayton Section 7.[26] The shares were divested, after a special law was passed in 1961 easing the tax burden on du Pont heirs from the forced sale.[27]

Vertical integration had only been partial, and the decision set a moderate limit on the market shares held by the firms.

Brown Shoe.   The Brown case had vertical aspects too. Brown made shoes and Kinney sold shoes. The Court looked less at the small market shares than at Brown's likely policy of requiring Kinney to carry only Brown Shoes. This would foreclose competition in a market which already had rising concentration.

The economic analysis underlying the problems—and these cases—must be complex and quantitatively imprecise. But the present policy lines do roughly reflect the best judgments about where the limits should be set. There is room for distinct economies to be proven and needed exceptions to be made.

CONGLOMERATE MERGERS

The backdrop of policy toward conglomerate mergers includes many old blue-ribbon conglomerates, established with major shares for many decades. The new conglomerates have mostly been corporate raiders (or

---

[26] *U.S.* v. *du Pont,* 353 U.S. 586 (1957).

[27] Despite asserted fears that the sale would send du Pont shares down, in fact the price tended more to rise than fall.

trivial houses of cards). An efficient policy will reap the efficiency-inducing effects of conglomerate mergers while filtering out the possible reductions in competition.

The share of new conglomerates in the 1960s wave was large but still less than half. Old conglomerates and unified firms dominated. But the new operators, working as outsiders in a slow-changing industrial scene, drew attention and criticism that were frantic at times. In financial circles and the business press, they were variously said to be wizards, hucksters and destroyers. In Britain, they are called "asset strippers." They really were part of the normal process of corporate renewal by new blood (recall Chapter 2). Their leaders included:

International Telephone and Telegraph. ITT was before 1960 a foreign twin of AT&T, operating many telephone systems abroad. After 1960 it shifted to take-overs of a string of dominant firms in middle-sized industries.[28] It acted only when cost savings of at least 20 percent could be foreseen. It tended more to redirect old managers than sack them. The leading raider of blue-chip firms, it rose to eighth largest industrial firm in 1970. It avoided reliance on weapons sales, and used private antitrust suits to challenge mergers by other firms. It survived a severe antitrust attack in 1969–71. When its political machinations were exposed in 1972–74, the corporate establishment predictably rushed *not* to defend it.

Litton Industries. An early and respectable science-based conglomerate, Litton began in the 1950s. It acquired second-echelon firms and added scientific capabilities. Slightly reliant on military sales, it had severe adjustment problems after 1966 but was still 36th largest in 1970.

Ling-Temco-Vought, (LTV), masterminded by James Ling, took over

FIGURE 8–4

New Conglomerates: Riding the Roller-coaster

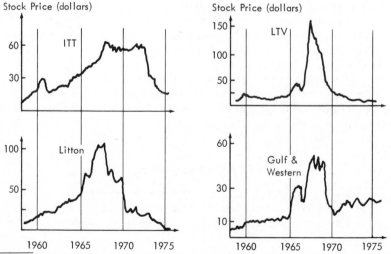

[28] See Anthony Sampson, *The Sovereign State of ITT* (New York: Fawcett, 1973) for a thorough, critical account.

a series of improvable and ever-larger firms during 1960–68, ending with Jones & Laughlin (6th largest in steel) in 1968. It was the 15th largest industrial firm in 1970. Ling was unique in keeping branches partly separate, with public accounts. Heavily reliant on military sales, it was broken after 1968 by a drop in weapons contracts and McLaren's anti-trust attack.

Gulf and Western Industries. This grew from auto parts and sugar to a wide variety of products, including movies, paper, and metals. It tried to take over Armour in 1968 and A&P in 1973, among various unconsummated deals. It avoided serious antitrust and management problems but not the general market disillusion with conglomerates. Its actions are highly publicized, though it was only 65th largest in 1970 and 79th largest in 1973.

The new conglomerates are usually built up by one remarkable founder, whose power and genius—and alleged villainy—come to be much exaggerated. Nearly all the new conglomerates have been hammered by share-price falls, caused in some degree by public policy actions.

There were sharp turns in policy, as the wave of mergers mounted. One doctrine after another was tried, by the Division and the FTC, all of them speculative. Before 1969, the agencies usually let the burden of proof favor the conglomerates, since direct effects on competition were not provably large. Though Turner was denounced for inaction—both by blue-ribbon corporate interests *and* by critics of big business!—his moderate line has been mostly vindicated by events.[29] In 1969, McLaren made a broadscale attack on conglomerat mergers, with LTV and ITT the main targets. This helped to stop the merger wave, but the attack was compromised before reaching the Supreme Court for a clear decision on the merits.

Therefore, policy remains unclear, a mixture of possible grounds upon which a conglomerate merger might be challenged. The agencies have focused on the danger of reciprocity, on potential entry, on size-disparity and the unfair advantages which a branch might acquire, on the toehold doctrine, and finally on a frank anti-bigness approach.

Reciprocity. An early case, decided in 1965, cited reciprocal buying. The Consolidated Foods Corporation, operating a nationwide chain of groceries and buying large quantities of processed food, had acquired Gentry, Inc., a small whoesaler making a third of the nation's sales of dehydrated onions and garlic (from such small cases large decisions often sprout!). Consolidated was thus enabled to require the food processors who sold to it to buy their onions and garlic from Gentry, thereby excluding Gentry's competitors from its market for these commodities. The Court held that the reciprocity made possible by the merger was anticompetitive. "We do not say," it went on, "that any acquisition, no matter how small, violates Section 7 if there is a probability of reciprocal buying . . . But where, as here, the acquisition is of a company that commands a substantial share of the market, a finding of probability of

---

[29] His basic position is given in "Conglomerate Mergers and Section 7 of the Clayton Act," *Harvard Law Review,* 1965.

reciprocal buying by the Commission should be honored."[30] The later big cases in 1969 broadened this, to urge that a gaint conglomerate could not escape the likelihood of *some* reciprocity and competitive loss in *some* of its markets.[31]

Reciprocity actually has only shallow roots and effects in most cases. Being a tangible act, it carries some weight in court, sufficient to tip some conglomerate merger cases. Yet—another irony—significant reciprocity by older existing conglomerates has never stirred major court action (instead, it usually occurs in single-industry firms, as in steel).

Loss of a Potential Competitor.   Recall that if a potential entrant X comes in by merger, a net loss of competition may result. Practical cases grow complex: was firm X *really* a potential entrant? Was competition reduced by enough to offset other gains?

The first case testing the doctrine failed. Pennsalt Chemicals and Olin Mathieson Chemical had formed in 1960 a joint venture, Penn-Olin Chemical, to sell sodium chlorate in the southeastern U.S. Since 1951 Pennsalt had considered entering this market; Olin had considered it since 1958. Would the joint venture prevent their entering separately? The Supreme Court ultimately said *No* in 1967, after a long series of appeals and remands.[32] But the vote was 4–4, and the case had distinctive features.

In Kennecott-Peabody, the FTC found evidence that Kennecott Copper Corp. had planned to enter coal-mining directly, before buying Peabody Coal (one of the largest producers) in 1967. The merger was finally prevented in 1974, even though the evidence on intent could be said to be inconclusive.[33]

More informally, a number of large mergers were stopped by threatening to bring suits based on potential entry. Two examples among many: in 1968, Bethlehem Steel's attempt to buy Cerro (the 5th largest copper firm) for $300 million was abandoned. Caterpillar Tractor's proposed merger with Chicago Pneumatic Tool—to fill out its product line—was also dropped when the Division said it would sue. Yet the appraisal of Bethlehem as "a leading potential entrant" into copper had to draw on speculative impressions and soft data.

There has been growing recognition that potential entry has complex relations to competition and is difficult to judge. Therefore, its role in conglomerate merger policy has rightly faded.

Toehold.   This has become the most general current doctrine.[34] Its rationale—that mergers with lesser firms will increase competition—

---

[30] *FTC* v. *Consolidated Foods Corporation,* 380 U.S. 592.

[31] E.g., LTV owned Braniff Airways. Airplane tail sections contain steel. If LTV owned Jones & Laughlin, it might buy planes only from aircraft companies that bought steel from J & L. This was only one specific charge, but it was alleged and accepted that other reciprocity was inevitable.

[32] *U.S.* v. *Penn-Olin Chemicals Co.,* 389 U.S. 308 (1967).

[33] A memo in Kennecott files discussing new entry into the coal industry—before the merger—was said by Kennecott officials to be only speculative and not part of company planning.

[34] It was advanced by a Presidential Commission on Antitrust in 1968, and in J. S. Campbell and W. G. Shepherd, "Leading-Firm Conglomerate Mergers," *Antitrust Bulletin,* 1968, pp. 1361–82.

was noted in Section 2 above. It was first strikingly applied in the P & G-Clorox decision of 1967. Procter & Gamble is the leading toiletries and detergents maker. It is also the nation's largest advertiser, spending over $175 million in 1967.

It bought Clorox, which held 50 percent of national bleach sales (71 percent in the Middle Atlantic region), compared to less than 15 percent for Purex, the next largest. Though bleach is a standard product, it is intensively advertised: Clorox spent 10 percent of revenues on advertising. P & G's TV advertising discounts and general power were held likely by the Court to entrench Clorox.[35]

The advantage was advertising, but the basic concept was the toehold. P&G could have purchased a lesser firm, to build it up. Clorox was divested in 1968. In 1968, the Court similarly required General Foods to divest S.O.S., the leading maker of steel-wool scouring pads.[36]

Toehold was a part of McLaren's 1969 attack on ITT, LTV, and Northwest Industries, which aimed to get a definitive ruling on conglomerates from the Supreme Court.[37] ITT's control of Canteen Corp., Continental Baking, Avis, Levitt, Sheraton Hotels, Grinnell, and Hartford Fire Insurance was held likely to entrench these leading firms (though only Canteen, Grinnell, and Hartford were formally challenged). With LTV, the dominance issue was far less clear, since J & L ranked only sixth in steel. As the cases moved along, there was intensive negotiations for compromise. McLaren urged appeals on up to the Supreme Court, to get a decision on the merits. But then compromises were reached, requiring some divestiture and curbs on future mergers.[38] LTV had to sell J & L and was, in any case, so damaged that it soon liquidated most of its holdings.

Therefore the toe-hold doctrine is not enshrined in precedent, but it is part of agency practice.

Bigness. This was also important in McLaren's attack, and in June 1969, it was even announced that *all* significant mergers by any of the 250 largest firms were likely to be challenged. This streched antitrust doctrine beyond competitive effects into the realm of global concentration and larger social policy. It also gave perfect safety from take-over for these large firms—a very large part of the corporate establishment. This rule has been relaxed moderately since 1969, but bigness is still one element which makes a merger more likely to be challenged.

To sum it up, a conglomerate merger is vulnerable if it involves: (1) a dominant firm, (2) a large firm, (3) a clear probability of reciprocity,

---

[35] *FTC* v. *Procter & Gamble,* 386 U.S. 568 (1967). This effect was affirmed by an episode in Pennsylvania, where P & G had helped Clorox defeat an attempt by Purex to enter the market significantly.

[36] *FTC* v. *General Foods Corp.,* 386 F. 2d 836; 391 U.S. 919 *Certiorari denied.*

[37] The cases cited nearly all of the possible doctrines against conglomerates. This kitchen-sink or scatter-gun approach was legally untidy, but it would have given the Court a full range of doctrines to choose among in setting the rules on conglomerate mergers. Northwest's inclusion reflected a frantic attempt by Goodrich to avoid take-over by an outside company. Here, and in resisting General Host's take-over of Armour in 1968, the Division was invoked to aid take-over targets, probably *against* the true social interest.

[38] ITT was given a Hobson's choice, between giving up Hartford and giving up Canteen, Grinnell, and four other holdings. It chose to keep Hartford, but that too has run afoul of more recent tax rulings and Congressional investigations. See Sampson, *op. cit.*

or (4) a potential entrant. Existing conglomerates are many, large, and untouched. In part these policy lines fit economic criteria. But they have virtually eliminated the influence of take-over from the main core of industrial firms.[39] To this extent, the normal market for assets and control has been abridged.

OTHER COUNTRIES

The U.K. offers interesting parallels, as usual.

Mergers have grown since 1960 (see Figure 8–5), with many of them horizontal. They have helped along a marked increase in concentration since 1958. Only since 1965 has the Monopolies Commission formally screened mergers, *if* the Board of Trade decides they need screening. During 1965–73 only 20 mergers out of some 833 total were referred, though 121 of the mergers would give market shares over 50 percent.[40] Of the 20 mergers studied, 7 were dropped before decision, 6 were opposed and 7 were found to be "not against the public interest."

Since 1973 the Office of Fair Trading pre-screens and refers mergers

FIGURE 8–5
Merger Trend in Britain since 1965

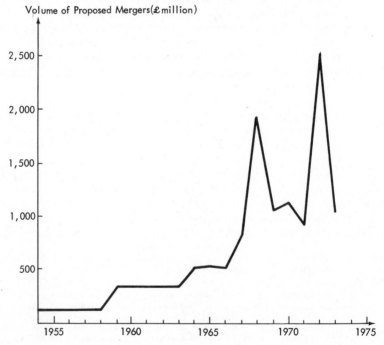

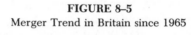

---

[39] Of course the very largest 25 or so firms are so large as to be free of real take-over threat in any case.

[40] J. D. Gribbin, "The Operation of the Mergers Panel since 1965," *Trade and Industry,* Her Majesty's Stationery Office, London, January 17, 1974, pp. 70–73.

more thoroughly. Mergers are investigated intensively if they involve large size (over $12 million) or market shares (over 25 percent).

Generally, dominant firms cannot make horizontal mergers, but the limits for smaller firms are not as tight as in the U.S. The cult of bigness—which fostered large mergers during 1964–69 to meet global competition—has faded. A variety of conditions are considered in screening mergers, and so no clear guidelines are possible.[41]

On the Continent, most dominant firms informally are aware that large horizontal mergers may be challenged in some way. But there is little constraint on other mergers, either in individual countries or in the Common Market as a whole. The Common Market Commission's Competition Department challenged Continental Can's merger with a Dutch firm, Thomassen En Drijver, in 1969. Continental dominates cans in the EEC, and Thomassen was one of its few rivals. The EEC court in 1973 let this merger stand, while finding for the Commission "in principle." So far, there is a thin shell of EEC merger policy but no practical content.

In Japan, there is little clear policy at all, beyond strict prohibitions on foreign take-overs of Japanese firms.[42] A 1972 merger, creating Nippon Steel with a dominant share and second rank among all steel firms in the world, was permitted. Matters are settled by informal negotiations.

In most countries, there is no arm's-length formulation of policy, but rather a complex process of private negotiation, often involving private firms, financial units, and government offices. Commonly, national power and sovereignty become elements in the solution. This makes for murky procedure and criteria.

SUMMARY

Since 1960, U.S. merger policy has been extended to nearly all sectors. It has also been made more strict and consistent toward new mergers. The existing structure largely predates this new policy set, and old mergers have not been touched. Therefore the equity and economic effects of merger policy are little known and highly debatable.

The lines are reasonably clear. Horizontal mergers may not appreciably increase market shares, especially if market concentration has been high or rising. Vertical mergers may not affect large shares, or otherwise be likely to reduce competition. Conglomerate mergers usually must not involve dominant, large or potential-entrant firms, nor make reciprocity likely. Yet there are frequent special exceptions, and the mass of smaller and local businesses are exempt in practice.

The policies are mainly rational in the small; constraining market shares and promoting entry. But they have come to exclude the take-over process from the main body of established firms. And they appear to harden industrial structure, by keeping smaller firms from merging to approach the positions which larger firms already have.

Once can regard U.S. treatment as seeming strict but still (1) permit-

---

[41] An attempt at guidelines was made in 1969; see Board of Trade, *Guidelines for Assessing Mergers,* H.M.S.O., 1969.

[42] See Eleanor M. Hadley, *op. cit.*

ting large exceptions and (2) tending to shield large and dominant firms. Or one can view it as much the strictest and—case by case—most procompetitive merger policy in the world. Once again, the critical factor is whether high market shares tend to fade away quickly, slowly or not at all (recall Chapter 2).

In any event, the antitrust agencies are still groping for the efficient margins and inner balance. A revival of conglomerate mergers could force more testing of their role and treatment. Meanwhile, the horizontal and vertical criteria seem likely to change little. The ultimate effects and wisdom of this remain speculative: make your own interpretation.

CHAPTER NINE

Patents

A patent is a monopoly grant to an inventor, giving control over the production and selling of a new product or technique for 17 years. The resulting monopoly is virtually absolute and often lasts long after the patent's formal life is over. Over 80,000 patents yearly are awarded in the U.S. Among this flood of new ideas is a small number of sensationally successful ones, many useful ones, and thousands of stillborn flashes of genius.[1]

The issue is important. Technical progress is the ultimate economic salvation from national and global scarcity. It derives from widespread processes of invention and innovation, which involve at least $30 billion

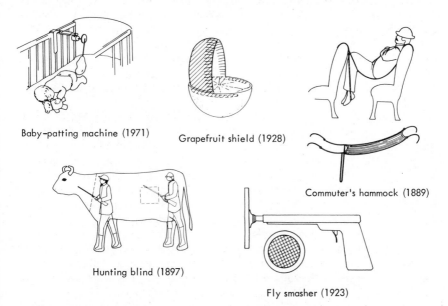

Baby-patting machine (1971)   Grapefruit shield (1928)

Commuter's hammock (1889)

Hunting blind (1897)

Fly smasher (1923)

---

[1] Table 9-2 lists some of the landmark inventions and patents.

yearly in nearly every nook and cranny of the economy. Patenting may enhance or impair this effort. In any event, it creates much monopoly profits, and it poses antitrust issues in several important industries.

Patents pose basic questions about the origins of progress and their relation to market power. Patents grant monopoly, which may last long. Yet patents may be an integral part of the process of progress and competition (recall Schumpeter). In this chapter, we first describe the patent system. Next we analyze the basic economics of patents. Then we consider the antitrust problems raised by patent policies, and possible reforms. Trademarks are also briefly reviewed.

The wisdom of the patent system is endlessly debated, but the system itself is highly resistant to change. Here the twin problems of progress and competition are brought together in the clearest possible focus.

THE PATENT SYSTEM

The U.S. system, like most others, gives a monopoly to the inventor. It processes and stores these new ideas, validating them (after a delay when they are "pending"), and making the invention public.

A patent is an exclusive right conferred on an inventor, for a limited period, by a government. It authorizes the inventor to make, use, transfer, or withhold whatever may be patented. This he might do in any case; what the patent adds is the right to exclude others or to admit them on his own terms. Without a patent, he might attempt to preserve a monopoly by keeping his invention secret; to get a patent, it must be disclosed.

The policy of promoting invention by granting temporary monopolies to inventors, a policy that had been followed in England for nearly two centuries, was written into the Constitution of the United States. The framers of the Constitution did not mention patents, but they did empower the Congress, in Article I, Section 8, Paragraph 8, "To promote the progress of Science and useful Arts, by securing for limited Times to Authors and Inventors the exclusive Right to their respective Writings and Discoveries. . . ."

Congress passed the first patent law in 1790, offering protection to all inventors of novel and useful processes and devices who would disclose their nature in sufficient detail to "enable a workman or other person skilled in the art of manufacture . . . to make, construct . . . or use the same." Under this law a committee composed of the Secretary of State (Thomas Jefferson, himself an inventor of some note), the Secretary of War, and the Attorney General granted 57 patents during the next three years.

In 1793 a second law relieved the cabinet officers of this burden, authorizing the Department of State to issue patents to everyone who might register inventions, without questioning their novelty or usefulness, leaving their validity to be determined by the courts. This act resulted in a flood of worthless patents and clogged the courts with litigation.

It was superseded in 1836, by a third law which set up a Patent Office under a Commissioner of Patents, required that applications be examined to determine whether the inventions claimed were really new, and

FIGURE 9-1

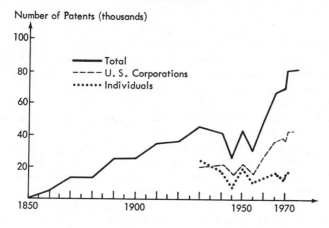

Number of Patents (thousands)

FIGURE 9-2

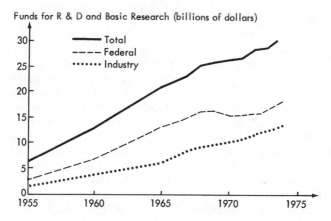

Funds for R & D and Basic Research (billions of dollars)

provided that patents should be issued only when such inventions were deemed by the Commissioner to be "sufficiently useful and important." The American patent system still rests upon the foundations established by the Act of 1836.

Patents have been obtainable in the United States since 1790 on any useful "art, manufacture, engine, machine," since 1793 on a "composition of matter," since 1842 on "ornamental designs," and since 1930 on botanical plants, and on improvements to any of them. The law thus covers processes of production (art, manufacture), the implements employed in such processes (engine, machine), and the products resulting from them (manufacture, composition of matter, and botanical plants). It covers, as a "composition of matter," not only such chemical products as dyestuffs, plastics, and synthetic fibers, but also foods and medicines—products to which the patent privilege is not generally extended under the laws of other countries.

Patents on "ornamental designs" may relate to the design of the article itself or to designs that are incorporated in it or affixed to it. Designs, however, may be protected more cheaply and for longer periods by obtaining copyrights. Design protection is afforded to products that are durable, such as jewelry and furniture. But fashions, in which the element of design is important, are neither patented nor copyrighted, not because the law exudes them, but because they change too rapidly to be protected by the usual legal processes. Patents are not granted on methods of doing business, or on fundamental scientific discoveries. But otherwise the law is generous in its coverage.

Patents are issued to individuals, not to corporations. under the law, a patent is granted only to a person called "the sole and true inventor." But patent rights can be transferred to others through assignment. An inventor may sell his rights in an invention he has already made. Or he may accept employment under a contract which binds him to transfer his rights in any invention that he may come to make.

In the usual case, he will file his assignment along with his application for a patent, and the corporation that employs him will be the assignee. In legal theory, patents are issued to individual inventors; in practice, 70 percent of them are assigned to corporations.

The territorial scope of a patent is limited to the jurisdiction of the country that grants it. An American who wishes to protect his invention in other countries must take out patents under their laws. Foreigners may likewise take out patents in the United States. A patent may be exploited in one country, in another, or in both, and rights in different countries may be assigned to different firms. Products that are patented may not be imported in violation of domestic patent rights.

Patent Life: An Historical Accident. In England in 1643 the duration of a patent was fixed at 14 years, a period sufficient to enable a craftsman to train two successive groups of apprentices. This term was adopted in the first patent law in the United States. In 1861, however, an effort to extend the term to 20 years resulted in a compromise that fixed it at 17, and 17 years is still the nominal duration of the monopoly conferred by the patent grant.

In most other countries the patent holder is required to put his invention to work. In some countries this requirement is absolute. In others, it may be waived if the holder can show good cause or prove that a reasonable effort has been made. Failure to work an invention may be penalized by revocation or by the requirement that it be licensed to others. Licensing may also be required where enforcement of one patent would prevent the development of an invention covered by another, where refusal to license would prejudice the trade of other groups, and where the output of patented goods falls short of meeting public needs.

No such obligations attach to patents issued by the United States. Within the limits laid down by the courts, the owner of a patent may refuse to work it, work it himself and refuse to license it to others, or license it on such terms as he may choose. In the lightness of its requirements, as in the breadth of its grants, the American patent law is extremely liberal.

How Patents Are Issued and Validated. It is the function of the Patent Office merely to accept or to reject the applications that are brought before it. Each application must describe, with some precision, the nature of the invention that is claimed. This description takes the form of drawings or formulae accompanied by exposition couched in technical phraseology; no working models have been required since 1890. The monopoly awarded to an applicant will be confined within the boundaries of his claims. These claims are usually formulated by a patent lawyer employed by the inventor or, more often, by the corporate assignee.

TABLE 9-1
Costs and Volumes of Patents Differ

Country	Minimum Amount of Fees and Other Costs of Patenting, per Patent, 1974	Numbers of Patents, 1971	
		Applied for	Granted
United States	$165	105,000	82,000
Britain	8	62,000	42,000
Holland	400	19,000	3,000
Sweden	130	18,000	11,000
Germany	165	64,000	19,000
Austria	14	13,000	10,000
Japan	43	107,000	38,000

Their preparation is an art in itself involving complex strategy decisions. The broader they can be made, without appearing to be limitless, the wider will be the area of the monopoly. The less informative they can be made, without appearing to withhold essential facts, the less is the likelihood that the technology involved will be disclosed to possible competitors. When the application, thus carefully prepared, is submitted to the Patent Office, it must be accompanied by a $65 fee. When the patent is obtained, another $100 must be paid. The fee or salary of the patent lawyer is the major cost of patenting. Comparative costs in various countries are given in Table 9-1.

Applications are not made public by the Patent Office. Persons who may hold patents on similar inventions are not informed of the proceedings. Persons who might be injured by a grant of monopoly are not notified. Agencies of government charged with the maintenance of competition are not represented. Interests adverse to the grant are given no opportunity to protest. Whether a patent shall be issued is determined as a matter not of public interest but of private privilege.

An invention is not supposed to be patented unless it is new and useful and actually works. But the number of applications presented to the Patent Office is so large, and the resources available for handling them are, by comparison, so small, that rigorous standards of appraisal cannot, in practice, be maintained. The Office does not undertake to determine whether an invention is workable; it has no laboratories or testing bureaus of its own; it lacks the funds and the time required to seek the technical advice of private agencies. With respect to usefulness, it adheres to the standard established by Justice Story in 1817. The word "useful," he said, "is incorporated in the Act in contradistinction to mischievous or immoral."[2] An invention is thus presumed to be useful unless there is evidence that it would do positive harm. Nor is there real assurance that the invention covered by a patent is new. The burden imposed on the Patent Office is so heavy and its resources, in comparison, so limited, that a thorough search of prior technology cannot be made.

Applications for patents run around 110,000 per year, with more than 200,000 pending at any one time, each of them being taken up in its turn. The Patent Office has a staff of about 70 examiners and 1,000 assistant examiners. The typical assistant examiner is an engineering graduate who is studying law at night, preparing to become a patent attorney. The turnover in this group, amounting to 20 percent per year, is one of the highest in the government. The Patent Bar is a thriving small army clustering in Washington, D.C., but also extending into every sizeable town.

Each assistant examiner handles 70 to 80 patent applications per year. In each case, he must analyze the application and search the prior art as revealed in Patent Office files and in scientific publications in the United States and abroad. In the case of certain chemicals, this process has been speeded by computerizing some of the relevant data; in other fields, however, mechanization is more difficult and has not yet been undertaken.

An examiner typically rejects one or more claims in an initial application, giving the applicant six months in which to file an amended application, which he then considers in its turn. He has, on the average, three working days in which to take all the steps that may be required from his first receipt of an application until a final determination can be made. Two out of five applications are finally abandoned or rejected; three are allowed. The typical patent, when granted, has been pending more than three years.[3]

If the examiner rejects an application, it may be carried to the Board of Appeals in the Patent Office where, in a third to a half of the cases, he is likely to be reversed. If the examiner is sustained, the applicant may go on to the Court of Customs and Patent Appeals where his chance of obtaining a patent may be one in five. Out of this flood of claims to monopolistic rights, granted as carelessly as must be the case, there will be many that will overlap.

The Patent Office does not guarantee its product. It does not warrant that the patentee is the true inventor or insure that his claim will be upheld. If he is sued for infringing another patent, he can argue that his own is different or superior. But the Patent Office will not come to his

---

[2] *Lowell* v. *Lewis,* 15 Fed. Cases, 1018, 1019.

[3] U.S. Senate, Committee on the Judiciary, Subcommittee on Patents, Trademarks, and Copyrights, Study No. 29, *The Examination System in the U.S. Patent Office* (Washington, D.C.: Government Printing Office, 1961). Each new Patent Commissioner vows to revolutionize (i.e., computerize, expand, etc.) the process, but progress is slow.

TABLE 9-2

A Selection of Major Patents

Period			Patent?	Battles over Patent?
1770–80	James Watt	Steam engine improvement	Yes	Yes
1793	Eli Whitney	Cotton gin	Yes	Yes (failed)
1834	Cyrus McCormick	Reaper	Yes	Yes
1839	Charles Goodyear	Vulcanizing rubber	Yes	—
1845	Elias Howe	Sewing machine	Yes	Yes
1868	C. L. Sholes	Typewriter	Yes	Yes
1875	A. G. Bell	Telephone	Yes	Yes
1879	T. A. Edison	Light bulb	Yes	Yes
1885	George Eastman	Commercial photographic film	Yes	Yes
1939–48	Chester Carlson	Dry copying	Yes	No

assistance. It leaves to him the burden and the cost of his defense. All that it gives him is a claim upon which he himself can enter suit. If another uses his invention without permission, he can seek an injunction and ask for damages. But the defendant may counter with a patent of his own, or may argue that the plaintiff's patent covers a process or a product that has long been common property. The resolution of such conflicts is the duty of the courts.

Judges have had their training, not in physics, chemistry, and engineering, but in the law. They are seldom expert in industrial technology. But they must decide if a patent covers a real invention, whether it was issued to the true inventor, and whether it has been infringed. And it is their judgment that determines the existence, the ownership, and the scope of the patent monopoly. Invention of the telephone was claimed by Daniel Drawbaugh, Elisha Gray, and Alexander Graham Bell. Gray's patents were acquired by the Bell interests when their suit against Western Union was settled out of court, and the telegraph company withdrew from the telephone industry. Drawbaugh's telephone was invented in 1869 and put to work in 1871; Bell's was patented in 1876. When Bell's suit against Drawbaugh reached the Supreme Court, two judges did not sit, three voted for Drawbaugh and four for Bell. It was on this foundation that the telephone monopoly was built.[4] More often, however, the courts have found that the plaintiff's patent was not infringed or that it was lacking in validity. Among 124 infringement suits brought before the Supreme Court from 1900 to 1960, 28 were found to be based on valid patents that had been infringed, 27 on patents that were valid but not infringed, and 69 on patents that were void.[5] It is a rare patent, however, that is taken to court, and an even rarer one that is appealed to the higher courts. The currency that is issued by the Patent Office thus passes at face value, save in those cases where the courts have found it to be counterfeit.

The decision to patent often involves close choices, and in numberless cases the choice is for secrecy or some other strategy instead. The choice depends on many things. Patents are a specific strategy fitted to certain conditions, *not* a universal stimulant to progress.

They cluster tightly in certain industries, especially in drugs, photocopying, aerospace, and electrical equipment. Over large areas of industry, patents are virtually absent and irrelevant.

Some patents are astronomically profitable (including some in Table 9–2). Often the inventor is so enriched that he ceases inventing altogether. Occasionally a patent serves to create a near-permanent monopoly (Table 9–2 contains some of those).

ANALYSIS

Does the system make good economic sense? One begins with the basic economics of technical progress.[6] The process divides into various categories:

---

[4] *The Telephone Cases,* 126 U.S. 1 (1887).

[5] E. Burke Inlow, *The Patent Grant* (Baltimore: Johns Hopkins Press, 1950), pp. 142–43; and 85th Cong., 2d Sess., Senate Report 1430, p. 19.

[6] See E. Mansfield, *The Economics of Technological Change,* (New York: Norton, 1968);

1. Invention; the new idea conceived and tested.
2. Innovation; the first application of the idea in production.
3. Imitation; spreading of the innovation to other producers.

Innovations are of two types:

a. Product innovations; new product, same production methods.
b. Process innovations; same product, produced differently (so that the average cost curve shifts down).

These conceptual distinctions often have blurred edges in practice, but they clarify the stages and incentives in the process.

Also, new ideas differ in scope. Some are small and specialized: a knob here, a notch there, or a stripe in toothpaste. At the other extreme, some are broad and basic concepts, such as the wheel and interchangable parts. Patents cluster in the middle range; significant ideas whose gains can be temporarily monopolized without intolerable social effects. Society must decide how far up the range of bigness it will let ideas be monopolized.

Much progress is autonomous, seeming to materialize from thin air as part of the great evolution of new ideas and technology.[7]

No one can say what actuated the inventors of the wheel, the wedge, the lever, the pulley, the mill, the screw, the drill, the lathe, the keel, the oar, the sail. Certain it is, however, that these contrivances emerged from cultures where the patent was unknown. Many men in later times have been driven to construct devices which could bring them no possible profit. Leonardo da Vinci, Benjamin Franklin, Thomas Jefferson never left off inventing things, never attempted to turn their inventions to practical account. Taussig, who studied the lives of the great utilitarian inventors found that they, too, "were constantly experimenting on all sorts of schemes, promising and unpromising. . . ." With these men, "schemes and experiments begin in childhood, and persist so long as life and strength hold. It matters not whether a fortune is made or pecuniary distress is chronic."[8] And when the Patent, Trademark, and Copyright Foundation asked a long list of inventors if the availability of patent protection had stimulated their inventive activity, one-fifth of those who replied said yes; four-fifths said that it was not essential or made little difference.[9] The nature and the motivation of invention have been something other than the law assumes. Other innovations arise strictly from the hope of private gain, often in frantic competitive efforts (as with Thomas Edison and the light bulb, and Bell and the telephone). More commonly, there is a mixture of incentive, eccentricity, opportunism, and random chance.

Invention requires *thought,* above all, plus large research resources

---

John Jewkes at al, *The Sources of Invention,* rev. ed. (New York: St. Martin's Press, 1968); and National Bureau of Economic Research, *The Rate and Direction of Innovative Activity* (Princeton: Princeton University Press, 1962), for good basic treatments.

[7] See J. Schmookler, *Invention and Economic Growth* (Cambridge: Harvard University Press, 1967); and Jewkes et al, *op. cit.*

[8] F. W. Taussig, *Inventors and Moneymakers* (New York: Macmillan Co., 1915), pp. 21–23.

[9] U.S. Congress, Joint Economic Committee, *Invention and the Patent System* (Washington, D.C.: Government Printing Office, 1964), p. 47.

in some cases. Despite recent rhetoric about team and large-scale research,[10] invention is usually a small-scale, personal activity. Innovation differs: it requires business skills and resources, sometimes on a large scale. Innovation therefore is usually done by firms, which may be entirely separate from the inventors who feed in the new ideas. *The incentives and resources needed for invention often differ from those for innovation.*

The *net* gains are the social criterion. Innovation destroys the old in creating the new. It can be too rapid. Its damage to one private group can exceed the private gains to another. And there may be wider external costs. The social goal is to optimize the net benefits from creative activity. This is more sophisticated and difficult than the usual goal of patents: getting as much innovation as fast as possible.

If all inventions were autonomous, there would be no social purpose in patents or related devices. Too, if capital markets functioned perfectly, no idea or inventor would lack the resources needed to optimize it. Therefore patents would be irrelevant or directly harmful. The case for patents rests on capital-market imperfections and on *inducement:* that the rewards of temporary monopoly will induce the optimal rate and direction of invention and innovation.

It is often urged that modern industry provides a new rationale for patents. Instead of the old handicraft economy, there is now large-scale, professional, *corporate* research underlying most new ideas. This R&D must be financed by profits on earlier successes, to keep progress going. Since patents yield profits, they are necessary to innovation.

This argument actually contains *non sequiters.* Much—not all—large corporate research is now realized to be bureaucratic and anticreative. The profits under patents may stray far from the optimum rewards that might be necessary. It is *future* gains that should properly induce R&D, not the financial flows from past actions.[11]

An "optimal" patent system will contain just the right (1) standards of patentability, (2) length of patent life, and (3) degree of control by the patent owner. These optimal conditions then depend in turn on three factual elements:

1. How much invention and innovation are actually induced by rewards,
2. How extreme the monopoly exploitation of patents is, during their life, and
3. How rapidly the monopoly fades after the patent life ends.

In short, there may be a social trade-off between net progress and monopoly. The trade-off may be constant in all markets, or it may differ

---

[10] Recall Jewkes et al; and Chapter 2, *supra.*

[11] In an objective survey of large corporations, one-tenth said that patents were important to investment in research, nine-tenths said they were not. See also A. E. Kahn, "The Economics of Patent Policy," in J. P. Miller, ed., *Competition, Cartels, and Their Regulation* (North Holland Press, 1962); Fritz Machlup, *The Economics of the Patent System* (Princeton: Princeton University Press, 1953); and F. M. Scherer, *Industrial Market Structure and Economic Performance, op. cit..*

sharply among sectors (with patents giving progress and competition in some sectors but stagnation and monopoly in others).

Around the core of simple issues are evidently a lot of complex relationships. All of them, simple and complex, may be hard to measure. The basic issues have been understood for generations, but there has been little clear analysis or estimation of the trade-offs.

Patent Life. The optimum patent life has been analyzed, under simplified assumptions.[12] Very roughly speaking, the more sharply a prospective innovation reduces costs, the shorter the optimal life of a patent will be. For a cost reduction of 10 percent and elasticity of demand anywhere in the range of .7 to 4.0, the optimal patent life appears to be in the range of 3 to 7 years. Broadly speaking, a long patent life is only optimal for the very largest and costliest innovations.

Yet such large innovations are precisely those which tend to create or recast an industry with full monopoly which may long outlast the patent. A correct analysis replaces *patent* life with *monopoly* life; an optimal patent life will be shorter—possibly much shorter—than optimal monopoly life.

Patent *life* and the degree of patent *control* are substitutable elements, for they both define the present value of—that is, the inducement for—the invention. The present patent system maximizes the control. It also makes the profits more secure, by giving a guaranteed monopoly. These profits may far exceed the optimal incentive by a large margin. Instead, there could be limits on the degree of profit, the terms of licensing, or other patent actions. In various countries, they are constrained.

Market Position. Generally, monopoly yields less inventive activity than does competition.[13] And firms with large market shares have incentives to follow rather than to innovate first.[14] They choose between speed and economy in innovation, often under conditions described by the curves in Figure 9–3. A rational dominant firm tends to go slow, imitating when forced to by lesser firms. A patent creating a dominant firm therefore tends to breed imitation, rather than future innovation.

Moreover, patentable activities are often related, so that one patent gives advantages in forming a cluster of newer patents which maintain or increase the firm's market share (as Xerox is seeking to do: recall Chapter 2 and see pages 278–79).

In short, there are often added costs of the patent monopoly beyond the direct profit rewards during the formal patent life. One should be alert for real cases where monopoly is extended. This accords with the research consensus that at market shares above 25 percent the degree of technical progress tapers off (recall Chapter 2).

The patent system exists on (1) an intuition that incentives breed progress, and (2) inertia, reinforced by interested groups. But we have now seen that incentives are a complex matter, where the net benefits

---

[12] The analysis is not simple. See W. D. Nordhaus, *Invention, Growth and Welfare* (Cambridge: MIT Press, 1969); and F. M. Scherer, "Nordhaus' Theory of Optimal Patent Life: A Geometric Reinterpretation," *American Economic Review,* 1972, pp. 422–27.

[13] Recall Arrow, footnote 12 in Chapter 2.

[14] Recall Scherer, footnote 13 in Chapter 2.

FIGURE 9–3

Typical Conditions for Innovations: Dominant Firms Tend to Follow

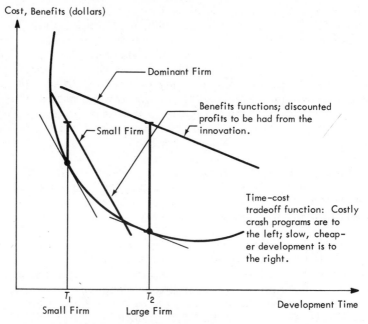

Cost, Benefits (dollars)

Dominant Firm

Small Firm

Benefits functions; discounted profits to be had from the innovation.

Time–cost tradeoff function: Costly crash programs are to the left; slow, cheaper development is to the right.

T_1
Small Firm

T_2
Large Firm

Development Time

Innovators maximize the gap between Benefits and Costs. The small firm normally innovates faster than the dominant firm.

Source: Adapted from Scherer, *Industrial Market Structure and Economic Performance, op. cit,* p. 367.

are easy to overstate and the total costs extend in time and space. There are plausible grounds for abolishing patents outright or modifying them sharply. There are good preliminary grounds for shortening patent life and limiting patent rights.

ABUSES OF PATENTS

So far, the analysis has not considered the ways in which patents can be used deliberately to suppress competition. These abuses are of several sorts.

Patent monopolies have been sought and granted on supposed inventions that have contributed little or nothing to the advancement of technology. In some cases, ownership of patents that cover the whole of an industry's technology has been concentrated in the hands of one or a few large firms. Patent litigation has been deliberately employed as a means of eliminating and excluding competitors. Common control of patents has been established by cross-licensing or through the operation of patent pools. Patent procedures have been so manipulated as to extend the duration of exclusive rights beyond the legal term of 17 years. The scope of patent protection has been extended horizontally to monopolize unpatented goods and vertically to control successive stages of production and distribution. Patent owners have refused to license their patents or have granted licenses on restrictive terms. Patent licensing has been employed as a means of controlling the output, dividing the markets, and fixing prices of entire industries.

Patents Without Inventions. The volume of patents has clearly been greater than the quantity of significant invention. Patents have been granted on mere gadgets, on contrivances expressing the lowest order of mechanical ability, and on ideas involving little in the way of novelty.

Patents have covered an indentation on the head of a screw, an eraser on the end of a pencil, rubber hand grips on bicycle handlebars, a bosom or dickie sewn onto the front of a shirt, the use of flat cord instead of round cord in the loop at the ends of suspenders, and the use of an oval rather than a cylindrical shape in a roll of toilet paper.

The patent that gave the Johns-Manville Corporation a monopoly of the business of insulating previously constructed buildings by blowing mineral wool into the space between the outer and the inner walls was one that applied, not to the manufacture of the wool itself, nor to the machinery used in blowing it, but to the process of "providing openings to afford access to the air spaces" in existing structures, "inserting the outlet end of a conduit through said openings, and forcing through the said conduit comminuted heat insulating material. . . ." In short, it was a patent on the idea of blowing through a hole.

When such patents reach the courts, they will rarely be allowed to stand. But until they do, they continue to afford a basis for industrial monopoly.

Suppression of Technology. Under American law the patentee is not required to work his patent. As a consequence, the law may be employed not to promote but to retard the introduction of advances in technology. It has frequently been charged—and as frequently denied—that new inventions are deliberately suppressed.

While proof is not sufficient to support this charge, it is certain that patents outnumber the inventions that are put to work. In 1959, there were nearly 600,000 patents outstanding. Of these, 150,000 to 300,000 were in use; half to three quarters were not.[15] But failure to work a patent need not involve suppression of technology. A patent may cover a product for which demand appears to be inadequate or a process that appears to be inferior to the one already employed. But a patentee's judgment as to these matters may well be influenced by the fact that he has substantial sums invested in a competing product or in a process that embodies an earlier technology. A vested interest may lead him to postpone an innovation that would otherwise be made. Under active competition, the rate of change is determined by the market. Under the patent monopoly, it is determined by the patentee. Insofar as suppression of patented inventions does occur, it clearly defeats the fundamental purpose of patent law.

The Monopolization of Patent Monopolies. Not only does a single patent confer a monopoly, but many related patents may be accumulated

---

[15] U.S. Senate, Committee on the Judiciary, Subcommittee on Patents, Trademarks, and Copyrights, Study No. 29, *The Examination System in the Patent Office,* pp. 36–37.

by one or a few large firms or brought together by agreement among them. There is no limit to the number of patents that may be held by a single company. The large corporation will usually obtain a steady flow of patents through assignment from members of its own research staff and will supplement them by purchases from outsiders.

Among the companies receiving patents from 1939 to 1956, there were 39 with more than 1,000 and 15 with more than 2,000 each; du Pont received 6,338; Westinghouse, 7,567; RCA, 7,894; AT&T 8,539; and GE 10,757.[16] The existence of competing patents, where their ownership is diffused, may be conducive to active competition. But concentration of patent ownership, on so great a scale, may place in the hands of a single firm control over each of the possible methods by which a good may be produced, enabling it to monopolize the technology of an entire industry.

Where a few large corporations hold patents that overlap, each is likely to share its rights with the others through cross-licensing. Such agreements may call for exclusive or nonexclusive licensing, and may cover future as well as present patent rights. The companies participating will usually agree to refrain from attacking the validity of patents held by other members of the group. Where the participants are engaged in different industries, each of them may be given an exclusive right, in his own field, to all of the patents that are involved.

The agreement that settled the contest between Bell and Western Union in 1879 divided the communications industry, leaving the telegraph to Western Union and giving the telephone to Bell. Some years later, AT&T entered into a series of agreements with RCA giving each interest an exclusive field within which to exploit the patents owned by both, RCA getting broadcasting, radio telegraphy, and other wireless services; AT&T getting wireless telephony and all the wire services, including wire facilities used in broadcasting. Where the participants in a cross-licensing arrangement are engaged in the same industry, all of the technology in the field may thus be brought under unified control. It was a series of treaties between Hartford-Empire, a company holding patents on machinery for making glass containers, and each of the major producers of such containers that enabled Hartford to establish its dominance over the container field.

Patent Warfare. Large firms have sometimes undertaken to fortify a position of monopoly by accumulating an arsenal of patents to be used in attacking possible competitors. Their lawyers have flooded the Patent Office with a constant stream of applications to cover every process, every machine, and every product that their technicians have invented or might conceivably invent.

Hartford-Empire, according to a policy memorandum taken from its files, applied for patents designed "to block the development of machines which might be constructed by others for the same purpose as our machines, using alternative means" and for other patents "on possible improvements of competing machines so as to 'fence in' those and prevent their reaching an improved stage." In addition to "blocking" and "fenc-

---

[16] U.S. Senate, Committee on the Judiciary, Subcommittee on Patents, Trademarks, and Copyrights, Study No. 3, *Distribution of Patents Issued to Corporations* (Washington, D.C.: Government Printing Office, 1957).

ing" patents, there are "umbrella," "accordion," and "drag-net" patents, drawn up with claims so broad, so expansible, and so effective as to cover and seize upon extensive areas of industrial technology. According to Alfred E. Kahn: "The great research laboratories are only incidentally technological centers. From the business standpoint they are patent factories; they manufacture the raw material of monopoly. Their product is often nothing but a 'shot-gun,' a basis for threatening infringement suit and scaring off competitors; or a 'scare-crow,' a patent which itself represents little or no contribution but seems . . . to cover an important part of a developing art and hence permits threat of suit.[17]

Litigation has been deliberately employed as a weapon of monopoly. Between 1877 and 1893, when the first Bell patent expired, the telephone company initiated more than 600 infringement suits.[18] Patent warfare was similarly employed to build the power of National Cash Register, Eastman Kodak, and United Shoe Machinery.[19] Hartford-Empire, in later years, repeatedly brought suit against competing manufacturers of container machinery, against the purchasers of such machinery, and against concerns that undertook to produce containers with their own machines.

In patent warfare there is no assurance that the adversary with the better claim will be victorious. Litigation is costly, and the outcome is likely to favor the party with the longer purse. Suits may be brought in different jurisdictions and under many different claims. A firm may see its markets vanish as suits are brought against its customers. Such litigation, moreover, may drag on for years. Its victim may well conclude that capitulation is preferable to bankruptcy. When Eastman Kodak sued the Boston Camera Co. in 1894, obtaining a temporary injunction against the sale of Boston's wares, Eastman was finally adjudged the real infringer, but Boston had by then been broken and was thereupon absorbed.[20] When the predecessor of the Aluminum Company of America sued the Cowles Brothers, it was found, after 10 years, to have infringed their patents, but they agreed to accept a cash settlement and retired from the field.[21] In many other cases, suits have been settled before the courts have passed upon the rival patent claims. A weaker firm with a valid patent may thus sell out to a stronger firm with a patent of dubious validity. Or it may recognize the latter's patent as valid, take out a license, and agree to abide by its terms. Exclusive rights thus tend to gravitate to large concerns, regardless of the legal status of their claims.

Extending the Boundaries of Monopoly.   The normal duration of the formal monopoly conferred under the patent system is not 17 years but over 20. An invention may be worked for a year before a patent is applied for, and the usual application remains pending in the Patent Office for three years more. The period of pendency has been further extended by

---

[17] Alfred E. Kahn, *op. cit.*

[18] Walton H. Hamilton, *Patents and Free Enterprise,* T.N.E.C. Monograph No. 31 (Washington, D.C.: Government Printing Office, 1941), p. 89.

[19] Floyd L. Vaughn, *Economics of Our Patent System* (New York: Macmillan Co., 1925), pp. 149-52.

[20] Hamilton, *op. cit.,* p. 47.

[21] George W. Stocking and Myron W. Watkins, *Cartels in Action* (New York: Twentieth Century Fund, 1946), p. 221.

the withdrawal and amendment of applications and through the initiation of interference proceedings by the Patent Office when two applications appear to cover the same ground.

The duration of monopoly has also been prolonged by dividing a complicated invention into several parts—the steps in a process, the elements in a compound, or the sections of a machine—and applying for separate patents at judicious intervals. During the life of a basic patent, its owner will seek to develop and patent improvements. He will also be the only buyer to whom patents on improvements made by others can be sold. When one grant of monopoly has expired, another will be ready to take its place. During its period of patent protection, moreover, a firm may have developed a productive organization, market outlets, control over materials, and a monopoly of skilled personnel that will make it difficult, if not impossible, for others to enter the field when its patents have expired. The patent system, in its operation, thus involves a longer tenure of power than that envisaged by the framers of the law.

The monopoly power afforded by patents has been extended in space as well as in time. Monopoly has been extended horizontally from one patented product to another and from patented to unpatented goods. Whether by contract or by persuasion, the shoe manufacturer who has leased one of his machines from the United Shoe Machinery Corporation has also obtained the rest of his machinery and supplies from United Shoe, the canner who has leased his canning machinery from American Can or Continental has also brought his cans from the same concern, and the office that has leased an IBM computer has often ordered its tabulating cards from IBM.

Monopoly has also been extended vertically from one stage of production and distribution to the next. The Hartford-Empire patents covered a machine used in making glass containers, but they were used not only to monopolize the container machinery business but also to cartelize the container industry itself. Machines were leased to manufacturers of jars and bottles, and each of them was licensed to turn out a certain quantity of a certain product and sell it in a certain market at a certain price. The jars and bottles were not patented, but their production and sale was effectively controlled. In these and other cases, extension of the boundaries of patent monopoly has been found to be illegal. But, in the meantime, the profits of wider monopoly have been obtained.

Restrictive Licensing. The patent holder may fail to work his patent himself; he may refuse to license others to do so. The Hartford-Empire Co. consistently refused to grant licenses to firms which undertook to enter into competition with its established licensees. According to its policy memorandum, the company "licensed the machines only to manufacturers of the better type, refusing many licensees who we thought would be price cutters. . . ." This policy was quite acceptable to manufacturers of the better type. "With the plans we now have," wrote one of them, "there is certain to be a curtailment of the promiscuous manufacture of milk bottles. . . ."[22]

---

[22] Wilcox, *op. cit.,* pp. 76–77.

The patentee who grants a license gives someone else the right to share in his monopoly. He promises, in effect, that he will not bring suit against the licensee. Licenses may be granted to one firm or to many. They may permit the licensee to produce and sell in any quantity, in any market, and at any price, or they may sharply restrict his liberty. Output may be limited by imposing quotas or by charging graduated royalties. Hartford-Empire's contract with the Florida Glass Co. provided "that the licensee shall not produce in any calendar year . . . more than 21,000 gross of such bottles."[23] Under its contract with General Electric, Westinghouse formerly paid a royalty of 1 percent on lamp sales which did not exceed 25.4 percent of the combined sales of the two concerns and 30 percent on sales made in excess of this share.[24] License contracts may authorize each licensee to sell in a different market, thus giving each of them a regional monopoly. Hartford's contract with the Northwestern Glass Co. permitted the latter to sell its wares only in Oregon, Idaho, Montana, and Alaska; the contract with the Laurens Glass works directed that concern to sell its bottles to two buyers in Spartanburg, South Carolina.[25]

A patent holder may also undertake to fix the prices that are charged by subsequent distributors. Thus, U.S. Gypsum required its licensees to sell on a delivered basis under a multiple basing point system and to observe the minimum prices which it prescribed, and Masonite licensed competing manufacturers of hardboard and fixed the prices they could charge.[26] In each of these ways, the patentee imposes restraints on competition. In some cases he may overstep the bounds of legality. In others, he may be within his rights. The alternative to restrictive licensing, it should be remembered, may be no licensing at all.

Patent Pools. In industries where essential patents are controlled by many firms, they may be brought together in a common pool. Under such an arrangement, patents may be assigned to a trade association or to a corporation set up for the purpose, and licenses granted to each of the participants under all of the patents in the pool. Licenses may be restricted or unrestricted; royalties may be collected and distributed, or patents may be licensed royalty free. A pool may be confined to patents relating to a single product or may include all those important to an industry. It may be limited to older patents, sharing the earlier inventions, but leaving to innovators, for a time, the advantage of exclusive use. But whatever its characteristics, the patent pool in every case will centralize control over a substantial segment of industrial technology.

Patent pooling may be employed either to liberate competition or to intensify monopoly. Under such arrangements, improvements resulting from invention are made available to all of the participants and costs are reduced by eliminating litigation within the group. If unrestricted licenses are granted to all applicants on reasonable terms, outsiders are afforded access to the industry's technology. In the automobile industry,

[23] *Ibid.,* p. 75.
[24] *Ibid.,* p. 104.
[25] *Ibid.,* p. 76.
[26] *Ibid.,* pp. 161–64.

since 1915, patents have been pooled and licenses freely given without restriction and without charge. Patents covering all but the more recent inventions are thus thrown open to the entire industry, and smaller and newer firms may use them without contributing inventions of their own. Since the pool was first established, no manufacturers of automobiles have appeared as plaintiff and defendant in an infringement suit.

But agreements combining patents may also be administered with less liberality. A pool controling all of the inventions in an industry will be the only purchaser of future patents and the only source of patent licenses. By refusing to license, by charging exorbitant royalties, and by drawing upon the combined resource of its members in prosecuting and defending patent suits, it may eliminate outsiders from the field. By including in its contracts provisions which restrict the quantity a licensee may produce, the area in which he may sell, and the prices he may charge, it may regiment an entire industry. Whether cross-licensing and patent pooling make for competition or for monopoly depends therefore upon the purposes for which they are established and the way in which they are administered.

PATENTS AND THE COURTS

Most of these abuses have been presented in cases brought before the courts. Decisions in such cases have dealt with the standard of patentability; with concentration of patent ownership; with the right of the patentee to deny licenses to others, and to grant licenses on restrictive terms; with his efforts to extend his monopoly to other products and to later stages of production, to control output, to divide markets, and to fix prices; with cross-licensing; and with the operation of patent pools.

In general, the earlier decisions were favorable to the patent holder. But the courts have come increasingly, in recent years, to limit the scope and check the abuses of patent monopoly.

The Standard of Patentability. Until 1835 no patent was found invalid for want of novelty. Thereafter a succession of cases involving patents on gadgets led to the development of a judicial standard of patentability. In 1850, the Supreme Court held that a doorknob made of clay or procelain rather than metal or wood was "the work of the skilled mechanic, not that of the inventor.[27] This distinction continued to govern the decisions handed down for the better part of a century, and patents were upheld if they were deemed to embody a degree of skill that was greater than that of the artisan. But as invention came increasingly to be the product of corporate research, the standard of patentability was raised. And finally, in the Cuno case[28] in 1941, the Court held that usefulness and novelty in a wireless lighter "does not necessarily make the device patentable."

Said Justice Douglas: "Under the statute, the device must not only be 'new and useful,' it must also be an 'invention' or 'discovery' . . . That

---

[27] *Hotchkiss* v. *Greenwood,* 11 How. 248.
[28] *Cuno Corp.* v. *Automatic Devices Corp.,* 314 U.S. 84.

is to say, the new device, however useful it may be, must reveal the flash of creative genius, not merely the skill of the calling. If it fails, it has not established its right to a private grant on the public domain."[29] The standard thus became one that distinguished, not between the skill of the mechanic and that of the inventor, but between mere skill and the flash of genius.

This standard rested upon nothing more than subjective judgment. It was rejected by Congress when it passed the Patent Act of 1952. Inventions still are not patentable if "the subject matter as a whole would have been obvious at the time the invention was made to a person having ordinary skill in the art." But "patentability shall not be negatived by the manner in which the invention was made." A flash of genius is no longer required; dogged research will suffice. A patent is to be issued if the differences between an invention and the prior art are substantial.[30] But the obviousness of inventions and the substantiality of their differences from the prior art is still a matter of judgment. Whether an invention is patentable depends, as it has always depended, on the opinion of the courts. In three cases decided in 1966, the Supreme Court found patents on two inventions (one that placed the shank on a vibrating shank plow above the hinge plate, and one that provided a leak-proof cap for a finger-operated spray dispenser) to be invalid, and a third patent (on a water-activated battery of a radically new design) to be valid, on the ground that the first two would have been obvious to an artisan having ordinary skill in the prior art, while the third would not.[31] The Court took note of the laxity of the standards employed by the Patent Office and cautioned the office to adhere more closely to the standards enunciated by the courts.

Concentration of Patent Ownership. Where a single company has clearly sought to monopolize an industry's patents as a means of monopolizing the industry itself, its action has been condemned. Thus, the Kobe company undertook to monopolize the rodless pump industry by buying up all the patents in the field and getting the sellers to agree not to compete. It then sued the Dempsey Pump Co. for infringement and organized a boycott among Dempsey's customers in order to eliminate it as a competitor. Here, a circuit court refused to find infringement, holding that Kobe's suit was an integral part of a scheme to monopolize the industry.[32] In itself, however, the ownership of many patents by a single company has not been found to violate the law.

The issue was raised in the United Shoe Machinery case. The company held nearly 4,000 patents, about 95 percent of them the product of its own research, only 5 percent of them purchased from others. The government charged that the company "has been for many years, and is now, engaged in a program of engrossing all patents and inventions of importance relating to shoe machinery for the purpose of blanketing

---

[29] *Ibid.,* p. 91.

[30] Patent Codification Act of 1952, Sec. 103.

[31] *Graham* v. *John Deere Co.* and *Calmar, Inc.* v. *Cook Chemical Co.,* 383 U.S. 1; *U.S.* v. *Adams,* 383 U.S. 39.

[32] *Kobe, Inc.* v. *Dempsey Pump Co.,* 198 F. 2d 416 (1952).

the shoe machinery industry with patents under the control of United and thereby suppressing competition in the industry."[33]

This was one among the factors that led to a finding of illegality. Here, the court found no evidence that the patent right had been abused. United had put a third of its patents to work; it had not suppressed the others or used them to threaten possible competitors. It had not offered or been asked to grant licenses, but it had not refused to do so. It had not resorted to litigation as a means of harassing competitors but had acted in good faith in bringing infringement suits.

It had adopted certain policies, however, that operated to handicap competitors. It had refused to sell its machines, making them available only on long-term leases. It had included in its leases provisions that discriminated against customers who might install competing machines. It had required them to use its own machines at full capacity on all the shoes they made. It had entered into blanket contracts covering not only the lease of machines but also the provision of supplies and services. None of these policies was held to be illegal *per se*. But their combined effect, given United's dominant position in the field, was found to prove monopolization, in violation of Section 2 of the Sherman Act.[34]

The issue of concentration of patent ownership was also raised in the 1950s Section 2 cases involving Western Electric and International Business Machines. But here the legality of such concentration was not determined, each of the cases being settled in 1956 by a consent decree. Apart from coercive tactics like those employed by Kobe or a complex of practices such as those followed by United, a monopoly of patents is yet to be condemned.

Tying Contracts. Many decisions of the courts have dealt with the efforts of a patentee to extend the scope of his monopoly beyond the boundaries of the patent grant. In some cases the patentee has sought to prevent a competitor from selling an unpatented product for use in a patented combination. In 1909, the Supreme Court held an unpatented record to be an integral part of a patented phonograph, licensed to users by the Victor company, and found that Victor's patent was infringed by the sale of Leeds & Catlin's records.[35] This position was emphatically reversed by the Court's decision in the Mercoid Case[36] in 1944. Mercoid had been sued by Minneapolis-Honeywell when it sold an unpatented switch to be used in connection with a patented combination of thermostats in controlling furnace heat. The Court found no infringement, holding Honeywell's effort to extend the scope of its patent to be illegal *per se.* "An unpatented part of a combination patent," said Justice Douglas, "is no more entitled to monopolistic protection than any other unpatented device."

In other cases the patent holder has included in his license contracts provisions requiring his licensees to purchase some other product that

[33] *U.S.* v. *United Shoe Machinery Corp.,* Civil Action No. 7198, District Court of the U.S., District of Mass., Complaint, December 15, 1947.

[34] *U.S.* v. *United Shoe Machinery Corp.,* 110 F. Supp. 295.

[35] *Leeds & Catlin* v. *Victor Talking Machine Co.,* 213 U.S. 325.

[36] *Mercoid Corp.* v. *Minneapolis-Honeywell Regulator Co.,* 320 U.S. 680.

he has for sale. Before the passage of the Clayton Act such tying contracts were upheld. Since that Act was passed, however, they have consistently been condemned. The courts have struck down contracts, among others, requiring radio manufacturers licensed under RCA patents to buy their tubes from RCA;[37] requiring lessees of International Business Machines to buy their tabulating cards from IBM;[38] and requiring the purchase of rivets by lessees of patented riveting machines.[39] In these cases, the contracts were found substantially to lessen competition, within the meaning of the Clayton Act, because the patentee dominated the market for the process or product to which the unpatented commodity was tied. But tying contracts have also been invalidated in cases where the patentee was far from having a monopoly. Thus, in the International Salt case,[40] the Supreme Court held that a contract requiring the users of a patented salt dispenser to purchase salt from its producer was unreasonable *per se*. It is evident that the courts will not now tolerate the use of tying clauses, under any circumstances, to extend the boundaries of a patent monopoly.

Restrictive Licenses. Where a patent owner grants a license to use a patented machine or process or to make and sell a patented product, the courts have generally upheld his right to limit the licensee to a certain geographic area[41] or a certain field of industry,[42] to restrict his output,[43] and to fix the price that he may charge when he sells the patented goods. The leading decision on the latter point was handed down by the Supreme Court in the General Electric case[44] in 1926. One of the issues raised in this case related to the right of General Electric, under its basic patents on the electric lamp, to fix the prices charged by Westinghouse. This right was upheld by the Court, and license contracts fixing a licensee's prices on patented products are still permitted by the law.

Surrender of title to a patented good, however, has long been held to terminate the patentee's authority over its subsequent use and sale. His right to control the price at which patented products, once sold by him, are resold by others has therefore been denied. In the case of *Bauer* v. *O'Donnell*[45] in 1913, it was held that O'Donnell had not infringed Bauer's patent on Sanatogen when he resold it for less than the price that Bauer had printed on the package.

This precedent has generally been followed since that time. General Electric, however, has circumvented this rule by treating its distributors as agents, shipping its bulbs on consignment, and retaining title until they are sold. The Court, in its 1926 decision, found this arrangement to

[37] *Lord* v. *Radio Corp. of America,* 24 F. 2d 505 (1928).

[38] *International Business Machines Corp.* v. *U.S.,* 298 U.S. 131 (1936).

[39] *Judson Thompson* v. *FTC,* 150 F. 2d 952 (1945).

[40] *International Salt Co.* v. *U.S.,* 332 U.S. 392 (1947)

[41] *Providence Rubber Co.* v. *Goodyear,* 9 Wall. 788 (1869).

[42] *General Talking Pictures Corp.* v. *Western Electric Corp.,* 304 U.S. 175 (1938).

[43] *Rubber Tire Wheel Co.* v. *Milwaukee Rubber Works Co.,* 154 F. 328 (1907), 210 U.S. 439 (1908).

[44] *U.S.* v. *General Electric Co.,* 272 U.S. 476.

[45] 229 U.S. 1.

274 *Public Policies toward Business*

be legitimate and permitted the company to fix the prices that its thousands of "agents" could charge.

Restrictive licensing of another manufacturer was permitted in the General Electric case, where it applied to a single licensee. But it has been held to be illegal when employed for the purpose of eliminating competition among many licensees. In the Gypsum case[46] in 1948, the Supreme Court condemned the establishment of common prices for manufacturers of gypsum board through provisions contained in separate contracts for patent licensing. The General Electric precedent, said the Court, "gives no support for a patentee, acting in concert with all members of an industry, to issue substantially identical licenses . . . under which industry is completely regimented." When each of several licensees accepts restrictive terms on the condition or with the knowledge that others will do so, they are guilty, in the eyes of the Court, of conspiracy in restraint of trade.

On a number of occasions, the government has asked the Court to reverse the rule of the GE decision permitting a patentee to fix the prices that may be charged by a single licensee. In the Gypsum case, in 1948, four of the judges were willing to do so, but this fell short of a majority. In the Huck case[47] in 1965, the Court split 4 to 4 on a similar request. Sooner or later, it is likely that the rule will be reversed.

Cross-Licensing and Patent Pools. Cross-licensing and patent pooling have never been held to be illegal *per se.* But their employment as a means of eliminating competition among patent owners and licensees has usually been condemned. In the leading case on patent pooling, the Standard Sanitary case[48] decided in 1912, where patents covering the production of enameled iron bathtubs and other sanitary wares had been pooled with a trade association, the inclusion in licenses issued to firms producing 85 percent of the output of such wares of provisions restricting output, fixing prices and discounts, and controlling channels of trade was held to violate the Sherman Act.

In the Standard Oil of Indiana case[49] in 1931, however, a pool controlling patents covering methods of cracking gasoline was allowed to stand. But here the Court was impressed by the fact that many other cracking processes remained outside the pool, that licensees under the pooling arrangement did little more than half of the cracking of gasoline, and that cracking provided only a fourth of the total supply. The pool, thus faced with competition, was found to be powerless to fix prices and was therefore held to be within the law.

In the Hartford-Empire case[50] decided in 1945, Hartford had employed the patents in its pool to dominate completely the glass container industry, curtailing output, dividing markets, and fixing prices through restrictive licenses; the Court found in Hartford's behavior, as a whole, convincing evidence of unlawful conspiracy.

---

[46] *U.S.* v. *U.S. Gypsum Co.,* 333 U.S. 364.
[47] *Huck Manufacturing Co.* v. *U.S.,* 382 U.S. 197.
[48] *Standard Sanitary Mfg. Co.* v. *U.S.,* 226 U.S. 20.
[49] *Standard Oil Co. (Indiana)* v. *U.S.,* 283 U.S. 163.
[50] *Hartford-Empire Co.* v. *U.S.,* 323 U.S. 386.

So, too, with cross-licensing. In the Line Material case[51] in 1948, the court was emphatic in its condemnation of a plan that eliminated competition through cross-licensing. Here, each of two small companies producing patented fuse cutouts had licensed the other and fixed the prices it might charge. Their agreement to do so was held to be illegal *per se.* "This price fixing scheme," said the Court, "does far more than secure to inventors 'the exclusive right' to their discoveries. . . . It gives them a leverage on the market which only a combination, not a patent by itself, can create." In the Besser case[52] in 1952, the Court held an agreement between two patent holders to refuse licenses to others to be a boycott and, as such, to be illegal *per se.* And in the Singer case[53] in 1963, where Singer had exchanged licenses with Swiss and Italian manufacturers of zigzag sewing machines and then brought infringement suits against importers of Japanese machines, the Court found the three concerns to be conspiring in restraint of trade.

Patent pooling was an issue in another suit which the government brought against the General Electric Company. The basic patents on the electric lamp had expired, and GE had undertaken to perpetuate its control of the industry by employing later patents on such parts of the lamp as the filament and the frosting on the bulb. To this end, it had formed a patent pool with Westinghouse and granted licenses to four other producers, controlling the output and the prices of all six companies. These arrangements, while similar to those approved in 1926, though involving different patents and a larger number of licensees, were found by a district court in 1949 to violate both sections of the Sherman Act. General Electric, said the Court, had conspired with its licensees and had "unlawfully monopolized the incandescent electric lamp industry in the United States."[54]

Among the most important cases involving the operation of a patent pool is that of the Radio Corporation of America. Here, in a civil suit brought in 1954 and a criminal suit brought in 1958, the government charged that RCA had entered into agreements with AT&T, GE, and Westinghouse and with firms in other countries that gave it the exclusive right to grant licenses under more than 10,000 radio-purpose patents in the United States. As a result, other manufacturers of electronic equipment were made to depend upon RCA. In granting licenses, moreover, the company refused to license patents individually, but insisted on licensing all of the patents in a packaged group. RCA pleaded *nolo contendere* in the government's criminal case, paying a fine of $100,000, and accepted a consent decree in the civil suit. Under the terms of this decree, the company agreed to license its existing radio and TV patents royalty-free, to license its new patents at reasonable royalties, and to permit its licensees to obtain patents individually instead of requiring package deals.[55]

---

[51] *U.S.* v. *Line Material Co.,* 333 U.S. 287.

[52] *Besser Mfg. Co.* v. *U.S.,* 343 U.S. 444.

[53] *U.S.* v. *Singer Mfg. Co.,* 374 U.S. 174.

[54] *U.S.* v. *General Electric Co.,* 82 F. Supp. 753.

[55] *U.S.* v. *Radio Corp. of America,* 1958 Trade Cases, Par. 69, 164.

Remedies in Patent Cases. Employment of patents to eliminate competition has repeatedly been restrained by the courts. This has been true, of course, in the many cases in which a court has found that a patent was not valid or was not infringed. In a number of cases, too, the Supreme Court has permitted defendants in infringement suits to show that patents had been used to violate the antitrust laws and then refused, on that ground, to enforce them.[56] The patents, though not invalidated, were rendered ineffective, and their use as an instrument of monopoly destroyed. The Court has also held that a defendant in an infringement suit, brought to enforce a patent that had been obtained through fraudulent representations, could sue the patentee for treble damages.[57]

One such case led to the heaviest penalty ever incurred through abuse of the patent right.

Here, Charles Pfizer & Co., a manufacturer of pharmaceuticals, had conspired with four other manufacturers to obtain a patent on tetracycline, an antibiotic, by misrepresenting its origin to the Patent Office. It had then licensed the other producers, forbidding them in its licenses to distribute the drug through packagers, who might compete in its sale. In this way, the group had been able to enforce a price of $30.60 for 100 capsules that had cost $3.87 to make. The companies were convicted of conspiracy in a criminal suit and fined $150,000 each. But, more important, they were sued for damages by governments, institutions, and individuals who had purchased tetracycline at the higher price, most of these suits being settled, in 1968, at a cost of $120 million.[58]

Judicial decisions and consent decrees in patent cases have been designed, not only to punish violators of the antitrust laws, but also to make markets more competitive by removing legal barriers to entry. The decree of the district court in the Hartford-Empire case[59] required the company to license all applicants under its patents, royalty-free. This decree was modified by the Supreme Court, in a 4 to 3 decision, to permit the collection of reasonable royalties, on the ground that their refusal would involve unconstitutional confiscation of the defendant's property. But the Court agreed, for the first time in history, to compulsory licensing.[60] In the National Lead case two years later, the government asked the Court to go beyond this precedent, reversing its position on the need for royalties. The Court, again by a 4 to 3 vote, refused to do so, but approved compulsory licensing, and intimated that it might agree to the elimination of royalties if this were the only way in which competition could be restored.[61]

---

[56] *Morton Salt Co.* v. *G.S. Suppiger Co.,* 314 U.S. 488 (1942); *B.B. Chemical Co.* v. *Ellis,* 314 U.S. 495 (1942); *Mercoid Corp.* v. *Mid-Continent Investment Co.,* 320 U.S. 661 (1944).

[57] *Walker Process Equipment Co.* v. *Food Machinery and Chemical Corp.,* 382 U.S. 172 (1965).

[58] See Peter M. Costello, "The Tetracycline Conspiracy," *Antitrust Law and Economics Review,* Vol. 1 (1968) pp. 13–44. Several years later, the decision was reversed on a legal point. But the conspiracy *had* existed and negotiated damages were paid. Yet these damages were tiny compared to the $1.9 billion which a trial victory could have yielded.

[59] *U.S.* v. *Hartford-Empire Co.,* 46 F. Supp. 541 (1942).

[60] *Hartford-Empire Co.* v. *U.S.,* 323 U.S. 386 (1945).

[61] *U.S.* v. *National Lead Co.,* 332 U.S. 319 (1947).

Royalty-free licensing was first required, by a district court, in the case of the General Electric Company in 1953. Following the company's conviction in a criminal suit in 1949, the government asked that it be required to dispose of half of its productive facilities; to abandon the agency system under which it controlled the prices charged by its distributors; to dedicate to public use all of its existing patents covering the manufacture of electric light bulbs and parts; and to grant licenses under future patents in this field, on a reciprocal basis, at reasonable royalties. The court refused to dismember the company or to ban the agency system, but it did order the licensing of patents, with future patents to be made available at reasonable royalties and existing patents royalty-free.[62]

Similar provisions have been incorporated in consent decrees. Scores of such decrees have been accepted, providing for the licensing of all applicants, many of them for licensing without royalties. Under the typical decree, existing patents must be licensed royalty-free and future patents at reasonable royalties. Royalty charges are determined by agreement between the patent owner and the licensee or, failing this, are established by the courts. A consent decree accepted by General Motors in 1965, in a suit attacking its control of 85 percent of the output of buses, provided for royalty-free licensing of future as well as existing patents. This provision, the first of its kind, was part of a program designed to open the industry to competition.

Decrees in antitrust suits have called not only for the licensing of patents but also for the provision of necessary know-how.

Owens-Corning Fiberglas was thus required to furnish its licensees, at nominal charge, with written manuals describing its machinery, materials, and processes. American Can was directed to provide any applicant, at cost, with "detailed working drawings, specifications of materials, prescribed production methods, and assembly blueprints," and if this should prove "inadequate to enable him satisfactorily to manufacture and assemble the machines and equipment covered thereby" to supply "further information, as the case requires, either (*a*) in writing, or (*b*) by making available a reasonable number of technical personnel for consultation . . . or (*c*) by permitting such applicant or his representative to visit defendant's machine shop where such machines and equipment are manufactured to observe the manufacture thereof."[63]

Eastman Kodak agreed to provide other finishers of amateur color film with manuals describing its processing technology, to keep the manuals up to date by issuing annual supplements, and to provide technical representatives to assist competitors in using the methods described.[64] International Business Machines agreed to train outsiders in the techniques of making and using tabulating equipment and to provide the trade with

---

[62] *U.S.* v. *General Electric,* 115 F. Supp. 835.

[63] *U.S.* v. *American Can Co.,* Civil Action 26345-H, District Court of the U.S., Northern District of Cal., Final Judgment, June 22, 1950.

[64] *U.S.* v. *Eastman Kodak Co.,* 1954 Trade Cases, Par. 67, 920.

its basic designs.[65] And General Electric was ordered to take similar steps to provide other manufacturers with the know-how required for the production of electric lamps.

LEADING INSTANCES

Key patents have helped to create a number of large and lasting positions of market power. These include the Bell System, General Electric, Eastman Kodak, Alcoa, United Shoe Machinery, IBM and, more recently, Xerox and certain drug companies. Though most gross abuses of patents have now been abated, patents still have power to make and reward monopoly on a large scale. Two prime examples—Xerox and drug markets—help clarify the outer edges of this continuing process.

Xerox. (Recall Chapters 2 and 7.) By 1948, Chester Carlson had invented and patented xerography. The key is a selenium drum which picks up electrostatic charges in the image of the original to be copied;

Courtesy Xerox

Chester Carlson (center) the original inventor of Xerography, with later collaborators John Dessauer (left) and Joseph C. Wilson (right), demonstrating an early dry-copying machine in Rochester, New York, in 1948. Carlson eventually realized over $200 million for his efforts.

---

[65] *U.S.* v. *International Business Machines,* Civil Action C-72–344, District Court of the U.S., Southern District of N.Y., Consent Decree, January 25, 1956.

this attracts powdered ink, and then deposits it on plain dry paper. Remarkably, several leading firms (including IBM) rejected the invention during the 1940s, and a tiny obscure firm, Haloid-Xerox, finally did the innovating. By 1959, the 914 copier was on the market, and the Cinderella story since then includes high growth, profitability and capital gains (a $10,000 holding in 1960 had risen past $1.1 million by 1970). "To copy" is now "to xerox."

Xerox's patent and pricing strategy has been complex and extremely rational for the long run. The main patent runs to 1978 and has given the firm about 95 percent of the dry-paper copy market. Xerox exploits it by providing all equipment on lease, with running charges per copy. This follows the old A. B. Dick, United Shoe Machinery, and IBM strategies of sophisticated price discrimination. It is reinforced by a large sales and support network. Xerox's new and more rapid machines are developed and priced to maximize customers' tendency to trade up to larger and better machines. Xerox has also developed a strong, patent position—with over 2,000 related patents—to continue its leadership after 1978. Even aggressive entry by IBM since 1970—with its powerful sales force and financial reserves—has scarcely touched Xerox's position.

Unless the FTC's action alters these basic elements, Xerox's dominance is likely to remain. (On the effects of the FTC action, see Chapter 7.) Evidently, the one key patent—gained by a lone genius and applied by a microscopically small firm—has had extreme effects. Monopoly of the first magnitude and near-permanence has been created. The actual and predicted monopoly losses appear to exceed the needed incentives by orders of magnitude. The innovation would probably have occurred nearly as soon if the patent had not existed. And it would have been more fully developed, at lower prices. Carlson's Xerox stock was eventually worth over $200 million when he died recently, but the rewards came more than two decades after his original work.

Drugs.   The drug industry illustrates another form of patent monopoly. Each firm operates in certain sectors or subsectors of the entire pharmaceutical industry. Although the industry's concentration is relatively low, the effective concentration is very high within many of the true markets. There is a certain amount of turnover in drug types, as new treatments and new medical problems come to the fore. The tendency is for a new drug to be introduced, to be priced very high during its patent life, and then eventually to drop toward competitive profit rates. During the interval, the monopoly profits are usually high (average rates of return on *all* drug sales run about 17–20 percent on equity). Effective monopoly often begins three or four years before the patent takes effect, and continues for several years after it has ended.

In short, there commonly is an extended interval during which one or at most two or three firms produce a patented drug and gain monopoly profits. The patent prolongs the life of the monopoly position, and increases the profits which can be reaped. There usually is deep price discrimination, with bulk prices at 20 percent or less of the retail price (instances of 2 percent are known). Other practices—large sales forces, insistence on brand names rather than generic names—are also used.

Accordingly, the drug firms jointly share a set of related markets in which patents create important monopoly positions. Many of these patents involve little more than small changes in mix, taste, or package design. Since 1960, the average and marginal productivity of drug industry research has gone down. New "miracle" drugs are few; the easy ones have been found.

The firms urge that the profit flow—augmented by patents—is essential to maintain research activity (recall the second section in this chapter). Patent monopoly on old and new drugs could therefore be necessary. This would fit the Schumpeterian hypothesis if the drug firms actually invaded each others' markets and had sharp shifts in position. In fact, there is very little shifting, less than a true Schumpeterian process would give. The alternative hypothesis is that drug firms are using patents rationally to create and exploit inelasticity of demand. This inelasticity arises from the life-or-death role of many drugs, and from the peculiar conditions in which most drugs are prescribed and paid for (see Chapter 27).

The drug industry is distinctive in these respects. In fact, specific patent reforms could be designed for the drug industry, involving more open licensing, cross-licensing, and changes in patent lives.

There is undoubtedly a tie between research efforts in the drug industry and *expected* profits. There is also a subjective sense of rivalry among at least some of the leading drug firms. And no one doubts that in the drug companies there is pressure on the R&D sections to come up with new drugs. Yet evidence is lacking that the duration of patent life, of actual monopoly, and of high rates of return are close to the optimal levels.

PATENT REFORM

Patent reform is always just around the corner. The courts have shaped the content of the law and limited many abuses. Congress has only made small changes, in 1939 and 1952. A large task force study proposed in 1967 mainly (1) a first-to-file standard and (2) confining Patent Office decisions to contested patents. Even these mild and obvious changes have been blocked—primarily by the Patent Bar, whose income they would reduce. Patent reform efforts usually exhaust all the participants and leave the system nearly untouched.

Still, patent reforms might offer large economic gains. Obvious ones include first-to-file and the obligation to use a patent or lose it (like the old homestead grants).[66] These have now been adopted in a number of countries.

---

[66] The number of patent monopolies might be reduced by legislative changes in the standard of patentability. Patents might well be confined to inventions representing really significant advances in technology or granted only to persons who could show that substantial sums had been spent on research and development. Designs might better be left to protection through copyrights. And the patent privilege might be withdrawn from foods and medicines. The multiplicity of patents might also be reduced through changes in procedure. Patent applications might be published and hearings given to competitors, consumers, and antitrust officials in opposition to the patent grants. The Patent Office might be equipped with a larger staff at higher salaries and thus enabled to take more time and exercise more skill in passing on applications. Larger appropriations for this purpose might be financed by increasing patent fees. All of these measures, or any of them, should operate to check the excessive creation of legal monopolies.

Patent Life. The issues are complex, but a shorter life—perhaps down to five years—now seems more efficient than the present 17 years. The precise change requires close study, and a range of lives—depending on the industry, subject, scope of patent, etc.—might be better than a single period. Patentors might be given a choice between long constrained patents and short unfettered ones. Or the limits might automatically begin after an initial period. One beauty of changing patent lives is that it could be applied to all new patents and soon (i.e., five or ten years) come to be universal without destroying present vested patent values.

Patent Restrictions. The patentor could be required to license all comers at a reasonable royalty fee. Such compulsory licensing is practical: it has been used in many consent decrees, and rarely have the courts needed to set the royalty rate.[67] When the would-be user can threaten court action, a "reasonable" royalty is usually agreed privately.

But there would be some burden on the courts or agencies. And compulsory licencing is a blade with two edges, not only making the strong firm license the weak one, but also the other way round. The proposal is a perennial, but its optimal use needs careful analysis.

Altogether, an optimal policy might be a sophisticated mix of periods and restrictions, perhaps with differing scope by types of inventions, etc. Yet a proliferation of ideal adjustments risks creating—in practice—a honeycomb of distortion by special interests. Somewhere between this and the simplicity of abolition is a yet-to-be-defined optimal patent system. Its conditions probably evolve as industrial conditions change. Could this optimum possibly be congruent with the present system, with its old and ancient origins?

TRADEMARKS

Readers will naturally be familiar with the trademarks of hundreds of goods. Specific company and product names can be made to signify extra product value, as well as simply to jog the memory. Trademarks are often built up by large volumes of advertising, and they often yield a large price premium. Like advertising generally, trademarks may serve as an entry barrier.

Trademarks are among all the kinds of identifying signs and words which firms try to use. By registering a trademark at the Patent Office, a person or firm gets 20 years (renewable) of formal evidence of ownership. After five years on the register, a mark cannot be contested.

Trademark rights, like patent rights, are enforced by bringing infringement suits. At first, such suits were entertained at common law. Statutory protection was subsequently given to trademarks by the legislatures of the states. The federal Constitution made no mention of trademarks. But Congress acted, in 1881, to protect marks used in foreign trade and, in 1905, to protect those used in interstate commerce. Infringement

---

[67] U.S. Senate, Committee on the Judiciary, Subcommittee on Patents, Trademarks, and Copyrights, *Compulsory Patent Licensing under Antitrust Judgments* (Washington, D.C.: Government Printing Office, 1960); Mark S. Massel, *Competition and Monopoly* (Washington, D.C.: Brookings Institution, 1962), p. 103.

suits were still decided in accordance with the laws of the states. The first effective federal trademark law, the Lanham Act, was not passed until 1946.

Trademarks inevitably cluster in consumer-goods markets, especially those with repeat buying of moderately complex and expensive goods, whose quality matters. Cars, film, beer, TV sets, and patent medicines are examples: vegetables and bricks usually are not.

Trademarks are frequently used to extend the market power created under a patent. They often are the only name by which customers know the product (examples: thermos jug and xeroxing. "IBM machine" has come close to standing for "computer." Try to list five other such names). Where names become generic, courts can defend the right of others to use the name. But this is often long, costly, and uncertain.[68]

Trademarks have been used successfully, where patents and copyrights failed, in the maintenance of resale prices, this practice having been approved by state and federal laws. They have been used to implement discriminatory pricing: methyl methacrylate was sold by Rohm & Haas to manufacturers as Lucite and Crystalite at 85 cents per pound, and to dentists as Vernonite and Crystalex at $45 per pound. They have been used to obtain exclusive markets: General Electric persuaded procurement agencies to establish specifications requiring Mazda bulbs, permitted Westinghouse to use the name, but denied its other licensees the right to do so.[69] Trademarks have also been used to effect a division of markets among the members of international cartels. Here, a mark is advertised throughout the world, each participant is given the exclusive right to use it in his own territory, and anyone who oversteps the boundaries assigned to him is driven back by an infringement suit.

Trademarks are more widely spread but usually weaker than patents. They reflect the underlying sales effort, which is often costly and must be refreshed by continuing efforts. Trademark reform is not a major topic or need, as long as abuses can be challenged in court. Any basic problem with trademarks arises from the advertising process which creates and maintains them.

Monopolistic practices involving trademarks have been enjoined in many cases by the courts. Contracts maintaining the resale price of trademarked goods were held to be unlawful in the Dr. Miles case[70] in 1911; their subsequent legalization has been discussed in Chapter 6. Decisions were rendered against the use of trademarks to promote discriminatory pricing in the Rohm & Haas case[71] in 1948 and against their use in excluding competitors from markets in the General Electric case[72] in 1949. In a number of cases involving the sharing of markets for

---

[68] Thus the patent on shredded wheat expired in 1912. But not until 1938 was the name found to be in the public domain: *Kellogg Co.* v. *National Biscuit Co.*, 305 U.S. 111. The case had been dragged out for more than a quarter of a century.

[69] See S. Timberg, "Trade Marks, Monopoly, and the Restraint of Competition," *Law and Contemporary Problems*, Vol. XIV (1949), pp. 323–61.

[70] *Dr. Miles Medical Co.* v. *John D. Park & Sons Co.*, 220 U.S. 373

[71] *U.S.* v. *Rohm & Haas*, Civil Action No. 9068, District Court of the U.S., Eastern District of Pa.

[72] *U.S.* v. *General Electric Co.*, 82 F. Supp. 753.

trademarked goods by international cartels, decided from 1945 to 1950, the courts found such arrangements to be in violation of the Sherman Act, rejecting trademark licensing as a defense.[73]

SUMMARY

Patents are a specialized device with obscure origins and many alternative forms. In the U.S., they grant 17 years of monopoly to any invention, small or great, often yielding huge returns. They are subject to abuse, and the resulting monopolies often last much longer than 17 years. Indeed, they have helped create some of the greatest and longest-lasting monopolies in the modern economy.

Yet literally nobody knows if they do induce invention and/or innovation. The optimal patent system—somewhere between abolition and a special grant tailored to each invention—is a matter for complex analysis of incentives, monopoly life, and monopoly effects. It may differ among sectors or types of inventions. It probably involves shorter patent lives, a first-to-file basis, and requirements to use the patent (directly or by licensing) or lose it.

The courts have steadily narrowed the range of patent abuses, but the monopoly-creating effect remains. Patent reform may be socially warranted, but it is unlikely to occur.

Trademarks pose similar but less severe problems. They can extend the life of patent monopolies and impede entry. But their power arises mainly from the sales effort which builds and maintains them, rather than the official grant itself.

---

[73] *U.S.* v. *Timken Roller Bearing Co.,* 83 F. Supp. 294 (1949). [Matched company names (from footnote 8, Chapter 2) follow: Swift and Co.: Esmark. Standard Oil (N.J.): Exxon. U.S. Rubber: Uniroyal. Sanitary Food Stores: Safeway. General Aniline and Film: GAF. Montgomery Ward (and Container Corporation): Marcor. National Dairy Products: Kraftco. Electric Storage Battery: ESB Industries. Corn Products Co.: CPC International. National Cylinder Gas: Chemetron. United Fruit Co.: United Brands. Standard Railway Equipment: Stanray.]

CHAPTER TEN

Antitrust Appraised

T he reader is now equipped to form judgments about "optimal" anti-trust policy and to compare them with what has actually occurred and seems likely to happen in the future. This chapter offers a guide to such an appraisal. No lessons can be drawn with certitude, but certain main lines have grown clearer in recent years. After nearly a century, U.S. antitrust may be ripe for revision. But in which ways, and how?

We review first its tasks and then its effects. This brings out the main causes of its difficulties. Possible "reforms" are then passed in review. The chapter considers finally the prospects for change.

THE CONDITIONS BEING TREATED

Recall that there are usually sizable net yields from abating market power—from market share or collusion—over a wide range. Loose oligopoly is the optimum market structure, except for the unusual cases with steep economies of scale. Yet tight oligopoly and near-monopoly occur extensively in present markets. The core of high market power in major industries has become increasingly stable in recent decades. Many of these dominant firms appear to have averted the normal erosion of high market shares, which usually occurs as industries go through a life-cycle. In these cases, and in oligopoly generally, the rate of decline of market power now seems to be low.

As the cult of bigness has gone the way of sarsaparilla and the penny beer, these market shares have had increasingly thin social justifications from economies of scale. In regulated sectors also, natural monopoly conditions are commonly receding, so that there is increasing scope for competition.

The costs of excess market power are not small. Prices and profits are increased. Efficiency is reduced. The fertility of invention and innova-tion declines. And the degree of inequality of wealth, income, and oppor-tunities is increased. The economy and society are put under avoidable burdens and stress.

Market power is endemic in many sectors and pathological in some. An optimal industrial structure would not go to the extreme of the pure competitive ideal, but it would possess markedly less market power in many industries.

EFFECTS OF ANTITRUST

Evidently, antitrust has not been perfectly optimal. Yet it may have had some strong effects and come close to the optimum in certain directions. In fact it has been, like the curate's egg, good in parts. One cannot be sure, for research on antitrust's economic effects has barely begun.[1] But some specific influences—and their composite effect on the whole structure of industry—are reasonably clear.

Cooperation has been reduced and altered. Formal cartel agreements have mostly been eliminated. What remains is covert, more fragile, and mainly among lesser firms in lesser industries. A degree of "fair trade" price fixing also remains, plus specific common practices in certain industries which avert price cutting (e.g., brand-name prescribing in drugs). Parallel pricing in shared monopolies is not treated directly. Large areas of the economy (regulated, local, exempted) are formally free of constraint, and other large areas are informally exempted by custom or lack of staff. The strict line against cooperation appears to be close to the optimal—*where* it applies.

Mergers have been tightly constrained since about 1963. Previously, mergers had been encouraged by the strict policy against cooperation. By the 1960s (recall Chapters 2 and 7), the main levels and lines of industrial concentration had been settled for decades. If the close limits on mergers remain, concentration *may* eventually taper down. Viewed in the small, horizontal and vertical merger limits now seem to fit efficient criteria reasonably well. The burden of proof and time are roughly in line with the economic factors.

Conglomerate merger policy is less efficient. Since 1969 it has protected the leading cases of industrial market power from take-over. This may avert some entrenching effects of mergers among leading firms in different markets. And the rate of rise in global concentration may have been slightly abated. But the loss in efficiency is likely to be appreciable. An efficient treatment would stop anticompetitive mergers but retain the pure conglomerate take-over process, at least in part. The ban on large-

---

[1] Earlier scholars looked only at legal results. The few studies of practical effects have had to be speculative. The most detailed is S. N. Whitney, *Antitrust Policies* (New York: Twentieth Century Fund, 1958), 2 vols. Yet his appraisal predates the Section 2 moratorium and the new merger strictness. His appraisal therefore stands in need of revision. Legal studies praising American antitrust are typified by two from the 1950s: U.S. Attorney General's Committee to Study the Antitrust Laws, *Report* (Washington, D.C.: U.S. Government Printing Office, 1955); and A. D. Neale, *The Antitrust Laws of the United States* (Cambridge: Cambridge University Press, 1959, rev. ed., 1970). Neale, a Briton, aims only to summarize U.S. antitrust, and he relies heavily on the Attorney General's Committee *Report* (which in turn reflects the views of its instigator, S. C. Oppenheim).

There exists no recent, full, analytical appraisal of antitrust's effects. The Nader group study (Green et al, *op. cit.*) is flawed and not analytical, but it has voluminous detail and its conclusions—that antitrust needs greater resources, powers, and economic consistency—may be valid.

firm mergers would be loosened to permit mergers by firms which are large but have modest market shares.

Established market power has been largely untouched for 20 years. Indeed, one could say it has scarcely been treated for 60 years. Certain leading cases were addressed and moderately revised during the first wave of Section 2 action (1906–20). The second wave recovered much of the doctrinal ground lost by the "rule of reason," but it had even more modest practical effects.[2] Since 1952, treatment has been nearly suspended, and the post-1968 actions have so far yielded only litigation (and fees), not effects. This moratorium arises from several causes (recall Chapter 7). It reflects rational choices by political appointees coping with biases in the system. The result: Section 2 cases likely to pose remedy problems are not even prepared or filed, to give the courts a chance to air the issues and set the margins of policy. Earlier, courts did define some monopolies and shared-monopolies as such, even if remedies did not ensue. Presently, even the process of evaluation—of thinking about what exists and how it might need change—has ground nearly to a halt. Even the several post-1968 suits face the same procedural blocks that have inhibited earlier treatments.

The eclipse of Section 2 is not really recent. Even the earlier actions came long after the original monopolization and scarcely touched the monopolizers' gains. Yet the present acquiescence tends neatly to regularize and legitimize market structure. And action which might touch the deeper financial structure surrounding these industries is simply beyond the reach of antitrust. Antitrust has itself become part of the industrial fabric, tending to preserve the existing industrial order and to limit change.

Again, there are positive effects. Absent antitrust, collusion and concentration would probably be greater. Recently, antitrust has been moving to reduce monopoly in regulated and exempt sectors. And the Division has had a better record than the FTC—and both rank above some regulatory and other agencies to be seen in later pages of this book. Yet the main lines of antitrust now appear to be off the optimum. There is need for a better balance among activities, a fuller use of antitrust powers, and a leaner use of agency resources. New tools and agencies may also be in order. Presently, antitrust relies on a narrow set of tools and procedures which seem incapable of treating the core problem.

CAUSES OF DIFFICULTY

At least five causes may be at work.

Procedure. The judicial process of "perfect justice" is slow and contains several important biases. Legal issues and evaluations supplant economic ones. Long, lucrative delay can be protracted deliberately, precisely where the social interests are largest. Weaknesses in judicial training can be exploited by fears and illusions.

Agency Resources and Powers. These may be far too small to treat

---

[2] The first series divided up several combinations and set implicit merger limits. The second series promoted entry (Alcoa, American Can) but did no important restructuring.

the breadth and severity of problems within the agencies' jurisdiction. These tasks are increasing in size and complexity, while real agency resources have scarcely grown for 25 years. Research is inadequate for lack of staff and access to information. Attorneys are routinely and steeply outmanned whenever treating major cases (pursuing small defendants is much easier). Fines are usually trifling and uncertain for the most important cases. And the agencies lack resources to carry out remedies efficiently, even if they were ordered. Pyrrhic victories are all too common, because (1) legal victories are about all the agencies have the resources to attain, and (2) the firms retain the power and information to control remedies.[3]

Expertise. Many agency officials lack skill in the issues of economics, finance, engineering, accounting, etc. which are the substance of the problem. As they pass through the revolving door of public office, they can hope only to learn the ropes and pull along a few prestarted actions. Basic changes are usually beyond their understanding or reach. Career staff members, on their part, are mainly lawyers attuned to courtroom standards, working to legal definitions rather than economic criteria.

Mistake and Waste. Agency officials are quite human (some of them moreso!) and so they often make errors and tolerate varying degrees of inefficiency. Most are not trained administrators, and their decisions are often made under extreme pressure. There are factions among parts of the agencies and often real deadwood among the staff and/or political appointees. Resources are often lavished on trivial activities, either by choice or in tasks imposed from outside. Powers are sometimes let rust, even those which operate with few resources (Section 2 is one example). The FTC has been the more wasteful, but the Division has had errors and inefficiencies too.

Political Economy. Perhaps after all, the root cause is the political economy surrounding antitrust. Power and interests play upon and around the agencies, using them and molding them as well as seeking redress in other forums. If so, the specific defects—procedural biases, scanty resources, inexpert officials, and errors, etc.—could merely be *effects* of the deeper real forces which distort antitrust and block *any* optimum solutions. Perhaps the bedrock of social and economic power is firmly set against what the economist would call optimal antitrust policy. This fits the view of, among others, both the libertarian and the radical left, as well as sceptical observers of moderate persuasion. *Classical liberal:* Given the unfriendly reality, one cannot expect policy to be more effective. The less of this maladroit interference there is, the better. *Radical left:* Finance capitalism underlies monopoly power and influences the political process. It has seen to it, and will continue to see to it, that antitrust serves—even expresses—corporate power rather than controls it. In the middle, some leading "moderate" scholars, too, are skeptical and disillusioned.

Each reader must judge (1) how far antitrust departs from optimality,

---

[3] See Walter Adams, "Dissolution, Divorcement and Divestiture: The Pyhrric Victories of Antitrust," *Indiana Law Journal,* 1951; and Kenneth Elzinga, "The Effectiveness of Relief Decree in Antimerger Cases, "*Journal of Law and Economics,* 1969.

and in which directions, and (2) what the causes are, specific or deep. American antitrust may be remarkably effective, even increasingly so. Or at the other extreme, it may be a pawn, controlled rather than controlling. The appraisal is determined by one's view of: (1) the economic conditions needing treatment, (2) the real effects of policies, and (3) the *realpolitik* surrounding policy. And these trace back, once again, to the natural rate at which market power diminishes.

Yet there is agreement that the procedures are slow and contain bias; that the agencies are bantams compared to their formal tasks; that officials often lack expertise; and that mistakes and waste occur. It is also agreed that antitrust is likely to continue largely as is, a system in political and economic equilibrium. There are no powerful groups seeking change. Most industrial interests who might be deeply hurt by antitrust have been exempted, formally or *de facto*. Nearly all sides engaged in the antitrust circus find something to gain from it—some very much indeed. Even the dominant firms who might be attacked gain legitimacy by the existence of agencies which *could* sue them for monopolizing but *don't*.

By comparison, some antitrust policies abroad have real substance and variety. Britain's agencies now have powers and resources comparable to those in the U.S., and Germany and Canada are not far behind. Certain British treatments—of resale price maintenance, formal agreements, and certain dominant positions—are at least as strict as in the U.S. Fact-gathering resources are also at least as adequate, compared to the apparent problems. And there is more use of supplementary treatments for the core cases: examples are public monopsony buying, price-screening bodies, and public enterprises of several sorts.

POSSIBLE REFORMS

U.S. antitrust has deep roots and great inertia, though its present twist has arisen mainly since 1952. The earlier favorable appraisals are out of date, and a wide variety of reforms have been proposed.

Two main directions for improving antitrust seem attractive:

Enrich and Enlarge. The agencies could be given more and better resources. Larger budgets, with less external control on their use, would give a freer hand for treating the core problems more thoroughly.[4] Appointees, especially those to the FTC, could be more broadly skilled and have longer tenure. Powers to get information and bring about basic changes could be added. In short, policy resources could be brought up toward parity with the problems to be treated.

This is a standard proposal, and it naturally has merit. But reallocation within the agencies and a more intensive use of existing powers would also increase effective resources.[5] And getting large increases

---

[4] Various observers suggest increasing agency budgets by as much as a multiple of five. See Green et al, *op. cit.*

[5] Recall Posner's analysis, *op.cit.* Also, the Division's sections could be realigned on a functional basis, with one specializing on price fixing, another on Section 2 cases, etc. Or, the trial lawyers could be used just as barristers, to try the cases, rather than as investigators and evaluators.

would require a major shift in the budgetary process as it is now handled both in the Executive offices and in Congress. As for officials, there seems little prospect of easing the grip of traditional lawyers upon the top positions.

Change the Tools. Several experiments could bring policy more into line with real incentives, power, and access to information. Amending the antitrust laws is a hazardous process, for it could easily be diverted into gutting them. But there is merit in these proposals:

1. Increasing and revising fines. The object is to set penalties and probabilities of conviction just high enough to induce optimal choices of behavior and structure. Optimal fines therefore can be lower if enforcement is more thorough. And for some offenses by small firms, fines are already steep enough. But for major offenses by very large firms, fines are presently too small. Even if used imaginatively by judges (e.g., X thousand dollars *per day* and per individual offense), they often leave even a convicted offender with large monopoly gains for every day the infraction lasted. The correct solution is to base fines on the degree of harm caused and/or the firm's ability to pay. This could be a percent of the monopoly profits, or of all profits, of the firm.[6] At present, fines are too small to be efficient in treating many problems. And their incidence— hitting smaller firms harder—often is palpably unfair.

2. Incentives. Section 2 treatment presently runs against the grain of corporate power, incentives, and information. Both managers and shareholders, and often workers too, believe that treatment would hurt their interests, even though in many cases it would actually benefit them. They are well set to resist study, trial, and effective remedy, as we have seen. If incentives could be reversed, so that corporate interests benefited by reducing dominance, the problem might become self-correcting. Various incentives could include:

a. Tax liability. Suppose that dominant firms were defined as such and given a deadline for reducing market power, and that share-price effects were given favorable treatment only if the deadline were met. Stockholders would then bring pressure on the managers to *achieve* the change, rather than serve as an excuse *not* to make it.

b. Direct tax. A light but real tax on market share over 30 percent could also induce firms to reduce them.[7] It would also yield appreciable tax revenues while abating monopoly profits. It would not tax efficiency or encourage expense-padding.

Other ways to align private and social incentives can be devised. None is perfect, and the most effective ones may be the most difficult ones to enact. But they could hardly be more out of alignment with corporate interests and power than Section 2 enforcement presently is.

3. Private suits. Private interests also are harmed by market power: competitors, customers, suppliers, etc. But they are commonly diffused, and they each suffer individual losses—e.g., a few dollars per purchase—

---

[6] See W. Breit and K. G. Elzinga, "Antitrust Penalties and Attitudes Toward Risk: An Economic Analysis, *Harvard Law Review,* Vol. 86, No. 4 (February 1973), pp. 693–713.

[7] See W. G. Shepherd, *The Treatment of Market Power* (New York: Columbia University Press, 1975), Chapter 7.

which do not justify a lawsuit. These potential plaintiffs usually have little legal skills or resources. Still, private suits can apply constraints in certain situations or even stir large changes (as in ITT-GT&E in 1972). To mobilize these interests, class-action suits are a powerful tool. They are brought by one victim on behalf of many, seeking penalties which can justify the cost of carrying the suit through. After brief efforts during 1968–73, class-action suits have met a stony reception in the courts. But if official antitrust continues as it is, class-action suits might provide the next best alternative, grounded firmly on private self-interest.

Several other ways to supplement antitrust have been noted, especially in Chapters 7 and 8. Trade barriers could be cut. This would affect several industries, but it is not a promising or general solution. Patents could be revised. This would affect a rather wider set of industries, but prospects for it are even less favorable. Nor would it abate the cases of settled market structure already created under patents. These and others will be discussed later in the book.

Finally, there are several "reforms" which seem more likely to be *harmful* than efficient.

Abolition.   This is occasionally suggested, on grounds that antitrust is (1) too powerful and harmful, or (2) a tool of corporate power. Sheer abolition, with no alternative, would probably bring about more collusion and concentration, plus possibly rather more flexibility in structure. Until other alternatives have been more fully tried, simple abolition seems extreme and crude.

Performance Criteria.   It is urged occasionally that antitrust act only where performance is poor, rather than treat behavior and structure directly. Thus, price fixing and monopoly would be treated only if performance could be shown to have been hurt. Chapter 3 helps us see that this proposal simply shifts the burden of proof and alters its content. Since performance data are hard to interpret and are controlled by the firms themselves, this proposal would bring antitrust nearly to a standstill and increase the load on the judiciary. In fact, it is precisely because performance questions have seeped into Section 2 actions that they have slowed to a crawl and become nearly unmanageable in court. To increase their role would paralyze antitrust policy behind a facade of economic rationality. Performance is already influential in policy, probably *too* influential.

More Consent Decrees.   Compromises do get half-loafs of remedy while sparing agency resources for other uses. Greater use of them could spread antitrust treatments further. Yet consent decrees have drawbacks (noted in Chapter 5) which caution against a shift toward them. *First,* they are often ineffective. They are routinely ignored after a few years, by the firm, courts, and the agencies themselves. Soon after a case is settled, the staff experts on it are gone or preoccupied elsewhere, so that a threat to reopen the case is often empty. Practices change to soften the decree's limits.

Second, they stifle private treble damage suits. No conviction is obtained, so private suits must start from scratch. They are also hobbled by the fact that the agency has not pressed for a conviction. Therefore a decree often throws away the one tool for treating the problem. *Third,* a decree immunizes. It legitimizes the situation, so that further action is presumed to be inappropriate for at least a number of years or decades. *Finally,* it leaves policy unresolved (as in conglomerate mergers in 1971). Precedential multipliers are not applied.

One Big Agency. Unifying antitrust under one agency is a perennial proposal. This would avoid overlaps and gaps. Responsibility would be focused and more accountable. Yet the change could be merely cosmetic, unless real resources and powers were changed. It would cause a seismic upheaval in treatment. And it could merely breed bureaucracy and political pressure, rather than efficiency. Only if the unified agency had increased powers to withstand the more focused interest groups might it be able to improve the actual treatment. Most experts prefer to retain two rival agencies—partly competing and emulating—in place of a monopoly agency.

Antitrust reform is a popular pastime, but it contains more quirks and illusions than is usually realized. Some reforms are palpably unwise, no matter how one appraises the present effectiveness of antitrust. Others are surely needed but, by any reasonable guess, unlikely to occur. Still others are untried and speculative. Devising optimal antitrust is a test of analytical skill, ingenuity and sophistication. One can expect the topic to persist unresolved for the next several decades, at least.

ACTUAL REFORMS

Little basic change is in prospect. The FTC was "revitalized" under Miles Kirkpatrick in 1970–72, but the main effect was only to raise truth-in-advertising slightly and start two actions toward Xerox and cereals firms. Even Turner has grown more ambivalent about how to treat shared monopoly; now he believes new law may *not* be necessary.[8] This not only recants on his earlier Kaysen-Turner proposal, but it also removes support for a similar proposal in 1968 by a Presidential task force (the *Neal Report*).[9] The one live, significant proposal is the 1972 Industrial Reorganization Act (appraised in Chapter 7). Its provisions for amnesty and flexible solutions make it a moderate strategy. Hearings on it are continuing intermittently, but it is regarded as extremely likely to be enacted in its present form. Even if it were, its subsequent funding and actual performance would be in doubt, under the same pressures which presently converge on the antitrust agencies.

---

[8] See Turner, *op. cit.,* 1969. This undercuts the Kaysen-Turner 1959 proposal and draft statute for deconcentration.

[9] The group included 12 leading lawyers and economists from a wide range of views.

Part III

THE FINANCIAL SECTOR

11.
Financial Markets

12.
Regulation of Banking, Securities Markets, and Insurance

CHAPTER ELEVEN

Financial Markets

Financial markets are the main control network of the modern econ-omy.[1] They stand above industrial, utility and trading enterprises, su-pervising and influencing their actions (recall Chapter 2). They allocate capital among enterprises in all sectors. They appraise performance and risk, and they fund new ventures and innovation.

Directly and indirectly, they influence managers, owners, consumers, and the other economic actors. They also shape the gaining and holding (and losing) of personal wealth. They can pool risks to insure against severe losses. Their degree of competition affects competitiveness in other markets. In short, they influence efficiency and equity throughout the economy.

Policies toward these markets have been distinctive and have had strong effects. There is much self-regulation, a degree of public regula-tion, and recently a marginal but growing role for antitrust. Public enter-prises also are important in parts of the sector (see Chapter 20).

The sector is complex and diverse. This chapter outlines the sector and its analytical properties (structure, costs, links with other enter-prises, etc.). We focus mainly on banking, investment finance, and insur-ance, which tie most closely to structure and performance in other mar-kets. Chapter 12 presents and assesses the policies toward these three areas.

Finance is highly sophisticated and flexible, often more elusive than

---

[1] Two splendid basic works on financial markets are Gerald Fischer, *American Banking Structure* (New York: Columbia University Press, 1968), and Irwin Friend *et al, Investment Banking and the New Issues Market* (Cleveland: World Publishing, 1967). An excellent survey is given by the set of reports by the Commission on Money and Credit, especially *Private Financial Institutions* (Englewood Cliffs, N.J.: Prentice-Hall, 1963); for a racy but sound introduction to stock-market realities, see Adam Smith, *The Money Game* (New York: Ran-dom House, 1967). See also the chapters by Phillips and H. M. Mann in Almarin Phillips, ed., *Promoting Competition in Regulated Markets* (Washington, D.C.: Brookings Institution, 1975). Extensive surveys of the stock market are given in Securities and Exchange Commis-sion, *The Structure, Organization and Regulation of the Securities Markets* (Washington, D.C.: U.S. Government Printing Office, 1971); and Senate Subcommittee on Securities, *Securi-ties Industry Study,* 93rd Congress, First session (Washington, D.C.: U.S. Government Printing Office, 1973).

quicksilver. It contains many of the country's most talented and intensely motivated commercial specialists, playing for the highest stakes of wealth and economic power. One must approach the issues with care, not expecting clear lines, full data, or optimal policies.

BASIC PATTERNS OF FINANCE

Among the varieties of business and consumer finance, our interest centers on the banking system and investment (or stock) markets.[2] These two sectors both bear closely on corporate control, and they both possess a core of large-volume processing operations.

Corporate Control. Private firms are embedded in close ties to their main financial backers (recall Chapter 2). This involves banking relationships, plus similar links to underwriters, investment houses, and other sources of support.[3] These ties are intimate and lasting, and they inevitably tend to link the larger banks with large and dominant firms. This in turn tends to reduce support for new and small firms, since their success would be at the expense of the larger banks' own clients. Through this process, financial imperfections tend to influence structure and performance in other markets.

Core Services. Both banking, stock trading, and insurance involve a large volume of routine processing. In banking, it is check-clearing and credit-coordinating among banks. In stock trading, it is reporting transactions, storage, and handling transfers. Insurance involves massive but simple data banks and retrieval systems. These core services are utilitarian and increasingly a matter of natural monopoly by large-scale computers and data transmission. A quasi-public enterprise (the Federal Reserve system) already handles the core banking services. Technology is forcing stock trading toward a unified meta-market, consolidating the present divided system. And various insurance programs (social security, accident, unemployment, etc.) have naturally shifted toward unified public systems. Though these economies are ripening, many familiar bank, brokerage and insurance activities at the *retail* level still have relatively small minimum efficient scale. Therefore the evolving technology leaves very wide policy options for future structure and control.

The basic policy problems in these three sectors are as follows:

1. The degree of monopoly is maintained above optimal levels, partly by official policies. Price competition is limited and the predictable losses of efficiency and equity result.
2. Layers of inside information are exploited to favor large and well-placed investors.[4] This reduces equity in the distribution of wealth, perhaps markedly.

---

[2] Such others as home mortgages and savings markets are interesting and important. But their problems are primarily "consumerist" and do not bear so closely on the structure and performance of the economy.

[3] Recall the first section of Chapter 2, and see Commission on Money and Credit, *op. cit.*

[4] Inside information is a fundamental problem. Changes in prospects for a company (a new product, or a downturn in profits, a new mineral discovery, etc.) are usually known first within the company, commonly to a handful of officers. They could obviously profit by trading

FIGURE 11-1
Financial Sectors

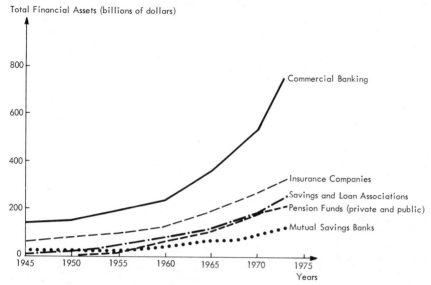

Source: Federal Reserve Board, *Flow of Funds Account,* annual.

These are not the only financial sectors with these problems. Nor do they dominate the whole of financial flows (see Figure 11-1). But their peculiar closeness to corporate control does increase their policy importance.

The policy questions are: (1) whether these monopoly restrictions are socially justified by providing safe banking and expert brokerage, and (2) whether policies provide investors with fair access to critical information. This depends in turn on the extent of the relevant markets, on economies of scale, on special risk factors, on the role of inside information, on the actual degree of competition, and on the performance of banking and stockbroker firms. We now turn to these technical conditions, taking banking first.

BANKING

The criteria for good banking include certain special attributes: (1) provision of funds to all borrowers on equal terms of access and price,

on their inside data, for the present stock price will change after the news gets out and affects expectations. The information then seeps out to the bankers, directors, friends of officers, and then to the more favorably placed brokerage houses, insurance companies, and other managers of investments. Eventually, usually, it reaches the man on the street. But it reaches him last, so that commonly all of the advantage of new information has been squeezed out before the news is announced. The news may be either bad or good for the company; one can gain from foreknowledge in either case. Much of the byzantine complexity and ingenuity in stock exchange devices and special funds can be viewed as simply ways of getting tips.

After all, investment—like all other speculative processes—boils down to a form of gambling against uncertainty. One is trying to outguess the *other* speculators, as much as to discover basic economic sources of company value.

TABLE 11-1
Banking Concentration in Selected U.S. Cities, 1970

Metropolitan Area	Total Deposits ($ billion)	Percent Held by Largest Three Banks
Largest Seven		
New York.	69.6	48
Chicago	23.7	43
Los Angeles.	15.4	70
San Francisco	13.2	78
Detroit	11.0	62
Philadelphia	10.3	46
Boston.	7.1	61
Others		
Phoenix, Arizona	2.0	90
Portland, Oregon.	2.0	80
Columbus, Ohio	1.7	93
Hartford, Conn.	1.5	89
Nashville, Tennessee.	1.4	90
Jacksonville, Florida	1.1	77
Albany, Georgia	.1	100
Lowell, Massachusetts.	.2	98
South Bend, Indiana	.6	56
Galveston, Texas	.3	50
National Total	433.4	

Source: Federal Deposit Insurance Corporation, *Summary of Accounts and Deposits in All Commercial Banks,* 1970 (Washington, D.C.: U.S. Government Printing Office, 1973).

and (2) avoidance of default on personal deposits. Some differences are acceptable, because certain genuine risks exist. But marked disparities in lending and large deposit risks are to be avoided.

Commercial banking actually involves several functions, the visible cashiering operations for personal checking being among the *least* important.[5] The core of banking activity and profits is in large-scale lending of funds to firms. These borrowers usually maintain large deposit and clearing accounts with their bankers: these, plus ancillary activities, are the elements of *full service* banking. This in turn is the core of transactions upon which long-lasting banking relationships rest. Banks also make consumer loans and mortgages: attract savings by large and small users; and operate trust departments which manage portfolios and other estate matters for citizens of ample wealth.

Banking markets are at local, regional, national, and international levels. Market edges are often blurred and controversial, but most of them can be defined reasonably well. Some seven large urban banking centers do 35 percent of the volume of all U.S. banking, but the mass of

---

[5] See Commission on Money and Credit, *Private Financial Institutions* (Englewood Cliffs, N.J.: Prentice-Hall, 1963); J. M. Guttentag and E. S. Herman, *Banking Structure and Performance* (New York: New York University Press, 1967); Fischer, *op. cit.;* and David Leinsdorf and Donald Etra, *Citibank* (New York: Grossman, 1973).

FIGURE 11–2
The Share of Large Banks has been Rising since 1950

Largest 50 Banks: Share of All Commercial Bank Assets

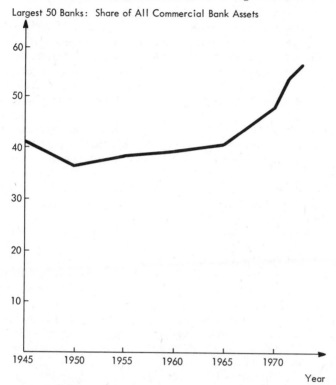

Source: *Fortune 500 Directory* and Federal Reserve Board, various years.

medium and small firms deal in hundreds of genuinely local banking markets.

The larger markets are moderate to tight oligopolies (see Table 11–1), while the smaller city markets run toward tighter structure.[6] Yet some small cities have surprisingly low concentration. Structure has been stable for decades, despite a modest degree of shifting and perhaps a very slow receding of the average degree of concentration. On the whole, banking structure is rather tighter than is usually found in other markets.

The total share of the largest banks has been rising strongly, both during the merger wave of the 1950s and more recently (see Figure 11–2). Mergers and differing regional growth rates have bred most of the changes in the large-bank list. The 50s merger wave strongly increased the degree of monopoly, creating anew the largest bank in Chicago and other large cities. Also, scores of one-bank holding companies were created, to permit banks to engage in related financial activities.

---

[6] City markets also contain various specialized submarkets, by type of industry and borrower. Within these, effective concentration is even higher.

Scale economies in banking could arise in any of the banking functions (loans, deposits, etc.), and so they are difficult to measure precisely. The best evidence suggests that average costs decline at small sizes but then are relatively flat over medium and large sizes.[7] This is reinforced by the low concentration in many small banking markets. One large loan can be made more cheaply than many small ones, because there is less processing and (probably) less risk. But this advantage is offset by various scale diseconomies, so that banking efficiency could be reached with a degree of concentration much lower than exists in most banking markets.

Formal banking structure is embedded in strong cartel restrictions and bankers' codes of behavior. These limit price competition and various other kinds of destabilizing behavior within the banking fraternity. They also tightly control new entry and other natural forms of corporate change, by making official bank charters difficult to get. Whether or not these restrictions are optimal, they do make the degree of monopoly greater than formal concentration suggests.

Banking has become almost free of the risk of failure. Since 1935 the rate of bank failures has dropped nearly to zero (see Figure 11–3), and it has remained low even during the stressful 1969–74 period. This is far below the business risks any other major sector. This reflects deliberate policy, including the restrictions on competition, the insuring of deposits, and Federal Reserve policies.

Banking relationships—between banks and their main client firms—are hard to discover, being highly sensitive facts which are not collected or published by any official agency. Patterns of banker directorships have been researched, and they reflect some of the underlying tissue of connections (recall Chapter 2).[8] They, together with financial folklore, indicate that there are strong and stable ties among leading banks and firms. Within the whole array, there are definite clusters around certain bank groups, especially the descendents of the original Rockefeller and Morgan interests.[9] The few extra-large international firms may relate to several or more major banks, partly for local connections and partly to play the banks off against each other. But for the greater mass of firms, a single strong banking relationship—reflecting the firm's own status—is normal.

Each bank can be regarded as relying primarily on a relatively few direct relationships with its major clients. It nurses these along, provid-

[7] See Guttentag and Herman, op.cit.; A. Phillips' chapter on banking in his Promoting Competition in Regulated Markets, ed. cit.; and D. Jacobs, Business Loan Costs and Bank Market Structure (New York: National Bureau of Economic Research, 1971).

[8] See U.S. House Subcommittee on Antitrust, Interlocks in Corporate Management, 89th Congress, First Session, (Washington, D.C.: U.S. Government Printing Office, 1965).

[9] See the excellent summary by James C. Knowles, "The Rockefeller Financial Group," in Ralph L. Andreano, ed., Superconcentration/ Supercorporation (Andover, Mass.: Warner Modular Publications, 1973). Also see U.S. House Committee on Banking and Currency, Commercial Banks and Their Trust Activities, 2 volumes, 90th Congress, 2d Session (Washington, D.C.: U.S. Government Printing Office, 1968), for a massive body of evidence. As for underwriters, the clustering is also strong. Thus Morgan Stanley & Co.—successor to part of the old Morgan group—has as clients six of the 10 largest U.S. industrial firms and 13 of the 25 largest, including auto, computer, electrical equipment, steel, chemical, photographic, and farm equipment firms.

FIGURE 11–3
Bank Failures Have Nearly Been Eliminated

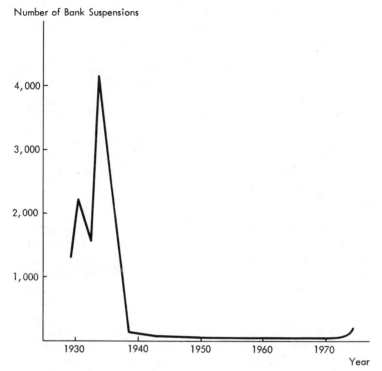

Number of Bank Suspensions

Source: Federal Reserve Board.

ing a variety of services and expertise, plus whatever insider and privileged information it can supply from any of the sources it can develop (including from these firms!). These ties are not formal, but they are often exceedingly strong. It is common knowledge, for example, that banks do not normally try to compete away each others' main clients. It is simply not done (with few exceptions), and in any event the ties resist most price-cutting inducements.[10] The key is the whole package of mutual trust and support which the banking relationship involves.

In short, banking tends toward very tight formal and informal market structure, much more than efficiency requires. In addition, its relationship to producing enterprises involves a degree of quasi-vertical integration and shared access, both to favorable credit terms and to higher-quality inside advice and information. Therefore, banking touches on both the efficiency of its own allocation and of its allocation of capital

---

[10] Thus, the failure of Franklin National Bank in 1974 traced back partly to its efforts to enter New York City banking in the 1960s. It could not hope to attract major new clients away from other banks. Only inferior lending activities were accessible, and so it was kept on the higher-risk fringe of the market from the start. This is the normal experience for new entrants. See Sanford Rose, "What Really Went Wrong at Franklin National," *Fortune* magazine, October 1974, pp. 118-21 and 220–27.

among other producing units. It also touches on the insider question, whereby those with better information are able to profit at the expense of others. Some of this insider problem arises in any market system, for the flow of information is inherently imperfect. Nonetheless, the problem inheres in banking relationships, and it raises serious questions for policy.

Banking behavior and performance fits these structural patterns. There is little direct price competition among banks. A degree of competition does occur on quality and fringe service features, much as it does among regulated airlines (see Chapter 17 below). But behavior closely fits the market structure and informal restrictions among banks. It has also been stodgy and sluggish, but partly for historical reasons.[11]

Banks record stable and rather high rates of return. Taking the top two banks in the ten largest banking centers, the average return on equity for these 20 banks during 1965–73 was 14 percent, quite a handsome level. There was little variation (either among the group or from year to year), reflecting a low degree of risk.

Interest rates differ by the size, market position, and banking relationship of the borrower. Large, dominant-firm clients pay lower interest rates, often by several percentage points. Interest paid on private deposits also varies, with larger depositors getting better terms. Interest rates on $10,000 and $25,000 certificates, for example are regularly 2 points or more above those provided for small accounts, more than costs or risk could justify.[12]

Also, bank trust departments normally cater only to large clients, usually with portfolios above $100,000. The best of the trust departments deal only in larger accounts, starting at $500,000 or more. These are the ones with large holdings, board-room positions and other sources of inside information. On the whole, bank trust operations favor the wealthier citizens.

The main recent change has been from foreign banks. By merger and growth, they increased their assets in the U.S. by sevenfold during 1966–74, to at least $3.5 billion or 5 percent of all U.S. banking assets. (By contrast, U.S. banks held $77 billion in assets abroad; but 68 percent of this was in Britain, Ireland, and the Bahamas.) British and Japanese banks have led the move into the U.S., which touches mainly the New York and California markets. They are free of two main restrictions on U.S. banks: they can operate in more than one state, and they can sell brokerage services. Moreover, they are free of federal regulation.

This modest incursion has stirred larger U.S. banks to seek equal freedoms for themselves to begin multi-state and brokerage operations.

---

[11] "Banking was a dead, dreary business in the days after World War II. Bankers were first stunned by the debacle of the 1930s and then dulled by years of doing little more than financing the massive U.S. war debt. A full generation of talented college graduates went into almost every business except banking" (*Business Week*, "The New Banking," September 15, 1973, pp. 88–92). Some change came during the 1960s, toward the degree of entrepreneurship common in other sectors.

[12] The official ceilings set by the Federal Reserve on interest rates for savings deposits were at 4 percent up to 1970, and not above 5½ percent during 1970–74; yet a variety of Treasury bills, short-term bonds and other certificates commonly used by the wealthy were paying as high as 10 percent.

FIGURE 11–4

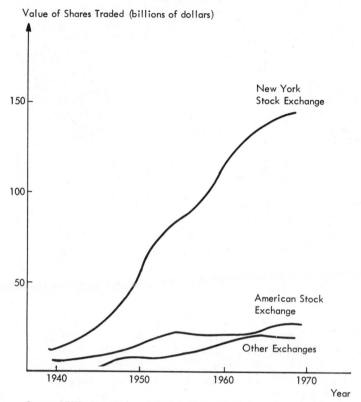

Value of Shares Traded (billions of dollars)

New York
Stock Exchange

150

100

50

American Stock
Exchange

Other Exchanges

1940   1950   1960   1970

Year

Source: NYSE *Fact Book,* and SEC *Statistical Bulletin,* various years.

It may eventually help erode the policy restrictions, which have induced the foreign entry. But the incursion, and the erosion, have taken decades to begin. The effect is still small, and any large changes appear remote.

SECURITIES MARKETS

Stocks are only one among the many kinds of asset values that are traded: bonds, commodities, futures, options, warrants, discounted paper, debentures, rights, etc. But the stock market is crucial for corporate evaluation and control.[13]

There are two levels to analyze. One is the narrow brokerage function; handling stock transactions for a fee. The other is the substance of trading, information and control over firms: the market for corporate control. Brokerage is handled by a hierachy of stock exchanges, shown in Figure 11–4. The basic moves in stock prices are shown in Figure 11–5. (The

---

[13] On basic conditions, see the sources noted in footnote 1 above; W. J. Baumol, *The Stock Market and Economic Efficiency* (New York: Fordham University Press, 1965); and Sidney Robbins, *The Securities Market* (Glencoe, Ill.: The Free Press, 1966). On the turbulent conditions of the 1960s, see John Brooks, *The Go-Go Years* (New York: Weybright and Talley, 1973).

FIGURE 11-5

Dow-Jones Industrial Average (monthly highs and lows)

1972–74 drop was much sharper for all stocks than this leading-firm average shows). The NYSE has the leading firms; the ASE lesser ones; while the regional and over-the-counter market includes the mass of small and new firms. They are the trading arena used by the hundreds of private brokerage firms.

Transactions are essentially simple housekeeping actions; finding the price, conducting a trade, recording the terms, and transferring the certificate. There must be an information network, so that traders at a distance can learn the going prices. The whole process is simple, standard, and increasingly computerized. Yet ordinary traders must have the transaction done—for a fee—by a broker, who has access to the exchange. This is usually a brokerage house, which has one or more memberships in (or seats on) the exchange, through which the trades are funnelled. Since NYSE members can only do brokerage business (by NYSE rule), they are neatly immunized from take-over by other firms.

The broker provides the access, the instant information, and the handling. The brokerage firms range from the dominant Merrill Lynch, Pierce, Fenner & Smith down to hundreds of small firms. Their ranks have been thinning with the fluctuations since 1966, by failure and mergers. The larger firms also do some market research and circulate advice to investors, but this printed material is of limited value to most customers.[14] The basic objective is to outguess the rest of the market. This involves much sheer gambling, since the impact of any new information depends on how well it has already been anticipated, plus many other

---

[14] See especially Adam Smith, *op.cit.*, and Mann, *op.cit.*

Drawing by Lorenz; © *1968 The New Yorker Magazine, Inc.*

Commercial Credit up nine and a half! Standard Oil tacks on a dozen! Ling-Temco-Vought closes at two hundred and one! Combined Dow-Jones at all time high!

influences; and those are anybody's guess in many cases.[15] (However, brokerage firms also try to get all possible inside information for their clients; some of this is important and also poses major policy questions; see Chapter 12.)

The broker's fee schedule is summarized in Figure 11–5: this is for the NYSE, but it is quite typical of others. The cost per transaction is relatively uniform, but the fee varies sharply by the *price* of the stock. Therefore, the pricing mixes cost and price discrimination. It must be paid, whether one gets various broker services (advice, research, etc.) or a mere transaction. The fee schedule is set by the exchange, acting as a cartel of its members. The policy question is whether any special features of stock brokerage justify such price fixing (recall Chapter 6).

The average costs per transaction are also illustrated in Figure 11–6. Small trades are done at a loss, while large trades are lucrative (i.e., the fee is above competitive equilibrium levels).[16] The large-trade profits

---

[15] Try to predict stock prices. Pick five firms, study their record and price trends using a 1970 *Moody's Handbook of Common Stocks,* and predict their stock-price moves since 1970. Or, pick and study five stocks as of now and then predict their level at the end of this course. See what help you get from brokerage house advice. Then try to analyze what forces did cause the actual changes in price. Good luck!

[16] The difference may be less, because brokers usually give large trades priority during rush periods. Therefore the marginal costs of small trades, made in effect off-peak, would be lower, more in line with actual fees.

In 1973, the direct costs per transaction were estimated at $30–$40; with all company costs averaged in, the average was reckoned at $94 by the NYSE. Yet the real costs would vary with peak load conditions and the degree of resources devoted to each transaction: these would differ sharply.

FIGURE 11-6

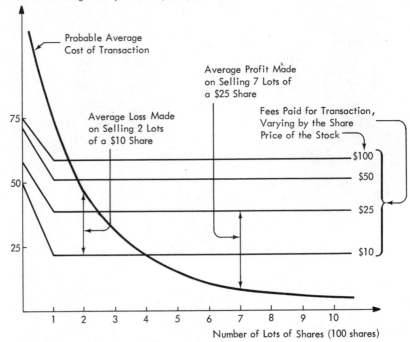

Price and Average Cost per Share (cents)

Probable Average
Cost of Transaction

Average Profit Made
on Selling 7 Lots of
a $25 Share

Average Loss Made
on Selling 2 Lots
of a $10 Share

Fees Paid for Transaction,
Varying by the Share
Price of the Stock

75

50

25

$100

$50

$25

$10

1   2   3   4   5   6   7   8   9   10

Number of Lots of Shares (100 shares)

stimulated the rise of special block trading—in the third market—and of semi-corrupt kick-back processes (so-called "give-ups") during the 1960s. These closely fitted the classic effects of discriminatory pricing by a cartel, including the steady shrinkage of the cartel's share of the market. The long-run trend is toward competitive pricing of broker services, as the shift from 1967 to 1974 rates shows (and see Chapter 12).

It is also toward computerizing and linking trades in one grand market. The separate stock exchanges will fade away in the process, and so will the cartel controls they maintain. Therefore they are retarding this evolution, so as to minimize their members' loss. Yet the members are also losing from the long-term shrinkage of business which the price fixing itself causes. The outcome is a vector of these cross-incentitives: some retardation, but with complex struggles among the various members, independents and other trading groups.

In all essentials, stockbroking is a potentially competitive industry.[17] Stock-exchange officials have claimed, instead, that it tends toward "de-

---

[17] See H. M. Mann, "Antitrust and the New York Stock Exchange: The Issue—Minimum Brokerage Commissions," Chapter 9 in A. Phillips, *ed. cit.;* Subcommittee on Securities, *Securities Industry Study, op.cit.;* and Irwin Friend and Marshall E. Blume, *The Consequences of Competitive Commissions on the New York Stock Exchange,* an excellent analysis included as Appendix A in "Stock Exchange Commission Rates," Hearings before the Senate Subcommittee on Securities, 92rd Congress, 2nd session (Washington, D.C.: U.S. Government Printing Office, 1972), pp. 259–404.

structive" competition, so that price fixing gives social benefits. The five main possible reasons for such destructive competition are as follows.

1. *Fluctuations.* Trading volume does shift from day to day and, to a degree, from year to year. But these are not the major cyclical swings which might force most of the industry into bankruptcy. Many healthy competitive industries have fluctuations sharper than those in stock volume.

2. *High fixed costs.* If fixed costs were a high percentage of all costs, any demand instability would make short-term price competition ruinous. Yet most stockbrokerage costs are variable, not fixed. At least 65 percent of costs are personnel, promotional costs, rents, utilities, and other adjustable items. There is little of the large, highly specialized technical equipment which high fixed costs usually involve.

3. *Atomistic structure.* Fluctuations might eliminate large numbers of firms. Yet entry is easy and firms could easily move in and out. Therefore, there would be no long-run loss of efficiency or capacity.

4. *Demand inelasticity.* If demand were inelastic, price competition would tend to be ruinous. But the slight evidence actually available suggests that demand is elastic, especially for the basic transaction service.

5. *Myopia.* Brokerage managers might be short-sighted, cutting back sharply in slumps and expanding too far in booms. This would raise long-run costs and destabilize supply. But these managers are not different from others. Even if they were, fixed fees would make the effects *more* severe.

Therefore, stockbroking is potentially quite normally competitive. One remaining argument for fee-fixing is that it makes valuable extra services possible: research, advice, etc. This point also fails; first, because these services could be separately priced and bought if customers did value them. Second, the services are actually of dubious value, as is increasingly clear.[18] A final reason for fixed commissions might be that they foster technological progress toward a unified market. But instead, as we have seen, the exchanges' cartel restrictions tend to retard it.

In short, there is little or no economic case for stock exchange price fixing. It has existed for over a century, only encountering policy resistance before the SEC in 1968 (see Chapter 12). Brokerage firms have had financial stress, especially since 1963; some have failed and many have been merged as failing firms (recall Chapter 8). The severity of these problems has probably been increased by the fixing of fees. And it has also reflected a degree of management inefficiency in many brokerage firms which is widely agreed—and which also arises from the cartel protections.

Now we turn to the deeper role of stock trading, in fostering efficient capital flows and giving fair access to information. U.S. conditions are know to be perhaps the best among the world's stock exchanges, but are still improvable. Stock holding and trading is by diverse units, including (1) large institutional investors (insurance firms, pension funds, endowments, bank trust officers, etc.); (2) small professional traders (expert,

---

[18] See Adam Smith, *op.cit.;* and Mann, *op.cit.,* among others.

well-placed, often specializing in esoteric operations); and (3) personal investors, ranging from large, experienced holders down to the masses of small investors. Institutions now do over 70 percent of all trading (in 1974 the share reached about 85 percent). The largest bank trust departments play a large role. In 1972, the top ten held $135 billion in trust assets and exerted strong influences on a broad range of share prices.[19] Small investors tend to earn small or negative gains, since (1) they are ignorant of basic trends, methods of evaluation, and timing strategy; (2) they get news after the professionals have already learned, acted upon, and discounted it;[20] and (3) brokerage fees are a higher proportion of the value of their trades.

The whole process performs several functions. It evaluates management (recall Chapter 2). It allocates capital among the whole range of firms. It rewards good and timely investment decisions and penalizes foolish ones. In a well-functioning capital markets, stock values move smoothly in line with the actual performance and prospects of the firm. And all (or at least many) investors have an equal chance to gain by making sound decisions. There is an inherent gambling element, but it operates moderately, as arbitrage to keep stock prices in line with the underlying industrial values.

Actual conditions diverge from this ideal in certain ways. The basic flaw is *insiderism:* the disparity in access to key information. There are layers of access to data, which systematically favor larger, well placed investors. This arises from the conduct of companies, in their strategies toward keeping or releasing information. Thus, most large firms have buried the details of their operations in company-wide totals: for highly diversified firms, this virtually suppresses all information from open view. Brokerage firms (and others) often discriminate in using the inside information they do get. There is a steady stream of cases involving favors to large clients: this is probably the small visible top of a large iceberg. Such insider problems are widespread and have strong effects. The small investor is forced to rely on mediocre advice and late information.[21]

There actually are two kinds of insider problems: short-run and long-

---

[19] Morgan Guaranty—which continues the old Morgan group trust activities—alone held $27 billion, with significant holdings in a cluster of major firms. See also Knowles, *op. cit.* Morgan Guaranty and Bankers Trust alone hold more than the total for all mutual funds.

[20] The advantages of professional stock specialists were neatly summarized by a successful trader: "As a trader, I had a terrific edge over the average investor because of all the electronics and direct lines to trading desks at my disposal. It gave me total information and market feel about various stocks, which is invaluable. Mainly I could get people to tell the truth about stocks." (*Wall Street Journal*, October 4, 1974, p.1).

[21] This is widely agreed among expert observers, and is frequently discussed in the *Wall Street Journal, Business Week, Forbes,* etc. As the small investor has realized that the market "is rigged against him in favor of the big institutional customers," (*Business Week,* November 17, 1973, p. 27), participation has decreased. In 1970, 30 percent of U.S. families owned some stock; in 1973, only 21 percent did. Companies routinely hold private meetings for institutional stockholders and security analysis at which advance information is given. This is used first for the best clients and then, if ever, disseminated. Repeatedly, the large traders' actions change the price by 25 percent or more before small investors have a chance to hear. Such cases in 1973 included Avon Products and Polaroid (down by more than 50 points) and Equity Funding (a 1969–73 drop from $80 to zero) with never a sell recommendation to small customers, though large customers were tipped off.

run. The short-run type has been discussed already. Long-run insiderism prevents the passage of information about basic conditions of a company out to the market generally and to competitors and potential entrants. An example: A company has ten branches, two of which are not profitable. Full knowledge of that pattern could well affect a wide range of financial choices and corporate strategies.

Short-run insiderism yields special gains to some at the expense of others, primarily from portfolio trading. Long-run insiderism reduces the scope of competition and new entry against firms. It also limits the possibilities of take-over, either of whole enterprises or of their parts. Further, by hiding basic information, it reduces the pressures upon company management to be efficient in all parts. Therefore, on the whole, long-run insiderism tends to abate the effectiveness of competition and managerial efficiency.

As for efficiency, stock markets deal in portfolio assets, not directly in productive investment. Their allocative effect is indirect and can be compromised by imperfections and extraneous disturbances. Market psychology can put whole classes of productive firms into disfavor, pushing their stock prices below levels at which efficient amounts of new capital can be raised. It is not clear that stock prices are brought into line with intrinsic values. Many experts believe that the allocative function is now poorly performed.[22]

In short, there are serious doubts about the structure, behavior, and performance of the stock market, both in its price fixing and its more profound effects. There may be large social losses under present policies.

INSURANCE

Insurance operations have two sides: (1) insurance proper (coverage of risks to life and property), and (2) investment (large-scale portfolio operations). Small net losses on the insurance are often more than offset by profits on the investment function (mutual firms have roughly zero net profits). The industry is on a large scale, with a range from large to medium-size firms. Life and property insurance are the main parts. To most consumers, life, home, and automobile insurance pose the main problems.[23] Though most operations are national, insurance is regulated only at the state levels (see Chapter 12).

As is common elsewhere, there are some economies of scale, but not beyond moderate size. The risk of the firm arises both in insurance and in investment operations, and so sheer size does not add greatly to stability.

Structure tends toward medium and tight oligopoly, with some variation among states. This is usually tighter than minimum efficient scale requires. Competition is also limited by various regulatory rules and by

---

[22] See Irwin Friend, "The Economic Consequences of the Stock Market," *American Economic Review,* Vol. 62, No. 2, (May 1972), pp. 212–19 and sources cited there.

[23] Health insurance is dominated by the Blue Cross-Blue Shield, Medicare and Medicaid systems (Chapter 27). Unemployment and accident insurance are largely public systems (Chapter 19).

the life insurance firms' practice of using the same mortality table as a basis for rates.

Profitability is difficult to assess. There is little fixed capital, but rather an array of salesmen and clerks plus large revolving funds for investment and policyholders' benefits. Expert opinion rates profitability at low to moderate; this can reflect efficiency in management, in portfolio choices, or in avoiding bad luck among policyholders.

There are four main criteria of social performance for insurance: (1) breadth of coverage, (2) efficient management, (3) reducing the cost of insured losses, and (4) security of coverage. *Breadth* of coverage need not be universal, but in a decent society it will not exclude large groups of needy and high-risk persons. This inherently conflicts with the economics of private insurance; to maximize profits, the firm will tend precisely to exclude persons with known high risks who are unable to pay premiums. This exclusion is not complete, but it is substantial. The large minority of the population which is left unprotected is primarily those who most need coverage, both on private criteria and social criteria.

Costs are substantial. Between 20 and 50 percent of premiums are absorbed in company costs (though much less for Blue Cross and Blue Shield). The sales cost are substantial, including about 600,000 salesmen. The more efficient firms hold sales and administrative costs to low levels; public, universal-coverage systems have especially low cost ratios.[24]

Constraints can be exerted by insurance firms on such costs as medical care and automobile design and repair. Special rates can be offered for healthy living and driving habits, and better automobile design. Hospitals can be pressured to increase efficiency and to price their services more efficiently. Instead, insurance firms have mainly been passive. Only a few firms have explored some of this ground, even though this aspect of automobile and medical insurance is widely known to permit unnecessary cost (see also Chapter 27).

Security is important, because the policy is a long-term commitment which becomes like a principal savings account to many policyholders. Failure of an insurance firm can cause devastating hardships for thousands of clients (unless the firm is reinsured, privately or publicly). Regulation permits various restrictions precisely in order to prevent insurance company failures (see Chapter 12). Actual failures are infrequent, but since 1970 several major collapses have occurred, which have had large impacts.

Performance in the main insurance markets therefore shows certain defects. These touch both on efficiency and equity, often with sharp impacts.

SUMMARY

In these key markets, there are certain marked departures from competition. The effects of this fit the standard predictions fairly well, and

---

[24] This partly reflects the greater variety of private policies, and so normative comparisons are hazardous. Yet some of the variety runs to excess, including gimmicks and obscure terms of coverage (the familiar "fine print").

performance appears to be inefficient and inequitable in several definite directions. These losses may be offset by other social gains, and so the three sectors may reflect a reasonable balance of public policies. But those gains would need to be large. In any event, we need to understand how the policies have evolved and how they now operate.

CHAPTER TWELVE

Regulation of Banking, Securities Markets, and Insurance

$\mathbf{P}$olicies toward these markets have tended mainly to reduce competition, as a way of reducing risk. The set of public regulatory agencies is large, complex, and fragmented—a patchwork, not a system. Tables 12–1 and 12–2 summarize the agencies and their roles. They were created after the private systems were in being (like most utility regulation; see Chapter 13), with large tasks but modest resources and powers.

TABLE 12–1
The Agencies Affecting Financial Markets

1. Banking	2. Securities
Federal Reserve Board	Securities and Exchange Commission
Comptroller of the Currency	3. Insurance
Federal Deposit Insurance Corp.	State insurance agencies
State bank regulatory agencies	
Antitrust Division, Dept. of Justice	

We begin with a brief history of regulation in these sectors. Then the sensitive points in banking regulation are reviewed. The SEC's treatment of brokers' fees and insider problems is considered next. The last section briefly assesses the regulation of insurance. Among the details of these three sectors run several common threads:

1. Regulation is designed to protect investors and depositors.
2. It adds (or acquiesces in) restrictions on competition and entry.
3. It applies only light constraints, or none at all, on prices and profits, tending more to raise than reduce them.
4. It tends to retard new efficient forms and methods.

TABLE 12–2
Regulatory Coverage in Banking

	Comptroller of the Currency	Federal Reserve	Federal Deposit Insurance Corp.	State Agencies
National Banks†				
Chartered by	*			
Examined by	*	*	*	
Reserves required by	*	*	*	
Subject to regulations of	*	*	*	
Mergers and branches limited by	*	*		
State Member Banks†				
Chartered by				*
Examined by		*	*	
Reserves required by		*		
Subject to regulations of	*	*	*	*
Mergers and branches limited by		*		*
Insured Nonmember Banks†				
Chartered by				*
Examined by			*	*
Reserves required by				*
Subject to regulations of		*	*	*
Mergers and branches limited by			*	*

† In 1971 the number and assets were as follows:

	Number	Assets ($billions)
National Banks	4,599	376
State Banks	1,128	136
Insured Nonmember Banks	7,875	124

EVOLUTION OF POLICIES

Financial markets have always mingled elements of (1) solidity and security, with (2) riskiness and turbulence. The essence of finance is to take risks and seek new ways of turning a profit (and a capital gain). This involves clashes of interest, as well as areas of rigid safety.

During 1865–1910, the unruly element was strong in American banking, stock trading, insurance, and other financial markets. This reflected the turbulence in the developing U.S. economy, as structural changes created large new openings for quick gains, risky ventures, battles for control, promotion of monopoly trusts, and fleecing of unwary investors. Gould, Fisk, Vanderbilt, Schiff, Morgan, the Rockefellers, and other financiers conducted spectacular struggles on many financial fronts. Even though their importance was exaggerated in current accounts, they did stir and shape the money markets. The operations deployed all the elements of finance, freely mingling banking, stock promotion, investment banking, etc., as the occasion required.

The basic thrust of policy has been to separate these subsectors, stabilize their structure, and reduce the risks from price competition.[1] Such

---

[1] See especially Fischer, *op. cit.*; Friend, *op. cit.*; and Phillips, *op. cit.*

trends were already under way by 1900–1920; recent policies have given them more form and force. This reaction against financial instability proceeded from about 1910 to 1960, with a sharp shift in the 1930s. The drift now appears to be reversing slightly under the pressure of events, toward permitting more competition among and within the sectors.

To 1929. Before 1910, banking was largely competitive and often tumultuous. With free entry, wildcat banking and other abuses often bilked depositors. Banks were also used as parts of the larger strategies of the leading investment bankers. Bank failures were common, especially during panics, when runs on banks could be triggered by the slightest of rumors. The basic social needs were to protect depositors against bank failures, and to develop the standard check-clearing system—the central banking operation—among banks.

The early Federal Reserve evolved some rudimentary capacity for these purposes during 1920–32, but it failed utterly to use its powers to save banks from the effects of the great crash of 1929–38.

In 1920, there were 30,000 banks in the United States; during the twenties more than 5,000 of these banks failed, most of them in small towns suffering from the effects of agricultural depression. At the same time, city banks, taking advantage of rising prices, made loans to finance speculation in real estate and in securities. When the market crashed in 1929, the value of their collateral declined. Their reserves were depleted; they were unable to meet the demands of their depositors. There were runs on the banks; 8,000 banks failed from 1920 to 1933. Bank holidays were declared by state after state and finally by the federal government. No depositor could get a penny from his account until the banks were reopened during the early days of the New Deal. Deposits in the stronger banks were unimpaired; depositors in the weaker banks suffered heavy losses. A Senate Report[2] revealed serious breaches of trust by bank officials. Certain large commercial banks had set up investment affiliates and sponsored dubious securities; instead of giving impartial investment advice to their customers, they had pressed them to buy securities in which they themselves had an interest. They had paid excessive compensation to their officers; had extended large loans, with inadequate collateral or no collateral, to directors and officers to enable them to finance their private speculations. In some cases, officials, acting on the basis of inside information, had sold short the stock of their own banks, reaping a profit as other stockholders lost. It was this experience that led to the creation of the Federal Deposit Insurance Corporation and to the passage of the Banking Act of 1933.

In the case of life insurance, a thorough investigation of the principal companies was made in 1905 by the Armstrong Committee of the New York State legislature with Charles Evans Hughes, later Chief Justice of the United States Supreme Court, serving as its counsel. The committee's report,[3] published in ten volumes, disclosed serious abuses. The compa-

---

[2] U.S. Senate, Committee on Banking and Currency, *Stock Exchange Practices* (Washington, D.C.: Government Printing Office, 1934), pp. 163–221.

[3] *Report of the Joint Committee of the Senate and Assembly of The State of New York, Appointed to Investigate the Affairs of Life Insurance Companies,* 1906.

nies were controlled, not by their stockholders or policyholders, but by self-perpetuating directorates. They had overpaid their officers and made lavish expenditures on unnecessary buildings. They had made extravagant investments, reported fictitious assets, and manipulated insurance funds. They had bought into banks, where they had maintained large inactive balances, reducing company earnings at the expense of shareholders and policy owners. They had refused to pay legitimate claims. They had maintained well-financed lobbies in state capitals to fend off corrective legislation. The Committee's recommendations for reform were embodied in the New York State insurance law of 1906, and this served as a model that was copied by many other states.

Stock trading involves many possible abuses, all of which occurred amply before 1929. The rigging of trading was endemic, and all manner of securities were issued, some worthless and fraudulent. Schemes to trick investors were legion, and the pyramiding that fueled the 1920s stock boom (see Chapter 15) was only one of many ways to turn small values into big—and shady—paper gains. Investors, especially small and gullible ones, were ruthlessly victimized by some bankers, by dealers and salesmen, and by investment advisors. They also were shorn by market manipulators influencing stock prices.

The distribution of securities has been regulated by the states since 1911, when Kansas passed the first of the so-called "blue-sky" laws, to prevent promoters, in the words of one legislator, from selling shares "in the bright blue sky itself." Such laws had been enacted by all states except Nevada by 1933. In a few states, these laws merely provide that the fraudulent sale of securities shall be a criminal offense, empower the Attorney General to prosecute offenders, and authorize the courts to grant injunctions and to impose penalties. In most cases, however, the laws require dealers in securities to obtain licenses, excluding nonlicensed dealers from the trade. They also require that securities themselves be registered before they can be sold within a state. Registrants must file extensive information, and registry may be denied where issues are fraudulent or registration statements falsified.

These laws have afforded scant protection to investors. The funds provided for their enforcement have rarely been adequate to finance a real analysis of the statements that are filed. Little effort has been made to censor security prospectuses, the only documents that buyers see. The laws do not prevent mismanagement of corporations, once their securities have been sold. Nor do they regulate the subsequent transfer of these securities. Many transactions escape control, moreover, since the jurisdiction of state authorities does not extend to sales across state lines.

As for securities markets, the speculative boom that followed World War I came to an abrupt end with the stock market crash in October, 1929. In the course of the next few years, the value of stocks listed on the New York Exchange fell from $89 billion to $15 billion and the value of bonds listed from $49 billion to $30 billion, representing a total loss to investors—on paper, at least—of $93 billion. At the same time, purchasers of stocks in public utility holding companies, investment trusts, and other ventures, and buyers of bonds issued by real estate promoters, foreign corporations, and foreign governments, took further losses as the issuers went bankrupt or defaulted on the payments that were due. Holders of stocks in the Insull companies, one of the great utility empires, lost nearly $740 million. Holders of shares in 22 investment trusts saw their value drop from $560 million to $50 million. Americans who bought debentures issued by Ivar Kreuger, the Swedish match monopolist, recovered $10 million on the $250 million they had paid. At the depth of the depression, three-fifths of the real estate mortgage bonds outstanding, two-fifths of the bonds of foreign corporations, and a third of those of foreign governments were in default.

This financial debacle led to a series of investigations: to hearings before the Senate Committee on Banking and Currency, running to 12,-000 pages of testimony and exhibits, on the practices on commercial banks, investment bankers, and the stock exchanges; to an inquiry by the Federal Trade Commission, filling more than 70 volumes, on the practices of public utility holding companies; and, subsequently, to studies by the Securities and Exchange Commission dealing with the practices of trustees who held the securities backing corporate bonds, and with those of investment advisers and investment trusts. Out of these investigations there came startling disclosures of misrepresentation, manipulation, incompetence, and irresponsibility on the part of many who had been conspicuous as leaders in finance.

Since 1929.   The traumas of 1929–33 led to several new regulatory steps. Their rationale has been to protect small consumers in their deposits and stock choices. Bank deposits have been made much more secure, and stock trading is marginally safer. But cartel restrictions have been strengthened, while regulatory supervision has ranged from moderate to zero.[4]

Banking was made secure by (1) creation of the Federal Deposit Insurance Corporation, a public firm (see Chapter 20) to insure deposits, and (2) a new readiness of the Federal Reserve Board to avert any severe monetary strains. Other controls were also added. The Federal Reserve began close inspection of member banks, and the Comptroller of the Currency was given power to grant national bank charters, control changes in status, and conduct examinations—removing officers and revoking charters where necessary. The Comptroller thus controls entry of new banks; few new charters were granted until the 1960s.

The main change in stock trading was creation of the SEC in 1934. Firms issuing new bonds or stocks must first file a report with the SEC, which the SEC verifies for accuracy. The report covers most items which might otherwise involve trickery.[5] SEC authority was extended to public

---

[4] See especially Phillips' chapter in A. Phillips, *ed. cit.,* for a summary of these measures.

[5] The report must disclose the provisions of the corporation's charter, outline its capital structure, explain the relation of the new security to others then outstanding, describe the scope and character of the company's business, tell how the funds raised by the new issue are to be employed, reveal any material contracts to which the corporation is a party, list its directors and officers together with the sums that they are paid, describe any cases in which such persons have had an interest in things the company has bought, list the principal holders of the company's stock, list those who have options to purchase its securities, tell what stock has been given for services or properties other than cash, name the underwriters of the issue,

utility holding companies in 1935 (see Chapter 15), associations of securities dealers in 1938, trustees of security issues in 1939, and investment companies and investment advisers in 1940. The SEC generally tries to bring about honest dealings, disclosure, and self-policing. In all cases, it seeks only to provide fair and full information, not to evaluate the value of securities. The SEC quickly became efficient in this informational role and has retained a reputation as "an outstanding example of the independent commission at its best."[6]

The SEC also took limited control over stock exchange practices. Registration of the exchanges, dealers, brokers, and listed securities is required. Certain manipulations (market pools, wash sales, false and misleading information, etc.) were prohibited, while others were put under regulation. Penalties can be severe: fines, closure, expulsion from trading, even jailing, plus damages to injured parties.

The New York Stock Exchange was transformed from a private club into a body with some public responsibilities. It was to self-police the SEC requirements and set new rules against other abuses. After prodding by the SEC, it did treat most of these matters.[7] But others remained, and its enforcement has been checkered (see below). And the core cartel privileges were kept: restricted membership and price fixing.

Insurance drew increasing efforts toward either federal regulation or antitrust coverage. In 1944, the Supreme Court held that the Sherman Act did apply, since there was much interstate sending of documents, letters, and money.[8] The insurance firms then took shelter under state regulation via the McCarran Act of 1945. It gave state regulation precedence over the antitrust laws, save for certain clear price-fixing actions and mergers. Many states then passed new regulatory laws for insurance, patterned on a model statute prepared by the insurance firms.

The bank merger wave of the 1950s finally provoked an antitrust response, which prevailed in 1963.[9] The policy limits quickly evolved after 1963 along lines similar to the general merger guidelines (recall Chapter 8), but appreciably more liberal. This antitrust breakthrough was closely confined to mergers. Previous mergers were let stand, and restrictive banking practices were not touched.

The one-bank holding-company movement of the 1960s also stirred reaction, for fear that it would let banks back into nonbanking activities. The issue came to a head in 1968 and was resolved in 1970 by amend-

---

reveal the size of their commissions, and show the yield of the security to the issuer as well as its cost to the purchaser. In the case of foreign bonds, similar information is required, including data on the purpose for which the funds are to be used, the legal status of the issue, the financial condition of the borrower, and his past record in making payments on his debts.

[6] It was so judged in 1949 by the Hoover Commission: Commission on Organization of the Executive Branch of the Government, *Task Force Report on Regulatory Commissions* (Washington, D.C.: U.S. Government Printing Office, 1949), p. 144. Its reputation is still strong.

[7] Among the NYSE's responses were its initiation of standards to govern the compensation of underwriters, its establishment of qualifications for securities dealers, its administration of rules fixing capital requirements for traders, and its enforcement of regulations regarding proxy solicitation, truthful disclosure, and financial reporting, which are prerequisite to the listing of securities.

[8] *U.S.* v. *South-Eastern Underwriters,* 322 U.S. 533.

[9] *The Philadelphia National Bank* case: recall Chapter 8.

TABLE 12–3
Bank Holding Company Movement into Nonbanking Activities, 1971–72*, as Affected by Fed
eral Reserve Board Policy

	Total de novo notifications	Proposed acquisitions			
		Total	Approved	Denied	Pending
Mortgage banking	90	26	11	5	10
Leasing personal property	69	6	3	2	1
Investment, financial, and economic advising	60	3	0	2	1
Insurance	56	39	7	2	30
Consumer finance	51	43	10	0	33
Data processing	26	2	1	0	1
Factoring	15	4	1	0	3
Commercial finance............................	12	†	†	†	†
Community development	12	1	0	1	0
Trust	10	2	2	0	0
Industrial banking	8	6	4	0	2
Other...	1	3	2	0	1
Total	410	135	41	12	82

* Through mid-September 1972.
† Combined with consumer finance.
Source: Federal Reserve Board.

ments to the Bank Holding Company Act. Holding companies were permitted, under certain restrictions. But they could engage only in lines
"closely related to banking." Table 12–3 shows that they are indeed
"closely related." A new wave of holding companies followed. In 1973
some 1,607 holding companies held about 65 percent of all bank deposits.

By 1960, stock trading was also ripe for review. In the years that followed World War II, there was a surge of speculative fever in the United
States, with investors demanding shares in unseasoned companies in
glamor industries in hope of realizing a quick rise in price. There was
a spectacular growth in the volume of business done on over-the-counter
markets. Much of this business was in new issues by small companies
not yet appropriate for popular participation. The securities involved
were not listed on organized exchanges; their issuers were exempt from
the reporting requirements imposed by the Securities Exchange Act of
1934. There was no evidence of the pervasive sort of fraudulent activity
that was disclosed in the 1930s. But there was evidence of grave abuses
requiring additional controls.

In 1961, stimulated by disclosures of manipulative activity leading to
expulsion of members of the American Stock Exchange and serious
shortcomings in the government of the Exchange itself, Congress directed the SEC to undertake a comprehensive investigation of the securities markets.[10] To make this study, the Commission employed a group

---

[10] The Commission's most serious failure occurred in the case of the American Exchange.
Here, control had been assumed by a self-perpetuating group of specialists. Attention was
centered on increasing the volume of listings without regard to their quality. American Exchange officials and members had profited from inside information given them by listed
companies and by purchasing the shares of these companies at prices lower than those

of lawyers, economists, and statisticians from outside its own staff. The result of their two-year investigation, published in 1963, was a report that ran to 5,400 pages, covering the distribution of new securities and its regulation by the NASD, the practices of mutual funds, trading on over-the-counter markets, trading on organized exchanges and its regulation by the exchange authorities, and the effect of exemptions granted under the securities law.[11] There were 175 recommendations for reform, only a few of them really important. Some were adopted voluntarily; some were ignored; others were included in the Securities Act Amendments of 1964.

After 1964, broker-dealers must meet certain SEC standards for competence and integrity. This screening (of over 23,000 employees of 450 firms) cannot be thorough, but it does give legal grounds for penalizing violations of ethical conduct. Since salesmen were paid by volume of sales, they had incentives to urge unnecessary trading. Since 1964 salesmen's commissions have been slightly adjusted to reduce this incentive, but it still remains.

Specialists drew special criticism. They are the men who handled actual trades in each stock, adjusting the price as conditions seem to warrant. They are supposed to stabilize prices within a narrow range by buying when the prices are falling and selling when they are rising. The specialist makes about half of his profit from the commissions he collects as a broker, half by trading for his own account. His position as a broker gives him an advantage in acting as a trader. He has exclusive access to his book of orders to sell and buy. These orders give him inside information on how the market is going to move. He may take a position as a trader in anticipation of market movements. He may even influence such movements. The specialist opens trading at the beginning of the day. When orders to buy exceed orders to sell and the markets should open higher than it closed the day before, he may start with a lower price and lead the market down. When orders to sell exceed orders to buy, he may do the opposite.

There is inherent conflict of interest in the specialist's situation, and abuses have occured. The rules on them were tightened by the SEC in 1964.[12] Similarly, the operations of floor traders (who trade only for their

---

charged on the Exchange. The rules of the American Exchange were neither observed nor enforced. The whole machinery of self-regulation broke down. None of this was detected by the SEC in time to be prevented. When the scandal was finally aired, the Commission required that the the American Exchange be reorganized and its rules revised. The Exchange, accordingly, adopted a new constitution, installed a new management, adopted stricter listing standards, imposed tighter controls on traders, and took disciplinary action against violators of its rules.

[11] *Report of Special Study of Securities Markets of the Securities and Exchange Commission* (Washington, D.C.: U.S. Government Printing Office, 1963), Parts 1–5.

[12] The rules require that specialists observe their obligation to buy and sell for their own account whenever it is necessary to maintain a fair and orderly market; that they refrain from selling their own shares on a declining market; and, when sales have been made, that they re-enter declining markets with price-supporting purchases. The rules forbid the specialist to make the first transaction of the day at a price which is inconsistent with the supply-and-demand situation revealed by his book. The rules, finally, require specialists to carry three times the previous amount of capital to support their market-stabilizing operations. Further extensive study of specialists was made in Senate Subcommittee on Securities, *Securities Industry Study, Part 4,* 92d Cong., 2d sess. (Washington, D.C.: U.S. Government Printing Office, 1972).

own accounts) and odd-lot dealers were limited to abate obvious chances for abuse.

The NYSE's cartel controls were challenged in the 1960s. In 1963, the Supreme Court held that a NYSE rule requiring members to sever private wire connections with nonmember brokers violated the Sherman Act.[13] But other private suits against NYSE fixed commission rates were denied, on the ground that Congress had exempted exchanges from antitrust by giving the SEC jurisdiction. The SEC then grasped the nettle and held hearings in 1968 on rate-fixing. The Antitrust Division and several distinguished economists argued instead for a competitive process. Block trading had already eroded rates for large sales, and so sales above $300,-000 value were soon set free. Much further controversy occurred, including extensive Congressional hearings and prodding toward competitive fees.

In March 1974 the SEC announced that all commissions would go on a competitive basis on May 1, 1975. This result partly reflected logic and SEC power; mostly it reflected the market realities. The SEC and Congress were also pressing for a unified market, in which the special status of the exchanges would eventually fade. In short, regulation was in the midst of a watershed period for stock exchanges in the 1970s. Though further delay seemed likely in 1975, both competitive fees and a unified market appeared to be fated within a few years.

Insiderism also came under marginal attack in the 1960s. Since the 1930s, trading by official insiders (executives and directors) in their own firms' stock has had to be reported, and is published monthly in the SEC's "Insiders' Report." This constrains part of the insider problem, but large areas of it are untouched. The SEC can act against abuses only when it has hard data, and before 1965 it had done little. Then in 1965 it caught one large violation cold in the *Texas Gulf Sulphur* case.[14] Conviction in 1970 was a major achievement, though penalties were moderate. In 1968 it charged Merrill Lynch, Pierce, Fenner & Smith—the largest brokerage firm in the country—14 of its officers, and 15 of its customers with insider violations.[15] Again penalties were light, but the principle of fair access

---

[13] *Silver* v. *New York Stock Exchange,* 373 U.S. 341.

[14] The company had discovered a rich deposit of copper and zinc on November 12, 1963; the insiders had then purchased or taken options on 127,000 shares of its stock and friends whom they tipped off had acquired 28,000 more. The company had put out misleading information on the strike on April 13, 1964; it had finally disclosed the true character of its discovery on April 16; and the price of Texas Gulf stock had thereupon risen from $17 to $34 a share. The SEC asked the court to require the insiders to make restitution to persons who, in ignorance, had incurred losses during this period by selling the stock to them or to their friends. In the final decision in the case, in 1970, the court ordered ten of the defendants to make restitution to the company in amounts ranging from $2,300 to $96,000 plus interest at 6 percent from the date of the offense. The decision also provided a basis for other suits against Texas Gulf by persons who had sold its stock to other buyers between April 13, when it had issued misleading publicity, and April 16, when it had told the truth.

[15] Merrill Lynch, acting as an underwriter for Douglas Aircraft, learned that Douglas earnings would decline in the last half of 1966. It passed this information on to 15 customers (large investment companies), enabling them to avoid losses by selling Douglas stock or to make profits, estimated at $4.5 million, by selling it short. It withheld this information from its other customers who presumably sustained losses. Following administrative hearings, Merrill Lynch accepted a consent order under which the firm's New York sales office was closed for 21 days and its West Coast underwriting office for 15, at a cost of around $1 million, nine of its officers were censured and six were suspended for three weeks without pay. The SEC could have imposed a much stiffer penalty.

was affirmed. Various other private and SEC cases have ensued, but there has been no broad-scale attack on the problem. The SEC has posed the issue and probably moved the margin of behavior slightly toward more fairness. But it did not—and could not, given its powers and resources—treat the basic causes. The insider problem remains serious, even though the SEC continues to bring several significant insider cases per year.

The 1960s also brought large Congressional studies of bank-company connections, both via boardroom positions and holdings by bank trust departments (recall Chapter 11). These clearly established that the influence was likely to be strong in scores of major industries. But the reports fell largely into a vacuum. There was little impetus for treating this sensitive area, and no clear solution was advanced.

The 1972–74 period brought several scandals, which had seemed unthinkable under regulation. The "Vesco affair" involved massive looting of a large off-shore fund—Investors Overseas Service—and attempts to corrupt the SEC's investigation of it. The Equity Funding scandal in 1973 exposed large-scale fraud in life insurance, which state regulation had quite failed to detect.[16] It also involved widespread insiderism, with informing of major customers while leaving small investors out in the cold. A sizable bank in San Diego went insolvent in 1973, from manipulations and its relations with a larger holding company. And the Franklin National Bank required massive salvage efforts to avoid collapse (recall Chapter 11).

These were all outsider firms, not part of the financial establishment. But the episodes did show that regulation in all three sectors was unable even to guarantee its minor housekeeping role.[17]

The one effort at conscious reform was the Nixon proposal for increased competition in banking. The Hunt Commission's proposals, prepared by financial interests and experts, were sent to Congress in August, 1973, in compact and workable form. They would have sped shifts which were already under way, and which experts had long been recommending. Certain entry barriers and restrictive practices would have been phased out. The package proposed to (1) remove, over a $5\frac{1}{2}$ year period, interest ceilings on time and savings deposits, (2) permit federally chartered thrift institutions and banks to offer checking accounts, (3) broaden the investment and lending powers of federally chartered thrift institutions and banks, with S&Ls getting power to make consumer loans up to 10 percent of total assets. (4) open up federal chartering to stock savings and loan institutions and mutual savings banks, (5) set up a central bank for credit unions, (6) remove FHA and VA interest ceilings, (7) take away the competitive edge that tax law gives savings and loan institutions over commercial banks and substitute a mortgage tax credit available on residential mortgage interest income earned by a taxpayer. But the proposal was stillborn, partly because of Watergate, partly because

---

[16] The *Wall Street Journal* noted that other scandals had occurred, and that state insurance regulation was widely regarded as a farce (August 2, 1973).

[17] A public firm (the Securities Investors Protection Corporation) was created in 1971 to protect investors against losses caused by bankruptcy of brokerage firms. Yet the unit is small and slow-moving, and it cannot unravel many of the complex cases. Its effect has largely been peripheral and of little use to the really small investor.

the package was so finely balanced that each side stood to lose as well as gain. Banks remain largely separated from savings and loan associations and from other major financial markets.

Current Status of Regulation. The basic policy apparatus presently seems firmly set. State bank and insurance regulation is known to be weak and incomplete, but it continues largely as is. The SEC continues to be regarded as effective and fair, though its resources are overstrained by the tasks it bears. It is able to conduct only forays into several major problem areas, setting examples and nipping some of the worst cases. Its surveillance of exchanges and irregular trading cannot be close or thorough, as shown by the American Stock Exchange, Vesco, and Equity Funding scandals. And it cannot order large basic changes. Still, its staff and leadership have been of high quality.

Banking regulation continues along lines similar to self-regulation. It mainly resists changes in structure and practices, yielding to them slowly only after natural economic forces become irresistible. The lines have softened in the 1960s but are still intact.

Evidently, the agencies and policies have evolved into stable patterns, but the underlying processes differ from the pre-1920s turbulence only in degree. The agencies bear much larger responsibilities than they can fully meet. Most of the current issues of policy are old ones, having been only gently touched by regulation. We now review these specific issues in banking, stock trading, and insurance.

BANKING POLICY ISSUES

The basic lesson is that banking is more restricted than is needed to meet the aim of secure deposits. The FDIC and Federal Reserve's support functions avert any serious hazards. The rest of the policy apparatus is superfluous and probably costly.

Restrictive Practices. These remain pervasive with official backing, and so banking competition is usually reduced and confined to peripheral service items. Large clients get more flexible treatment, via full-service banking. But pricing is obscure within these banking relationships, and competing for major clients is largely against the unwritten code. The limits vary from state to state, where state laws do apply at all, but the effects are similar. The restrictions often just formalize the more complete underlying cooperation within the banking fraternity.

These roles do not erase all competition. And the larger firms often play banks off against each other. Even under free competition, interest rates would vary among customers. But they would be more flexible and open to innovation and change.

Structural Controls. There are four main parts:

1. Entry into banking markets can occur only with official approval, which is influenced by the interests of established banks,
2. Banks cannot be taken over by nonbanking enterprises.
3. Mergers among banks now are limited to relatively small market shares, after a period when many large-share mergers were freely permitted, and,

4. In many states, banks' ability to set up multiple branches in different cities is limited or prohibited.

Entry control has been at the heart of banking policy for 40 years. The decisions to permit entry are made by the Comptroller, the Federal Reserve, and various state banking regulators. An aspiring entrant must prepare a case which proves a concrete need for additional banking services, beyond what is already being supplied by banks or is likely to be supplied in the future. The burden of proof is mainly against the entrant (recall Chapter 3). Proof is usually difficult, and the prior banks can often take actions to make capacity seem adequate. The criteria for showing an "unmet banking need" are subjective, involve debatable predictions, and can always be disputed.

Entry has been more liberally permitted since 1961, but the net effects have been modest. Entry was mainly into the smallest city markets, but even so the degree of concentration remained high. In the larger cities, new banks had a negligible impact.[18] In line with Chapter 2, entry is not the key to competition.

The controls reduce new entry *and* the formation of new banks by experts presently working in the established banks. This second effect probably is the more important. Upper bank officials might otherwise tend to form new banks, taking the better corporate clients with them. Banking economics would yield a fluid banking structure, more efficient and adaptable. By comparison, entry by small inexperienced outsiders is likely to be peripheral in any event.

The 1930s rules ended certain abuses by sealing off banking from nonfinancial activities. But this also immunized banks against take-over or other outside influences. Since banking and regulatory motives strongly favor security, the lack both of take-over discipline and of competition would naturally foster inefficiency. The degree of inefficiency is, by objective appraisal, not small. The recent rise of one-bank holding companies does not correct this, because the really powerful nonfinancial groups are excluded. The barrier between banking and other markets is still intact.[19] There are losses of efficiency both in banking *and* in the nonbanking markets which bank holding companies might diversify into.

Mergers have been a prominent issue but are of moderate importance. The 1950–63 wave was stimulated partly by the hope of getting in under the wire before the Celler-Kefauver Act could be tightly applied. This worked, in fact, and so the 1963 *Philadelphia* case and its aftermath has had the same effect as merger policy in industry (recall Chapter 8): it tends to ratify and harden a tighter structure. In 1973–74 the Supreme Court at last found against the Antitrust Division in two small bank merger cases. Yet these were marginal cases, involving small market

---

[18] D.A. Alhadeff and C. P. Alhadeff, "Bank Entry and Bank Concentration," *Antitrust Bulletin* (Spring 1975). New banks (all those entering during 1948–66) had in 1970 only about 2 percent of deposits in the large-city markets.

[19] Blurring the line does pose risks, as foreign experience suggests. Also, the 1973 failure of the San Diego Bank demonstrates the possible abuses. But these can be limited in various ways while retaining the refreshing effects of some outside influence.

shares and merely potential competition from banks presently in separate cities. Competitive effect has now become the ruling criterion for bank mergers (superseding various banking factors cited in earlier agency approvals). But the net effect of the whole tilt and timing of policies may be anticompetitive.

Branching is a natural form of banking, with local units spread out within cities and among towns. Yet it remains prohibited or closely limited in many states. The main valid reason for these restrictions is to foster local interest and support by banks. This could be important on Jeffersonian grounds, if absentee-owned banks did systematically ignore local clients in favor of large impersonal firms. Yet some of the local banks, thus shielded, tend to be inefficient and restrictive, so that the net effects of branching rules are probably negative.

Branching appears to improve bank performance, if the branching does not involve increased local market shares. These two elements are quite separable. In nonbranch states, old banks in the smaller cities live cloistered lives and their clients have restricted choices. The loss is: (1) allocative inefficiency, for rates are not competed down and service expanded, and (2) X-inefficiency, for the banks are often isolated from modern management techniques and portfolio criteria.

The old branching prohibitions are slowly eroding, but they are still extensive. Moreover, branching *among* states is also outlawed (except presently for foreign banks), and this limits competition even more severely. Still further, banks and quasi-banks—savings and loan societies, credit unions, etc.—also cannot compete directly, under official policies. These add up to a balkanization of markets similar to franchised utilities (see Chapters 13 and 15), with the predictable negative effects.

Banking Relationships.   Policy toward banking relationships scarcely exists. There is no policy or means for disclosure of them. Little is done to offset the advantages which they give to established firms against small and potential entrants. No agency presently has the resources or political standing to press the issue.

It may be the effects are not deep, especially compared with those in other countries, where bank-company ties are usually closer. Yet the rise of the newer conglomerates in the 1960s suggests otherwise (recall Chapters 2 and 8). They responded to the passiveness of many banks in letting their clients persist in sluggish behavior, which in turn made them good take-over targets. The sheer volume of the 1963–69 conglomerate wave—even against the grain of resistance by many of the target firms and the main banks—indicates that the problem was a large one, and it continues. But the neatness with which the conglomerate bud was nipped also suggests that there is little chance for basic reform. Presently there is a vacuum: close regulation (or even simple disclosure and study) and normal market forces have both been averted.

Summary.   The main effect of banking policies is toward rigidity, inefficiency, and retardation of progress. Most of the restrictions could be removed (perhaps gradually) without reducing the security of deposits and of banks. Rather, it would improve banking performance in several directions. Why such reforms are not occurring is understandable, given the structure of interests. But the economic case for a marked revision of policies is valid and clear.

STOCK MARKETS

There are three main issues: (1) fixed commissions, (2) insiderism, and (3) the SEC's role.

Fixed Commissions. Policy long tolerated cartel behavior by the stock exchanges, which held brokerage prices above their long-run levels. This fostered inefficiency in the brokerage houses, which the stresses of the 1960s quickly exposed. The inefficiency is widely agreed to persist. The exchanges have also retarded evolution toward an efficient unified market. The SEC's shift toward the 1968 hearings and then the planned 1975 termination of fixed rates was partly a shift toward improved regulation. But mostly it reflected the shift in the basic interests, as trading moved off the exchange floors into the large-volume third market and the NYSE's members own interests altered. The SEC (and Congress) nudged; it also—or instead—was carried along by the underlying realities.

Insiderism. Recall (from Chapter 11) the two levels of insider problems: (1) inside information used improperly for personal gain, and (2) long-term secrecy about company performance.

The SEC abates gross instances of insider trading, via its "Insider Report" and occasional cases. But the basic problem remains, with no new policy treatment in prospect. And even the occasional suits usually rely on special tips and complaints, and so the many unreported offenses slip by. Experts regard the volume of unprosecuted insider abuses as extensive. The SEC has also acquiesced in other practices (such as special briefings for institutions and analysts) which favor some investors at the expense of others. Nor has it studied the problem in depth.

Long-term secrecy has been reduced by the SEC's recent requirements for divisional reporting. Since 1970, firms must disaggregate on *Form 10–K* all "lines of business" over 15 percent of company revenues. The definition of "line of business" is often slippery, and costs and assets can often be freely allocated among lines of business to fit company objectives. Form 10–K has therefore reduced secrecy only marginally. Moreover, it was a response to pressures from the investment community to offset the growing secrecy which the spread of conglomerates naturally brought. Therefore, the SEC was—as in other matters—making only a moderate change, which really reflected a shift among the basic interest groups. The net effect has been moderate—much of it merely moves back toward the previous degree of openness—and it falls far short of full disclosure.

The SEC's Role. The SEC emerges as part mediator, part innovator. It is superior to most other regulatory commissions (see also Chapters 13–18), though it treats some problems only moderately and others not at all. This reputation can be credited to several factors. (1) It has a diverse constituency; large and small investors, the exchanges and brokers, industrial and other firms, etc. It can balance among these, nudging toward changes which are already begun. It need not become dependent on just one regulatee (see Chapter 13).

(2) It focuses its efforts. Since its resources are thin compared to its ultimate tasks, this means that large problems go untreated. But it also preserves the SEC from entering various troubled waters. (3) The tradition of high-quality chairmen has become fairly firm. As in antitrust, the constituency has come—since 1960 especially—to expect sophistication, honesty, and energy in the appointed chairman.

INSURANCE REGULATION

State regulation of insurance involves a severe disparity between agency resources and tasks. The supervision tends to lag well behind events, as the few evaluators struggle with masses of material. Though California and Illinois are regarded as among the better regulatory units, it was they who conspicuously failed to detect the brazen Equity Funding abuses of 1970–73. Like other state regulators (see Part IV), they tend to become passive toward the larger firms they regulate and to be unable either to regulate or to achieve reform for their own awkward situation.

The regulators supervise (1) financial soundness, (2) the fairness of trade practices, and (3) rates.

Soundness. State insurance commissioners determine the capital a company must have, require the maintenance of adequate reserves, prescribe accounting methods, check on the value of assets, and control investment policies. They enforce these controls by requiring companies to make deposits of securities, by calling for annual reports, and by conducting examinations of company accounts. Processing often lags two years behind the filings.[20]

Trade Practices. Brokers and agents are required to obtain licenses, and those who cannot satisfy administrative standards are excluded from the field. Tying clauses, requiring one party to a transaction to purchase insurance from the other, and the rebating of premiums to favored purchasers of insurance, are banned. Policy forms are simplified and standardized or limited to those that the commissioner may approve. An effort is made to assure fairness in the settlement of disputed claims, some states seeking to avoid the time and cost of litigation by providing machinery to arbitrate disputes.

Rates. Here the choice lies between competition, on the one hand, and cooperation under public supervision, on the other. Cooperation has been chosen on the ground that competition might drive rates down to a level that would impair the ability of the companies to pay their claims. The laws provide only that rates shall not be excessive (whatever that may mean) and shall not discriminate among the purchasers of policies.

---

[20] In the *Wall Street Journal's* words, "The picture the audit presents has all the freshness of the Dead Sea Scrolls." The regulatory units are usually financed by the insurance firms themselves, and officials move freely between the firms and official positions. "Commissioners often negotiate for and announce new jobs in the industry while they are still in charge of regulating it." Regulation is also shallow and inefficient in various ways, and commissioners are of doubtful quality and have high turnover. And the regulation of state-size parts of large national firms is inevitably incomplete. *Wall Street Journal,* August 2, 1973.

The rates of fire and casualty insurance companies are prepared by private rating bureaus, filed with the state insurance commissioner, and made effective when approved by him. Commissioners have sometimes succeeded in preventing increases and bringing about reductions in rates. Membership in rating bureaus is required in a few states but not in most. Some states forbid agreements by the insurers to adhere to bureau rates. Independent filing is generally permitted, and deviations from bureau rates have increased. In the case of life insurance, rate bureaus are not needed. All of the companies use the same mortality table as the basis for their rates.

This supervision may marginally abate the risk of financial failures and avert some sharp trade practices, but it tends more to stabilize premiums than to constrain them.[21] As in stock trading, the conditions that might cause destructive competition are absent or weak. Risks of default could be covered—as in banking—by direct insurance (or reinsurance) of the firms. Therefore the present regulation is an alternative to (1) genuinely strict and thorough regulation, or to (2) effective competition.

---

[21] For a lucid analysis of the reasons for removing regulation, see Paul L. Joskow, "Cartels, Competition and Regulation in the Property-Liability Insurance Industry," *Bell Journal of Economics and Management Science,* Vol. 4 No. 2 (Autumn 1973), pp. 375–427.

Part IV

REGULATION

REGULATION

Regulation—optimism's form;
Small craft sent out to bind and bend the storm,

Yet roughly tossed. Survival is their hope;
By trimming sail and lying low, they cope.

Conceived in compromise, it's oddly made,
Beset by trivia and hopes betrayed,

Yet tries to fit the public interest;
The bender bent, not worst but scarcely best.

CHAPTER THIRTEEN

Tasks and Forms
of Regulation

Regulation is what regulators do. It is an American experiment, reflecting such native traits as a trust in independent authority and skill, and a reliance on private capital. Like other policies, regulation is a core of conventional practices and sectors, surrounded by mixed and marginal cases.[1]

To "regulate" has at least three definitions. One is the tough and unilateral: "to govern or direct according to rule." Another refers to compromise and smoothing over: "to reduce to order . . . to regularize." And another is superficial, perhaps empty: "to make regulations."

The classic, optimistic image of regulation fits the first definition, as follows. A utility sector is an natural monopoly, and so its firms are given franchises as exclusive suppliers to their areas and put under a regulatory commission. This Commission has full information on the utility and great skill in analyzing it. The Commission sets "fair" ceilings on the utility's prices and profit rates, and ensures that the utility price structure is "just and reasonable." The utility must supply all customers at those constrained prices. The Commission monitors service quality and, if necessary, prevents the utility from being inefficient.

Regulation therefore aspires to ratify monopoly where—and only where—it is necessary in the public interest, to prevent exploitation by the producer while reaping economies of scale, and yet to avoid using public capital, subsidies, or guarantees against risk.[2] The aim: maximum public control with minimum public resources. The Commission is lean, omniscient, powerful, and quick.

---

[1] The best treatises on it include A. E. Kahn, *The Economics of Regulation*, 2 vols. (Wiley, 1970), 1971; C. F. Phillips, Jr., *The Economics of Regulation: Theory and Practice in the Transportation and Public Utility Industries*, rev. ed. (Homewood, Ill., Irwin, 1969); and J. C. Bonbright, *Principles of Public Utility Rates* (New York: Columbia University Press, 1961). These are heavy books; one might best look into them *after* reading Chapters 13 and 14 here. Phillips provides a goldmine of details of actual regulation.

[2] Regulation is also appropriate for *public* firms (see Part V). The economic criteria are the same for both public and private enterprises. But in the U.S., it is often regarded as "an alternative to" public enterprise.

Credit: Cornell University	Credit: MIT	Credit: Michigan State Universit

Alfred E. Kahn (born 1917) of Cornell University, a leading scholar of regulation, who urges that regulation, though imperfect, is workable and often effective. He was made chairman of the New York State Public Service Commission in 1974. (Shown 1955.)

Paul W. MacAvoy (born 1934) of MIT suggests from research that the regulation of natural gas, railroads, and electricity has been unnecessary and costly.

Walter Adams (born 1922 has stressed that regulated firm are often given too muc monopoly. A leading scholar o industrial competition and anti trust, he has also criticall analysed military purchasin policies.

Such *perfect* regulation never existed and never will. It might, even if it were perfect, have costly side effects, as we will see. Our job is to learn how actual regulation differs from the ideal, why it differs, and what effects it has had.

There are obvious hazards in regulation. (1) It is part of a larger social bargain, which grants a very real monopoly in exchange for a possibility of regulating it (see below). (2) Technology and demand change as the years go by, and the regulatory treatment may not adapt well to this. (3) Since regulation deals with large and tightly focused interests (the suppliers and their main customers), the political economy may see to it (in Congress, state legislatures, etc.) that regulation is weak or biased (recall Chapter 4). And (4), it relies on personal judgments about complex, often obscure issues, rather than on clear laws or formulas.

So one approaches regulation hoping for the best but braced for the worst.

Regulation's true character is warmly disputed. Consider this sample of expert opinions. Henry Simons (1936): "Unregulated, extralegal monopolies are tolerable evils; but private monopolies with the blessing of regulation and the support of law are malignant cancers in the system." Walter Adams and Horace Gray (1955): "Among all the devices used by government to promote monopoly, public utility, or public interest, regulation is in some respects perhaps the worst." Donald Dewey (1974): "I put it to you that as citizens we wish the regulatory agency to serve as a forum for group therapy, a better business bureau, a check on bureaucracy, and a brake on economic and social change." Richard A. Posner (1969): "Public utility regulation is probably not a useful exertion of governmental powers." Ben W. Lewis (1966): "Public-utility regulation has not lived up to its early-twentieth-century promise." Roger Cramton (1964): "Much regulatory activity has little economic significance." John Bauer (1950): "Under the conditions that have existed, the wonder is that regulation has worked as well as it has."

The topic requires a thorough coverage in this book, because regulated industries are important, and because it is such a complex, thriving, and spreading phenomenon. This chapter sets the stage by laying out regulation's environment and basic forms. The next chapter sets forth the analytical problems involved in trying to control the *level* of prices and profits and the *structure* of prices for regulated services. Then we take up—in separate chapters—the power sector, communications and transport. These include the core, standard utility sectors under regulation. The larger lessons from the regulatory experiment are drawn in Chapter 18.

In this chapter, we will first outline the scope of utility sectors and of the basic things which regulators do. Then the social objectives and the special economic features of utilities will be assessed. Next, the normal evolution of utility sectors and of regulation over time will be laid out. There is a brief historical review of regulation, and then a summary of the chapter.

SCOPE AND METHODS OF REGULATION

Regulated firms have *rights* and *duties,* usually as follows:

Rights. (1) They are entitled to "reasonable" prices and profits. (2) They are given complete or partial protection from competition (via a franchise). (3) They can exercise eminent domain in acquiring property, even by coercion. (4) Rules governing them must be reasonable.

Duties. (1) Prices and profits are to be no more than "reasonable." (2) At those prices, all demand must be met, even at peak times. Service must be adequate in quantity and quality. (3) All changes in services (adding *or* dropping them) must be approved in advance. (4) The safety of the public is to be protected.

Coverage

At each point of time, every economy has a set of sectors which possess "utility" characteristics in varying degree (these are defined below). This set changes over time, as utility life-cycles proceed (recall Chapter 2 and see a later discussion in this chapter). Natural monopoly status is often a temporary detour from normal conditions. The set of utilities in 1975 differs from those of 1900; and those of the year 2050 will probably differ even more sharply.[3] The present sector of regulated utilities is subject

---

[3] These past and future sectors are considered below in "Utilities and Regulation Both Evolve."

TABLE 13-1
Present Utility Sectors

Primarily Monopolies	Partially Competitive
Telephone service	Railroads
Electric power	Waterways
Natural gas	Pipelines
Postal services	Airlines
Urban transit	Broadcasting
Water	Cable television
Sewage	Hospitals
Ports	

TABLE 13-2
The Scope of Certain U.S. Utility Sectors, 1973

	Percent of National Income Originating in These Sectors	Percent of Total Fixed Investment Going to These Sectors
Electric, gas, and sanitary services	0.9	10.4
Communications: telephone and telegraph	2.1	6.6
Transportation	3.7	
Railroad		1.0
Other		2.1
Total	7.7	20.1

Source: *Survey of Current Business*, May 1974.

to change, and indeed there is endless argument about whether—each one, and collectively—they do have "utility" conditions deep enough to justify the apparatus and protection of regulation.

The present consensus on utility sectors in the U.S. is summarized in Table 13-1. There are three broad classes; the energy sector, communications, and transport. Within each of these sectors certain parts are more clearly utility functions than others; for example, certain telephone services are clearly natural-monopoly utilities, while other portions are not (see Chapter 16). Still, Tables 13-1 and 13-2 outline the utility sectors reasonably reliably. Note that despite their relatively small share of national income, these sectors absorb a substantial portion of national investment. These sectors have mostly shown rapid rises in labor productivity during recent decades (thanks to labor-saving investment). Some of them are rapidly growing. Some also combine activities which are highly monopolistic with others which are highly competitive. And of course, some are publicly-owned, in whole or part: examples are postal services and urban transit and water systems.

Commissions now exist to regulate—in one or all of the three defini-

TABLE 13-3

The Main Federal Commissions, 1973

Commission	Year Established	Number of Members	Term of Office (years)	Number of Staff Members	Expenditures Fiscal Year 1973 ($million)	Jurisdiction
Interstate Commerce Commission.............	1887	11	7	1,770	29.4	Railroads; motor carriers; water shipping; oil pipelines; express companies, etc.
Federal Power Commission.................	1920, 1935	5	5	1,191	22.8	Electric power; gas and pipelines; water-power sites
Federal Communications Commission	1934	7	7	1,785	32.8	Telephone; television; cable TV, radio, telegraph
Civil Aeronautics Board	1938	5	6	708	13.5	Airlines (passenger and cargo)

Source: Adapted from Table 4–4 in C. F. Phillips, Jr., *The Economics of Regulation*, rev. ed. (Homewood, Ill.: Irwin, 1969); and *Budget of the United States Government, Fiscal Year 1973, Appendix* (1972).

TABLE 13-4

Basic Conditions of Regulatory Commission Budgets (1972–73)

	Total ($1,000)	Sources — General Tax Funds	Sources — Taxes and Fees from Utilities	Salary of Commissioners ($1,000)	Economists	Accountants and Auditors	Engineers	Inspectors	Rate Analysts
Federal Power Commission	21,836	100%	0%	38	31	102	70	0	0
Federal Communications Commission	30,382	100	0	38	15	50	33	0	0
Alabama	910	0	100	18	—	—	—	—	—
Alaska	583	100	0	27	0	3	4	0	2
Arizona	1,170	100	0	14	0	2	4	29	1
Arkansas	438	0	100	18	0	6	2	2	1
California	12,175	51	49	32	5	46	18	83	83
Colorado	997	50	50	20	0	—	—	14	7
Connecticut	712	—	—	20	0	8	2	1	1
Delaware	—	—	—	24	—	—	—	—	—
District of Columbia	450	0	—	5	0	7	1	1	0
Florida	2,881	0	100	36	0	20	17	52	11
Georgia	773	100	0	23	0	4	4	11	2
Hawaii	581	100	0	—	0	6	0	3	2
Idaho	357	30	70	17	2	3	0	4	1
Illinois	2,330	0	100	30	2	21	1	5	2
Indiana	1,152	—	—	23	0	—	5	3	0
Iowa	695	0	100	15	0	11	5	4	2
Kansas	2,259	75	25	18	0	5	9	5	1
Kentucky	—	0	100	16	0	7	3	4	2
Louisiana	585	0	100	18	0	6	2	7	2
Maine	296	—	—	16	0	5	3	0	1
Maryland	966	100	0	12	0	8	9	24	2
Massachusetts	1,632	100	0	14	0	3	1	55	3
Michigan	3,513	27	73	27	2	12	13	112	2

Minnesota	838	92	8	21	0	4	2	10	0
Mississippi	—	—	—	20	0	2	4	30	1
Missouri	2,200	0	100	24	1	23	3	9	5
Montana	270	100	100	14	0	5	0	7	1
Nebraska	715	0	0	14	0	2	1	21	3
Nevada	460	0	100	18	1	10	5	10	1
New Hampshire	462	0	100	17	0	2	2	4	1
New Jersey	2,124	3	97	22	0	18	10	53	4
New Mexico	924	100	0	17	—	—	—	—	—
New York	12,758	100	0	38	8	91	58	92	13
North Carolina	1,008	100	0	—	0	8	16	9	4
North Dakota	790	100	0	16	0	2	2	6	3
Ohio	3,100	0	100	—	1	15	6	43	2
Oklahoma	—	—	—	—	—	—	—	—	—
Oregon	2,550	1	99	25	3	36	8	13	4
Pennsylvania	4,839	0	100	24	2	11	3	44	47
Rhode Island	859	53	47	9	0	2	1	5	0
South Carolina	1,137	0	100	17	0	5	2	25	0
South Dakota	292	100	0	13	0	1	1	11	0
Tennessee	1,217	0	100	24	0	5	2	35	1
Texas	4,984	0	100	31	—	—	—	—	—
Utah	327	0	100	18	0	4	1	4	0
Vermont	533	0	100	4	0	3	4	0	1
Virginia	—	—	—	30	—	—	—	—	—
Washington	2,459	—	—	23	0	16	3	0	2
West Virginia	1,172	0	100	22	0	—	7	28	19
Wisconsin	3,183	30	70	28	0	21	15	5	14
Wyoming	347	100	0	—	0	1	1	2	1
Totals					74	486	354	989	255

Dashes indicate data were not supplied.
Source: Federal Power Commission, *Federal and State Commission Jurisdiction and Regulation* (Washington, D.C.: U.S. Government Printing Office, 1973).

TABLE 13–5

The FCC's Allocation of Funds, 1973

Activity	Funds ($1000)
Common carrier (the core regulating activity)	3,408
Commissioners	1,651
Broadcast (licenses, technical, etc.)	6,793
Safety and special (ham operators, etc.)	3,091
Field engineering	7,794
Research and planning	4,539
Cable television	1,114
Support	4,256
Total	32,800

Source: *Budget of the United States Government, Fiscal 1973* (Washington, D.C.: U.S. Government Printing Office, 1972).

FIGURE 13–1

Actual Regulatory Coverage May Differ from Formal Coverage—and from "Natural Monopoly" Areas

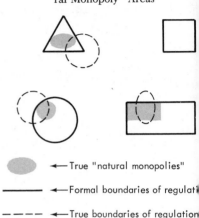

- ◀— True "natural monopolies"
- ◀— Formal boundaries of regulation
- ◀— True boundaries of regulation

tions listed earlier—most of these sectors.[4] Telephones, electric power, gas, and railroads have been the classic core cases. But coverage is commonly in a patchwork of state and federal commissions—there is an ongoing struggle among them—each over part of these interrelated systems. The main lines of federal and state commissions are given in Tables 13–3 and 13–4. State commissions control prices and profits mainly of electric, gas, and telephone companies. For the rest, they mainly issue licenses and supervise technical conditions.

The standard commission has (1) members, (2) a staff with various specialized functions, (3) a budget, and (4) various legal powers. The members are appointed by an executive (President, governor, or mayor) and often have little prior skill in the industry. The pay of both commissioners and staff is usually moderate to low, far below the private-utility officials they face. Much of the agency's budgets usually go to secondary duties and small technical tasks (bookkeeping, inspecting, etc.).

For example, the FCC's core task is to regulate the telephone systems (in Chapter 16). Yet only about one-tenth of its budget actually goes to that purpose (see Table 13–5). Such things as ham operators, aviation and police services, radio licenses, etc., take up the rest. The state commissions have a not-so-small army of accountants and clerks processing information, but only a handful of well-trained economists.

Not only do commissions overlap in some areas, and in other parts leave gaps. They also vary in the quality of their work and strictness of control. In fact, one cannot safely speak of a *system* of regulation. Instead, there is simply a bundle of state and federal commissions—of varying forms and resources—which have evolved down the years and are still changing.

---

[4] Yet several of the sectors are treated by other forms of supervision; government departments, or elected bodies.

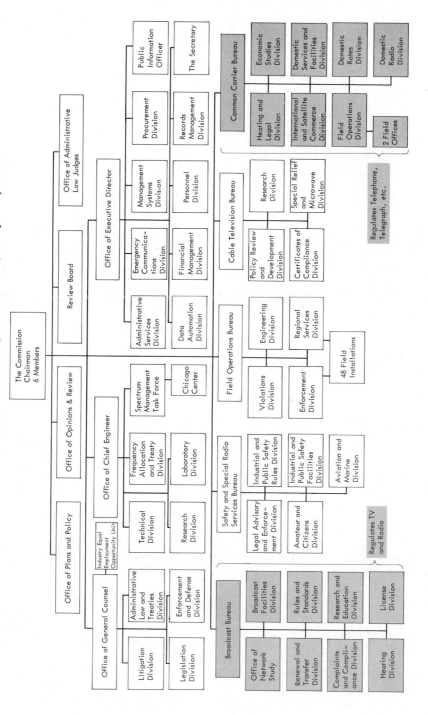

FIGURE 13-2

Federal Communications Commission Organization Chart, as of January 1974

FIGURE 13–3

Michigan Public Service Commission Organization Chart (with number of employees circled) as of May 1974

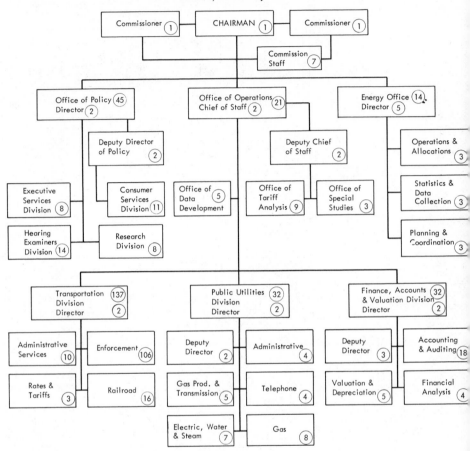

Their formal coverage includes genuine public utilities *plus* others; see Figure 13–1. Their actual coverage—the real exertion of control—is much smaller, as Figure 13–1 also illustrates.

Nature of Commissions

The typical commission structure is illustrated by Figures 13–2 and 13–3. As in antitrust, the top officials come and go, often speedily, while the career staff works on along conventional lines. Also, as in antitrust, the private resources routinely dwarf the agencies. The degree of strictness of commissions is loosely, but only loosely, related to the ampleness of their resources.[5] Some larger state and federal commissions (the ICC

---

[5] The folklore regards several state commissions as being relatively strict (California, Wisconsin, New York, Massachusetts, Michigan, Illinois). The rest range down to total passivity. These conditions do change occasionally.

FIGURE 13–4

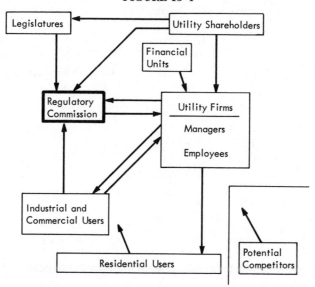

is a common example) manage to dissipate ample budgets on side issues.

The basic relationships of commissions to their interest groups are outlined in Figure 13–4. Some commissions direct their companies, other negotiate. Still others virtually rubber-stamp the companies' decisions (see Figure 13–5). Some commissions are strictly autonomous; others live from hand to mouth, dependent on legislative approval. Others go through alternating phases of dependence and independence from executive control.

Commissions act by hearings and decisions.[6] Usually, the hearings are precipitated by the utility, requesting a price change or a change in service offerings. Occasionally, a crescendo of complaints by the public stirs action. The typical sequence is summarized in Figure 13–6. It involves: (1) open hearings, offering opposing rationales for a decision, (2) setting the range of possible compromise, and then (3) picking the compromise and explaining it by one or more rationales. Like most social decisions, regulatory actions start off with a range of choice, and all that follows is simply a roundabout way to pin down the exact splitting of the difference. In some cases, the hearings become a mere ritual, often long and dreary. In others, they are head-on collisions among the parties, with great drama and suspense about the outcome. But the normal process is simply to find the range of reasonable compromise, split it (often right down the middle), and then justify that split to interested parties.

The actors are a special group. Most commissioners are not experts, of the high caliber envisioned by regulations' proponents. Instead, they usually are politicians, either young and trying to rise, or old and on the

---

[6] Also, much is done informally, in adjusting small complaints by users and even in negotiating price changes. But the standard format for airing and deciding an issue is the public hearing and decision.

FIGURE 13–5
Commissions May Control, Negotiate, or Acquiesce

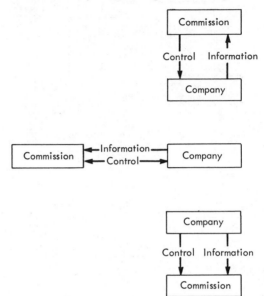

FIGURE 13–6

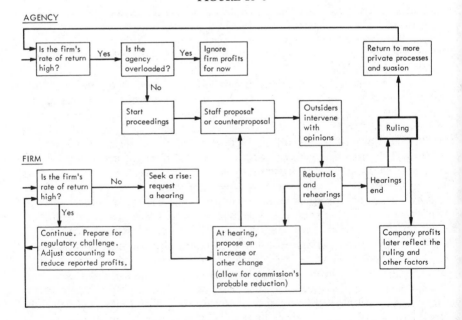

way out to pasture. Often there is a peppering of eccentrics, minority members, or even economists, but the standard type is a lawyer with political ambitions or experience. The hearing process is conducted by lawyers, following legal rules. Economists are used only in preparing some features of the staff proposal; some may also be used as expert witnesses by the companies to defend their side. Since there are economists of all persuasions to choose among for expert witnesses, even the economic input tends to become ritualized and wooden. The regulators soon learn to try mainly to maintain their public image and minimize public criticism (discussed below). The commissions tend to identify with the success of their utilities, and so they usually mingle a sense both of control and of dependency.[7]

Their powers do not permit them to apply either the ultimate penalties—taking away the franchise—or even specific instant feedbacks. Their task is economic in character. Yet most regulators, even in the more advanced commissions, do not fully understand this economic content. If their decisions still somehow grope along toward or at the optimal, this is often merely a lucky accident.

Basic Choices

Now we can summarize the basic choices which commissions have to make (Chapter 14 gives more detail) and analysis of the criteria for decisions. *Private* utilities will be considered first, but the basic issues are similar for regulated *public* firms.

The distinctive fact about regulation of private firms is that the utility firm issues equity stock *with voting control*, in addition to bonds. Directors and managers are creatures of these shareholders alone; no regulatory agency controls who is on the board or how they supervise their managers *nor* how self-selecting and self-controlling the managers may be. The capital and management—and therefore the motivation—are private.

Yet the State creates the utility too, by making it the sole franchised supplier in its area.[8] This hardens and often extends the economic basis of the monopoly, and it excludes entry. Thus shielded from actual *and potential* competition, the private utility has the tightest of possible monopolies. This franchise raises the value of the enterprise; the regulatory commission's constraints on profits and the price structure are intended to reduce the value toward the bare-bones minimum. In all this, the management is under two layers of supervision, but the supervision is usually not close. These private and public constraints are not entirely divergent; both, for example, induce managers to avoid gross inefficiency. But certain important divergences also occur.

The Level of Prices and Profits. The big effort of regulation has been

---

[7] Ask a regulator what his commission has accomplished. The usual answer will cite various actions and results *by the company*. But where are effects—and credit—to be assigned?

[8] In multiple-firm regulation—airlines, etc.—the firm is one of several, but it still enjoys advantages.

to restrain total profits to some efficient—the usual jargon is "fair"—rate of return on the utility's investment. It is still a preoccupation of most commissions. The basic choice is in these terms:

$$\text{Rate of Return} = \frac{\text{Total Revenue} - \text{Total Cost}}{\text{Capital}}$$

Capital is supposed to include all fixed assets actually used—and necessary to use—in supplying the utility service. The rate of return includes the return to all investors, in both equity and debt.

A Glossary of Regulatory Terms

Affected with the public interest. Defined by the legislature as being eligible for public regulation. The grounds for inclusion are almost limitless.
Common carrier. A franchised utility required to serve all customers at the regulated prices.
"Fair" rate of return. The criterion the regulators are supposed to meet: avoids confiscation of owner's value while not gouging consumers.
Franchise. Legal definition of a common carriers market position. It usually excludes some or all competitors and is enforced by public agencies.
"Just and reasonable" rates. The ideal price structure; blending several considerations.
Marginal-cost pricing. Setting price strictly in line with specific marginal costs (not in line with demand differences).
Natural monopoly. In concept, a case in which average costs decline over such a wide range of output that only one firm will survive.
Original cost. The value of utility investment when first installed. (Now commonly used instead of reproduction and historical cost.)
Price discrimination. Prices set in line with demand. Often called "value of service pricing."
Public utility. Vernacular phrase for a common carrier. May be privately or publicly owned.
Rate base. The asset value which the commission accepts as the utility firm's investment, for rate-setting purposes.
Tariff. The published set of regulated prices charged by the firm (also called prices or rates).

Commissions can be liberal in fixing the rate base and/or the rate of return; or neither. The normal range for "fair" ceiling rates of return (after tax) has been about 6 to 10 percent, or about 2 points above the rate of riskless Treasury securities (see Table 13–4). Normally the commission attempts to find the "cost of capital," a weighted average of bond rates of interest and roughly a 10–12 percent "cost" imputed to equity capital (that is, stocks). The "fair" rate is then set just above this "cost of capital." The process of decision often appears to be—and is—merely a compromise between the proposals of the company and the commission's staff.[9]

Cost of capital ought to be reckoned looking ahead: at what the real

---

[9] Cost of capital has drawn endless controversy, much of it arid and hair-splitting. And the "true" rate base stirred quite genuine sophistry all through the 1920s and 1930s, enough to bring regulation nearly to a standstill. See Irston R. Barnes, *The Economics of Public Utility Regulation* (New York: Crofts, 1942); Bonbright, *op. cit.,* and Kahn, *op. cit.*

cost of new investment will be. But rather than the marginal cost of new investment, commissions instead look backward at the average past cost of existing capital. The two are indirectly linked, of course; "new" investors look at how well the senior capital is being treated. Yet, in principle, the usual regulatory determination of cost of capital looks at the wrong quantities, and ignores the truth that sunk costs should not govern present and future decisions.

The tradition is followed because (1) it has a surface plausibility, and (2) there are definite numbers to tie it to (the old interest rates being paid on bonds are quite definite; future ones can only be estimated). Yet— wheels within wheels—new capital costs do usually get worked in informally, when the commission makes its final decision with an element of intuition and realism.

The Structure of Prices. *The second task is to get an efficient structure of prices.* Utilities supply many different consumers, in residences, shops, industry, offices, etc. The outputs also vary, in times, amounts and terms of supply, but they are usually supplied via direct physical connections to the users. The utility usually has a lot of elbow room to price-discriminate; that is, to set prices in line with demand elasticities. The regulators' task is therefore to prevent undue discrimination. This means setting prices in line with the true costs of service; *that is what efficient allocation means* (recall Chapter 1). These real costs, properly defined, are marginal costs. The objective is to set

$$\text{Price} = k \,(\text{Marginal Cost})$$

where k is some ratio which is similar among outputs and which is as close to 1 as possible. The utility, of course, wishes k to vary, setting it highest where demand is most inelastic, so as to maximize its profit potential and avert any possible competition. The customers will press at rate hearings for lower rates. Caught between consumers and the utility managers, who know their own cost and demand conditions best (though not always very well), the regulators usually settle on compromises which reflect both cost and demand conditions. Or—more commonly—they may just leave these complex issues to the utility to settle, acquiescing in the proposed rates.

Since the hearing is called normally at the utility's request, the issues and timing are usually set by the company, not the commission. In inflationary periods, these requests come frequently. Stable and deflationary periods often pass with no formal hearings at all.

The prime motives of utility officers are three. *One* is to raise the permitted profit ceiling. Such rises can have potent effects on shareholder capital, since a "mere" one point rise in the rate of return—say, from 8 to 9 percent—can add 10 or 20 percent to the price of the company's stock. A *second* motive is to set low prices where there is actual or potential competition, covering the balance of costs from its more captive markets, where demand elasticity is low. This minimizes long-run risk and enlarges the rate base upon which profits can be earned (Chapter 14 discusses this further). The *third* motive is to avoid, at almost any cost, a service failure (e.g., a blackout), for that stirs public resentment and endangers—as no other event can—the utility's privileged status.

The regulators share the third motivation, for service failures call *their* role into question too. This bears repeating: *service breakdowns are the great fear of firms and regulators alike.* The other two motives are partially shared by regulators, for they provide healthy and expansive service. Certain consumer groups also share these motives, in varying degrees and patterns.

In short, the regulatory process contains shared interests among utilities, regulators, and the major user and supplier groups. In the process of negotiation and compromise, commissions often behave as mediators, or even more passively. Their objective is to make it appear to work well, so as to minimize the sum total of outside criticism and avert a resort to public enterprise. Any resemblance between this and thorough public control—with clear scientific decisions based on full knowledge and economic criteria, and which have the force of directives—is often coincidental, or even contrived.

WHAT SHOULD BE REGULATED?

In this regulatory activity, the economic objective is as before: to optimize efficiency, innovation, and equity. *Natural monopolies* are eligible for regulation. Yet the conditions of *natural monopoly* are often obscure. And other cases may also need regulating.

The classic regulated utility is a natural monopoly, which has steep and extensive economies of scale, out toward the whole of the market. Therefore, at least in some core activities, competition is not viable and the enterprise is inevitably a monopoly. This is illustrated in Figure 13–7.

The capacity of the utility is finite; that is expressed by the rise in marginal and average cost beyond the minimum cost size. Over-capacity levels mean sharply rising costs. Off-peak levels (say at QB) have much lower real costs. Any enterprise which attempted to sell at levels below QA would unable to match the costs at QA and therefore could not survive. Utilities of course sell more than one output. They often use much the same capacity—a generating plant, a telephone switching system, a subway line—for many outputs, going to many different kinds of consumers, under differing conditions. The basic division can be crudely represented in Figure 13–7 by the difference between peak output at QA and off-peak output at QO. These are different outputs *by time;* they differ even though they are from the same capacity and are measured in the same physical units. Also, obviously, the true costs differ for these two sets of output. This poses the second task of regulation: to set an efficient and fair structure of prices between these two differing outputs. This simple two-part case is only a microexample of the really complex situations—with hundreds of definable outputs—in most utilities.

The further objective is to achieve this balanced price structure while also keeping the total revenue of the utility in line with total costs, thereby avoiding too much or too little profits. In short, the main condi-

FIGURE 13-7
Typical Cost and Demand Conditions for a Utility

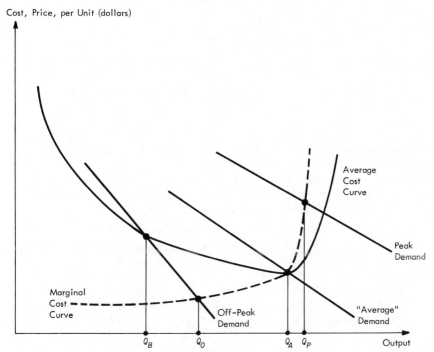

tion for regulation—the special structure of costs—also poses difficult problems for it. Chapter 14 explores these matters.

One simply identifies the natural monopolies and sets regulation over them: that is how it looked during 1900-1940. Yet it turns out to be much more complicated.

1. *Natural monopoly is often mingled with competitive conditions in "utility" sectors.* How can the *whole* of such a mixed enterprise be regulated? Moreover, this mixture changes over time, as technology evolves. Telephones, electric power, and railroads pose this problem acutely.

2. *Scale economies range along a spectrum,* with many gradients between "natural competition" and "natural monopoly" (recall Chapters 2 and 7: Are computers and canned soup almost natural monopolies?). And these conditions also evolve. Where does one draw the line, and how adjust it?

3. *Actual cost conditions are usually hard to measure* (recall also Chapter 2). This plagues decisions to apply regulation or—especially—to remove it from an erstwhile natural monopoly.

In practice, utility status is often not explicitly rationalized at all: it just happens in a vote of the legislature. Or it may be pegged on a number of specific conditions. Regulation certainly is not confined to natural monopolies. Rather it usually occurs where technical conditions enable the supplier to exploit users and discriminate sharply. It can be regarded as an extension of antitrust supervision; a degree of constraint is simply made more formal.

The common features of such utilities are:

1. Demand elasticities vary sharply among users, with some very inelastic.
2. Output fluctuates regularly and steeply; hourly, daily and/or seasonally (e.g., rush-hour bus loads, electricity peak load: see Chapter 14–17).
3. Users are connected physically to suppliers, by wires, pipes or other means. Users therefore cannot change suppliers easily, and suppliers can control use more thoroughly.
4. The output *from this supplier* is regarded as vital in some sense. (This is a slippery criterion; many goods and services are vital but have many alternative suppliers.)

These conditions recur in Chapters 14–17. They actually boil down to *scale economies plus price discrimination:* They make a single producer "natural," and they increase his power to discriminate and to victimize some or all users. In short, they make inefficiency and inequity likely.

In practice, each utility has its own bundle of these conditions, and the bundle evolves (see below). There is no universal or simple formula for applying regulation. Also, regulation is often applied or retained where it is *not* socially needed; and often it is absent where it *is* needed. What to regulate is a matter of judgment, not mechanical tests. The old legal phrase was "affected with the public interest" (discussed in later section). Until the 1930s (and especially during 1876–1934), this limited regulation to certain hard-core public utilities. But since 1934, the courts have held that regulation may be applied wherever it appears to be needed. Our task is to learn to judge where it is needed, in light of its probable benefits *and* costs. These needs, alas, do not stand still.

UTILITIES AND REGULATION BOTH EVOLVE

To understand regulation, you must see it as part of a Basic Social Contract: *a monopoly is officially granted, in exchange for a degree of public control.* This basis largely predetermines the outcome, as the industry and its regulation evolve. The usual result fits the following nine points.

1. *Utility sectors commonly proceed through four stages.* A regulated utility is usually a *system* providing many services to a spectrum of users, whose levels and elasticities of demand vary greatly. The network has permanence, often uses public facilities, and often is attached physically to the user. The utility's technology can change or be supplanted by rival modes.

Most utilities pass through 4 stages, as follows (in skeleton form):

In *Stage 1,* the system is invented, often leading to control by patents. This period is usually brief but decisive for the future form of the system.

In *Stage 2* the system is created and grows, often displacing a prior utility (e.g., buses replace trolleys, telephone displaces telegraph). Cross-subsidies among users, and a separation of creamy and skim markets, become embedded in the price structure.[10] The new service *seeks to get itself regulated,* in order to achieve permanence, legitimacy, and market control. The new regulators act as promoters, doing what they can to make the service available to all households.

In *Stage 3* the system becomes complete as a matter of technology and market saturation. It now shifts from an offensive to a defensive stance. Competing new technologies arise beyond the utility's control to substitute for it in its basic and peripheral markets. Its physical layout and pricing structure increasingly are out of fit with evolving city patterns. Users in creamy markets challenge the prices they are charged, and traditional external impacts (e.g., air pollution, proliferation of poles and wires, etc.) become less acceptable. The utility finds itself increasingly trying to obstruct new technology or to warp it to fit its own private interests.

Finally, in *Stage 4,* the system with its monopoly attributes bends and yields to these new pressures of competition and technology, and the sector reverts back—no longer a utility—to conventional competitive processes. Or, in certain cases where externalities, equity, or other social effects are peculiarly important, a degree of public ownership may be adopted.

Table 13–6 estimates very roughly the stages for a number of present and past utilities. During these stages, the basic technology prescribes *different* optimum structures and policy treatments.

2. *Regulation usually starts in Stage 2, in harmony with the preexisting interests of the utility and its larger industrial customers.* The structure of mutual interests, the profit expectations, and the basic terms of exchange (especially the supplier's rate level and structure) therefore

TABLE 13–6
Stages of Utility Life-cycle: Approximate Intervals

	Stage 1	Stage 2	Stage 3	Stage 4
Manufactured gas	1800–1820	1820–1880	1880–1920	1920–1950
Natural gas	1900–1930	1930–1950	1950–	
Telegraph	1840–1850	1850–1916	1916–1930	1930–
Railways:				
All	1820–1835	1835–1910		
Passenger			1910–1935	1935–
Freight			1910–1960	1960–
Electricity	1870–1885	1885–1960	1960–	
Street railways	1870–1885	1885–1912	1912–1922	1922–
Telephone	1875–1880	1880–1947	1947–	
Airlines	1920–1925	1925–1965	1965–	
Television	1935–1947	1947–1965	1965–	
Cable TV	1950–1955	1955–		

---

[10] Under price discrimination, some markets are highly lucrative (creamy) and others barely profitable (skim). See Kahn, *op. cit.*

precede regulation. This has been true of railroads, electricity, telephones, banks, and now the Postal Service. Thus placed atop the preexisting situation, regulation naturally tends to legitimize, reinforce, and smooth these interest-group compromises—recall the middle definition of regulation: ". . . to regularize." Regulation can alter the preset conditions—"to govern or direct according to rule"—only marginally. And often the new commission can only fit the third definition: "to make regulations." Rate structure is not thoroughly assessed and changed. *Regulators operate within the Contract.* They cannot really change it (e.g., rescind the franchise or cut rates sharply), though some observers wrongly think they can.

They are often called Public Service Commissions, and the rates they set are supposed to be "fair, just and reasonable." Yet by contract as it were, regulation promotes and protects the utility and its larger customers, on into Stages 3 and 4.

3. *Regulation has (barring the odd exception) inadequate funds and mediocre talent for its true economic tasks.* So those at its center usually have little motivation, or even understanding, to change the basic contract and the process.

4. *The Contract excludes seller competition from the Service area, in exchange for a review process. The efficacy of the review tends to atrophy, from lack of funds, expertise and powers. The exclusions spread and become absolute.* The contract is formally with utility owners, and so the franchise itself often becomes a large equity value in Stage 3. But its key effects are on managers.

The exclusions protect management from evaluations, controls, or take-over. Few managements have ever been so privileged, and isolated. They (and their Boards) occupy a strange position between shareholders and commission. What they are maximizing is unclear. Such a vacuum leaves incentives and responsibility—and the public interest—unclear.

The managers find it natural to maximize along both dimensions of profitability: (1) the rate of return (by influencing the commission as well as decisions in the marketplace), and (2) avoidance of risk (to do this, they take steps to keep their market shares high and avert new competition). Since profit rates are formally limited, the regulated firm is encouraged to devote resources (or sacrificed profits) instead to market-share-maintaining activities of many kinds (see Chapters 15–17). There may also be a degree of nonpecuniary maximizing (translate: waste). From these two diversions, the loss of efficiency may be large.

In any event, formal profit limits induce hypercontrol of the market and hyperreaction by the firm against new entry. The franchise and regulatory process themselves become manipulated by the managers as part of their whole efforts to maximize the utility's value and minimize the risk and uncertainty of their positions. And since the utility's share prices capitalize the value of the franchise, any threat to their value—such as by unilateral new entry—is regarded as "confiscation," *ergo* intolerable to the *regulators* as well as the utility.

So regulation is not neutral toward new competition: the bias arises from the very contract itself, and it is accentuated by the profit constraints. Oddly, this bias further increases the utility's bargaining power against the commission: the utility, seeming to be irreplaceable, must be catered to. So regulation tends to prevent the natural evolution of new competition. That might be appropriate for Stage 2, but it is not for Stages 3 and 4.

   5. *The Contract turns out in practice to allot responsibility and service liability increasingly to the commission.* Penalties and rewards are not applied—either in general or specific directions—to the utility's performance. Instead of asserting or imposing the public interest, the commission often ends up accepting responsibility for service, good or bad. Under it, too—and this is perhaps the crowning oddity—there are few practical, specific penalties which can be applied to the utility for specific lapses (e.g., brownouts, crossed wires, late planes or trains) or for general failures of management. The regulatory contract lacks explicit performance standards, and it lacks mechanisms for enforcing any possible standards. The only penalties which can really be applied to a utility are political ones—e.g., open criticism—and these usually hurt the regulators as much as the utilities. The utility's and commission's objective therefore becomes simply to minimize political repercussions, to avoid facing basic issues, to gloss over. The strangeness of the managers' role is matched by that of the regulators'.

   6. *So the Contract hyper-excludes, in at least eight ways.*
       a. It excludes seller entry from primary markets and often even from secondary and tertiary ones.
       b. It excludes inter-area competition for major customers.
       c. It excludes take-over or any lesser change in managerial and financial control, either by private interests or ultimately by the commission itself or other public groups.
       d. It excludes service-liability claims by legitimate plaintiffs.
       e. It excludes rivalrous innovation, of Schumpeterian or other types.
       f. It excludes regulatory choices which would cause significant reductions in utility share prices.
       g. It excludes thorough, neutral treatments of third-party effects of utility actions (e.g., on the environment).
       h. And it excludes future revisions or termination of the contract itself.

   Taken together, these exclusions are often large and long lasting. Few of these exclusions, and their likely costs, have been clearly recognized for what they are. And the regulatory contract breeds mutual vested interests against change, even among potential entrants.

   7. *In short, there is a reversed evolution of regulation, in the opposite direction from what utility evolution calls for.* Regulation comes to shield firms, rather than permit the proper degree of competition.

   8. *This Contract and regulatory process tend to induce inefficiencies of several sorts.* Research on these effects is only beginning, and so the

relative importance of these costs is unclear and probably will never be known precisely (see Chapter 14). The three leading costs probably are:

a. internal inefficiency, because of the lack of financial or regulatory constraints.
b. the design of utility technology is made more exclusive to the established utility. This induces innovation to be below optimal levels and in nonoptimal directions.
c. excess peak demand and capacity is induced by inefficient price structures. Promotional rates encourage use (see Chapter 14). But, especially with new scarcities of resources and capital, the resulting levels of use may be greatly excessive and costly.

Regulation does not just permit these. It often induces them with powerful incentives. The costs are insidious because they are piecemeal, difficult to detect, and *officially* are not to be permitted or admitted (few regulators admit to permitting inefficiency, much less inducing it!). The effects often increase utility and commission security from breakdowns, and so they can be protrayed as "high-quality" service even if they are wasteful. There is also little inherent pressure from regulation toward equity, to protect poor, politically-weak users from being overcharged relative to wealthy powerful ones.

These costs are likely to increase during Stage 3. The normal constraints on management are reduced or absent. And the utility's incentives are to tighten the exclusions further.

9. *The exclusions tend to be stable and self-perpetuating.* Entry by new sellers is difficult to force unilaterally upon a utility. Any severe such depressant on utility stock prices is asserted to be confiscatory. Also, large firms are commonly reluctant to try to enter, partly because their other profit opportunities exceed those which regulation formally permits (recall Chapters 2 and 7). Small entrants are vulnerable and usually of trivial effect. "Better" regulation of rates—by hiring more brilliant commissioners or staffs, giving them bigger budgets, etc.—does not correct the basic contract, the structural conditions, nor the inefficiencies.

The upshot can be anti-Darwinian with a vengeance: regulation is often ill-fitted from the start, evolves the wrong way to fit its proper economic function, and survives only too well. Abolition is usually too simple and abrupt an answer, except for some Stage 4 cases. What is needed is regulation which (1) lasts only as long as is appropriate, (2) contains inducements for its own termination, and (3) while it lasts, induces optimal choices by those in the regulated firm.

These tendencies are universal, but they can be offset on occasion. Some commissions avoid them, at least for a period, and so regulation has a checkered performance. Yet the tendencies do exist.

A BRIEF HISTORY OF REGULATION

Regulation has developed slowly and fitfully—and often stormily—during the last 100 years. Its history helps explain its present crisis of identity and its uncertain future. Despite its hoary atmosphere, regulation had—and still has—intensely controversial origins.

Commission regulation exists partly by default, because its earlier close alternatives have proven unsuitable. Control by courts is inherently erratic, negative, and amateurish. Franchises and charters are clumsy and inflexible. Ordinances and statutes are also too rigid. What is needed is a continuing, detailed expert supervision, backed by powers to require behavior to fit optimal criteria. Independent commissions appeared— during the watershed 1890–1930 period—to offer just that. They are the vector of two concepts: (1) public regulation as a system of economic constraints, and (2) the natural monopoly, with just *one* franchised utility. Both concepts, we will see, are routinely overstated and warped.

Variants of regulation—giving favor to an enterprise and setting limits on it—trace back into prehistory. It evolved from medieval Europe as part of mercantilism (recall Chapter 4). Monopoly grants by the sovereign came to carry varying rights and duties. The great laissez-faire rollback of many of these interferences during 1750–1850 cleared away many quasi-regulatory devices.

The legal origin of modern regulation traces back to 1670, when Lord Chief Justice Hale in Britain summarized the law of businesses "affected with a publick interest."[11] Speaking of ferry boats, as well as port facilities, he noted that they were not merely private, because—as monopolies—they had public effects and public duties. This concept of *public interest* has been the pivot upon which all later setting of *public* constraints upon *private* capital have turned.

During 1820–70, there was much local experience in America with rate regulation: for example, private wharves, chimney sweeping, bread, and horse-drawn transportation in Washington, D.C., and in other cities. By 1860, five eastern states had tried advisory commissions for regulating railroads: they relied on competition plus supervision. By 1870, a variety of small-scale utilities—gas workers, water works, railroads, etc.—existed and were being loosely treated in many ways. Competition was still commonly part of the approach.

It was railroads and the newer utilities—electricity, telephones, and city transit—which crystallized the modern regulatory method during 1880–1920.

Transcontinental railroads evolved during 1850–70. They had great bargaining power in the Midwest, dealing with individual farmers. In contrast to many eastern lines, where a degree of competition was possible, farmers out on the plains usually had no alternative ways to get their products to market. Grain elevators also exercised monopoly power, often tied directly in with the railroads. Therefore, by the mid-1870s, a deep-going set of discriminatory practices had been developed by the railroads, to charge all that the traffic would bear (see Chapters 14 and 17). The resulting wave of opposition took form as the Granger movement, and was the origin of what we now recall as "prairie populism."

By 1874, many Midwest states had created regulatory commissions to

---

[11] Sir Matthew Hale, *De Portibus Maris* and *De Jure Maris*, London, 1670.

control railroad rates. Most of them quickly reverted to passive status, for railroad power was really a regional problem. The landmark *Munn v. Illinois* case in 1877 established that States could assert regulatory authority over trades (in this case grain elevators) "affected with the public interest."[12] The criteria of "public interest" were: (1) *necessity* of the service, and (2) *monopoly*. The decision set the general precedent that regulation can be applied wherever a public interest can be perceived.[13] Yet it fatefully set *monopoly* as the prime target of regulation, and that still persists in the orthodox image.

By 1887, pressure had risen to redress the monopoly power of Midwestern railroads. This meshed neatly with the Eastern railroads' wish to create a cartel device to prevent periodic bouts of price competition among them.[14] The result was the Interstate Commerce Commission, created in 1887. Despite its apparent position of control, the fledgling ICC was blocked by the courts from settling effective rate ceilings until about 1910 (see Chapter 17). By the 1920s, the railroads were already under heavy new competition from road carriers. The ICC therefore failed to regulate when it was appropriate and then did regulate after it became largely unnecessary.

By 1900, electric and telephone utilities were already well advanced and evolving toward regional and national scope. Initially, open franchising had been the rule, with cities often having several—or even scores—of little "utility" systems. But then the doctrine of natural monopoly took hold. During the watershed period of 1907–25, most states created public service commissions to franchise and regulate these private firms. In many cases, the firms lobbied hard to create regulation, as preferable to public ownership or federal regulation. Most state commissions had little leverage until the 1930s. Powers and resources were lacking, and/or firms created long, sterile controversy over the proper rate base, and these staved off action during the 1920s (see Chapter 14). Most state commissions are still passive.

Federal regulation of electric power and telephones was formally established only in the 1930s, in reaction to severe scandals in utility stock manipulations during the 1920s stock-market craze. The federal commissions have had perpetual conflict with state agencies over Who Controls? From the start, state commissions have sided with the firms, against what is seen as the common threat of the (marginally) stricter federal commissions. This overlap and conflict is a basic and troublesome fact of regulatory life, creating large practical problems in assigning utility operations among state and federal jurisdictions. They also enable the utilities to play off the commissions against each other on many issues. Often what a federal commission denies, state commissions will give back; and vice versa.

---

[12] *Munn* v. *Illinois,* 94 U.S. 113 (1877).

[13] There were departures during 1920–34. But the *Nebbia* decision of 1934 (291 U.S. 502) firmly settled that regulation can be freely applied.

[14] See Gabriel Kolko, *Railroads and Regulation 1877–1916* (Princeton: Princeton University Press, 1965), and Paul W. MacAvoy, *The Economic Effects of Regulation* (Cambridge: MIT Press, 1965).

State regulation has been used openly as a haven from federal regulation in insurance (the McCarran Act of 1945) and other trades.

The state commissions have done little to control the quality of utility services, in general leaving initiative to the companies and acting only on complaint. Most of them have manifested little interest in the structure of rates, accepting cost analyzes advanced to rationalize discrimination, or entrusting the formulation of particular charges to the discretion of managements. All of them have been concerned with the level of rates. But few have sought to control operating expenses, the largest element in the rate level, by passing on them in advance. All have prescribed accounting systems, essential to rate control, but few have attempted to enforce them by audits in the field. Few have undertaken to develop criteria of equity or efficiency to govern earnings.

And none has sought to maximize consumption by reducing rates to the lowest level that would yield a fair return. Instead, attention has been centered, in the past, on determining and preserving the value of utility properties. Some commissions, in making valuations, have accepted reproduction costs. Others, while giving such costs little weight, have made obeisance to the courts by going through the mumbo jumbo of the valuation ritual. Energy has been diverted from the purpose for which the laws were passed and the commissions formed.

Formal action is through a rate case. Some commissions initiate such cases. Others are passive, waiting for cases to be brought. In 1967, it was reported that four states had had no rate cases for eight years; that four others had had none for 13 years; that Delaware had had none since its commission was established in 1949; and that South Carolina had had none since 1933.

In rate case proceedings the contest between the company and the consumer is not an equal one. The company is represented by able lawyers, well paid, fortified with facts, and supported by a staff of expert witnesses. In some states the commission assists the consumer in preparing his case. In others, it does not. In both, his lawyers are poorly paid and inadequately reinforced.

And if the consumer wins, the company can appeal—and appeal—and appeal. In the past, protracted litigation has been the rule. One telephone case dragged through the courts for 13 years. In such a situation, the commissions despaired of making progress through formal procedures and sought to salvage what they could by entering into negotiations with the companies.

Negotiation is faster and cheaper than litigation. And it may lead to cuts in rates. But there is no assurance that it will always protect the public interest. The negotiators meet behind closed doors; no record of their proceedings is released. The outcome will depend upon the zeal of the contending parties and on their skill in bargaining.

The commission has certain advantages: it can threaten formal action, appeal to public opinion, or deny requests for extensions or abandonments or for the issuance of new securities. But the companies have the support of greater knowledge, financial resources, and staying power. They are therefore unlikely to concede as much as the law would have required. The rates agreed to may still be well in excess of costs; the profits they yield may be exorbitant.

Responsibility for the failures of regulation cannot be charged to the commissions alone but must be shared by the courts, the legislatures, the executives, and the public at large. The *courts* asserted their right to review the work of the commissions, stripped them of necessary powers, and reversed their decisions, always to the end of preventing or canceling reductions in rates. The *legislatures* have impeded regulation by denying the commissions adequate jurisdiction, powers, and funds. The errors of courts and legislatures have been matched by those of the *executives*. Governors have made poor appointments, filling commissionerships with political hacks, unqualified by experience or interest for the work. In some cases they have even appointed men chosen by the utilities or have otherwise discouraged real enforcement of the law.

In short, the concept and legal basis for effective regulation ripened in good time—in 1877, before electric, telephone, and other modern utilities emerged. But actual regulation has lagged far behind, by decades. As noted, it has been set atop existing structures of firms and interests.

Formal regulation has existed for over a century. Actual regulation has been tried, under adverse conditions and only in scattered areas, only for several decades.[15] From the start, most commissions have had scant resources. Also, the utilities have gained by using obtuse doctrines and procedural tactics to congest and fend off regulatory efforts. In the early 1910–35 period, this led to a morass of stupefyingly complex debates over reproduction cost as the value of the rate base. The whole effect of it has made much regulation into arid ritual.

Still, an image of adequate regulation somehow persisted after 1940. New sectors evolved (natural gas, airlines, TV, cable TV, etc.), each with mixed motives toward being regulated. Slight as its known effectiveness was, regulation was extended to new areas. By the 50s, it covered—formally—nearly the whole of the economic infrastructure of the U.S. economy. This was probably the peak coverage of conventional regulation, and most economists—from optimism or ignorance—assumed that it actually did *regulate*.

Yet by the 50s no one could say in any detail or depth what the effects of regulation had been and how well they conformed to the public interests. Research on regulation had nearly ceased. During the 60s, the more searching economic questions about regulation began to be asked again: What, if anything, should be regulated? What are its effects? What levels and patterns should it follow? The possibility that regulation was a charade, a cloak for utility interests, or itself a source of unnecessary monopoly, came to the fore.

Therefore, in the 70s regulation is at a crossroads. Its economic worth can no longer be assumed, and may fairly be doubted (see Chapter 14). The ways in which it could be costly are now increasingly clear and possibly important. The most forceful defenders of utility regulation are

---

[15] Recall, only several states are strict, in some degree. The FCC has had formal rate hearings and decisions only since 1964. And FPC regulation became (moderately) forceful only after 1960.

the regulators themselves and the companies supposedly under strict constraint.

There is much intriguing folklore about regulation. For example, only a handful of utility regulators stand out as being effective and forceful, from among the vast numbers of those which have held office down the years. Among state commissions, a few are known to be strict or at least creditable (recall footnote 5 above). Meanwhile, there is a rich folklore about utility performance and management. For example, electric power managers since the 30s are agreed to have been relatively stodgy and insulated: hence their severe difficulties in meeting the new problems since 1965 (see Chapter 15). Bell System management is widely regarded as thorough, uninspired, and tenacious in its defense of Bell System interests. During the 20s there were widespread efforts by utilities to influence academic and public discussion of utility interests.[16] In some cases this reached the level of open scandal. Since then, utilities have been more careful to avoid even the appearance of trying to twist debate their way. Nonetheless utilities are also anxious to have a favorable image, and the Bell System in particular cultivates academic and public approval in a wide variety of ways. Some of these—e.g., a sponsored journal—have social value. But the persuasive and social power of these large, settled enterprises can be great, and it serves genuine private interests. One result is that the newer problems since 1965—scarcities, service breakdowns, and new rate-structure pressures—have come more from the onrush of unexpected events rather than from careful academic research or far-sighted commissions.

In fact, the late 60s mark a sharp break with the previous several decades. Ecological problems came to the fore, stopping some utility development patterns in their tracks and causing a near crisis in energy

---

[16] Irston R. Barnes, *op. cit.,* Chapter 23, covers this seamy episode thoroughly.

In hearings conducted by the Federal Trade Commission in the early 30s, trade associations of gas and electric companies were shown to have spent millions of dollars every year to influence public opinion. These bodies fed news and editorials to the press and used their control of advertising to prevent unfavorable publicity. They supplied friendly speakers for public meetings and kept unfriendly speakers from getting a hearing. They provided teaching materials to schools and colleges and sought to censor textbooks that they disapproved. They planted their propaganda in labor unions, granges, women's clubs, churches, and Sunday schools. According to one of their officials, they employed every means of communication but skywriting. And so they spread the word that tighter regulation was not required. It took financial scandals of the greatest magnitude to overcome the confidence that they created and to arouse consumers from the lethargy this confidence induced.

After the disclosures of the 30s, the utilities were more discreet. But, according to Bauer, they continued their efforts to influence regulation.

First, they have maintained close and insistent political connections with both major parties. Second, they have watched constantly for their own interest along the entire political front so as to get favorable actions and avoid unfavorable. Third, they have watched and promoted, or opposed, appointments, not only to the commissions but to the technical staffs. Fourth, they have sponsored favorable legislation and headed off unfavorable. Fifth, they have participated in quasi-public organizations and through them extended their influences into the communities and into political channels. Sixth, they have used extensive advertising and other means of publicity to stimulate favorable attitudes, and to prevent unfavorable news articles and editorial comments; seldom have newspapers printed squarely the public side in utility controversies. Seventh, the companies have kept close contact with the commissions, spreading graciousness and lures for their private advantage.

While originally the companies were vigorously opposed to regulation, they have come not only to accept it but largely to convert it into an instrument of protection for themselves. John Bauer, *Transforming Public Utility Regulation* (New York: Harper & Bros., 1950), p. 193.

supply. The first serious breakdowns ever in Bell System service quality appeared, especially in New York city. New center-city groups came forward to assert their interests, for the first time. And the cost of capital rose sharply, faster than utility profit rates. In fact the whole promotional ethic of the utility managers, which has led to low prices for service and intensive efforts to raise the levels of customer usage, came head-on against the new scarcities of urban and national life after 1965.

Therefore, from a large number of directions, the institution of regulation and the activity of the regulated companies have come under severe new doubts and stresses. And still it seems to flourish and spread! The 70s are likely to be a genuine watershed for the further fate of regulation. Yet, even if any sharp changes in it do occur, they are likely to fit within the process of evolution outlined earlier.

CHAPTER FOURTEEN

Rate Level, Rate Structure, and Efficiency

Regulatory commissions ideally try to apply two criteria: the fair rate of profit, and a just and reasonable price structure.[1] These are exercises in applied microeconomics which, elsewhere in much of the economy, are performed by competition. The ideal economic result would be: (1) precisely the efficient level of capacity and output in each part of the utility and in its total, (2) no X-inefficiency, (3) the optimal rate of innovation, no more, no less, and (4) a fair division of burdens and rewards among investors, consumers, managers, and others.

Most commission work ignores these four points, instead centering on rate level and structure. Indirectly, these might then bring about the optimum results. But this is not assured; mistakes may occur, the indirect influence may not be tight enough, or the regulatory process itself may insert new biases. And one goal may conflict with another: e.g., prices which maximize *efficiency* may not be *fair*.

So in this chapter, we consider rate levels and rate structures. In each section, we first define the optimum and then compare it with what is actually done. The likely effects on performance are explored. The special problems of regulating several firms at once are taken up. We will then be equipped to look for the sensitive points and past results in electric, gas, telephone, and other utilities.

PROFIT LEVELS

Criteria

Assume first that the utility's price *structure* is efficient. At what *level* should that whole structure be set, so that the total profit rate is consistent with efficient allocation? Recall that the profit rate is simply:

---

[1] The best and deepest modern treatments of these issues are in Bonbright, *op. cit.;* and Kahn, *op. cit.* These issues are never settled. For the flavor of the continuing debates (and some of their forbidding—and often meaningless—technical complexity), dip into several issues of the *Bell Journal of Economics and Management Science.*

$$\text{Rate of Return} = \frac{\text{Total Revenue} - \text{Total Cost}}{\text{Invested Capital}}$$

$$\pi = \frac{TR - TC}{K}$$

Some profit rate ceiling is to be set, but how high? The firm cares intensely about this. The market value of the firm (i.e., the price of the stock) will rise if the profit rate (π) can be raised, even by just a little.[2] If large capital gains are at stake, the utility will be willing to use large resources—and virtually any line of argument—to persuade the commission to raise the ceiling on π. There is a vague range within which reasonable π could fall: 6–12 percent is a good estimate.

The main issue resolves down to two simple diagrams. Figure 14–1 shows the simplest utility case, with one output and economies of scale large enough to make a natural monopoly. The firm prefers point QA; restricted output and maximized profits. The social optimum is at a

FIGURE 14-1

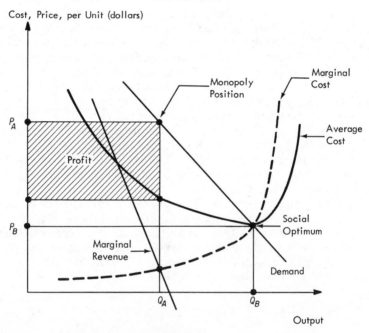

Cost, Price, per Unit (dollars)

---

[2] Example: a utility with $2 billion in total asset value at a π of 10 percent (there are quite a few larger than this). Leverage is 50 percent (half equity, half debt), and the current market value of the stock is $1 billion, or 8.3 times the net income flow of $120 million per year (i.e., a price-earnings ratio of 8.3: quite normal). Interest on bonds is at eight percent, and the estimated cost of equity is 12 percent.

If π is raised to 11 percent, then, *ceteris paribus,* net income must rise to $140 million per year. This will capitalize into stock prices at 8.3 times the extra $20 million, equal to $166 million in the total market value of the equity—a 16.6 percent capital gain. These are large stakes, to which the utility might commit $166 million or more in the effort to raise the permitted π (recall Chapters 3 and 4).

FIGURE 14-2

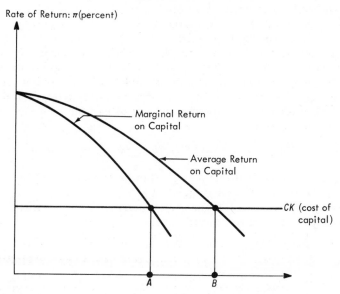

Rate of Return: π(percent)

Marginal Return on Capital

Average Return on Capital

CK (cost of capital)

A   B

Amount of Capital Invested (dollars)

higher output level, at or near point *QB.* The recurring struggle—repeated in scores of commissions year by year—is over the size of that sliver of price which goes to profit.

So, what *should* π be? Answer: it should be at the level which attracts the efficient rate of new investment into the firm. This depends on the marginal productivity of capital, both in this firm and in the rest of the economy. The decision looks ahead to new investment, not to past investments. The basic choice is shown in Figure 14-2. There is a range of future projects to invest in (plants, networks, offices, etc.) with varying returns. Funds for them can be acquired at a cost shown by *CK* (for cost of capital). The regulator's job is to set the profit rate ceiling so that investment occurs at just the efficient level. If that ceiling is too high, the supply of capital will be too large and actual investment will be too small. And vice versa; if π is too low—so that the utility's prices are all too low—then demand for services will be too high and capacity will have to be larger than the supply of capital permits.

Note where the strain arises: the utility firm prefers point *A,* where its monopoly profit is maximized. The competitive—generally, the optimal—result is point *B.* These points correspond to points *QA* and *QB* in Figure 14-1, which is the familiar cost and demand situation under monopoly. The commission endeavors to press π (and prices) down to costs (barebones costs, minimum costs, or by any other name) but not below. The firm tries to show that costs are really much higher, especially when the true costs of capital are allowed for.

Actually, the efficient level is roughly in line with competitive levels, but not rigidly.[3] The utility's profits and investments are to be fitted within the efficient allocation among all markets. Profit and risk conditions elsewhere influence the correct answers here. If profit rates elsewhere are high, even for secure firms, then this regulated firm's π should not be too low, or it will go begging for funds and will soon run short of its optimal capacity. Thus arises the conventional regulatory concern about the cost of capital and capital-attraction; company lawyers try to scare the commissions with forecasts that capacity will lag and breakdowns will occur if π is set below the cost of capital.

Specific criteria include:

1. *Cost of capital.* The measured average cost of past and/or new investment.
2. *Capital-attraction.* Returns high enough to induce capital markets to supply at least the efficient level of new capital.
3. *Comparable earnings.* Returns commensurate with returns in other enterprises having comparable risks.

These seem sensible and mutually consistent. But they are Pandora's boxes, full of theoretical and practical problems. They are circular and ultimately empty, though commissions regularly seek to apply them.

More on Comparable Returns. If regulatory doctrine has progressed at all on the definition of a fair return, it has been toward a concept of comparable returns. That utility rates of return and risk criteria should be in line with risk-return conditions in the rest of the economy is prescribed, approximately, by second-best analysis. This point cautions against a blind limiting of utility returns to minimal levels. And it may be, as many company witnesses in rate hearings have maintained, that utilities bear substantial long-term risks, despite their apparently secure positions.

Yet comparable returns will not do as a criterion for setting profit ceilings, for several reasons. *First, it is not practical.* Acceptable definitions of "comparable" have not been forthcoming, even after concerted efforts. Risk, in particular, has defied reliable definition and measurement. Cross-section and time-series variation in profit rates have been hypothesized as estimators of risk. But they are highly dubious and incomplete in concept. And in actual measurement they have not displayed the expected properties (recall Chapter 2).

Therefore, *second, the conceptual risk-return basis for a comparable-earnings standard has not yet been verified.* Moreover, when risk is high, capital possibly should not be attracted, but, instead, withdrawn. Therefore a *low* rate of return may be prescribed by high risks, rather than a high rate of return to compensate for the risk-bearing. In fact, the refusal to recognize that many utilities reach a phase when capital should be *depleted* is the blind spot which afflicts most of the simple criteria for fair rates of return.

Third, actual earnings of a firm should relate to relative efficiency, not to a guaranteed, if comparable, return. Since utilities are monopo-

---

[3] To be precise, the regulated levels should also allow for deviations from competitive results elsewhere. These are called "second-best" criteria. See Kahn, *op. cit.,* and the sources cited there at Vol. I, pp. 195–99.

lies, their attainment of the target comparable return could happen even if they were inefficient, uninnovative, and possessed of a markedly irrational price structure. This proviso would hold even if the previous two problems were somehow solved. Therefore, the relation of comparable earnings to allocative efficiency is remote.

A *fourth* problem simply adds to the remoteness. This is that *the regulators themselves create much of the utilities' risk, so that the criterion is quite circular.* The regulators do not find the degree of risk; they make it. If they are strict, the risk of a low profit rate is very high. And vice versa.

In short, a comparable earnings criterion for regulation of fair returns is a will-o'-the-wisp, with little substance. This is not to deny that the optimal rate of return may bear some relation to risk, and that it may be roughly in line with what commissions often set as a criterion in the belief that they are using a comparable earnings standard. But there should be no illusion that the standard has much scientific or practical substance.

Are there other criteria which are clearly superior? Not on economic grounds, for the criterion depends on the social objective. Rather than try to derive a universal criterion, one should incorporate the net after-tax rate of return into the whole strategy of social control. The optimal net rate of return can be said, in any event, to be somewhere between 15 and 5 percent on equity capital. The precise rate attained should depend *not on regulatory choice but on company performance.* That has been one great fallacy of regulation; that by making the profit results *look* like competition, the other results of competition—efficiency, equity, innovation, etc.—could be guaranteed. Instead, several opposite effects may have come about. An optimal strategy will need to have a more direct incentive mechanism.

The optimum rate of net investment may be high, low, or negative: in some cases—shrinking industries; utilities in Stage 4?—capital should not *be* attracted. That holds for over-built utilities which, for the time being, have excess capacity (see Figure 14–3). Examples include eastern railways in the U.S. and urban trolleys in the 1950s. During the disequilibrium period of adjustment back to a smaller system, net investment should be negative, and π should be below the opportunity cost of capital (and possibly below zero).

The opposite case of excess demand (see Figure 14–3 also) requires a very high π, to choke off excess demand and reflect the true scarcity of output. Both of these disequilibrium cases may be temporary, but in some industries the transition lasts decades or more. The regulators are then faced with the need to require chronic losses or excess profits. Generally, the excess demand case is early Stage 2, while losses may arise in late Stage 3.

The mainstream cases are down the middle, with an equilibrium growth path or level of output which keeps capacity roughly in line with demand. The utility plans this growth sequence; the commission sets π so as to make the investment possible, without allowing excess profits. Apart from fine points, setting π is not excruciatingly difficult. It will range between 5 and 15 percent, depending on (1) broad capital-market

FIGURE 14-3

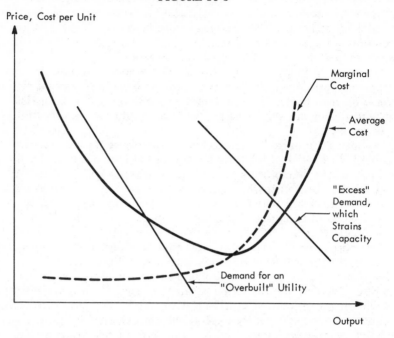

Price, Cost per Unit

Marginal Cost

Average Cost

"Excess" Demand, which Strains Capacity

Demand for an "Overbuilt" Utility

Output

trends in interest rates, and (2) the degree of inherent technical risk in this utility. A delicate test is the price trend of the utility's common stock. If it has been sharply up compared to the whole market, then investors are probably getting and/or expecting excess profits. And vice versa. The utility's risk will depend both on its technology (is it in Stage 2, 3, ?) *and* on the regulator's decisions. The mainstream utilities in Stages 2 and 3 have very low risk, because their solid monopoly permits them to raise prices to cover virtually any foreseeable cost problems. In fact, therefore, the exercise is circular. *The regulators themselves* set much of the risk factor precisely while they are setting the ceiling on π. They do not find the profit-risk conditions: they *make* them.

All this means that the 5–15 percent range is a battleground which matters keenly to the firm but not much to allocation. If π is really too low, it will quickly be seen. Otherwise, the decision largely reflects the regulators' liberality to investors and their prudence in leaving a margin for safety.

ACTUAL METHODS

How do commissions set rate levels? They make three main evaluations: costs, rate base, and the fair rate of profit.[4] The firm urges a high

---

[4] Full information is necessary (if not sufficient) for a good regulatory decision. Yet early regulators lacked good data for decades (e.g., the ICC for 20 years). Even now, accounts are often deficient and good figures on critical costs are often unavailable. Regulation does force much vital data out into public view. But the effort to get full information is a continuing one.

π, on one criterion or another; the staff rebuts, favoring a low π. The Commission gravely picks some π in between, almost always less than the firm's request.

Setting Allowed Costs

The firm will gain by padding costs: (1) by sheer waste, (2) by transferring nonutility costs onto the utility operations, and/or (3) by accounting methods which make utility costs look bigger than they are.

Waste can arise in many forms, since utility managers have great discretion (see Chapters 13 and below). Costs of any or all types may not be minimized. And specific types—managers' rewards and perquisites, benefits for favored groups, propaganda activities—may be enlarged.

Nonutility expenses can be transferred outright or, more subtly, when the firm's overhead costs include utility and nonutility items. This can occur (1) statically, among coexisting operations, and/or (2) dynamically, when a new nonutility service might be added to the preexisting utility services.

The problem of allowable costs has long been recognized.[5] Some commissions scrutinize costs closely and disallow certain items. Usually this requires showing an abuse of discretion by managers.[6] The burden of proof favors the managers, in practice; their good faith is assumed. Most commissions routinely accept all utility expenses as valid.

None of them has promulgated rules or established standards to govern expenditures. Nineteen state commissions have the power to require that budgets be submitted in advance. But these lack budgetary control; they cannot prevent unwise expenditures from being made. Most commissions examine the reports that are periodically submitted on expenses incurred in the past. If certain items seem improper, they may warn the companies concerned that they will not include them in computing future rates. But the warnings may be ineffective. When rates are formally contested, expenses may be questioned. Yet the company will present its accounts as a record of established facts. And the representatives of the public are seldom equipped to challenge the propriety of the items they contain. Upon occasion, certain items may be disallowed. But such control, at best, is indirect and weak.[7]

Where it is exercised, the supervision of expenditures is selective. The prices and wages paid for goods and services bought in the open market are accepted as given. Inquiry is confined to matters where the interests of consumers and investors are obviously in conflict, and where the prices paid do not result from arm's-length bargaining.

On balance, specific expenses—and efficiency as a whole—are immune from thorough regulation.

Depreciation offers great discretion to managers in setting their accounting levels of cost. Assets decline in value as time passes, mainly

---

[5] *Chicago & Grand Trunk Railway Co.* v. *Wellman,* 143 U.S. 339 (1892).

[6] *West Ohio Gas Co.* v. *Public Utilities Commission of Ohio,* 294 U.S. 63 (1935), and *Acker* v. *United States,* 298 U.S. 426 (1936).

[7] Recently, certain salaries, public relations, and advertising costs have been disallowed in a few cases. But the totals have been small.

from (1) wear and tear (physical depreciation), and (2) obsolescence (functional depreciation), as innovations render old plant inferior and, therefore, destroy their value. Yearly depreciation is a valid cost of business. It is entered as a cost. Its summed totals appear in the balance sheets, where total fixed assets minus accrued depreciation reflects the *net* value of assets actually in use.

Key point: the level of *costs* is thus connected to the *rate base* via depreciation. A high rate of depreciation (e.g., writing off an investment in five years rather than 20) will *increase* the current cash flow—permitted profit plus yearly depreciation. *But* it will also keep the rate base *lower* in later years. The utility naturally optimizes by choosing a depreciation method which attunes present cash flows versus its future rate base, in line with the firm's motivation. The common choice favors a high rate base, and so slow depreciation—with long assumed asset lives and small yearly depreciation—is common.

Depreciation involves (1) salvage value, (2) asset life, and (3) the method of write-off during the life.[8] A short life with no assumed salvage value will give large present write-offs. A long life with high salvage value gives small yearly write-offs. Accounting methods—straight-line, declining-balance, and sum-of-the-years-digit are three common ones—give further choice. Figure 14–4 illustrates the discretion.

These sharp differences do not exaggerate the real cases. Plausible estimates of service life and salvage value can differ by multiples. Most

FIGURE 14–4
The Choice of Depreciation Method Can Sharply Affect the Value
of Capital

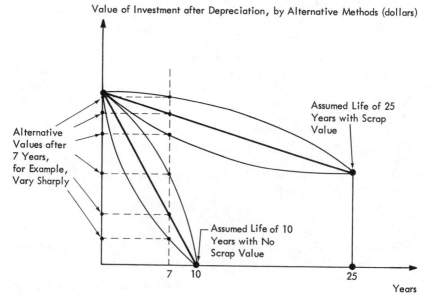

Value of Investment after Depreciation, by Alternative Methods (dollars)

Assumed Life of 25 Years with Scrap Value

Alternative Values after 7 Years, for Example, Vary Sharply

Assumed Life of 10 Years with No Scrap Value

7   10   25

Years

---

[8] Any good accounting textbook will explain these choices.

utility accounting ignores obsolescence. Yet it may actually be rapid, and a major innovation can quickly render valueless a utility's entire plant. (That, indeed, is precisely what can and does happen in Stages 3 and 4: e.g., trolleys, manufactured gas.)

Therefore, despite its seeming dullness and obscurity, depreciation is intensely controversial and keenly argued. It is mostly guesswork. Engineers can measure useful life (20, 30, even 40 years), but these are really only rough estimates. And innovation can falsify them quickly; so can changes in demand and in official requirements.

In practice, utilities are usually permitted to choose their preferred depreciation method, which they must then stick with. After long debate, the *original* cost of assets is almost universal as the required basis. But any reasonable service lives and depreciation techniques are permitted. And if unexpected changes arise, commissions usually permit utilities to handle them as they wish.[9]

Taxes are treated as a cost. They are not an important regulatory issue.

The Rate Base Problem

The utility is permitted to earn profits (at π) on the full value of the rate base. Regulators need to prevent it from being padded or overstated: to limit it strictly to prudent investment actually needed for utility service.

Rate base can be enlarged in three ways: (1) accounting devices which overstate its value, (2) assigning nonutility assets to the utility services, and (3) actual expansion of real investment.

Accounting valuation is, again, partly a matter of optimum depreciation strategy by the utility.

It was also—during 1898 to about 1940—a morass of empty dispute about reproduction versus original cost of assets. The Supreme Court opened the floodgates in the landmark *Smyth* v. *Ames* case in 1898.[10] Rejecting a Nebraska attempt to regulate railroad rates (William Jennings Bryan argued for the state), the Court added a dictum on valuation:

We hold . . . that the basis of all calculations as to the reasonableness of rates to be charged by a corporation . . . must be the fair value of the property being used by it for the convenience of the public. And, in order to ascertain that value, the original cost of construction, the amount expended in permanent improvements, the amount and market value of its bonds and stocks, the present as compared with the original cost of construction, the probable earning capacity of the property under particular rates prescribed by statute, and the sum required to meet operating expenses, are all matters for consideration, and are to be given such

---

[9] A special problem since 1954 has stirred sharp debate. Accelerated depreciation (under a special tax rule of 1954) permits faster write-offs and shifting of taxes over time. Utilities could either pass these benefits on immediately, or normalize them over time. A complex debate has ensued. Immediate flow-through of the benefits is possible, but it might negate the stimulus to investment. Normalization would preserve that incentive but also permit higher real profits and neglect a chance to cut prices to consumers. The state and federal commissions have divided about evenly on the issue: the FPC, ICC, and 23 state commissions require or favor flow-through. See Phillips, *op. cit.*

[10] 169 U.S. 466.

weight as may be just and right in each case. We do not say that there may not be other matters to be regarded in estimating the value of the property. What the company is entitled to ask is a fair return upon the value of that which it employs for the public convenience. On the other hand, what the public is entitled to demand is that no more be exacted from it . . . than the services rendered . . . are reasonably worth.[11]

This was a meaningless fruitcake, containing indefinable and conflicting principles (Try critiquing it before reading the next footnote).[12] During 1920–40 it was cited to justify long and tortured arguments against the *original* cost rate base approach, which is palpably the only workable method.[13] Not until 1944 did the *Hope Natural Gas* case lay it firmly to rest.[14] The rate base could at last be settled, and attention could rightly center on the rate of return.[15]

This detour is now mostly closed (though many states still follow it; see Table 14–1 below), but it did deep damage to regulation while it lasted. And it ensured that regulation had little effect on railroads, telephones, electric and gas utilities until well into Stage 2 or even Stage 3.

Intangibles were another bogus tactic used to inflate the rate base. Intangibles have been claimed to include good will, franchise value, water rights, leaseholds and value as a going concern. All of these—and especially good will and going concern value—are inappropriate, for they are not productive assets, and their value depends—circularity again!—on the commission's own decisions. Yet these values were solemnly asserted during 1898–1935 to be valid parts of the rate base.

---

[11] *Ibid.*, pp. 546–47.

[12] Actually, (1) operating expenses are irrelevant, having nothing to do with the determination of the rate base; (2) earning capacity and (3) the market value of stocks and bonds are logical absurdities, since these depend upon the rates that are being fixed; (4) original cost and (5) present cost, while relevant and logical, are inconsistent, since the values to which they lead are far apart. What is fair value: original cost or present cost or some compromise between the two? The Court does not say. Both must be considered, and each must be given "such weight as may be just and right. . . ."

Some of the errors in the doctrine of *Smyth* v. *Ames* came to be corrected in the next few years. Operating costs were quietly dropped from the factors to be considered in appraising property. Earning capacity and the value of stocks and bonds were rejected as factors by the Court. [*Minnesota Rate Cases,* 230 U.S. 352, (1913), and *Knoxville* v. *Knoxville Water Co.,* 212 U.S. 1 (1909)]. Deduction for depreciation, overlooked by Justice Harlan, was added to the "matters to be regarded" in 1909. Original cost and present cost remained as determinants of value.

It should be noted that the rule of *Smyth* v. *Ames,* in its time, was not calculated to justify excessive rates. Consideration of construction costs afforded a wholesome corrective to the tendency to set rates at levels that would validate inflated capitalizations. And consideration of "the present as compared with the original cost" provided a check for use in cases where original cost had been too high. The conversion of this rule into a device for raising rates was the work of later years.

[13] Reproduction cost appears to fit economic analysis, since it seems to reflect what the assets are *now* worth. Yet it ignores the bedrock fact that the regulators *make* the value of the assets by their own decision. And reproduction cost invites endless differing estimates. The assets can't actually be sold to anybody (perhaps regulators *should* permit such bidding and take-overs: but regulatory policy would still influence value). And estimates of cost can be made in at least four different major ways, which give varying values. That the Supreme Court was willing even to entertain the sophistry of reproduction cost during 1920–40 was inexcusably bad economics.

[14] *FPC* v. *Hope Natural Gas Co.,* 320 U.S. 591 (1944).

[15] Still, some state commissions are willing to use reproduction cost. But many of them compensate by setting lower profit-rate ceilings.

FIGURE 14–5
Simplified Illustration of the Rate-Base Effect

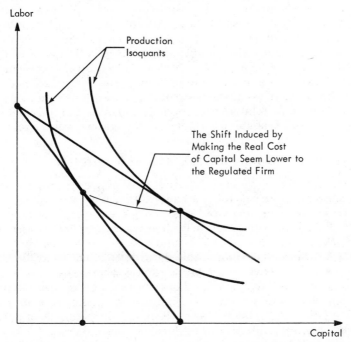

Actual investment may also exceed efficient levels, either by mistake, design, or a natural response to regulatory incentives (see below). Justice Brandeis urged during the 1920s that only "prudent investment" be allowed, excluding unwise, extravagant or fraudulent investment. Some commissions do examine utility investments for prudence, though exclusions are rare. But the problem is now recognized to be more subtle and, probably, insoluble.

Managers usually have a wide degree of choice in designing their systems and innovating new technology. Rate-base regulation routinely induces these choices to favor capital-intensity.[16] The effect operates quietly, and pervasively, to shift the margin of choice toward capital-intensive plant (see Figure 14–5). By making capital cheaper, in effect, regulation may induce some extra use of it, large or small.

This effect is ingrained in the situation and unarticulated by the managers—most of whom stoutly deny that it could even exist, though common sense plainly says otherwise. It is scarcely recognized by regulators as a natural effect of their efforts, and it would be virtually impossible to factor out from actual investments. Therefore, it remains untouched by regulatory discussions and actions.

---

[16] The landmark analysis of this is H. Averch and L. L. Johnson, "Behavior of the Firm under Regulatory Constraint," *American Economic Review,* 1963, pp. 1052–69. A stream of later articles has left its main point intact.

State and Federal Coverage. Separating the rate base between state and federal jurisdiction is a necessary and hugely complex operation for telephone, electric, railroad, and certain other utilities. (Costs and revenues must be allocated, also.) Further, utilities which operate in several states must divide their assets, costs, and revenues among those states.

The task is an economist's nightmare, for large volumes of true overhead and joint costs have to be arbitrarily sliced up into economically dubious portions. The firms try to maximize the share assigned to the states (and, among states, to the more liberal states). The resulting allocations may bear some relation to economic categories, but the whole process is suspect and probably routinely biased against federal coverage.

Setting the Fair Rate of Return

The efficient π is never clear. It needs to be above the rate on riskless assets (e.g., the treasury prime rate), for utilities have some risk (depending on their life-cycle stage and regulatory treatment). But how much higher? The *Bluefield* decision early cited several possible criteria.[17] But like *Smyth* v. *Ames,* it left priority and weightings among the criteria unresolved. In practice, comparable earnings has not controlled. Competitive industries have *lower* profits and *higher* risks. As Chapter 2 noted, a general positive relation between risk and return has not yet been scientifically shown. Instead high profits appear to relate mainly to market power or—in some cases—economies of scale. And practical measures of comparable risk are difficult to prepare.

Commissions instead usually look to the cost of capital. Estimates of the cost of past capital are prepared. There are also guesses about the cost of new capital. And the commission usually adds a safety margin. The resulting figure, artificial and inelegant as it is, does give a safe and sane approximation roughly in line with reasonable judgments.

Leverage. The leverage (or capital structure: the debt-equity ratio) of the utility can influence the estimated cost. The cost of debt is taken to be the interest rate paid, usually around 6 to 9 percent. The cost of equity is usually reckoned at least 4 points higher. Therefore, the orthodoxy has it, high leverage gives cheaper capital. And each firm has an ideal capital structure for its risk situation.

Yet the capital structure is probably broadly irrelevant. The true economic cost of capital is mainly determined by the firm's basic risk condi-

---

[17] *Bluefield Waterworks and Improvement Co.* v. *Public Service Commission,* 262 U.S. 679 (1923). "The rate of return . . . must be determined by the exercise of a fair and enlightened judgment, having regard to all relevant facts. A public utility is entitled to such rates as will permit it to earn a return . . . equal to that generally being made at the same time and in the same general part of the country on investments in other business undertakings which are attended by corresponding risks and uncertainties; but it has no constitutional rights to profits such as are realized or anticipated in highly profitable enterprises or speculative ventures. The return should be reasonably sufficient to assure confidence in the financial soundness of the utility and should be adequate, under efficient and economical management, to maintain and support its credit and enable it to raise the money necessary for the proper discharge of its public duties. A rate of return may be reasonable at one time, and become too high or too low by changes affecting opportunities for investment, the money market, and business conditions generally."

tions.[18] The issue is complex, but the nub is that higher leverage—because it increases risk—tends to *increase* the cost of both equity and debt, rather than just substitute cheap borrowing for expensive equity.

Normally, risky utilities should have lower leverage.[19] Electric firms have had high leverage, too high for the new uncertain times since 1965. And Bell System leverage was moved up at regulatory insistence after the 1950s, on the ground that the firm's risk was relatively low. Put generally, leverage should peak in early Stage 3 and then move down as normal risks arise.

The resulting estimates of fair return lack clear guidance.[20]

The rate actually allowed by the commissions and the courts has been conventional or arbitrary to a degree. It has usually been based on expert testimony and rules of thumb, with little pretense of economic analysis. There has been no real study of the conditions governing investment decisions, the character of alternative investment opportunities, or the expectations that must be satisfied if new investments are to be made. Bankers and brokers appearing for the companies give their opinion that future risks are likely to be great and that earnings, consequently, must be high if securities are to be sold. Witnesses for the public point out that risks, in the past, have been small. The commissions and the courts have exercised judgment as best they can, coming up with a figure that they rarely attempt to explain. Usually, this figure has fallen somewhere between 6 and 10 percent. The allowed return differs from state to state and from industry to industry, and it varies over time (see Table 14–1).

The use of judgment is not *per se* incorrect at all, for differing complex conditions cannot efficiently be settled by crude uniform rules. Rather, it is the seeming shallowness of the exercise which is disturbing. Perhaps nothing better could be expected, even from Solomon: the political pressures are great, the facts are obscure, and the principles clash. Fortunately, the precise choices do not appear to have strong effects. The actual π levels often stray from the ceiling, and a strict decision often merely provokes a quicker return for the next rate request.

Viewed whole, the rate decisions usually reflect the commissioners' feelings about the utility's general prospects.

---

[18] A leading statement of this point is F. Modigliani and M. H. Miller, "The Cost of Capital, Corporate Finance and the Theory of Investment," 48, *American Economic Review,* 261 (1958).

[19] This accords with basic principles of company finance.

[20] One example shows how the estimates can vary. In a 1968 telephone rate case in New Hampshire, five witnesses gave these estimates:

	Debt Ratio	Cost of Equity	Cost of Capital
McIninch	—	9.5–10%	—
Conrad	35%	10–11	8.0%
Barker	35	10	7.75–8.5
Lowell	35–40	10–11	8.0
Kosh	45–50	6.95–8	5.5–6.05
Commission decision	45	7.75	6.11

Re *New England Telephone & Telegraph Co.,* 42 PUR 3d 57, 60–61 (N.H., 1961), summarized in Phillips, *op. cit.,* p. 288.

TABLE 14-1

Rates of Return Prescribed or Approved by State Commissions as of 1973 (in the most recent case)

State	Electric Rate of Return on		Gas Rate of Return on		Telephone Rate of Return on		Valuation Standard Generally Applied to Assets (often with some adjustments)
	Assets	Equity	Assets	Equity	Assets	Equity	
Alabama	—	—	—	—	8.58%	10.5%	Original cost
Alaska	9.24%	11.25%	—	—	—	—	Original cost
Arizona	6.75	15.65	6.75%	15.65%	7.32	11.68	Fair value
Arkansas	—	—	10.50	15.32	8.04	11.0	Original cost
California	7.9	11.9	8.0	11.88	7.85	9.50	Original cost
Colorado	7.46	12.82	8.6	12.4–13.2	8.625	11.4	Original cost
Connecticut	8.01	14.5	8.0	12.0	8.1	9.6	Original cost
Delaware	6.0–7.0	—	6–7	—	—	—	Fair value
District of Columbia	7.1	12.55	—	10.08	8.0	9.5–10	Other
Florida	7.93	12.13	8.46	14.0	8.25	10.55	Prudent investment
Georgia	7.95	11.5	8.5	11.5	8.3	11.3	Original cost
Hawaii	8.25	—	7.94	—	—	—	Original cost
Idaho	6.9	11.5	7.6	10.73	6.31	—	Original cost
Illinois	7.74	—	8.43	—	7.33	—	Elect. & gas: OC. Telephone: FV
Indiana	6.49	13.89	6.75	14.2	6.43	10.53	Fair value
Iowa	7.172	11.72	8.23	10.0	4.3	12.15	Original cost
Kansas	7.45–7.75	11.0	7.6–8.0	11–12	8.1–8.5	9.9–10.6	Original cost
Kentucky	8.0	12.2	—	—	—	—	Various
Louisiana	8.39	13.5	8.33	11.29	8.3–8.5	10.5	Original cost
Maine	7.7	11.25	—	—	8.65	11.0	Original cost
Maryland	8.2	—	8.6	—	8.4	—	Fair value
Massachusetts	7.91	12.0	8.59	11.25	7.8	10.0	Original cost
Michigan	7.47	12.12	7.58	12.0	7.96	9.3	Original cost
Minnesota	—	—	—	—	7.5	—	Other
Mississippi	8.65	14.32	9.0	13.94	8.01	—	Fair value
Missouri	7.22	11.9	8.14	12.66	8.11	9.4	Fair value
Montana	6.125	7.4	6.5	8.2	6.23	7.3	Fair value

Nebraska	—	—	—	—	7.76	—	Other
Nevada	8.13	12.0	8.0–8.25	12.0	8.12	12.0	Original cost
New Hampshire	8.5	12.0	8.5	10.0	7.8	10.0	Original cost
New Jersey	7.85	—	7.85	—	7.93	9.9	Other
New Mexico	7.25	15.16	7.25	11.4	—	—	Fair value
New York	7.96	12.10	8.37	16.5	9.25	11.6	Original cost
North Carolina	7.82	12.0	7.68	—	8.16	8.94	Fair value
North Dakota	6.97	—	6.77	—	7.44	—	Prudent investment
Ohio	6.49	—	6.86	—	6.93	—	Reproduction cost
Oklahoma	6–6.12	—	6–6.37	12.0	6–6.37	—	Original cost
Oregon	8.0	12.0	8.0	10.0	8.6	10.5	Original cost
Pennsylvania	7.25	12.8	6.8	11.5	7.75	10.5	Fair value
Rhode Island	7.25	12.0	7.5	—	7.6	10.0	Original cost
South Carolina	7.56	—	7.56	—	8.9	12.0	Other
South Dakota	—	—	—	11.5	7.0	9.0	Original cost
Tennessee	—	—	—	9.25	8.50	10.5	Original cost
Texas	7.9	13.0	7.375	10.0	—	—	Fair value
Utah	8.25	13.8	7.0	9.22	9.1	8.88	Original cost
Vermont	8.56	—	9.22	—	7.93	9.75	Various
Virginia	—	—	—	—	8.61	—	Original cost
Washington	7.2–7.5	10.8–11.5	8–8.3	10.8–11.8	8.2	10–10.5	Other
West Virginia	6.173	—	7.0	—	7.5	—	Original cost
Wisconsin	—	—	—	—	—	—	Original cost
Wyoming	7.15	10.89	7.15	10.89	8.05	10.81	Original cost

Dashes indicate that data were not supplied, or that the commission decision did not prescribe a specific rate of return.

Source: Federal Power Commission, *Federal and State Commission Jurisdiction and Regulation* (Washington, D.C.: U.S. Government Printing Office, 1973).

What really matters—when all the sophistries and details of the rate presentations are over—often includes these things:

1. The general financial condition of the utility.
2. The recent trend of the utility's stock price.
3. How well the utility has been performing (a composite of many things: service complaints, adequacy of capacity and expansion plans, trade commentary on managerial and service quality, etc.)
4. General price and wage trends, by comparison with the utility.
5. The degree of strictness of *other* commissions in setting π, rate base, allowable costs and—in general—price levels for their utilities.
6. The intensity of pressures and of expected criticisms.[21]

FIGURE 14–6

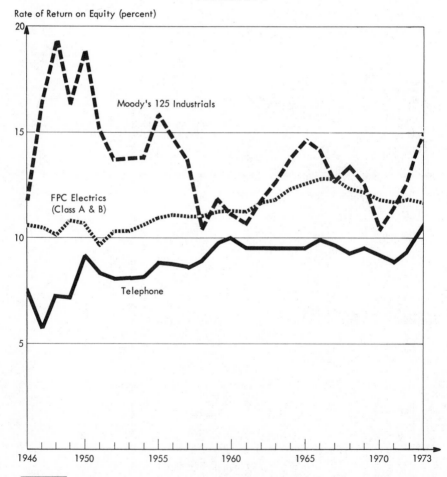

Rate of Return on Equity (percent)

---

[21] An interesting attempt to model and explain commission actions by these and other factors is made by Paul Joskow in "Inflation and Environmental Concern: Structural Change in the Process of Public Utility Regulation," M.I.T. Working Paper in Economics, No. 128, March 1974.

The rate hearing is only the visible ceremony at which familiar issues are presented. Actual decisions draw on the wider understanding and responses which commissioners inevitably—and usually rightly—apply.

Results

Regulated profits seem to reflect a degree of restraint, but there is naturally much variety. Table 14–1 gives recent ceilings for π in most state and federal commissions. Figure 14–6 gives some broad averages, in comparison with some industrial profit rates.

Actual rates of return do not follow the ceilings rigidly; some shift or stay above, while others move below. Figure 15–10 (below) will show the spread among about 190 private electric firms in recent years. And Table 14–2 gives recent returns for a selection of leading regulated firms.

The spread reflects utility life-cycles and efficiency (see below) as well as regulatory limits. Broadly, the mainline utilities have had returns surprisingly close to the average for all large firms, and some have done even better. Others have done poorly—eastern railroads, Consolidated Edison, etc.—not only from known blunders but also because of underlying life-cycle determinants.

During about 1945–65, average costs in some utilities (e.g., telephones, electricity, airlines) were stable or declining, as scale economies were explored (see the following chapters). This was a golden age of regulation: few rate hearings, steady or falling utility prices, good service quality, simple issues, and handsome profits.

Regulatory lag favored the firms, and the excess profits were not recaptured. But it seemed not to matter, for utility finance, performance, and price trends all seemed favorable. There was even a boom in AT&T stock and many other utility stocks during the 50s.

TABLE 14–2
Rates of Return, 1970–73, for Selected Large Regulated Firms

Rank among 50 Largest Utilities in 1973	Service	Assets 1973 ($million)	Average Rate of Return on Equity 1970–73
1 AT&T	Telephone	67,051	9.1%
2 Consolidated Edison	Electric, gas	5,968	7.3
3 Pacific Gas & Electric	Electric, gas	5,471	9.7
5 American Electric Power	Electric	5,071	13.4
6 Commonwealth Edison	Electric	4,649	10.6
10 Detroit Edison	Electric	3,061	8.4
17 Florida Power and Light	Electric	2,400	11.4
18 Texas Utilities	Electric	2,351	13.8
22 American Natural Gas	Gas	2,113	13.3
23 United Telecommunications	Telephone	1,959	12.4
25 Baltimore Gas and Electric	Electric, gas	1,871	9.7
33 Northern Natural Gas	Gas	1,595	11.4
39 Houston Lighting and Power	Electric	1,425	12.9
41 Western Union	Telegraph	1,402	4.6

Since 1965, regulatory lag has crimped the firms. The pressure of events has forced a drastic shortening of the old prolonged regimen, but the delays still matter. Even so, commissions have been quite able to force out decisions on large increases in a small fraction of the time formerly needed to decide small changes.

The probable effects of rate-level regulation on efficiency are noted later in this chapter.

RATE STRUCTURE

We now turn to the inner structure of prices. The problem is important and complex. The utility—private or public—usually has much latitude in designing its prices. A great variety of price structures will be consistent with any single global objective (profit rate, efficiency, innovation).

Some price structures will enhance the utility's financial security: others will increase its capacity; still others, its political leverage; and still others will deter new competition, of the sorts we have already discussed. Pricing is usually too complex for public policy to treat in detail. The cost and demand conditions are complicated and obscure, knowable mainly by expert feel and study rather than easy research.

The price structure can be—and is—used to entrench the firm and exploit consumers. The social impact may be great, when some users pay multiples of other users' prices for a staple utility service. Inefficient and unfair price structures can have major economic and social effects.

As usual, there is a core of relatively simple concepts, which can be—and often are—refined down to the point of hairsplitting. The basic objective is simple and direct: individual prices should normally be as close to marginal cost as possible (recall Chapter 13). The intriguing and baffling problems arise (1) in deciding what marginal costs are and in measuring them, and (2) in deciding how much price discrimination may be necessary. The alternative basis is to discriminate in prices according to elasticity of demand. That can be done extensively, it suits the companies' interests, and it is part of their effort to maximize profits while minimizing long-run risks.

A basic strain therefore arises from the commissions' objective to put prices in line with *costs,* against the companies' efforts to fit them to *demand* conditions. Much of the early impetus for regulation has come in reaction to gross discrimination by utilities among their consumers. And so the commission decisions on price structure can be an acid test of their effectiveness. Yet, commissions have tended instead to be preoccupied with rate *level* questions, leaving most or all of the price structure decisions to the companies. Only recently, since the 50s, has there been an awakening of concern over price structure.

In some parts and services, cost and demand conditions will be parallel, so that marginal-cost pricing and discrimination are congruent. In those cases, no explicit regulatory control is needed (though supervision is still needed). The greater difficulty arises when the two diverge. The difficulty also arises when marginal cost is nearly or quite impossible to define.

FIGURE 14–7
Efficient Pricing Often Can Smooth
Loads and Reduce Needed Capacity
(A, B, C, and D correspond to the
same letters in Figure 14–8)

FIGURE 14–8
Efficient Price Structure: Prices in Line with
Marginal Costs at B and C

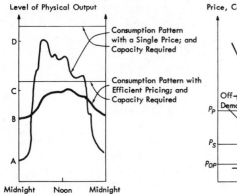

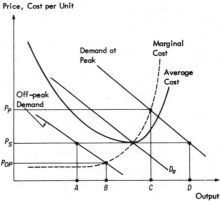

Figures 14–7 and 14–8 sum up the key points. Use fluctuates, and so costs vary. Figure 14–8 simplifies down to two periods, such as peak and off-peak. Demand for each period is in different range of marginal costs. These correspond to peak conditions commonly found in the electricity, transit, telephones, and others. Costs and demand may also differ among consumer types, such as residential and industrial. In those cases, high elasticity of demand often goes with low marginal costs of supply. Still, Figure 14–8 does convey the gist of rational pricing.

How can marginal costs vary so sharply among periods? There are three main causes:

1. The last margin of capacity is used only at peak, and so the total costs of installing, depreciating, and maintaining it year-round are focused on just a few units of use. This cost properly falls on peak-load use, which is responsible for requiring the capacity.[22]
2. Utilities use their best capacity for base load, using their worst units (e.g., old buses, inefficient generators) only at peak times. Their variable costs are high.[23]
3. At off-peak times, fixed (capacity) costs are zero and variable costs may be low (e.g., slight costs from using an idle telephone exchange or line).

These factors can set peak costs an order of magnitude or more above off-peak costs. A telephone call, an extra subway ride, a light switched on, or a letter: at peak times they are much more costly than off the peak.

---

[22] This responsibility holds despite lengthy efforts to justify allocating it among all users. See Kahn, *op. cit.,* Vol. I, pp. 87–103; and Bonbright, *op. cit.*

[23] Moreover, peak or congestion operations often impose external costs, such as from old, smoky generators.

These short-run cost differences are parallel to long-run costs, for a succession of capacity-straining peaks ultimately means that peak costs are high in the *long* run.

If a utility is on an efficient growth path, it will usually have peak and off-peak conditions similar to Figure 14–8. Its aggregate revenues from all periods will balance out to cover total costs. Marginal-cost pricing will not cause chronic deficits or surplus, unless the utility gets seriously overbuilt or short of capacity. (Such disequilibria do occur: witness the eastern railroads and electricity in New York.) *Normally, marginal-cost pricing is fully compatible with private ownership and fair rates of return.*[24]

For efficient allocation, price should be in line with marginal cost for each individual class of output. This results in a peak level price at P_p which is much higher than the off-peak price P_{op}. When costs differ, prices should differ in line with them. If demands are at all elastic, efficient pricing will smooth fluctuations and raise the load factor (as in both Figures 14–7 and 14–8). If D_a represents some kind of average demand conditions and the commission required a single price to be set at P_s, the resulting levels of output demanded would diverge sharply and perhaps disastrously from the efficient levels, as shown in Figure 14–8. Peak level demand would be far to the right, straining capacity so severely that true marginal costs would be almost infinitely high. In practical terms, the utility would be short of capacity and some demand would *not* be met. Meanwhile off-peak usage would be less than the optimal.

Evidently, marginal-cost pricing can be of critical importance, for it may avoid gross and chronic overload on the system. Before 1970 this point often fell on deaf ears; the new scarcities have at last driven it home. Without it, the inherent tendencies of regulated utilities to overinvest will be aggravated (see below). Therefore peak-load pricing is an essential offset to the other distortions which regulation may induce. Figure 14–8 is for a balanced-growth utility, in which capacity and the spectrum of demand are roughly in line. The price structure shown in Figure 14–8 would result in an overall level of revenue which would cover total costs. Again, marginal-cost pricing will be perfectly consistent in most cases with overall rate-*level* objectives.

Marginal-cost pricing in practice faces difficult problems in defining peak-load responsibility and cost. In some cases, peak-load costs are relatively easy to determine, while in others they are virtually beyond measurement. Still, the principle is the same: during peak-load periods pricing should be up in line with costs, while off-peak prices should be relatively low.

Net Revenue Erosion.   Not only do promotional rates often conflict with static criteria of rational pricing. They also can erode the firm's

---

[24] It is not tied to socialist firms or deficits, despite a common impression to the contrary. That arose from the belief—traceable back to Alfred Marshall—that all "utilities" have decreasing costs even in the short run, and from the 1930s literature on pricing of public enterprise. As we will see, U.S. private utilities do a great deal of marginal-cost pricing, call it what they may.

FIGURE 14–9
Promotional Pricing Pays When Costs Are Declining

FIGURE 14–10
Promotional Pricing Does Not Pay When Costs Are Constant or Rising

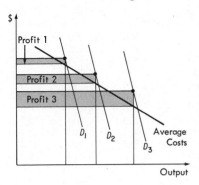

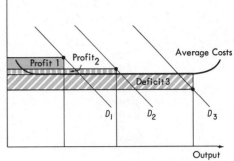

profits over time, when long-run marginal costs cease to decline. In Stage 2, there may be decreasing costs (see Figure 14–9). As long as promotional rates are not—roughly speaking—even more sharply downward sloping, then both net revenues will grow over time and rate-base incentives will be fulfilled. But let costs become constant or even rising—with capital shortages (see Figure 14–10). Growth will now automatically erode net revenues. When capacity is tight, the profit erosion can become calamitous; peak load is grossly underpriced at a time when its cost may even undermine the firm's financial standing. It is these private *profit* effects of socially irrational pricing which are finally inducing firms to shift toward more efficient price structures.

The Case for Discrimination

In some cases, where genuine decreasing costs prevail throughout the range of demands, it may be necessary to add a margin to price in order to reach a total profit level that is large enough. In those cases, the added price margin on each kind of output may need to reflect demand elasticity in some degree.[25] To that extent in that special case—usually early Stage 2—efficient pricing may involve some degree of discrimination.

Discrimination may have certain marked advantages. First, it may bring about a fuller employment of facilities and a wider consumption of services. Thus, in Table 14–3 we see that output is raised from 400 units to 2,000 units. Second, discrimination may result in lower prices for all consumers. The price reductions in the lower groups need not be offset by price increases in the upper groups. At every level in the scale, including the highest, the price charged can be lower than would be the case if the seller did not discriminate. But this gain is unlikely to be realized unless rates and earnings are controlled.

---

[25] See Kahn, *op. cit.,* Vol. I, pp. 131–50. Recall that utility conditions—fixed connections, variety of demands, overhead costs—make deep discrimination easy and natural. They are prime social reasons for regulation in the first place.

TABLE 14–3
An Unregulated Monopolist Discriminating in Price

Price	Sales	Sales in Each Class	Revenue from Each Class	Total Revenue	Total Cost	Profit or Loss
$9.00	100	100	$ 900	$ 900	$1,400	—$ 500
8.00	200	100	800	1,700	1,750	— 50
7.00	300	100	700	2,400	2,050	350
6.00	400	100	600	3,000	2,300	700
5.00	500	100	500	3,500	2,500	1,000
4.00	700	200	800	4,300	3,000	1,300
3.00	1,000	300	900	5,200	3,400	1,800
2.50	1,400	400	1,000	6,200	4,100	2,100
2.00	2,000	600	1,200	7,400	5,000	2,400
1.50	2,800	800	1,200	8,600	6,400	2,200
1.00	3,600	1,200	1,200	9,800	8,000	1,800

Let us refer again to Table 14–3. Here, the monopolist obtained $2,400 beyond the fair return that we assumed to be included as a cost. He did so by taking from each class of customers all that the traffic would bear. He cut some prices from $6 to $5, $4, $3, and $2; he raised others from $6 to $7, $8, and $9. Now let us assume that rates are regulated. The regulatory agency limits earnings to a fair return. Suppose the law permits discrimination. The results are shown in Table 14–4. Here, again, the prices, sales, and costs are the same as those previously shown. As in Table 14–3, consumers are classified and a different price charged in each class. But here, a fair return is obtained from a scale of prices that begins at $1.50. The volume of output is raised to 2,800 units. And every price in the scale, up to the top price of $3, is well below the $5 that would have to be charged if discrimination were not allowed. The customer who pays $3 is not harmed when the same service is sold to another for $1.50. On the contrary, he is helped, since this enables him to save $2 himself.

It is on this basis that discrimination has long been permitted in railroad and public utility rates. If the railroads, for instance, were to establish a uniform rate per ton at a figure that would cover average total costs, they would not improve the position of shippers whose commodities now bear the higher rates. In fact, they would worsen it. For producers of heavy and bulky low-value goods, that are now carried at low rates, could

TABLE 14–4
A Regulated Monopolist Discriminating in Price

Price	Sales	Sales in Each Class	Revenue from Each Class	Total Revenue	Total Cost	Profit or Loss
$3.00	1,000	1,000	$3,000	$3,000	$3,400	—$400
2.50	1,400	400	1,000	4,000	4,100	— 100
2.00	2,000	600	1,200	5,200	5,000	200
1.50	2,800	800	1,200	6,400	6,400	0
1.00	3,600	1,200	1,200	7,600	8,000	— 400

no longer afford to ship them. The volume of traffic would decline. All of the railroads' fixed charges would have to be met by the traffic that remained. The rates paid by high-value traffic would have to be raised. Shippers who now pay high rates should therefore be happy that other shippers are served at low rates.

For discrimination to be so justified, however, certain conditions must obtain. First, there must be a heavy investment entailing high fixed costs *and a substantial amount of capacity standing in idleness,* so that costs per unit can be reduced by spreading the fixed costs over a larger volume of output. Second, the lower rates must be needed to get business that would not otherwise exist. Third, they must be high enough to cover variable costs and contribute something to overhead. And fourth, the whole scale of rates must be regulated to keep earnings reasonable and to keep discrimination within bounds.

The situation can be stated in more practical form. Sticky problems arise where large overhead costs must be allocated among users who share the same utility network. In railroads and telephones, such cases abound (see Chapters 16 and 17). The responsibility for capacity is not at all as clear as it is with peak–off-peak patterns. One or more users then appear to have low marginal costs and declining average costs throughout (see Figure 14–11). Each user can help spread the overhead, by being priced somewhere above marginal costs. The utility simply optimizes by setting the ratio of prices to marginal costs for various users so as to ensure that enough total revenue comes in.

FIGURE 14–11

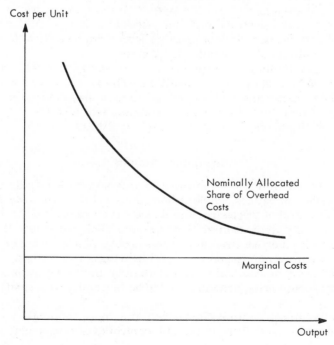

Cost per Unit

Nominally Allocated
Share of Overhead
Costs

Marginal Costs

Output

This is the practical rationale for discrimination: total costs must be covered. It does not apply where peak–off-peak price patterns—in line with marginal costs—can generate sufficient total revenues. And it does not give adequate guidance about *which* discriminatory structure should be permitted. Therefore the general rule remains that prices should be aligned with costs, keeping discrimination to the bare minimum. Cases justifying high discrimination are relatively unusual, even though the utilities have an interest in claiming that they are pervasive. Commissions will therefore need to look critically and with sophistication at the true cost conditions of the utility, in judging whether long-run marginal costs are genuinely declining. As we saw earlier, they are likely to be declining only where the system as a whole is just forming or is overbuilt temporarily, and needs actually to run financial losses for the time being. Genuine decreasing-costs utilities are relatively few: they occur usually only during Stage 2 and tend to vanish during Stage 3.

An added complication is that many services provided by utilities are not part of the genuine *natural monopoly*. These often are newer services with more inelastic demand. The utilities' rational strategy would be to skim the cream off the services, while letting the rest sell at prices close to their bare-bones cost. More generally, a utility will commonly have a core of services with relatively inelastic demands, which it wishes to price at a large profit margin compared to the rest of the services. These core services it will regard as essential to its entire system, and it will resist any possible new competition for them. Efforts to permit new competition will be resisted, on the sound reasoning that new entrants will only skim the cream off these markets, leaving the utility with insufficient profits to support the entire system. In short, price discrimination breeds its own self-destruction, *if* the regulators permit. To that extent, the regulatory decisions about price structure can be critical to the life cycle and viability of the whole utility system.

In short, optimum price structure sticks close to marginal costs, with deviations only under unusual conditions. The pressure for such deviation will be intense and widespread. But unless they hew to the unified principle of marginal-cost pricing, regulators will give free play to the utilities' ability to charge what the traffic will bear.

Regulatory Actions

The actual commission treatment of rate structure usually departs from the efficient pattern. On the whole, there is little specific or general study and control of price structure. Price structure is largely set by the firms, with only slight commission revisions. This is because the commissions lack expertise, time, and access to data. Also, they are tied down by the company emphasis on rate-level hearings. And further, commissions tend to act on complaints rather than on their own initiative, and complaints about price structure tend to be few and have a spotty coverage.

Therefore most commissions—even the most thorough and best-equipped ones—exert little systematic control over rate structures: this has always been true. There will be occasional cases posing rate structure directly, but these are usually limited in scope and relatively shallow in effect. The most pressing problems arise when a new market arises adjacent to other utility services. Or, alternatively, new entrants may seek to compete with a utility service. Then commissions have to consider what the marginal costs are, what the effect of entry and new pricing will be on the entire utility system, and the terms under which entrants may (if at all) enter the market. If entry is permitted, the utility usually cuts its prices to reflect, meet, or undercut the new competition. The result is to align prices more closely with cost, but this also reflects the genuine change in demand elasticities under new competition. *The play of partial or actual competition does tend to drive prices more into line with true costs.*

Where such pressures are absent, and there are only consumer complaints or commission initiatives to go on, then price structures may stray very far from efficient criteria. There are exceptions, of course, and something like marginal-cost pricing can be observed in a handful of utilities over a relatively small part of their business.[26] Moreover, these marginal instances of marginal-cost pricing occur as much under private ownership as under public. Regulation tends slightly to modify price discrimination by utilities, preventing some of the steeper instances of it. But it fails utterly to bring prices into line with real costs on a standard basis. (Actual prices will be reviewed at some length in the next chapters.)

The effects of this are relatively simple and clear. Peak-load use and capacity are usually too great: off-peak use is overpriced. The burden of prices does not fall fairly on those who incur the costs. The lack of efficient pricing has accentuated the effects of rate-base incentives on the use of capital. It took decades to get some utilities to use promotional pricing in order to stimulate demand.[27] Now it is clear that much promotional pricing runs squarely against efficient pricing. As we will see, promotional prices are usually well below below the peak costs and so peak-load use and capacity are raised—and so are service crises and breakdowns. Therefore the price structure often accentuates the other deviant incentives, rather than correcting them. This is partly a matter of commission preoccupation with other problems; it also reflects the inability of many commissioners even to perceive the problem. Earlier, when capital was abundant and utilities were regarded as simple, isolated technologies, the cost of these deviations seemed insignificant. Now they are recognized to pose serious issues. Two sectors display them currently, for differing reasons.

In electricity and gas, the apparent fuel crisis has combined with ecological problems to prescribe a *reversal* of the promotional rate struc-

---

[26] See W. G. Shepherd, "Marginal Cost Pricing in American Utilities," *Southern Economic Journal,* 1966, pp. 58–70, for a survey of telephone and electricity rates. See also Chapters 15 and 16.

[27] Samuel Insull was the leader in this effort in electric power, despite a bad reputation as a stock trickster which he unfairly was given in his dotage. See Forrest McDonald, *Insull* (Chicago: University of Chicago Press, 1962). AT&T adopted promotional pricing (e.g., flat monthly rentals) from the start.

ture (see Chapter 15). A reversal of this sort had long been in order, so as to align prices with true costs, as much as possible.[28] Marginal-cost pricing of this kind would accord with other performance objectives, including adequate profits for the entire firm. Now an even sharper reversal may be needed, to reflect the true increasing costs of supply in most directions. This is accentuated by equity considerations, since the effective prices to innercity users—who are generally of low income—are regularly double those of affluent suburban users. Yet the resulting shift toward rate reversal has been only slight, so far.

In telephones, marginal costs have been only partly reflected in prices, and so extra demand and capacity have been induced in a number of directions (see also Chapter 16). As telephone service quality and capacity have come under increasing stress in the 1960's, the firms' interest in fitting prices to true costs has grown. This is limited by the design of much local equipment, which does not permit close metering of calls. That design in turn reflected the earlier promotional motives, by which metering of calls was irrelevant. Abroad, pricing has been more rational, with costs more closely allowed for. In telephones in the U.S., regulation has been largely peripheral to the firms' own recent interests in a socially more rational price structure, fitted closely to costs. But regulation could press it further.

One should not be dogmatic. In many cases the level and character of marginal costs are controversial and unsure. Accordingly, the extent of misallocation, waste, and inequity are honestly debatable. Still, the general tendency is broad and powerful.

PROBABLE EFFECTS ON EFFICIENCY

Regulatory treatments are a crazy quilt of inaction, partial controls, and fallible choices, with much slippage between the formal and the real. Several main effects on performance are likely to occur from all this.

Bear in mind that the firms usually benefit from having an extra margin of capacity and quality, to avoid all breakdowns and to project an image of high-grade service. Regulators often share these benefits, and so they are not diligent in estimating this margin and trying to keep it from being wasteful.

Recall also that utility managers routinely lack pressures and incentives for efficiency. During Stages 1–3 the degree of internal efficiency is partly a matter of choice. Only if the regulators somehow manage to maintain the possibilities of take-over or of other close outside supervision (either by themselves or by other private entities) will there be a normal kind of efficiency constraint. In fact, they do not, as we have seen. Therefore, the cost curves shown in Figures 14–2 and 14–8 may not be as low as possible. If they are shifted upward by a margin of inefficiency, then prices will be higher and output levels will be lower.

In short, serious questions about the level of capacity and the effi-

---

[28] See Shepherd, *op. cit.;* and James R. Nelson, ed., *Marginal Cost Pricing in Practice* (Englewood Cliffs: Prentice-Hall, 1964).

ciency of management arise under regulation and seem to have no easy solution. Regulation might well hit the efficient overall profit levels right on the button, while also fostering thick layers of inefficiency, excess capacity, and unfairness.

There are five main probable effects. *First,* the process tends to extend and harden the degree of monopoly held by the utility during Stages 2 and 3, and even Stage 4. The commissions come to defend the companies against potential competition. They control procedures which exclude take-overs or other changes in supervisors. And they preside over hearings which serve primarily—though not always—a safety-valve function, in letting complainants against the utilities believe that they have been thoroughly and effectively heard. The utility's monopoly is double: it has an actual or virtual monopoly, and it is protected by official barriers against possible new entry.

Second, the process encourages inefficiency, by applying a cost-plus incentive system (basically similar to much weapons purchasing: see Chapter 29). The managers are remarkably free of constraints, and so the resulting degree of inefficiency is likely to be significant. These tendencies can affect all inputs, labor, capital, materials, and services.

The *third* effect stems from the peculiar focus of regulation upon the rate of return on *capital.* This causes two special effects. *One is that the firm prefers a higher level of capital than it otherwise would.*[29] As long as the permitted rate of return is above the true cost of capital, the firm gains a margin of extra profit on any additional investment that it can get into the rate base. Therefore it will prefer to write up its accounting capital, or to invest in higher levels of physical capacity and capital, to buy rather than lease, and/or to choose technology which is more capital-intensive. This so-called Averch-Johnson effect—or rate-base effect —was a prime topic of debate in the 60's. But it goes back to 1920 and earlier, when the interest of regulated utilities in overinvesting was already recognized. This effect may increase the utilities' capital-intensity by a great amount or perhaps by a fairly slight margin.[30] But the direction is clear: towards higher levels of investment.

A related impulse is toward capturing adjacent markets at below-cost prices. Recall that most utilities operate across a variety of markets, some of which are core natural monopolies, others which are partly natural monopolies, and still others which are related but could be quite competitive. Because of the rate-base effect, utilities will have a steady incentive to reach out into the further markets as long as the capital for the production can be included in the rate base. The urge may be very strong, even leading to prices which are below cost. For the utility, the strategy is simple: merely file a new set of low prices for the new service. If ratified by the commission, this quickly and officially gives the utility a monopoly in that service. Again and again, commissions have gone along with this tactic by which old utilities capture new markets.

Both of these effects arise from the rate-base focus of regulation, in

---

[29] Recall Averch and Johnson, *op. cit.*

[30] Actual conditions are considered in the next chapters.

which a regulated utility will normally wish to expand its capital and market coverage. Both of them require sophisticated and resolute resistance by the commission, in order to offset the incentives (examples follow in the next chapters). The extent of this effect is still a matter of debate, but it is probably significant in a variety of cases.

The *fourth* probable side effect of regulation is upon innovation. Where the utility also makes its own capital equipment, it will have incentives which are different from those operating upon free-standing, competitive suppliers. This is true for telephone equipment in the United States. As Chapter 7 noted and Chapter 16 will explore further, the Bell System owns Western Electric Co. and buys virtually all of its equipment from it. The resulting incentives tend to increase the total expenditure on invention, but also to inhibit the application of these results. The system also applies incentives to arrange innovation so as to keep out competitors. Across the wide range of choices among alternative technology, the firm therefore has more complete control. The result will probably be a different and nonoptimal pattern of innovation.

(Note that these doubts about regulation arise mainly where regulation is effective, and puts a real bite on company earnings. In fact, regulation often is so loose as to be virtually absent. Where that happens, some of the negative side effects will also be absent. Thus some argue that regulation is benign and tolerable precisely where, and because, it is ineffective. Perhaps its results are worse where regulation is tightest.)

Fifth, capacity and peak use are enlarged where peak-load pricing ignores true marginal costs.

These effects of regulation depart from the optimum. Yet one can instead take a more optimistic perspective on them, suggesting that even if they do occur they may tend to promote long-run efficiency rather than retard it. In particular, Kahn has argued that the rate-base effect will tend more to promote long-run innovation than to waste capital, as long as innovation requires new investment.[31] The monopoly conditions tend to encourage utilities to restrict, while the rate-base effect induces them to overexpand. To that extent, the rate-base effect may be a productive— though unintended and poorly understood—side effect of the regulatory process.

So far, unfortunately, the sketchy studies on the topic are quite unable to resolve this question. The optimists are few, compared to the many analysts who believe that regulation tends on balance to strengthen monopoly and increase the use of capital and other inputs.

Ways to Abate Inefficiency

The efficiency problem has long been recognized by experts, though regulators and firms prefer to ignore it. There are frequent calls for incentive regulation to correct the biases, but it is not clear that any practical relief can be expected. Several treatments to avert the possible inefficiency have been aired or tried, and these we will now assess.

The *first* one is incentive regulation. Regulators could determine

---

[31] Kahn, *op. cit.,* Vol. II, pp. 49–59.

which utilities are the more efficient—it has recently been said—and then reward them. This will restore incentives for efficiency.[32] The treatment must have two parts: (1) a method for making objective estimates of efficiency, and (2) a method of applying rewards and penalties.

The most promising method of estimating efficiency has been applied to private electricity systems by William Iulo.[33] It shows both the strengths and the limits of the approach. The aim is to factor out exogenous and other influences on enterprise activities, leaving a residual, presumably representing true performance and not just insufficient specification or weak data. The distinctive trait of this work—its reliance on outside information—puts it at one remove from the actual processes in the utility enterprises. If the available data do not happen to include the true determinants (economic or other) or elements (what about fairness?) of performance, then performance will be neither measured nor explained.

Even if the principal variables are included and properly specified, the data at hand are likely to mask much of the real processes and differences. They will be averages, often grossing up disparate quanta, and even more often they will not closely fit the economic elements sought. Iulo's study shows not only his skill in handling these problems, but also the stubborn data difficulties which nonetheless remain.

There are also four general points. First, whatever success it may achieve with power supply, cross-section statistical analysis will not be easy to extend to other utilities, whose products are even more heterogeneous than in electric supply. Not only are the basic variables (such as output of telephone or transport services) difficult to specify, but also their determinants and interrelations are likely to be more complex and shifting than in the case of power.

Second, these econometric appraisals of performance are likely to confirm the preexisting informal folk-knowledge in management and regulatory circles. Most commissions already know fairly clearly, even without metrical tests, how efficient the firms in their juridiction are. In the profession of utility management generally, the appraisals of who the best managers are may be even sharper. Therefore econometric analysis is likely to systemize, double-check, and spruce up the folklore with scholarly coloration. But much of its results are perfectly (if privately) well known already. We will all be especially interested in those unusual cases where the objective data clash with the folk-knowledge. Yet, given the difficulties in the statistical analysis, feeding as they do on outside data, the first presumption may unusually be that the folklore is right.

Third, this may account for the slightness of impact which studies of this sort have had upon regulatory activities. Where the data are right, their message is probably already known; where they challenge the folklore, they are presumed wrong and, often laboriously and wrongly, ex-

---

[32] See Kahn, *op. cit.*

[33] See his pioneering study of electric utility efficiency, in *Electric Utilities—Costs and Performance,* Washington State University, (Seattle: Washington State University, 1961); but efficiency does not seem to yield higher profits (see W. G. Shepherd, Chapter 1, in Shepherd and T. Gies, *Utility Regulation* (New York: Random House, 1966).

plained away, if not ignored altogether. Further work in this vein, therefore, is not likely to evoke or force a greatly enlarged response, no matter how definitive the findings may be.

Yet, fourth, these studies do bring the inside opinion out into the open. Inefficiency becomes a published fact, not a private opinion. This gives commissions a new weapon to use in seeking improvements, if they have the resolve and wit to use it effectively. Accordingly one can applaud these research efforts, even though the approach inherently contains a number of severe limitations and is unlikely to succeed in other utility industries.

A *second* tactic is to order direct audits of managerial performance, to fill the void of control. These outside audits would be a basis for specific changes in the firm's form, staffing, and activities. They would also give the regulators and directors a basis for differential rewards.

Managerial evaluation is a well-developed professional field, with a great variety of unbiased assessors to choose among. The problem requires expert, sophisticated judgment. Efficiency includes not just allocational niceties, but also research and innovations, hard bargaining over supplies, attention to consumer preferences, and the rest. The lonely academic, feeding published data into a computer, can neither capture the whole of this, nor fully evaluate the cause, nor appraise the enterprise's prospects for future performance.

The mere possibility of undergoing an audit may inject strong incentives for minimizing costs and searching out new technologies. It would clarify the regulatory role too, by fixing responsibility for performance. These points hold equally for private, public, or mixed ownership. So far audits have only been tried once or twice (in New York and Michigan), with no reinforcement. If the practice became routine, its effects could be thorough. If the regulatory process continues to create the incentive void, direct audits may be the only practical way to fill it. The two trial audits occurred since the new pressures arose after 1965. If the pressures intensify, we may expect more audits to occur.

The *third* strategy is to permit entry; that is, to relax regulatory bars to entry by new sellers, competing against the utilities. It is optimal and natural to do this in Stages 3 and 4, and recently it (and its extreme form, deregulation) has been seen as the main route for regulatory reform. Actually, there are three forms of seller entry: by new firms against old utility sellers, by the old sellers against each other, and by revisions of the old sellers themselves. Recent commentary has favored the first, but the second and third are more promising in a wider range of utilities. (Chapter 18 considers this in more detail.)

REGULATING OLIGOPOLY

When regulation is applied to several firms rather than just one, some of the main problems and results change. There is some degree of natural monopoly, but not enough to prescribe just one utility firm. If overhead costs are high enough, then there may be a tendency towards destructive and unstable competition. That is the reason for which such companies usually try to get regulated. In general, the conditions are those like Stage 4 in which the utility would—if unshielded—become competitive.

In this setting, regulation tends to apply price floors as well as price ceilings, as part of the effort to stop or contain price competition. Usually, the regulation of oligopoly applies little or no ceiling to the rate of return.

The main features and effects of such regulation are four, as follows:

Cartel Support. Regulation becomes a support for cartel price fixing and the prevention of new entry. Prices tend to be higher than they otherwise would, because regulation sets minimum prices in order to avert ruinous competition. Strict bars to entry are set up, and routes and and market portions are set officially. In some cases, ceiling prices are also set. These then tend to become a *floor* price. The effects on price levels are roughly the same as under private cartels, though the official support makes the cartel tighter.

The Shift to Nonprice Competition. Competition naturally turns to nonprice features of service or product, which are often quite numerous. They include the reliability of service, quality, frequency, and still other features: airlines and broadcasting exemplify these varieties. In airlines, service is made more reliable and convenient. It is made fancier, with meals, personal service, decor, etc. Service is also made more frequent, as airlines add flights at small intervals throughout the day in order to match each others' takeoff times.

However, this does not guarantee that service diversity will be optimal, or even very large at all. Rather, the diversity of offerings tends to be less under regulated oligopoly than under either monopoly or unregulated oligopoly. This is because regulation reduces uncertainty and makes experimentation more difficult. The well-known tendency for oligopolists to match each others' offerings—rather than to explore the demands of minority customers—is sharpened.[34] The result is clear, for example, in the case of television (see Chapter 16). The breadth of offerings tends to be narrowed by the effects of regulation.

Price Discrimination. Even if profits are constrained by the regulators, a degree of price discrimination usually continues. This is because the regulated oligopolists still have strong incentives to exploit differences in demand elasticities among the consumers. Because the sellers are multiple rather than single, regulators may have even more difficulty securing valid data on costs. Therefore, even if regulatory strictness is great, price discrimination is likely to occur. The degree of regulatory control may be irrelevant to the degree of discrimination.

Regulatory Hangover. The extent of regulatory control against competition will tend to exceed what is optimal, especially as the technological need for regulation fades away in Stage 4. Such regulation is too valuable to the firms to be let go. Regulators will think of their controls as being coexistent with the public interest rather than against it. There-

---

[34] H. Hotelling, "Stability in Competition," *Economic Journal*, Vol. 39 (1929), pp. 41–57; Arthur Smithies, "Optimum Location in Spatial Competition," *Journal of Political Economy*, Vol. 49 (1941), pp. 423–39; and P.O. Steiner, "Program Patterns and Preferences, and the Workability of Competition in Radio Broadcasting," *Quarterly Journal of Economics*, Vol. 66 (1952) pp. 194–223.

fore they will defend their partitioning of the market strongly, permitting new entry and the loosening of control only reluctantly. Especially because the companies are not monopolies, the commission will take an avuncular interest in keeping them secure. Therefore the tendency towards excessive regulation will be as strong or stronger than under the regulation of single-firm utilities.

In short, regulation of several firms tends to be excessive, anticompetitive, conducive to excess service quality, and skimpy or negative in net public benefits. Some of the direct effects do differ from those which the regulation of monopoly yields.

SUMMARY

We have now outlined the basic conditions and effects of regulation, as it is normally done in the United States. We now turn to specific regulatory commissions and industries. We will look especially at:

1. Actual levels of profits rates and prices permitted under regulation.
2. Evidence about price-cost structures.
3. Control against entry by new competitors.
4. Incentives towards efficiency or inefficiency.
5. Indication of possible excess service quality.
6. Possible excess capacity or other indication of expanded rate base.
7. Anticompetitive regulation of oligopoly cases.

In all, we will expect to observe the basic struggle, which is common in other sectors and policies. This is the effort by one or several firms to get themselves designated as *the* official supplier, as a regulated monopoly. Failing that, each will try to get itself designated as one of several official suppliers, under an official cartel. In addition, the firms will endeavor to gain subsidies either directly or by the public's absorbing their risks.

If we see regulation clearly and honestly, without illusion, we can then perceive its true effects and effectiveness. We will bear in mind that the alternatives may be less satisfactory, but at the least we will see what is really there. And in some cases we may be pleasantly surprised.

CHAPTER FIFTEEN

Regulation of Electricity and Gas

E lectricity is a doubly typical regulated industry. It is conventional in its origins, regulatory status, profit rates, and price structures. And it is an old case. Yet it also has new problems of scarcity, an ill-fitting price structure, and potential competition.

Gas regulation is conventional at the piping and local selling levels, but it is caught in unique problems at the wellhead where gas is fed into the pipelines. Both are now part of an "energy crisis," which—whatever

Credit: Consolidated Edison Co.

Edison's Pearl Street Station was an early step toward electricity as a utility. Though tiny in size and service area, it embodied the elements that still affect the policy status of electricity supply.

FIGURE 15-1   **FIGURE 15-2**

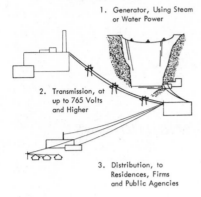

1. Generator, Using Steam or Water Power

2. Transmission, at up to 765 Volts and Higher

3. Distribution, to Residences, Firms and Public Agencies

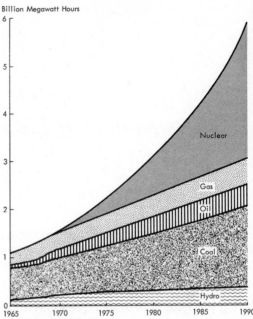

Source: Federal Power Commission, *National Power Survey, 1970.*

its true severity may be—surfaced about 1968 and may persist for years. Both are well advanced in Stage 3, and so competitive issues are on the rise, including the long-standing competition *between* electricity and gas.

ELECTRICITY

Structure

Electricity is a three-stage sector.[1] The basic technology is shown in caricature in Figure 15-1. The first stage is *generation.* This may occur from conventional sources of heat, such as coal, oil, or gas. Recently nuclear energy has begun to be a significant generation source.[2] The shares of the different sources are shown in Figure 15-2, which also includes pre–energy-crisis predictions by the FPC about future trends.

---

[1] For good summaries of the sector see Russell E. Caywood, *Electric Utility Rate Economics* (New York: McGraw-Hill Book Co., Inc., 1956); Edwin Vennard, *The Electric Power Business* (New York: McGraw-Hill Book Co., Inc., 1962); and Federal Power Commission, *National Power Survey* (Washington, D.C.: U.S. Government Printing Office, 1979), 4 volumes.

[2] Predictions about energy are risky. The share of future nuclear power has been routinely exaggerated, especially by the Atomic Energy Commission. The Federal Power Commission frequently overstates the likely total growth of consumption.

By now, most of the good hydroelectric sites are occupied, and the future sources of power lie mainly between coal and nuclear energy—with possibly fusion and solar heat further ahead (see Chapter 26).

Transmission is the bulk carriage of electricity from generating sites to final-use areas. The pylons and huge towers which march across the countryside carry these connecting lines. Figure 15–3 gives a sample view of the importance of transmission in one sector of the United States. As transmission scale has increased, the country (and certain sources in Canada) has become partly interconnected.

The *distribution* level is local: from the substation to the final users. (Try to identify the firm supplying your electricity. Can you locate the local substation?) This involves wires, either overhead or underground, to a great variety of users, including residential, commercial, industrial,

FIGURE 15–3

TABLE 15–1

Leading Electric Utility Firms

	Area Served	Also a Large Gas Supplier?	Number of Customers (1,000)	Revenues ($ million) 1960	1973
1. Consolidated Edison	New York City	Yes	2,866	655	1,736
2. Pacific Gas and Electric	North and Central California	Yes	2,633	647	1,490
3. Southern Company	Ala., Georgia, Miss., Fla.	No	1,908	319	1,165
4. American Electric Power	Ohio, W. Virginia, Indiana, etc.	No	990	338	966
5. Commonwealth Edison	Northern Illinois	No	2,593	469	1,266
6. Southern California Edison	California	No	2,467	305	1,079
7. Public Service Electric and Gas	New Jersey	Yes	1,619	393	1,076
8. Philadelphia Electric	Philadelphia	No	1,182	273	766
9. Detroit Edison	Southeast Michigan	No	1,542	279	753
10. General Public Utilities	N.J., Pennsylvania	No	1,323	206	662
11. Virginia Electric and Power	Eastern Virginia	No	1,016	160	550
12. Duke Power	Western N. and S. Carolina	No	1,110	166	600
13. Consumers Power	Michigan	No	1,095	281	834
14. Middle South Utilities	Ark., Miss., Louisiana	No	1,140	214	658
15. Florida Power and Light	Florida	No	1,340	172	714
16. Texas Utilities	Central Texas	No	1,139	202	615
17. Northeast Utilities	Conn. and Mass.	No	998	336	536
18. Niagara Mohawk Power	Upper New York State	Yes	1,234	299	671
19. Baltimore Gas and Electric	Baltimore	Yes	693	174	473

FIGURE 15–4

Service Areas of the Largest Private Electric Utilities

Adapted from map supplied by *Electric Light and Power,* Cahners Publishing Co., Boston.

and public agencies. There are the end points of electricity supply, which require much servicing and change, as customers and uses shift.

In addition to this technical structure of electricity, the ownership structure is important. About three-quarters of the industry is privately owned in the U.S., in about 200 firms; leading ones are given in Table 15–1 and Figure 15–4. The conventional pattern is for all three levels of operation to be integrated vertically within the same firm. This condition has been common since the very beginning of the industry.

During about 1930–60, the publicly owned share of the industry rose, but now it is stable. It exists in (1) hundreds of small local municipal systems, in (2) one statewide public power system (Nebraska), (3) in hundreds of Rural Electric Cooperative systems, and (4) in the bulk gen-

TABLE 15–2

Federal Electricity Systems, 1970

	Capacity (1,000 Kw)	Investment ($ million)
TVA	17.3	3,703
Columbia Basin	9.0	3,080
Missouri Basin	2.7	1,222
Southeastern Power Administration	1.9	644
Hoover and Parker-Davis	1.7	225
Southwestern Power Administration	1.5	494

FIGURE 15–5

Private and Public Power

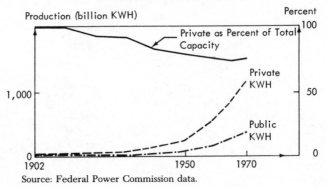

Source: Federal Power Commission data.

eration and transmission of power by the federal government, mainly from hydroelectric sources, and primarily in the Tennessee Valley and in the Northwest and Southwest of the country. These are indicated in Table 15–2 and Figures 15–5 and 15–6. This parallel role for public and private power is in contrast to the conventional situation in other countries, where public ownership is virtually complete and unified. In some countries, the primacy of public ownership dates from generations ago, but in several main European countries it has existed only since 1945–50 (see Chapters 19 and 21).

FIGURE 15–6

Nonfederal Publicly Owned Systems (municipal, state, county, and power districts)

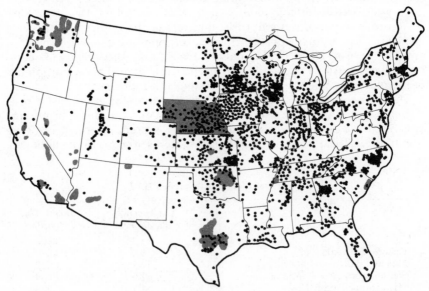

Source: Federal Power Commission, *Prevention of Power Failures* (Washington, D.C.: U.S. Government Printing Office, 1967), vol. I, p. 33.

American electricity supply is decentralized into a patchwork of geographically separate operations. Dotted among the private systems is the swarm of small public and rural systems and the occasional large federal system. There is no overall control over coordination of the system, by contrast with the unified electricity supply in most other countries. There is a degree of coordination among many neighboring electric firms, in order to pool capacity and supply for peak loads. The trend towards such coordination is strong and rising, but the suppliers are still separate.

Technology

There are relatively moderate economies of vertical integration. More important are the economies of scale at each level. At both the generation and transmission levels the scale economies are large, and these have favored an increasingly large size of apparatus during the last several decades. Yet it is *distribution* at the local level where natural monopoly most clearly exists. There the inefficiency of duplicating the supply network is clearest, and so distribution is *the* core of natural monopoly in electricity supply.

In *generation*, the last four decades have seen a rise in size of units; this rise has explored the properties of larger boilers, turbines, and other components. This was not strictly a technological advance, but rather the realization of preexisting economies of scale. In the last decade, it has become apparent that the limits of scale economies are being reached, and so generation no longer seems to present endless economies of scale.[3] Therefore generation is characterized by economies of scale which are definite but limited. In the future, new plants will tend to be about the same size as the biggest ones now being built, rather than ever larger.

Transmission has been at increasing scales also, and further economies seem to be large (see Figure 15–7).[4] Large-scale transmission offers major new opportunities for carrying bulk supply over long distances and in high volume. The present partial network is shown in Figure 15–8. Transmission is therefore the most sensitive area for future adjustments in the scope of local monopoly and regulation. This trend is creating new opportunities for competition among electric firms.

On the whole, the technology is evolving so as to permit realignments of the old service areas and competitive strategies.[5] The core of natural monopoly at the distribution level will continue, but the pressures for detaching it from the rest of the sector—so that new structures can evolve—are growing. Electricity is currently at a watershed, from which new structures and regulatory treatments are evolving. Therefore the conventional regulation which held from about 1935 to 1970 is likely to change appreciably, toward dissolving the old airtight boundaries. The direction of change may also include a basic evolution toward regional

---

[3] Federal Power Commission, *National Power Survey,* 1970, *op. cit.,* vol. 1.

[4] FPC. *ibid.*

[5] See especially Leonard W. Weiss, "An Analysis of Antitrust in the Electric Power Industry," in Almarin Phillips, *ed. cit.*

FIGURE 15–7
Cost of Electric Energy Transmission for 200 Miles (under certain assumptions)

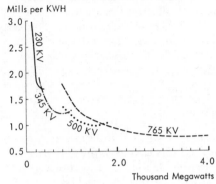

Mills per KWH
3.0
2.5
2.0
1.5
1.0
0.5
230 KV
345 KV
500 KV
765 KV
0
2.0
4.0
Thousand Megawatts

Source: Federal Power Commission, *National Power Survey, 1970,* pp. I–13–9.

FIGURE 15–9
Utility Stock Price Movements

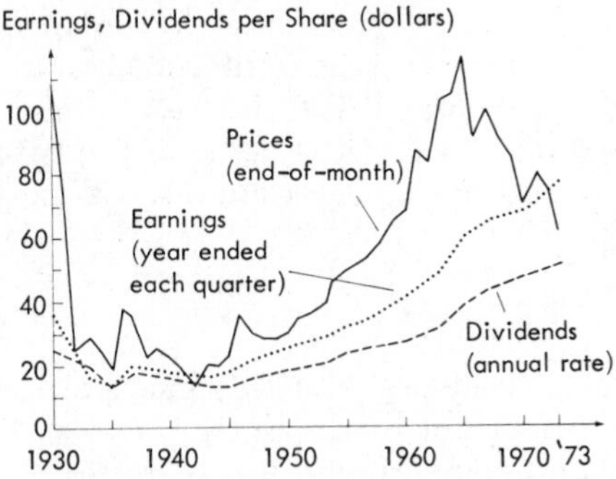

Earnings, Dividends per Share (dollars)
100
80
60
40
20
0
Prices
(end-of-month)
Earnings
(year ended
each quarter)
Dividends
(annual rate)
1930
1940
1950
1960
1970
'73

Utilities include mainly electric and telephone companies.

FIGURE 15–8
U.S. Transmission System

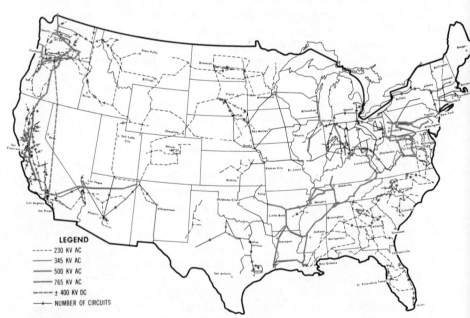

LEGEND
230 KV AC
345 KV AC
500 KV AC
765 KV AC
± 400 KV DC
NUMBER OF CIRCUITS

or national grids of bulk supply. In short, the technological options are widening.

Historical Background

The sector originated in the 1870s, when the basic technology of generating and illuminating was invented and applied. During 1890–1920, electricity evolved from a luxury of the rich into a more broadly used service. It also developed from a small local service to intercity and statewide systems. But this evolution was not easy or quick. Among the early leaders of the industry, Samuel Insull pushed his colleagues towards a wider supply system and a promotional pricing system to stimulate demand. The result was growth and falling costs.[6] By 1910, the basic groundwork of the industry was in place, with suppliers in most areas already in being and fully related to their main customers. There followed a further growth and unification of the industry among cities, and then the great rise, peak, and crash of holding companies in 1920–33. The great stock market boom which ended in 1929 was fed in large part by intricate schemes to pyramid control and profits from the base of ordinary electric companies. The resulting abuses of utility holding companies were fully exposed in the early 1930s, after the stocks had plummeted (see Figure 15–9). Ironically, Insull was pilloried as the symbol of the manipulator. But the trickery had been much more widespread and cynical than his, and the whole scandal and its effects led to a drastic reorganization of the industry.

Holding company abuses were so severe—and so akin to holding company activities which still continue—that they deserve recounting. Control could be pyramided over several levels, with a small stake at the top giving control over vastly larger investments.[7] There were as many as

---

[6] Forrest McDonald, *Insull* (Chicago: University of Chicago Press, 1962).

[7] For example:

1. Assume that there are 64 operating companies, each capitalized at $4 million, divided as follows: $2 million in 4 percent bonds, $1 million in 5 percent preferred stock, and $1 million in common. The total investment in these properties is $256 million. Each operating company can be controlled with half of its common, requiring an investment of $500,000. All 64 can be controlled with $32 million. This is $1/8$ of the total investment.
2. Now divide the 64 operating companies into 16 groups of four each. Over each group set up a Father Holding Company. Each Father controls each of its operating companies with $500,000; all four with $2 million. It is capitalized at $2 million; of this, $1 million is in 5 percent preferred and $1 million in common. Each Father company can thus be controlled with $500,000. All 16 can be controlled with $8 million. The controlling share is $1/32$ of the total investment.
3. Now divide the 16 Father companies into four groups of four each. Over each group set up a Grandfather Holding Company. Each Grandfather controls each of its Father companies with $500,000, all four with $2 million. Half of its capitalization of $2 million is in 5 percent preferred and half in common. Each Grandfather can thus be controlled with $500,000; all four of them with $2 million. This is $1/128$ of the total investment.
4. Now set up a Great-Grandfather Holding Company to control the four Grandfather companies. It does so with an investment of $2 million. Its capitalization of $2 million is half in 5 percent preferred and half in common. It can be controlled with $500,000. This is $1/512$ of the total investment.
5. Finally, set up a Great-Great-Grandfather Holding Company. Capitalize it at $500,000. Sell half of it in 5 percent preferred. The half that remains is $1/1,024$ of the total investment.

12 layers, and one Insull operating company was controlled by an investment of one two-hundredths of one percent. Profits were correspondingly pyramided, often over 100 percent of the top-level investment.[8] But pyramiding was also risky, for a small dip in operating profits could plunge the holding company into bankruptcy.[9] The holding company operators thus took control of an industry that was guaranteed a legal monopoly of a necessary service and turned it into a highly speculative enterprise. From the soundest investment in the market, they converted utility shares, at the upper levels, into counters in a game of chance.[10]

The investing public puts up $255,750,000. John Dough puts up $250,000 and runs the show.

If anything, this illustration understates the case. A larger part of the total capitalization could be in nonvoting securities. Control could be obtained with less than half the common. The money needed to buy the stock of one company could be borrowed, putting up the stock of another as security. The number of holding companies between the controlling interest and the operating properties could be multiplied indefinitely.

[8] Continuing the example in Footnote 7:

1. Assume that the 64 operating companies are allowed a return of 6 percent. On $256 million, this gives them $15,360,000. Of this amount, 4 percent must be paid on $128 million in bonds, or $5,120,000. Then 5 percent must be paid on $64 million of preferred, or $3,200,000. This leaves $7,040,000 to be distributed as dividends on $64 million of common, a return of 11 percent.
2. Half of this, or $3,520,000, goes to the 16 Father companies. They pay 5 percent on $16 million of preferred, or $800,000. This leaves them $2,720,000 to distribute on $16 million of common, a return of 17 percent.
3. Half of this, or $1,360,000, goes to the four Grandfather companies. They pay 5 percent on $4 million of preferred, or $200,000. This leaves them $1,160,000 for $4 million of common, a return of 30 percent.
4. Half of this, or $580,000, goes to the Great-Grandfather Company. This company pays 5 percent on $1 million of preferred, or $50,000. This leaves it $530,000 for $1 million of common, a return of 53 percent.
5. Half of this, or $265,000, goes to the Great-Great-Grandfather Company. It pays 5 percent on its $250,000 of preferred, or $12,500. It has $252,500 left for John Dough. On his investment of $250,000, he makes more than 100 percent.

Actual profit rates often ranged above 50 percent in equity during the 1920s. Federal Trade Commission, *Control of Power Companies* (Senate Doc. 213, 69th Cong. 2d. sess.) (Washington, D.C.: U.S. Government Printing Office, 1927).

[9] Let the operating firms in footnotes 7 and 8 earn only 4 percent instead of 6 percent:

1. The 64 companies get $10,240,000. They pay $5,120,000 on their bonds, and $3,200,000 on their preferred. They have $1,920,000 left for their common, a return of 3 percent.
2. Half of this, or $960,000, goes to the Father companies. They pay $800,000 on their preferred. They have $160,000 for $16 million of common, a return of 1 percent.
3. Half of this, or $80,000, goes to the Grandfather companies. They cannot meet the dividends on their preferred, let alone their common.
4. The income of the Great-Grandfather company and that of the Great-Great-Grandfather company is zero. They pay no dividends. They cannot even pay their bills. The companies go bankrupt. The house of cards comes tumbling down.

[10] In this situation, there was an insistent drive for dividends. These could be obtained in one way, through higher rates. Every dollar by which rates were changed was reflected in the dividends of the upper holding companies. These companies, therefore, were vigorous in resisting rate reductions and ingenious in finding ways by which rates could be increased. To this end, they padded the valuations of the operating companies, by making excessive charges for construction services, by causing properties to be sold back and forth at rising prices, by failing to make deductions for depreciation, and by writing up the value of the assets on the books. Dividends could be obtained, too, by reducing charges against income. And here, the holding companies indulged in fair-weather finance, neglecting to maintain their operating properties, failing to set aside reserves for depreciation, and building up fictitious surpluses. Dividends were thus paid out of capital, and the strength of the underlying enterprises was impared.

Profits on such activities were often extraordinary, ranging over 200 percent of the actual *expenses.*

The holding companies also raised their profits by manipulating intercompany transac-

In 1928 the Federal Trade Commission had been directed by Congress to investigate electric and gas utilities. In 1935 it published its final report, summarizing more than 70 volumes of hearings and exhibits. Many holding company abuses were thus brought into glaring light. Meanwhile the largest holding company systems—Associated Gas and Electric, Insull, and Foshay in Minneapolis—had come down in ruins, scores of others were bankrupt, in receivership, or in default, and hundreds of thousands of investors had seen their savings disappear. The country was ripe for reform.

The Public Utility Act of 1935 had two parts. Title II for the first time gave jurisdiction over interstate transmission of electricity to the FPC. Title I was the Public Utility Holding Company Act. This was the most stringent corrective measure ever applied to American business. It required the reorganization of corporate structures and forced divestment of property. It made the Securities and Exchange Commission a potent regulator of electric and gas holding companies. Wherever abuses had been disclosed, it provided powers of control.

The Act defined a holding company as one holding 10 percent or more of the voting stock of another holding company or an operating company or having a "controlling influence over the management or policies" of such companies. The main provisions of the law fall into five categories: (1) The most severe provision was that of Section 11(b)(2), generally known as the "death sentence," which provided for the elimination of the third and upper layers in the holding company structures, permitting Father and Grandfather companies, but forbidding Great-Grandfathers, Great-Great-Grandfathers, and remoter generations in the sequence of control. (2) Section 11 also empowered the SEC to effect the simplification of the remaining holding company structures through financial reorganization. The law then provided for the regulation of the reorganized concerns, authorizing the SEC to control (3) the operations of holding companies, (4) the dealings of their officers and directors, and (5) their relations with their subsidaries.

The Commission was instructed to confine each holding company organization to a single system of integrated operating companies and other businesses economically necessary or reasonably incidental thereto. It was authorized, however, to permit a holding company to control more than one system if (1) such control was needed to preserve substantial economies; (2) the systems were contiguous, being located on both sides of state or national borders; and (3) the resulting structure would not be so large as to impair local management, efficient operation, and effective regulation.

Extensive regulatory powers were conferred upon the SEC. Among others, the firms were required to obtain the Commission's approval

---

tions. They borrowed money from the operating companies and loaned money to them. They handled the sale of their securities. They sold them equipment and supplies. They set up subsidiaries to provide them with engineering and managerial services. The prices paid in these transactions did not result from arm's-length bargaining. The officers of the operating companies depended on the officers of the holding companies for their jobs. If they were asked to pay excessive prices, they did not complain. They did as they were told. In this way, holding company profits were hidden in operating company costs. And they were covered, of necessity, by the state commissions in setting the level of rates.

before buying or selling assets or floating securities. Their officers and directors were required to file their stockholdings and to make reports on changes. Bankers were denied directorates unless such appointments were approved by the SEC. Holding companies were forbidden to borrow money from operating companies; their loans to these companies were subjected to control. Holding companies were forbidden, too, to perform various services for operating companies. For this purpose, mutual service companies, subordinate to the operating companies, were to be formed. All intercorporate contacts within a holding company system were brought under Commission control. And the Commission was further authorized to protect the operating companies against exploitation by controlling the declaration of dividends. Some of these powers have withered from nonuse, but others have had force.

The Commission approached its task with caution.[11] It was not until 1940 that voluntary disintegration plans were submitted and formal proceedings begun. By 1951 the Commission had undertaken the reformation of corporate structures including more than 200 holding companies and nearly 2,000 other companies. In 1952 it reported that 85 percent of the job was done.[12] In the upper levels some holding companies had reduced their holdings of operating company voting stocks to less than 10 percent, becoming investment companies. Others had merged with their subsidiaries. Still others had distributed their holdings to their stockholders or had sold them in the market and distributed cash, thus liquidating their affairs.

Where were holding company systems to be dissolved and where allowed to stand? The Commission was strict in its enforcement of the principle of integration. It favored a compact system, confined to a single area, its facilities interconnected or capable of interconnection, its operations coordinated, and its management unified. It opposed the common control of electricity and gas, and the operation of companies providing other services, unless they could be shown to bear a functional relationship to the provision of electricity or gas. In this way the many-tiered holding company systems with widely scattered properties were eliminated and the simpler, closely integrated systems were preserved. There are about 20 regional holding company systems remaining under Commission control (including six of those listed in Table 15-1).

The method by which divestment was to effected had not been specified by law. Here initiative was left to the companies. Some holding companies sold their properties to other holding companies, to indepen-

---

[11] The constitutionality of the Holding Company Act was promptly challenged. The Electric Bond and Share Company refused to register, the SEC brought suit to compel it to do so, and the registration requirement was upheld by the Supreme Court. The North American Company resisted reorganization, arguing that the disintegration provisions of the Act exceeded the powers conferred on Congress under the commerce clause and violated the Fifth Amendment by depriving the company of property without due process of law. This argument was rejected by the Court. The American Power and Light Company then contested the simplification of its corporate structure, advancing the previous arguments and also contending that the law involved an unconstitutional delegation of legislative power. Again, the Court did not agree. The SEC thus found itself on solid ground.

[12] *Report* of the SEC to the Subcommittee on Monopoly of the Select Committee on Small Business, U.S. Senate (83d Cong., 2d Sess.), Subcommittee Print No. 4, 1952.

dent operators, or to local governments. Some sold their security holdings on the market. Some divided them among the owners of their shares.

Along with the simplification of holding company systems went reorganization of the capital structures of individual companies. Here, the Commission scaled down overcapitalization, eliminated write-ups, required competitive bidding for new securities, and strengthened depreciation reserves.

This sweeping reorganization of the electric and gas utility industries was a significant accomplishment. It did not in itself make the regulation of rates and services effective. But it removed a major obstacle to control.

This decentralizing of financial control assured a continuing decentralization of operations; this continues despite a series of mergers since the 1950s. It also assured a trauma in management and ownership during the 1930s and 1940s from which the industry is only now emerging. The senior management in electric utilities during the 1950s and 1960s had started out during 1930–50, when the industry was scarcely attractive. Therefore, it is not surprising that the relatively simple and undemanding decisions required of electric utilities between World War II and 1965 fitted well the urge for managerial security.[13] From 1930 on, the industry engaged primarily in a push for growth by means of promotional pricing and the realization of scale economies at generation and transmission levels. It was a rather easy ride during that period, with all growth signs upward and with a underlying technology which permitted electricity prices to move down relative to general price trends in the economy.

This golden era came to a rude halt in the late 1960s, as scarcity and complexity recurred. There were several special problems. One was the narrowing leeway in picking sites for generation and in setting transmission lines. Urban problems and concern about pollution made the siting problem critical in the largest utilities. As nuclear power came on in a rush after 1963, it too encountered a rash of unexpected problems, of (1) delay in completing plants, and of (2) public resistance to possible dangers from nuclear plants. Moreover, the growth of electricity demand was higher than had been expected, and this accentuated the capacity crisis in which many utilities suddenly found themselves by 1970. The old push for sheer growth was no longer appropriate or indeed possible. Further, the new awareness of urban problems generated a new concern about the equity of electric pricing structures. The old promotional schemes now could be shown to be only inefficient but also probably inequitable. And to top it all off, the prices of conventional fuels surged upward, especially in 1973, as the fuel crisis sharpened.

The whole effect was to plunge a mature and settled growth sector into crosscurrents of new forces, which required not only a new delicacy and sophistication in handling but also fundamental changes in the old ways of doing business. Like many a crisis, this one may turn out to be less severe and chronic than feared at first, but it has already had marked effects. It has arisen under regulation, in ways which—if one understands what regulation has and has not been doing—are predictable. But

---

[13] This is clear in Jeremy Main, "A Peak Load of Trouble for the Utilities," *Fortune* (November 1969) pp. 116 ff.

they are clear only when one understands the history of the sector. The most basic features has been the way in which regulation has fitted conventionally into Stages 2 and 3; from the start it has served the companies as well as—in part—constraining them.

Profits and Price Structures under Regulation

Regulation was first developed on the state level, with some commissions becoming tolerably effective by middle 1930s. A federal regulating group was created in 1920 but it dealt only with hydroelectric projects and had little regulatory content. The FPC did gain power in 1935 to regulate interstate transmission, but for three decades it did little more than enforce a uniform system of accounts.

The FPC was revived after 1960 by Joseph C. Swidler (Chairman 1961–66). Rate hearings became markedly more thorough, meaningful, and strict. And a massive *National Power Survey* was made, with industry cooperation. Published in 1964, the *Survey* showed that large savings were to be had from fuller pooling and coordination. The *Survey* was sophisticated and foresighted; a second *Survey* was finished in 1970. By tackling both rates and technology, the FPC at long last began to achieve the modest targets that were possible.

Wide World Photo

Joseph C. Swidler (born 1907) revived the Federal Power Commission while chairman during 1961–66 and chaired the New York Public Service Commission during the turbulent years 1969–1974. He is shown in 1965 testifying to a House Committee about the great electrical blackout of the Northeast in November 1965.

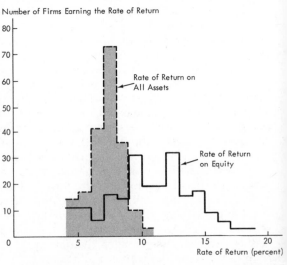

FIGURE 15–10

Rates of Return in Private Electric Utilities, 1971

Number of Firms Earning the Rate of Return

Source: Federal Power Commission, *Statistics of Privately-owned Electrical Companies* (Washington, D.C.: Government Printing Office, 1972).

The companies still strive to keep as much of their operations as possible under state regulation, because it usually is more liberal. In some cases, company activities and pooling have been confined within state borders, despite the gains from connecting across state lines.

The leading electric companies summarized in Table 15–1 and Figure 15–4 therefore reflect certain dramatic episodes and moderate regulatory efforts. These firms differ. Some are tied to old, slow-growth areas, while others are in booming regions. Some have been growing by mergers, while most have not. Some are known to have first-class managerial quality, while others display mediocrity or eccentricity.

The trend of electric-firm profits under regulation was noted in Figure 14–6. Differences among company profits arise both from regulation and from underlying economic conditions (see Figure 15–10). There are big differences also in the profits earned by public power systems (see also Chapter 21). These are nominally not under regulatory control, and so they exhibit the full range of purpose and levels which the variety of cities and state authorities follow.

During the 1920s and 1930s, the reproduction-cost controversy and the holding company phase effectively deprived regulation of any real profits control. By the 1960s the FPC and some state commissions had put a degree of constraint on some company profit rates. But the constraint was not tight, and it was made more tolerable before 1965 by the natural decline in relative electricity costs over the years. More recently the rise in the cost of capital has raised the possibility that permitted rates of return are below the true cost of new capital. Among the lowest profit rates had been Consolidated Edison of New York, thanks both to its own inefficiency before 1968 and an acute squeeze of costs, rate ceilings, and plant siting problems. By 1974, it appeared to be sliding toward public ownership under the pressure. Two of its largest plants were sold to the State of New York, and further financing was in doubt.

Figure 15–11 shows the shift toward rate increases since 1965. There is some tendency for commissions which are strict on rate base concepts to be relatively liberal in setting rates of return. Therefore the overall differences in the bite of regulation on profitability are not very great among the states. One could fairly conclude that state regulation has little effect at all in most states, and that federal regulation has applied only a mild constraint.

Price structures have evolved towards a standarized pattern, in which users pay either according to declining-block or two-part tariffs (and some tariffs combine both). Table 15–5 gives samples of each of these in recent years, and Figure 15–12 illustrates them. The key *promotional* feature is that the effective price declines as usage rises, in the familiar pattern of bulk discounts. This may reflect some degree of cost difference, as the user takes more units via a constant set of supplying apparatus. This classic promotional price structure of electricity evolved over decades of many years of effort, debate, and intense controversy during 1890–1930. It means that large users get electricity cheaper than small users. The differences can be sharp, up to a multiple of 3 or 4. As for the comparisons among different user classes, large-scale industry and com-

FIGURE 15–11
Electric Companies' Rate Actions 1960–73

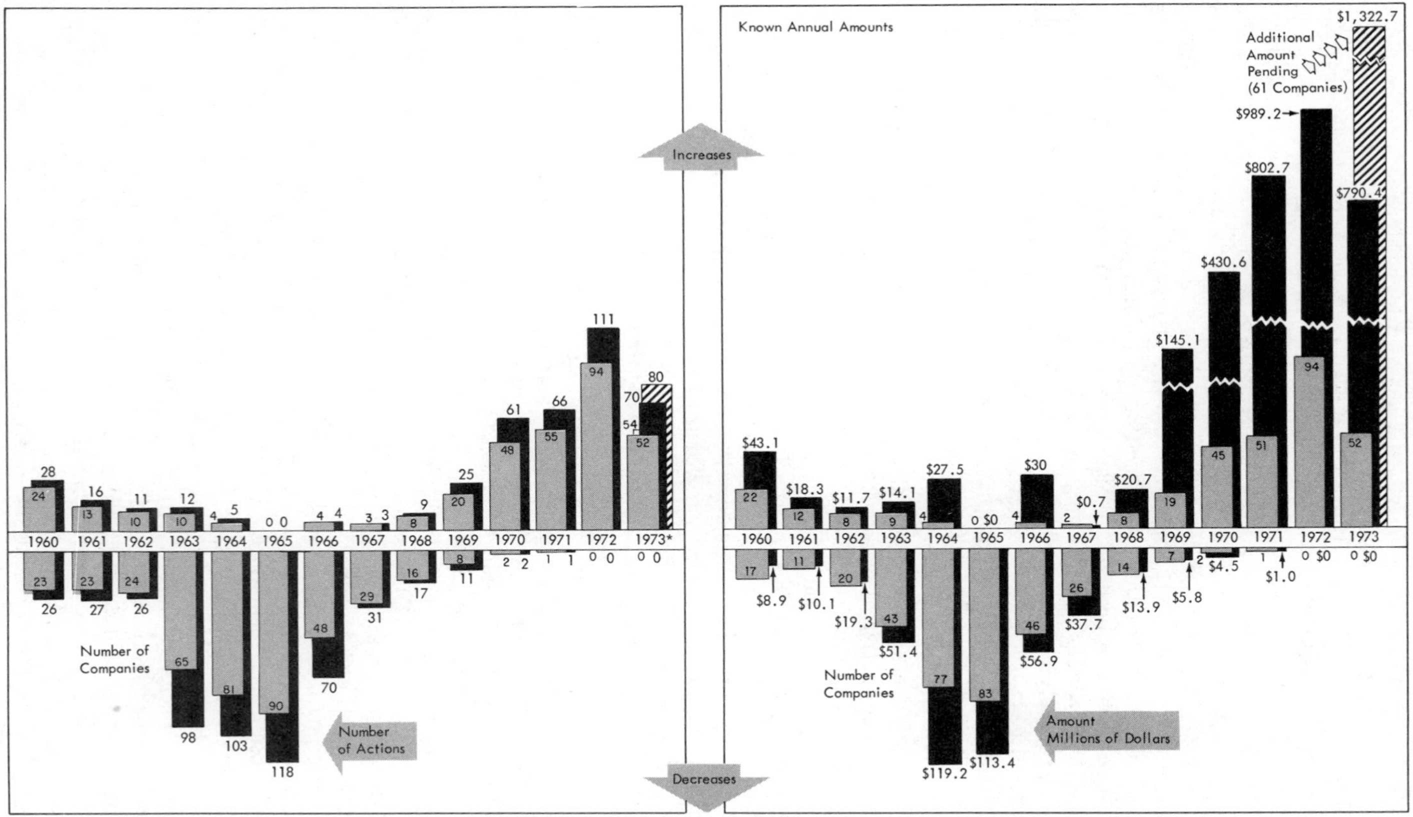

Known Annual Amounts

Increases

Additional
Amount
Pending
(61 Companies)

$1,322.7

$790.4*

52   1973   0 $0

$989.2 →

$802.7

94   1972   0 $0

51   1971   1 $1.0

$430.6

45   1970   2 $4.5

$145.1

19   1969   7 $5.8

$20.7

8   1968   14 $13.9

$0.7

2   1967   26 $37.7

$30

4   1966   46 $56.9

$0   1965   83 $113.4

$27.5

77   1964 $119.2

$14.1

43   1963 $51.4

$11.7

9   1962   20 $19.3

$18.3

12   1961   11 $10.1

$43.1

22   1960   17 $8.9

Number of Companies

Amount
Millions of Dollars

Decreases

Number of Actions

80   1973*   0
70
54
52

111   1972   0
94

66   1971   1
55

61   1970   2
48

25   1969   8
20   11

9   1968   17
8   16

4   1967   29
3   3   31

4   1966   48
4   70

0   1965   90
0   118

5   1964   81
103

12   1963   65
10   98

11   1962   24
10   26

16   1961   23
13   27

28   1960   23
24   26

Number of Companies

Note: Some companies had more than one action in the same year in one or more jurisdictions.
* As of September 30, 1973

TABLE 15–3
Sample Electric Rates

Residential Service

Pacific Gas and Electric Co. (after August 13, 1973)
1. Monthly customer charge: 50¢
2. Energy charge:

4.029¢ per kWh	first	50 kwh
3.029 " "	next	50 "
1.829 " "	"	"
1.629 " "	"	"
1.529 " "	"	"
1.329 " "	all additional "	

Los Angeles Department of Water and Power (public) (after June 12, 1972)
1. Monthly customer charge: $1.19
2. Energy charge:

2.75¢ per kWh	first	150 kWh
1.79 " "	next	250 "
1.65 " "	"	600 "
1.35 " "	all additional	"

Primary Light and Power (industrial users)

Detroit Edison
Character of service:
A-c; 60 cycles; 3 phase; nominally 4,800, 13,200, 24,000, 41,600 or 120,000 volts at the utility's option.
1. Demand charge:

$4.20 per kW	first	200 kW demand
3.75 " "	next	800 " "
3.15 " "	"	9,000 " "
3.00 " "	all additional	" "

2. Energy charge:
0.7¢ per kWh plus fuel adjustment per kWh.

FIGURE 15–12
Typical Rates, 1973

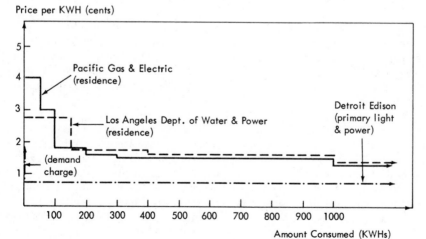

Price per KWH (cents)

merce will obviously get electricity more cheaply than do small residential users. On average, the residential user pays 2.1 times the price charged to large industrial users. The fundamental question is whether this fits true cost differences among users, or instead is simply price discrimination.

Consider Costs, First. An electricity system has large overhead costs in supplying a great variety of users. There are wide fluctuations in daily and seasonal loads (see Figures 15–13 to 15–15). Actual costs can vary sharply, by time and other conditions of supply.

The accountants divide costs into three categories: output costs, customer costs, and demand costs.

Output costs are those incurred in the operation of a plant; the costs of labor, fuel, materials, and supplies. They vary with the volume of production. *Customer costs* are those incurred in reading meters, sending and collecting bills, keeping accounts, and the like. They vary with the number of customers. *Demand costs* are also known as readiness-to-serve costs. They are the overhead costs of capital and management involved in providing a plant that is large enough to meet the peak demand that may be made on it at any day and hour. They are thus a function of capacity.

Differences in total cost per kilowatt-hour cannot be attributed to output costs, since they are roughly the same for each unit produced. They can be attributed, to some extent, to customer costs, since these costs decline, per kilowatt-hour, as a customer's consumption grows. Such differences, however, are not large enough to be of major significance.

It is in demand costs, therefore, that the explanation for differences in cost per kilowatt-hour is mainly to be found. Investment in electric plants is heavy and overhead costs, accordingly, are high. The investment required depends upon the peak demand. A kilowatt-hour taken at the peak adds to the overhead; one taken at another time does not. The cost of the first, therefore, is higher than that of the second, often by a multiple (recall Chapter 14).

Utility accountants, in their analysis of costs, speak of the load factor of a utility system, the load factor of an individual customer, and the diversity factor of the system as a whole. The *system's load factor* is its average load expressed as a percentage of its peak load. Thus, if the average load over a period is 6,000 kilowatts and the peak at any moment is 9,000 the load factor is 66-2/3 percent. The *customer's load factor* is his average consumption expressed as a percentage of his maximum consumption.

The *system's diversity factor* is determined by adding up the maximum demands of all of its customers, whenever they occur, and dividing this sum by the maximum demand made on the system as a whole at any one time. Thus, customer A may take one kilowatt at 8 A.M., customer B two kilowatts at noon, and customer C three kilowatts at 4 P.M., a total of six kilowatts; the maximum demand made on the system at any hour, however, may be three kilowatts; the diversity factor, therefore, is 2.

The average cost per kilowatt-hour will be reduced if the system's load factor can be raised. This may be accomplished in two ways; by improving the load factor of each customer or by raising the diversity factor.

FIGURE 15–13
Typical Daily Load Patterns

Load–Thousand Megawatts

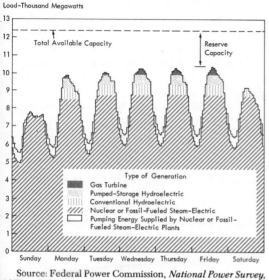

Source: Federal Power Commission, *National Power Survey, 1970*, p. I–7–5.

FIGURE 15–14
Estimated 1970 Monthly Peak Demands

Thousand Megawatts

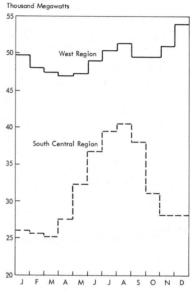

Source: Federal Power Commission, *National Power Survey, 1970*, p. I–3–3.

FIGURE 15–15
Regional Load Patterns (estimated difference between August and December peak loads, within each power supply area, 1970)

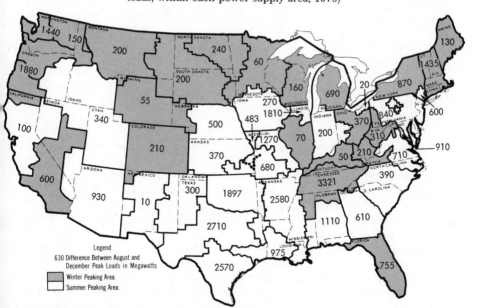

Source: Federal Power Commission, *National Power Survey, 1970*, p. I–18–22.

The customer's load factor may be improved by encouraging him to increase his consumption, using more power at off-peak hours. The diversity factor may be raised by attracting groups of customers whose maximum demands will be scattered, also coming at off-peak hours. Thus, there is in the nature of electricity costs a basis for differentiating rates, setting them at different levels for different classes of customers, and reducing them as a customer buys in larger quantities. Such rational pricing uses marginal costs as the basis.

Actual rates do not fit marginal costs closely.

In the early years, electricity was sold at a uniform rate per kilowatt-hour. Then as producers sought to extend their operations, they began to discriminate. In order to sell to groups who were unable or unwilling to buy at the established rate, they classified their customers, fixing a lower rate for the new customers, maintaining the higher rates for the older ones. And in order to encourage greater consumption by present customers, they fixed lower rates for larger quantities, maintaining the higher rate for smaller ones.

In fact, electricity rates became a patchwork of special deals; some customers squeezed better terms from the utility, while others provided creamy markets. Regulation came after these deals took form and has tended only to ratify them. The process continues: rates are adjusted to meet competition (e.g., against gas for new apartment blocks or industrial users) and to gain preferred customers. Regulation often leans against it but does not eliminate it.

The structure of electric rates has long been highly differentiated. Different classes were established for residential use, commercial light and power, industrial power, etc., and rates were differentiated from class to class. Within each class, moreover, consumption was divided into blocks. Thus, the average rate per kilowatt-hour charged for residential use might be 4 cents, for commercial use 3 cents, and for industrial use, $1\frac{1}{2}$ cents. And among residential users, the charge for the first 50 kwh. per month might be 5 cents per kwh.; for the next 150 kwh., 3 cents; and for everything above 250 kwh., 2 cents. As a consequence of these distinctions, the spread between between the upper and lower rates came to be substantial, industrial users being favored over residential users and large consumers over smaller ones.

The differences thus created have been modified with the passage of time, the ratio of domestic to commercial and industrial rates dropping from 1.93 to 1 in 1951 to 1.53 to 1 in 1972. But discrimination persists, the differences corresponding, in general, to differences in the elasticity of demand. Many big industrial users have the alternative of generating their own power; their demand, therefore, is highly elastic; their rates are low. Other users lack this alternative; their demand is less elastic; their rates are higher.

Householders can use gas rather than electricity for cooking; for this purpose their demand is elastic; the additional kilowatt-hours used in cooking fall in the quantity blocks where rates are low. Householders, on the other hand, are unlikely to substitute gas, kerosene, or candles for electricity in lighting; their demand for this purpose is inelastic; the hours used in lighting fall in the first block where rates are high. Both customer classes and quantity blocks are set up by the utility companies on the basis of their judgment of what the traffic will bear.[14]

The companies deny that they discriminate, defending their rates by presenting analysis of costs. Output costs (for labor, fuel, etc.) are distributed among customers in proportion to their consumption as measured by meters. Customer costs (for billing, collecting, etc.) are charged equally to each customer. And demand costs (for the investment necessitated by readiness to serve) are also calculated for individual customers. These costs may be measured by the number of switches a customer can turn on, the number of appliances he uses, or, more precisely, by a meter that has recorded his consumption at its half-hourly peak during the previous year.

Peak-Offpeak Conditions are Crucial. Such demand charges rarely are based on the customer's use *at the system's simultaneous peak.* Therefore they fail to encourage users to use off-peak service.[15] The firms nonetheless argue that these demand charges—and the first high blocks in the residential tariff—recover the customer and capacity costs. The low prices for higher usage are said to fit the operating costs, which are low.

Such a rate structure, however, is clearly discriminatory. The amount of money that must be invested in a utility business depends upon the size of the plant it must build, and the size of the plant is determined by the quantity of service it is called on to render during periods of peak demand. Those who use the service during such periods should therefore contribute more heavily than off-peak users toward meeting its capital costs. Under the usual block rate system, however, rates are not varied according to time of use. Some of those who pay the higher rates in the earlier blocks may consume this power off-peak, while some of those who pay the lower rates in the later blocks may consume this power on-peak. The system thus encourages wastefully high levels of peak use.

The crucial question, in judging the discriminatory character of a rate structure, is how the costs of capital (the demand costs of utility accounting) should be allocated. Most economists contend that discrimination is not to be avoided unless all such costs are charged to on-peak users and none of them to off-peak users. (This is easily done by installing twin meters controlled by a time switch and charging a higher rate for the consumption shown by the on-peak meter than for that shown by the off-peak meter.)

Other economists object that periods of peak demand are subject to constant change, and that allocation on this basis would therefore necessitate frequent and disturbing changes in the structure of rates. This difficulty could be overcome, however, by announcing changes in advance, at stated intervals, and making them gradually.

More serious is the objection that the utility plant is required for the

---

[14] See R. K. Davidson, *Price Discrimination in Selling Gas and Electricity* (Baltimore; Johns Hopkins Press, 1955); and Kahn, *op. cit.*

[15] The demand charge is usually based on the user's own peak rate of usage during the previous month, no matter when that peak occurred.

service of off-peak as well as on-peak users and that they should there-fore contribute something toward its cost. But how much? The difficulty is that there is no correct method of distributing the costs of capital among the different classes and quantities of service. Any method em-ployed will depend upon the judgment of the person who adopts it. And his judgment is likely to be influenced by his purposes.

The utilities now employ the *noncoincident demand* method of al-locating overhead. For this purpose, they compute an aggregate max-imum demand by adding together the separate maximum demands of all classes of buyers, although these demands may come at different times. Then they determine the percentage of this aggregate that is at-tributable to each class. And then, finally, they distribute their overhead costs in accordance with these percentages.

The method is based upon two fallacies. *First,* it involves circular reasoning. The differences in demand that are used as a guide in allocat-ing costs are not independent of differences in rates, but are themselves determined by these differences. The companies first fix the rates they want to charge. These rates, in turn, affect the quantities demanded. These quantities are then used to govern the distribution of costs. And the costs are presented, finally, to justify the rates. Q.E.D.

Second, the method does not make proper allowance for the factor of diversity. The concept of maximum coincident demand for a utility sys-tem as a whole is meaningful. The concept of aggregate noncoincident maximum demands of customer classes is not. A company will need to build a plant big enough to meet the peak of coincident demand. It does not have to build one big enough to meet the aggregate of noncoincident demands. For such demands, by definition, occur at different times. If a customer's maximum comes at the same time as the system's maximum, he may properly be charged with more responsibility for the size of the investment that is required. If it comes at any other time, he should be charged with less. The so-called demand costs assigned to individual customers under the noncoincident demand method of allocating over-head are arbitrary in character and are not to be accepted as justifying present differences in rates.

In short, electricity rates are permeated with discrimination. Some rates of some utilities do fit marginal-cost criteria. But these are a small minority, and they are slight compared to the extensive marginal-cost pricing done abroad in various public systems (see Chapter 22). Recent pressures are forcing some utilities to dilute the promotional character of prices. But such tariff inversion has not yet reached a positive tilt, and only a few hard-pressed firms have done it. It is likely to be decades before rates reflect the true costs of service.

Self-interest—not regulation—is governing these choices.[16] The com-missions continue to be mainly passive to rate structure. It was the firms

---

[16] Declining-block rates now generally tend to erode revenues as the level of customer use rises. Inverted—that is, "rising-block," rates will automatically raise the utility's revenue per unit as growth occurs. Such an automatic rate increase is a powerful attraction to suppliers and is likely to induce the change in tariffs. That it also fits true costs is a happy, but secondary, side effect.

FIGURE 15–16

State Average Monthly Bills—500 Kwh Residential Service—Jan. 1, 1971 (United States average bill—$11.13) (cities of 2,500 population and more)

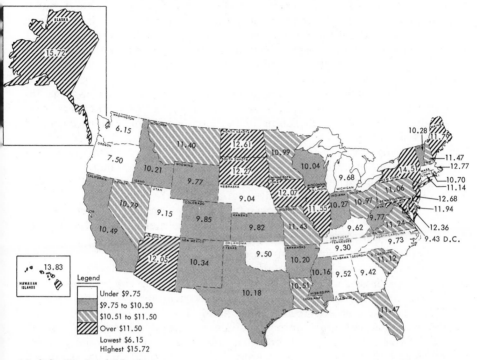

* Includes District of Columbia.

Source: Federal Power Commission, *Typical Electric Bills* (Washington, D.C.: U.S. Government Printing Office, 1971), p. xi.

which offered special rates and an advertising campaign in the 1960s to encourage "all-electric homes," and it was their choice more recently to cancel the program in many states, as new scarcities made them highly irrational.

Actual prices (Figure 15–16 shows some of the differences among states) therefore reflect a mixture of costs and discrimination—and possibly some modest effects of regulation in some states. Regulation has also induced a margin of extra costs and rate-base in many firms.

Main Current Issues

From this background emerge four main questions about regulation and its results. We will consider these now in turn. They all relate to the performance of utilities under regulation, and therefore they help us form an impression of the role, if any, of regulation itself.

Performance.   A main dimension of performance in electricity supply is the trend in costs over time. This has been downward relative to prices in the whole economy, and so regulation may share the credit for this gain. We will talk about it on two planes. Both of them suggest that the role of regulation is not great.

The decline in relative costs of electricity has been marked, but it cannot be credited either to the utilities or to the regulators. It has arisen mainly from the inherent scale economies embodied in new equipment, as larger scale frontiers were explored. Therefore, the long-run trend in costs cannot be clearly credited to utilities, regulators, nor perhaps even to the equipment makers.

But differences in real efficiency can be compared among the individual utilities at each point in time. This has been done in several studies, which factor out some of the basic economic determinants of cost, leaving the rest to be "explained" by real differences in managerial skill.[17] During the 1950s and 60s, there were sharp contrasts among private utilities on this basis, some showing remarkable efficiency, while others were notorious for inefficiency. Regulation has induced costs and rate-base levels to be marginally higher.[18] But the effect is not uniform. The cases of gross inefficiency have usually come to be corrected by natural market forces or changes in the management, rather than by any direct regulatory effort. So the effects of regulation on utility efficiency are marginally negative, but not conclusively known.

One result is that the factual basis for "incentive regulation" is weak. Of course, cross-section analysis can tend to confirm the folklore which regulation and industry experts already share about the relative quality of utility managements (recall Chapter 14). But an objective basis would make it more workable. Moreover, since state regulators tend to face only one or two utility firms, their ability to use economic sanctions to pry efficiency upward is limited, even if they had the will and data to do so.

Marginal-Cost Pricing.   As we have seen, the structure of utility prices tends to be antimarginalist and discriminatory. There are exceptions. But on the whole, promotional pricing has prevailed and continues, both for residential and industrial users. This clearly worsened the shortages of capacity and pinch on profits during the late 1960s and early 70s.

A few firms are beginning to reverse the structure of price towards genuine peak-load pricing, but the changes come slowly. Several firms have switched their advertising effort from promotional to "economy."[19] But the basic price incentives still are working to increase peak loads, at prices far below real costs.[20]

---

[17] Recall Iulo, op. cit., the leading study of this sort.

[18] Recent studies affirming these costs include R. M. Spann, "Rate of Return Regulation and Efficiency in Production: An Empirical Test of the Averch-Johnson Thesis," and L. Courville, "Regulation and Efficiency in the Electric Utility Industry," both in the Bell Journal of Economics and Management Science (Vol. 5, No. 1: Spring 1974), pp. 38–74; and H. C. Peterson, "The Effect of Regulation on Production Costs and Output Prices in the Private Electric Utility Industry," Memorandum #151, Center for Research in Economic Growth (Stanford: processed, 1973).

[19] In many cases "marketing men" have simply been retitled as "customer service representatives" or "energy utilization consultants."

[20] Adjusting peak rates upward can be difficult and stressful. During March 1973 to March 1974, all-electric homes in Westchester found their average monthly bills rising from $137 to $252. This partly reflected a flattening (not rise) in the declining-block tariff. Full peak-load pricing would sharply increase the bills further, and provoke even more picketing and pressure tactics than did occur in 1974; see Business Week, (April 1, 1974), p. 36.

Competition in Bulk Supply. The bulk supply of electricity has now reached the end of Stage 3 (thanks to growing scale economies) and is now technologically capable of effective competition in most areas. This is raising—in practical *and* theoretical form—the prospects for a major change in regulatory standing. Many utilities could compete, and would compete, vigorously among themselves for at least their major customers. Each utility would gain by raiding its neighbors' main clients. And nearly all major urban centers have at least two or three alternative suppliers. Therefore the technical basis for competition—at least as open and complete as in many industrial oligopolies—now exists in bulk electricity. It will evolve *away from the traditional tight vertical integration of the three levels within each geographic monopoly*. This, too, simply restores normal economic behavior.

The gains from this change could be large. Inefficiency would be under direct constraint, for the first time in decades. Service standards and cheapness would both be used to gain customers, as they should be; this would ease the probable present bias toward excessive service quality. Utilities would be induced to develop and use the technology of large-scale supply more fully, in order to penetrate each other's markets for bulk electricity.

The change would offer net gains to many utilities, since it widens their opportunities. It is bilateral, not a unilateral threat to their managerial security and share values. Therefore it would gradually dissolve, or at least reduce, the patchwork of market divisions which now prevails. In many cases possibly it will be welcomed, not resisted, by utilities.

In bulk electric power, these possibilities have been evolving rapidly during the 1950s and have been present during the last 15 years. Their legal aspects have been discussed by Meeks, and Weiss is among those who have treated some of their economic aspects.[21] They were extensively reviewed in the Otter Tail case in 1973, involving the town of Elbow Lake, Minnesota. There, the Supreme Court affirmed that antitrust rules do hold for bulk supply. And a series of cases in other areas reflects that the sector has become technologically favorably to competition. In various areas, hundreds of major customers are within range of alternative suppliers and presumably would seek bids. Some are cities; others include large private firms and large public agencies. In Michigan, for example, about one-third of the largest commercial accounts at single locations are close enough to alternative suppliers to take bids, even if wheeling (the carrying of power for others) were not required. If wheeling were mandatory, the fraction would be much higher. Other industrial areas are similar.

Although this inter-area competition would only affect the larger customers, many smaller users could pool their demand to become large joint buyers. It would naturally introduce complex game conditions into the present rigidity. Pooling and mergers would become strategic ele-

---

[21] James E. Meeks, "Concentration in the Electric Power Industry: The Impact of Antitrust Policy," *Columbia Law Review*, Vol. 72:64 (1972), pp. 64–130. A thorough economic analysis is by Leonard W. Weiss, "An Analysis of Antitrust in the Electric Power Industry," in Almarin Phillips, *ed. cit.*

ments in the process, since many adjoining utilities would be both competing and cooperating. It is possible that much discrimination, and possibly collusion, would result, because the competitive situation would not be perfect. But this danger does not warrant stopping competition. The possibilities can be tried as part of a learning process. Even a moderate shift toward competition could yield large gains. And it seems clear that a great deal more than moderate competition is viable.

As a general matter, only a simple basic revision in the regulatory contract is needed: contracts with an outside supplier would be unregulated. The rest of the utility's business would remain its service area and subject to regulation. Wheeling at reasonable charges—or as part of exchange agreements—could be required, within certain distances. Separate transmission lines could be built at will for outside supply, even though it is not clear whether the usual powers of eminent domain should apply for them. Horizontal mergers among electric firms which would adversely affect this competition (and most of them would) should require overriding evidence of scale economies. Indeed, many of the larger systems are probably already too large, by this criterion.[22]

The result of this competition would be a more complicated and yet more efficient industry. The mass of smaller contracts would still be regulated, but by a streamlined and focused regulation process. The terms of service and the liability for all service would be explicit. Structure and contracts would be more flexible, in some cases the outcome of intricate and evolving strategy. In short, part of this industry would evolve properly through Stage 3 toward economic normality, where it belongs. The current strains and capacity problems of some utilities do not affect this basic trend. Some electric power firms would not have sufficient capacity to move strongly into inter-area competition at this time. But competition can proceed now for many firms. Moreover, off-peak excess capacity is often great even for firms with tight peak-load conditions; even these firms would be eager to add off-peak sales. For antitrust and regulatory policy alike, bulk power has the preconditions of a competitive market.

At this point, the main obstacle is regulation itself, which maintains the balkanized set of markets. Much ingenuity and pressure will be needed, in reshaping regulation to fit this new range of competition, and the process of change will probably be arduous and slow. But the delay will reflect mainly the inertia of regulation itself, rather than the underlying economic realities.

In short, this is a watershed period for the structure and performance of the electricity sector. How further change occurs will show much about how regulation operates and evolves.

Environmental Problems.   Until the 1960s, the main problem of environment—or amenity, as it was called—was the location of the high voltage lines in the countryside. These questions involved a small drumfire of debate and social pressure, but on a minor scale. Since 1965 there

---

[22] A plan by seven New York private utility firms in 1974 to form a joint corporation to build shared electric plants—a form of partial merger—would tend to suppress such new competition.

have arisen major problems with the siting of utility plants, the use of nuclear fuel, and the operation and pollution from old plants. These have run straight against the industry's old habit of solving problems by ample investment. On the contrary, the investments themselves have become the problem.

The basic problem arose when environmental groups discovered the ease with which the regulatory process could be used to block investment projects by the utility companies. Here again, the critical importance of the burden of proof and the advantage of time worked strongly in favor of one side, in this case the environmentalists. By 1974, a whole range of investments in conventional and nuclear plants have been slowed or stopped, by a skillful use of regulatory delay.

The problem was further compounded by the technical delays in completing many nuclear projects, often years beyond the original target date. These could be blamed on the handful of equipment suppliers (mainly General Electric, Westinghouse and Combustion Engineering), who had their own strategies for maximizing their long-run market shares and profits. Caught in the middle were the electricity firms, stopped in front by the environmentalists in regulatory proceedings, and undercut from behind by the equipment suppliers. To some, it seemed that regulation now stood squarely and awkwardly in the path of necessary utility expansion. (The irony of the price structure inducing *extra* peak-load use should not be forgotten.)

Yet these hitches are likely to be a relatively temporary phase. It is not the regulatory process which is at fault, but only the surprise with which its delays have been suddenly exploited by a new interest group. Eventually the processes will adjust, and smooth handling will prevail.[23] But it has been a shock for the utilities and the regulators, and in some cases the process has nearly ground to a halt. For a period, regulation was not even performing its minimal safety-valve function of smoothing over the compromises among interest groups.

Effects of Regulation

Standing back from the whole sector, what lessons about regulation does electricity show? *First,* even here where it is most likely to be possible, measuring regulation's effects is virtually impossible. The whole apparatus of regulation in this sector has operated and grown for six decades. Yet nobody can say with much precision what its results have been (although some inefficiency has been estimated).

Second, a few possible effects can be discerned. One is the tendency towards excess capacity and peak use. Another is the tendency to hold off new competition in the major old markets which are nearly in Stage 4. Indeed, regulation may now stand in the way both of (1) the formation of an efficient national grid for bulk supply, which technology may now

---

[23] Thus the Storm King plant of Consolidated Edison, delayed since 1964, now appears to be headed for approval; A. R. Talbot, *Power Along the Hudson* (New York: E. P. Dutton, 1972). (Yet still other factors—including high interest costs—are leading the company to abandon it!)

justify, and (2) a competitive bulk-supply market. *Third,* regulation has proven brittle and unable to cope smoothly with large new problems.

All of this reflects regulation's peculiar origins and biases. It is tracing the conventional evolution of regulation; late and weak in starting, it is strong in resisting its own withdrawal.

THE SUPPLY OF GAS

The technology of gas supply has changed sharply in the last 50 years, shifting from local manufactured gas to interregional piping of natural gas. The technology has three stages. Gas is a joint product with oil. It is bought at the wellhead, then piped to cities and towns, and then distributed to final users. As with electricity, the three stages are distinct and separable. The final distribution level has been nominally regulated for decades (in some towns, as early as 1830), before natural gas and then since. The pipelines originated mainly since the 1930s, as natural gas came in. They are very numerous; there are ten or more between some major areas (see Figure 15–17). The great majority, which cross state lines, are regulated by the Federal Power Commission. The supply level has also been regulated by the FPC since 1954, under intense controversy.

Natural gas, obtained as a by-product in the search for oil, was wasted for many years, being blown off, burned, or devoted to inferior industrial uses in the vicinity of the oil fields. Then, in the 1930s, big new oil and

FIGURE 15–17
Major National Gas Pipelines

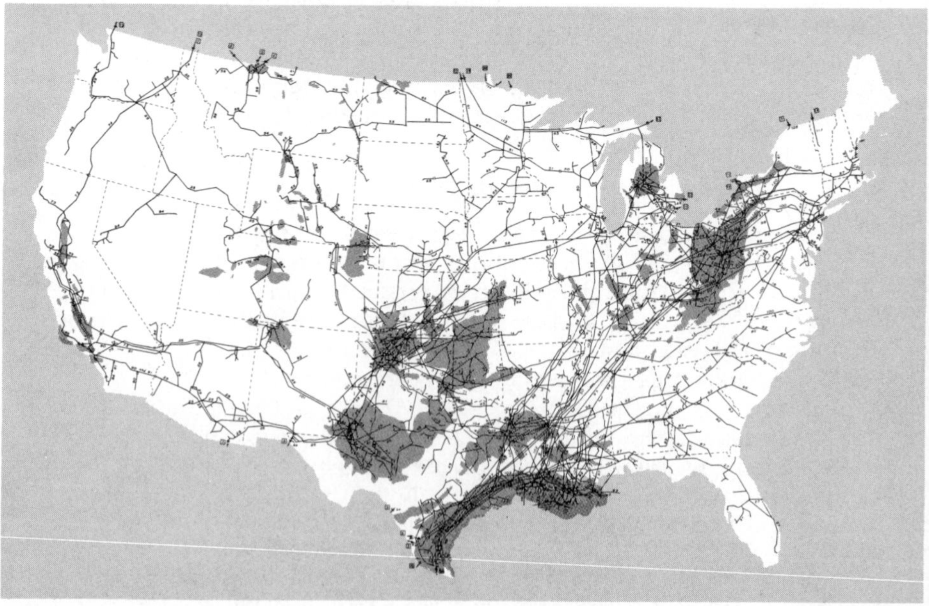

Source: Based on maps and reports filed with the Federal Power Commission; U.S. Government Printing Office, 1971.

gas fields were developed in regions remote from markets for gas. And, at the same time, the introduction of seamless pipe and other improvements in pipeline construction extended the distance over which gas could be economically transported from around 200 miles to 1,000 miles or more. High-pressure pipelines were build from the fields in the Southwest to every corner of the country. Now the major part of the gas produced moves in interstate commerce. Natural gas provides a third of the nation's energy. Of the gas that leaves the field, around two-thirds goes into industrial uses; more than one-third goes to 40 million commercial and residential consumers.

The gas industry has three levels: production, transport, and distribution. Gas is *distributed* to consumers by local utility companies, under conditions of natural monopoly. Their operations are regulated by state or city governments. It is *transported* by pipeline companies, some of the lines being owned by producers and some of them by distributors. There are some scale economies, but not enough for natural monopoly along major routes.

Gas is *produced* by oil and gas companies; roughly a score of them corporate giants conducting integrated operations, some thousands of them being independents selling their output in the field. The pipeline companies produce a tenth of the gas they carry and obtain nine-tenths of it from producers (including large oil firms). At the wellhead level, there has long been a degree of competition. Some say that it approximates pure competition, though others would rate it as oligopolistic, with much collusion.[24] The need for regulation, therefore, at this level is highly debatable. The great issue in gas regulation at the well-head is: should it be done at all?

Of the industry's three stages, distribution involves the largest costs, transport far less, and production least of all. Of the price that the distributor pays the pipeline, two-thirds to four-fifths—depending on distance—if for transport; only a fifth to a third for the gas itself. But the cost of gas to the pipeline company and the company's charge for transport enter into the costs of local distributors and must be reflected in their rates.

State-Commission Regulation of Distribution

Regulatory treatment follows the standard regimen and criteria, and it is no different in strictness.

The pattern of gas rates is similar to that of electric rates. Customers are classified and rates are varied in accordance with differences in the elasticity of demand. Lower rates are charged, for instance, for industrial than for domestic use, and for space heating and air conditioning than for cooking and water heating where competition is not so stiff. Overhead

---

[24] Effective competition is seen by, among others, P. W. MacAvoy, *Price Formation in Natural Gas Fields* (New Haven: Yale University Press, 1962). For a counter view, see D. A. Schwartz and John W. Wilson statements to the Senate Antitrust and Monopoly Subcommittee, *Hearings* on the Natural Gas Industry, June 27, 1973 (Washington, D.C.: U.S. Government Printing Office, 1974). They show 4-firm concentration at each gas field to be above 60 percent, and averaging over 80 percent.

is allocated on the basis of noncoincident demands. Consumption is measured by meters, and rates usually are of the declining block type. Many sellers have a general service tariff for most or all customers.

But the pattern is simpler than with electricity, and the differentials involved are not as great. This may be attributed, in part, to an important difference in the character of two services. Electricity must be produced as it is used; gas can be manufactured or imported and kept in storage. With gas, therefore, operations can be carried on with greater regularity. The load factor is less important, and there is less need to improve it by manipulating rates. Yet gas faces stronger and wider competition than electricity, and so the degree of discrimination remains high.

Federal Regulation

Until 1938 state and local authorities were powerless to control the price that distributors paid for imported gas. Interstate pipelines, the Supreme Court held, were beyond their reach.[25] As a result, they were confined to regulating distribution charges. Controlled gas rates floated on top of the uncontrolled prices charges at the city gates. This escape, similar to the one found until 1935 in the interstate transmission of electricity, was closed by the Natural Gas Act of 1938.

The Act brought the interstate transmission of natural gas and its sale for resale under the control of the FPC. It exempted the production and gathering of gas and its retail distribution. It established the usual pattern of rate control, requiring the pipeline companies to publish and adhere to their charges, given prior notice of prospective changes, and empowering the Commission to suspend such changes, to fix "just and reasonable" rates, and to eliminate "undue" preferences.[26]

Regulation of Pipeline Rates.   It is in the regulation of over 220,000 miles of gas pipelines that the FPC has done its most important work. The Commission, over the years, has made substantial reductions in pipeline rates. In doing so, it has adhered to the principle of making valuations at original cost. It was the Commission's defense of this principle that led to the decisions of the Supreme Court in the Natural Gas Pipeline case in 1942 and the Hope Natural Gas case in 1944, repudiating the "fair value" doctrine of *Smyth* v. *Ames* and breaking its hold on the regulation of gas and other utilities.

Before money can be raised to build a pipeline or permission obtained from the FPC for its construction, the pipeline company must be assured a lasting supply of gas. To this end, it enters into contracts with producers for periods running as long as 20 years. Since market conditions for such a period cannot be foreseen, these contracts contain clauses providing

---

[25] *West* v. *Kansas Natural Gas Co.,* 221 U.S. 229 (1911); *Haskell* v. *Kansas Natural Gas Co.,* 244 U.S. 217 (1912); *Public Utilities Comsn.* v. *Landon,* 249 U.S. 236 (1918); *Pennsylvania* v. *West Virginia,* 262 U.S. 553 (1923); *Barrett* v. *Kansas Natural Gas Co.,* 265 U.S. 298 (1924).

[26] It also authorized the Commission to prescribe and enforce methods of accounting and to ascertain the "actual legitimate cost" of pipeline properties. As amended in 1942, the law requires the companies to obtain certificates from the FPC for interstate construction, acquisitions, extensions, and abandonments, and gives the Commission limited power to order extensions. The law carries no authority to regulate financial practices or combinations. And, unlike the Act of 1935 relating to electricity, it confers no power to order interconnections and makes no provision for studies directed toward the possible unification of facilities.

for escalation of producer prices. Some of the escalation clauses are definite, requiring specific price increases on specific dates or reimbursement for larger taxes on production. Others are indefinite, requiring price increases whenever the contracting pipeline or another pipeline pays more to another producer or collects more from a distributor.[27] Some provision for price adjustment is necessary in contracts running as long as 20 years. But indefinite escalation makes for spiraling inflation. In 1961, therefore, the FPC forbade all indefinite escalation clauses in future contracts save those providing for renegotiation of prices at five-year intervals.

Setting pipeline prices raises the old state-federal problem, and so complex allocations of pipeline costs have to be made. The standard method is the so-called "Seaboard formula," which has five steps.[28] There are various adjustments to it in practice, but its basic form is common. It does tend to assign too few actual peak costs to peak sales, and so it encourages excess peak use and capacity.[29] Once again, the rate-base effect is reinforced by irrational price structures.

Practical rate cases get into mind-numbing detail, as sellers optimize their private gains by complex discrimination. The FPC hears a spectrum of intervenors—each with its special interest—and then usually strikes a compromise giving something to all sides: that is, letting much discrimination occur. The resulting rates reflect costs (from different fields and differing pipeline conditions) only partly. Table 15–4 shows

TABLE 15–4

Wholesale Gas Prices for Several Large Cities, 1966 (per million cubic feet)

	Average Cents per Mcf *Charged by Pipeline to Distributor*
Baltimore	44.5
Boston	57.9
Chicago	33.1
Los Angeles	31.9
Newark	44.2
San Francisco	31.2
Washington, D.C.	49.6

Source: FPC, *Annual Report,* 1966.

---

[27] There are five types of indefinite clauses and two types of definite clauses. For the details, see Phillips, *op. cit.,* pp. 620–22.

[28] The steps are:
1. Costs are placed in main categories; production, transmission, etc.
2. These are further subdivided into fixed and variable costs.
3. These are then reclassified as "commodity costs" (variable costs plus half the fixed costs) and "demand costs" (the other 50 percent of fixed costs).
4. Demand and commodity costs are assigned between state and interstate. Demand costs are related to peak volumes; commodity costs are related instead to annual volumes.
5. Finally, demand and commodity costs are similarly alloted among market areas, again in line with peak and annual volumes, respectively.
The basic method arose in *Re Atlantic Seaboard Corp. et al,* 43 PUR (NS) 235 (FPC, 1952); see also Phillips, *op. cit.,* pp. 624–5.

[29] The tendency is lucidly analyzed in S. H. Wellicz, "Regulation of Natural Gas Pipeline Companies: An Economic Analysis," 71 *Journal of Political Economy* 30 (1963), pp. 30–43.

how prices to several large cities vary. It is universally realized that the regulation is largely arbitrary and subjective, with little scientific basis. Not only are its effects virtually unknown; even its content resists a clear evaluation.

Regulating the Field Price of Gas

It is at the first level, in regulating the field price of gas, that the most intense current debate focuses. Such regulation might seem ridiculous, for there are many suppliers of gas, and so neither the cost basis nor the fact of monopoly seem to exist. In fact regulation of gas at the wellhead came about by a series of surprising events, and was virtually thrust upon the FPC.

The pipeline companies do not function as common carriers, transporting goods for others. They own the gas they carry, producing some of it themselves, buying most of it from independent producers. The FPC, in determining the charges made for transport, had to start, therefore, with the price of gas at the city gate, and then subtract from it the cost incurred or the price paid in obtaining gas in the field. It thus became involved not only in regulating the transport of gas but also in fixing the price of gas itself. And this stirred up a hornet's nest of politics.

At first the Commission confined itself to determining a value for gas produced by the integrated companies. For this purpose, it considered two alternatives: one was to use the price that was paid to independent producers; the other was to use the production costs of the integrated companies. It chose the second, computing the cost of producing gas by taking the companies' operating expenses and adding a return of 6 percent on the depreciated original cost of their producing properties.

Its authority to take such action was challenged on the ground that the production and gathering of gas were exempted from control by the wording of the law. In 1945, however, the Supreme Court held that this exemption did not prevent the Commission from including the value of producing and gathering facilities in the rate base when fixing the transport charges of integrated companies.[30]

This decision protected consumers against increases in the price of gas where it it was produced by integrated companies but not where it was produced by independents. The Commission's duty to take action in such cases was made an issue in a case involving the Phillips Petroleum Company. Phillips was the largest of the independent producers of gas. The company raised its price and was brought before the FPC upon complaint by the state of Wisconsin and the municipalities of Milwaukee, Kansas City, and Detroit. The Commission decided that it lacked the power to act.

The plaintiffs appealed, and in 1954, the Supreme Court found Phillips to be a natural gas concern within the meaning of the Natural Gas Act, holding that exemption of the functions of production and gathering did not involve exemption of subsequent sales. It was therefore the Com-

---

[30] *Colorado Interstate Gas Co.* v. *FPC,* 324 U.S. 581.

mission's duty to determine whether the prices charged by Phillips were just and reasonable.[31] Thus, for the first time in U.S. history, the Court directed a regulatory agency to increase the scope of its activities.

The FPC was faced with the unwelcome task of fixing the prices charged by thousands of producers of an extractive product—one whose profit is mainly economic rent. The task was both mountainous and devoid of clear criteria.[32] The traditional rate-base and cost method of regulation will not work for gas, which is (1) an extractive product, and (2) a joint product (with oil). Cost is a mare's nest, and rate base is a chimera.

Costs. The quality of gas is not uniform. The cost of producing it varies from field to field, from well to well, and from level to level in the same well. Part of the supply of gas comes from oil wells where it appears as a joint product along with oil. Part of it comes from gas wells, but much of this is a by-product of the search for oil. Determination of a cost for gas therefore involves an allocation of joint costs.

Of the costs incurred in exploration, all are joint; of those incurred in development and production, as much as half are joint; of the total costs of such an operation, less than a third are clearly separable and more than two-thirds are joint. The cost determined for gas is thus dependent upon the method chosen for use in allocating joint costs.

Under one method, annual costs are allocated in proportion to the respective revenues received from sales of oil and gas, and fixed costs according to the respective values of reserves remaining in the ground. Under a second, joint costs are allocated in proportion to the British thermal unit content of these products. Under a third, they are divided in proportion to the respective costs of producing gas and oil from wells where they are produced alone.

None of these methods is really defensible. Nor, in the very nature of the case, can costs so calculated ever be anything but arbitrary in character.

Further difficulties are encountered when an attempt is made to fix a value for a rate base and to find an appropriate rate of return. Evaluation of investment again involves the allocation of joint costs, and requires that proper allowance be made for depletion. Selection of a rate

---

[31] *Phillips Petroleum Co.* v. *Wisconsin,* 347 U.S. 672.

[32] Within a month, the Commission issued an order freezing the wellhead price of natural gas sold for interstate transmission, requiring producers to apply for certificates and file their prices, and establishing control over future increases. By 1963, nearly 18,000 producers had applied for certificates. To lessen the burden of regulation, some 17,500 of the smaller producers were excused from keeping records and submitting reports in accordance with the system of accounting prescribed for other regulated concerns, and were allowed to file their applications for rate increases on simplified forms. As a usual matter, such increases were allowed to go into effect without objection by the FPC.

Regulation of the price of gas was vigorously resisted not only by gas producers but also by other members of the oil industry who saw in it an entering wedge to price control for oil. Efforts were made to negate the Court's decision by action in the state legislatures and the federal Congress. Laws were passed in Oklahoma and Kansas empowering state commissions to fix minimum prices that might be higher than the maximum prices fixed by the FPC, but these were held to violate the federal Constitution. A bill was passed by Congress in 1953 exempting independent producers from control, but was vetoed by President Eisenhower when it was revealed that an oil company lawyer had attempted to influence a Senator's vote by offering a contribution to his campaign fund.

of return depends upon opinion as to risk and the inducement that is needed to overcome it.

The price that is finally set will reflect a summation, not of objective facts but of subjective judgments. In this industry, moreover, the amount of money invested bears little relation to the amount of service rendered: a large investment may open dry holes; a small investment may produce a gusher. Whatever the usefulness of this procedure in fixing the rates of a producer of electricity, its application to an industry as competitive and as risky as the production of natural gas is hazardous.

The Method Used. After several abortive attempts and years of growing paralysis in coping with a massive caseload, a workable method involving area prices was revised.

In 1960, the FPC had 3,200 requests for rate increases, filed by 570 producers, awaiting action. It estimated that, with a tripled staff, it would not be able to hear and decide these cases in less than 82 years. Finding the traditional method of fixing prices to be unworkable, the Commission announced that it had adopted an alternative approach. Under the new approach, known as area pricing, it delimited 23 producing areas and published tentative ceiling prices for each of them, based upon the prices that had prevailed from 1956 to 1958. It announced that requests for new prices and for escalated prices that were below these levels would be approved, but that producers asking for prices above them would have to bear the burden of proof. The effect was to lighten the Commission's burden by facilitating price adjustments below the ceiling while concentrating on those cases where the ceilings would be breached.

The FPC made its first area price determination for the Permian Basin of Texas and New Mexico in 1965. Here, it set two ceiling prices. One of them applied to gas from wells already in production and to gas produced in association with oil. The other applied to gas to be brought into production in the future, not in association with oil. Both ceilings were based on an average of costs plus a fair return on the investment in producing properties. The first ceiling was based on the average costs and the average investment reported in 1960 by all producers in the area for gas from wells already in production, no separate calculation being made for associated gas.

The second ceiling was based on an industry-wide average of the costs incurred in producing new gas unmixed with oil. In calculating the investment base, the Commission assumed depletion over a period of 20 years. And it allowed a return, above costs, of 12 percent on investment. Using these methods, the Commission established a maximum of 14.5 cents per thousand cubic feet for old gas and for gas associated with oil; a maximum of 16.5 cents for new gas unmixed with oil. The first of these maxima was designed to prevent the realization of monopoly profits. The second was designed to afford an incentive for exploration and development.

The Commission required producers to make refunds where prices had been above its maxima since 1965, and barred the operation of escalator clauses that would put future prices above its maxima. The price determination was promptly appealed to the courts and, in a decision handed down in 1968, the Supreme Court held that the Commission's method of establishing its ceilings did not exceed its authority, and that the resulting prices did not deny producers a reasonable return.[33]

In a second determination, for the Southern Louisiana Area, the FPC employed the same method, establishing a triple ceiling that set a maximum of 18.5 cents for old gas and for gas produced along with oil, a maximum of 19.5 cents for gas produced alone from wells opened before October 1, 1968, and a maximum of 20 cents for such gas from wells

FIGURE 15–18

Area Price Levels for Independent Producer Natural Gas Sales

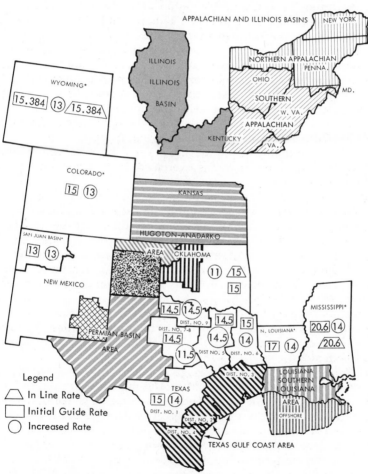

In cents per thousand cubic feet at 14.65 psia, except as noted.
At 15.025 psia.
Notes: (1) Increased rate ceilings 0.6¢ per Mcf (at 14.65 psia) higher than those shown are applicable under rate schedules from which favored nation and price redetermination provisions have been eliminated, and 1.0¢ per Mcf higher under rate schedules from which all escalation provisions have been eliminated. (2) All rates shown above include tax except North Louisiana 14.0¢ and 17.0¢ rates.
Source: Federal Power Commission, *Annual Report*, 1972, p. 39.

[33] *Permian Basin Area Rate Cases*, 390 U.S. 747.

opened after that date. The Commission also announced that it would use the Permian Basin method in pricing new gas produced by the integrated companies and would reconsider its method of pricing their gas from wells already in production. The most recent patterns are illustrated by Figure 15–18.

An Evaluation

The FPC finally developed a method of fixing maximum field prices for gas and its method was accepted by the courts. But serious questions remained. It may be asked, first, whether price control is needed to protect the consumer against monopoly. This would be the case if control over supply were concentrated in the hands of a few producers. But it is not. Producers number in the thousands, the degree of concentration seems low, new entry is unobstructed, and there is little hard evidence of concerted action among producers to push prices up. Among the buyers of gas in any field, however, there are no more than two or three pipeline companies. When new fields are opened, more buyers bid for the supply. But the successful bidders are the only ones to lay in their lines. It may be possible for other buyers to enter, but such an occurrance is rare. The buyers' side of the market is thus characterized by oligopsony.[34] But if oligopsony power is exercised, it should operate to push prices not up but down.

Another factor, however, must be considered: gas is sold, as we have seen, under long-term contracts containing escalator clauses. The only prices being freely negotiated, therefore, are those between the buyers and sellers of new supplies. With demand growing and new supplies small, their prices tend constantly to rise. And these increases are communicated to the rest of the supply through escalation under the contracts. A price that is fixed in this way may be unfair to consumers in the sense that it affords producers a higher return than would be needed to induce new exploration and development. If the market is workably competitive, however, the price will not be much too high. Therefore, there is sharp controversy about the degree of monopoly, with plausible data on both sides.

Has Regulation Caused a Shortage of Natural Gas? More recently, regulation has been blamed for cutting the incentive to explore for gas and hence aggravating the recent energy shortages. The regulated prices set in the 1960s did follow a long period of sharp rises in gas prices. Gas prices stayed virtually steady for a decade, well into the recent fuel crisis. During this period, the rate of exploration and discovery slipped compared to the consumption of gas, leading some analysts to blame the gas price ceiling for cutting the incentives for discovery. By 1974 massive pressures had arisen for a sharp rise in the price of gas, *in order—it was said—to restore the inducements for adequate exploration.*[35]

---

[34] Schwartz and Wilson also stress that oligopoly is tight within the relevant markets, and that the integrated firms do exercise considerable market power; see footnote 24 above.

[35] See P. W. MacAvoy, "The Regulation-Induced Shortage of Natural Gas," *Journal of Law and Economics,* Vol. 14, No. 1 (April 1971), pp. 167–99.

On the other side, it was argued that the prospect of a price rise was inducing suppliers to hold back new finds until the new higher prices were set. Therefore the case for higher gas prices was alleged to be quite circular, hanging by its own bootstraps (i.e., from expectations). If price rises were explicitly renounced, the holdback would cease and gas supplies might well turn out to be adequate. Moreover, it was urged that the actual structure of gas markets within the relevant regional submarkets was highly concentrated rather than virtually competitive. This would make the withholding of gas supplies more possible (though this was not necessary: expectations alone *could* induce the holdback).

Further, the price rises would confer a massive windfall capital gain to the holders of gas reserves, not only of the new reserves but also all old reserves. The gas price rise would therefore have a large redistributive effect on wealth, perhaps shifting several tens of billions of dollars in a sharply disequalizing direction. This was the basic case against a major rise in the price of gas in order to raise incentives for exploration. The gist of it was that *much of the "regulation-induced shortage of natural gas" was in fact a self-fulfilling mirage, based on expectations and some market power.* A rise would be neither efficient nor equitable.

In the event, the political pressure for gas supplies and the industry pressure for specific gains proved more than the FPC could resist, and nearly a doubling of the price of gas was permitted during 1973–74. The effort to de-regulate gas at the wellhead entirely has not succeeded, but it will surely continue. Much of field price regulation could be withdrawn without causing large long-run losses, because the sector does have a degree of competition. But once regulation was established, de-regulating has been an awkward process. Letting the regulated price rise does cause a large disequalizing shift of wealth. But once that has occurred, the basis for dissolving the controls on field prices are relatively sound.

One gains perspective on this by looking at the use of natural gas abroad. There the supply system is almost universally under public ownership on a national scale. In Britain there are decentralized levels of controls in the system. But in any case, the national systems in Europe operate as monopsonists in buying supplies. Therefore, they are able to drive a hard bargain and acquire gas at virtually the lowest possible economic cost. This has shifted much of the rents, which producers might have gathered, to consumers. To this extent, public monopsony has substituted much more effectively for the FPC effort to establish direct regulation. And it has prevented expectations from forcing—by circular processes—a rise in price and producer surplus.

SUMMARY

The energy sector illustrates the problems arising when regulation occurs on several levels and by overlapping agencies. The regulated firms seek out the line of least resistance, and they exert a wide degree of choice in their own internal management and performance. It becomes virtually impossible to factor out the effects—and often even the content—of regulation.[36] The main virtue may be that large errors are probably, on the whole, avoided because of the fragmented variety of decisions. Moreover it is conceivable, though not likely, that the rate-base inducements towards extra investment have speeded along the progress of technology in the sector, rather than caused a degree of waste.

Nonetheless, regulation has not made use of its opportunities either for (1) control, or for (2) reintroducing competition. At present, it tends to block a number of processes which would improve both structure and performance in the sector. In short, it has evolved in the standard directions and had checkered performance, much as would be expected. The sector as a whole is headed towards more competition and an erosion of the old service-area concept. How it adjusts to this—or even helps it along—may ultimately be the prime test of the effectiveness of regulation in the sector. Meanwhile it remains complex, often obscure, and economically dubious.

---

[36] Stephen Breyer and Paul W. MacAvoy, *Energy Regulation by the Federal Power Commission* (Washington, D.C.: Brookings Institution, 1974) urge that the FPC's costs have exceeded benefits in most of its activities.

CHAPTER SIXTEEN

Regulation of Communications

The communications sector has three distinct parts: telephones, broadcasting, and postal services. The first two are instant communications —or telecommunications—and are quite different: telephone is point-to-point, while broadcasting is from one point to many. They are treated in this chapter. Postal systems are normally public enterprises (see Chapter 21).

The main actors in U.S. telecommunications are familiar: the Bell system, the television networks, and the FCC. But the sector is suffused with actual and potential competition, and these conditions shade into bigger issues of political and social power. Many classic points of pricing and investment criteria do crop up on the telephone side, but the hardest regulatory choices in both telephones and broadcasting deal with competition.

TELEPHONES—POINT-TO-POINT TELECOMMUNICATIONS

The Sector

The core is local telephone service, familiar to everyone. The newer parts—long-distance service and business services—are growing faster than the older local-exchange services. U.S. telephone capacity is more advanced than other countries (see Table 16–1), both in the coverage of households and in the range of services provided. The question: Do regulatory policies enhance or hinder the sector's performance, or perhaps not affect it at all?

The telephone system—primarily the Bell System—is actually part of a wider set of activities, as shown in Figures 16–1 and 16–2. There are two main levels: (1) design and *production* of equipment, and (2) *operation* of equipment. The Bell System does both, as a virtually closed system of vertical integration. So do GT&E and, to a degree, ITT (in its foreign operations). But there are large areas of competition and choice.

Equipment producers can be divided into two distinctive categories:

Courtesy James Flora and Fortune

Up, Up and Away, the FCC regulates the unruly communications sector in this 1967 view. The problems and interests have gained even more stress since then. Their onrush is shown in Nicholas Johnson and John Dystel, "A Day in the Life: The Federal Communications Commission," *Yale Law Journal,* July 1973, pp. 1575–1634.

group 1, those owned by regulated carriers, such as the Bell System and General Telephone and Electronics; and group 2, all other equipment-making firms, large and small. Group 2 firms generally innovate and market their equipment under competitive, or at least rivalrous, conditions, although there are tendencies toward tight rather than loose oligopoly and Western Electric is excluded from competing in these markets. There are many buyers of broadcasting equipment (networks and individual stations), even though one buyer is owned by a major pro-

TABLE 16–1
Telephone Patterns in Selected Countries, 1973

	Total Telephones (*1,000*)	Telephones per 100 Population	Share under Private Operation (*percent*)
United States.....................	131,606	62.8	99.9
Canada..........................	10,987	50.0	83.2
France	10,338	19.9	0
Germany	16,521	26.8	0
Italy............................	11,345	20.8	100
Norway..........................	1,262	32.0	0.2
Sweden..........................	4,829	59.3	0
Switzerland	3,404	54.0	0
United Kingdom	17,570	31.4	0
Israel...........................	619	19.4	0
Brazil	2,190	2.2	11.6
Australia........................	4,399	33.9	0
Japan...........................	34,021	31.5	97.9

Source: American Telephone and Telegraph Co., *The World's Telephones, 1973* (New York: 1973).

ducer—Radio Corporation of America (RCA) owns the National Broadcasting Company—and both RCA and International Telephone and Telegraph Corporation (ITT) have a variety of carrier operations abroad. Since the networks' earnings are not regulated, rate-base preference is not a factor in their purchasing policies. Some items are affected by international competition. Market structure is particularly competitive in the smaller, peripheral products, such as terminal attachments for data transmission.

FIGURE 16–1
The Complex Communications Sector

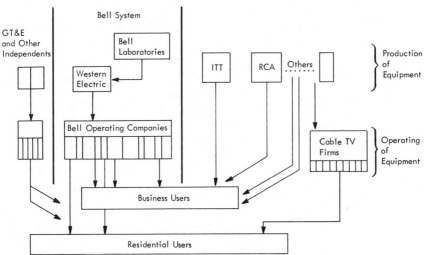

FIGURE 16–2
The Bell Telephone Companies

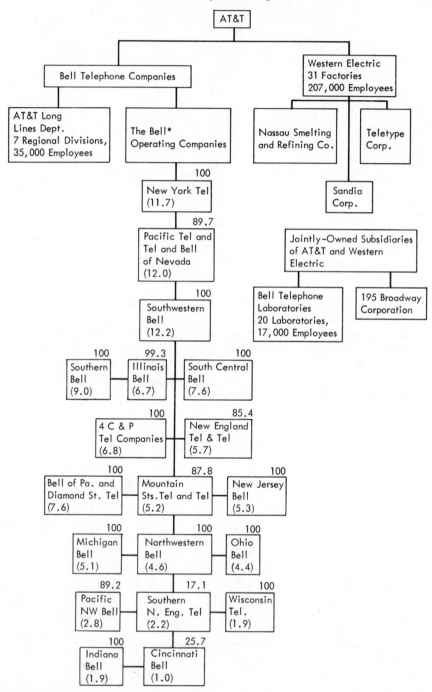

* In descending order of 1972 total operating revenues.
Numbers are percent ownership by AT&T.

Telephone operations involve three main parts: the switching subsystem, the transmission equipment, and the terminal devices. *Switching* is the process of selecting a local or intercity message path; it involves electromechanical and electronic equipment. (Try to locate the local telephone exchange building in your town.) Intercity *transmission* is by cable, land-based microwave, and terrestrial satellite, at selected levels of message-transmission quality. *Terminal devices* (*e.g.,* display units, feed-ins for data and computers, private exchanges, printing devices, etc.) are of great and growing variety, and their interconnection with the system must provide safeguards against damage to the system's functioning.

A key variable in choosing technologies in all parts of the system is the standard of reliability, a probabilistic criterion which encompasses the determination of both optimum *quality* of service and optimum *capacity* during peak loads. The decision to alter technology or service offerings in any of these dimensions often embraces complex interactions within the system. By the same token, the innovating carrier commonly has a high degree of choice among technological modes, service offerings, and spatial configurations. This latitude is enhanced if research and equipment design are vertically integrated with the provision of services, as they are in the major communications carriers.

The telephone system is indeed a *system,* but it is also partly a mosaic of separable parts. *How* separable they are has been the recurring basic question since telephony began 100 years ago. AT&T's dominance of telephony—and how regulation has dealt with it—can best be evaluated in light of its origins.

Background. Briefly, Western Union came to control telegraphy after 1855; telephony was quickly dominated by the Bell System in the 1880s; and telephony has far surpassed telegraphy and gone into new areas (data transmission, satellites).[1] But the basic common-carrier business is still transmittal of the human voice, locally and among cities. Regulation was applied gradually after 1935, well after all of the basic patterns were set in late Stage 2. Table 16–2 and 16–3 lists the milestones of the sequence.

Signals were first transmitted electronically by wire by Samuel F. B. Morse in 1835. The first telegraph line was strung between Washington and Baltimore in 1843. Thereafter, telegraphy soon came to be used in the dispatching of trains and the transmission of news, 50 companies being engaged in this enterprise by 1851. Many of these concerns were subsidized, being permitted, without charge, to string their lines along the rights-of-way of land-grant railways. A number of these enterprises were combined to form the Western Union Telegraph Company in 1856.

Invention of the telephone was claimed by Daniel Drawbaugh, Elisha Gray, and Alexander Graham Bell (recall Chapter 9). Drawbaugh's telephone was invented in 1869 and put to work in 1871. Bell first transmitted

---

[1] For an outline of the development of the industry and public policies toward it, see Charles F. Phillips, Jr., *op. cit.,* Chap. 17. See also the landmark study by the then-new U.S. Federal Communications Commission, *Investigation of the Telephone Industry in the United States,* H. Doc. 340, 76 Cong. 1 sess. (1939).

TABLE 16–2
Milestones in Point-to-point Telecommunications

1869.	Daniel Drawbaugh invents the telephone.
1875.	Alexander G. Bell invents the telephone.
1876–94	Basic Bell patents apply.
1879.	Western Union and Bell interests agree to stay out of each other's area.
1882.	Western Electric Manufacturing Co. partially merged in.
1881–85	Early growth and consolidation.
1890s.	Rapid growth of the Bell system.
1875–87, 1902–20.	Theodore Vail in charge of Bell policies.
1900–1907	Independent systems grow rapidly.
1907.	Bell gains control of Western Union.
1907–1913	Rapid Bell acquisitions of independents.
1913.	Kingsbury Commitment.
1921.	Bell System resumes merging of small systems.
1924.	Bell Laboratories established.
1930s.	FCC and state regulation acquires standing.
1948–50	Bell System secures control of microwave transmission.
1949.	Antitrust suit filed seeking divestiture of Western Electric.
1951.	General Telephone acquires suppliers.
1956.	Western Electric case settled.
1959.	"Over 890" issue raised.
1961–1974	Telpak issue drags on.
1962–1974	Capabilities for domestic satellite exists, but are not implemented.
1965–67?	First formal rate hearings (Phase 1, 1965–71, phase 2, 1972–).
1965–67	New Western Electric suit prepared; not filed.
1967.	First electronic switching station.
1968–69	MCI and Carterfone decisions by FCC, contested further.
1972.	GT&E ordered by District Court to divest its suppliers and all operating systems acquired since 1950s.
1974.	Major Section 2 case filed against AT&T.

voice by wire in 1875. Patent litigation ensued. The Bell interests acquired the Gray as well as the Bell rights and sued Drawbaugh for infringement. Bell won its suit in the Supreme Court in 1887. It then proceeded with the construction of telephone lines.

A war for survival followed. Western Union, then the stronger company, barred Bell's lines from the railway rights-of-way and sued Bell for infringement of its patent. But Bell successfully resisted the attack. The patent suit was settled out of court in 1879. The communications business was divided between the two concerns, Western Union taking record communications for itself and leaving voice communications to Bell.

Bell then went on to establish its dominance over the telephone industry. Up to 1898, it brought infringement suits against 600 small local companies, converting the losers into licensees. It refused to sell telephonic equipment manufactured by Western Electric to independent companies, refused to connect them to its long distance lines, and drove them out of business by undercutting their rates. Bell bought the shares

TABLE 16–3
Early Growth of Telephone Capacity

1876....... Invention.
1877....... First telephone exchange: New Haven, Connecticut. First overhead telephone line: Boston to Sommerville, Mass.
1880....... 47,900 telephones in the U.S.
1881....... Boston and Providence connected.
1884....... New York and Boston connected.
1889....... Dial telephone invented by Almon B. Strowger.
1895....... First dial exchange: La Porte, Indiana.
1902....... 1,002 of 1,051 U.S. cities over 4,000 population have service: 137 independent, 414 Bell, and 451 both.
1907....... Bell has 3.1 million telephones, independents 3.0 million.
1915....... First transcontinental service.
1920....... 8.1 million Bell telephones in service.
1927....... Transocean radio service begins.
1962....... International communications satellite orbited.

Credit: Culver Pictures

Theodore N. Vail (1845–1920), driving force in the founding and development of the Bell System, he established the structure and policies that continue even now. (Shown about 1910.)

of its licensees and those of independent companies. Where no such companies existed, it encouraged local promoters to establish them, assisted their development, and then acquired control. Proceeding ruthlessly over the years, it virtually monopolized the business of telephony.

In 1913, the threat of antitrust attack produced the "Kingsbury Commitment," in which Bell agreed (1) to interconnect other telephone systems, (2) not to acquire competing telephone companies, and (3) to separate out Western Union and stay out of telegraphy.[2] In return, it was permitted to keep Western Electric as its exclusive supplier. The present structure was thus established and legitimized over 60 years ago. The driving force in creating this system was Theodore N. Vail, president after 1901.

Bell then had just over half the telephones in use, but all long-distance operations. During 1921–40, a series of selective mergers increased it to about 90 percent of telephones. Since then, the growth of suburbs has favored the independents' rural areas, and so the Bell share of telephones has receded to about 80 percent. During the 1950s, GT&E (the second largest, about one-tenth's Bell's size) also acquired its own suppliers and launched on a series of mergers of small systems. This was successfully challenged in 1972 by ITT (recall Chapter 7).

---

[2] The letter was sent by N. C. Kingsbury, Vice-President of AT&T, to the U.S. Attorney General.

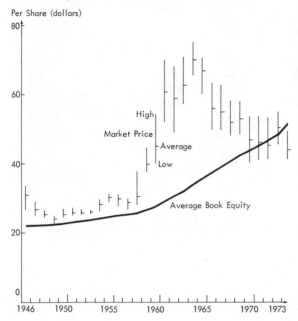

FIGURE 16–3
Bell System: Book and Market Value of Shares

Nicholas Johnson (born 1934) an outstanding maverick FCC commissioner during 1966–73. Often a lone dissenter, he eventually brought the commission round to improved policies toward competition, satellites, cross-media ownership, and other areas. He had previously shaken old maritime subsidy policies (see Chapter 25) during a short period as Maritime Commissioner.

In 1948–50, Bell reached out to monopolize the new microwave technology (those towers at 30-mile intervals which carry the television and other signals). A 1949 antitrust effort to divide Western Electric out was abandoned in 1956 (recall Chapter 7). The 1960s brought major new issues of competition, on trunk routes and in the supply of terminal apparatus. New technology also seemed fruitful, in satellites, optical fibers and lasers, electronic switching, and other directions. But some expected breakthroughs—such as "Picturephone"—turned out to be slow and slight. Instead, the pedestrian problem of service quality became acute in some areas in the late 1960s (especially New York). Large parts of the system were in classic late Stage 3 conditions: new competition, changing city patterns, capital scarcities, pressure on the rate structure.

During 1958–64 Bell's successes caused AT&T stock to rise from $30 to $70. But since 1964, the pressure of rising capital costs has grown. Figure 16–3 shows the effect, as AT&T shares have gone down by 30 percent. Still dominant, powerful, and only marginally regulated, the Bell System has faced new stresses since the middle 1960s.

Technology and the Role for Regulation.   A telephone system must stand ready to provide connections among its subscribers, and service standards may require unified control over all components and possibly self-supply of key apparatus. Hence, the telephone carriers (particularly the Bell System) have argued that there will be large costs from reducing "systemic integrity," and the Bell System has resisted interconnection with other systems and the attachment of terminal devices not produced and serviced by itself.

If the technology of telecommunications prescribed a natural monopoly, total and integrated control by one system under appropriate public constraints might be economically justified. Yet the technological margins between necessary monopoly and possible competition have been in a state of flux, particularly in the last two decades, and the newer optional services have tended to be both more lucrative and more capable of supporting a fully competitive market structure. Where these new markets are not already carrier-controlled (as in optional handset features), the common carriers have had an incentive to capture the entire markets for these services by persuading the regulators to classify them as exclusively carrier activities. Failing that, the carriers may have been able to offer newer services at prices that independent firms, lacking the carriers' established earnings base, cannot meet. Meanwhile, independents have been arguing that the carriers (again, primarily the Bell System) could permit terminal attachments and interconnection with private systems much more freely than they do without significantly reducing system integrity and service quality. These and related changes could greatly enlarge the scope for competition, or at least rivalry.

There is thus a large public stake in the technological trade-offs: in the degree of alternative costs and gains from reducing monopoly barriers, and conversely in the losses of efficiency and innovation that are likely to be caused by overextending the franchise for monopoly. In all of the variables in question, one needs to consider alternative gradations of change rather than simple comparisons between the status quo and extreme alternatives. For example, simple assertions about technological requirements or claims that vertical integration yields great economies of coordination do not suffice as a basis for public policy, especially where they come from carriers with an interest in excluding competition.

Not only may the carriers' own internal perception of the trade-offs be conditioned by their interest in increasing the reach of their control, but in addition the very nature of the innovations they adopt may tend to be selected so as to maximize the exclusivity of their systems. This will indeed be so if the carrier is behaving rationally and if it has a significant degree of choice. The more integrated the system, the more scope there may be for selection among innovations, and the harder it is, even for alert regulators, to perceive, anticipate, and offset the bias. As noted earlier, reliability of service frequently plays a key role in the carriers' strategy for innovation and profit maximizing.

The strong incentives of carriers to increase the reliability and quality of service may shape the whole direction of technology. Regulators share some of these inducements (for example, to avoid embarrassing stoppages in service), so they must be particularly alert to the likelihood that the degree of reliability and exclusivity will be extended beyond the technological optimum.

The natural monopoly conditions and limits are roughly similar to those in electricity. Local operations are virtually a true natural monopoly. Transmission technology has improved greatly over the decades, including the onset of microwave and now newer modes. The scale is rising sharply and marginal costs are low. This gives a rising scope for choice about the forms of supply, the variety of service types and qualities, and the degree of possible competition. Satellites, particularly, offer sharply wider choices for transmitting all kinds of signals. They can act as large trunk circuits; they can also pin-point areas, beaming specific signals under a variety of special limits. A few big domestic satellites could radically alter the present system. That is one reason their use has been delayed since 1962 (see page 447 below).

Generally, the United States has offered exceptionally favorable conditions for innovation in communications. Its great size, scattered large cities, and extensive commercial use of telecommunications have all favored the creation of high-density trunk routes that can exploit the major potential advances in transmission technology. These have been the main cost-reducing innovations in the last 40 years. Also, at least a large portion of demand is probably income-elastic. Rising incomes have brought about high and rising levels of demand for basic and optional services, so that many other innovations have been relatively easy to prepare, test, and carry out.

Regulation

Nominal regulation came only after 1907, well into Stage 2. Real regulation began during the 1930s but has had a definite constraining effect only since the 1950s. The sharpest issues have concerned competition, although there is much formal regulation of rates of return at the state level.

As state commissions were created after 1907, telephones were among the standard utilities covered. In 1910, interstate telephone and telegraph service was added to the ICC's responsibilities, but little was done. During the next 24 years, the ICC did not once have a formal proceeding to reduce rates. In 1927, a Federal Radio Commission was created. Then in 1934 the Federal Communications Commission was established, covering telephone, telegraph, and radio (and later television). The FCC's main task is to regulate the common carriers, now principally the Bell System. But from the start it has been loaded with many other technical operations (recall Table 13–5), which absorb the main part of its resources.

The FCC's first five years were engrossed with a massive study of the telephone system. In sharp contrast with electricity, no major abuses were found, and only relatively small changes were later negotiated. The accepted *Report,* therefore, tended to ratify the whole structure of the industry, as it had already evolved for more than half a century.

The FCC Study and Basic Bell System Conditions. The FCC study was large. Some 300 lawyers, accountants, and engineers were engaged in the work over a period of four years. The basic record included 8,500 pages of testimony, 2,000 exhibits, and 77 staff studies. The Commission's final report was published in 1939.[3] It disclosed no such financial scandals as those found by the Federal Trade Commission in the electrical industry. But there were real problems. AT&T had taken advantage of its opportunity to increase profits, at the expense of the consumer, by padding the operating expenses and the property valuations of the associated companies.

AT&T rendered various services to its associated companies, giving advice on the construction and operation of their properties, carrying on research through the Bell Laboratories and obtaining patents, raising and holding funds to meet their financial needs, and managing the assets of the parent company. For these services, it charged the associated companies a license fee amounting to 1.5 percent of their gross revenues. (This was later reduced to 1 percent.)

The Commission found that the parent company, in prescribing methods of accounting, had required its subsidiaries to include in operating expenses depreciation charges known to be in excess of actual requirements but had forbidden them to deduct more than a part of depreciation reserves in arriving at the valuation of their properties. Annual charges for depreciation had not been reduced by an amount sufficient to compensate for the increasing length of life of the telephone plant.

These charges were close to a fifth of the expenses involved in operating the system and thus significantly affected the consumer's bill. Reserves, built up out of such charges, represented nearly 30 percent of the investment in the telephone plant. But only observable depreciation was deducted in determining the rate base, and the depreciation observed amounted to only 7 to 12 percent, instead of 30 percent, of property values. To the extent that reserves, accumulated from rates paid by subscribers, were not deducted from the base upon which further rate payments were computed, the subscribers were compelled to pay the company a return on money which they themselves had contributed.

AT&T handled the financing of the whole system. It made advances to the associated companies, supplied them with the capital which they required, and charged them for the costs incurred in the process. Year after year, the company collected interest at a fixed rate, neither altering its charge with fluctuations in the rates charged by other lenders nor permitting its subsidiaries to enter the money market on their own. Insofar as its policy increased the price they had to pay for capital, it was reflected in the telephone subscriber's rates.

AT&T was found to have issued instructions which compelled the associated companies to purchase practically all of their apparatus, equipment, and plant materials from Western Electric. Six small independent producers of such supplies, subsisting largely on the business which Western gave them, were in no position really to compete with it. Since Western obtained its orders without competitive bidding, it was not forced to sell at a competitive price.

The company's cost accounts did not afford an authentic basis for testing the reasonableness of the prices which it set upon specific prod-

---

[3] Federal Communications Commission, *Investigation of the Telephone Industry* (Washington, D.C.: Government Printing Office, 1939).

ucts. Its prices, moreover, bore no apparent relation to its own statement of costs. Both costs and prices for many items were above those reported by independent firms. Western Electric profits had never been subject to any sort of public control.

From 1882 to 1936 the company realized a net income on its paid-in capital that exceeded 20 percent in 41 years, 50 percent in 25 years, and 100 percent in 6 years. To the extent that Western's charges were excessive, the excess entered into the property valuations and operating expenses of the associated companies and thus compelled the state commissions to fix rates that yielded something more than a fair return.

Finally, the facilities employed by AT&T and its subsidiaries in rendering long-distance service so overlapped that it was virtually impossible to determine how much of their cost should be charged to the Long Lines Department of the holding company and how much to the associated local companies. And it was therefore practically impossible to judge either the reasonableness of the tolls charged or the fairness with which the resulting revenues were divided. The tolls may well have been too high. And they may have been so divided as to divert revenues from the associated companies to the Long Lines Department, thus necessitating higher local rates.

By negotiation, the FCC has abated some of these problems. Rate base was revalued on original cost, and depreciation was altered. Western Electric has eventually been indirectly regulated; each year it reports its results under several functional headings. The reported returns on telephone production are always in range of 9–11 percent on equity. Though full outside control of cost allocation does not exist, this sideways, pressure-less process may have removed the possibility that Bell rate base is padded by excess prices for supplies (see below). A massive "separations" system for allocating between intrastate and interstate was also developed.

Regulation since 1935: From Passive to Mainly Passive. From 1935 to 1966, the FCC's role was mainly passive; a tiny agency facing enormous economic and political power. It held no public hearings on rates, instead relying on informal discussions with Bell officials which occasionally yielded price reductions. These reductions mostly flowed from the natural technology and growth of the system, not FCC strictness. In relying on negotiation, the FCC gave up the leverage and initiative that public hearings provide in dealing with powerful interests and complex issues. And it left both the character and the results of its actions unavailable to outside study. "Continuous surveillance" has prevented the rigidities and formal posturing that regulatory hearings too often create—an important gain. Moreover, a series of rate changes has emerged from these informal negotiations. Possibly the FCC has significantly influenced those changes; but outside observers are left with neither descriptive data nor normative guidelines for appraising them or for factoring out the FCC's role, if any, in bringing them about.

Until 1965, there had been no public FCC review at all of the profit criteria, the price and cost structure, the equipment purchasing policies, and the interconnection and terminal equipment policies of the telephone industry.[4] Since 1965 there has been some review of some of these, but the FCC's posture is still basically passive.

Since 1948, and especially since 1960, the FCC has been forced to review prickly issues affecting the structure of communications markets. These include particularly spectrum allocation, microwave access and interconnection, the division of data transmission between Western Union and the Bell System, foreign attachments, and satellite transmission. Most of these have been lengthy, perhaps befitting the depth of the problems. Some have been mind-numbing, full of jargon, "boiler-plate" arguments, tactical delays, and procedural strategies. In nearly all cases, the Bell System holds and controls the information about key variables, with the FCC striving to get an adequate, neutral picture of its choices.

State regulation is even more passive. Commission resources in telephone matters are especially slender. States can aspire to regulate no more than a small piece of the entire system, in which great volumes of overhead costs can be allocated arbitrarily. Worse, 36 states, with about half of all Bell telephones, are served by *multistate* Bell operating firms (such as Southwestern Bell Telephone, which provides Missouri, Kansas, Arkansas, Oklahoma, and Texas a total of 40 million telephones). The scope for effective state regulation has been reduced as the distinction between interstate and intrastate operations has become increasingly blurred.[5]

The states are more passive *both* on profit rates, rate structure, and market control. The carriers find it natural to try to regain at the state level what the FCC may have denied them (as in terminal attachments: see below).

On the whole, regulation of telecommunications came late, has never been effective, is caught among powerful interests, and is unable to make the major adjustments which may be needed in Stage 3.

Current Issues

The optimal policy treatment would balance (1) the profit and price constraints and (2) the various new competitive policies with the need to keep the carriers viable. In practice, the carriers have dominated these choices, so that the degree of social control has been low. Several current issues may be altering this situation.

The Great FCC Investigation (Phases 1 and 2). During 1962–65, the FCC studied Western Union's plight and possible remedies. A prime question was whether the Bell System competed unfairly, using price discrimination to optimize its monopoly position at the expense of West-

---

[4] Meanwhile the Bell System's ability to manage its large system efficiently was being eroded: see Jack Ross and Michael Kami, *Corporate Management in Crisis* (Englewood Cliffs, N.J.: Prentice-Hall, 1974).

[5] There is no clear technological basis in the pattern of single-state and multiple-state companies; single-state companies range from very large (New York, with 11 million telephones) to very small (Delaware, with only 300,000). The situation appears to be ripe for revision, with perhaps a major extension of FCC jurisdiction. Yet the FCC has made no move to assert this jurisdiction, and indeed it does not have the staff to do so.

ern Union and others.[6] This led the FCC to plan its first full hearings on rate of return (Phase 1A), rate structure (Phase 1B), and Western Electric's role, etc. (Phase 2). Despite vehement AT&T resistance, Phase 1 began in 1966 and the rate-structure hearings in 1967. In 1971 the FCC announced that it would abandon Phase 2, for lack of resources. A sharp public outcry and quick promises of more funds followed, and the study was reinstated. It has yet to produce visible results, though it may have encouraged the Antitrust Division's 1974 suit against AT&T.

Rate of Return.   The main outcomes have been to debate the criteria for profits and price structure at length. Permitted rates of return have been raised, much as new conditions would have warranted in any event.[7] It was apparent that actual profit rates had moved out of line with permitted rates for long periods.To this extent the FCC followed events, not controlled them.

Further rises in profit rates have been permitted since 1970, as the cost of capital has risen, and the promotional rate structure has continued to erode revenues. The FCC and state commissions have had leverage, but they have used it very sparingly, as before. They have also proven to be nimble in granting increases far more briskly than in the earlier eras. That the rates of return have been tightened is clearly seen in the decline of AT&T market value toward book value (Figure 16-2).

State regulation of Bell System profit rates has a certain surreal quality. The operating companies are only parts of a larger system, and so their risk and performance are virtually impossible to assess. Only AT&T stock is on the market, and so state regulators have little to compare their own appraisals with and no direct way to test the financial effects of their actions.

Rate Structure.   Rate structure resolved into the old basic contest. The FCC staff favored cost as the standard. Bell officials and witnesses favored "value-of-service" pricing (discrimination); long-run marginal cost plus a variable margin based on differing degrees of competition.

Local Pricing.   None of this touched the local price structures, which the states regulate. This pricing—your phone bill—has always been promotional, with a flat monthly fee and *zero* price for each call. This has induced extra use, including added peak load and indifference to the length of the call (see Figure 16-3). This also erodes revenues, by reducing the average revenue per unit as growth occurs. The degree of inefficiency depends mainly on the elasticity of demand and on the cost gradients.

Since 1965 the burden of this has slowly been recognized, and message unit pricing has spread from business use and large cities down to residence use in medium-sized cities. With smaller monthly fees and roughly a 5 cents charge per call, the rates now fit cost conditions more

---

[6] Also, the FCC's effectiveness was very much in doubt. Booz, Allen & Hamilton, a firm of management consultants, in a report prepared for the Bureau of the Budget in 1962, asserted that the FCC was not organized, staffed, or equipped to do a thorough regulatory job; that its investigations of costs were superficial; that it had developed no criteria to govern rates of return; and that it was therefore unable to determine the reasonableness of telephone rates.

[7] But this involved some actual *cuts* in long-distance rates during 1967–70.

FIGURE 16–4
Illustration of Local-Service Telephone Pricing

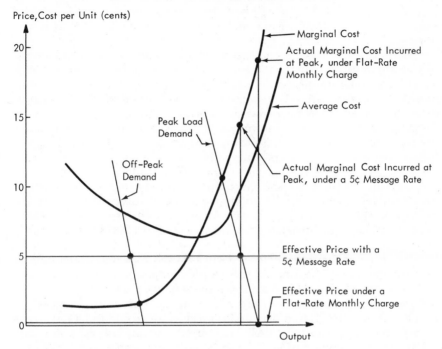

Price,Cost per Unit (cents)

closely. But they still usually ignore the timing and length of calls, so that peak use is still enhanced.

In most European systems, pricing has long been more rational. Metering is usually precise, so that prices can be closely fitted to the true costs of peak and off-peak use.[8] Only now are U.S. metering equipment and pricing beginning to move toward the sophistication which has long existed abroad.

In the U.S., prices also vary between users (business rentals are higher) and among basic and optional services.[9] Discrimination is common. The monthly rentals charged for added equipment, for instance, ($1 to $1.25 for a "Princess" phone, 90 cents for an extension phone, and 35 cents for an extension cord) are based, not on costs ($4.20 a year yields an astronomical return on the company's investment of a few pennies in a length of wire), but on the subscriber's docility. Business users are charged more than domestic users because they find the service indispensable. Domestic users are charged more for single party lines because they are willing to pay for added convenience. They are charged less for

---

[8] See W. G. Shepherd, "Residence Expansion in the British Telephone System," *Journal of Industrial Economics,* 1966, pp. 263–74.

[9] Also, rates have long been higher for cities than towns, with steep gradients across the range of sizes. This made good political sense, but it did not fit cost patterns. Recently, these differences have been narrowed, and rough equality is likely to be reached eventually.

multiple-party lines because low rates are needed to bring about the widest possible use of the service. And the more widely the service is used, the more valuable it will be to those who can be made to pay the higher rates. The structure of telephone rates is deliberately discriminatory.

Yet there are marked recent shifts toward costing services and charging for them. Most of this is at company initiative, under the new scarcity conditions. The prices are increasingly—often bewilderingly—complex.[10] The commissions have simply approved, often despite bitter protests that the changes harm various worthy groups.

Long Distance Rates. Intercity call prices, of course, fit costs much more closely. Costs are higher during busy hours and with operator help; prices are too. The carriers' thoroughness and ingenuity in this area contrast with their clinging to discrimination at the local level.

Until the 60s there was no sharp differentiation in the rates charged by AT&T for various types of interstate services, those for each service bearing a similar relation to its costs. During the 40s, Western Union and AT&T had each constructed a microwave (radio-relay) system to carry a portion of its messages. Then, in 1959, the FCC ruled that airspace in the band above 890 megacylces might be used for communication by private operators. This opened the door to competition with the private carriers. And it led AT&T to overhaul the structure of its rates. Rates for telephonic communication were not changed. But rates for teletypewriter service (TWX) and private line service were cut and a new class of private line service (TELPAK) was introduced, providing volume discounts for the full use of packages of channels between specific points for a month or more at a time. As a result, rates for these services were set at 51 to 85 percent of their previous levels.

This differentiation in the pattern of Bell's rates led Western Union to complain that AT&T was engaging in unfair competition, using its monopoly of telephonic service to subsidize its TWX and private line telegraphic services. Consequently, as a part of its investigation of the telegraph industry, the FCC requested AT&T to report to it on its investment, expenses, revenues, and earnings in each of seven categories of interstate service, showing its net earnings, in each case, as a return on the portion of its investment allocated to that service.

Bell's report on its seven-way cost study was submitted in 1965. It revealed a wide discrepancy in earnings from the different services. The average rate of return for all of the services stood at 7.5 percent. The rate for the telephone service was 10 percent; that for TWX was 2.9 percent; that for TELPAK was 0.3 percent. These figures lent support to Western Union's charge that Bell was engaging in undue discrimination in its competition for the private line business.

The Commission's staff shared this view. Bell, they argued, should be required to set its rate for each service at a level that would cover its fully-allocated costs and yield a fair return on its investment. The FCC would therefore set higher rates on TELPAK and others like it.

---

[10] Thus the new rates announced by the New York Telephone Company on November 27, 1974, filled 1 2/3 pages of the New York *Times* with small print. There were 18 different categories of prices.

The staff's fully-allocated-cost rule may go too far, but it does try to offset the carrier's ability to discriminate so as to eliminate competition entirely. Predictably, TELPAK has attracted hundreds of major customers, and these form a powerful opposition to increases in TELPAK rates. After 12 years of efforts by the FCC to get adequate revisions by the Bell System—and of amazing procedural delays and tactics—TELPAK rates are still the subject of sharp controversy, and the issue is not resolved. The whole episode shows the ability of a monopolist even—or especially—under regulation to enter or capture a market at below-normal pricing (recall Chapter 14).

Western Electric. The continuing FCC study also includes the role of vertical integration. An antitrust solution was begun in 1949 and 1965–67, and twice aborted (recall Chapter 7). In the 1956 decree, no way was provided for outside suppliers to compete in the sale of equipment to Bell operating companies, and little has been done in this direction since. At the same time, Western Electric agreed to produce only telephone equipment, for sale largely in the Bell System and to government agencies; since then it has not bothered to enter competition in foreign markets, regarding itself as fully occupied with domestic responsibilities.

Thus the consent decree of 1956 operates as a détente, which at one stroke eliminates two possibilities for new competition. It leaves intact what is probably the country's largest industrial monopoly (in Bell System supplies, currently about $5 billion annually) and at the same time it excludes Western Electric from competing in other communications and electronic equipment markets, many of them substantial. Even if the Phase 2 FCC study recommends major changes, the FCC probably lacks powers to enforce the changes. AT&T regards retention of Western Electric as supremely important, and it has the proven skill and resources to get its way. At the most, some modifications toward outside purchasing might gradually be required.

The new Antitrust Division suit filed in 1974 opens up the issue for an airing at trial and possibly a real change (recall Chapter 7). The suit makes no detailed suggestions for remedy. The optimal changes will depend on the conditions as they are brought out—at long last—at trial. The process seems likely to be long and intense, lasting 15 years or more, unless cut short by compromise or surrender.

Parallel Systems. The carriers have always been paralleled by a variety of private specialized operators (railroads, certain large firms), but they have always avoided letting them interconnect. Yet—as technology ripens and Stage 3 continues—the basis for connected and competing systems has evolved. This is already true of the main intercity routes (e.g., New York-Chicago), and it appears to be evolving with cable TV in the cities. The FCC first permitted the Bell System to capture microwave in 1948–50, then decided in 1968 to let some competition in. Many Bell officials regard the issue as crucial to the system's survival. Its handling tells much about FCC policies and powers.

Microwave during 1946–69. Microwave technology dates back to well before its first public demonstration in 1915, and a variety of public and private groups—American and British—participated in its development during the 1930s and World War II. By 1944, microwave had emerged as the obvious technique for meeting the massive increase in broad-band intercity transmission capacity that television would require in the post-war years. By 1946, several firms had created or planned microwave capacity between major eastern cities and had applied for an FCC franchise, with further expansion in prospect.[11] The Bell System recognized the advantages it could gain in displacing these independent systems, and it proceeded to do so with utmost thoroughness.

It mounted a large, rapid two-stage innovation effort between 1946 and 1950 to create a nationwide microwave relay system—called the TD-2—to preempt the microwave field. This involved a crash program to make the technology operational quickly. The new system also displaced much of a large expansion of coaxial cable capacity that had been projected by the Bell System in 1946. The program was extensive and costly, and some specific expenditures no doubt yielded a low social return, even though they evidently generated high private returns to the Bell System by helping to assure its control of this crucial area. The development was telescoped into about three years. By this quick, costly stroke, the Bell System had acted quickly enough to take over virtually the entire domestic microwave carrier field.

Meanwhile, AT&T unremittingly refused to interconnect with rival microwave systems. As on other issues, the refusals were not supported by quantitative evidence about quality of service and other marginal costs and benefits that might be involved. By the period 1949–50 the Bell System had succeeded in maneuvering the FCC into converting the microwave field—with much potential for fruitful competition—into a monopoly, not only of transmission operations but also of equipment manufacturing. Indeed, control extended even further. The FCC excluded all private microwave until 1959. Only when the FCC's "Above 890" decision removed that exclusion did the Bell System respond with the TELPAK offering and related data-transmission services.

After 1952 microwave innovation reverted back from costly and uncharacteristic revolution to the System's traditional approach of evolution. The subsequent improvements have involved frequent cost overruns and slippages of schedule, in contrast to the extreme speed and precision with which Bell established TD-2 under competitive pressure.[12] Yet for low-density-route, short-haul radio systems, which are under competitive pressure, the Bell System has again responded quickly, with tight scheduling and generous R&D resources. During the 1960s, renewed efforts to open trunk-route microwave transmission have

---

[11] F. M. Scherer, "The Development of the TD-X and TD-2 Microwave Radio Relay Systems in Bell Telephone Laboratories," Weapons Acquisition Research Project, Harvard Business School (October 1960; mimeographed); A. C. Dickieson, "The TD2 Story: Changing for the Future," *Bell Laboratories Record,* Vol. 45 (December 1967), pp. 357–63; and Donald C. Beelar, "Cables in the Sky and the Struggle for Their Control," *Federal Communications Bar Journal,* Vol. 21 (January 1967), pp. 26–41.

[12] Weapons Acquisition Research Project, "Development of the TD-X," Chap. 6; and "Development of TH and TJ Microwave Radio Relay Transmission Systems." The TH system "slipped approximately five years from the original completion date of December, 1955, established in August, 1952." The lack of competitive pressures for TH appears to have been partly responsible for the difference.

been deflected by the FCC's reluctance to order the Bell System to interconnect with independent systems. And Bell has imitated consistently —and filed exclusive tariffs for—new service offerings by potential entrants wherever they have begun to attract the serious interest of the FCC.

MCI and Competition since 1969. By the middle 1960s, mainline data traffic had grown so large that new competition was quite feasible. The Bell System resisted, charging that parallel systems would merely skim off these markets the cream which was needed to support the whole system. When a small firm—Microwave Communications, Inc. (MCI) —applied for FCC approval, Bell refused to let MCI interconnect. MCI sought to provide cheaper economy-grade service. This challenged both the pricing and the quality criteria of long-standing Bell System practice.

In 1969, the FCC approved MCI's entry, reversing decades of protective policy. Further delay ensued as the Bell System exhausted its tactical opportunities for rearguing, etc., but MCI has eventually begun carrying signals. Predictably, it has joined with Bell in resisting further entry by *other* new firms! The Bell System has also responded with sharp price cuts in certain services; this is well within its ability to allocate overhead costs among these and other services. The FCC's impossible task is to determine if these price cuts are "just and reasonable."

Satellites. Even deeper changes may be brought by satellites (as noted above). By 1969, seven *international* satellites were in orbit, tied in with 40 ground stations in 25 countries. Much larger new ones have been added more recently.

Their use over the U.S. has waited for more than ten years, as the many interests have contended and regrouped. Against the natural Bell System interest in adding this to their system, there are such others as Western Union, Comsat (which operates international satellites), the TV networks, various electronics firms, IBM, public broadcasting, the Ford Foundation, etc.[13]

The problem was, in fact, too big for the FCC to decide—or even arbitrate—and in 1970 a remarkable White House initiative set an open-access policy for domestic satellites. All qualified applicants will be able to send up and operate satellites. By 1974, several had gained approval. Though the Bell System still held the trump card of interconnection, new technology is reducing its power. In any event, the Bell System will be only one among several operators, by contrast with the earlier microwave outcome.

In short, the Bell System's grip on mainline transmission is no longer fully exclusive, though the inroads are only marginal so far and can still be closely influenced by the Bell System. Whether this will seriously affect the system's viability is in doubt. Despite Bell alarums, the impact seems likely to be modest, partly because Bell still controls the tech-

---

[13] Comsat is a mixed private corporation, created in 1962 after efforts to use a public enterprise form were defeated in Congress. It has a franchised monopoly, is under FCC regulation, and does earn a profit. It has tried and partially succeeded in capturing the U.S. domestic satellite market. It competes with transoceanic cable (owned by the Bell System) and has had excess capacity for most of its life so far. Its shares were issued at $20, rose as high as $70, but have settled at about $30.

nology. Also, the FCC is ready to avert any harmful effects, if they should emerge.

Terminal Equipment. Until 1969, the Bell System forbade its subscribers to attach to their phones—by *any* means, electrical, inductive, or acoustical—any equipment not provided by Bell, contending that such attachments might impair the quality of its service. The company thus attempted to prevent the use of one-piece Swedish handsets, of antique handsets, of simple "Hush-a-phone" mouthpieces that enabled users to converse without being heard by other persons in the room, and of other non-Bell devices. Such restrictions curbed the growth of independent phone systems and helped AT&T to maintain its monopolies of the long-distance telephone and television transmission markets.

Bell's rule was challenged in the 1960s by the Carterfone Company, a tiny Texas firm making a coupling device that plugged two-way mobile radio communications systems into subscribers' telephone lines, so that any phone could be used to communicate with radio-dispatched vehicles. AT&T had put Carter out of business by harassing its customers. Carter brought suit under the antitrust laws and the court referred the question to the FCC. In 1968, the Commission outlawed Bell's attachment rule, holding it to be unreasonable and discriminatory. The telephone subscriber, said the Commission, has the right to attach any device that serves his convenience without detriment to others.

This decision made possible the use of a variety of devices, not only those that tied radio communications systems into telephone lines but also units such as tape recorders, push-button phones, small-business switchboards, and closed-circuit TV, and devices that permit abbreviated dialing, talking by phone through speakers located anywhere in a room, switching office calls to home phones, and the like. The decision appeared to put an end to Bell's monopoly in all such fields and opened the way to competitive development. Users now have a much wider choice of apparatus. They must pay for an interfacing device provided by the Bell System (there are over 70 specific devices, for varying conditions). This monthly fee is not small, and so it does limit the range of terminal equipment which can be used.

Bell officials had warned that systemic integrity would be harmed by permitting "foreign attachments," as it called them. Instead, no severe effects have occurred, and the financial impact on the Bell System has been slight.[14] Innovation and choice in the apparatus market has been greatly stimulated.

Bell resistance to competitors' attachments is still strong, often leading to sharp tactics and pressures upon customers to reject non-Bell

---

[14] By 1973, interconnect sales by outsiders will still be less than 3 percent of all Western Electric sales. Yet the Bell System has begun to try regaining its control by asking *state* commissions to prohibit "foreign attachments."

In Canada, an intense struggle has arisen since 1970 over IBM's efforts to supply equipment for the growing data processing network. Trans-Canada Telephone System (a national company owned by Canada's eight largest regional telephone companies—two of which are owned by provincial governments) will choose the system format and apparatus. Bell Canada and other telephone companies are competing with IBM for a large part of the most lucrative service and equipment markets.

equipment. This helped stir the Division's 1974 suit, which seeks to end such abuses. For this, too, separating Western Electric from AT&T would be necessary.

Summary

Regulation has recently begun to reverse its long passivity to the carriers' policies on pricing, profits, and market control. The new scarcities are also inducing the carriers to revise pricing more in line with costs. Discrimination is at last coming under analysis. And the margin of competition is being drawn more carefully and tightly than before.[15]

The FCC's awakening has, however, yielded only marginal changes so far. And it has not been matched at the state level. This may reflect that the basic problems are beyond their scope. But it also reflects the limitations of state regulation, in resources and perspective, as it is forced to deal with small parts of national problems.

BROADCASTING

Regulation of broadcasting is a hybrid. There are several suppliers, not one. Regulation deals with market control and, obliquely, program content, not with profit and price constraints. It reviews and renews franchises, rather than leaving them frozen as in other utilities. Part of its sector—radio—is now in Stage 4, on a competitive basis. Regulation is strictly at the federal level. And it is now entangled in the stressful introduction of new forms (cable TV, pay TV, public broadcasting) which touch on deep vested interests.

In all this, the FCC is mainly an arbiter or compromiser, dividing up the cake, not an expert group applying clear criteria to functional economic problems. The basic economics of broadcasting would support a great degree of diversity, among modes and within each mode. Yet the FCC has consistently reduced that diversity—first in radio and then in letting the radio networks come to dominate television—and helped to retard the use of new technology. The FCC was added on after the basic structure was set, and it has inevitably had a protective role.

The social goals are of two kinds: (1) *economic efficiency,* in meeting consumer preferences, and (2) *content,* especially local interest, diversity, and culture. These further divide into (a) *localism,* fitting local interests, (b) *diversity,* servicing the whole range of social and cultural interests, and (c) *minimum quality,* avoiding harmful effects, such as inculcating violence or exploiting ignorance in children. The main reason for regulation would be a divergence between the two, and indeed the FCC *has* tried to influence content. The whole social impact of this

---

[15] The Bell System has responded since 1972 with a campaign against "competitive experiments" in microwave, terminal equipment, and other areas. The state commissions' interest group—the National Association of Regulatory Utility Commissioners—joined Bell's effort, with a 95 page report and a legal challenge to the MCI decision before a state commission in 1973.

Bell officials knew, of course, that the Division's suit was in the works. Their campaign could neatly anticipate the filing, or even make it less likely to occur.

regulation could—in a society where people watch more than 3 hours *per day* on average—far surpass any regulatory result in other sectors. The actual impact is obscure and possibly even negative.

First we need to understand the economics of the sector. Then the nature and effects of regulation can be assessed.

The Sector

Broadcasting is mainly television, both by size and by public impact (see Table 16–4). Television is primarily the three private networks (ABC, CBS, and NBC), plus some 438 affiliated stations. Revenues are primarily from advertising; exceptions are cable TV (mainly subscriptions) and public broadcasting (public and foundation funds). Advertisers, in turn, choose freely among all types of media (newspapers, magazines, TV, radio, etc.), and other selling devices (sales networks, discounts, etc.). Therefore the demand for broadcast advertising is —usually—highly elastic. Moreover, television especially attracts mass advertising, because the other media and devices are more attunable to specific groups.

TABLE 16–4
Revenues ($ million)

	1961	*1971*
Television	1,318	2,750
Radio	591	1,258
Cable TV	20	150

Broadcasting mingles city and national markets. Viewership appears to be roughly constant, regardless of the number of stations. Profits therefore depend critically on the number of stations in each market and on the ability to stretch overhead costs. The present structure—with three dominant networks and a relatively few stations even in the largest cities—reflects the pressure to achieve scale economies and to limit competition. Technology is not close to natural monopoly, and content is more responsive when there are at least three sources. But more stations would be viable in most of the larger markets than are now permitted.

Background. The present TV structure grew directly from the early radio patterns of the 1920s. Communication by radio dates from the discoveries of Guglielmo Marconi in Italy around the turn of the century and from subsequent developments by Ambrose Fleming in England and by Lee De Forest and E. H. Armstrong, among others, in the United States. The first public broadcast in this country, using the method of amplitude modulation, occurred in 1920 when Westinghouse station KDKA in Pittsburgh announced the election of Warren G. Harding. Other stations were soon established by Westinghouse, General Electric, and AT&T. It was assumed, at this time, that broadcasting was to be financed by manufacturers of receiving sets and, perhaps, by educational institutions and city governments. Then, in 1922, commercial broadcasting was inaugurated by the AT&T station, WEAF in New York, and radio shortly became an advertising medium. The first network was set up by AT&T in 1923. Then, following an agreement with GE, Westinghouse, and their patent-holding company, RCA, in 1926, AT&T withdrew from the field, its network being taken over by an RCA subsidiary, the National Broadcasting Company. The Columbia Broadcasting System was set up in the following year. Network domination of the broadcasting business dates from this time. Frequency modulation broadcasting, on a commercial basis, was authorized in 1940, television in 1941, and color television in 1951. The business has grown phenomenally. There were 7,500 broadcasting stations in the United States in 1974 and receiving sets in more than 60 million homes. Radio and television programs were reaching almost all of the country's population. Cable TV has also grown since 1950, toward real importance by the early 1970s.

Early radio had no fixed frequencies for stations, until in 1927 regulation was imposed to allocate the radio spectrum. The new Federal Radio Commission accepted and favored the commercial network structure; it had few powers and slight resources. R. A. Coase has noted that this spectrum allocation was inappropriate, since spectrum was not in fact scarce and the net effect was to create unjustified monopoly.[16] By the time the FCC was assigned broadcasting regulation in 1934, the situation was the conventional one: regulation added after the industry is formed, increasing the degree of monopoly.

Radio's heyday was 1925–50. Its rigid structure dissolved during 1950–65 back toward effective competition. The radio networks predictably influenced the FCC to extend their dominance into television, when it arose after 1945. At first the FCC allotted to television only the very high frequency band (VHF) of 54 to 216 megacycles per second, which has room for only 12 stations in any area. (In practice no more than six stations can operate well, because of mutual interference.) Television was structured around these few channels. Though 70 ultrahigh frequency (UHF) channels were later authorized (1952), it was only in 1962 that the FCC began requiring new sets to have UHF tuning. UHF stations, dominated by the networks, have therefore dominated commercial broadcasting. Network and VHF station profits fully reflect this market position (see Table 16–5). The really big profits (including most of the networks' profits) are creamed off in the few very largest cities: rates of return there are probably over 300 percent yearly.[17]

Cable TV began in 1950, simply to help small town viewers pull in distant signals. It grew and by 1960 was ready to offer better pictures and newer services in major cities. But the FCC blocked it entirely from the 100 largest cities until 1972, primarily in order to protect TV broadcasters' interests, though assertedly to protect the more vulnerable UHF stations. Though cable TV could greatly enrich intracity communication —and offer local and national programming now neglected by

---

[16] R. A. Coase, "The Federal Communications Commission," *Journal of Law and Economics,* Vol. 2 (October 1959), pp. 1–40.

[17] Roger G. Noll, M. J. Peck and J. McGowan, *Economic Aspects of Television Regulation* (Washington, D.C.: Brookings Institution, 1973), p. 17.

TABLE 16-5

Profitability in U.S. Broadcasting, 1971

	Number of Stations	Broadcast Revenues	Broadcast Expenses	Net Profits before Tax	Net Tangible Investment	Profit Rate on Net Investment (percent)
		($ millions)				
Television						
3 networks and their 15 stations....	15	1,378	1,237	144	142	101
Other VHF stations.................	438	1,223	946	277	466	59
UHF stations.....................	145	148	181	−33	122	−27
Radio						
AM, AM-FM stations (partly network related)	6,040	1,176	1,059	118	406	29
Independent FM..................	548	82	47	−15	47	−32

Source: Federal Communications Commission, *Annual Report*, 1972.

broadcasters—it is only now being permitted tc develop. Eventually it may breed complex two-way communications, a variety of special-interest pay TV, and social programming (see below).

It is clear that TV and radio broadcasting generate consumer benefits which greatly exceed the costs of their (1) production and of (2) consump-

TABLE 16–6
Network TV Offerings, Fall 1974

		8:00	8:30	9:00	9:30	10:00	10:30	11:00
SUNDAY	ABC	Sonny Comedy Review		Movie re-run ──────────────────────▶				
	CBS	Apple's Way	Kojak (crime)		Mannix (crime)		Protectors (crime)	
	NBC	Disney	TV Movie (mystery) ──────────────────▶				Profiles in Black	
MONDAY	ABC	The Rookies (crime)		Professional football game ─────────────▶				
	CBS	Gunsmoke (western)		Maude	Rhoda (comedy)	Medical Center		
	NBC	Family Theatre (drama)		Movie re-run ──────────────────────▶				
TUESDAY	ABC	TV Movie ───────────────────────────▶				Marcus Welby, M.D. (medical)		
	CBS	Good Times (comedy)	M.A.S.H. (comedy)	Hawaii Five-0 (crime)		CBS Reports		
	NBC	Adam 12 (crime)	TV Movie ───────────────────────────▶					
WEDNESDAY	ABC	That's My Mama (comedy)	TV Movie ──────────────────▶			Get Christie Love! (crime)		
	CBS	Sons and Daughters (drama)		Cannon (crime)		Manhunter (crime)		
	NBC	Little House on the Prairie		Lucas Tanner (drama)		Petrocelli (drama)		
THURSDAY	ABC	Odd Couple (comedy)	Paper Moon	Streets of San Francisco (crime)		Harry O (crime)		
	CBS	The Waltons		Movie re-run ──────────────────────▶				
	NBC	Sierra (drama)		Ironside (crime)		Movin' On (drama)		
FRIDAY	ABC	Movie re-run ───────────────────────────▶						
	CBS	Planet of the Apes		Movie re-run ──────────────────────▶				
	NBC	Sanford and Son	Chico and the Man (comedy)	Rockford Files (crime)		Police Woman (crime)		
SATURDAY	ABC	The New Land (drama)		Kung Fu (western)		Nakia (crime)		
	CBS	All in the Family	Friends and Lovers	Mary Tyler Moore	Bob Newhart	CBS Reports		
	NBC	Emergency (medical)		TV Movie ───────────────────────────▶				

tion (sets, electricity, etc.).[18] Yet it clearly operates below its social potential. Its technology is too narrow, and its offerings are also culturally narrow, neglecting a variety of viewing interests.

The basic reason for this lies in advertising as the source of TV revenues. TV offerings are a side effect of—or a vehicle for—advertising messages. These messages, in turn, are most efficiently delivered to mass audiences on a nationwide basis. It is well-known that oligopolists will cluster at the center of a market (e.g., the middle of a town), and so TV advertising and programming tends toward identity at the *cultural* mean reflecting the most viewers' *tastes.*[19] These tastes are, in turn, subject to molding by the media and advertisers. The outcome—as shown in the fall 1974 network offerings, in Table 16–6—tends toward standard light fare. And networking, with its ability to spread costs over a large audience, has crowded out most local content.[20]

The fewness of networks adds to the narrowness. If there were five or six networks rather than three, the willingness of some of them to cater to specialized audiences would be much greater.[21] Oddly, at the other extreme, collusion or outright monopoly would probably *increase* the variety of content, compared to the three-network competition for the center of the mass market. Figure 16–5 illustrates the general pattern.

FIGURE 16–5
Diversity Varies with the Degree of Competition

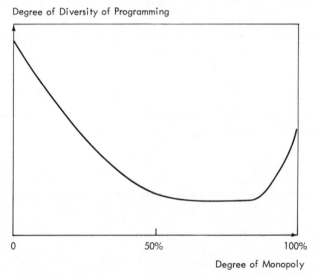

Degree of Diversity of Programming

0   50%   100%

Degree of Monopoly

---

[18] *Ibid.,* pp. 20–26.

[19] See P. O. Steiner, "Program Patterns and Preferences, and the Workability of Competition in Radio Broadcasting," *Quarterly Journal of Economics,* Vol. 66 (May 1952) pp. 194–223.

[20] Extensive studies of Oklahoma, New York, the District of Columbia, Maryland, Virginia and West Virginia were made by FCC members Kenneth Cox and Nicholas Johnson during 1969–72. They showed "local" programming to be less than 20 percent, often much less, and to be mainly weather, sports, and news. Noll, Peck and McGowan, pp. 108–16.

[21] Noll, Peck and McGowan, *op. cit.,* pp. 49–54.

The freeness of advertising-based broadcasting further cramps diversity. Viewers cannot directly respond to existing programs. Rating services do reflect viewing, and purchases may vaguely respond to the program content as well as the advertisement. But intensively felt preferences go unrecognized. And one—or a group—has no direct way to foster programs that are not offered. Some device for "pay TV" therefore is needed to supplement the present system.[22]

Further, social impacts of TV content—violence is the most obvious possibility, among many—are simply irrelevant to advertising-financed choices. External costs may occur and external benefits be ignored, though—in a society with near-saturation viewing—they are likely to be large.

In short, the present network structure and financing basis are probably close to the least favorable economic setting for program diversity, even though U.S. citizens' interests are astonishingly diverse!

Policies

FCC "policies" have caused—or at least facilitated—much of this narrowness. The FCC has tried to promote a balanced degree of competition and innovation, while encouraging localism. Nobody's appraisal is definitive, but it seems probable that the FCC has maintained too much market control, retarded innovation, and achieved little local content.

Allocating Spectrum. From the start in 1927, the FCC's spectrum allocation has been crucial. In TV, the primacy of the scarce VHF channels is an FCC artifact, which consigned the great mass of UHF slots to limbo. And within VHF, the scarcity operates to create especially large economic rent for stations in the largest cities (see Table 16–7). The 15 next largest cities have the highest profit margins—around 30 percent. This reflects their fewer stations: 4.3 on average. But the return in capital is highest in the largest cities.[23] These profits have naturally been capitalized: probably half of the asset value of stations is the value of the franchise itself. The FCC's contrived scarcity created the value as a gift to the lucky ones who got franchises. And the FCC has no powers to limit the resulting profits or pricing behavior. It is widely agreed that some version of an auction system for franchises would be more efficient and fair, with proceeds going to the public purse or to enriching the content of broadcasting. Yet the past excess profits are effectively out of reach, being part of present value. And the FCC has not responded to the many authoritative and sophisticated proposals for auctions or other ways of skimming off the excess profits it has created. The alternatives are noted in Table 16–8.[24]

---

[22] There is of course an extensive process by which network personnel try to predict viewers' interests, select programs, and then interact with station managers in trying to sell them. That such a massive process *still* gives forth bland, narrow content indicates that the basic incentives are defective.

[23] See Harvey J. Levin, "Economic Effects of Broadcast Licensing," *Journal of Political Economy,* Vol. 72 (April 1964), pp. 151–62.

[24] See Harvey J. Levin, "Spectrum Allocation without Markets," *American Economic Review,* Vol. 60 (May 1970), pp. 209–18; and sources cited there for a full discussion of the alternatives.

TABLE 16-7

Broadcasting in the Largest Cities

	Number of Stations per City	Sales of Time		Total Broadcast Revenues	Profit before Tax	Profit as a Percent of Broadcast Revenue
		Total	Local Only			
		($ million)		($ million)		(percent)
New York	8	133	28	140	32	22.8
Los Angeles	11	90	40	110	22	22.0
Chicago	7	75	21	84	20	23.9
Philadelphia	6	45	22	57	12	21.1
San Francisco	7	45	15	49	13	26.5
Boston	5	43	14	47	15	32.0
Detroit	5	36	14	43	16	37.2
These 7 TV markets	7	467	154	530	130	24.6
All other TV stations	658	1,413	483	1,126	205	18.2
15 next largest cities	4.3					

Source: Federal Communications Commission, *Annual Report*, 1972

TABLE 16–8

Alternatives to the Current System of Spectrum Allocation

A. Freely-transferable Rights.
   1. Rights created in the courts under tort law, through inclusion and exclusion, with spectrum bought and sold outright, like land.
   2. Federal designation of rights, leaving them freely-transferable after their subsequent sale outright.
   3. Federal designation of rights, periodic competitive leasing for limited periods, with lessees substantially free to transfer at will.
B. Auctions of Federally-designated Radiation Rights.
   1. Interband contests to determine reallocation as between different services, in addition to intraband contests limited to like users within the same service.
   2. Interband contests to ration grants among like users, within different services competing for the same spectrum, with managers free to utilize the resultant values in further reallocation of spectrum between the two services.
   3. Intraband contests within a single service to ration rights there, with results used to set user charges elsewhere too.
C. User Charges.
   Applied on occupied three-dimensional spectrum as measured by some index of physical usage.
   1. Per unit rates derived from intraband auction values.
   2. Per unit rates derived from estimated shadow prices.
   3. Per unit rates set at some arbitrary flat dollar rate.
D. Shadow Prices.
   Derived from maximum sums that current spectrum users and systems designers would be willing to pay rather than do without some small amount of spectrum.
E. New Administrative Techniques.
   Greater role for frequency clearance,* secondary rights,† and a heavier burden of proof on spectrum managers where they deliberately override economic considerations.

---

* The requirement that federal government users secure prior authorization to use particular frequencies (from the Director of Telecommunications Management) before disbursing funds to develop or build any communications system.

† Rights to share or borrow frequencies contingent on noninterference with rights of the primary user.

Source: Harvey J. Levin (see footnote 24)

Meanwhile UHF continues unprofitable. Its development is one prime way to increase diversity. The other main way is cable TV.

Cable TV. The FCC prevented the growth of cable TV in the major city markets during the 1960s. Yet the economics of cable (see Figure 16–6) offers decreasing costs and an escape from the scarcity of channels. The cost function for over-the-air service rises, because UHF channels are more costly and less efficient than VHF. But cable costs per channel fall, because the marginal cost of added channels on an existing system is virtually zero.[25] Cable can replace the high economic rents created by over-the-air TV with low cost and a technologically richer service. Cable TV offers special possibilities for *local* service. Ultimately, wired cities systems—with refined two-way signalling, information and entertain-

---

[25] Harold J. Barnett, "Perspectives on Cable TV Regulation," in Shepherd and Gies, *Regulation in Further Perspective, op. cit.*

FIGURE 16–6
Broadcast and Cable TV Costs Diverge, as Demand Rises

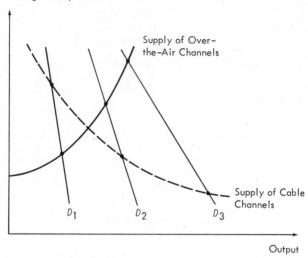

ment banks, free public access, news and other local services—may result. Indeed, if and as cable technology matures, *it may converge with local telephone technology.* In the 1980s, an eventual fusion of cable TV and telephone systems may be a major policy issue: who will own it, what content and access will it provide, and how might it be regulated?

Meanwhile, the FCC impeded cable TV growth until 1972, claiming that it would undermine free TV. In 1962, 1963, and 1965, it forbade importing programs for use on cable. In 1966 it affirmed that cable TV was to be supplementary and proposed prohibiting cable systems from originating programs. In 1966 and 1968 the FCC virtually prohibited cable systems in the largest 100 cities, and it limited the cable firm's own program origination to just one channel.

This protective policy changed partway in 1972. Cable TV can at last import signals, originate multiple programs, and operate multiple channels. But a host of restrictions remain, to protect the older TV interests: indeed, the new policy is roughly a compromise struck between the old and new interests and stamped "Approved" by the FCC.[26] Regulation is

---

[26] Thus, the FCC has still

1. limited CATV imports of commercial station signals to two in the 100 largest markets; and in smaller markets which are served by three networks and one independent station, denied commercial station imports altogether;
2. required that the two imported signals, where authorized, be from nearby cities, rather than leading stations from New York, Los Angeles, Chicago, or elsewhere;
3. imposed program exclusivity protection for local stations, whereby CATV may not duplicate local station programs for a year or two, and must black out such programs on imported signals;
4. imposed strong blackout restrictions on CATV importation or carriage of sports programs;
5. denied carriage by CATV of the signals which can, in fact, be received over-the-air from nearby "overlapping" markets;

still extensive and protective, though a complete FCC withdrawal from regulating cable TV would make economic sense.[27]

Cable TV is not yet thriving in the larger cities. The 1970–74 vintage firms are expected to have hard financial times, and perhaps only in 1978–85 will the technology ripen, as subscription TV, specialties, and two-way capabilities are developed. Networking of cable systems may develop, mingling national with local programming. Open public use of several channels offers large external benefits: it gives the only free access to media for all shades of local social and political opinion. Cable can eventually supply much of the balance to network TV by adding pay cable TV, which provides content in direct response to viewers' preferences.[28] This plus the developing public network will at last provide an approximation of efficient broadcasting performance.

Cross-media Ownership. The FCC has permitted a byzantine and monopolistic world of combined newspaper and TV ownership to evolve. By 1971, 231 daily newspapers were jointly owned by broadcast licenses in the same city.[29] In many cities, the one radio or TV station is owned by the one newspaper. In most major cities there is an important degree of joint ownership. This clearly creates monopoly in the local markets for advertising, news, and entertainment. This in turn has monopoly effects in these markets.[30] This policy continues largely unmodified.

License Renewals. The FCC hands out and renews valuable prizes which its own market controls have created. Grants have been a highly charged and—in the 1950s—partly corrupt process. Renewals have been mostly automatic; yet they offer an unorthodox regulatory opportunity to enforce "good" performance. The criteria officially include residence, experience, the nature of proposed programs, and past performance. But the choices, even at best, are subjective and speculative, often involving grandiose claims, counterclaims and promises.

In practice, it has been a murky business, with little content or consist-

---

6. emasculated cable pay-TV by prohibiting programs which TV stations or networks usually buy. Thus FCC denies to cable pay-TV the showing of films between 2 and 10 years old; sports programs which are less than 2 years old; or any series programs with interconnected plots or using the same cast of principal characters. And it further constrains pay-TV by not permitting revenue advertisements before or after, as well as during programs;
7. required concurrence by the local ETV station and educational authorities before permitting importation of outside ETV signals; recommended and endorsed provisions for the new copyright statutes which greatly extend protection of stations, networks and copyright.

Barnett, *op. cit.,* pp. 87–88.

[27] The Sloan Commission on Communications, *On the Cable* (New York: McGraw-Hill, 1972); and Barnett, *op. cit.* An important Cabinet Committee *Report on Cable TV* (January 1974) urged freeing cable TV from virtually all restrictions. It is a brilliant and balanced approach (reprinted in *Television Digest,* Vol. 14, Jan. 21, 1974).

[28] For analysis of cable TV economics, see R. W. Crandall and L. L. Fray, "A Reexamination of the Prophecy of Doom for Cable Television," *Bell Journal of Economics and Management Science,* Vol. 5, No. 1 (Spring 1974), pp. 264–89 and the other research which they cite.

[29] FCC, *Annual Report, Fiscal Year 1972* (Washington, D.C.: U.S. Government Printing Office, 1972).

[30] Advertising prices are probably 10 percent higher, at least: see B. M. Owen, "Newspaper and Television Station Joint Ownership," *Antitrust Bulletin,* Vol. 18, No. 4 (Winter 1973), pp. 787–807.

ency. Despite activist efforts since 1960 to block renewals of stations with "poor" social performance, only six TV renewals were denied during 1960–72, none of them because of citizen protests about performance. Most of them were in small towns. Burdened by the hundreds of renewals it must decide (plus all its other tasks) and beset by political and special interest pressures, the FCC scarcely uses its renewal powers at all.[31]

SUMMARY

Broadcast regulation fits the standard patterns both for (1) regulatory evolution and protection, and (2) multiple-firm regulation. Regulation has consistently limited competition too tightly. The FCC has created (or arranged, by compromise; or largely acquiesced in) a structure which does provide a degree of competition, diversity, and localism. Yet the system and its financing tend to minimize diversity and local service. New technology has been retarded. Large excess profits have been made and become fixed in property rights. Antisocial effects of programming have gone uncorrected.

This outcome has been predictable, since the FCC has been quite out of its depth from the start. It will presumably continue more to arbitrate interest group conflicts—and protect the established interests—than to put broadcasting firmly on optimal lines. Given its modest powers, resources, and bargaining position, that is about all it can do.

---

[31] Recall the scathing analysis by Nicholas Johnson and John Dystel, *op. cit.*

CHAPTER SEVENTEEN

Regulation of Transport

Transport is a patchwork of a sector. From a railroad-dominated phase during 1870–1910, it has evolved into a mingling of competitive and monopoly parts, laced with subsidies and external effects.[1] Railroads were the first regulated part of the economy; many of them have since been forced back into competitive status, and yet some of them are now also going into public ownership. In this sector, regulation seems to have scored its most resounding failures, and yet it lives on and on.

The variety of the sector is apparent in Tables 17–1 and 17–2, in the

TABLE 17–1

Operating Revenues, by Type of Transport: 1940 to 1971 (excludes Alaska and Hawaii, except as noted)

TRANSPORT AGENCY	1940	1945	1950	1955	1960	1965	1969	1970	1971
REVENUES (mil. dol.)									
Electric railways	53	87	79	60	23	13	13	11	11
Railway Express [1]	120	284	223	241	248	316	270	313	263
Railroads [2] [3]	4,519	9,284	9,924	10,590	9,955	10,738	11,951	12,511	13,321
Waterlines [4]	113	173	330	452	427	426	450	502	525
Pipelines (oil) [5]	226	304	442	678	770	904	1,103	1,188	1,249
Domestic scheduled air carriers [6]	77	215	558	1,215	2,129	3,609	6,857	7,131	(NA)
Motor carriers of property [3]	898	1,840	3,737	5,535	7,214	10,068	13,958	14,585	(NA)
Motor carriers of passengers	176	652	539	552	667	885	1,007	[7] 882	[7] 911

NA Not available.
[1] Through 1969, data are after deducting payments to others for express privileges.
[2] Includes pullman (for 1940 to 1965), line-haul, and switching and terminal companies.
[3] Beginning 1960, includes Alaska and Hawaii.
[4] Includes only revenues from domestic traffic of carriers under jurisdiction of the Interstate Commerce Commission.
[5] Beginning 1960, includes 1 pipeline operating in Alaska.
[6] Revenues for scheduled passenger cargo operations.
[7] Excludes Class II and III passenger carriers.
Source: *Statistical Abstract of the United States,* 1973.

---

[1] Good analysis of transport problems is given in D. P. Locklin, *Economics of Transportation* (6th ed.; Homewood, Ill.: Richard D. Irwin, Inc., 1966); at various points, Kahn, *op.cit.;* and National Bureau of Economic Research, *Transportation Economics* (New York: Columbia University Press, 1965).

TABLE 17-2

Class I Railroads and Motor Carriers of Property: Revenue Freight Originated, by Commodity Group: 1971 (carloads and tons in thousands; revenue in millions of dollars)

COMMODITY GROUP	RAILROADS			MOTOR CARRIERS		
	Carloads	Tons	Revenue [1]	Truckloads	Tons	Revenue [1]
Total	25,172	1,390,960	$12,247	17,871	395,776	$9,500
Farm products	2,066	121,601	1,042	381	7,552	115
Metallic ores	1,375	110,404	329	26	570	5
Coal	4,646	360,554	1,336	16	455	2
Nonmetallic minerals, except fuels	2,113	157,834	430	268	5,679	31
Ordnance and accessories	48	2,341	91	31	559	26
Food and kindred products	2,547	106,392	1,472	1,649	29,254	658
Basic textiles	63	1,241	39	318	4,136	115
Lumber and wood products, exc. furniture	2,071	104,687	1,000	216	4,094	52
Furniture and fixtures	205	1,730	103	52	477	22
Pulp, paper and allied products	1,157	42,166	802	681	10,505	217
Printed matter	21	595	19	143	2,057	61
Chemicals and allied products	1,488	90,821	1,243	2,122	39,734	634
Petroleum and coal products	630	34,185	324	4,521	109,456	405
Rubber and misc. plastic products	239	3,839	130	311	3,816	141
Stone, clay and glass products	1,186	69,912	557	1,287	26,199	227
Primary metal products	1,266	72,088	819	1,598	29,873	463
Fabricated metal products [2]	349	10,109	214	445	5,948	151
Machinery, except electrical	171	3,821	146	398	5,523	197
Electrical mchy., equip. and supplies	309	4,156	179	271	3,030	122
Transportation equipment	1,274	29,453	1,029	2,065	23,828	584
Waste and scrap materials	746	37,483	250	58	1,022	14
Freight forwarder traffic	217	3,828	147	74	852	23
Small packaged shipments	(X)	727	33	(X)	66,876	4,911
Other	984	29,991	514	941	14,282	329

X Not applicable.
[1] Gross.
[2] Except ordnance, machinery, and transport.
Source: *Statistical Abstract of the United States*, 1973.

maps in Figure 17-1, and in Figures 17-2 and 17-3. Some modes are mutually competitive for at least parts of their markets: trucking and railroad freight haulage, for example. Pockets of market power also exist, including some (taxis, airlines) which regulation has created and preserved. The common themes are: (1) regulation tends to be a cartel device, to exclude entry and to maintain prices, and (2) regulation follows the classic protectionist path.

Here we will focus on U.S. railroads and airlines, with a brief look also at trucking, waterways and taxis. Urban transit is reserved for Chapter 21, because it is commonly under public enterprise. Foreign railroads and airlines are also taken up in the public enterprise chapters.

BASIC ECONOMIC ISSUES

There are four basic issues: (1) natural monopoly, (2) allocation of costs within each mode, (3) the equalizing of subsidies and costs among modes, and (4) the optimal way to help a sick industry (e.g., certain railroads) to shrink. The larger drama is the great rise and then decline of railroads, as road and air traffic have grown. The ultimate social aim is to evolve an efficient mix of transport capacity and traffic. Since 1960, events have moved swiftly to change the status of some railroads, but the

FIGURE 17–1
U.S. Railroad Trackage

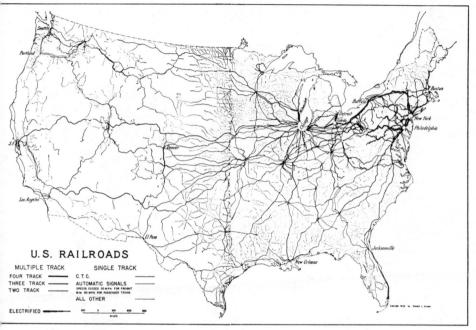

Source: E. L. Ullman, *American Commodity Flows* (Seattle: University of Washington Press, 1957).

Waterways of the United States

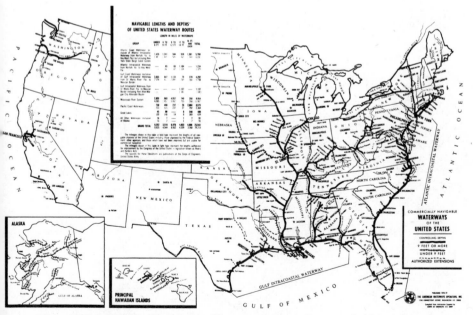

Source: Published 1970 by The American Waterways Operators, Inc.; compiled from information supplied by Corps of Engineers, U.S. Army.

FIGURE 17–1 (continued)
The National System of Interstate and Defense Highways (status of improvement as of March 31, 1971)

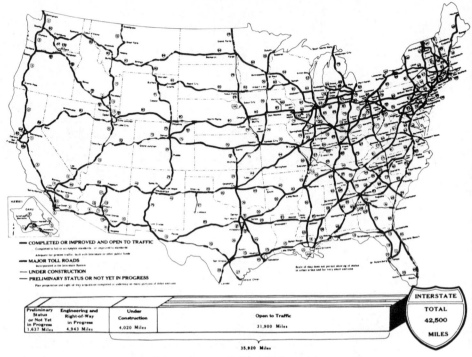

Source: U.S. Department of Transportation, Federal Highway Administration.

United States Air Transportation System—Routes Certificated to Trunk-line Carriers, December 31, 1970

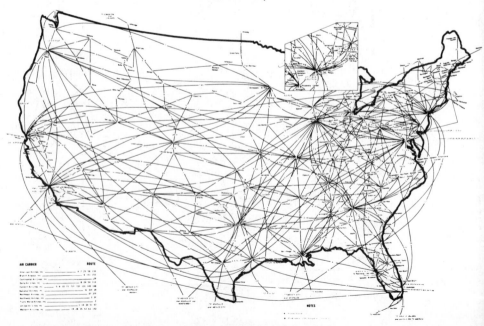

Source: Civil Aeronautics Board, Office of Facilities and Operations.

FIGURE 17–1 (concluded)
Product Pipelines in the United States

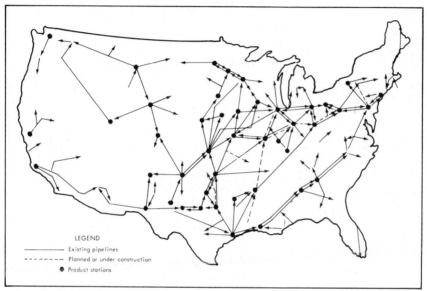

LEGEND
——————— Existing pipelines
– – – – – – Planned or under construction
● Product stations

Source: National Petroleum Council, December 31, 1966

FIGURE 17–2
Intercity Freight by Modes* (Including Mail & Express) (Billions of Ton-Miles)

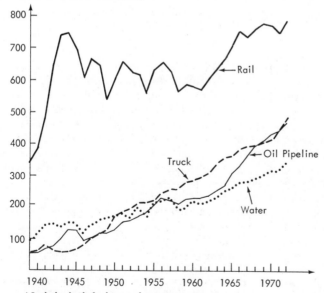

Amount (billions of ton-miles)

* Includes both for-hire and private carriers.
Source: Transportation Association of America, *Transportation Facts and Trends* (Washington, D.C.: October 1973), p. 8.

FIGURE 17-3
Passengers Carried by Public Transportation: 1950 to 1972

Millions of Passengers

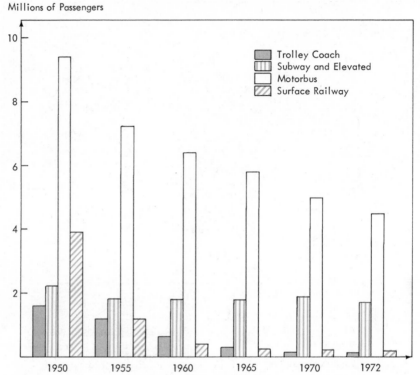

Source: Chart prepared by U.S. Bureau of the Census. Data from American Transit Association, Washington, D.C.

larger evolution is slow and perhaps costly. It is not easy to perceive and/or to bring about an optimal transport mix.

Natural Monopoly and Costs. The modes differ sharply in cost conditions. Railroads, with their heavy track costs in fixed patterns, usually have low marginal costs and extensive ranges of decreasing average costs.[2] Also, the eastern lines are mostly larger than dwindling demand requires. While they are operating below capacity (recall Figure 14–8), the efficient price would be below average cost, and deficits would result.

Railroads have natural-monopoly conditions on many train routes. But the parallel highway and airline services provide severe competition on other routes. The cost structure is very complex to unravel. But the basic patterns fit common sense.[3] Costs for *freight* favor trains for bulk, low-value, long-haul cargo, above 200 miles, but trucks for short-haul, high-value shipments with diverse destinations. For passengers, airlines

[2] See J. R. Meyer *et al.*, *The Economics of Competition in the Transportation Industries* (Cambridge: Harvard University Press, 1959).

[3] *Ibid.*, Chapters 2–6.

are superior for long trips (except for the many persons who fear flying) and buses and trains for most short trips.[4]

Each of the modes of transport has its particular advantages. Motor carriers are best adapted to moving light goods in small quantities, making short hauls, providing feeder services, and meeting the need for flexibility. Water carriers have the lowest costs where freight is hauled in bulk for long distances and speed is not required. The airlines enjoy superiority in carrying passengers and valuable goods for long distances at high speeds. The railroads are needed to carry passengers where distances are too short for travel by air and traffic too congested for travel by road. They are at their best in hauling freight for long distances in carload lots at intermediate speeds. Here, their scope, speed, and dependability are greater than those of the water carriers and their costs lower than those of the motor carriers. The railroads get three times as many ton-miles per worker and more than three times as many ton-miles per gallon of fuel than do the trucks.

The decreasing-cost features of railroads thus leave them with limited actual cases of natural monopoly. Still, these cases—and the variety of partial competition on other routes—do induce price discrimination. Table 17–3 shows how steep the differences can go.

Cost Allocation and Rate Patterns.   Railroads have always posed cost-allocation problems with a vengeance. The same track is used for freight and passenger service, for cannonball expresses and milk runs. How to apportion the capital and maintenance costs among them? The

TABLE 17–3

Ratio of Rail Carload Revenues to Out-of-Pocket and Fully Distributed Costs for 20 Commodities, 1960

Commodity	Out-of-Pocket Costs	Fully Distributed Costs	Commodity	Out-of-Pocket Costs	Fully Distributed Costs
Sugar beets	54	42	Cotton, bales	152	123
Straw	64	57	Automobiles, passenger	187	171
Fruits, fresh	66	60			
Petroleum, crude	67	54	Iron, pig	187	139
Vegetables, fresh	69	63	Rubber, crude	201	160
Dairy products	69	65	Cigarettes	223	185
Pulpwood	75	57	Liquors	246	200
Oranges, grapefruit	82	73	Military vehicles	328	256
Gasoline	93	77	Magnesium metal	367	254
Flour wheat	97	77	Explosives	413	324
Bituminous coal	110	82			

Source: Interstate Commerce Commission, Bureau of Accounts, Cost Finding Section, *Distribution of the Rail Revenue Contribution by Commodity Groups—1960*, Statement No. 2–62 (Washington, D.C.: U.S. Government Printing Office, 1962).

---

[4] T. E. Keeler shows that railroads offer lower passenger costs for short-haul high density routes than all other modes, if they were run well. For 1968–70, the average estimated costs per seat-mile were: bus 1.4 cents, airline 2.7 cents, automobile 4 cents, and train 1.1 cents. See his "The Economics of Passenger Trains," *Journal of Business,* Vol. 44, No. 2 (April 1971), pp. 148–74.

answer can and does determine whether whole classes of service make big profits or sharp losses. Thus passenger service has been run down since the 1930s precisely because railroads believed it to be inevitably unprofitable, after dividing track costs between it and freight.

The problem has no clear solutions. Overhead costs can only be assigned with some degree of arbitrariness.[5] Yet some rules apply. (1) Off-peak, residual use should carry little or no capacity costs. (2) If a service is being phased out, it should also carry little capacity costs. Therefore, railroads which are becoming mainly freight lines, and are giving freight trains priority over passenger trains, should set passenger fares roughly at only variable (out-of-pocket) costs.

Their large overhead costs leave railroads wide latitude for (1) price discrimination or (2) simply price confusion. Actually, railroad prices are extraordinarily complex and cumbersome, with thousands of specific rates. Some of these are nonsensical, retained only by inertia or ICC rigidity.

Where new efficient services can be offered at no extra capacity costs, rates can be cut low and still reflect true costs. But these may be blocked by public policy, out of fear that the price-cut is just discrimination. Since cost-allocation is such an occult art, such cases may provoke endless dispute and be difficult to settle efficiently (see the Ingot Molds case below).

Equalization of Costs. If some modes are subsidized compared to others, then prices based on private costs will bias traffic choices away from the unsubsidized mode. That is the railroads' lament since the 1920s: that their competitors have tax and subsidy privileges. Table 17–4 gives details of the railroads' view. The others reply that gasoline taxes and other payments offset this, so that any net subsidy is zero or the other way.

The issue is murky, but the net balance of subsidies does appear to go against the railroads. The railroads have to cover all their costs. Their competitors are not always required to do so. Diesel trucks and tractor-trailer combinations fall short of meeting their full share of highway costs. Water carriers are not required to pay for the use of the waterways. Air carriers do not cover the costs of the airports or the airways. And local airlines, in addition, are paid an outright subsidy. As a result, facilities are expanded where costs are high and traffic is diverted from carriers whose costs are low. To equalize, the motor, water, and air carriers could be charged for the use of public facilities. Or the railroads could be given aid that would be comparable to that now given their competitors.

User charges have the advantage of collecting the cost of transport facilities from the people who use them instead of imposing it on the general taxpayer. Their effect on competition among the different media depends upon the way in which they are computed.

Here, there are three possibilities: (1) The other carriers might be asked to pay charges equivalent to the burden borne by the railroads. In this case, they would be expected not only to meet their share of the costs

---

[5] Kahn, *op. cit;* Locklin, *op. cit.*

TABLE 17–4

Disparities among Modes of Domestic Transportation

Item	Railroad	Highway Freight	Highway Passenger*	Air	Water
Right-of-way:					
Financed and built by	Railroads	Government	Government	Government	Government
Maintained by	Railroads	Government	Government	Government	Government
Investment cost paid by	Railroads	Government	Government	Government	Government
Property taxes paid by	Railroads	Tax free	Tax free	Tax free	Tax free
Traffic control provided by	Railroads	Government	Government	Government	Government
Terminals:					
Financed and built by	Railroads	Truckers (some by government)	Bus operators (some by government)	Government	Water carriers (some by government)
Maintained by	Railroads	Truckers	Bus operators	Government	Water carriers
Investment cost paid by	Railroads	Truckers	Bus operators	Government	Water carriers
Property taxes paid by	Railroads	Truckers (some tax free)	Bus operators (some tax free)	Tax free	Water carriers (some tax free)
Cash subsidy paid by government	None	None	None	Some airlines (all certificated carriers eligible)	None
Transport diversification restricted:					
Railroads	No	Yes	Yes	Yes	Yes
Truckers	No	No	No	Yes	No
Bus operators	No	No		Yes	No
Airlines	No	No	No		No
Water carriers	Yes		No	Yes	
Rates regulated	Yes	33 1/3 percent	Yes	Yes	10 percent
Payment for facilities used	100 percent	Partial	Partial	Only nominal	None

* Excluding private automobile.

Source: *Problems of the Railroads* (Hearings before the Subcommittee on Surface Transportation of the Committee on Interstate and Foreign Commerce, Senate, 85th Cong., 2d sess.) (Washington, D.C.: U.S. Government Printing Office, 1958), Part 1, p. 297.

incurred by the government in providing them with facilities but also to cover costs the government had not incurred: interest on land though no land had been bought, interest on investment though it had been financed in whole or in part by taxation rather than by borrowing, interest at commercial rates though money had been borrowed at government rates, and taxes on property though no such taxes had been paid. This method of computation would protect the railroads, but it would subject the other carriers to an artificial handicap.

(2) The users of public facilities might merely be required to pay their own share of the costs actually incurred by the government. Such costs would not include the imputed interest or taxes mentioned above. Their allocation among different purposes and among different classes of users would be difficult. But once this problem was solved, the subsidization of competing carriers through government outlays would be brought to an end. This, however, would not require the users of public facilities to meet their full economic costs. For these include the cost of capital, not only when borrowed, but also when provided by the taxpayer.

(3) User charges could be set to cover economic costs, including interest actually paid by the government and interest imputed, at the same rate, on capital provided by the taxpayer. But even here, the competitors of the railroads would enjoy an advantage. They would have to meet only a part of the cost of jointly used facilities. This cost would include interest but at the low rate paid by the government. It would include no taxes.

If the users of public facilities were required to pay tolls that would cover their full share of the costs of construction and maintenance, the allocation of traffic among the different transport media would change. The motor carriers and the water carriers could pay such charges and continue to compete. The airlines could continue to serve the major cities. But air service to hundreds of smaller cities would be dropped. If this service is desired, it must be subsidized.

Competition might be equalized, alternatively, by aiding the railroads. Local governments might exempt them from taxes on their roadways, or the federal government might give them money to offset the taxes that they pay. Or the government could purchase their facilities, assuring them continued use. It could then provide ways to all types of carriers without charge, or impose charges that would result in comparable costs. Even if the railroads were required to finance the government's outlay, their fixed costs would be reduced: the interest rate would be lower, and there would be no property taxes to pay. This suggestion raises many problems that cannot now be explored. It is opposed by the railroads, who see in it an entering wedge for public ownership.

Efficient Shrinkage. Many eastern railroads have been overbuilt and out of equilibrium since the 1930s: they have excess trackage for their demand.[6] This reflects (1) irrationality, (2) limits on the rate of depletion of capital, and (3) outside limits on their efforts to stop service and aban-

---

[6] Estimates of excess trackage run as high as 200,000 miles; see T. E. Keeler, "Railroad Costs, Returns to Scale, and Excess Capacity," *Review of Economics and Statistics,* Vol. 56, No. 2 (May 1974), pp. 201–8; and Anne F. Friedlaender, "The Social Cost of American Railroads," *American Economic Review,* Vol. 61 (May 1971, pp. 226–34).

don routes. Optimal pricing requires incurring deficits during the transition toward an efficient, shrunken network. Social policy should prescribe such a transition, plus specific measures to retain services that have clear social benefits. Abroad, such reorganization has occurred in many countries, usually under public ownership (see Chapter 21). In the U.S., it has only moved ahead on a national basis since 1965, with Amtrak for passenger service and the Northeast system changes of 1974–75. The need is both for some shrinkage and some shifting into new kinds of railroad traffic.

The Department of Transportation now treats much of the transport sector, though the ICC, the CAB, and other groups have much independence. Transport policy is still an Irish stew of old taxes and subsidies, controls, interest groups and compromise. But a basis for consistent policy now exists, and the outlines of an optimal—or at least reasonably balanced—system are widely agreed. Later in this chapter, we will consider the parts of the system and their policy status.

RATE STRUCTURE

But, first, we need to learn the strange world of pricing in the transport sector. It reflects costs, discrimination, and sheer nonsense. There is much mutual cream-skimming, plus some regulatory restraints.

Railroad Rates. Passenger fares show relatively little discrimination. Higher fares are charged in parlor and Pullman cars and lower fares on commutation trains. But the principle of classifying service, so common in Europe, is little used in the United States. Circuitous lines meet the fares of direct lines for service between competitive points, and lower fares are offered for special trips. But, in general, the railroads charge a uniform fare per mile. They practice discrimination, chiefly, in the structure of rates for freight (Figure 17–4 gives an example). The ICC's methods and criteria in "setting" these rates are presented in the Appendix to this chapter.

More than 10,000 different commodities are hauled on the rails. These appear as some 25,000 commodity descriptions when differences in packing and manner of shipment are taken into account. There are freight stations at some 35,000 locations in the United States. Goods can move between these stations by scores or even hundreds of different routes. As a result, if rates were specified item by item and haul by haul, there could be tens of millions of separate rates. The structure of rates has been simplified, however, in two ways.

First, the railroads have adopted systems of classifying commodities. Three standard systems were developed before 1890 by committees representing the carriers: one known as the "Official Classification" in the northeastern states, one in the South, and one in the West. There were seven regular classes in the Official Classification, twelve in the southern, and ten in the western, identical commodities being differently classified in the three regions. In 1952, regional classifications were superseded by a uniform classification, with 31 classes, in the area east of the Rocky Mountains. Under such systems, particular commodities

FIGURE 17–4

Railroad Rate Differentiation Due to Competition from
Competing Mode of Transport

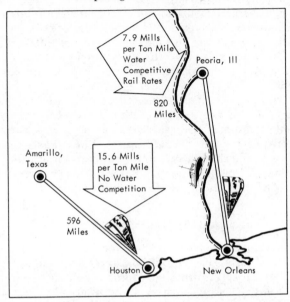

Shipping Blackstrap Molasses from Houston to Amarillo, Texas and from New Orleans to Peoria, Ill.

Source: *Proposed Amendments to Federal Transportation Laws*
(Hearings before the Committee on Commerce, U.S. Senate, 87th
Cong., 2d sess.) (Washington, D.C.: U.S. Government Printing Office, 1962), p. 365.

packed in particular ways are assigned to particular classes and all commodities in the same class pay the same rate.

Second, the computation of rates for different distances is also simplified. Rates based on cost would be less than proportionate to distance, as we have seen, since long hauls cost less per mile than short hauls. But distance rates are not made to conform precisely to differences in cost. Instead of being tapered mile by mile, they are reduced in mileage blocks. And rates for several points of origin or destination may be combined in common groups. In spite of these devices, the structure of rates remains a complicated one. There are some 75,000 freight tariffs in use in the United States. And a single tariff may run to more than a thousand pages.

The rate structure discriminates among commodities. The classes of freight are numbered from 400 to 13. Goods in classes above 100 move at multiples of the Class 100 rate. Those in classes below 100 move at fractions of that rate. But discrimination does not stop here. Most of the goods carried in less-than-carload lots pay the class rates. But some of them pay "exception ratings" which are much lower. These are ratings that were established for the purpose of meeting the competition of motor carriers in hauling light weight, valuable goods.

Around 85 percent of all freight moves, in carload lots, at "commodity rates." These apply to the transportation, in large quantities, of specific commodities between specific points. Ton for ton, they are set far below other rates. This has long been done to make possible the movement of heavy, bulky, low-grade goods and, in particular, to meet the competition of water carriers. In the structure of rates as a whole, therefore, the differences between commodities are great. And these differences bear little relation to differences in cost. Table 17–3 shows a few of these striking differences.[7]

The rate structure discriminates, too, among hauls. Some discrimination is incidental to the practice of simplifying the structure by using distance blocks, relating rates to key points, and grouping points of origin and destination; more is a consequence of the policy of so fixing rates on particular hauls as to meet those charged by competing carriers and so fixing rates for particular locations as to equalize their competitive opportunities. Thus, a circuitous line will match the rate charged between two points by a direct line, and a railroad will match the rate charged between ports by a water carrier, maintaining higher rates at other points. And where two producing points are at unequal distances from a common source of raw material or a common market for their product, the more distant point will be given the same rate as the nearer one. These differences have nothing to do with costs: rates are lower where demand is made elastic by competition, higher where it is not.

The Rates of Other Carriers. Among other carriers, discrimination has been a serious problem only in the case of *oil pipelines*. These lines are owned and operated by the major refiners. But they also carry oil to independent refineries. In this situation there is danger that the majors may handicap the independents by charging high rates or imposing unreasonable restrictions on their services. The problem presented is a special one, having to do with competition in the oil industry.

With *water carriers* along the coasts and on the Great Lakes, the fixed costs of vessels and terminal services are substantial. The marginal cost of handling a particular shipment thus falls below its total unit cost. The shiplines are therefore under pressure to increase their cargoes by discriminating in their rates. They charge less where they meet the competition of rail and motor carriers; more where they do not. With inland water carriers, the fixed costs of barges and terminals are lower than with the others and there is less temptation to discriminate. Here, the freight classification established by the railroads is used and rates are based on railroad rates. Most traffic moves, however, on commodity rates. To compensate for slower service, these are set at a fixed differential —usually 20 percent—below rail rates. The discrimination found in the

---

[7] See also the discussion in C. F. Phillips, *op. cit.,* pp. 311–326; and M. L. Fair and E. W. Williams, *Economics of Transportation and Logistics* (Dallas: Business Publications, Inc., 1975).

railway rate structure is thus reflected, at a lower level, in water rates.

In the case of *motor carriers,* where investment in rights of way is unnecessary and investment in rolling stock is smaller than with the railroads, fixed costs are low and marginal cost is close to total unit cost. It would thus be possible for these carriers to establish a nondiscriminatory rate structure—one that would closely conform to their unit costs. Instead of doing so, they have patterned their structure after that adopted by the railroads, with rates set at or near the discriminatory charges made for hauls by rail. The motor carriers discriminate, too, by using railway rather than highway distances in making rates, and by making greater reductions in rates for more-than-truckload shipments than are justified by savings in costs.

The *airlines,* like the truckers, need not invest in ways or terminals. But their investment in aircraft is substantial. They therefore have a strong incentive to establish a structure of rates that will keep their planes in the air rather than on the ground and flying well filled rather than poorly filled. Until 1948, all passengers were carried at a common rate, fares being determined by multiplying distances by a common charge per mile. Thereafter, different types of service were introduced and fares were differentiated to promote traffic. At present, lower fares are charged for coach services than for first class, and recently there were lower fares for youth, family, stand-by, and shuttle services. The structure of fares is discriminatory, favoring short hauls over long hauls, routes where the density of traffic is low over those where it is high, and first-class service over coach service. Air express rates are made proportionate to distance, in mileage blocks, but are subject to arbitrary minima for small shipments and for short hauls. Lower rates are charged for certain commodities, such as newspapers and securities. Air freight, offering slower service, is carried at lower rates than air express. Here, rates are higher for directions in which traffic is heavy and lower for directions in which it is light.

Some fare differences fit cost differences. Yet many do not, and so the structure of rates contains much discrimination.

RAILROADS

The railroad was born into competition, acquired regulated status as a cartel system, and them underwent new competition in the 1920s just when regulation began to be effective—and superfluous. As a result of this and other influences, ironically, many eastern railroads now are slipping into public ownership.

By 1887, railroads were the dominant mode of haulage in large parts of the country. In the West, there was monopoly; in the East, powerful competition among two or more roads along most routes. Possibilities for abuse and price fixing were large and routinely taken. Price discrimination was set deep in the system, especially in the Plains.

As the network grew toward maturity in the 1880s, the ICC was established to "regulate" it. Several forces created the ICC. One was Granger resistance to western railroad monopoly. Another was the desire of eastern railroads to stop rate-cutting competition.[8] Another was a complex of financial interests seeking to merge railroads further. The ICC was thus born of uncertain parentage, in a new form recently made possible by the 1876 *Munn* v. *Illinois* decision. It could be expected to have, on balance, light effects in limiting railroad monopoly.

This in fact occurred. The Supreme Court soon emasculated the ICC's powers.[9] More than 20 years were spent before Congress gave the ICC authority to get data and to set effective ceilings on prices. During this interval, the ICC did help to keep rates up against railroad price cutters. But not before World War I did the ICC possess more than shadow powers. Therefore, when railroads were most powerful, regulation was a

TABLE 17–5
Milestones of Transportation Policy

1840–60	Several states build railroads (Pennsylvania, Illinois, Indiana, Michigan, Georgia, and others).
1870s	Granger Laws.
1887	Interstate Commerce Commission created.
1888–1906	ICC powers are gutted by the Supreme Court.
1906–10	Hepburn and Mann-Elkins Acts gives powers to ICC.
1917–20	Railroads are taken over for war operation by the U.S. Railroad Administration.
1920	Transportation Act sets ICC powers and criteria still used now.
1935	Regulation extended to motor trucking.
1938	Civil Aeronautics Board created to regulate airlines.
1940	Reed-Bullwinkle Act legalizes railroad cartels.
1958	Transportation Act modifies regulation.
1966	Department of Transportation created to "coordinate" policy.

mere pretense or even a prop for railroad cartels. When the need for strict regulation had passed, it began.

Strengthening the ICC 1906–10. The Hepburn Act of 1906 undid some of the damage that had been done by the courts. (1) It authorized the Commission, when rates were found to be unreasonable, to specify the legal maxima. (2) It contained many provisions designed to prevent personal discrimination. It gave the Commission jurisdiction over industrial railroads and private car lines and empowered it to control divisions of rates and charges made for switching and for special services rendered by shippers and by carriers. It forbade free passes, except to railway employees. It increased the liability of recipients of rebates and the criminal penalties that could be imposed.

(3) The law forbade railroads to haul (except for their own use) goods they had themselves produced. This provision, known as the commodities clause, was designed to remove the advantage in car service and

---

[8] See P. W. MacAvoy, *The Economic Effects of Regulation: The Trunk-Line Railroad Cartels and the Interstate Commerce Commission before 1900* (Cambridge: The MIT Press, 1965); and Gabriel Kolko, *Railroads and Regulation* (Princeton: Princeton University Press, 1965).

[9] The main cases were *Counselman* v. *Hitchcock*, 142 U.S. 547 (1892), *ICC* v. *Cincinnati, New Orleans and Texas Pacific Railway Co.*, 167 U.S. (1897); and *ICC* v. *Alabama Midland Railway Co.*, 168 U.S. 144 (1897).

rates enjoyed by railroad-owned anthracite mines over their independent competitors. (4) The law sought to prevent railroads from refusing to interchange traffic with water carriers by empowering the Commission to require the establishment of joint routes, to fix joint rates, and to determine how they should be divided.

(5) The law strengthened the ICC in other ways. It required that all accounts be kept in such forms as the Commission might prescribe. It provided heavy penalties for delay and falsification in the submission of reports. And it made the Commission's orders effective after 30 days, with noncompliance punishable thereafter by a fine of $5,000 per day, thus putting on the railroads the burden of appealing to the courts.

The Mann-Elkins Act of 1910 made other significant changes in the law. (1) Under the Act of 1887, the ICC had been unable to pass upon a rate until after it had been put into effect. When rates were rising and complaints were numerous, this meant that unreasonable charges could be collected for many months before the Commission was able to act. When action was finally taken, moreover, these charges would have been passed on in product prices and restitution was therefore difficult if not impossible to effect. The new Act corrected this situation by giving the Commission power to suspend proposed increases, for a stated period, while it considered their legality. The burden of justifying higher rates was thus put on the carriers.

(2) When one rate was cut, under the original Act, the railroads could compensate for the reduction by raising another. Now the Commission was empowered, on its own motion, to consider the schedule of rates as a whole. (3) The Commission was also authorized to control the system used in classifying freight. And finally (4) the loophole found by the court in the long-and-short-haul prohibition was closed. The phrase "under substantially similar circumstances and conditions" was dropped from the law. The effectiveness of the prohibition was thus restored, and the formulation of policy to govern exceptions was left, in the main, to the ICC.

The new laws rehabilitated the Commission. Its orders, in general, came to be accepted by the courts. Other legislation followed. In 1912 the railroads were forbidden to own or operate vessels passing through the Panama Canal. In 1913 the ICC was directed to determine the value of railway properties. In 1917 it was authorized to require the roads to establish reasonable rules to govern the provision of freight cars and, if need be, to prescribe such rules itself.

World War I. The war brought a strange interval of government operation of the railroads. The strains of war transport overloaded the existing system, and so the government had to take them over in order to apportion capacity and unify operations. The fragmented private railroad system was incapable of meeting these stresses. Each railroad sought profit for itself. It therefore hoarded cars when they were needed on other lines, and routed shipments over its own tracks and terminals even when other lines made it possible for other terminals to be bypassed. Congestion resulted and a near breakdown of the transport system. The government took over the railroads on December 1917 and operated them until March 1920.

The U.S. Railroad Administration operated the railway system as a single unit. It pooled rolling stock, and economized equipment by establishing priority for freight and assuring that cars were fully loaded by fixing sailing days. Compared to the previous operations under war conditions, the unified handling was much closer to an optimum use of the railroads. The government paid rental for the use of properties, maintaining these properties and returning them in equally good condition. Actual management of operation was left to the officials of the roads. Only the larger allocation of railroad resources were controlled by the government. The experiment was costly to the public purse. But this loss occurred because railway rates were held down despite the rise of costs. This episode in public ownership was quite a specialized event. It proves more about the benefits of unifying railroads than of public ownership.

Railway regulation was drastically tightened with the Transportation Act of 1920. This act gave new authority to the Commission over service, securities, and rates. The Commission could establish minimum as well as maximum rates. Its powers to control prices and operations were firmed at the level at which they have remained ever since. The Act also grappled with the problem of weak and strong railroads, whose costs differ. Many railroads faced more competition than others from road traffic, and the Commission could not guarantee survival with adequate profits for any railroad. The Act empowered the Commission to look into the honesty, efficiency, and economy with which the railroads were managed. It also set the "fair" rate of return at 6 percent.

Weaker roads were to be assisted. They were now encouraged to pool their resources or even merge. During 1921–29 the ICC prepared a comprehensive plan for consolidating stronger and weaker railroads in a system of about 20 competing railroads. But the stronger systems, instead, merged with the better of the weak systems, leaving the main problem unsolved.

The Depression.   The Great Depression hit the railroads hard. Car loadings fell off; from 1929 to 1932 gross revenues were cut in half. If their capitalization had been in stocks, the roads would have been in a better position to sustain this loss. But 56 percent of their capitalization, in 1932, was in bonds, bearing an average interest charge of 4.58 percent. In many cases, though operating costs were covered, interest could not be paid. By 1938 as many as 111 railroads, with more than 30 percent of the country's mileage, had become insolvent and were in receivership. Railway bonds had been a major outlet for conservative investment. Nine-tenths of them were held by institutional investors: savings banks, insurance companies, university endowments, and the like. The railway problem thus became, not that of protecting the shippers against the railroads, but that of protecting the holders of railroad securities against financial loss.

In 1932 the Hoover administration set up the Reconstruction Finance Corporation and empowered it to make loans to the railroads, among others (see Chapter 20). In the next ten years such loans reached a total of $850 million, enabling many roads to stave off bankruptcy.

The financial shifts of the railroads are reflected in the stock-price movements in Figure 17–5. The 1929–31 fall was never made good, even with rises during 1949–56 and 1962–68.

World War II restored traffic for awhile. But the long-term malaise persisted, and the new interstate highway system—mostly complete by 1965—plus the spread of airline travel steadily eroded the position of most eastern railroads.

FIGURE 17–5
Movements in Railroad Stock Prices

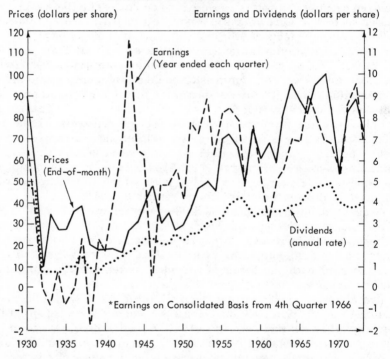

The railroad problem partly reflected special subsidies to the competing modes, and the ICC also repeatedly blocked the railroad's efforts to compete by price cutting. Yet there were also efforts to use regulation to help the railroads.

Regulation was extended in 1935 to trucking, airlines and waterways. The methods were conventional. But the motivation was different: to contain competition, not constrain monopoly. Also the rate bureaus, which had long served as private railroad cartels, were legalized in 1948.

This is how the process works. A road proposing a new rate takes its proposal to one of these bureaus. The proposal is examined by bureau employees, who forward it to large shippers and to competing roads. If any object, the rate is considered by a committee of traffic officers. Their decision is subject to a series of appeals. The final action of the bureau takes the form of a recommendation to the carriers concerned. Legally, each of them retains the right to make a change, even though the bureau disapproves. In practice, none of them is likely to do so. Rates will not be changed unless competing roads agree. This machinery operates as a cartel, removing the making of rates from the hands of individual managements. Its effect is to make rates higher and more rigid than they otherwise would be. Rate bureaus, long used by the railroads, have also been set up by other types of carriers.

In 1944 the Department of Justice brought a suit against the Western Association of Railway Executives, the American Association of Railroads, and a number of western roads, charging that the establishment or rates through bureaus was a violation of the Sherman Act; and the state of Georgia brought another suit in which the legality of such activities was attacked. In the light of existing precedents, there was little doubt that the bureaus would be held to violate the law. The railroads therefore turned to Congress for exemption. The Reed-Bulwinkle Act, granting their request, was passed over the veto of President Truman in 1948.

The new law made rate agreements subject to approval by the ICC. It left shippers free to carry complaints to the Commission, and authorized the Attorney General to take cases before that agency. The law was defended as maintaining order in the making of rates and bringing all aspects of the process within the jurisdiction of a single body. It was attacked as assigning further responsibilities to a body that lacked the ability and the inclination to discharge them in the public interest. The Commission could scarcely begin to review the thousands of individual rates on which the bureaus might act. And it was less likely than competition to force reductions in such rates.

The Railroad Problem. The railroads enjoyed good earnings during World War II. Traffic was heavy and, with the war being fought on two fronts, it moved to the West as well as to the East. Expansion of motor carriage was limited by shortages of trucks, parts, and tires. Coastwise water haulage was curtailed as ships were sunk and, until more pipelines could be built, the railroads had to carry oil from the producing regions to the refineries. The great bulk of wartime freight was moved by rail.

Earnings were down again in the 50s; the railroads' return on their investment averaged 3.6 percent during the decade. It stood at 2.8 percent in 1958, the railroads ranking at the bottom of the list of major industries. With earnings low or nonexistent, the roads could not attract the capital required to maintain or improve their plants. In the South and West, where business was good and hauls were long, the problem was not quite so serious. In the Northeast, however, where hauls were shorter and highway competition heavy, it was acute.

The railroads made money hauling freight, but they sustained heavy losses in hauling passengers. According to the method of accounting used by the ICC, which charges part of the annual cost of tracks, signals, property taxes, etc., to the passenger service, these losses amounted to $724 million in 1957. If no charges were made for the use of the railway plant, they would still have amounted to $370 million. In other words, the railroads would have been $370 million better off if they had quit carrying passengers. But most of this drain was imposed by commutation services, requiring multitrack stations on costly downtown sites, hundreds of cars, and hundreds of employees, all of them being fully employed for only 20 hours a week and mostly standing idle for the other 148. For some roads, there was danger that the losses on passenger traffic would exceed the profits on freight. This could bankrupt the railroads.

The major cause of declining earnings was the continued loss of traffic to competing carriers. The railroads' share of freight traffic dropped from 75 percent in 1929 to 45 percent in 1959. Intercity movements of passengers were only one-tenth by common carrier, nine-tenths of them being effected by private automobile. Of the common-carrier business, the railroads' share dropped from 77 percent in 1929 to 29 percent in 1959.

The railroads were caught in a vise.[10] They were not entirely free either to increase their earnings or to reduce their costs. They might obtain permission to raise the level of their rates, but competition would prevent them from doing so. They could not get more business by reducing particular rates because the ICC would limit their cuts. Some of their competitors were subject to similar regulation, but large numbers of carriers were exempt. The railroads could not escape the losses incurred in carrying passengers because they were forbidden to discontinue unprofitable services without obtaining the permission of the ICC or—in the case of intrastate services—that of the state utility commissions. They were compelled, under union work rules, to employ workmen they did not need. The cost of such featherbedding was said to run to more than

---

[10] A brace of studies and hearings during 1945–65 clarified these problems. They include:

Dearing, C. L., and Owen, W., *National Transportation Policy* (Washington, D.C.: Brookings Institution, 1949).

Revision of Federal Transportation Policy. A report to the President prepared by the Presidential Advisory Committee on Transport Policy and Organization (Weeks Report). Washington, D.C., April, 1955.

Problems of the Railroads, Hearings before the Subcommittee on Surface Transportation of the Committee on Interstate and Foreign Commerce, Senate, 85th Cong. 2d sess., Parts 1–4. (Washington, D.C.: U.S. Government Printing Office, 1958); and *Problems of the Railroads,* Subcommittee Report (Smathers Report), 1958.

Nelson, J. C., *Railroad Transportation and Public Policy.* (Washington, D.C.: Brookings Institution, 1959).

Transportation Diversification, Hearings before a Subcommittee of the Committee on Interstate and Foreign Commerce, House, 86th Cong. 2d Sess., (Washington, D.C.: U.S. Government Printing Office, 1960).

Richmond, S. B. *Regulation and Competition in Air Transportation.* (New York: Columbia University Press, 1961).

Proposed Amendments to Federal Transportation Laws, Hearings before the Committee on Commerce, Senate, 87th Cong. 2d sess., Parts 1 and 2. (Washington, D.C.: U.S. Government Printing Office, 1962).

Conant, M., *Railroad Mergers and Abandonments.* (Berkeley and Los Angeles: University of California Press, 1964).

Kuhn, T. E. *Public Enterprise Economics and Transport Problems* (Berkeley and Los Angeles: University of California Press, 1965).

Transportation Economics. (New York: National Bureau of Economic Research, 1965).

The Crisis in Passenger Train Service, Hearings before the Committee on Commerce, Senate, 89th Cong., 1st sess. (Washington, D.C.: U.S. Government Printing Office, 1965).

$500 million per year, and this cost could not be cut without running the risk of a paralyzing strike. The railroads could not cut costs by merging their operations without first obtaining the approval of the ICC. They could not avoid the federal excise tax of 3 percent on their freight rates, the tax of 10 percent on their passenger fares, or the heavier burden of real estate taxes imposed on them by state and local governments.

The Rate-Making Rule of 1958. The ICC had long forbade the railroads to undercut the rates charged by the trucks or the barge lines, even though lower rates would have more than covered the railroads' out-of-pocket costs. Its purpose was to limit the use of rate discrimination as a means of diverting traffic from the highways and waterways to the rails. But in serving this purpose, it denied the railroads their principal opportunity to increase their revenues.

This limitation was modified by Congress when it passed the Transportation Act of 1958. The new law amended the 1933 rule of rate making by adding this provision: "Rates of a carrier shall not be held up to a particular level to protect the traffic of any other mode of transportation, giving due consideration to the objectives of national transportation policy. . . ."

The new rule was intended to help the railroads by enabling them to compete for a larger share of traffic. But the ICC and the courts have blunted its effect. The Commission has approved rate cuts on competitive shipments, but its orders have sanctioned few cuts that went below the railroads' average total costs, including a full allocation of overhead.[11] In 1963 the Supreme Court set aside the Commission's rejection of a cut made by the New Haven Railroad, saying,"If a carrier is prohibited from establishing a reduced rate that is not detrimental to its own revenue requirements merely because the rate will divert traffic from others, then the carrier is thwarted from asserting its own inherent advantages of cost and service."[12] But the Court did not say how inherent advantages were to be measured, whether by average total costs or by out-of-pocket costs, including no charge for overhead.

Big John. The next case to come before the Court involved the rates set by the Southern Railroad for carrying grain. Most of this traffic had been handled by trucks and by barges that were exempt from rate control. In an effort to compete for the business, the railroad designed a new hopper car, known as the Big John. Made of aluminum, it had twice the capacity and half the weight of the old box car and could be loaded and unloaded more easily and at lower cost. In 1961 the Southern proposed to cut its rates on movements of grain in trains of such cars by as much as 66 percent. Its proposal was fought by southern elevators and millers who saw grain moving more cheaply to the East, by the truckers and the barge lines, and, on behalf of the barge lines, by the TVA. The issue was disputed before the ICC and the courts for the next four years. In 1963 the Commission disapproved Southern's rates, holding them to be insuffi-

---

[11] This is much the same as the FCC's insistence on "fully distributed cost"; of course the Bell System is a more powerful monopolist than most railroads and capable of deeper discrimination.

[12] *ICC* v. *New York, New Haven & Hartford R.R. Co.,* 372 U.S. 744, 759.

ciently compensatory. In 1965 a district court rejected this decision, finding the evidence on which the Commission based its action to be inadequate. The Supreme Court agreed, returning the case to the ICC for further consideration.[13] And finally, the Commission reversed itself, deciding that the rates were legal after all. They were thus allowed to take effect.

Ingot Molds. This was a victory for the railroads. But a defeat soon followed. Ingot molds had been moved from Pittsburgh to Steelton, Kentucky by barge and truck for a charge of $5.11 per ton. In 1963 the Pennsylvania and the Louisville and Nashville Railroads cut their joint rate on this shipment from $11.86 to $5.11. The barge and truck lines complained, contending that the railroads' move violated national transportation policy by depriving them of their inherent advantage. The ICC found that the railroads' out-of-pocket costs on the shipment were $4.49; their fully allocated costs $7.59. It rejected their argument that rates were legal if they covered out-of-pocket costs, holding that they must cover fully allocated costs. The Commission was reversed by a district court that found its choice of fully allocated costs to have inadequate support. But it was finally upheld, in 1968, by the Supreme Court, which ruled that the selection of a method of costing whereby to determine inherent advantage was within the authority of the ICC.[14] Given the policy of the Commission and the Court's reluctance to call it into question, it would appear that the railroads' freedom to compete for traffic by cutting rates is to be strictly limited.

By 1959 it was clear that partial or complete deregulation of the railroads was in order.[15] The Ingot Molds and other 1960s cases simply dramatized how firmly the ICC was blocking the adjustment toward an efficient total transport system.

The ICC's method for deciding price questions is presented in an Appendix to this chapter. The detail conveys some of the suffocating effect which the ICC applies to the railroads' efforts at price competition.

Support and Adjustment. In other directions, railroads have been given more support and leeway. The 1958 Act made abandonment easier. During 1958–68 the number of scheduled intercity passenger trains was cut by three-fifths. On more than a third of the routes served in 1958 the service was completely eliminated. Two states were left with no passenger service by rail.

The 3 percent excise tax on freight rates was discontinued in 1958, the 10 percent tax on passenger fares in 1962. At the same time, a number of states and cities moved to reduce the burden of commutation services. The featherbedding problems were put to effective arbitration starting in 1964.

Perhaps the biggest shift was toward permitting railroad mergers.

---

[13] *Arrow Transportation Co.* v. *Cincinnati, New Orleans, and Texas Pacific Ry Co.,* 379 U.S.642 (1965).

[14] *American Commercial Lines* v. *Louisville & Nashville Ry Co.,* 392 U.S. 571.

[15] Meyer, Peck, Stenason, and Zwick, *op. cit.* The issues are complex: see Kahn, *op cit.,* Vol. 1, Ch. 6 and Vol. 2, Ch. 5. Yet the need to remove many ICC controls and equalize the competitive basis is now widely agreed. Major proposals for deregulation were advanced by President Kennedy in 1962 and President Nixon in 1970.

The ICC permitted 33 of 38 proposed mergers during 1958–68. Most of them did eliminate competition, and the massive Penn-Central merger eliminated "useless duplication" over scores of routes in the north central region. But the merger wave did not correct the more basic problems, and some mergers promptly belied the grandiose claims that they would yield greater efficiency. The merged Penn-Central system was a colossal muddle, with lost trains and near-chaos before bankruptcy occurred in June 1970.[16] The problems continued after 1970, amid growing deficits. By 1973–75, it and seven other troubled eastern railroads were being reorganized into public ownership.

An efficient consolidation had been needed and proposed since the 1920s. Instead, much too late, an erratic series was permitted in the 1960s, and still others are being processed through. But 40 years of regulation and disequilibrium had put the eastern roads beyond cure by merger.

The railroads' share of intercity traffic continued to decline in the 1960s, their share of ton miles dropping from 45.5 percent in 1959 to 41.5 percent in 1967; their share of common carrier passenger miles from 28.8 percent to 11.7 percent. They made money hauling freight but continued to lose money hauling passengers. In 1929, there were about 20,000 passenger trains in the United States; in 1970, there were only 420 and the railroads had petitioned the ICC for permission to discontinue more than 100 of these.

During the traumas of 1970–75, two big shifts toward public enterprise occurred. Passenger service was transferred to Amtrak (the National Railroad Passenger Corporation) in 1971. And in 1974 the Consolidated Rail Corporation was created by Congress with up to $2 billion in funds, to salvage the finances and operations of eight bankrupt eastern railroads. At first the banks and other creditors balked, but this was partly maneuvering to improve the terms for the owners (the classic process in which private interests resist, and then profit by, a shift to public ownership: see Chapter 19). Out of the muddle will evolve some degree of public financing and control.[17] The Department of Transportation is already providing loans, guarantees, and extensive planning resources toward the salvage. Further issues are treated in Chapter 21.

The railroads are thus a classic case of regulation persisting after the need for it has passed. It has presided over dubious railroad mergers without being able to guide the whole system toward stable optimal long-run arrangements. On the contrary, the ICC has tended to keep the railroads from adjusting to Stage 4. It is clearly an institution whose time has passed, and the main question is how to arrange its withdrawal

---

[16] The inefficiency continued under bankruptcy during 1970–74. By February 1974, derailments were occurring at 1,179 per month (*New York Times,* March 22, 1974).

[17] The creditors (mainly large banks and insurance firms) challenged the Reorganization Act in court, as a means of forcing the government to pay them more for their Penn-Central securities. After an appeals court held the Act unconstitutional on June 25, 1974, the issue was headed for a long period of appeals, Congressional struggles, and further revisions, perhaps lasting many years.

In Canada, public subsidies for passenger service had reached $125 million by 1972 and a shift toward a public firm similar to Amtrak was in process during 1974: *New York Times,* June 19, 1974.

cleanly. The ICC has helped to cause a loss of efficiency and a crisis of financial solvency for a large share of current railroads. This parallels the earlier transition in many other countries from private to public ownership. The government has been left with residual control and responsibility for a major number of railways and their creditors. The railroad problem will continue under public or private ownership, as long as present ICC behavior continues.

AIR TRANSPORT

Air travel retains some of the aura of derring-do with which the industry was born just after World War I. The airlines' daily and yearly activities are marked by change, there are several firms competing in most markets, their capital is mobile in the extreme (even literally), and the government has provided a large slice of the fixed capital in the sector.[18]

The basic setting, in fact, is provided by public resources. Airports are public enterprises. The air safety and control system is run by a large public agency, the Federal Aviation Administration. There are public subsidies for certain airlines. And the new plane types have often been developed in relation to government-sponsored military planes.[19]

An airway is a route, ten miles or more in width, equipped with aids to navigation: beacon lights, radio ranges, communications facilities, weather reports, and emergency landing fields. The airway system is maintained and operated by the federal government. It is used not only by common carriers but also by military aircraft and private planes. The airlines contribute to its support by paying a federal tax on gasoline. This payment falls short of their share of airway costs, and so there is a degree of public subsidy.

Airports, too, are publicly financed. Half of their construction cost is provided by local governments, half by the federal government. The airlines make no contribution toward interest or amortization. Operating costs at the largest airports are nearly met by revenues from landing fees, rentals, and the sale of fuel. But elsewhere, these revenues fall far short of costs; deficits are met by local governments. In 1970 $5 billion in federal funds were authorized to be used over the next five years, to automate air traffic control and to match local expenditures for the construction and modernization of airports.

Airlines are also subsidized directly through payments designed to cover the amount by which a line's revenues fail to cover its costs and yield a fair return on its investment. From 1938 to 1957, such subsidies were paid to all the airlines in the United States. Since then, they have been confined to local-service, territorial, and helicopter operations. In

---

[18] See R. E. Caves, *Air Transport and Its Regulators: An Industry Study* (Cambridge: Harvard University Press, 1962); George Eads, *The Local Service Airline Experiment* (Washington, D.C.: Brookings Institution, 1972); and W. A. Jordan, *Airline Regulation in America: Effects and Imperfections* (Baltimore: Johns Hopkins Press, 1970).

[19] See the chapter by Almarin Phillips in W. M. Capron, *Technological Change in Regulated Industries,* (Washington, D.C.: Brookings Institution, 1971).

1965, this subsidy stood at $84 million, in 1968 at $59 million, and in 1970 at $40 million.

Routes. Within this setting, the trunk carriers have held and fought over the major routes among largest cities, and the local service carriers have operated along the threadbare minor routes among little cities. There are in addition the international air operations which also reach into all major cities within the country. The scope of competition and cooperation has been set both by the carriers and the regulatory groups.

The main format of air service is shown in Table 17-6. The operators in this sector are (1) the larger scheduled carriers, (2) local service carriers, (3) nonscheduled and other chartered groups, and (4) general aviation, including private and personal operations. Regulation has centered on the major carriers, and here it has become a classic case of multiple-

TABLE 17-6
Airline Competition on the 31 Main U.S. Routes, 1973

City-pair Route (ranked by volume) (*indicates intrastate)	Airlines Offering Flights (parentheses indicate 2 or less flights daily)
New York–Boston	American, Delta, Eastern, (National, TWA)
New York–Washington	American, Allegheny, Eastern, National (Ozark, Southern, TWA)
New York–Chicago	American, Northwest, TWA, United
New York–Miami	Eastern, National, Delta
Los Angeles–San Francisco*	Air California, Pacific Southwest, Western, Hughes Airwest, United, TWA, Holiday
New York–Los Angeles	American, TWA, United
Los Angeles–Las Vegas	Hughes Airwest, TWA, United, Western
New York–Detroit	American, Northwest, United, (TWA)
New York–San Francisco	American, TWA, United
New York–Pittsburgh	American, Allegheny, TWA
New York–Cleveland	American, United, (TWA)
Los Angeles–Chicago	American, Continental, TWA, United
New York–Buffalo	American, Allegheny
Boston-Washington	American, Allegheny, Delta, Eastern
Chicago–Detroit	American, Delta, Northwest, United
Chicago-Miami	Delta, Eastern, Northwest
Chicago–Minneapolis	North Central, Northwest, United
San Francisco–Seattle	United, Western
Chicago-St. Louis	American, Delta, Ozark
Chicago–Philadelphia	Northwest, TWA, United
Los Angeles–Seattle	Continental, United, Western
Atlanta–New York	Delta, Eastern, United
Boston–Philadelphia	Allegheny, Delta, (Eastern)
New York–Rochester*	American, Allegheny
Chicago–Washington	American, Northwest, TWA, United
Chicago–San Francisco	American, TWA, United
Chicago–Cleveland	Northwest, United
Dallas–Houston*	Braniff, Texas International
New York–Syracuse	American, Allegheny
Boston–Chicago	American, United, TWA
Los Angeles–San Diego*	American, Delta, Pacific Southwest, United, Western, (Holiday, National)

Source: *Official Airline Guide,* 1973 (Washington, D.C.).

firm regulation, with the predictable consequences (recall Chapter 14).

There are certain scale economies from network scheduling and deploying fleets of aircraft. But these are limited. The airlines make no investment in airways or airports. But planes are costly and depreciate rapidly. The annual cost of capital, therefore, is lower than for railways and higher than for motor carriers. Investment, however, is flexible: planes can be shifted from route to route or transferred to other lines by lease or sale. Operating costs vary with volume, but not directly: flying expenses, half of the total, decline with size of plane and length of flight; ground expenses, the other half, are more nearly constant. Given the level of fixed costs, there may be some tendency toward destructive competition and the emergence of monopoly. But the industry is not one in which economies of scale are such as to demand great size. Entry, unless restricted by law, is quite possible. Without regulation, it is likely that the industry would be effectively competitive.

Demand. Demand is specialized. Most passengers are businessmen, at company expense. They are mostly indifferent to cost, concerned rather with scheduling convenience and comfort. Other passengers are mainly infrequent travelers, also with relatively inelastic demand. The great market for economy travel has never been tapped, and so airlines remain for the middle and upper income groups, buses for the rest.

The main outlines of air transport history and behavior are as follows. Traffic has grown very rapidly over the last few decades, though more normal growth rates may have set in since 1970. This growth reflected (1) the rise of new rapid service, offset partly by (2) the slow introduction of minimum prices to explore the mass market for air travel. New plane types have been introduced in waves, beginning with the first passenger transports in the 1930s, then the postwar use of planes developed during World War II, then turboprops which were shoehorned in between the propeller and the jet planes, then jet aircraft around 1960. Since then, variations on the jet principle have been introduced, including widebodied, giant, short-haul, and other types. There has been no new wave of plane types since 1965, even though short-takeoff-and-landing technology has become developed. Each wave of new plane types has tended sharply to displace the previous one, rather than being phased in (with the older type being held on at lower fares).

The air carriers' reported profits have fluctuated, as shown in Figure 17-6. These shifts have reflected both (1) fluctuations in demand, and (2) the periodic effects of adding new aircraft, which are so rapidly depreciated that profits are low in the first few years. Compared to some other regulated firms, air carriers have unstable profit rates. Meanwhile, the total investment in aircraft has risen, but leasing has also taken a rising share of the aircraft in use. In fact, airline operations are partly a venture in speculation about aircraft innovation and finance.[20]

Recently, charter and other nonscheduled traffic has eaten into the total share of normal scheduled flights. Charters operate at both peak and off-peak periods, and their rise reflects the ability of outside groups

---

[20] Thus many of the large Boeing 747 planes, introduced in 1969, have become surplus capacity and are being leased and mothballed in a variety of ways.

FIGURE 17-6
Airline Profits Vary

FIGURE 17-7
Airline Load Factors Have Declined to about 50 Percent (load factor is revenue passenger miles as a percent of available seat miles).

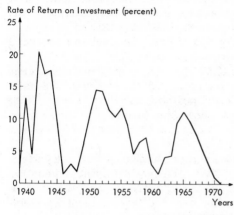

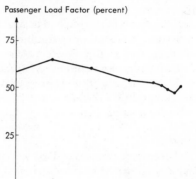

to take advantage of artificially high prices set for the scheduled services. The result is that actual pricing of flight services involves extensive discrimination.

The structure of competition along the major routes has been rigid. Nonprice competition does occur to a degree, but it does not cause much change in the relevant markets. Meanwhile, the level of congestion at major airports has become significant, with peak-hour delays. This has arisen partly because the airlines have found it rational to focus their services at the peak hours.

Meanwhile, the planes have been flying with an increasing share of seats empty. This is shown in Figure 17–7. At higher load factors, the average price of a ticket could be much below present levels. The economic analysis of the optimal load factor is a complex trade-off between (1) frequency of service, (2) costs, and (3) the ease of booking with assurance at the last moment. By most criteria, the optimal load factor is in the range of 70 to 80 percent.[21] Therefore recent levels are well below the optimal rate of usage of plane capacity.[22]

In short, air transport is an unusual regulated sector, where certain competitive elements are rigid and several forms of inefficiency have arisen and persist. Regulation has been part of the evolution of these patterns.

Regulation. The CAB has had powers since 1938 to (1) control entry and schedules, (2) set subsidies, and (3) control prices. It has controlled

---

[21] See George Eads' chapter in Almarin Phillips, *ed. cit.*

[22] This holds even though the 1973–74 "energy crisis" (see Ch. 25) has stirred collaboration among the airlines (at CAB urging) to trim hundreds of parallel flights, reduce frequency, and use smaller planes, so as to raise load factors. The changes also raised airline profits, while reducing service by about one-fourth. They may mark a permanent shift toward cartel control of service offerings, under passive CAB approval.

entry tightly, phased down subsidies after 1957, and done more to raise fares than reduce them.

Until 1957 it coexisted in the Department of Commerce with the Civilian Aeronautics Administration, which promoted airports and safety. This CAA became the FAA in 1958, and both agencies were made more independent.[23] All along, CAB members have mostly been airline boosters. Their main concern is to protect the airlines' viability, not to enforce "abstract" criteria of cost, efficiency and equity. The level and structure of fares are set primarily at the airlines' initiative.

Entry has been controlled since 1938. The 16 existing lines were certified, but the 150-plus applications for new trunk lines since 1938 have *all* been denied. These main trunk airlines now number 11, with TWA, American, and United the largest. Local and feeder lines have been freely let in, by contrast; they are of course less profitable and have been subsidized.[24]

Entry into nonscheduled service (on any route) was originally open, but growth mushroomed after World War II. The CAB tightened control after 1947, turning them into "supplemental carriers" by 1962, mainly for charter flights. Also the Board has certified five all-cargo carriers. These concerns have difficulty in meeting the competition of the passenger lines, which transport cargo in the bellies of their planes. They account for a sixth of air cargo ton miles, the supplemental carriers for around a fourth, and the passenger lines for three-fifths.

Routes are also controlled. The CAB's criteria are vague and shifting, but the basic preference is for two or more lines (but not many more) on main trunk routes.

The Board devotes a major part of its time and energy to consideration of route applications. The numbers of carriers it admits to particular routes are usually less than the numbers there would have been in the absense of regulation. The Board's control over routes has clearly operated to delay adjustment to shifting demand. And it has done so at a considerable cost in manpower and in money.[25]

Control of Service.   The CAB has primarily discouraged competition in service. When coach service was introduced, it feared that lower fares would impair the carriers' financial strength. It therefore sought to limit

---

[23] The FAA employs 45,000, including 15,000 traffic controllers at over 300 airports and a score of control centers. FAA services are not priced—peak, off-peak or otherwise—and so the efficiency of their allocation and use cannot be appraised. They simply attempt to cope with whatever traffic burdens are placed on them. This fits the "passive" model of public firms (see Chapter 19).

[24] See George Eads, *The Local Service Airline Experiment* (Washington, D.C.: Brookings Institution, 1972). Many of these carriers were operated by former Army pilots, flying second-hand planes. They were attacked as affording inferior safety and skimming the cream off the market to the detriment of the scheduled lines. They were defended as exemplifying the virtues of small competitive enterprise.

[25] Richard E. Caves, *Air Transport and Its Regulators* (Cambridge, Mass.: Harvard University Press, 1962), chap. ix. The CAB also limits competition on all international routes which relate to U.S. locations. In one recent example, Laker Airways, a small British firm, prepared "Sky train" shuttle service at $125 year-round one-way fares between London and New York. CAB approved fares were $326 during the peak tourist season. The CAB, under pressure from TWA and Pan American Airways, simply delayed action from 1972 on, preventing entry and causing Laker large current costs. (*New York Times,* June 27, 1974, p. 65).

the quality of the service, requiring high-density seating and confining flights to night hours. The Board, in controlling routes, has permitted fewer types and classes of service than might otherwise have been available. Shuttle services, for instance, and cheaper flights in older and slower planes have been barred or limited. Its policies, on the other hand, have speeded the introduction of new equipment. The Board has allowed rapid write-offs for the depreciation of new planes, permitted their owners to charge higher fares, and forbidden them to cut their fares on older planes. It has also used its control over routes as leverage in promoting modernization. As a result, the industry's rate of innovation may well have been more rapid than it would have been in the absence of regulation. But the competition thus fostered has been competition in comfort, convenience, and speed, not in economy.[26] Only a small percentage of citizens use airlines, in large part because the CAB has helped to limit the offering of low-cost air services.

Subsidies were important until 1957, both in value and in the CAB's attention. Now only local service carriers are directly subsidized, at a dwindling rate. Still, the benefits given to the original carriers were large. They—and the indirect subsidies—have had a regressive impact, since the owners and users of the favored airlines have been mainly high-income groups.

Fares. Originally, air fares were based on first-class rail fares, so that the airlines might compete for passengers. They have borne little relation to costs, since deficits, if they occurred, would be covered by subsidies. When earnings have been low, an increase in the general level of fares has been requested by the carriers. When earnings have been high, a reduction in the general level of fares may have been made by the CAB. Initiative in proposing changes in particular fares is taken by the carriers. In aviation, the procedure differs from that followed by the railroads and the trucking companies. Collusion in fare making is not explicitly condoned by the CAB. Most requests for changes in fares are not formally discussed and agreed upon before they are presented to the Board.

The CAB paid little attention to the level of fares before 1957. Airline earnings could be controlled by allocating routes and by fixing subsidies. But when the trunk lines went off subsidy in 1957, it became necessary to adopt a policy regarding fares. The Board therefore made a General Passenger Fare Investigation, announcing its results in 1960.[27] The investigation dealt only with the general level of fares.

Here, procedures were prescribed and standards established to govern the computation of allowable earnings. The airlines had proposed that earnings be computed, as they are for motor carriers, as a percentage of revenues. The Board rejected this approach, calculating earnings, as is generally done, as a return on investment. To determine the needed rate of return, the Board ascertained the respective shares of debt and equity

---

[26] A classic instance is the CAB's approval for the airlines' jointly limiting 747 layouts to 350 rather than nearly 500 seat capacity. Also, efficient innovation would retain older planes at lower fares; instead, only newer planes are offered, at uniform higher fares.

[27] A similar investigation was done in 1970–73 also. See G.W. Douglas and J. C. Miller, III, "The Domestic Passenger Fare Investigation," *Bell Journal of Economics and Management Science,* Vol. 5, No. 1 (Spring 1974), pp. 205–32.

in the capital structures of the airlines and estimated the rate that was needed to attract each type of capital. As the rate to be allowed, it took a weighted average of the two. The resulting return for the Big Four was 4.5 percent on debt, 16 percent on equity, and 10.25 percent overall; for the other trunk lines, 5.5 percent on debt, 18 percent on equity, and 11.125 percent overall; for the local carriers, 5.5 percent on debt, 21.35 percent on equity, and an average for the different carriers, running from 9 to 12.75 percent overall. The Board thus established—perhaps more elaborately and precisely than good sense required—a measure of reasonableness for earnings.

In the mid 60s, when the average earnings of the trunk lines had climbed above 10 percent, they requested an increase in the level of fares. The CAB refused to grant it. In the late 60s, however, when heavy investments had been made in jumbo jets, when labor and material costs were inflated, and when planes were flying partly full, airline earnings fell. The CAB approved two fare increases, totalling more than 10 percent, in 1969. By 1975, the CAB was prodding the airlines to adjust their routes and fares so as to increase their earnings. This was unusually open cartel pricing, even for the CAB. In short, rate levels are only very loosely controlled.

For many years, the Board's control of the structure of fares was sporadic, casual, and uninformed. It had no demand or cost data on which to base its decisions; no standards by which to judge the propriety of particular rates. The fare structure was modified from time to time, on an ad hoc basis, at the initiative of the carriers. Lower charges were fixed for coaches than for first-class flights. Promotional fares were introduced for family groups, for military personnel, for youths, for excursions, and for stand-by services. But there was no consistent pattern. As a part of its passenger fare investigation, made before 1960, the Board announced its intention to examine the structure as well as the level of fares. But its report on this part of its study did not appear until 1968. The Board then proposed that fares be based on costs, beginning with a common terminal charge for each trip, to cover the costs of takeoff and landing, and adding a charge per mile, tapering with distance, with first-class fares set at 125 percent of coach fares and promotional fares continued at their current discounts. A foundation for a rational structure of fares has thus been laid.[28]

Yet the basic flaw remains: the CAB mainly sets *floors* under fares, not ceilings upon them. It prevents the airlines from price competition as neatly as could a perfect cartel. Entry is also limited. Therefore, rivalry is diverted into service quality, including many frills, some of which soak up profits as a form of X-inefficiency.

---

[28] Still, rates involve much discrimination and are often extremely complex; "filled with jargon, double-talk, strange phraseology and catch phrases" (according to a CAB official in 1974: *New York Times,* April 30, 1974). For some simple trips between two cities, the applicable tariff provisions were six large volumes of printed matter.

Also, the fixed fares breed extensive secret rebates and kickbacks from airlines to travel agents who handle large-scale orders. Such discounting, though illegal, runs as high as 50 percent of the ticket price, with 10 to 20 percent a common level. The CAB floor under prices automatically induces such discrimination and payoffs, *and* it keeps the final consumers from getting the lower prices which would be available in long-run equilibrium (see *New York Times,* May 14, 1974, p. 1).

TABLE 17-7
1972 Fares and Costs

Route	1972 Flying Time (minutes)	Estimated Long-run Marginal Cost 1972 (dollars)	Actual Fare 1972 (dollars)	Percent Markup
Boston–New York	62	14.31	22.22	55.3
New York–Washington	69	15.96	24.07	50.8
Chicago–New York	128	35.66	54.63	53.2
Miami–New York	170	41.76	76.85	84.0
Los Angeles–San Francisco	65	15.70	15.28	−2.7
Los Angeles–New York	340	90.21	150.93	67.3
Las Vegas–Los Angeles	58	13.83	25.00	80.8
Detroit–New York	105	25.56	41.67	63.0
New York–San Francisco	345	93.49	150.93	61.4
Chicago–Los Angeles	245	64.34	101.85	58.3
Boston–Washington	90	22.93	35.18	53.4
Chicago–Miami	180	44.73	84.42	84.3
Chicago–St. Louis	63	17.36	25.93	49.6
Atlanta–New York	130	36.37	56.45	55.2
Chicago–Washington	118	30.97	47.22	52.5
Chicago–San Francisco	252	67.38	113.88	69.0
Dallas–Houston	58	15.41	18.52	20.2
Boston–Chicago	140	40.54	62.96	55.3

Source: 1972 flying times and fares came from the *Official Airline Guide* (5), February, 1972 edition; T. E. Keeler, "Airline Regulation and Market Performance," *Bell Journal of Economics and Management Science*, Vol. 3, No. 2 (Autumn 1972), pp. 399–424.

Effects.   The results have fitted the predictable effects of multiple-firm regulation. It has supported airline prices against competitive cutting. It has not put tight constraints on overall earnings. It has largely ignored the optimal rate structure, especially the use of off-peak fares to optimize the time pattern of travel. It has, in short, presided over the airlines' setting of a discriminatory fare structure. Moreover, it has almost totally ignored the scope for mass marketing of airline services, either by chartering, by the use of older planes, or by the use of bare-bones service offerings.

The result has been several kinds of inefficiency. Also there have been major costs to the public through subsidies of various sorts, including those for operations, airports, and new plane types.

This effect is clear in comparisons of federal regulation with the experience of intrastate operations in California.[29] Carriers compete without regulation on the San Francisco–Los Angeles route and elsewhere (Table 17-6). The costs and rates are sharply lower, and service offerings are at least as good. There are some fine points about the comparison, but the simple lesson is that CAB regulation has had costs well above the benefits provided. Table 17-7 shows that the mark-up has been as high as 40–60 percent of costs, on average. There is no indication that the CAB is sufficiently aware of this to begin major changes to alleviate the ef-

---

[29] See Jordan, *op. cit.*

fects. On the contrary, all indications are for continuing or intensifying the past treatment, strictly in line with the perverse evolution of regulation in Stages 3 and 4.

Reforms. There are two main choices. One would be towards fostering a series of mergers among the carriers to reduce their number to about 6 to 8 comparable-sized firms, which would operate on a more balanced set of routes throughout the country. Conceivably, this could result in wider service overlaps and a general rise in the degree of competition and efficiency. Yet the more realistic analyst would expect that a new wave of mergers would tend to increase the market power and the imbalance of competitive conditions, rather than the opposite. Also, the cartel effects of fare regulation would continue. Pressure for more mergers has come mainly from the airlines themselves, whose interests lie in tighter market controls rather than more competition.

The second line of change—supported by nearly all objective analysts —is to deregulate air transport in several major directions. The first is to take off the control on entry on the major routes. The resulting period of adjustment would bring about changes in offerings, as in normally competitive markets. This shift would then make it possible for the CAB to stop its passive "regulating" of minimum prices. The results would be—as California suggests—several improvements: prices would fall and align better with costs, costs themselves would be more tightly controlled, load factors would improve, and congestion at airports would abate. Market shares would shift more flexibly, and the offering of services would become more diverse, as airlines kept on older planes at lower fares in parallel with the newer models.

TRUCKING

There are about 15,000 trucking companies, and the industry would —without regulation—be highly competitive and efficient.[30] Trucking has none of the standard utility features (recall Chapter 13), nor any likelihood of chronic destructive competition.

Regulation in this situation is bound to be weak, restrictive and a morass of bureaucracy. It covers only about one-third of highway freight. It was imposed in 1935 partly in order to benefit the railroads by restricting their competitors. It has lived down to its worst possibilities since then, largely functionless and obscure but burdensome and rigid.

There are various insurance, accounting, and merger rules under the Motor Carrier Act of 1935. The main controls are on entry and rates. In both areas they tend to reduce competition and increase prices. And their slowness further stifle normal market forces. Altogether, trucking regulation flouts nearly every criterion of optimality.

In controlling entry, the Commission's policy is restrictive. Applicants for new operating authority, for alternate routes, and for extensions of existing routes are required to prove that the proposed service is really needed, that the services already available are inadequate, and

---

[30] Exceptions include household movers (4–firm concentration near 50 percent) and automobile carriers (25 firms have 70 percent nationwide, more in specific regions).

that adequate service cannot be provided by carriers already in the field. They are asked to justify their applications in detail: to defend the financing they propose, the equipment they intend to use, and the schedule they plan to follow. For small concerns, the obstacles created by this procedure are almost insurmountable. Decisions, moreover, may be delayed for months or years. Certificates may then be refused on the ground that adequate service can be rendered by established truckers, or even that rail service is available.

Where operating rights *are* granted, they may be strictly limited. Operators may be confined to hauling particular goods between particular points. They may be required to follow circuitous routes, forbidden to serve intermediate points, and denied the right to carry cargo on the return haul.[31] They are thus prevented from reducing costs by filling empty space. By cutting operating rights into bits and pieces, the ICC condemns the carriers to inefficiency. In considering whether to issue a certificate of public convenience and necessity, the Commission directs its attention only to "necessity," ignoring convenience. Its purpose is not to serve the interests of shippers but to protect the position of established trucking companies.[32]

With regard to rates, too, the effect of Commission action has been to make the industry less competitive. In passing on requests for changes in the general level of rates, the Commission concerns itself, as in the case of the railroads, not with individual companies, but with the carriers as a whole. But here, its standard is a different one. It does not judge the rate level by measuring the return upon the carriers' investment, since investment in the industry is so small in relation to revenue that rates calculated to yield a fixed return might not suffice to cover costs. Instead, it seeks to insure an operating ratio that will afford a safe margin of revenues over costs, generally holding a ratio of 95 (costs being 95 percent of revenue) to be reasonable.

In acting on particular rates, the Commission employs the same principles, in the main, that it does with the railroads. But here it is more concerned with fixing minima than maxima. To prevent "destructive competition" within the trucking industry, it has put a floor under rates. In doing so, it has placed less emphasis on marginal costs and more on covering fully allocated costs. But it has acted tardily, permitting rates to drop a long way before it has called a halt.

Changes in motor carrier rates, as with the railroads, are agreed upon in rate bureaus before being proposed to the ICC. Here, the burden of proof is on the carrier who proposes to cut a rate.

The structure of rates conforms, not to costs, but to that established, on a value-of-service basis, by the railroads. In considering individual

---

[31] Thus, a carrier operating between New York and Montreal has to detour 200 miles via Reading, Pennsylvania; a carrier operating between the Pacific Northwest and Salt Lake City can have cargo eastward but not westward. Walter Adams, "The Role of Competition in the Regulated Industries," *American Economic Review,* Vol. XLVIII, No. 2 (1958), pp. 527–43 at p. 531.

[32] See *Competition, Regulation, and the Public Interest in the Motor Carrier Industry,* Report of the Select Committee on Small Business, U.S. Senate (84th Cong. 2d Sess., Senate Report No. 1693, 1956).

rates, therefore, the Commission has been influenced less by motor carrier costs than by competing railway rates. As a result, traffic is allocated uneconomically, much intercity freight moving by truck that could be carried more cheaply by rail, and much freight being hauled by private truck that could be handled more cheaply by common carrier.

The Commission has generally followed the rule of maintaining parity of rates between competing media. With rates held equal, competition is confined to service, and this gives an advantage to the trucks. But the Commission's purpose in fixing rates, as in controlling entry, has been to protect established interests in both the trucking and the railroad industries.[33]

WATER CARRIERS

Most traffic is in the Great Lakes and the Mississippi River system. The cargo is mostly minerals and grain, high-bulk goods with little need for speed. Only about 15 percent of waterborne traffic is actually regulated by the ICC. Its level and mix shift strongly, as trade patterns change. The basic routes and terminals are mostly provided by public resources. The shippers can therefore adjust rapidly, even shifting into foreign operations.

Regulation here suffers from the same deep flaws as it does in trucking. Entry control is unnecessary and biased to protect older firms. Price regulation is quite passive. The water carriers set their rates at a fixed differential—often about 20 percent—below those charged on competing hauls by rail. This saving keeps shippers from asking that rates be lowered; rail competition prevents the carriers from asking that they be raised. The Commission (as we saw above) has tended to cuts in rail rates in order to keep competing water carriers in business. If both waterways and trucking had been unregulated, the ICC might even have fostered railroad competitiveness in the 1960s and earlier rather than blocked it.

TAXIS: A TEST-TUBE CASE

In all major cities, taxis are private operations under some kind of public regulation. The variety of systems is great, but the lines of regulatory treatment are similar. The basic issue is how tightly the market is restricted. The treatments differ widely, and so do the economic results. New York taxis are scarce and expensive, while in Washington, D.C., and London, England, they are plentiful and cheap. In many foreign cities, there are official taxis, plus a wide range of other vehicles.

The underlying technology makes possible a variety of services, ranging from chauffeured limousines on through radio-dispatched taxis, through roving taxis, on through semibus carriers traveling routes more or less at will—often called jitneys—on to the large buses covering major routes at fixed intervals, and then to subways, trolleys, and other fixed-rail carriers. Yet the actual choices have become narrow, providing only

---

[33] See Ernest W. Williams, Jr., *The Regulation of Rail-Motor Rate Competition* (New York: Harper & Bros., 1958).

taxis plus the larger bus or subway services. This is common to the U.S. and to major cities abroad but not in less developed countries.

The reasons for the differences lie primarily in regulatory treatments, and particularly the prohibitions on entry. Taxi regulation illustrates how economic regulation closely reflects the quality of its political setting. In most cities, this political quality is low, or even corrupt. The taxi interests evolve out of earlier livery operations, preceding regulation. The regulatory agency or department can only compromise within this setting. The established taxi operators are numerous and assertedly vulnerable to any reduction in their position, so that their interests are a prior constraint on regulatory decisions. The best-known result of this is the taxi medallion in New York which has had a value as high as a seat on the New York Stock Exchange, because their number is fixed (i.e., entry is excluded); in Toronto taxi licenses are traded at $14,000 each. In Chicago too the controls are tight, virtually as if arranged in the interests of already existing taxi operators.[34]

The economic results of this are predictable. The extent of service is less than would be efficient. Fares are higher than costs. Potential taxi drivers are prohibited from operating. The existing operators tend to cluster in more lucrative areas and routes and to neglect low-income areas. The variety of vehicles used as taxis is narrow and often quite inappropriate. And, finally, the situation is economically stable, with no powerful group pushing to change it towards more optimal conditions. These results contrast with those in the few cities where regulation is different. In Washington, D.C., for example, entry is virtually free by a deliberate policy choice. Rates are low and service is more flexible and complete.

This subsector illustrates the common tendency of local regulation to stray far from the economic optimum. Moreover, much of the loss is sustained by relatively poor and unorganized citizens, many of whom do not even realize that they are being mistreated, both as riders and as potential drivers. Both on equity and efficiency grounds, therefore, taxi regulation illustrates the pathological results which regulation yields in so many parts of the transportation sector.

REFORM?

As these deviances have been increasingly recognized over many decades, the economic case for reform or abolition has grown strong. The main lines for change are (1) coordination and (2) deregulation.

Coordination. If companies (private or public) embraced the full range of modes—rail, road, air, and water—they could organize services more efficiently. Terminals, "interfaces," and scheduling could be integrated, so that each mode was used where its cost advantages lie. Excess capacity and needless duplication would be cut.

Such "transport coordination" has long been proposed, and in some

---

[34] For an excellent analysis of the Chicago situation, see E. W. Kitch, M. Isaacson, and D. Kasper, "The Regulation of Taxicabs in Chicago," *Journal of Law and Economics,* Vol. 14, No. 2 (October 1971), pp. 285–350.

countries it has been tried. But it has conceptual and practical limits. It increases the degree of monopoly, with all its likely costs in efficiency. Transport performance has been worst precisely where monopoly has existed. Possibly several multimode transport firms could compete side-by-side, but that would take careful design and management of the natural monopoly parts.

In practice, U.S. laws prevent integration, and so an arduous legislative process would be needed to make integration possible. The actual outcome—if the past is any guide—might tend to maximize monopoly and minimize the actual basic integration.

Deregulation. The expert consensus now strongly favors removing most or all regulation, letting competitive forces work. Basic costs and burdens would also have to be equalized. Both that and the process of deregulation would be difficult and complex, but the direction of change is widely agreed.

The case for deregulation has many specific parts.[35] (1) Restriction of entry into the motor transport industry should be abandoned. The industry's economic characteristics are not such that destructive competition would occur if entry were free. (2) Limitations on trucking rights should be removed. Truckers should be permitted to haul any cargo in either direction over any route, cutting their costs by filling empty space. (3) Control over air routes should be discontinued. Supply should be free to adjust to changes in demand. The energy that is wasted on route proceedings should be devoted to more vital tasks.

(4) The railroads should be given greater freedom to abandon unprofitable services. (5) Railroads should not be permitted to suppress the competition of air or water carriers by bringing them under control, but combinations of rail and water and motor carriers should be approved to the end that coordinated motor-rail-motor and motor-water-motor services can be supplied.

(6) Rules that obstruct innovations in technology should be abandoned. (7) Collusion should be forbidden in fixing rates; rate bureaus should be made subject to the antitrust laws. (8) Where agricultural commodities and goods moving in bulk are exempt from rate control, the same exemption should be extended to the railways as to motor and water carriers. The scope of regulation for each mode of transport should be the same.

(9) The power to fix minimum rates for truckers should be withdrawn; the structure of costs in this industry is such that there is little temptation to discriminate. Maximum and minimum rate controls for the railroads,

---

[35] Outright abolition of regulation is not indicated, at least not yet. This is mainly because competition is not complete. There are many hauls that can be made only by rail. And though competition has changed the pattern of discrimination, protection against undue discrimination is still required. The railroads, moreover, possess much greater resources than their competitors. In the absence of regulation, they might engage in unfair competition, driving their weaker rivals from the field. They might refuse, for instance, to interchange shipments with other carriers. They might slash rates on competing traffic or establish competing services, conducting them at a loss. With their competitors eliminated, they might then proceed to regain and to exploit their position of monopoly.

At the least, full deregulation would set large new burdens upon the Antitrust Division, to appraise behavior and stop anticompetitive actions.

however, should be retained. Otherwise rates on noncompetitive traffic may be set too high and rates on competitive traffic too low. Control is needed if discrimination is to be kept within bounds. (10) The clause in the 1933 rule of rate making that required the ICC to consider "the effect of rates on the movement of traffic" should be repealed. Decisions concerning the probable effect of rates on revenues should be returned to transport managements, eliminating duplication of the managerial function with its consequent delays.

All of these proposals point toward less reliance on regulation and more on competition. And this is the direction in which official recommendations for changes in policy have moved in recent years.

Actual changes have been ambivalent. The Department of Transportation could increase coordination. But its coverage is incomplete, and so policies and intermodal competition are far from unified. Public ownership of railroads is increasing rapidly, but the optimal criteria and form for the whole transport patchwork remain unclarified. There may be some occult method in this muddle, and draconian solutions might be worse. Still, there are large known losses in various parts, where policies clearly need revision.

APPENDIX

Regulation of Railway Rate Structures

When it is said that a regulatory agency "fixes" rates, this does not mean that the agency takes the initiative in setting each of the many particular rates that go to make up the rate structure. Such rates are initiated by the companies themselves. Railroad rates, for instance, are originated by the railroads, acting through their traffic associations. Proposed changes, usually involving reductions in particular rates designed to meet the competition of other carriers, are filed with the ICC. Unless the Commission suspends them, in response to protests or on its own motion, they take effect in 30 days.

Individual shippers or organized groups of shippers may always complain concerning particular rates, and the Commission will review them. But the rates that come to it for action, though large in number, are probably less than 1 percent of all those in effect. When it acts in such cases, the Commission takes the other rates in the structure for granted, not questioning the propriety of the pattern as a whole. When a carrier applies for an increase in the general level of rates, however, the Commission may effect substantial modifications in the rate structure, permitting some rates to be raised more and others less.

The Interstate Commerce Act contains a number of provisions with respect to the structure of rates. Section 1 requires that the rates charged on particular goods and between particular points be "just and reasonable," and that the systems used in classifying goods be "just and reasonable." Section 2 prohibits discrimination between persons. Section 3 covers other forms of discrimination, making it illegal for a carrier to give any "undue or unreasonable preference or advantage" or to impose any "undue or unreasonable prejudice or disadvantage." Section 4 applies to a particular form of discrimination between places, forbidding a carrier, without express permission of the ICC, to charge more "for a shorter than for a longer distance over the same line, in the same direction, the shorter being included within the longer distance." Section 6 requires that rates be published and adhered to and forbids changes in rates without prior notice.

These requirements were first applied to the railroads. They have since been copied in regulating other carriers. But the ICC, in their enforcement, has concerned itself mainly with the structure of railroad rates. For it is here that the problem of discrimination has been most serious.

Particular Rates. A shipper may complain that the rate charged for a particular commodity or a particular haul is unjust or unreasonable, in violation of Section 1 of the Interstate Commerce Act. Such a complaint does not allege discrimination: it has to do, not with the relation between one rate and another, but with the propriety of a rate in and of itself. But the ICC has no absolute standard by which justice and reasonableness may be judged. It does not attempt, for instance, to determine the cost of carrying a particular commodity or making a particular haul. Instead, it compares the rate that has been questioned with some other rate in the structure, taking as its standard an analogous commodity or a haul of equal length.

The Commission will approve a difference in rates if it can be justified on either of two grounds. *First, it may be shown that it corresponds to a difference in costs.* Here, it should be noted, the determining factor is not the absolute cost of handling a particular shipment, but the difference in the cost of handling two. *Second, a difference in rates may be justified by a difference in the value of the service to shippers.* Thus, the Commission has long held that it is just and reasonable to charge more for handling finished goods than for handling raw materials and more for valuable goods than for cheaper goods.

And since 1933 the agency has taken elasticity of demand into account under an amendment that requires it to consider the effect of rates upon the movement of traffic. In a few cases, finally, the Commission has based its decisions upon considerations of public welfare, approving lower rates, for instance, to encourage the shipment of such commodities as fertilizers and building materials. But this is the exception rather than the general rule.

When it finds a rate to be unreasonable, the ICC prescribes a maximum that may be charged. Before 1915 the Supreme Court permitted such maxima to be set low for particular goods, provided a railroad was able to obtain a fair return on its business as a whole. Thereafter, the Court held that maxima could not be set below the full cost of the service rendered, including overhead, since this would deprive the roads of property without due process of law.[36] In 1953, however, the Court appeared to return to its earlier position, not explicitly reversing its previous deci-

---

[36] *Northern Pacific Railway Co.* v. *North Dakota,* 236 U.S. 585 (1915).

sions, but holding that "the Due Process Clause should not be construed as a bar to the fixing of noncompensatory rates for carrying some commodities when the public interest is thereby served."[37] The railroads may not charge more than the maximum rates that are prescribed; they may charge less. But here, too, their freedom is limited. The ICC has power to fix minima as well as maxima. It may permit a road to set a rate at a figure that fails to cover its full costs. But it requires that all rates be reasonably compensatory. To this end, it forbids the setting of any rate at less than out-of-pocket costs. A just and reasonable rate, therefore, is not a specific figure but is one that comes within the limits that may be prescribed, not rising above a maximum that may cover or more than cover fully allocated costs, not falling below a minimum that covers only out-of-pocket costs.

Classification Systems. The three major systems of classifying commodities for the purpose of establishing class rates—the Official Classification in the Northeast, the Southern, and the Western—were developed by the railroads in these regions before the turn of the century and were influenced by the economic conditions prevailing at the time. In each region the roads undertook to establish the structure of rates that would maximize their revenues. And this led to the adoption of different principles of classification and to the establishment of different rates for the same goods.

The Northeast was a manufacturing region, and here the classification was so arranged as to encourage the exportation of manufactured goods. The South and the West were exporters of foodstuffs and raw materials, and here, with rates set low for such commodities, the roads augmented their revenues by setting them high for manufactured goods. As a result, class rates were higher in the South and much higher in the West than in the Northeast, though the cost of hauling goods was actually lower in the South and only moderately higher in the West. These discrepancies in the geographic structure of rates persisted for many years. They made it easier for manufacturers in the Northeast to ship to the border states and to the South and West, harder for those in the South and West to ship to the border states and to the Northeast and imposed an artificial handicap on industry in the South and West.

With the beginning of large-scale industrial development in the South and West during the 30s, the geographic discrimination in the classification systems came under vigorous attack. Complaints were made by the State of Georgia, by the Tennessee Valley Authority, and by the Antitrust Division. The fight was carried to the ICC, to the courts, and to the Congress. Action was opposed by the manufacturing interests and the railroads in the Northeast and by the railroads in the South and West. But in the Transportation Act of 1940 Congress provided explicitly that railroad rates should give no unreasonable preference to any region, district, or territory.

In 1945 the ICC found the three existing classification systems to be unreasonable and issued a temporary order raising class rates in the

---

[37] *Baltimore & Ohio Railroad Co.* v. *U.S.,* 345 U.S. 146, 150.

Northeast and reducing them in the South and West, pending hearings on the establishment of a uniform classification for the country as a whole. Its action was challenged by the railroads but was upheld by the Supreme Court in 1947.[38] A uniform classification was then prepared and was finally put into effect, in the territory east of the Rocky Mountains, in 1952. It has operated to encourage the location of industry in accordance with factors other than discriminatory elements in railroad rates.

Control of Discrimination.   Railroads have discriminated in three ways: between *persons,* between *commodities,* and between *places.* Discrimination between persons was once extensive. It is now forbidden by law. Rebates are no longer given to favored shippers at the expense of their competitors. There may still be some favoritism in the performance of service. But when it is disclosed, it is enjoined. Discrimination between commodities and between places is not forbidden as such but only when it is "undue" or "unreasonable." It is one of the principal functions of the ICC to determine the meaning that is to be assigned to these words, thus establishing the limits within which discrimination is to be permitted.

An action charging discrimination may be brought before the Commission by a shipper who complains that he is required to pay a higher rate than another shipper is permitted to pay. If he is to obtain a favorable decision, the complainant must show three things: (1) that there is a competitive relationship between his own commodity or location and the one that enjoys a lower rate, (2) that he has suffered (or is likely to suffer) serious injury as a result of the difference in rates, and (3) that the same railroad charges the two rates and would be able to correct the situation by changing one or both of them.

The railroad, on the other hand, may argue that the difference in rates is nondiscriminatory, corresponding to a difference in costs. Or it may defend discrimination by presenting evidence that its service is more valuable to one shipper than to another, or that it encounters competition in serving the one and not the other. If the Commission fails to find undue discrimination, it will allow the rates to stand. But if it makes such a finding, it will order the railroad to remove the discrimination, permitting it to do so by reducing the higher rate, by raising the lower rate, or by doing both.

Cases involving discrimination between commodities arise where goods that may be substituted for one another compete in the same market and where competition between fabricators is affected by the relation of rates on raw materials to those on finished goods. With respect to substitutes, the Commission usually requires comparable rates. It has acted, for instance, to forbid higher rates for benzol than for gasoline, for linseed oil than for cottonseed oil, and for lard substitutes than for lard. With respect to raw materials and finished products, the relationship of rates may affect the location of industry, giving plants that are close to raw materials an advantage over those that are close to markets, or doing the reverse. The fortunes of different flour mills, for instance,

---

[38] *State of New York* v. *U.S.,* 331 U.S. 284.

will depend upon the rates fixed for livestock and meat. In such cases the Commission tends to eliminate any artificial advantage or disadvantage by relating differences in rates to differences in costs. In either type of case, however, exceptions may be made, the railroads being allowed to fix lower rates on commodities where they face competition than on those where they do not.

Discrimination between places had been built into the structure of freight rates long before the Interstate Commerce Act was passed. In the Northeast, rates were generally related to distance. But in the South, they were so established as to meet the competition of water carriers to various ports, and these ports served, in turn, as basing points in fixing rates to inland towns. As a result, rates throughout the South declined as traffic approached a waterway. On transcontinental traffic, moreover, rates were computed by taking the water rates from Atlantic to Pacific ports and adding to them rail rates for hauling goods back toward the East. Transcontinental rates therefore declined as traffic moved on toward the Pacific Coast. The Act forced a revision of this structure. Under its provisions, the ICC has adopted the principle of relating rates to distance. But it has permitted many exceptions to this general rule.

Cases of place discrimination fall into two categories. Those involving a higher charge "for a shorter than for a longer distance over the same line, in the same direction, the shorter being included within the longer distance" come under Section 4 of the Act, known as the long-and-short-haul clause. All other such cases come under Section 3, which deals with discrimination in general. Long-and-short-haul discrimination is forbidden unless expressly permitted by the ICC. In Section 4 cases, therefore, the burden of proof is on the railroad that seeks relief from this provision of the law.

In Section 3 cases, however, the procedure is the same as that for discrimination among commodities. A shipper who complains of a higher rate than that charged at another place must show that the two places are in competition, that he is injured by the difference in rates, and that same railroad charges both rates and has the power to change them. And the railroad may defend itself by showing differences in the cost of service, in the demand for service, and in the competition faced on the two hauls. The considerations that influence the Commission's decisions in cases brought under either Section are much the same.

Discrimination may be permitted where there is competition between railroads and other carriers, between two railroads, or between two producing areas obtaining their raw material from a common source or selling in a common market. Thus, as shown in Figure 17–8, a railroad that runs from *A* to *B* may be permitted to meet the low rate of a water carrier operating on the river between these points without fixing an equally low rate on the equidistant haul from *C* to *B*.

And, as shown in Figure 17–9, a railroad that runs from *D* to *E* may be permitted to meet the rate of a water carrier between these points, even though it would then be charging more for the shorter haul from *D* to *F* than for the longer haul from *D* to *E*. Similarly, as shown in Figure 17–10, railroad *W* that follows a circuitous route from *G* to *H* may be

FIGURE 17–8

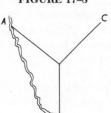

FIGURE 17–9

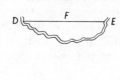

FIGURE 17–10

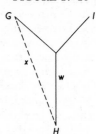

FIGURE 17–11

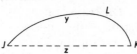

FIGURE 17–12

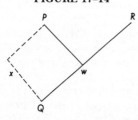

FIGURE 17–13

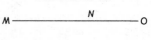

FIGURE 17–14

FIGURE 17–15

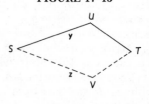
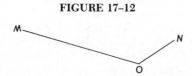

permitted to meet the rate of railroad *X* that follows a direct route, without fixing an equally low rate for the equidistant haul from *I* to *H.*

As shown in Figure 17–11, railroad *Y* may be permitted to meet the rate of railroad *Z* from *J* to *K,* even though it would then be charging more for the shorter haul from *J* to *L* than for the longer haul from *J* to *K.* And finally, as shown in Figures 17–12 and 17–13, a railroad that serves the competing industrial centers *M* and *N* that draw their raw materials from the common source *O* or sell their product in the common market *O* may be permitted to reduce the rate at *M* to the figure charged at *N.*

Such discrimination has its limits. A railroad may fix a lower rate for one of two equidistant hauls or for a longer than for a shorter haul only when it is forced to do so to meet competition that arises from some natural advantage, such as that of a water carrier or a shorter rail line.

Thus, as shown in Figure 17–14, railroad *W* will not be permitted to charge lower rates between *P* and *Q* where it competes with railroad *X*, a line of equal length, than between *R* and *Q*, where it has no competitor. And, as shown in Figure 17–15, railroads *Y* and *Z* will not be permitted to charge less for the longer haul from *S* to *T* than for the shorter hauls from *S* to *U* and *V*, merely because they compete at *T* and not at *U* and *V*.

A railroad may be permitted to equalize the competitive opportunities of different places, as was done in Figures 17–12 and 17–13. But it cannot be required to do so. Thus, the producers at *M* have no legal right to demand that their rate be made the same as that at *N*. And opportunities can be equalized only by offsetting natural disadvantages, not by canceling natural advantages. In the cases shown in Figures 17–12 and 17–13, the railroad may reduce the rate at *M* to the level of that at *N*. It may not raise the rate at *N* to the level of that at *M*.

The decisions made by the ICC and reviewed by the courts, in cases such as these, determine when discrimination will be permitted and when it will not. But the line thus drawn between legality and illegality is not always clear. The limits of discrimination, at any time, will depend upon the composition and the judgment of the Commission and the courts.

Consequences of Discrimination. Discrimination among commodities, where it involves the establishment of lower rates for goods that otherwise would not move at all, may be of general benefit. It is of benefit to the carriers, since it enables them to enlarge their revenues, make fuller use of their facilities, reduce their unit costs, and improve their position with respect to earnings. It obviously benefits the producers of commodities that pay the lower rates. It even benefits the producers of those that pay the higher rates, for if the low-rate traffic did not move, they would have to pay all the overhead costs and provide all the earnings by themselves, and their rates would be higher still. It benefits the community as a whole, since goods are thus made generally available that otherwise would be confined to local areas.

Discrimination among commodities, however, is frequently designed, not to increase the volume of traffic, but merely to divert existing traffic from one carrier to another. Discrimination between places, also, usually has this effect. Such discrimination may benefit a particular carrier, enabling a railroad, for instance, to obtain traffic that would otherwise have moved by water or by highway or over another line. It obviously benefits the commodities and the places that enjoy the lower rates. It may even be said to benefit those that pay the higher rates. Thus, in Figures 17–8 through 17–11, the people of *C, F, I,* and *L* are better off than they would be if the railroads serving them got none of the traffic between the competitive points, and were therefore forced to turn to them for more of the revenue required to cover costs and provide a fair return.

But it cannot be said that such discrimination is of benefit to the community as a whole. What one carrier gains, another loses. The discriminating carrier gets more traffic and more revenue; the competing carrier gets less. With the former, costs and rates will be lowered. With the latter, they will be raised. The practice, moreover, has a social cost. It obstructs the allocation of traffic among different media in accordance with their relative economy. And it results in wasteful transport by roundabout routes.

Discrimination between places has another effect. It exerts a powerful influence on the location of industry. Where the disadvantage of distance from materials and markets is offset by lower rates, one community (such as M in Figures 17–12 and 17–13) may grow in importance while another (such as N) may be denied the growth it would otherwise have attained. Production may thus be diverted from more economic to less economic sites.

The less desirable consequences of discrimination are to be attributed to the competitive character of the transport industry. If transport were monopolized, goods would not be moved by rail where water was cheaper or by circuitous routes where direct routes were available. Nor would a transport monopoly, under public regulation, be so likely to promote the development of one community at the expense of another. But where transport is provided by many different carriers, each of them must be given an opportunity to go after competitive business and to develop new sources of revenue. And the forms of discrimination thus permitted will lead to waste. Competition, however, may have offsetting advantages.

CHAPTER EIGHTEEN

Regulation Appraised

No final appraisal of regulation is possible, now or perhaps ever. Its real content and effects are not yet known, beyond rough estimates. It may, indeed, never have been tried properly and scarcely ever with the force which it nominally has. Perhaps it never will be fully applied. Moreover, regulation *as it is* must be compared with alternatives, not just judged as regulation, *Si* or *Non*. It may be just an American Dream Machine, but its alternatives may be worse.

REGULATION: ACTUAL AND IDEAL

Regulation has been tried (1) formally since 1870, (2) in some practical degree since the 1930s, and (3) under reasonably favorable conditions since the 1950s. Its lessons are mixed and sobering.

It usually conforms to the evolutionary process outlined in Chapter 13. Most utilities go through life-cycles with four phases. Most commissions are added late, and they then evolve in ways which retard the natural evolution of their utilities back toward normal conditions.

Actual regulation has passed through distinct periods. During 1888–1910, the ICC demonstrated that regulation can be an empty shell. During the 1920s, the valuation controversy stalled regulation further. The 1950s brought the taint of corruption and ineptitude. A partial revival in the 1960s coincided with powerful new doubts about regulation's economic effects. The new stresses since 1965—scarcity, ecology, competition, high interest rates, inflation—have placed regulation in a crisis—or watershed—situation.

But there have also been constants since 1870. Regulation has been passive, overburdened with tasks, and weak in treating the really critical matters.[1] State commissions have fought federal regulators. Actual regulation conforms more to the pessimistic image of it as a mediating device

---

[1] For more favorable views on regulation, see Kahn, *op. cit.;* and C. F. Phillips, *op. cit.* More critical evaluation have been noted frequently during Chapter 13–17; see also James M. Landis, *Report on Regulatory Agencies to the President-Elect* (Reprinted by U.S. Senate, Committee on the Judiciary [Washington, D.C.: Government Printing Office, 1960]), pp. 5–6.

to carry out political compromise, rather than to the ideal applier of economic criteria. And perversely, regulation thrives on adversity: the more it is criticized, the more it seems to grow and spread.

Ideally, it applies expert, independent judgment, briskly, with clear principles. It induces progress and clarity. In practice:

1. *Expertness* is the exception among commissioners, while political loyalty is the rule. Quality is mediocre. Turnover is high, so that most commissioners barely learn the industry and the issues before they move on. For some decisions, political skills are helpful; but for the most important ones, one needs to grasp the deeper issues before tempering them with political "realities."

2. *Independence* is diluted. Commissions are influenced by legislatures and executives, on virtually all issues that really matter. And really big issues are taken from the commissions for settling elsewhere. The commissions also become industry-minded and protective. Pure independence may exclude some suitable political influences and—in any event—be impossible to get. But most commissions are so dependent as to serve only as compromisers or industry promoters.[2] This often worsens as the industry and the commission age.

3. *Briskness* is rare. Procedures are usually slower than molasses and often manipulated. Regulation usually delays changes, often for decades.

4. *Principles* are usually fudged and obscured. Even when sound criteria do have an influence, they are usually diluted with fine points and judgment. Commissions usually just compromise rather than clarify or impose criteria.

5. *Progress* is often retarded or twisted. Regulation often impedes not only innovation but also the evolution of new suppliers and services. The delays often last for decades; some major ones continue right now.

These departures are, in the extreme, serious defects of regulation. Actual regulation conforms more closely to the *realpolitik* version than to the ideal model.

PROBABLE EFFECTS: GAINS AND LOSSES

Nobody knows, beyond guesses, what effects actual regulation has had. The likely effects can be summarized, with *good* and *bad* effects in that order. Most of the analytical predictions about regulation's direct and side effects (in Chapters 13 and 14) have been borne out in practice. What is the main picture?

At the least, regulation is likely to give the following benefits:

1. It is a safety valve, which lets all parties have the impression—even if it is often only an illusion—that their interests and logic have been heard and considered in the official decisions. It also provides a forum for returning with further complaints.

---

[2] See William L. Cary, *Politics and the Regulatory Agencies* (New York: McGraw-Hill Book Co., 1967), chap. 1; John Bauer, *Transforming Public Utility Regulation* (New York: Harper & Bros., 1950), pp. 137–38; Marver H. Bernstein, *Regulating Business by Independent Commission* (Princeton, N.J.: Princeton University Press, 1955), pp. 294, 296.

2. It brings about compromises among the parties at issue. This smoothes the adjustment process, perhaps as efficiently as is possible. Also, it eliminates most of the gross abuses which could occur under unfettered monopoly conditions.

3. It is occasionally quite strict and in line with optimum criteria—in some periods and on some issues. These high points might justify the mediocrity and costs of all the rest.

4. Where it is ineffective or slow, the resulting lag may provide just the right positive or negative incentives for efficiency, in line with effective market processes. This is part of the regulatory-lag hypothesis, by which regulation does *best* for efficiency when it is doing *least.*

5. And finally, the rate-base effect may promote technical progress in the long run in these capital-intensive sectors, offsetting the restrictive tendencies which would otherwise prevail.

These benefits would not be trivial, especially by the realistic standards which we have learned to apply in this book. In some cases, they could easily justify the costs of regulation, as they are ordinarily measured. And indeed, the best commissions during their best periods are hard to beat. If public ownership were the only alternative, regulation's uncanny ability to conserve on public capital and direct subsidies might put it ahead in most cases.

But now for the costs.

1. The first cost is in the grant of monopoly greater than would be necessary or natural in the absence of the franchise. This is a loss in itself and a cause of many of the other costs.

2. The direct costs of managing the regulatory process, and of private efforts to resist and twist it, are not small.[3] Nor, are these costs closely correlated with effective regulation: some of the largest commissions are among the least effective, or perhaps most harmful. Especially in the older commissions, which have persisted and grown during their industries' Stages 3 and 4, the costs tend to be greater than the possible benefits.

3. The internal inefficiency which arises under the regulatory franchise and process may be large.[4] This has proven difficult to assess, but the likelihood of its occurring is very great, and there is growing evidence that indeed it is significant, perhaps ranging over 10 percent of costs. It varies from case to case, but it is a normal part of the regulatory outcome.

4. The rate-base effects, in enlarged capital investment, are probably of medium but real scale. They relate to the lack of marginal-cost pricing; together, these two induce excess peak load and capacity and other directions of extra investment.

5. The level of service quality probably tends to be higher than is efficient. It also tends to be less diverse, offering a narrowed range of consumer choice in most regulated sectors (especially communications and transport). This reflects both the shared anxiety of regulators and

---

[3] They probably range well over a billion dollars annually; see also R. A. Posner, "Natural Monopoly and Its Regulation," *Stanford Law Review* (February 1969), pp 548–632; and Breyer and MacAvoy, *op. cit.*

[4] On points 3–6, Capron *ed. cit.,* and A. Phillips, *ed. cit.,* give valuable appraisals.

firms to avoid service breakdowns, and the inherent tendencies under multiple-firm regulation to converge on a narrow set of offerings.

6. And finally, where the supply of equipment is vertically integrated with the utility operating level, the rate and direction of innovation tends to be altered from the optimal.

These are tendencies which appear to be borne out objectively in practice, in a variety of utility sectors. They have not been proven conclusively, but logic and the burden of proof now rest against those who deny them. So far, counter-proof of this sort simply has not been forthcoming.

ALTERNATIVE IMAGES OF REGULATION

One has a wide range of plausible images about regulation's nature and effects. The choices include at least the following:

Success. Regulation is the best possible treatment, in the world as it is. The monopoly is inevitable, at least at the start, and it disappears over time; and the regulatory controls do have some effect. It is cheap, effective enough, and foolproof, because even—or especially—where it is loose and lagged, it is a tonic for efficiency.

Defective. It needs reform or at least more vigilance. Regulation works from time to time, especially when appointees are excellent and staff resources are abundant. But it requires vigilance plus a high order of political support and resources. Various minor and major reforms are needed, including a strong expansion of regulatory budgets. Generally, economists should replace lawyers as key operators of regulation.

Irrelevant. Regulation is unnecessary and of little consequence in either direction. It does not alter the basic economic outcomes. Instead, it simply provides a series of rituals, at which solemn dignitaries pretend to be deciding issues which, in fact, they neither control nor understand.

Ineffective. Regulation usually gets diverted and mired down in side issues, while the main economic conditions go untouched. The side effects are costly, even when regulation is performing as advertised. On balance its costs exceed its benefits, save in the rare cases of early and inspired regulatory leadership. But such cases are rare, partly because the interests involved will see to it that regulation is tardy and starved of resources.

Hoax. Finally, regulation may be a sham, invoked by powerful and wealthy firms, their investors and main customers, in order to enlarge their ability to exploit. Not only does it further disequalize wealth, income, and opportunity, by serving as a tool of the private interests. It also stands squarely in the way of other, more effective treatments for the basic conditions.

There are still other images, which the reader may explore now or which may arise in the future. But these six images do include the main current interpretations of regulation. They are all plausible, and evidence can be adduced for all of them.

Despite this wide range of images, there is a narrower set of technical features which regulation does seem to display consistently. It does seem to evolve perversely, during the broad utility evolution from Stage 1 to 4. It does seem to induce large costs of resistance or evasion by the private firms. And it does induce a variety of side effects, which alter the levels of resource use. And finally, it often creates an impression of effective public action when, in fact, there is little—or even antipublic—action.

ALTERNATIVES TO STANDARD REGULATION

A number of alternatives or supplements to regulation have long been considered or are live possibilities for the future. Their urgency varies inversely with one's image of regulation's success. We will consider several of these now in turn. The possible changes come under three main headings: more and better regulation, deregulation, and new hybrids of regulation.

More and Better Regulation. The most obvious first step would be to shift most regulatory attention from profit rates to price structure. Some of this is already occurring, by necessity. But more is needed. Also, more attention is needed on market structure and the possibilities of new competition. State regulation is barren ground for this improvement, though federal commissions might be more receptive. The FCC is already shifting, and the FPC and ICC may adjust further.

Next, more resources are needed for most commissions. At the state level, this is often a high multiple of the present levels. But where are such resources to come from? From the legislatures? There the utilities themselves will resist strongly. Perhaps the only method is to draw extra resources from the utilities themselves, as is being done in several states. Even so, the prospects for adequate resources are slight.

Further, better commissioners and staffs may be sought. One proposal is to replace lawyers with economists.[5] But, good as this idea is in principle, it suffers from the thinness of the ranks of available economists.[6] At the most, an infusion of economists could happen at the federal level only. The political economy of the sector assures that state regulation will continue to be managed by lawyers and politicians.

Still, as long as regulation is as extensive and obscure as it is, calls for better quality and talent are in order and may lead to marginal gains. But no major improvements up to optimal levels can reasonably be expected.

Deregulation. Regulation may be withdrawn, either partially or entirely. Partial deregulation, down to a core of regulatory activities, is a realistic goal. Indeed it is the proper sequence for regulation to follow during Stages 3 and 4. In most sectors, the core of natural-monopoly activities can be defined relatively clearly as it evolves over time, and regulatory constraints could be adjusted to those without major legislative effort. The result would be closer attention to the key utility prob-

---

[5] Recall Charles F. Donahue's argument, *op. cit.,* from Chapter 13.

[6] Perhaps a score of present economists are sufficiently trained and mature to be capable, expert regulators. This reserve would be easily absorbed by the federal commissions and largely finished in the course of five years. Meanwhile their research and independence would probably be reduced.

lems, and a gradual withdrawal from irrelevant and harmful activities. But this too is caught in the crosscurrents of utility and large-customer interests. It would take resolute, clear-minded and powerful commissions—with supportive legislatures and executives—to follow this route.

Complete deregulation is another matter. It requires a legislative act withdrawing both the constraints and the monopoly franchise. Consider the legislative sequence. Some party must introduce legislation and get it a fair hearing on its economic merits, despite its threat to powerful and focused utility interests. By Stage 4, the commission is a protector, not a limiter. Therefore support must be rallied from a wide range of potential gainers against the strong interests of the central parties. These parties include the regulators themselves, as a threatened group, who will naturally resist. Therefore the phasing out of regulation will usually be ardous and confused. In principle, abolition of regulation is clean and efficient. In practice, it is usually the opposite, as the ICC demonstrates.

Recall from Chapter 15 that there are several kinds of new entry which can be fostered as part of deregulation. Those include new entry by sellers, take-over, revision of the present structure, and new interutility competition. A skillful commission might anticipate the needed changes and foster them. But most commissions can be expected to resist and divert them, as they have in the past.

New Hybrids. Supplements to regulation can be of several sorts. One is to review the franchises, in contrast to the present *de facto* perpetual grant of monopoly. Actually an old idea, this device would provide incentives for efficiency, if renewal required a showing of good performance.[7] It has worked with at least a slight effect in television broadcasting. The key need would be to give it the proper time structure. Thus, if renewal were a last-minute decision, risk would be so high toward the end of the period that proper efficiency and investment would suffer. This might be averted by periodic or open bidding situations, in which an effective take-over could be permitted at any time. The prospective new owner would bid for the franchise and would get it unless the current utility bid even higher. The excess—or possibly a portion of that excess—of the bid over the original rate base of the utility could go to the public purse. This would provide incentives for good performance and also let the public share in the value created by the utility franchise. It would also ease the need for regulatory constraints on utility profit rates.

Second, profit constraints may be tied directly to performance. Rate increases can be made conditional on specific actions or results.[8] This elides the difficulties of estimating total performance (recall Chapter 13) or of letting regulatory lag give loose rewards for cost-cutting—and/or for evading, or postponing—regulation. It would face the disincentive problem and apply clear incentives.

Third, direct audits of utility performance could be ordered (recall

---

[7] On early renewal experiments, see Martin G. Glaeser, *op. cit.;* Emery Troxel, *Economics of Public Utilities* (New York: Rinehart & Co., Inc., 1947); and Paul J. Garfield and Wallace F. Lovejoy, *Public Utility Economics* (Englewood Cliffs: Prentice-Hall, 1964).

[8] An example is the ICC's granting a railroad rate increase in June, 1974, on condition that the revenues be applied to new rolling stock.

Chapters 13 and 14). These could appraise general management performance or specific actions. Such studies—whether published or not—could help fill the partial vacuum now surrounding managerial behavior.

Other supplements can be devised and tried. Presently regulation is settled in conventional lines. It attempts to do more than is possible, in ways which lack feedback from performance and which stir strong company resistance. Reforming regulation by increasing its quality and quantity is not enough. The incentive structure also needs changing, including ways to induce regulators to withdraw from Stage-4 former utilities.

Reformed or not, regulation will continue and probably spread, and it is needed for public as well as private utilities. Your image of the optimal design of regulation—as a device or package of devices—depends on your image of the actual effects of regulation. These effects may include a wide array of positive and negative influences.

It also depends on your image of the changing group of utilities. One can view them as brief departures from normal markets, requiring little unusual treatment. Or the distinction between utilities and other industries may seem sharp and permanent. Whatever images you form, they govern your policy judgments. In all the utility sectors, these questions are intensely debated, for the stakes are high and the policy issues continue to be open. Form your own images and policy lessons carefully *and* independently.

Part V

PUBLIC ENTERPRISE

19
Fields and Forms
of Public Enterprise

20
Public Enterprise in Finance and Industry

21
Public Enterprise in Utility Sectors

22
Public Enterprise in Urban and Social Sectors

23
Public Enterprise Appraised

CHAPTER NINETEEN

Fields and Forms
of Public Enterprise

Recall again that *public ownership* is a substitute for *private ownership*, not for the economic content of antitrust or regulation. And ownership is only one dimension of the publicness of public enterprise; others include control, subsidy, risk-bearing, and localism.

The scope and variety of public enterprise often surprise students, who have been taught to regard it as peripheral and alien, at best an occasional necessary evil. In fact, it is a varied and increasingly refined set of tools. Like other treatments, it is capable of good use or misuse. We will first note its range of types and causes. Then we set public enterprise in historical context, for its origins help to clarify its content and directions. The next section treats its main economic issues, and finally the chapter contrasts the main "efficient" and "inefficient" types of public enterprise.

Public enterprise is common abroad, and so this part of the book offers more global flavor and comparisons than the other parts. Yet the U.S. economy also has a variety of public enterprises, some of which are as American as apple pie. Public enterprise has definite forms and properties, which fit it to certain social uses. In practice, some public enterprises are costly, others are fruitful. Nearly all could be improved by revisions of form and criteria. To understand public enterprise is neither to blame or praise, it, nor to advocate or oppose it, but only that: to understand it.[1]

---

[1] There is no full, balanced treatment of the economics of public enterprise. Such sources as there are center on British experience. For background, see W. A. Robson, *Nationalized Industry and Public Ownership* (London: Allen & Unwin: 1960); W. G. Shepherd, *Economic Performance under Public Ownership* (New Haven: Yale University Press, 1965); R. Pryke, *Public Enterprise in Practice* (New York: St. Martin's Press, 1972); F. L. Pryor, *Property and Industrial Organization in Communist and Capitalist Nations* (Bloomington, Ind.: Indiana University Press, 1974); and M. Einaudi, M. Bye, and E. Rossi, *Nationalization in France and Italy* (Ithaca: Cornell University Press, 1955).

For lucid treatment of certain economic issues, see W. A. Lewis, *Overhead Costs* (London: Allen & Unwin, 1949); W. A. Lewis, *Principles of Economic Planning* (London: Allen & Unwin, 1950); and Ralph Turvey, *Economic Analysis and Public Enterprises* (London: Allen & Unwin, 1971).

SCOPE AND VARIETY

The present scope of public enterprise was outlined in Tables 1–1 and 4–2. The variation is wide, from near-totality in "command" economies to a variety of lesser or minor roles in "western" economies. In less-developed countries the patterns are even more mixed and rapidly changing. The U.S. differs from other western industrial economies chiefly in the low share of public enterprise in its utilities, industry and finance; these are the cores of market power (recall Chapter 2). Otherwise U.S. patterns are not peculiar. The typical pattern in western economies is: (1) *utilities,* entirely or mainly publicly owned, (2) *finance,* one or several public banks, (3) *insurance,* large social insurance programs, (4) *industry,* several major industries under partial public ownership, (5) *social services,* mainly under public ownership, and (6) *distribution,* little public enterprise.

Public enterprise exists in many parts of the U.S. economy. It takes a great variety of forms and behavior patterns. It includes a wide array of public firms, projects, departments, and programs which produce goods or services. It ranges from conventional utility cases, such as TVA, to industrial and service areas, over into certain subsidy programs, and into important *social* enterprises such as public schools and universities, mental hospitals, the courts, and prisons. Public enterprise goes far beyond TVA, British Railways, and the local municipal water works. We are surrounded with public enterprises of many sorts. Yet they tend to be a phantom presence in the U.S., often not recognized for what they really are.

One defines "public enterprise" by several elements; ownership is only one of them. Table 19–1 arranges a variety of cases roughly by the two criteria of public *control* and public *sponsorship.* One also needs to look at the degree to which the public enterprise is national or local in scope, since local units are usually more responsive. Also, one needs to know if the enterprise is a monopoly or, instead, faces tight competitive or countervailing constraints.

Public sponsorship is burdensome, since it draws on public resources. This involves tax friction and, often, regressivity; also, the tax revenues could be devoted to other public programs which have high yields. Therefore, sponsorship *per se* is to be minimized. For any given degree of sponsorship, effective control is to be maximized (except in certain unusual cases—broadcasting, education—where independence may itself be a desirable feature). Therefore, cases to the upper left of Table 19–1 are socially more optimal than those toward the lower right. Subsidy without public control is the worst of both worlds. Almost always, too, local controls are preferable to national ones and a competitive situation is superior to setting up a monopoly.

In short, the main dimensions of public enterprise are:

1. Cost to the public (in subsidies, capital, risk guarantee, etc.).
2. Control by the public.
3. Degree of monopoly.
4. Degree of localism versus national scope.

TABLE 19-1

Selected Public-Enterprise Activities in the United States, by Approximate Degree of Control and Subsidy

	Degree of Effective Public Control		
Degree of Public Sponsorship	*Full Control*	*Partial Control*	*Slight Control*
No Subsidy	Municipal utilities (water, sewage)	State liquor stores	Port of New York Authority
	AEC enrichment plants	National land management	Federal Reserve Board
	U.S. Government Printing Office	Amtrak	FHA housing program
		SBA programs (including minority support)	Tennessee Valley Authority
	Social Security	FAA programs	Performing arts centers
	Municipal parking facilities	Airports	Sports stadiums
		Highway construction and maintenance	Public housing
	Municipal transit	State courts	Medicare
		Local courts	Medicaid
	Federal courts	Federal maritime program	Public universities
		Mental hospitals	SST program
	Public law programs	State and local law enforcement agencies	Military R&D contracting
	Child-care programs	Prisons	Veterans Administration hospitals
		Corps of Engineers	Weapons purchasing and management
Full Subsidy	Primary education	Census Bureau	

These can vary sharply. The sectors and tasks facing public enterprises also differ sharply, such as between a sick coal industry and a booming electrical sector, a jail and a National Theater, or a university and a subway. In some public enterprises, only a small but controlling share of stock is publicly owned. In others which are wholly owned by the public, management is done for a fee by *private* firms. The range of choices and combinations is wide.

THREE BASIC TYPES

Among the varieties, three basic types are common: (1) The classic older public corporation, in a declining and/or utility sector with a national monopoly, and with its capital and perhaps some subsidy provided directly by the Treasury. (2) A public investment bank. It has working control of several industrial firms, earning profits and operating flexibly to influence a range of behavior. (3) Social enterprises, which produce services (e.g., education and health care) but which draw little or no revenues from users.

The Conventional Older Form.   This is the "autonomous public corporation." Furthest developed in Britain, it is found in utility sectors throughout western Europe and, less frequently, North America. It is commonly regarded as *the* alternative to the regulated *private* utility. Normally it is similar to a private firm except: (1) its capital is all from the public Treasury or backed by public guarantee, and (2) it is not formally regulated, but is supervised by a government department.[2] This

FIGURE 19–1

The Setting of a Typical Public Enterprise

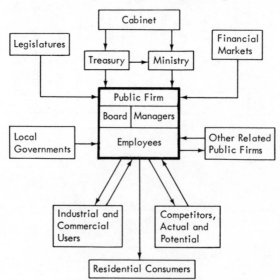

---

[2] See Shepherd, *op. cit.;* Robson, *op. cit.;* and C. D. Foster, *Politics, Finance and the Role of Economics: An Essay on the Control of Public Enterprise* (London: Allen & Unwin, 1971).

is shown in Figure 19–1. Its board members are public appointees, but they and the managers are often undistinguishable from their counterparts in private firms. Indeed, they are commonly drawn from the same pool of talent, move freely between public and private positions, and often hold directorships in other firms of both kinds.

Such public firms cluster in utility sectors, or in others with a special social impact. They sell products and/or services, and are required to take in enough revenue to cover costs plus some degree of profit on capital. They are also usually burdened with a variety of social policies, to perform tasks which the government is not willing to do directly. These social burdens are heavy in some cases, so that the firm's profit targets are often entangled in definitions of its *commercial* and *social* activities. Also, their capital usually comes at reduced costs, from the Treasury, or with a public guarantee, so there is some possibility that it

Which of these industrialists manage private firms and which ones manage public firms? See footnote 1 in Chapter 23 for the answer.

will be used beyond the margin at which its returns cover the true opportunity costs of capital to the State.[3]

The classic public firm unifies—i.e., monopolizes—its industry, often backed by franchise and entry protections as ample as those of private firms under regulation. Its target or *minimum* rates of profit are set in the same range (6–10 percent) as regulatory *ceilings* on rates of return. This often leaves the price structure questions at least as indeterminate as they are in private firms under regulation.

This classic form tends to enlarge the public's commitment of capital and limit its control over what the enterprise does. Even so, the public subsidy element may be small compared to the firm's total revenues.

Public Investment Banks. This type has no subsidy element at all. The objectives are more strictly economic: to allocate investment and control so as to improve performance in industrial firms. Public banks take partial holdings where profitable change can be made, often where private finance is not enforcing efficient management or requiring needed restructuring. Such banks may play a strong take-over role. They work best when not overloaded with ailing industries which have large social impacts. They work mainly through competitive market processes.[4]

Social Enterprises. These have large or complete subsidies. They also often pose important questions of monopoly and X-efficiency, which are, however, commonly ignored. Their motivation is often distinctive or indeterminate; they do operate under budget constraints, but their maximand is not clear. Hospital managers or university administrators, for example, may optimize among several criteria, including (1) quality, (2) size, (3) minimizing subsidy, and (4) maximizing autonomy. These may ultimately resolve into a larger net revenue maximand which is quite similar to long-run profit maximizing in private firms. And bureaucracy appears to be about the same, whether in large subsidized social enterprises or in large private enterprises with large profit margins.

Therefore these three types of public enterprise (and others) are merely variants of the more conventional forms of behavior which antitrust and regulation deal with. Their responses and yields may differ slightly, but they need social scrutiny and constraints fully as much as private firms. As a first approximation, most public-firm managers behave similarly to private managers. The constraints may differ, but they usually involve (1) budgetary limits on costs and revenues, (2) a definite profit target, and (3) a degree of financial supervision akin to what actually occurs in large private firms.[5]

Our proper objective is not to reach some grand Teutonic judgment between public and private enterprise. Rather, it is to analyze the variety in public enterprise, to identify the more efficient types, and to learn how to combine them with other strategies. Evidently, "nationalization" and "public ownership," in the classic British and TVA style, are special cases, not representative of the whole. There exists no nationalization in

---

[3] See Shepherd, *op. cit.;* and Pryke, *op. cit.;* and the references noted there.

[4] They are discussed in S. Holland, ed., *The State as Entrepreneur* (White Plains, N.Y.: International Arts and Sciences Press, 1973), among other sources.

[5] Foster, *op. cit.;* Robson, *op. cit.;* Turvey, *op. cit.;* Pryke, *op. cit.;* and Holland, *op. cit.*

any Western economy which is comparable in scale to "nationalization" in the giant U.S. economy. Abroad, even the largest public firms are only on a regional and local scale by U.S. standards. And public ownership is only one choice within the whole public enterprise toolkit.

REASONS FOR PUBLIC ENTERPRISE

The valid economic reasons for public enterprise all boil down to some form of external benefit. The main categories are:

1. *Social preference.* Society may simply prefer public to private control, especially for certain prominent sectors. Such cultural preferences seem to explain much of the great variation in Tables 4–1.

2. *Inner nature of the firm.* Public firms may modify the power structure and working conditions of private management. Such changes may be significant even if they do not magically transform the social content of the firm.

3. *External impacts.* Public firms may allow for outside social harms or benefits which private firms ignore. There may be a structural disequilibrium (e.g., shrinking railroads) with transitional social impacts, or a continuing social benefit that justifies continuing subsidy. In the extreme, the service may be a *pure public good* calling for a full subsidy.

4. *Scale and risk.* A new industry or project may be indivisible, large and risky, so that private firms will not finance it. If total discounted benefits (private and social) really do sufficiently exceed discounted costs, then a degree of public enterprise and/or subsidy may be efficient. Some such infant industry cases are valid; some are notoriously exaggerated. A backlog of such candidates is on tap at every point, each with its backers and beneficiaries. Only some, or possibly none, will deserve public support.

5. *Incomplete coverage of needy users.* Universal coverage of some services (e.g., old-age funds, health care) is often regarded as part of a *good* society. Private firms may supply only the more lucrative groups of customers, leaving needy groups unprovided. Public programs may be the most efficient way to give complete coverage on a fair and decent basis.

These and other conditions for public enterprise are often valid. But they are often misrepresented and usually controversial. Even where an external effect exists, it can often be treated more efficiently by incentive devices, partial public control or ownership, direct public programs, or other packages, rather than a conventional fully public firm.

Viewed broadly, public enterprises are best fitted for sectors where (1) goals are multiple, hard to measure, transcend efficiency, and pose hard choices of equity, and (2) pricing choices are discretionary and have a large effect on equity. So public enterprise suits soft, complex, and culturally important sectors. This fits its richness of forms and tactics.

HISTORICAL ROOTS

The history of public enterprise is checkered. One line is autocratic, from ancient statecraft through to the Organic State of Italy, Soviet-type economies, and other nondemocratic political systems. Another is sentimental British and Continental socialism, which is embodied in national firms in certain utility and sick-industry cases. Still another line is the pragmatic city utility, common throughout history and increasingly widespread in the United States.

From the earliest tribal days, there have been tools and productive units which were held and operated in common. No society has been devoid of them, though few have relied wholly on public units.

In ancient days, many varieties occurred. Athens' theaters were the city's, but many plays were sponsored by wealthy citizens.[6] The mines were state-owned and profitable. Some naval expeditions were sponsored collectively; in others, private sponsorship was central. Public entities were numerous and important; their atrophy coincides with the postclassical decline of Athens. In dynastic Egypt, the state dominated, partly by religious power. Production was organized about the great collective resource—the Nile—and the common system of irrigation. In the code of Hammurabi and the Old Testament alike are references to various communal workings. But the ancient lines are often blurred and not translatable into the modern forms.

The Roman empire at its peak had a variety of "public enterprises."[7] Armaments and defense arrangements were one part. Another was the provision of public facilities for trade, shipping, religion, water and bathing and—of course—popular games and circuses. Land was the prime element of official control, often to be disposed of or controlled by the current authority. As always, coinage and weapons were primarily under direct control.

The descent into the Dark Ages was sped by the disintegration of the great public works and enterprises—port, aquaducts, courts, markets—which had given order and support to the flow of trade and the fabric of society. Only local seigniorage and almonry remained, together with the growing church ownership of lands, and simple production and basic services. Under feudal hereditary rights or church control, land remained a staple quasi-public factor in the medieval economy.

Later, European cities rose and thrived with a variety of public entities and related forms. As the power and scope of hereditary aristocracy and monarchs then grew, the church receded into a rentier role, owning but not operating. By the 16th Century, kingship had prevailed in much of Europe, and the regional scope of much trade and production was ripe for efforts to induce development.

Mercantilist policy came to stress manufacture and trade, including a range of devices to stimulate new (if primitive) industries. Along with patents, a common device was the state-sponsored works.[8] The State also commonly made at least some of its own weapons and monopolized trade in such items as salt and tobacco. At the local level, public works and

---

[6] See A. Boeckh, *The Public Economy of Athens* (London: John Murray; 1828).

[7] Edmond Gibbon, *The History of the Decline and Fall of the Roman Empire,* 5 vols, 1776–1788.

[8] C. W. Cole, *Colbert and a Century of French Mercantilism* (New York: Columbia University Press, 1939).

enterprises in the growing infrastructure—ports, highroads, water and sewage, courts, etc.—helped to induce the rise of early mining and manufacture.

As the Industrial Revolution (1770–1850 in Britain) advanced, the relative scope of private enterprise naturally rose. But a variety of new public enterprises also evolved in Europe and the United States. Finance and industry were primarily private—with attendant consequences both in growth and in social impacts—while much infrastructure was public.[9] As new utilities evolved during 1830–1900, the European and American choices began to diverge. The post, the mint, and the arsenal were alike public. But in railroads, canals, and then electricity, telephone, and city transit, America went largely private, while Europe went mainly public. This reflected partly the low state of American political management at all levels during about 1870–1900, in which public enterprises were liable to deep abuse. But larger traditions were also at work: collective experience, unabashed private acquisitiveness, and standards of amenity.

The contrast is only partial, for the full scope of western European public ownership was only reached as late as 1945–50 and much public enterprise has existed all along in the U.S. But there were real differences, especially after the U.S. veered sharply toward regulation of private utilities from 1900 onward. In social infrastructure too, Europe developed earlier than the U.S.: public schools (after 1870 in Britain), social insurance, health care, public housing, museums, etc.

By 1930, public enterprise was extensive. It has continued and spread since then. To summarize:

For more than a century governments have monopolized certain industries, operating them as sources of public revenue. From 10 to 20 countries, in each case, have thus monopolized tobacco, matches, alcoholic beverages, and salt. In the Latin countries of Europe and America, in Australia, in various states of the U.S., and elsewhere, governments finance themselves in part by conducting public lotteries, having nationalized the gambling industry.

Another long-established field of public enterprise is transport and communication. Highways and port facilities have been publicly provided nearly everywhere. The railroads of Belgium, Italy, Germany, and Switzerland were taken over by governments in the latter years of the 19th Century. All those of France were taken over by 1937. The railroads of more than 50 countries, including all the major powers but Britain and the United States, were nationalized before World War II. Urban transit systems have been public undertakings; the telegraph systems, in most countries, have been developed by the postal authorities. In Germany the

---

[9] One example, among many, of important state-owned railroads is detailed in Robert J. Parks, *Democracy's Railroads: Public Enterprise in Jacksonian Michigan* (: Kennikat, 1972). The courts have not barred public enterprise. The Supreme Court of the United States upheld the establishment of a municipal fuel yard by the city of Portland, Maine, in 1917, socialization of banking, grain storing, milling, and other enterprises by the state of North Dakota in 1920, initiation of a wholesale and retail gasoline business by the city of Lincoln, Nebraska, in 1927, and the right of the federal government to engage in the business of generating, transmitting and distributing hydroelectric power in 1936. See *Jones* v. *City of Portland,* 245 U.S. 217; *Green* v. *Frazier,* 253 U.S. 233; *Standard Oil Co.* v. *City of Lincoln,* 275 U.S. 504; and *Ashwander* v. *TVA,* 297 U.S. 288.

telephone service was developed by the state telegraph system. Elsewhere in Europe the telephones were taken over around the turn of the century.

Public utilities, throughout the world, have long been owned by governments. Water supply, in nearly all large cities, is a public responsibility. Gas and electricity were publicly provided in more than three-fourths of the cities of Germany and in more than half of those in Great Britain before 1930. Regional systems for the generation and transmission of electricity were operated by governments in Canada, New Zealand, and South Africa. The Central Electricity Board, in Great Britain, was given a monopoly of transmission lines by a Conservative government in 1926.

Housing has been supplied by governments for longer periods and in greater quantities in Europe than in the United States. In England public housing was first permitted by law in 1851. In Germany and the Netherlands, it dates from 1901. Elsewhere it has its origin in the shortages that followed World War I. In most countries, the governments undertook to stimulate construction by cooperatives, limited-dividend societies, and other private builders by providing subsidies in the form of cheap land, tax exemption, and low-interest loans. But in some cases—notably in the city of Vienna—housing was built and operated by the governments themselves. In Great Britain, between the two world wars, a fourth of the new housing, including virtually all of the rental housing, was constructed by local authorities.

Since 1930, four main further increases in public enterprise have occurred. (1) Whole economies were shifted, as in China and eastern Europe after 1948, and Yugoslavia developed a hybrid set of "worker-managed" enterprises. (2) A nationalization wave in western Europe rose during the 1930s and crested during 1945–52, touching mainly utility sectors. (3) Rising urban and postindustrial problems in the U.S. have bred a series of pragmatic new public enterprises (mostly in utilities and social sectors). And (4) Many less-developed countries have tried new public enterprise for sovereignty, infant-industry, and other reasons.

In Italy, industries were made public less by design than by default.[10] An Institute for Industrial Reconstruction was set up during the depression of the 30s to extend financial aid to ailing industries. This agency, with its subsidiaries, came to hold the shares of many Italian companies. These holdings, moreover, were continued and increased during and after the war. As a result, IRI controls a substantial part of Italian industry, owning nearly all of the stock in shipbuilding, most of that in iron and steel, and a large part of that in the manufacture of transport equipment, electrical equipment, tractors, and machine tools. In addition, the government owns the country's five largest banks, the railroads and the airlines, the telephone, telegraph, radio, and television systems, the motion picture studios, the coal mines, and the petroleum industry. Public enterprise, though adopted without reference to any logical pattern, is

---

[10] See Holland, *op. cit.;* and M. J. Posner and S. J. Woolf, *Italian Public Enterprise* (London: Duckworth, 1967).

thus as extensive in Italy as it is in Britain or in France. Since 1960 IRI's coverage and effects have spread still further. IRI now operates partly as a new kind of public investment bank (see Chapter 20).

The nationalization program of the Labor Party in Great Britain, effected through measures adopted in 1946–50, included finance (the Bank of England), Commonwealth communications (civil aviation, cables, and radio), public utilities (gas and electricity), transport (carriers by rail, by water, and by road), a depressed industry (coal), and another industry that fell into none of these categories (iron and steel). Some of these measures were not controversial. But others, such as those relating to road haulage and to iron and steel, were highly so. Each case was argued on its merits. The argument for public enterprise ran in terms of its possible contribution to productive efficiency and public responsibility. But Britain was to remain a mixed economy, a fifth of it—more or less—being under public ownership, four-fifths of it still in private firms.

In France the postwar nationalizations included the Bank of France and the four largest commercial banks, the 34 largest insurance companies, as much of the coal, gas, and electrical industries as still remained in private hands, the Renault works, and a company manufacturing engines for airplanes. In addition, the government extended its participation in mixed companies in a number of different fields: aviation, shipping, motion pictures, broadcasting, news service, chemicals, and petroleum. Nationalization was to promote economic reconstruction, transfer economic power from the capitalists to the workers, and in some cases, such as the Renault works and the airplane engine company, it was to punish collaborators.

Elsewhere in Western Europe, public enterprise was also expanded in utility areas before 1955. Then patterns stabilized. More recent shifts have been instead toward public banking and social enterprises. Among industries, only sick firms (e.g., aircraft, ship-building) have drawn much new public ownership.[11]

---

[11] Less developed countries deserve a brief analysis. They illumine the U.S.'s own heritage, from its development period. Among the 100 or so LDCs, there is great variety. Some are developing steadily, others are oil-rich, still others are new tiny microstates with slender economic prospects, and others seem hopelessly mired in failed development efforts. A common basic question is: Can development occur under private ownership and free markets, or are public ownership and planning necessary?

The critical points on which industrial policies turn appear to be:

1. Official levels of income per capita are very low.
2. Production is mainly agricultural and from other earth resources, such as mining or oil. Exports are often important, primarily of agricultural and mining output. These products range from bananas, rubber, coffee, and livestock on over to raw chemicals, oil, and metal ores.
3. There is a small modern sector, usually with three or four main industries.
4. The LDCs often have a very wide choice among types of industries to create. Moreover, many of these industries offer a range of economies of scale.
5. There are often several or more large multinational firms operating visibly in these countries. Commonly they hold very high market shares in their local operations.
6. Capital markets in these countries are usually quite rudimentary and small. The cost of capital—in terms of interest rates or other required payments—is usually very high.
7. Managerial talent is usually quite scarce, either for managing enterprises or for public administration.
8. There are a few leading families, with a large share of local wealth. Their assets are often

The main lines of public enterprise are now stable. U.S. patterns are summarized in Table 19–2. The fields in which public enterprise is most common, in the noncommunist world, are banking, transport, communications, and public utilities. In nearly all countries, the central banks are owned by governments; in some countries, other banks and insurance companies have been nationalized. Almost all of the railroads outside of the United States are public undertakings. Commercial airlines, with few exceptions, are government-owned. Telephone and telegraph services, too, are usually governmental. Radio and television broadcasting is a public enterprise in most countries. Urban transit and electricity are characteristically provided by governments. Rental housing, in cities, is widely accepted as a public responsibility.

---

held abroad for safety. There also are usually major problems of ethnic discrimination within the society.

9. A development sequence in these countries usually requires a series of major structural changes. Some of these shifts may be beyond the scope of private interests to perceive and to carry out.

10. Many underdeveloped countries get large volumes of economic and military aid from the *big powers*. This aid is given with a variety of strings and requirements, often serving the national and commercial interests of the givers.

11. Political leaders in these countries often believe in the desirability of monopoly in industry. They also believe in their own ability to control and guide such monopoly.

The main scarcities are therefore primarily in administrative talent, in investible resources, and in foreign exchange. The problems are recognized to be large and difficult, but current officials evince confidence in their ability to make and impose the right choices. The political setting normally runs to a high degree of autocracy. The social and economic strains seem to make it necessary to hold and exert tight and thorough controls from above. There is often a high degree of instability, in which regimes come and go in rapid succession.

These contrast with the economic and political stability which make marginal analysis and solutions valid in industrial economies. Such turbulence means that a wide range of strategies are about equally advisable. There is a strong urge to control the industrial and finance sectors, to *plan* development, and to control activities. This contrasts with a private market model. Ordinarily it involves a stress on heavy industry which, once in place, produces for the *planned growth* of other sectors. It may oppose or suit the strong interests of the leading families, whose control it might displace.

Each of these strategies has its own merits, but it also is vulnerable at several points to the special problems of development. Apart from the oil-rich states—which have the means to choose almost any development strategy—the *normal* underdeveloped country will often find it optimum to pursue an opportunistic mixed strategy. This would involve some substantial aid from outside, both in funds and in technical assistance of various kinds. It will wring concessions from multinational companies as much as possible, without actually banishing them. It will also include a degree of joint ownership and be forced localism in employment by these firms. And finally, it will include both a degree of central planning and anticipation of the major events in the development sequence, plus a deliberate creation of competition in infant industries from the start. Such a strategy will have a variety of offsetting stresses within it, rather than a committal to a single device.

Many LDCs resort to a large amount of public ownership, both for local and foreign enterprise. Ordinarily this has little economic analysis or clear economic objectives behind it. It is more a political and social device, aimed at establishing local independence and limiting the power of the established groups. In the case of oil companies, the recent rise in public ownership is more an effort simply to capture profits for the home countries.

The range of enterprises thus taken over is wide and often inconsistent. It would seem likely to foster waste and inequity on a large scale. Yet the actual results are not clear. The performance of public enterprises in LDCs is a large new frontier for research. The public ownership itself is not a solution to any of the problems, but it does offset certain biases in the classic development conditions, including the role often played by the main prior holders of economic power. In certain ways, monopoly under public enterprise can be more tolerable than under private ownership. The enterprises often become targets for other efforts to control the development process in favor of one group or another. Still, there is no basis yet for concluding that public enterprises perform more poorly than the alternative methods of economic control and incentives.

TABLE 19-2
Local, State, and Federal Public Enterprises in the United States

1. *Local*	*Extent of Public Enterprise*

1. *Local*

Utilities

Transit (bus, subway, trolley . . . . Most large cities
commuter lines)
Water and sewage . . . . Virtually all large cities
Garbage disposal . . . . Most cities
Electricity . . . . Many smaller cities, several large cities
Ports . . . . Most port cities
Airports . . . . All large cities

Social Units

Schools . . . . All cities and towns
Libraries . . . . Virtually all cities and towns
Parks, golf courses, pools . . . . Virtually all cities and towns
Sports stadiums . . . . Many cities
Museums . . . . Many cities
Zoos . . . . Some large cities
Cemeteries . . . . Most cities and towns

2. *State*

Prison facilities . . . . All states
Insurance services . . . . Unemployment: All states
                                     Workman's Compensation: 18 states
Parks . . . . Most states
Liquor retailing . . . . 16 states
Electricity . . . . Nebraska, New York
Ports . . . . Port of New York Authority (transport and
                                     urban facilities); New Orleans; other
                                     ocean ports
Toll roads, bridges and tunnels . . . . 29 states
Health care . . . . Mental and old age institutions

3. *Federal*   *(expenditures in 1973)*

Electricity . . . . Corps of Engineers, $1,803 million;
                                     Bureau of Reclamation, $519 million;
                                     Tennessee Valley Authority
Postal service . . . . $11,679 expenditures; $1,391 subsidy
Lands . . . . Forest Service, $320 million;
                                     National Park Service, $82 million
Commodities stockpiles . . . . Value, $653 million
Transport . . . . Alaska and Panama Canal railroads;
                                     Military air and sea transport services;
                                     St. Lawrence Seaway
Loans and guarantees . . . . About 100 agencies, includes housing,
                                     farming, rural electricity and telephones,
                                     Export-Import Bank, Small Business
                                     Administration
Insurance . . . . Many agencies: banks, housing, crops,
                                     shipping, foreign investment, stock
                                     markets, veterans life and annuity
                                     insurance, old age pensions
Health care . . . . Medicare, Medicaid, veterans hospitals
Industry . . . . Various: Government Printing Office,
                                     Military production, etc. (World
                                     War II aluminum, steel, rubber and
                                     other plants)

Several governments are engaged in mining, in manufacturing, and in foreign trade. Great Britain, France, and Italy operate coal mines. Turkey is in the business of mining coal, copper, chrome, and manganese. Tin is produced by Bolivia, and oil by Mexico. The oil resources of South America and the Middle East are owned and their exploitation controlled by governments. Fifteen of the 200 largest industrial enterprises in noncommunist countries outside the United States are government-owned, being engaged in the production of chemicals, petroleum products, and iron and steel. Public enterprise in manufacturing and trade is found most often in less-developed countries.

Still, there is much debate and change at the margins. Table 19–3 gives a selection of changes during just the short 1970–74 period. There is much fluidity, and there are powerful practical reasons and interests at work tending to enlarge the scope of public enterprise.

The 1930s brought hopes that public firms could provide *yardstick* competition for private firms, setting criteria of performance. But the hope has come to little.

Comparable private and public units often are not available. It is possible, for instance, to compare the railroad, airline, telephone and telegraph, and radio and television services provided privately in the United States with those provided publicly abroad. It is possible, too, to compare private transit, water, gas, and electric utility services in some American cities with similar public undertakings in others. But so many variables are involved, in every case, that sweeping generalizations concerning relative efficiency cannot be justified.

When quality of service is compared, the judgments have to be mainly subjective. It would be possible, of course, to measure the speed and frequency of trains, planes, and transit vehicles, their adherence to schedules, and their records of accidents, the time required to make a telephone connection or to deliver a telegram, the pressure and purity of water, the heating value of gas, the constancy of electric current, the number of stations providing broadcasts, the number of hours they are on the air, and the frequency and duration of interruptions to all these services. But such comparisons are seldom made. And objective standards are often lacking.

Rates can be compared, but such comparisons may be misleading. Where the quality of service differs, there is no comparable unit to which the rates can be applied. Rate structures are complicated; charges vary with customer classes, with types of service, and with quantities consumed. It is therefore difficult to find, in different schedules, particular rates that are properly to be compared. And even though services and rates were standardized, comparisons might not be meaningful. A high rate might cover costs and yield a profit; a low rate might be subsidized.

So, too, with comparisons of cost. The conditions under which private and public enterprises provide their services may differ in many respects, and these differences will be reflected in differences in costs. Transport costs, for instance, will be influenced by the density of traffic and the character of the terrain, telephone costs by the size of the exchanges, and water costs by the accessibility of adequate supplies. Elec-

TABLE 19-3
Selected Changes in Public Enterprise, 1970–74

U.S.

Finance.................. Securities Investor Protection Corp. created to ease impacts of stockbroker failures on investors. Federal National Mortgage Assurance (Fannie Mae) converts to semiprivate status, grows rapidly. A new RFC is proposed, to support private firms.

Utility .... Post Office shifted to public corporation basis, 1970. Amtrak begins, 1970; subsidy grows to $200 million (much smaller than comparable systems abroad). Consolidated Rail Corp. created to absorb 8 failing eastern railroads; hits legal snags; future in doubt in 1975. Long Island Railroad sharply improves service quality. Public urban transit expands further. Major airports continue expanding (Dallas–Ft. Worth, others); Puerto Rico buys ITT telephone system. Many cities build large sports stadiums. State universities increase share of students by undercutting private tuition. Legal aid put in a public corporation, 1974. Public TV system decentralized, put on firmer financial footing, 1973–74. Public housing shift to owner-occupied basis fosters massive corruption; large projects continue.

Other..................... State lotteries emerge. Public off-track betting is created in New York, others. U.S. General Service Administration extends operations to apply monopsony power.

Canada..................... Canadian Development Corp. is created to assert national ownership. Takes over TexasGulf Sulfur Company. Alberta takes over the main airline in the province. National health system is extended, refined. Railroad passenger service is put in a public firm.

U.K......................... Rolls-Royce nationalized following insolvency: car operations left private. Concorde program continued, despite great costs. Channel Tunnel given public backing for 90 percent of capital. Attempt to "hive off" secondary activities of public firms is abortive. Government uses public firms heavily to raise wages, restrain prices, 1973–74; large deficits result. British European Airways and BOAC merged into British Airways. Private broadcasters permitted in radio. Public shares in aircraft and British Leyland are planned.

Sweden .... A state holding company is set up to manage 22 various public firms.

France...................... Public tobacco monopoly sets fees for all cigarette sales. Renault takes leadership in French auto production.

Germany .... Public holding company for oil distribution evolved in 1973. Volkswagen faces severe problems.

Finland..................... Public holding company controls diverse enterprises.

Middle East Oil Countries..... Extend public ownership to oil production facilities in most countries.

Pakistan .... Nationalizes 31 large companies and cotton and rice trades in 1973; also various others. But subject to rapid reversals.

Other LDCs .... Zaire, Ethiopia and others plan to nationalize nearly "all" industry and commerce.

---

tric costs will vary with differences in the method of generation, the scale of operation, and the degree of physical integration. In the case of multipurpose projects, they will depend upon the principle used in allocating some part of the joint costs to the business of producing power. Costs will be affected, too, by differences in the burden of taxes, in the charges for capital, and in the policies adopted in depreciating assets and retiring debts. As a consequence, where the costs of private and public enterprises differ, it is difficult to determine how much of the difference is properly to be attributed to factors such as these and how much to differences in the efficiency of managements.

The main lessons of history appear to be:

1. Virtually all types and extents of public enterprise have occurred within our cultural mainstreams.

2. The specific set of enterprises is largely a cultural matter, varying widely in line with social traditions and preferences.

3. Many public enterprises are residuary; filling gaps or assuming responsibilities unmet by private interests. This often includes only the burdens and poor risks left after private groups have skimmed the cream off the market. There is strong, continuing pressure on public resources to sponsor or protest private interests via forms of public enterprise.

4. Public enterprise is extended in or after crisis periods, which tip the old balance of interests. A major war almost always increases public enterprise, often permanently. Depressions create corporate orphans requiring support (e.g., by the Italian IRI and the American RFC).

5. Resistance to public take-over is mainly a matter of the price offered for the private firm. Almost every private enterprise will agree to becoming publicly-owned if the terms are favorable enough. *Ideological* battles against public enterprise are often merely a tactic in the underlying *economic* contest over the price to be paid.

6. The economic purposes and operations of public enterprises are highly varied, from high profits to high subsidies and from narrow financial targets to broad social effects.

7. The form and operating policies of a public firm—*not* its public ownership *per se*—largely determine its performance.

8. Comparisons of performance between public and private firms are usually difficult and inconclusive.

ECONOMIC ISSUES

The criteria for guiding and evaluating a public firm's performance are the same as before (recall Chapters 1–3). Ideally the firm operates at quantity and quality levels which bring marginal social benefit into line with marginal social cost. Its investment policies also fit such efficient lines. Equity, progress, and other criteria are included in the appraisal. In conventional public firms, commercial criteria will usually suffice, with only small adjustments for social-private divergences. In wholly social firms, social benefit-cost analysis should apply to the core decisions.

There are several economic questions to be asked in defining a public enterprise and its likely performance.

Origins. Is compensation above, at, or below the unit's true economic value? Overpayment is usually both inefficient and unfair. It sacrifices the potential social benefits in advance, and it usually saddles the new public firm with heavy, irrelevant interest costs.[12]

Is it a genuine take-over, in which old methods, managers, and content are changed? Or is it a friendly way for existing shareholders and managers to shelter their interests and jobs?

Structure. Is ownership completely public, or partial? Is the enterprise larger than scale economics require? What degree of monopoly does it have (market share, entry barriers)?

Operation and Criteria. What motives and incentives are in effect? Profit or budget targets? Or output, market share, engineering targets? What profit rate is targeted and/or reached?

Is the price structure efficient? What are its effect on equity (i.e., who gets the benefits of public enterprise): regressive or progressive?

What external effects and social objectives are laid upon the enterprise? Are they paid for directly from the fisc, or cross-subsidized (with profits on some operations covering losses on others)?

LESSONS AND POLAR TYPES

Though there has been much experience with public enterprise, only a handful of studies have been made of its effects. These will emerge in Chapters 20–22. They can be summarized in advance:

1. The greatest yields arise in firms which take an *active* role in changing structural conditions and their own content. Thin or negative yields are common when the public firm merely tries to mirror commercial behavior.

2. The benefits of any public enterprise will normally tend to become *less progressive* over time. The public firm is, like any other social device, a target for interest groups to use their advantage. Large firms and affluent citizens will normally be able to adjust more fully, to reap the benefits of public enterprises (e.g., low-price outputs). Over time, this means that the benefits will shift toward less needy groups.[13]

3. *Social burdens* will be laid on the public firm more heavily than private firms. Many of these need, instead, direct treatment by public programs. (Yet the whole budgetary stress laid on the public firm by these burdens *may*—if it is not too severe—also tend to assure that operations are kept efficient and output quality is not excessive.)

---

[12] See W. A. Lewis, *op. cit.,* among others. Much of the Western European shifts since 1930 have involved very generous compensation (partly yielding to ideological strife: recall point 5 just above). This has usually caused seeming financial losses, from interest payments on worthless "capital." The struggles since 1970 over "rescuing" bankrupt U.S. railroads are mainly about the degree of compensation.

[13] Examples: TVA at its creation had a variety of progressive effects on rural poverty. Now it primarily sells bulk electricity to large private firms and utility systems. The U.K. National Coal Board's output has shifted from households primarily to industry and electricity generation.

4. Cheap guaranteed capital supplied by the Treasury *may* induce an increased level of investment (but this may also promote optimal progressiveness in the long run).

5. Inefficient pricing may be less frequent than under regulated private ownership, and so the antimarginalist effects on output and investment may be less.

In short, public enterprise often involves certain incentives and processes, but they also tend to avoid some deviances which arise in private firms under regulation. From this wide field of types and results, we need to focus on the main groupings. One way to do this is to identify those types of public enterprises which have (1) relatively low social yields, and (2) others which have relatively high yields.

The Low-Yield Cases.   There are at least four types.

The *first* is high sponsorship with low control. This shades into straight subsidies, often from poor to rich, often via State guarantees against private risks. A few examples are capital loaned free of charge to military suppliers, various loan guarantees for large private corporations, and portions of the U.S. maritime and agriculture subsidy programs (see also Chapter 24).

Second is subsidy for activities used mainly by those with above-average income and wealth. Possible examples include certain subsidized programs for performing arts, much suburban commuter service, and tax support of university education for children from upper economic levels. The several systems of courts—in the context of unequal access to the best legal counsel—can be regarded as a complex set of public enterprises with primarily a regressive incidence, including their treatment of commercial and consumer matters. These cases include some of what are regarded as our finest institutions, in the arts, education, and the law (see also Chapter 22).

Third is the syndrome of the *sick* industry, often using large amounts of capital and often selling to (and buying from) large private firms (see also Chapter 21). Since the "sickness" is often industry-wide (with severe dislocations which invite a unified treatment), the common strategy is a centralized monopoly, financed directly and extensively by the Treasury. British experience suggests that these cases should be handled differently. Many of the social impacts are external to the industry. But governments routinely fail to treat them directly, instead leaving them as a burden on the public firm, to be met by slowing down closures and by cross-subsidizing the losing parts. The public firm is also often prevented from raising its prices, and it is usually expected to raise wages rapidly. The main beneficiaries usually are industrial users and equipment suppliers. The resulting financial losses, redundancy and demoralization in the public firm are often interpreted to discredit all forms of public enterprise. The drain from all this on public supervision, public funds, and public administration talent is often large.

A *fourth* type is the nationwide public firm in a *healthy* utility sector, such as electric power and telephones. "Health" means that revenues cover costs (often because of excess demand) and that there are few big external effects (such as pollution) or social impacts. Yet these enterprises still absorb large amounts of capital and administrative talent. The gains are often minor and mainly taken by private firms and upper economic groups. Moreover, the lack of competitive constraints can induce internal inefficiency.

These are categories of public enterprises which perhaps should—on criteria of efficiency and equity—be revised in form and objectives.

High-Yield Cases. By contrast, certain other kinds of public enterprises have tight constraints (by competition or budgetary control), minimum use of public funds and talent, a progressive incidence, and flexibility in arrangements.

One such type is the public-firm competitor, with a quarter or less of the market and some mixture of private-public ownership and motivation. It can cause improved pricing and efficiency in tight-oligopoly markets. Its take-over threat to firms in other tight-oligopoly markets could indirectly induce increased efficiency in them too.[14]

A *second* group is the public entity as countervailer against private market power which may be immune to other constraints. An instance is the British National Health Service as a buyer of drugs from private companies (see Chapter 27). It is paralleled on a small scale in the U.S. by the Veterans Administration and certain hospital groups. Defense weapons purchases occasionally, but not consistently, are done on this basis (see Chapter 28).

Third are activities with high progressive benefits spread throughout society. A downtown public library is one example, as is the provision of good-quality legal services to poor people. Programs stopping contagious disease are another; so is universal primary schooling, if properly structured. The social-critic and innovator aspects of public universities also are of this sort.

Fourth are units whose outputs go mainly to upper-wealth groups *and which maximize profits.* Prime examples are state universities, performing arts programs, and high quality medical care, *if* they were operated to gain large profits. This can be done by using price discrimination, on a means test or some other basis.

A more basic division is between *active* and *passive* public enterprise. An active firm operates to cause structural change, either reorganizing its industry or causing change in other firms. It has independence of control and finance and leeway to change fields. It is aggressively managed and competes with other firms. By contrast, a passive public firm accepts its environment and clings to its monopoly position. It tends to subsidize corporate interests—as a milk cow—while staying confined to its original markets.[15] These subsidies are commonly regressive. Generally, active firms tend to evolve toward passive behavior as time passes.

---

[14] See W. C. Merrill and N. Schneider, "Government Firms in Oligopoly Industries," *Quarterly Journal of Economics,* 1966, pp. 400–412.

[15] See Pryor, *op. cit.;* and M. Shanks, ed., *Lessons of Public Enterprise* (London: Jonathan Cape, 1963), especially Chapter 7, "Relations with Private Industry," by John Hughes.

SUMMARY

Public enterprise is varied and integral in the modern economy. It takes many forms and roles, ranging from commercial-like to social. It ranges also from partial to complete public ownership, and in other dimensions too.

It has deep historical roots, which reflect pragmatic social needs as well as cultural preferences. Abroad, it occurs in utility, finance, and social sectors, with scatterings in industry and trade. There is less of it in U.S. finance, utilities, and industry, but versions of it are more widespread than is usually recognized. It is tending to spread and evolve in new directions.

It has certain economic properties, which can be clinically analyzed. The conventional form is the public corporation in a utility sector, under pressure to mirror commercial behavior. Improvement of content, equity, and other social objectives have been increasingly neglected in practice and the literature. Yet the potential of public enterprise is broader and richer. New public banking and social enterprises are exploring new ways to yield social benefits while easing the drain on public resources.

Social criteria for public enterprises are the usual ones. Antitrust, regulation and other treatments are as suitable for public firms as for private ones. Managers of public firms usually have problems and criteria essentially similar to those in private firms, and bureaucracy has common properties in both. The origins, constraints, and criteria usually define the economic performance which public firms will show. Several low and high yield types of public enterprises can be identified.

These economic properties of public enterprise can be tested and evaluated in practice. We now look at several groups of public firms, in finance and industry, and in utilities and social sectors.

CHAPTER TWENTY

Public Enterprise in Finance and Industry

There is much variety of form and experience. Some of this variety will be presented, and common lessons will be drawn. Public banking has recently grown, with increasing linkage between finance and industry. Many of these public units are passive (recall Chapter 19), but in some countries there is a gradual shift toward active behavior. As ideology has waned, the ability to design practical units adapted to specific purposes has improved.

FINANCE

Public firms participate in the three main types of financial operations: commercial banking, investment banking, and insurance (recall Chapters 10 and 11). Some of these public units have been brief experiments, while others are large and permanent.

Banking

The functions are mainly three: to clear checks, to make short-term loans and hold savings, and to set the terms of banking competition (recall Chapters 11 and 12). Much of this is done by public central banks throughout the world, except for the U.S., where the Federal Reserve Board is quasi-private.[1] There are also public operating banks in some countries: in France, for example, the four largest banks are public. Table 20–1 gives some detail on these banks.

Their clearing, lending, and savings roles are largely passive and mechanical. They also shape the structure and terms of banking activity. In the U.S., the Federal Reserve does this partly in conjunction with state banking agencies and the Comptroller of the Currency (recall Chapter

---

[1] Surveys are in R. L. Sayers, ed., *Banking in Western Europe* (London: Macmillan, 1962), and D. Alhadeff, *Competition and Controls in Banking: A Study of the Regulation of Bank Competition in Italy, France, and England* (Berkeley: University of California Press, 1968).

12). Elsewhere, it is done directly. Bank mergers are screened; charters for new branches are meted out or withheld; and the ways in which banks can compete are limited, directly or indirectly. In some cases, the public central bank merely approves and enforces the terms set by the bankers' own groups.

The scope of direct competition among public and private banks is large in some countries. But the public banks often behave much like private ones; France is a striking example. Only in marginal areas do public banks differ, and deliberate price competition by public banks is not common.

TABLE 20–1
Large Publicly-owned Banks outside the U.S. (other than central banks)

Ranks by Assets among All Foreign Banks	Bank	Country	Assets 1973 ($ million)
2	Banque Nationale de Paris	France	32,927
10	Credit Lyonnais	France	24,461
11	Societe Generale	France	24,202
13	Banco Nazionale del Lavoro	Italy	22,844
18	Westdeutsche Landesbank Girozentrale	Germany	19,889
19	Banco di Roma	Italy	19,385
22	Banco Commerciale Italiana	Italy	18,617
25	Banco do Brasil	Brazil	16,523
34	Credito Italiano	Italy	13,738
36	Bayerische Landesbank Girozentrale	Germany	13,082
37	Hessische Landesbank-Girozentrale	Germany	12,917
46	Norddeutsche Landesbank Girozentrale	Germany	10,191

All are 50 percent or more publicly owned.
Source: The *Fortune Directory*, August 1974.

Public Holding Companies

Public investment banks take a more direct role toward company management, mingling long term loans and financial support with a degree of supervision and control.[2] Their economic potential is great. They can fit their holdings in private firms to the social need. They can change these holdings freely. They can focus on small growth companies as well as on established firms. Since they are a roving presence, their threat or promise of action can often have effect beyond their actual holdings. They can support take-overs, in which investment banks operate upon, rather than with, established firms. They can seek capital gains as well as dividend income. In short, investment banks can directly alter structure and change management behavior, while also drawing earnings. Public benefits arise especially where (1) private banks are not adequately supervising or constraining industrial management, and (2)

---

[2] See especially Stuart Holland, *op. cit.*, and the sources he cites.

where financial markets create or maintain inequitable distributions of wealth.

Several public investment banks are summarized in Table 20–2. Each has had a distinctive role and result. The Italian IRI acted as a type of corporate and banking receiver after 1933 for three major banks. Through their stock-holdings, IRI was given full or partial control of half the Italian steel industry, two-thirds of telephone service, 80 percent of shipbuilding, one-third of electricity supply, and lesser shares in several other engineering industries.[3] Specialized holding companies for each industry were created within IRI, and the holdings were aligned. After

TABLE 20–2
Four Public Investment Banks

Country and Bank	Year Established	Purpose	Size (assets, at peak)	Nature of Holdings
Italy IRI..............	1933	Rehabilitation, growth, regional balance	~9 billion lire	Wide range of industrial and utility firms
US RFC	1932	Avert failures during the depression	Over $10 billion	Wide range of industrial firms, utilities, banks, farms, etc.
UK IRC..............	1965	Restructure industries	£150 million	Temporary holdings in smaller firms
Canada CDC..............	1971	Assert Canadian control	$150 million	Selective; natural resources, others

severe wartime damage and postwar reorganization, IRI has stabilized and its holdings have gradually grown.

It has always followed commercial forms and criteria, with modifications. Standard management and profit guidelines are adjusted to fit such social criteria as (1) regional balance (especially improving southern Italy) and (2) easing the social impact of closures. Capital is raised mostly from private sources (60 percent during 1958–69), and company securities are traded in private markets. This applies a degree of external supervision. Investments mostly undergo a conventional screening for yields. There is both growth and reorganization among the constituent companies.

Mistakes and distortions have occurred. There was delay in reorganizing engineering and shipbuilding after 1945. Regional development has only been modestly promoted. Vague public-interest notions have induced (or excused) some wastes of investment and current resources.

---

[3] Posner and Woolf, *op. cit.;* and Holland, *op. cit.*

Yet the whole record is remarkably good. IRI has been flexible and responsive to the main criteria of performance. It has fostered change and growth, while easing certain social costs. Much IRI success derives from a handful of gifted officials. But the main lines of reasonably efficient policy now appears to be firmly set. It may be "a machine without a driver," lacking tight social direction.[4] Still, it has become an important innovation in public enterprise.

In the United States, the Reconstruction Finance Corporation was created in 1932 to supply credit to distressed firms during the Depression. It become the country's largest single source of industrial credit. It did not assert management control, though it did act to some degree as a financial adviser to some firms. For 20 years the Reconstruction Finance Corporation was the largest lender in the United States. The RFC was established, on a temporary basis, in 1932, to check financial disaster by extending emergency aid to such enterprises as railroads, banks, and insurance companies. But its life was repeatedly extended and its powers enlarged. During the 30s, it was employed to finance relief and recovery programs; during the war, to finance the procurement of strategic materials and the construction of industrial facilities.

In 1948, its powers were again enlarged, enabling it to lend to any state or local government, to any public agency, to any financial institution, and to any business enterprise in the United States. According to the investigators who reported to the Hoover Commission in 1949, the Corporation's record during the Depression was highly satisfactory and the functions assigned to it during the war were well performed. Soon thereafter, the RFC came into bad odor; it appeared that the quality of its management had declined and that dubious loans had been made on the basis of political influence. As a consequence, a bill was passed in 1953 putting the agency into liquidation. In 20 years, the RFC had made 640,-000 loans and lent or spent $48,740 million. It had suffered defaults on only 1 percent of its loans, and had paid more than a billion dollars into the Treasury; its remaining assets were valued at $700 million.

In 1974–75, there was strong new interest in creating an investment bank like the RFC (a key proponent was Felix Rohatyn: recall Chapter 8). It would use up to $10 billion to support firms against unusual stresses during rapid inflation, high interest rates, a lack of equity finance, and materials shortages. It could be just a costly prop for mismanaged firms. Or instead it might fit the *active* mode discussed above.

Two agencies still make business loans. The Export-Import Bank lends to American traders and their foreign customers. The Small Business Administration lends to meet the capital needs of small concerns. Here, as with the loans to farmers, there is an element of subsidy.

Since 1965, several small experiments along IRI lines have been started in other countries. They are small and mostly begin without a large prior portfolio of holdings. Britain's Industrial Reorganization Corporation (1966–71) was to use its £150 million to arrange mergers to improve international competitiveness. It marginally encouraged a se-

---

[4] Posner and Woolf, *op. cit.*, p. 128.

ries of mergers, but it did not exert control. The Canadian Development Corporation by contrast, was created in 1970 with several holdings and is adding others. It aims to assert Canadian control in key resource and "science-based" industries, following the IRI pattern.[5] Sweden is creating a larger IRI-type firm, with 22 holdings from pre-existing public firms. In all of these newer cases, the utilities and social enterprises are left outside the holding company, in separate firms supervised by the government.

The public holding company is still experimental, its potential not yet proven. Nowhere has it had a free run for control and take-over. Rather it has been assigned specific functions: reorganizing, asserting sovereignty, regional development, encouraging mergers, etc. Still, it has shown that effective control can be exerted with minimal burdens on public resources. High commercial skill can be combined with a concern for social aims. The U.S. is conspicuous among industrial countries for lacking any such public entity. Various subsidies (especially to weapons and ship producers: see Chapters 25 and 29) have not been linked with public controls.

INSURANCE AND RISK-ABSORPTION

Public insurance enterprises divide into two broad groups: those providing services directly to persons, and those insuring other enterprises. The distinction is not an absolute one, for some personal insurance is done by programs which operate by insuring private firms: and vice versa.[6] Table 20–3 shows the main such units that now operate in the United States: there are also many other small ones. They are a remarkable array, ranging from services for the poorest citizens to coverage for powerful corporations. The effects on equity also differ widely. Some have a broadly equalizing effect (although even these usually contain some regressive elements). But others strictly disequalize.

Their scope is remarkable. The familiar social security and housing insurance units are only the core of a large and diverse group. Their scope has been growing and their operations are increasingly varied. Some are quasi-public. Most cover their direct costs with revenues, on standard insurance principles. A few of them are partially subsidized. Yet even where there are no direct subsidies, there is a cost to the public from absorbing private risks. This cost can be large, though it is hidden.

The performance of these units varies widely. In the narrow sense of administrative efficiency, most of them have done well for several decades. There is little evidence of *X-inefficiency* in their operations. But in *allocational efficiency,* their effects are less clear. The programs have increased the level of risk-taking, perhaps well beyond optimal levels. For example, in house buying and farming, the levels induced by mortgage and other guarantees may be above the social optimum. Investor

---

[5] During 1972–74 it adroitly acquired working control of Texasgulf, a leading sulfur company with extensive Canadian operations.

[6] For example, the FDIC insures *personal* accounts, but this indirectly stabilizes the banks' own position.

TABLE 20–3
Leading U.S. Federal Insurance Entities

	Indicators of Size, 1973 ($ billion)	
Personal Security		
Old Age and Survivors Insurance (Social Security)	41.3	(benefits paid)
Federal Disability Insurance Trust Fund	4.5	(benefits paid)
Federal Unemployment Insurance	5.8	(benefits paid)
Federal Employees Life Insurance	39.9	(insurance in force)
Veterans Special Life Insurance Fund	5.3	(insurance in force)
Federal Hospital Trust Fund	7.0	(payments)
Federal Supplementary Medical Insurance Trust Fund	2.5	(payments)
Housing		
Federal National Mortgage Association	26.3	(loans insured)
Federal Home Loan Bank Board	13.8	(loans insured)
Federal Home Loan Mortgage Corporation	3.1	(loans insured)
Federal Housing Administration	78.2	(mortgages insured)
Veterans Administration	42.4	(mortgages insured)
Finance		
Federal Deposit Insurance Corporation	5.6	(funding)
Federal Savings and Loan Insurance Corporation	3.3	(funding)
Securities Investors Protection Corporation	1.0	(authorized capital)
Overseas Private Investment Corporation	11.0	(face amount of insurance
Export-Import Bank	8.2	(loans insured)
Agriculture		
Banks for Cooperatives	2.3	(assets)
Federal Intermediate Credit Banks	8.2	(assets)
Federal Land Banks	9.3	(assets)
Federal Crop Insurance Corporation	1.0	(assets)
Other		
Student Loan Insurance Fund	4.0	(loans insured)
Federal Insurance Administration (urban, other)	.1	(assets)

Source: *Budget of the United States Government, 1973*, various pages.

protection by the Securities Investor Protection Corporation since 1971 is likely to be either inefficient (by overinducing small traders to take risks) or inequitable (protecting only larger investors); or possibly both.

The *equity* effects are especially doubtful. Social Security is largely *regressive* because of the way it is financed. The federal government insures the risks of a large range of commercial operations in this country and abroad. There may be some benefits for all from abating these risks. But the direct benefits focus tightly among upper economic groups.

On the whole, public insurance enterprises are strongest by narrow performance criteria (e.g., X-efficiency) and weakest by the major social criteria. Their administrative costs are usually a much smaller share of

TABLE 20-4

Large Public Firms in Industry, Outside the U.S.

Rank (by Sales) among Large Industrial Firms Outside U.S.	Company	Country	Industries	Sales, 1973 ($ million)	Employees 1973 (1,000)
17	Renault	France	Automobiles, tractors, machine tools	4,655	170
21	British Steel Corp.	Britain	Iron and steel	4,289	225
28	National Iranian Oil	Iran	Oil products, gas, petrochemicals	4,000	46
46	ELF Group	France	Oil products	2,866	22
52	National Coal Board	Britain	Coal, by-products	2,537	268
59	Petroleo Brasilerro	Brazil	Oil products, petrochemicals	2,337	36
75	Italsider	Italy	Iron and steel	1,861	49
76	Salzgitter	Germany	Steel, shipbuilding, machinery	1,852	56
84	DSM	Netherlands	Chemicals, fertilizers, plastics	1,660	30
90	Petroleos Mexicanos	Mexico	Oil products, gas, petrochemicals	1,564	78
96	Charbonnages de France	France	Coal, electricity	1,511	101
97	VOEST-Alpine	Austria	Iron and steel	1,511	80
104	Yacimientos Petroliferos	Argentina	Oil products	1,345	40
108	Statsforetag Group	Sweden	Mining, paper products, steel, tobacco	1,287	40
123	Zambia Industry and Mining	Zambia	Mining, chemicals, manufacturing	1,158	87
142	Codelco Group	Chile	Mining	1,012	32
164	Saarbergwerke	Germany	Coal mining, electricity, oil	895	29
165	Aerospatiale	France	Aircraft	890	41
179	Viag	Germany	Aluminum, electricity, chemicals	831	23
184	Pertamina	Indonesia	Oil products	800	40
186	Indian Oil	India	Oil products	794	15
206	Entreprise Miniere et Chemique	France	Chemicals, mining	741	17
225	Hindustan Steel	India	Iron and steel	652	131
238	Alfa Romeo	Italy	Automobiles	604	42
244	ISCOR	South Africa	Iron and steel, mining	585	46
259	SEITA	France	Tobacco and matches	553	11
281	OMV	Austria	Oil products, gas	517	9

Source: Fortune, Directory of the 300 Largest Industrial Corporations Outside the U.S., August, 1974.

insured value than is true for private insurance. Reforms in this sector should mainly be directed not at the inner functioning of these agencies but rather at their size, their incidence, and—in some cases—their very existence. The negative effects—especially on equity—could be altered if the charges for these services were set differently. These are set by the political process, not by the public enterprises themselves. Once again (as with antitrust and regulation), the main defects lie in the setting within which the policy tools operate.

INDUSTRY AND SERVICES

The sprinkling of public firms in American industry, trade, and services was shown in Table 19–3. The largest public firms in other countries are given in Table 20–4. The U.S. cases lie outside the core industries, especially those with market power. Elsewhere, public firms hold large shares in a number of major industries. Elsewhere, too, there is much variety in mixed private-public firms, while nearly all U.S. public firms are wholly public.

Some of these firms are monopolies, while others are under stiff competition. Some are old, some new. Here we can only start with several broad points and then review a few U.S. and foreign examples.

Basic Points

These points will emerge from the following details.

1. The firms have no systematic economic origins. They are *not* carefully preplanned and coolly made public.
2. They do not cover the core problem industries (recall Chapter 2) in Western economies—and least of all in the U.S.
3. There is no broad tendency to inefficiency among them. Managerial performance varies more by nation and sector than by the type of firm.
4. There is also no clear equity gain from them.
5. Their source of investment funds does seem to influence their performance. A degree of funding from private markets induces the firm to behave more commercially and responsively to the market.
6. The firm's success depends closely on its individual leaders, at least as much as on impersonal conditions and criteria.

Case Studies in the U.S.

AEC Uranium Enrichment Plants.   The AEC was created to promote and control the development of nuclear power.[7] A public monopoly, it has

---

[7] At the start, it acquired establishments with a capital investment of $1,400,000,000, including a weapons research laboratory and town of 9,000 at Los Alamos, New Mexico, production plants, a research laboratory, and a town of 36,000 at Oak Ridge, Tennessee, and another plant and town of 17,000 at Hanford, Washington. It inherited a contract system with 5,000 government employees and 50,000 contractor employees. It was entrusted with the knowledge required to produce fissionable materials and atomic bombs. It was given custody of the nation's stock of bombs. The facilities controlled by the AEC now represent an investment

relied on incentives and subsidies to private contractors. It has restricted activities to a relatively few established firms (especially General Electric and Westinghouse), and so the new nuclear power equipment industry is matching the tight oligopoly structure of the older electrical equipment industry (recall Chapter 7). Development lagged well behind U.K. and other advances. Then in 1963 the seeming success of a test plant at Peach Bottom, New Jersey, triggered a rush of private-utility orders for nuclear plants. Major hitches have plagued this expansion, and the future role of nuclear power is quite uncertain. The AEC now retains only its research facilities plus three plants which enrich uranium.

These plants bridge all three main policy contexts: antitrust, regulation, and public enterprise. They pose the economic choices about public enterprise with remarkable clarity. And these issues are not yet resolved.

The three giant plants are at Oak Ridge, Tennessee; Portsmouth, Ohio; and Paducah, Kentucky. Using electric power in large quantities (partly from TVA), these plants raise the uranium content of ore from less than one percent to about three percent, using the "gaseous diffusion" process. The plants cost about $2.6 billion when built in the 1940s. Having armed a vast stockpile of nuclear bombs for military use during the 1950s, the plants have now been turned toward providing uranium for atomic power plants. They are the only source of commercial enrichment services in the U.S. and, indeed, the world. These plants illustrate how the desirability of public ownership depends closely upon the operating and pricing policies adopted.[8]

In the 1960s and 1970s the demand for uranium has gradually risen towards full use of the three plants' capacity (augmented by an expansion during 1966–73). Demand is expected to reach capacity by the late 1970s. Yet the predictions are hazardous, since many conditions elsewhere can throw them off.

The government has sold enrichment services at $26 per kilogram until 1970, when they were raised to $32. In 1973, a further rise to $38

---

of close to $10 billion. Its annual budget exceeds $2 billion. It has installations in more than half of the states. To supplement the plants at Oak Ridge and Hanford, it has built large plants for processing of nuclear materials at Portsmouth and Fernald in Ohio, at Paducah, Kentucky, and on the Savannah River in South Carolina, and smaller plants at other points. The Commission has a plant to manufacture weapons at Sandia in New Mexico, a number of testing ranges, and a score of centers for research and development.

Of the total amount spent on the atomic energy program in a year, less than 5 percent goes to support the AEC and more than 95 percent goes to its contractors. In 1970 the Commission itself had 7,000 employees, its contractors 125,000. Research was carried on, plants were constructed, ores were processed, fissionable materials were produced, components of weapons were manufactured—all by contractors. The Commission's research work has been done, largely, by universities, by independent agencies, and by industrial laboratories. The plants have been operated by such concerns as Union Carbide, General Electric, Goodyear, du Pont, Bendix, and AT&T. The government has provided the facilities, the raw materials, the working capital, and the overall direction. The contractors have supplied the labor and the management.

[8] During World War II, the forced-draft development of atomic bombs required creating a large enrichment capacity in jig time. The best technology then was unknown, and so the three close alternative methods were applied in a competitive "tournament." The gaseous diffusion process (at Oak Ridge) won out. This process involves a physical membrane, through which uranium particles pass by an osmotic process. By continual repetition of the filtering process, the uranium content of the ore is gradually raised. The membrane technology is highly classified, but is not believed to be highly complex.

was announced. The plants are managed by *private* firms on contract: two by Union Carbide Corporation and the third by Goodyear International. This is an unusual hybrid of public enterprise, but it appears to function well. The AEC does continue to manage research and development in enrichment technology.

This is the last part of the atomic power cycle remaining under the AEC, the others having been sold off to private enterprise. After 1963, as orders for reactors suddenly blossomed, the interest of private groups in taking over these plants also bloomed. Concurrently, the Budget Bureau grew restive at providing over $500 million to build a fourth plant.

The decision about the future ownership of these plants—and of additional future plants—is a vector of all the lessons about public policy choice we have been exploring. There is wide agreement that the management of the plants and of innovation in the sector has been efficient. All agree, too, that the $26 price for services was a partial subsidy. Therefore, this public enterprise was fitting the passive version of public enterprise, in which benefits are extended to large commercial customers.

The question of transferring ownership related directly to the pricing policy for enrichment services. A private market price would be much higher, but how much? If a new monopoly or tight oligopoly under private control were created, would not the price be excessive? Could it be regulated? If a transfer were approved, who should be permitted to own the plants, and by what criteria should the choice be made? The basic question is whether any transfer at all can be designed which is better than the existing ownership *plus* an optimal pricing policy. If a high price were to be charged by the AEC for enrichment services, that would favor keeping the plants in public hands.[9]

Among the potential bidders for the plants are the operators—Union Carbide and Goodyear—plus other firms already in the nuclear power sector, such as General Electric, Westinghouse, and uranium ore firms. The latter group would gain from vertical integration, but this might also increase their market power, which already is substantial. If the two operating firms acquired the plants, then the entry of other firms would be less probable. Yet these two groups of firms would be likely to offer the highest bids for the plants, precisely because they would reap special advantages! The contradiction is inherent: those with most to gain in public expense would be willing to offer the most to get it. Therefore a delicate choice would have to be made, in which the highest bids would probably be denied in place of lower ones. That optimal choice might not be possible in practice. Also, some regulation would be necessary if the plants were highly monopolistic; yet Chapters 13–18 have shown the hazards of that treatment. The question also turns on the pricing policy to be followed. On balance, the optimum treatment is to keep the plants

---

[9] The issue is further complicated by the possible rise of an alternative enrichment technology: the centrifuge. This involves spinning a solution of uranium so that the heavier particles separate out. This can be operated on a small scale, with low capital requirements, by a range of large and small nations or firms. There are signs that it will ripen to economic use by 1980. If it does, it could lop off the demand growth for the existing gaseous diffusion plants, turning them into an instant sick industry. Therefore the question is a dual one: not only who might share the benefits of future growth, but who should risk future failure?

public. At the new going price of $38 per kilogram the plants do earn at least an efficient return on the investment.

In 1970, it was decided to retain the plants as a separate public corporation. This and the current price closely fit the optimum treatment for the time being. More recently, private firms have shown an interest in building the fourth plant which rising demand may make necessary. This, too, fits the optimum, for it means that private funds will bear the risk inherent in the marginal plant. That this is being induced by the AEC price umbrella is both natural and acceptable. The future price and investment strategies will adjust as events mature and centrifuge technology is developed further.

Government Printing Office. The Government Printing Office is the largest printing plant on earth, doing about $300 million of business each year. By common agreement, it is run efficiently, and it covers costs with revenues. Its content is unusual, including both the Congressional Record and other high-speed operations, and the vast outpouring of government publications, across a wide spectrum. Some of its publications are of limited interest and have little sale or circulation. Unlike private printing houses, the GPO does not select its own titles; instead it passively produces what is required by other agencies.

Still, it somehow manages to surmount its vast publishing tasks with efficiency. Sales are made by the Superintendant of Documents, which buys documents at cost and resells at a markup of about 50 percent. This operation currently turns a $20 million profit for the Treasury. Despite its core of specialized publishing, the GPO has a variety of offerings which do overlap with private issues. Here the quality is at least comparable to that available elsewhere, and the management of inventory and product strategy is also comparable. In this sense, the GPO is an efficient public enterprise which meets the standard commercial tests of performance. It also is a conduit for social benefits from some of the publications it produces.

The Post Exchange System. As all ex-GIs know, the PX system markets an immense array of goods at military bases throughout the world. The PX system is in fact one of the largest retail systems operating anywhere in the world. It sells at a discount, it buys in very large volumes, and it covers direct costs with revenues. PX privileges are eagerly sought, for the PX undercuts prices almost everywhere else.

Its main economic advantage is volume buying, by which it obtains discounts on many of its purchases. But there are also other elements at work. These include the avoidance of certain taxes and the use of military base and warehousing facilities (this is a prickly problem in allocating joint costs; the true costs and subsidy elements are not clear). PX discounts therefore are partly an illusion, resting also on indirect subsidies from the taxpayer though the military budget. Still, the PX system is a notably aggressive and successful marketer. Its purchasing is at least as effective as large private chains, and its inventory and retailing operations are widely considered to be efficient. Its flexibility in setting its composition of shelf items is also high.

In short, the PX system is a skillful, aggressive, and efficient marketing organization, the opposite of the classic image of public-enterprise distributors as slow and rigid. The benefits of its operations do not offer large equity gains. Rather, they are merely a supplement within the whole strategy of military pay and hiring policy. The PX system is a well-performing operation as a public enterprise, though its setting does not permit it to generate large equity gains.

Several Case Studies Abroad

Renault. Before 1945, the Renault company was one of the three largest automobile makers in France. It had been established for many decades, but its owners collaborated with the Germans in World War II. In retaliation it was expropriated in 1945, and it has continued under public ownership to the present.[10] It had been one of the leaders in the French market, specializing in medium-range cars. Its competitors included Citröen (which has models both in the luxury class and the utility level) and Peugeot. Renault under public enterprise continued to get its funds primarily from the private market.

Its operations have been efficient and competitive, by wide agreement. During the 1950s its behavior was distinctive in several ways which reflect its public-enterprise status.

The social objective for French industry during 1945–55 was to recover and grow rapidly. Therefore Renault was especially under encouragement to expand. It responded, and by 1955 it was the largest in the industry. This it did both by normal competitive growth and by a deliberate attempt to develop a small economy car for lower-income buyers. This conscious effort partly reflected social criteria, as well as private returns to the firm. More recently, increasing competition from German and Italian cars has confined Renault's ability to modify commercial objectives, and it has evolved towards a standard commercial approach. Though its labor relations are unusually good, this is not a drastic difference and is in line with private criteria.

Renault therefore is one of those public enterprise which have, at least for a period, adapted to distinctive social criteria which were also consistent with commercial guidelines. This fits the general pattern that social criteria are usually followed only temporarily by public enterprises, especially if they are under competitive pressure. In any event, Renault shows that a public firm can perform well in a major, changing, and competitive industry.

The British Steel Corporation. Among all public enterprises abroad, you are most likely to have heard of the British Steel Corporation. Created in 1967, it manages over half of the British steel industry and is the fourth largest steel firm in the world. Its origins are intensively controversial. The industry stagnated during 1920–40 and was a leading instance in Britain's 1930s cartel craze.[11] Its labor relations were poor,

---

[10] J. B. Sheahan, *Promotion and Control of Industry in Postwar France* (Cambridge: Harvard University Press, 1963).

[11] D. L. Burn, *The Economic History of Steelmaking, 1867–1939* (Cambridge: Cambridge University Press, 1940); and *The Economic History of Steelmaking, 1940–1956* (Cambridge: Cambridge University Press, 1957).

and so nationalizing it was formally proposed as early as 1920. It was the only deeply divisive case in the postwar British nationalizations, when it was finally done in 1951. The new Conservative administration in 1953 put most of it back under private ownership, under a supervisory Iron and Steel Board. It is a marginal candidate for public enterprise, a mingling of industrial power, industrial dislocation and social burdens; a small dose of public ownership might suffice. Labour returned about two-thirds of the industry to public ownership in 1967, under the single BSC. This basis now appears permanent.

During 1953–67, the Iron and Steel Board's activities boiled down to setting maximum prices which, in practice, soon became minimum prices. Therefore it operated with the standard multifirm regulatory effect of stabilizing cartel prices. It also presided over industry that was moderately progressive but too fragmented to achieve major economies of scale and slow to close down its obsolete plants. In 1965–67, Labour government officials erred on the other side; they probably overstressed a "need" for coordination and rationalizing. This led them to create one wholly public dominant firm, rather than several competitive ones or a mixed firm. The BSC emerged in 1967 looking remarkably like the U.S. Steel Corporation at *its* creation in 1901. It had about two-thirds of the basic capacity of the industry, but by no means a complete monopoly. It centered in the older and less lucrative basic steels rather than in the newer, specialized, and more lucrative submarkets of the industry (see Table 20–5). Moreover, it includes disparate units, many of them obviously facing closure. Therefore, like U.S. Steel, it seemed fated for a long period of indifferent financial results, arduous structural change, and a steady decline in its market position.

Since 1967, BSC has retained most of the previous managers, while attempting major changes in organization and capacity. The manage-

TABLE 20–5
Selected Market Shares of the British Steel Corporation, 1967–68

Product	BSC share of	
	UK production	*All deliveries to UK users*
Nonalloy		
Tinplate	100	100
Ingots, blooms, billets and slabs	95	85
Plates	91	83
Hot rolled strip	83	55
Wire rods	57	48
Castings	11	9
Alloy (including stainless steel)		
Ingots, blooms, billets and slabs	70	72
Tubes and pipes	27	22
Hot rolled and cold rolled strip	26	6
High speed steel	11	11
Castings	5	3

Source: British Steel Corporation, *Annual Report and Accounts 1967–68* (London: Her Majesty's Stationery Office, 1969), pp. 40–41.

ment has been developed partly into functional and regional groups, and after two stressful years a number of hostile holdover managers were let go. Over seven years, BSC has derived a consolidation strategy with large units and fairly severe changes. The plan is widely agreed to be efficient. Changes have been slowed by worker resistance; but this may fit social criteria for easing local impacts (especially in South Wales).

BSC's price strategy has evolved towards a substantial degree of price discrimination among customers. This is inevitable and probably socially optimal. BSC is selling a major industrial commodity to a wide range of corporations. Therefore its ability to improve equity by passive policies is probably close to zero. In this situation, it is probably desirable that it gain sizable profits with some degree of price discrimination, as long as gross abuses are avoided. Since its prices are quasi-regulated by a government ministry, the basic effect is likely to be close to an efficient pricing policy. Its investment funds and risk-absorption come in part from the government, but there are no indications that this has encouraged overinvestment or giantism.

BSC's problems are severe and the constraints on it are close. The social impacts which limit its changes are part of the wider economic problem of Britain, and so the impacts could well be treated more directly by the government. By modifying its evolution, BSC is making a variety of direct social contributions, at the expense of its own solvency. Also it has bought domestic coal at somewhat higher prices than it could arrange for imported coal.[12] This burden has provided an indirect social contribution.

The management style of BSC has been active and sophisticated, at least comparable to what might have been expected under continuing private management. The present managing director (Monty Finniston: shown on page 519) is particularly forceful. All in all, BSC has done a creditable job, both by short-run and long-run criteria. A different treatment—with three or four competitive public firms, or with several joint ventures—might provide comparably good results. Simple re-privatizing is not now a viable choice, at least until the main changes have been made. Even then, some degree of quasi-regulation or antitrust limits would be in order, and this would have its own side effects. Presently, there is a close scrutiny of the commercial effectiveness of BSC and of its use of investment resources as it strives to maintain its market positions. That market position may well dwindle naturally, perhaps over the next decade or two.

Therefore, BSC is a good example of a tightly constrained public corporation facing much competitive pressure and with major economic and social disequilibrium conditions. That it has performed reasonably well reflects both the resiliency of the basic instrument and the sophistication with which it is being used.

---

[12] The National Coal Board, created in 1946 as a monopoly, has consolidated the coal industry by a remarkably efficient long-run program, especially during 1956–65: see W. G. Shepherd, *Economic Performance under Public Enterprise, op. cit.;* and Shepherd's "Alternative for Public Expenditure," Chapter 9 in R. E. Caves and Associates, *Britain's Economic Prospects* (Washington, D.C.: Brookings Institution, 1968); and Pryke, *op. cit.*

Yugoslav Enterprises. Midway between East and West, and yet with its own peculiar brand of public enterprise, the Yugoslav economy offers a distinctive set of lessons about the structure and uses of public enterprise. We will consider the *general* forms of Yugoslav enterprise, rather than specific branches of it.[13]

There are several distinctive features. (1) Enterprises are owned variously by the central and regional governments. (2) Many firms hold great monopoly power in regional or national markets. (3) They are funded in part by central banking and fiscal resources, and by retained earnings. (4) Management is both by professional managers and, in part, by workers. Although the degree of worker participation varies from case to case, it is not merely formal. (5) It governs certain key economic choices about wages, finance, and investment. The net surplus of the enterprise for each period is divided among those participating in the firm, particularly the workers. This is like a year-end bonus in some private firms, which the participants will naturally wish to maximize.

There may be a doubly restrictive effect from this method of deciding the worker's share of the profits. Workers will prefer that net revenue be maximized. And they will prefer to have it shared out rather than be reinvested. Accordingly, the enterprise will tend to have smaller capacity *and* smaller output levels in the future. Since this occurs across a wide range of Yugoslav enterprises, the national levels of growth and investment may be reduced. This poses intriguing parallels to private monopoly in Western economies.

The degree of monopoly held by most Yugoslav enterprises is not small. Most of them operate in regional submarkets or with substantial market power in the national markets. The central authorities take a relatively passive role toward the monopoly power of most firms, and so most Yugoslav markets are correctly seen as a series of tight oligopolies or near-monopolies. This gives a crystal-clear demonstration that public ownership need not reach the underlying economic problems, nor substitute for antitrust, regulation or still other treatments. Still, the Yugoslav economy has performed well. This may show that the grass-roots initiative and control is neatly balanced by key centralized policy levers, especially constraints on investment budgeting and prices.

In any event, the Yugoslav public enterprise offers distinctive attributes. As before, the mere fact of public ownership may matter much less than the forms and policies which are used. And even Yugoslav firms only begin to explore the variety which public enterprises may follow.

SUMMARY

Despite the great diversity of actual public enterprises in finance and industry, there are large areas of experimentation yet untouched. Even

---

[13] See Jaroslav Vanek, *General Theory of Labor-Managed Market Economies* (Ithaca: Cornell University Press, 1966); and the excellent survey by Joel B. Dirlam, "The Yugoslav Economy," in U.S. Senate Subcommittee on Antitrust and Monopoly, *Hearings on Economic Concentration,* 90th Congress, 2nd Session, Part 7 (Washington, D.C.: U.S. Government Printing Office, 1968), pp. 3758–74.

if the scope of public enterprise in these sectors does not grow in the future, there are likely to be more trials of hybrids and new forms. More likely, the scope of public enterprise will continue to rise in these sectors, although only gradually and under close constraints and burdens. In this process of learning by doing, old methods are tried and often discarded in favor of new ones. Since there is only modest impetus in the U.S. for enlarging the role of public enterprise in industry and trade, new experiments are likely to be *ad hoc* and for special purposes. For these, we have seen that public enterprise offers flexibility and variety and—in some cases—quite good performance. One can also learn from the negative cases. At any rate, there is no scientific general case against public enterprise in finance and industry. As industrial conditions continue evolving, public enterprise offers certain scientific possibilities for treating a variety of—not all—problems.

CHAPTER TWENTY-ONE

Public Enterprise in Utility Sectors

$\mathbf{B}$y tradition, public enterprise clusters most closely in utility sectors. The variety of firms, criteria, and results is too large to lay out fully here. This chapter will summarize the broader patterns and then touch on several sectors (electricity, railroads, and communications: certain urban services are held over to Chapter 22). Chapter 19 has summarized the conventional public corporation in utility sectors. Here we will consider more detailed lessons.

GENERAL FEATURES

Utilities are commonly under public ownership elsewhere—but with exceptions (see Table 21-1). Sweden is one, despite common opinion. Canada also has mixed patterns. These details reflect oddities of historical chance and cultural traditions, rather than tight economic laws. Some economic determinants do exist. Being capital-intensive infrastructure, utilities have often been created publicly as a means of guiding development and stabilizing total investment levels. Public ownership gives more direct control over these "natural monopolies." It also can assert social and national control over these crucial units of the economy. Further, failing private utilities in Stages 3 and 4 are often salvaged under public ownership (e.g., U.K. railroads, eastern U.S. railroads). The U.S. stands out with its low share of public enterprise, but the economic determinants that might increase the share are complex. If a rise does come, it will probably evolve out of impersonal chance and policy cross-currents—rather than by a clear design.

The lessons can be put briefly:

1. Public enterprise is extensive in utility sectors.
2. It tends to be in the conventional form of the public firm, with full ownership, risk-absorption by the public, and a natural monopoly.
3. The costs in capital, managerial talent and policy supervision—and subsidy, in some cases—are high.

551

TABLE 21–1
Public Firms in Utility Sectors, 1971 (Figures indicate share of the sector publicly held, and employees. Many figures are estimates.)

	United States	United Kingdom
Energy		
Electricity	Various Federal, state, and local units. 25% of supply; 90,000 employees	Electricity authorities. 100% of sales; 100,000 employees
Gas	None	British Gas Corporation 100%; 110,000 employees
Transport		
Railroad	Amtrak, Alaska, Panama, eastern railroads shifting	British Rail 100%; 202,000 employees
Airline	Military (large operations)	British Airways 100%; 58,000 employees
Intercity	None	National Bus Corporation 100%; 77,000 employees
Transit	Most large cities have complete systems; also many other cities. 70–90%; 200,000 employees	City systems. 100%
Waterways	New York State and certain others	British Waterways Board 100%; 3,000 employees
Ports	Port of New York and certain others	Various city ports; 100%
Communications		
Postal	U.S. Postal Service. 100%; 708,000 employees	Post Office 100%; 234,000 employees
Telephone, telegraph	Defense system	Post Office 100%; 173,000 employees
Broadcasting	Public broadcasting network; educational stations. 5%	British Broadcasting Corporation TV 50%; Radio 90%

Sources: European Center for Public Enterprise, *The Evolution of Public Enterprises in the Common Market Countries* (Brussells: May 1973); Stuart Holland, *The State as Entrepreneur, op. cit.;* annual *Reports* of public firms; and various other sources.

4. The net benefits—compared to some alternatives—are usually real but marginal. They arise mainly from unification, better content and work relations, and stricter economizing on capital and service quality than in regulated private firms.
5. Profit rates and price structure closely resemble those of private regulated utility firms.
6. These public firms yield little of the deep social gains to which some of their creators aspired. They are simply large, investment-absorbing public firms doing highly technical, narrow functions.
7. The benefits do become more regressively distributed as time passes, in line with the general hypothesis (recall Chapter 19). The net gain in equity is, at best, modest. *If* public ownership is applied early, it does avert the large capital gains which have usually arisen in some private utilities during Stage 2 under regulation (recall Chapter 13).

TABLE 21-1 (continued)

France	Germany	Italy
French Electricity 100%; 94,000 employees	A large number of separate and combined systems, under varying controls 80%; 98,000 employees	ENEL 100%; 106,000 employees
French Gas 100%; 26,000 employees	Systems under varying con- trols 80%; 98,000 em- ployees	Various gas units 100%; 10,000 employees
French Railways 100%; 293,000 employees Air France 100%; 28,000 employees Various public systems	German Railways 100%; 419,000 employees Lufthansa 100%; 23,000 employees	State Railways 75%; 156,000 employees Alitalia 100%; 14,000 employees Various systems
Paris and other cities 100%; 80,000 employees	Various city systems 100%; 110,000 employees	Various city systems 100%; 115,000 employees
Various maritime units 100%; 7,000 employees Various ports 100%; 3,000 employees	Various waterway units 100% Bremen and others 100%	Various maritime units 100%; 11,000 employees Venice, Naples, Genoa and others, 100%; 8,000 employees
Postal and Telegraph 100%	German Post Office 100%; 469,000 employees	Postal and Telegraph 100%; 142,000 employees State Telephone System 100%; 60,000 employees
Radiodiffusion-Television Francaise. 100%	A Federal System and a set of provincial systems	Radiotelevisione Italiana 100%; 11,000 employees

International comparisons—say, between U.S. private firms and public firms elsewhere—are always hazardous. U.S. private utilities are in an economy with unusually high personal income levels. Therefore high levels and standards of utility service fit the underlying income levels and elasticities. With lower incomes would go lower consumption of utility (and other) goods.

Thus, telephone service is not, and *should not be,* as high-grade or extensive in most of Europe as it is in the U.S. (see Figure 21-1). American superiority in electricity or telephone supply carries no direct normative meaning. The real question is: are U.S. utility service standards in line with the *U.S.* economic norm, set by marginal allocation conditions throughout the economy?

Utility standards could be *too high* (indeed Part IV suggested they may be, in certain directions) as well as too low or just efficient. Reflect on this

FIGURE 21-1
Utility Service Varies with Income Levels

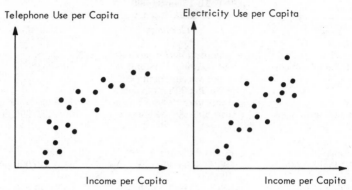

problem of comparison before continuing: it means that there can be few easy lessons about the relative optimality of public and private enterprise in various countries.

Public-firm utilities have provided certain distinctive outcomes, but at significant costs. The rest of the chapter gives details for these interpretations.

ELECTRICITY

U.S. experience is in (1) TVA and other federal power programs, (2) New York and Nebraska, and (3) the many local electric systems scattered around the country (recall Chapter 15). Table 21-2 adds detail on them (see also Table 21-3 below).

Abroad, public enterprise arose first at the local level, during 1890–1930. As national systems matured, national grids became publicly owned. Gas and electricity were publicly provided in more than three-

TABLE 21-2
Selected Data on Public Power Systems in the U.S.

	Assets (net utility plant) ($ billion)	KWh Sold To First Users (billion kw hours)	For Resale (billion kw hours)	Residence Revenues as a percent of Total (percent)
Tennessee Valley Authority	2.8	36	55	0
New York Power Authority	1.2	4	17	0
Los Angeles	1.2	15	0	38
Nebraska (total)	.8	10	1	41
All Public Systems	(18.1)	220	175	28
All Federal Systems	(9.5)	68	117	.01
All Municipal Systems	8.6	153	58	39

(Estimate)
Source: Federal Power Commission.

TABLE 21-3

Rates of Return on Net Utility Plant in Selected Public Power Systems, 1971

	Assets ($ million)	Net Income as a Percent of Assets
Alameda, California	4	26
Ames, Iowa	15	1
Burlington, Vermont	12	54
Columbia, Missouri	18	3
Eugene, Oregon	76	1
Ft. Collins, Colorado	6	11
Gainesville, Florida	49	6
Jacksonville, Florida	291	12
Kansas City, Kansas	85	4
Knoxville, Tennessee	73	3
Lafayette, Louisiana	33	4
Lansing, Michigan	75	4
Logan City, Utah	2	31
Los Angeles, California	1,299	3
Mishawaka, Indiana	4	25
Nebraska Public Power District	181	3
Oberlin, Ohio	3	4
Omaha, Nebraska	362	4
Paducah, Kentucky	9	5
Pasadena, California	39	8
Rochester, Minnesota	20	5
Sacramento, California	466	4
Salt River, Arizona	272	2
San Antonio, Texas	291	11
Seattle, Washington	342	1
South Carolina Public Service	138	2
Springfield, Illinois	66	2
Stillwater, Oklahoma	5	21
Wallingford, Connecticut	9	9
Wellesley, Massachusetts	6	5

Source: Federal Power Commission, *Statistics of Publicly Owned Electric Utilities in the U.S.*, 1971.

fourths of the cities of Germany and in more than half of those in Great Britain before 1930. Regional systems for the generation and transmission of electricity were operated by governments in Canada, New Zealand, and South Africa. The Central Electricity Board, in Great Britain, was given a monopoly of transmission lines by a Conservative government in 1926.

The present patterns were set by 1950 (recall Chapter 19). The structure of these units, and their policies on profit rates, price structure, and investment, have stabilized along lines closely akin to those in private U.S. utilities.

In the U.S., thousands of city power systems evolved from the start, followed—mainly in the 1930s—by federal and state agencies. The Tennessee Valley Authority is the leading case of federal power.

TVA. The Tennessee River is the fourth largest river in the U.S. Rising in the Blue Ridge Mountains, it flows 800 miles to the Ohio, draining parts of Virginia, North Carolina, Kentucky, Georgia, Alabama, and Mississippi, as well as Tennessee. The first federal installations on the river, consisting of two nitrate plants, a steam power plant, and Wilson Dam at Muscle Shoals, were constructed during World War I. After the war private companies offered to buy the properties, but their bids were rejected as inadequate. At the same time, Senator George W. Norris, Republican, of Nebraska was urging public operation of the facilities at Muscle Shoals and further development of the resources of the Tennessee.

Bills embodying this program were passed by Congress but were vetoed by President Coolidge in 1928 and by President Hoover in 1931. For years, the power and nitrate plants stood idle and the power contained in water falling over Wilson Dam was allowed to go to waste. Then, with the New Deal in 1933, a bill was enacted by Congress and signed by President Roosevelt to carry out the program that Senator Norris had proposed. The first of the new dams to be planned and built under the program was named Norris Dam.

The primary purposes of the new law were flood control and navigation. The third purpose stated was that of providing for "the maximum generation of electric power" insofar as this was "consistent with flood control and navigation." It was declared to be public policy to use the plants at Muscle Shoals to "improve, increase, and cheapen the production of fertilizer and fertilizer ingredients." And a broader aim was to conserve and develop the resources of the valley and to promote the economic and social well-being of its people, many of whom were poor and isolated.

To carry out this program, the law created a semiautonomous agency in the form of a corporation, designed to combine the prerogatives of government with the flexibility of private enterprise: the Tennessee Valley Authority. The policies of the Authority, within the law, are determined by a Board of Directors consisting of three members appointed by the President, subject to approval by the Senate, for overlapping terms of nine years. Detailed administration is delegated to a General Manager who is appointed and held responsible by the Board. The Authority is freed from Civil Service regulations in selecting and managing its personnel. TVA's physical layout is shown on the facing map

Operations. Unlike some other federal enterprises, it does not depend on annual appropriations to cover its costs in producing power but meets them from its own commercial revenues. The Authority must obtain approval from the Bureau of the Budget for its administrative expenses and on its plans for new construction and from the Treasury for the terms on which it borrows. Its books are audited by the General Accounting Office. But its operations are not regulated by state or federal utility commissions. Compared with most federal enterprises, it is generally free of external controls.

The TVA operates an integrated multipurpose water system. It maintains its reservoirs at levels that leave room to store floods. It releases

FIGURE 21-2

Extent and Complexity of the TVA System

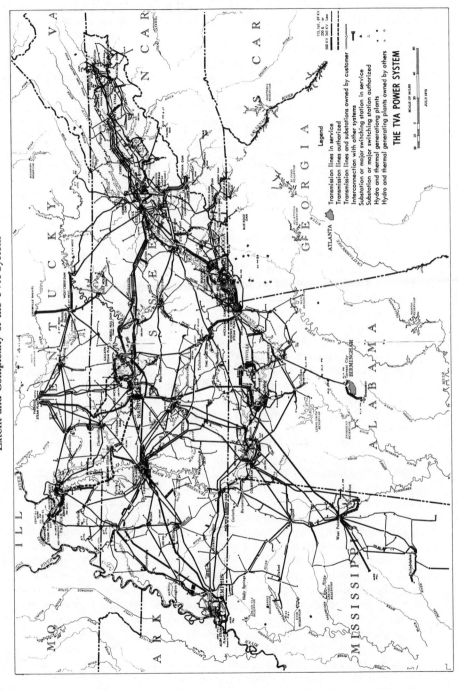

Legend

ATLANTA ▲ Transmission lines in service
Transmission lines authorized
Transmission lines and substations owned by customer
Interconnection with other systems
▲ Substation or major switching station in service
△ Substation or major switching station authorized
● Hydro and thermal generating plants
○ Hydro and thermal generating plants owned by others

115, 161, 69 KV
230 &   or
500 KV 345 KV Less

SCALE OF MILES
20   10   0   20   40   60   80

JULY 1972

THE TVA POWER SYSTEM

water in the quantities needed to maintain navigation. Within these limits, it uses water to produce power. Under its enabling act, the agency was instructed to put its power activities on a self-supporting basis. It was required to give preference to public and cooperative nonprofit bodies in selling its power. It was authorized to lease, buy, or build transmission lines to reach the market. It was permitted to control prices charged by its distributors.

In building up its transmission and distribution systems, the TVA encountered determined resistance from the Commonwealth and Southern system, whose subsidiaries were already operating in the valley. These companies wanted TVA to sell its power to them, but this would have violated the clear intent of the law. TVA did not undertake to duplicate their facilities; in cooperation with the cities in the region, it sought to buy them out. But its offer to purchase the properties at original cost less depreciation, as determined by an independent audit, was rejected as inadequate, their owners demanding prices that would cover the capital value of their earning power.

TVA then proposed that public and private power be pooled and sold at a common rate. The companies refused, demanding a division of the field. Negotiations ended in disagreement. TVA then embarked on an aggressive sales campaign, making contracts with large industrial users and promoting the formation of competing municipal systems and rural electrification cooperatives. The companies brought a number of suits, seeking to prevent the TVA and the cities from going into the business of distributing power. To check the growth of cooperatives, they built spite lines designed to skim the cream from the rural market.

The TVA was finally victorious, winning its lawsuits, building up its rural market, and purchasing private facilities at prices between those it had offered and those their owners had asked. It thus acquired a territory of 80,000 square miles, twice as large as the drainage basin of the Tennessee, with a population of 5,000,000 of whom 1,500,000 were then consumers of electricity.

The TVA inherited the dam and steam plant at Muscle Shoals and bought six dams from private companies. Its first new dams—Norris and Wheeler—were designed by the Bureau of Reclamation. The Authority then organized its own engineering staff and built 20 more dams itself. In addition to the dams it owns, TVA exercises control, by agreement, over the storage and release of water at six dams owned by the Aluminum Company of America. The Authority has built a number of steam plants to meet the growth in demand. Its installed capacity in 1968 was 18.2 million kilowatts. Less than a fourth of the power it sells is hydroelectric; more than three-fourths is produced by steam. New thermal plants now under construction, all larger than any in operation, two of them using atomic fuel, have carried the system's capacity to 28 million kilowatts by 1974. The TVA sells 22 percent of its output to other federal agencies, the most important being the Atomic Energy Commission, 23 percent of it to private industries, and 55 percent to distributors, 157 in number, 102 of them municipalities, 53 rural cooperatives, and two small private companies.

In answer to a question at a press conference in the summer of 1953, President Eisenhower cited the TVA as an example of what he meant by "creeping socialism." In a sense, the characterization was justified. The project is certainly socialistic. And it has moved from place to place. The TVA started with a series of multipurpose dams. To transport incidental power, it built transmission lines. To obtain an assured market, it promoted public ownership of distribution facilities. To avoid duplication, it bought out private companies, thus obtaining a regional monopoly. To "firm up" its power supply, it built steam plants. To keep pace with growing demands, as any private enterprise would have done, it built more steam plants. Far from creeping, it proceeded at a walk or even at a run.

Pricing. In fixing its initial rates, the TVA sought to promote expansion in the use of power, assuming demand to be elastic and setting its charges at a level designed to create a market that would enable it to produce at full capacity. In regulating the rates of its distributors, too, it required that they be set at levels designed, not to yield a profit that would finance the other activities of local governments and reduce their taxes, but to increase the use of power and contribute to the valley's economic development.

The low-rate policy, thus established, has been continued. In 1967 residential consumers in the Tennessee Valley bought electricity for just over half of the nation's average rate: 1.28 cents per kilowatt-hour compared with 2.47 cents. The policy has been successful. From 1933 to 1972, in the region, the number of farms electrified rose from 3 percent to more than 99 percent. The use of domestic power, per customer per annum, rose from an average of 600 kilowatt-hours to 14,040, a figure more than twice as high as that for the nation as a whole. The total consumption of power rose from 1.5 billion kilowatt-hours to 91 billion.

Subsidies Are Small. It is often charged that the customers of TVA are subsidized, because (1) the Authority does not pay taxes, (2) it does not pay a proper share of the joint cost of the multipurpose facilities or charge to power a proper share of joint administrative costs, and (3) it does not pay the market rate of interest on capital provided by the government. Each of these points requires examination.

The TVA itself pays to state and local governments, in lieu of taxes, 5 percent of the revenue it collects from customers other than the federal government. Its distributors make such payments as the laws of their states require. In 1972, these payments, taken together, amounted to more than $53 million. This was 8.3 percent of total revenue. The taxes paid by neighboring private utilities ranged from 4 to 10 percent of revenue. The TVA does not pay the federal tax on corporate net income, which is a tax on private profit rather than a cost. But it is repaying the government's investment in its plant, a charge the private companies are not required to meet.

There is no question that TVA rates have covered the costs of building and operating the facilities that are used exclusively in producing power. This includes the steam plants that turn out three-fourths of the power, the hydroelectric plants, and the transmission lines. The only question that can be raised is whether the Authority is paying its proper share of the cost of the multipurpose dams and charging enough of the cost of general administration to power. It has arrived at a distribution that allots 27 percent of the cost of the dams to navigation, 31 percent to flood control, and 42 percent to power. Correspondingly, it charges 30 percent of the cost of general administration to navigation, 30 percent to flood control, and 40 percent to power. Whether this is the proper allocation is a matter of opinion. Since this issue is now relevant only to a minor part of the cost of a minor part of the supply of TVA power, it has lost whatever importance it may once have seemed to have.

On the bonds that it issued to finance the purchase of private properties and on those that it may issue to finance the construction of new facilities, the TVA must pay the rate of interest that the market requires. On the capital provided by the Treasury, it need only pay the rate at which funds are borrowed by the government. Since this is lower than the rate that private companies must pay, they may argue that the difference amounts to a subsidy. The use of the term in this connection can be questioned, but the advantage given the Authority cannot. The private companies, on the other hand, when granted the privilege of accelerated amortization receive what amounts to an interest-free loan from the government. The pot, in this case, is calling the kettle black.

The subsidy given consumers of TVA power, if any, is small indeed. In the 25 years from 1933 to 1958, the Authority earned an average return of 4 percent on the government's investment in its power establishment. It invested $470 million of its earnings in new facilities and paid more than $250 million into the Treasury. Under legislation enacted by Congress in 1959, the Authority must pay off the remaining $1 billion of its debt in the next 45 years. Its annual payments since that date have run well ahead of those required. The repayment—which private firms do not do—tilts TVA's finances even further away from subsidies.

Since 1953, Congress has made no appropriations to finance new power facilities. But in 1956 it authorized TVA to invest its earnings in such facilities, and in 1959 it gave the Authority permission to raise new capital by selling up to $750 million in revenue bonds. At the same time, it forbade the agency to extend its operations more than five miles beyond its existing boundaries. TVA is thus allowed to grow but not to spread.

Long-time friends of TVA complain that its character has changed. It is now more interested in the production of electricity, they say, than in the other purposes for which it was originally created. There is some basis for this criticism. But it should be noted that many of the social activities initiated by the Authority have been taken over by the region's state and local governments. The environment in which the agency now operates differs markedly from the one into which it was born in 1933.[1]

---

[1] See G. R. Clapp, *The TVA: An Approach to the Development of a Region* (Chicago: University of Chicago Press, 1955); J. R. Moore, ed., *The Economic Impact of TVA* (Knoxville: The University of Tennessee Press, 1967); and Richard Hellman, *Government Competition in the Electric Utility Industry: A Theoretical and Empirical Study* (New York: Praeger Publishers, 1972).

Over half of TVA power now goes ultimately to private industry. Its rural development aims have been met, and it is now much like any other large power system. Its rate structure has little or no peak-load pricing features.[2]

Other River Valley Developments. These—Colorado, Columbia, and Missouri (recall Chapter 15)—have provided navigation, flood control, urban water supply, irrigation, and recreation, along with electric power. These gains have often been used to justify the cost involved, when electricity revenues would not cover costs of capital and operation. Such joint costs are, of course, virtually impossible to assign, and the actual cost allocations have been something of a black art.[3] In many cases, the agencies have overstated the benefits and ignored real costs (such as capital costs, and the destruction of natural sites and ecology: see Chapter 26).

These are engineering—dam-building—agencies: the Bureau of Reclamation (Interior Department) and the Army Corps of Engineers. Their huge projects in the 1930s have nearly exhausted the good possibilities, but they continue seeking rationales for new ones. Local groups also continually seek pork-barrel financing for such projects. Benefit-cost analysis has long been used to select proposals and justify them. But it routinely overstates net benefits; and the crucial choices are usually made politically, in any event. The whole situation illustrates how cost-benefit analysis can be misused, either deliberately or by neglect.

Biases in Cost-Benefit Choices (recall Chapter 3). In estimating benefits, these agencies have established three categories: tangible benefits—primary and secondary—and intangible benefits. Tangible benefits are

---

[2] See W. G. Shepherd, "Marginal Cost Pricing in American Utilities," *op. cit.*

[3] At one extreme, there is the view, sometimes expressed by the private companies, that all of the cost of these dams should be charged to power and none of it to other purposes. This would transfer from the taxpayer to the power consumer the cost of subsidizing navigation, irrigation, and flood control. At the other extreme, there is the view, once espoused by proponents of public power, that all of the cost should be charged to the purposes for which the dams were supposedly built and none of it to power. This would compel the taxpayer to subsidize the power consumer. Between the two extremes, a number of methods have been proposed for allocating to power its proper share of the joint costs.

Each of these methods is open to criticism. (1) An equal charge might be made for each of the purposes for which a dam is used. This would be workable but purely arbitrary. (2) Contributions to joint costs might be made proportionate to the separable costs of the various uses of common facilities. This, too, would be workable but arbitrary. (3) The contributions might be made proportionate to the benefits received by the users of different services. This is justifiable but unworkable. The benefits of some services are difficult to measure. The benefits of others can be measured by the prices which they bring. But since these prices are in question, this method would involve circular reasoning. (4) The alternative cost of building a single-purpose dam for each of the purposes served by a project (where this would be economically justifiable) might be computed, and contributions to joint costs might be made proportionate to their respective shares in the total of single-purpose costs. The use of alternative possibilities as a basis for allocation has a certain logic. But this procedure necessitates an estimation of the cost of imaginary projects, an exercise in which personal judgment has free play and differences of opinion are certain to result. (5) The share of joint cost charged to each purpose might be made proportionate to its use of reservoir capacity. This, too, makes sense. But the cost of different layers in a reservoir is difficult to estimate. The use of reservoir capacity for different purposes is even more so, since it differs from season to season and from day to day. The usefulness of a reservoir in producing power depends, moreover, not only on the volume of water that passes through the turbines, but also on the head of water behind the dam. If this procedure were to be used, costs would have to be allocated, in the end, in accordance with an arbitrary rule. Choice among the methods of allocation is a matter of judgment. The final decision, whatever its nature, will be open to dispute.

those that flow indirectly from a project. In the case of irrigation, for instance, they include the gains of the millers and the bakers who would turn an added supply of wheat into flour and bread, the gains of the carriers and the distributors who would handle these products, and those of the other businessmen who would sell to them. Intangible benefits, finally, are those to which a monetary value cannot be assigned. Included in this category are such matters as the saving of life that would result from the prevention of floods.

Direct benefits are valued at the prices that the beneficiaries would presumably be willing to pay to obtain them, these prices being determined, where possible, by finding those of the cheapest alternatives.

The estimation of costs follows the same pattern. Primary costs are those that would be incurred in constructing, operating, and maintaining a project, taken at the prevailing market rates, plus the value of properties that would have to be abandoned if land were flooded and the amount of taxes that would have to be foregone. Secondary costs are those associated with secondary benefits. In the case of irrigation, cited above, they would be the added costs of the millers, bakers, carriers, distributors, and other businessmen.

In appraising a project, the agencies compute a ratio of tangible benefits and costs, with benefits as the numerator and costs as the denominator. If the ratio is greater than 1, the project is said to be justified. Intangible benefits are described in writing, but their role in the guidance of investment is a minor one.

Use of the ratio of benefit to cost as a criterion for investment is open to question. A favorable ratio shows that some return will be realized, but it does not show what the rate of the return will be. It does not distinguish, for instance, between an investment that will yield 6 percent and one that will yield 3 percent. It therefore discriminates against projects where capital requirements are low and operating costs high in favor of those where operating costs are low and capital requirements high.

Favorable ratios can be manufactured by overstating benefits and by understating costs. *Benefits* may be overstated by including secondary benefits. In the case of irrigation, for instance, the gains of the millers, bakers, etc., can properly be counted if these producers would not otherwise have been employed. They can be regarded, under any circumstances, as a benefit to the region in question. But in times of full employment they should not be counted as a benefit to the economy as a whole. Primary benefits, too, can be overstated. Generous estimates can be made of the increase in crops that will result from irrigation, the increase in traffic that will follow improvements in navigation, and the amount of damage that will be prevented by controlling floods.

Costs, on the other hand, may be understated. Here, the most important item is the cost of capital. In figuring this cost, the development agencies use the rate of interest that must be paid by the government. The Corps of Engineers, in years past, has used 3 percent; the Bureau of Reclamation, 2.5 percent. Such rates did not cover the real cost of the capital employed. The real cost is measured by the interest that would have been earned if the capital, instead of being taken by the government, could have been invested in the private sector of the economy. Measured in this way, the cost would have been closer to 8 percent.[4]

If benefits and costs could be measured with greater accuracy, the benefit-cost ratio would be a better guide. This might be done if the task were transferred to an agency that would have no selfish interest in the findings it would make. As it is, the process operates to justify such projects as groups with political influences may desire.

The net social returns on much of these federal projects is probably below the true opportunity cost of capital. The systems tend to be bureaucratic, rigid, and insensitive to social impacts. This reflects their pork-barrel sources of revenue and support, their age, and the completion in the 1930s of the better projects.

City Power Systems. These systems have been permitted no such ossification, for power technology has shifted sharply to curtail their discretion. Most systems are now small dependent clients of large private suppliers, merely managing local distribution. In certain cases—especially in New England and the Eastern seaboard—large private joint projects for generating plants have excluded them. This would cause their prices to be higher, and the incentives to be absorbed in the private systems would be strong.[5] Public systems have therefore been embedded increasingly in hostile and powerful arrangements. The *Otter Tail* decision and related changes may reverse this trend (recall Chapter 15), but that is yet to come.

Meanwhile, the city systems are diverse, some skimming off high profits for the city treasury (as a hybrid taxing device), others supplying strictly at cost, as Table 21–3 shows. There is no hard evidence about their efficiency compared to private systems. The continuing inducements to sell off to private utilities applies a steady pressure toward efficiency on many city systems. In many cities, the public power system is active and spirited.

Public Power Systems Abroad. These are also diverse but show generally good performance.[6] In Britain and France, marginal-cost pricing is advanced and sophisticated both in bulk and retail supply.[7] This reflects both the greater scarcity of capital and the presence of several gifted economic analysts in the systems (especially Marcel Boiteaux in France and Ralph Turvey during 1963–67 in Britain). Also, the objective price structure is a valuable device to deflect political pressures for special rate cuts to backward regions, powerful customers, and other claimants.

Coordination is effective, and there appears to be no tendency toward excess capital-intensity (compare Chapters 14 and 15). Pooling of capac-

---

[4] See John V. Krutilla and Otto Eckstein, *Multiple Purpose River Development* (Baltimore: Johns Hopkins Press, 1958).

[5] See A. E. Kahn, *The Economics of Regulation, op. cit.,* Vol. 2, pp. 317–23.

[6] See Pryke, *op. cit.;* J. R. Nelson, *Marginal Cost Pricing in Practice, op. cit.;* W. G. Shepherd, *Economic Performance under Public Ownership, op. cit.*

[7] Both Britain and France apply marginal-cost pricing in bulk and retail markets: in France, it is the green tariff, in Britain, the White Meter tariff. See Nelson, *op. cit.;* Ralph Turvey, *Optimal Pricing and Investment in Electricity Supply* (London: Allen & Unwin, 1968); and *Annual Reports and Accounts* of the U.K. Electricity Council.

ity is thorough. The forecasting of demand has been no better than average, and they too have exaggerated the gains which nuclear power might offer.[8] Most of them face *other* public firms as coal suppliers, rail shippers, and gas competitors. In Britain, electricity officials have professed to want to shift away from coal more swiftly than the government has permitted, and so this has been claimed as a social burden on the power system (after 1969 it has been modestly compensated by the Treasury).

The siting and safety of nuclear plants has not posed a crisis such as the U.S. has had. This reflects the closer supervision which the systems get. Amenity, too—the routing of transmission lines, and pollution of air and streams—has been better handled than by the American commissions, preoccupied as they are with rate of return, rate base, and price questions. Therefore, in those social-economic issues which have recently plagued American utilities, public systems abroad have routinely shown superior performance.

TRANSPORT

Railroads. Railroad systems abroad are nearly uniform in two surface respects: they are mostly public, and they run large financial losses. But the more basic economic lessons are more diverse.

First, most of the systems are national monopolies, which combine commuter, intercity passenger, and a variety of freight operations. (Canada differs, both because there is direct competition between a private and public systems and because the system is mainly a long-distance one rather than the compact sizes common elsewhere.) As noted in Chapter 17, the optimal range for railroad freight operations is 200+ miles, which exceeds most operations in these small-country systems. Yet these countries also suffer serious problems of urban congestion and amenity which road transport burdens aggravate. Also, rail passenger service is optimal for *less* than 200 miles.[9] Therefore, the economic case for a railroad system as an important mode in these countries is strong.

The common pattern of these systems is

1. An overhang during 1945–55 of excess capacity, especially in nontrunk parts, which has required trimming of trackage, rolling stock, and work force.
2. A concurrent effort to "modernize" via high-speed trains, containerization, and other engineering devices. This effort often approaches messianic levels, both as an engineering challenge and as a diversion from more pedestrian financial problems.

The systems commonly have had very low short-run marginal costs, exactly parallel to the conditions of overcapacity in certain eastern U.S. railroads. Therefore, even if operations were conducted with internal efficiency—as, on the whole, they are—the correct pricing basis is to set rates at levels below average costs and thus incur a deficit.

---

[8] See Shepherd, Chapter 9 in Caves and Associates, *Britain's Economic Prospects, op. cit.*, and sources cited there.

[9] Recall footnote 4, Chapter 17.

Moreover, pruning the system involves closures, some of which impose serious social costs. The socially optimum rate of shrinkage is therefore below what profits alone would dictate. In fact, closures are invariably required to pass governmental screenings, which are usually slow. Meanwhile, the railroads themselves have no choice but to maintain loss-making operations which enlarge their deficits.

Finally, there is the basic issue of road-bed subsidy. The large carriers in other modes tend to be subsidized via road, airport, and other programs, while railroads must finance their own tracks (recall Chapter 17). The true comparative costs are usually unclear, but the railroads usually carry some degree of net burden (though they are often permitted to write off part of their capital, to ease their interest payments).

These factors together explain on economic grounds at least part—and perhaps all or more—of the losses run by most public railroad systems, especially on passenger services. The deficits are endemic partly because they do fit optimal criteria. This does not excuse the occasional inefficiency in pricing and/or investment.[10] But on the whole, performance compares well with U.S. railroads during recent decades.

Meanwhile, the efficiency and innovativeness of these systems has not been deficient (with exceptions). If anything, there has been a fixation on new traction, containerizing, and similar engineering improvements (which some U.S. railroads, under regulation, have tended to slight). But the upshot has probably been reasonably close to the long-run optimal pattern of innovation, in many cases.

The rate structure of these public systems tends to avoid clear inefficiencies. The degree of discrimination is probably less than in private systems. The scope for peak-load pricing is relatively slight, compared to the commuter and transit systems (see Chapter 22). On the whole, public systems have developed price systems more rational than those common in regulated private railroads.

Airlines. Public airlines are nearly universal elsewhere (several British lines are the main exceptions). These entities, many of them quite large indeed, are also stand-by military carriers for their governments. But they follow commercial policies and join fully in the international price cartel. This involves extensive price discrimination and pricing against marginal-cost criteria. High peak-season fares do approximate marginal costs; but genuine off-peak pricing is rigidly excluded by the international cartel.

All face international competition (though not in fares) but hold important monopoly positions on their home routes. They adhere to the international airline rate cartel as closely as the private airlines do.[11] Britain since 1971 has deliberately added a degree of competition, but

---

[10] The 1956 British Railways modernization Plan, for example, contained certain economically irrational parts which can best be explained by the lingering attachment to the 19th century "iron horse" image of railroads. See Select Committee on the Nationalized Industries, *Report on British Railways,* H. of C. 254 (London: H.M.S.O., 1960) for a searching appraisal; see also Pryke, *op. cit.*

[11] See M. Straszheim, *The International Airline Industry* (Washington, D.C.: Brookings Institution, 1969) for a thorough analysis.

this is exceptional.[12] The lines appear to be comparable in total efficiency (X-efficiency, pricing, and innovation in planes and ticketing systems) to private airlines.

COMMUNICATIONS

We will consider—briefly—postal, telephone, and broadcasting activities.

Postal Service

The basic postal system is everywhere a public enterprise. The postal service, wrote Adam Smith in 1776, "is perhaps the only mercantile

Costumes and architecture change, but the basic postal operation of sorting is much the same as in the 1840s at the British main Post Office in London, seen at the time when Rowland Hill was establishing the "penny post" uniform letter charge. This principle continues even now.

project which has been successfully managed by, I believe, every sort of government. The capital to be advanced is not very considerable. There is no mystery in the business. The returns are not only certain, but immediate."[13] Congress was given the power by Article I, Section 8 of the Constitution "To establish Post Offices and Post Roads," and a postal

---

[12] See the "Edwards Report," *British Air Transport in the Seventies,* Committee of Inquiry into Civil Air Transport, Cmnd. 4018 (London: H.M.S.O., 1969).

[13] *The Wealth of Nations,* Book V, chap. ii, Part I.

system, including 74 post offices, was established by the first Congress in 1789. The system was originally set up as a separate agency under the President. In 1829, the Postmaster General was admitted to the Cabinet. And in 1872, the Post Office was made a department of the government. In 1971 it was revised into a public corporation.

In the early days of the republic, the postal service had a vital function to fulfill. In the absence of modern means of communication, it afforded the only tie that bound the country together, uniting the wilderness with the capital, scattered settlements with centers of trade and finance. It contributed to a sense of national identity, to economic and political unity. It was a basic instrument of public policy.

Today the Post Office is one of many media of communication. It is big business—one of the biggest on earth—with 44,000 offices, over 700,-000 employees, and a budget of $9 billion a year. It delivers mail each weekday to nearly every business and household in the land, handling 110 billion pieces each year. Only 14 percent of this is personal correspondence. A tenth is newspapers or magazines. More than a fourth is advertising matter. Over half involves business transactions: orders, invoices, bills, checks, and the like. The volume of such materials is twice as great today as it was 20 years ago. And it promises to keep on growing at an increasing rate.

In the U.S. and Britain, it has recently been converted from department status into a public corporation. The common pattern abroad is for postal services to be combined with telecommunications (the French PPT, the British Post Office, etc.). This corresponds to combining the Bell system and other telephone independents with the Postal Service and telegraph service—*but* also splitting it into five regional systems. Since these foreign systems are all less than one-fifth as large as the U.S. system, the total monopoly effect is rather less than it might seem. Also, the services are usually operated, accounted, and evaluated separately.

In the U.S., as elsewhere, the postal service is among the country's largest employers. In fact, the postman (or woman) on his rounds is part of a network which constitutes the core of natural monopoly conditions in this industry. Repeat: the universal delivery and pick-up system is the one clear element of natural monopoly. Related to it, of course, are the sorting and bulk shipping parts of postal service. But these are more separable and less marked by decreasing costs.[14] Indeed, they are a focus of new competition.

Deficits. Postal services commonly run a financial deficit.[15] This stems from a variety of political and social factors, possibly related to

---

[14] President's Commission on Postal Organization, *Towards Postal Excellence* (Washington, D.C.: U.S. Government Printing Office, 1968); and Morton Baratz, *The Economics of the Postal Service* (Washington, D.C.: Public Affairs Press, 1955).

[15] For a quarter of a century after the Post Office was established, it was operated as a business and returned an annual profit. But since that time, Congress emphasized expansion of the service and made little effort to insure that rates should cover costs. In all but a few years the Department has operated at a deficit. During the 60s the deficit exceeded $8 billion; in 1967, it stood at $1.2 billion. And these figures understated the loss, since the Department's accounts included no allowance for the government's contribution to the pension fund, no interest charge on the sums invested in postal facilities, and no provision for depreciation.

external benefits which postal services may provide. An informed and well-communicating populace is an important precondition for functioning democracy. First-rate and thorough postal service may contribute to this, and therefore its values may ultimately be far greater than the individual users may be willing to pay. That is the apparent rationale behind the subsidies which have been extended traditionally to such postal users as magazines, newspapers, and senders of educational materials. Yet postal services are overwhelmingly *business* services: 70 percent of all mail is business mail (bills, ads, reports, etc.). The system routinely subsidizes the circulation of advertising and other strictly commercial items. Therefore, the basic question about postal service is what its marginal costs are on the different kinds of service, and whether social effects justify direct or indirect subsidies to cover any of the true marginal costs.

Cost Structure. The structure of costs arises from the special rhythm of postal activities, primarily in the sorting facilities and the delivery networks.

In every post office—in every country—there are two sharp peaks of activity during the day; these fit the standard analysis of peak-load costs (recall Chapter 14). Post offices are merely arenas within which mail is handled. In the early morning hours, the mail comes in from other cities. There follows a rush of handlings: emptying of bags, sorting of mail, and packaging for the deliverers to take out in the early morning. Next there follows a slack period during the middle of the day. Then comes the late afternoon rush, during which the mail sent by people in the city piles up and is sorted and packaged for sending outward. These rush periods commonly strain the capacity of the post office and its employees.

Obviously, postal services bear the same sharp fluctuations which are common with other utility services. These peaks and valleys cause sharp variations in real marginal costs; peak costs are sharply above off-peak costs. This underlies the common schedule of postal rates. First-class mail is presumably handled at the peak and is charged a high price—perhaps in line with its true marginal costs—while other types of mail may be set aside for handling during the low-cost, off-peak periods. If postal operations were in fact closely costed, the proper level of peak and off-peak cost (that is, basically, first versus second and third-class rates) could be ascertained within reasonable boundaries. But this is not regularly done. Rather, it is occasionally done in detail but on highly arbitrary assumptions.

Price Structure. Instead, the tradition of uniform postal rates still governs postal operations. Designed under Rowland Hill in the early 19th century to foster circulation of messages within the British Isles, the standard "penny post" rate has been extended into the present on the philosophy that all mail should share in covering the costs of the system. Therefore, most postal rates are averaged among users rather than fitted directly to the real costs involved.

Do first, second, and third class postal rates fit the true costs involved? In all probability, they tend to overcharge first class mail and to undercharge the lower groups.[16] These prices reflect both actual costs and the political power of these groups which have been able to gain preferential postal rates. Nobody really knows the true cost patterns. They could be decisive to the financial health of the postal systems, both in the U.S. and abroad. Most of the postal deficits arise from cheap handling of high-weight, low-class mail. If there are external benefits from circulating advertisements, they must be very large to justify the subsidy which has been given in the past.

Management. Postal management has faced severe problems under the old departmental basis.[17] Critical decisions were limited from outside. This external control also bred excessive internal caution, and decisions were overcentralized in a rigid process.[18] Key personnel had to be selected on political grounds.[19] Worker morale was low.

These problems reached crisis proportions in 1966, when the Chicago post office—the largest in the world—was virtually paralyzed for three weeks. Several factors caused the breakdown: a rise in bulk mailings, equipment failures, labor problems, and the like. But the problems were recurring and cumulating elsewhere too, under the old rules.

---

[16] Airmail letters, according to the Department's estimates, have recently been carried at 121 percent of cost, other letters at 103 percent, advertising matter at 67 percent, and periodicals at 25 percent. In a recent year, the Post Office is said to have made a profit of $162 million in carrying first class mail and airmail; incurred a loss of $922 million in carrying other classes of mail and in maintaining rural services. The inadequacy of the rate level and the character of the rate structure forced the taxpayer and the letter writer to subsidize other users of the service.

[17] It could not select its own personnel. The upper positions were filled through political patronage; the remaining jobs were controlled by the Civil Service Commission. The Department did not set the rates it charged. All rates but those for parcel post were fixed by Congress. Parcel post rates were fixed by the Interstate Commerce Commission. The Department did not determine the amounts it spent. Salaries were fixed by Congress. Funds for post office buildings were included in the annual appropriations for public works. The Post Office made contracts with private carriers for transport of the mail. The amounts it paid the railroads were fixed by the Interstate Commerce Commission. The sums it paid the airlines were fixed by the Civil Aeronautics Board. Postal Revenues could not be used to defray the costs of the service; they had to be paid into the Treasury. To finance its activities, the Department had to present its budget requests to the Bureau of the Budget and to appropriations committees of the House and Senate and have funds voted it by Congress in appropriation bills. Funds for the Post Office were broken down, by purposes, into some 60 different appropriations, and each expenditure had to be charged against the appropriation under which it had been authorized. The Department's books were checked by the General Accounting Office to make sure that no unauthorized expenditures were made.

[18] The individual postmaster could not operate his office as if it were a business. He was bound hand and foot by the rules contained in *Postal Laws & Regulations,* a book that weighed nearly three pounds and ran close to a thousand pages. The Commission on Postal Organization in 1968 found the management structure of the Post Office to be "archaic" and "inappropriate": that "In appearance, many people are responsible for running the Post Office; in fact, no one is" and that "the nominal managers of the postal service don't have the authority to run the postal service," and concluded that "the present organization of the Post Office prevents it from being managed properly."

[19] The Postmaster General, with few exceptions, was appointed, not because of his experience in postal administration, but as a reward for his service as a politician. He functioned, traditionally, as the chief patronage dispenser of the national administration. Candidates for individual postmasterships could establish their eligibility by passing a Civil Service examination. But the candidates appointed by the President were selected, with the advice of Congressmen and local politicians, from among the top three found eligible. A third of the postmasters appointed in the 60s came from the career service; two-thirds were political hacks. Workers employed at lower levels were, in general, poorly educated and inexperienced.

FIGURE 21-3
Competition for Parcels Service

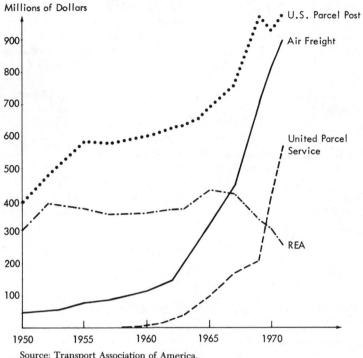

Source: Transport Association of America.

To free the postal service from the bureaucratic paralysis and rising deficits, a special Commission in 1968 recommended turning it into an independent postal corporation. It would have normal personnel policies, thorough cost accounting, and the ability to set postal rates (under regulatory—not Congressional—constraint). It would draw capital by selling bonds in private markets. This was done in 1971, paralleling a similar change in Britain in 1969. The new Postal Service is to be self-supporting within 15 years, as management and pricing are reformed.

The new Postal Service has much to gain by aligning its price structure with true costs. Further, in the U.S. there is a new regulatory authority—the U.S. Postal Rate Commission—which might lead postal pricing along efficient lines. Yet three years of experience already have proven unimpressive.[20] The new management of the postal service has shown itself zealous mainly in cutting staff rather than in adopting a rational price structure. To some extent, this can be blamed on the private-enterprise bias of the new managers. As always, managers of com-

---

[20] It is already a mediocre commission; though staff members have tried to develop economic issues, the commissioners have scarcely understood them and exerted little constraint on the key elements of postal pricing.

plex public organizations with dubious histories have difficult tasks in adapting their operations towards economic criteria.

Competition. To some extent, the postal system is under stress from growing competition with telecommunications and package delivery systems. The Postal Service is best regarded as a large system of people ready to continue the old ways of sorting and delivering. But new technology is taking away some of these activities and offering alternative ways of doing others.

The handling of parcels is partly a natural joint product of the main sorting and shipping operations. It can be fitted partly with off-peak operations at low cost. But even so it does not really share in the core natural monopoly of the system—the final delivery and pick-up network. Therefore it is arguably eligible for an open competitive approach. In fact, United Parcel Service Co. has already built up a private near-monopoly of its own in small, high-value, high-speed parcels (see Figure 21–3). Its high profitability fully reflects its market position. REA and various air delivery firms also compete for parts of this market. In this and other areas, the post office monopoly is actually under close constraints.

A fair evaluation would be that U.S. postal managers are slowly emerging from a politicized managerial situation, and that many of their more lucrative markets are being skimmed. Beset by inherited deficits and traditions, they are not doing poorly. Still, the moves toward rational pricing—both in the U.S. and abroad—have been slow.

Point-to-point Telecommunications

This is the provision of telephone service plus the growing new role of data transmission. Abroad, this is commonly combined with postal services. There the degree of monopoly is great (compare Chapter 16). Yet the supply of telephonic equipment is nowhere fully integrated with the operating system, as it is in the Bell and GT&E systems.

Naturally, the extent of penetration of residential and business markets is lower abroad than in the United States, because the standards of income and consumption are lower (recall above). Moreover, the quality of service is usually lower abroad than in the U.S., as indeed are the standards of other consumption items. In many European countries and nearly all LDCs, the home telephone is still largely an upper-class device. Yet normative lessons from this are slippery.

One can make useful policy comparisons between Britain and the U.S. The U.K. system aims broadly at a rate of progress comparable to that in the U.S. under regulation. The price structures have differed but are converging slowly. British pricing has long been more closely cost-based (recall Chapter 16).[21] Business rentals are only slightly above residential rentals. The metering of local telephone usage is far more thorough in Britain than in the U.S. Usage is charged by units of time—often with peak–off-peak differentials—so that prices quite closely approximate the

---

[21] See W. G. Shepherd, "Residence Expansion in the British Telephone System," *op. cit.*

costs of service. Moreover, this extends through to long distance usage, where the degree of fineness in pricing has been greater than the United States. As U.S pricing is refined (recall Chapter 16), these differences are receding. But British pricing has set the norm for efficient pricing.[22] A prime reason is that capital has been scarcer and rate-base effects have been absent under public ownership.

The innovation policies broadly correspond to those in this country, with a few exceptions. The Bell System has followed a deliberate evolutionary policy (recall Chapter 16), avoiding marked shifts in telephone technology in favor of gradual changes. This has normally been true in other countries, including Britain, except for the 1960s. Then, the British system attempted to innovate directly from electro-mechanical switching to electronic switching, a move which turned out to be difficult and caused special problems in the late 1960s. This was a response to the tight economic constraints on the system during 1950–65; an attempt to bridge difficult financial and engineering conditions at a stroke. The key lesson is that the public enterprise was willing to innovate much *more* rapidly than regulated private systems.[23]

On the whole, public telephone systems in western Europe have not been inferior in internal efficiency or innovative ability. Though not as promotional in marketing, they have been experimental and quick to try new technology.[24] Their local-service price systems have been more refined and efficient than those in the U.S., although this gap is closing under the new financial and urban pressures on the Bell System. Service quality is marginally lower abroad, but the normative lessons from that are not clear.

Broadcasting

The main comparison is between the state-owned television systems which are common elsewhere and the private broadcasting networks in the United States. The issues are complex, turning in large part on the program content and local service, rather than on narrow economic criteria. Even so, certain comparisons can be ventured.

There have been three main distinctive features in most other systems: (1) public ownership, (2) monopoly, usually in a single entity, and (3) financing by a television tax plus a degree of direct subsidy, rather than advertising. These differences have helped cause the clear differences between U.S. and other television fare. Abroad, broadcasting hours are much shorter. There are only one to three channels to choose among. Program content is of higher quality: less light material and violence, more culture and local-interest programming. Instead of the oligopoly convergence on mass appeal (recall Chapter 16), the monopoly choices

---

[22] Other European systems have also followed marginal cost criteria.

[23] See Shepherd, Chapter 9 in Caves and Associates, *op. cit.*

[24] During 1920–55 they tended more to lead than lag in new technology and service offerings. See John Sheahan, "Integration and Exclusion in the Telephone Equipment Industry," *Quarterly Journal of Economics,* Vol. 70 (May 1956) pp. 249–69. And recall the appraisal of Bell System management noted in Chapter 16.

cover the spectrum of special interests more fully. Advertising is either absent, or where it is presented, it is spaced and presented less obtrusively. News coverage, however, is usually less complete and independent than U.S. news broadcasting has become since 1960.

These basic differences of ownership, form, and finance have receded since 1955 (see Table 21–4). Britain and Canada have private broadcasting systems. Some state networks carry a small amount of advertising. Public entities now usually offer two or three channels, with differences in emphasis and level. The U.S. now has a small public broadcasting system. Yet where the public system is larger and well financed, the basic contrasts in programming remain.

The economic lessons are predictable. In both systems, the viewer —once the set, antenna, and any TV taxes are paid—receives programs at virtually zero prices, which is roughly in line with the marginal cost of the broadcaster. When separate systems compete, they are mutually

TABLE 21–4
Television Broadcasting in Selected Countries

	Type	Regional Units?	Regulated?	Advertising Revenues, Share of Support
Canada				
Canadian Broadcasting Corp. .	Public	Yes	Indirectly	25%
Canadian Television	Private	Yes	Yes	100%
U.K.				
British Broadcasting Corp. (2 channels)	Public	Yes	No	0
Independent Television	Private	Yes	Franchise renewals hinge on program "performance"	100%
Sweden				
Swedish Broadcasting Corp. ...	Public	Yes	Yes	Part
France				
Radiodiffusion-Television Francaise (3 channels)......	Public	Yes	Indirectly	Small
Italy				
Radiotelevisione Italiana (2 channels)	Public	No	Indirectly	Part
Germany				
Federal network.............	Public	No	Indirectly	0
Nine regional systems (which also pool programs)	Public	Yes	Indirectly	Part
Australia				
Australian Broadcasting Commission	Public	Yes	Indirectly	0
Private stations..............	Private	Yes	Lightly	100%
Japan				
Noncommercial, nongovernment system (based on subscription fees)	Semi-public	No	?	0
Commercial.................	Private	Yes	?	100%

Sources: World Television *Fact Book,* periodical; and Walter B. Emery, *National and International Systems of Broadcasting* (East Lansing: Michigan State University Press, 1969).

induced toward mass programming, whether they are public or private. Thus when new commercial TV in Britain in the 1950s forced BBC toward lower program quality, this reflected more than just the invasion of U.S.-style "wasteland" fare. It also forced BBC to compete for maximum viewership, rather than focus on "elevating" taste and culture. Differences do remain: BBC and other public networks deliberately offer better and more varied content, while commercial TV inevitably maximizes its audience exposure to advertising messages.

On the other side, U.S. private networks benefit from having a minor —even passive—public network to cater to specialized interests. This leaves them politically freer to program for maximum private returns. Private networking and large-city franchises are highly profitable abroad, just as they are in the U.S. (recall Chapter 16).[25] But stricter franchise-renewal criteria have induced them to maintain program content at least marginally above the U.S. levels.

The steady revenues for public systems permit them to treat programming in larger and longer perspective. This has fostered a series of major high-quality serials (The Forsyte Saga, Shakespearean plays, etc.) which U.S. networks find profitable to show but do not finance or produce.

The public and mixed conditions abroad do unquestionably yield more varied and especially responsive program content (except, in many cases, for news coverage). The optimal situation appears to include a strong public system with two or more channels, genuine competition with one or more private networks, and reasonably strict criteria for franchise renewal.

SUMMARY

Evidently, public enterprise in utility sectors is firmly fixed abroad and has established a performance record that is, in some respects, superior to that of regulated private utilities. Yet the cost of these units (especially in electricity, railroads, and telephones) is not small—in public capital, risk-absorption, managerial talent, and subsidies in some cases. They are usually small firms by comparison with the national counterparts in the entire U.S. Moreover, there are other national differences in culture and public traditions which may affect their performance. And finally, their performance is often affected by a degree of competition. Therefore, public enterprise is often less important than its setting, criteria, and constraints. Public firms in utility sectors often perform better when they *depart* from the conventional model, rather than fit it closely.

---

[25] One British franchisee candidly described his franchise as "a license to print money."

CHAPTER TWENTY-TWO

Public Enterprise in Urban and Social Sectors

These units usually have definite social effects and are partly subsidized. Yet their management, competitive status, and economic criteria are also important. The basic industrial policy analysis applies to them, much as it does in other sectors.[1]

The enterprises have seven common features:

1. They are diverse and integral in modern life.

2. As city size and density increase, the role of public enterprise in urban services also increases. This is because natural monopoly and social elements deepen.

3. Their role has therefore grown naturally, as urban size and density have risen.

4. These units offer economic and social yields which may rival or exceed those which antitrust and regulation offer in the standard industrial and utility sectors.

5. Their economic conditions vary. Some of them yield mainly private benefits, but under natural monopoly conditions (subways, water, sewage, garbage disposal). Some also offer large benefits from externalities and improved equity (e.g., parks, libraries). Some involve subsidies which may be highly regressive (frequently: airports, theaters, sports stadiums).

6. Their pricing and investment policies vary. The degree of subsidy ranges from total down to zero (even to negative, in some profit-earning units). Some price structures are simple, some sophisticated; and some have quite irrational parts. The cost of capital is treated variously, in some cases scarcely being considered at all.

7. The *nature* of service itself is often the main problem. What coverage, frequency, and reliability should bus and subway service have? What kinds of parks and libraries should there be, and where located?

---

[1] See the excellent volume by S. J. Mushkin, ed., *Public Prices for Public Products* (Washington, D.C.: Urban Institute, 1972) for basic discussion and applications in several areas.

Often services have become narrow and rigid (e.g., bus systems which exclude jitneys and informal routes). Operations may be profit-earning, or internally efficient, but not fully optimal.

We will·look first at the core urban services, which are now mostly under public enterprise. Then we turn to several major *social* enterprises: schools, courts, public housing, and parks. With so many cases, one risks losing the main points amongst the details. But each one shares the same basic problem: optimizing performance by applying a mix of competition, budget constraints, and specific criteria.

URBAN ENTERPRISES

Units supplying essential urban services range from subways and water systems to zoos, parks, and libraries. Many of them are quite necessary and utilitarian—and as *dull* as only sewage, garbage disposal, and cemetaries can seem. But others pose wider choices and raise hot controversies: airports, for example, enclosed sports stadiums, and hospitals. Some of them are treated in other chapters. Here we will consider transit, water, garbage, and libraries.

Transport

This includes a variety of operations, from cross-town transit (bus, subway, etc.), bridges and parking, to commuter lines, ports and airports. Despite their range, the key feature is their mutual dependency. They interrelate, both as *alternatives* (buses versus subways; commuter lines versus bridges and tunnels for private traffic) and as *supplements,* which feed into each other. This mutual externality—the need to "integrate" them technically and economically—makes them both difficult to optimize and also natural for a public treatment. With adroit pricing, tax and subsidy criteria, one could conceivably mesh them as private firms and minimize their external costs (noise, air pollution, and other destruction of amenity). But that is usually not possible; instead, the choices need to be applied directly via public enterprise and combined treatments. In any case, the remaining private transit systems have been going into bankruptcy in droves, to be taken over by city transit enterprises.

Public systems often follow deviant policies, but they possess the preconditions for perceiving and applying an efficient treatment. They can see interactions among the parts of the urban transit system (e.g., how parking fees relate to subway fares and bridge tolls) and set the prices in line with that—*and* arrange the necessary subsidies of some units. Their broader social effects (e.g., service to ghetto areas; and easing noise and air pollution) can be fitted into other criteria for decent city life.

The main allocation issues concern pricing and subsidizing of the various modes. These also tie in with equity questions, for the subsidies are often big and—on balance—regressive.

New York City.   New York City illustrates how the elements mesh. Figure 22-1 shows some parts: the basic bus and subway network is surrounded by PONY parts plus various commuter railroads. The core facts are the 3.2 million people and the 700,000 vehicles which pour into Manhattan Island each workday morning and leave in the late afternoon (see Figure 22–2). On average, there are about 1.3 persons per car; that is, a driver plus an occasional passenger. They use streets and highways which are free, plus bridges and tunnels charging various tolls. They park in the streets, in company garages, or in paid lots. Result: the rush-hour crunch, a daily double crisis.

FIGURE 22–1
The Transit System in New York City

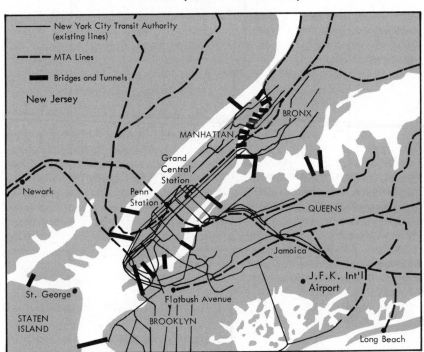

Meanwhile, the subways, buses, and commuter lines—even the Staten Island Ferry—are jammed with their riders twice a day. The airports, too, have rush hours which strain capacity.

Because of the fluctuations, true costs are high at peak and low at other times. As in all big cities, the private cost per car-rider is a multiple of the cost for the others; and the additional social costs (from congestion, disamenity, and the paving over of urban area) are often large.[2] If transit capacity is expanded to the optimum level, then the efficient level of

[2] The problem is heavily researched. See Wilfred Owen, *The Metropolitan Transportation Problem* (Washington, D.C.: Brookings Institution, 1962); and J. R. Meyer, J. F. Kain, and M. Wohl, *The Urban Transportation Problem* (Cambridge: Harvard University Press, 1965). The most thorough analyst has been William Vickrey, in a series of theoretical and practical papers.

FIGURE 22-2

New York City Traffic Fluctuates (The hub is the lower half of Manhattan Island).

Hourly Fluctuations in People
Entering and Leaving the Hub, 1971

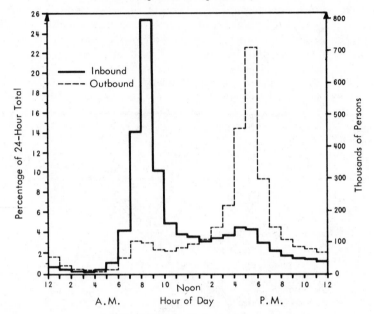

Hourly Fluctuations in Vehicles
Entering and Leaving the Hub, 1971

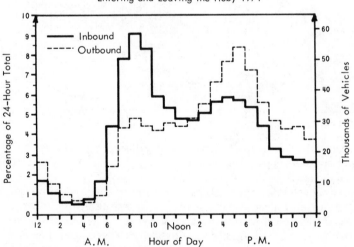

subway fares is (at long-run marginal cost) much lower than private costs. It would eventually induce travelers to shift to public transport. Conversely, car drivers should be set a high effective price; but how can this be applied? Toll booths at all entrance roads are impossible, or at least preposterous. Bridge and tunnel tolls, and parking fees by curbside meters and at parking lots and structures, are the main practical hope. Total "road pricing" is not feasible and perhaps never will be, but the other devices can give a rough approximation. These extra revenues would be pooled against the financial deficits which efficient pricing prescribes for some of the mass transit units.[3]

Under combined public ownership, the planning and design of systems and their prices can be coordinated, or at least not limited by strictly private interests and warring factions. And the subsidy flows can be managed more smoothly and avoid causing functionless and inequitable capital gains. In practice, this is often done defectively and incompletely, but some rough degree of efficiency can be seen and may perhaps be increasing.

Subways. There is a partial deficit. The flat 35 cent fare (as of 1974) rewards longer trips, and so it does tend to help induce commuters not to use their cars. But it should be cut sharply for off-peak use.[4] And there is expert agreement that the system's capacity is below both optimal size and the efficient level of service quality. This is reflected by comparative costs and by peak-hour congestion.

Commuter Railways. Peak-hour fares are set appreciably above standard fares. This is roughly in line with an efficient fare structure. But the whole structure may be too high compared to the prices set—presently or ideally—to motorists.[5]

Bridge and Tunnel Tolls. These are constant throughout the day, though peak-hour congestion is severe and off-peak use is low: therefore prices do not fit cost patterns. (A wrinkle: one pays 50¢ on the George Washington Bridge going *in,* but zero going *out.*) But the rates are probably above average cost, and so they slightly induce less total traffic.

Parking. Parking fees are high, reflecting classic urban land rent. But they are still below the true social cost from the cars' use in the city, and their reduced monthly rates tend to reward just those commuters who regularly add to peak congestion. Also, even the low metered prices for on-street parking are poorly enforced (there is much double parking, infrequent ticketing, and scofflaw behavior toward tickets). Therefore a key pricing device—parking fees—to make motorists pay real costs is neglected; this is partly because most parking lots are private. Complete

---

[3] In a landmark case, a British study recommended that a new London subway line (the Victoria line) be built, even though direct fare revenues might never cover all costs. It would remove enough traffic from London roads to justify its economic costs. The line has been built, as have others in some cities, on the same reasoning. See *The Victoria Line,* Ministry of Transport (London: H.M.S.O., 1963).

[4] Fares scaled by distance and differing between peak and off-peak periods are efficient. Most European fares are so scaled; most U.S. fares are not. Flat fares actually discriminate, often sharply, and tend to aggravate both congestion and deficits. See Mushkin, *op. cit.,* Chapters 10 and 11.

[5] Since commuters are mostly at or above average income levels, subsidies for commuter service tend to be regressive. Equity may therefore clash with efficiency.

public ownership and adequate enforcement could generate large financial surpluses from optimum parking fees. These and other traffic-abating net revenues could then subsidize the enlargement and improvement of the basic carriers.[6]

The network of pricing and investment levels therefore deviates from efficiency in many directions, but it is not far off in some others. The greatest difficulty is in getting: (1) the efficient structure of effective prices between cars and public transit, (2) sharp peak and off-peak price differentials, and (3) a smooth flow of subsidies among the modes. Instead, average-cost pricing and budget-balancing by individual modes is often sought. Still, some roughly efficient pricing results, and the public units do avoid most of the price discrimination and windfall private gains which certain private entities (e.g., parking lots) provide.

Water and Sewage

Drab as they may seem, these systems have become key urban problems, as many cities reach ecological limits for clear water and sewage disposal.[7] They are public enterprises (indeed, city departments) almost everywhere, and they often (with major exceptions) set prices somewhere near their average operating costs. Price structure and ecology are the main economic problem.

The technology virtually requires public ownership. Here is a rare permanent natural monopoly (not a life cycle: recall Chapter 13). It is closely related to public health, and there are deep possibilities for price discrimination. For decades, water and sewer systems have been quietly ignored as an economic problem. They have simply been built big enough to allow growth and then priced with utmost simplicity (and usually some dgree of subsidy). Water metering has been strictly at fixed prices, and in many cities the final user pays no price per unit at all. Thus, New York users pay fees unrelated to the amounts used, and in all cities many apartment dwellers pay no individual price at all. Such zero pricing induces use out to levels of zero marginal utility, even though water is often urgently scarce.[8]

City growth often causes the long-run marginal costs for these systems to be well above true average and short-run marginal costs. New suburbs and major apartment buildings are routinely planned, approved, and supplied with water and sewage service at going rates (often zero unit prices), even though these additions impose new capacity and service costs at levels sharply above the average costs of the existing system. Such pricing and its effects are often grossly inefficient. They accentuate urban sprawl and burden the finances of central city areas.

Ecological problems often require regional solutions, which in turn

---

[6] They are being explored and applied to a degree in Britain.

[7] See Mushkin, *op. cit.,* Chapters 6 and 12 for analysis and actual patterns.

[8] During the 1968 water shortage, a dirigible lit with giant letters "SAVE WATER" floated over New York City, while down below the lack of efficient prices encouraged a flood of wastage. Many cities endure such summer crises regularly, never even considering a higher price for water during the scarce season.

involve struggles among public units at various levels up to federal agencies. Public ownership is virtually a necessary (not sufficient) condition for internalizing these effects. Bureaucratic stress and political struggles over these solutions often involve groups and criteria which direct economic criteria cannot reflect. This seems to be the inevitable process, imperfect though it is. No large role for private ownership seems to be at all feasible.

On the whole, these systems operate with tolerable internal efficiency, avoid conscious price discrimination, and are part of a system for solving the larger problems of supply. But they often need sharp revisions in price levels and structures, to align them with true scarcity levels.

Garbage Disposal

This humble operation also has suddenly encountered new problems. Recently relabelled as "solid waste disposal," it now faced a growing avalanche of solid wastes, for which the dumping places are getting few and costly. Moreover, newer packaging materials (plastics, metals, non-returnable bottles, etc.) are less biodegradable, which worsens the difficulty. The basic problem is also growing in other advanced economies.

Once again, the old ways—primarily, a unit price of zero—worsen the problem. Though operating costs and scarcities of dumping space make long-run marginal costs high and probably rising, the service is usually given away, even to many very heavy users. The obvious answer is to set prices at costs, based on volume, frequency, and other conditions of service. Where private service remains, it at least charges a price in line with private cost (though the use of public dumping space is often not properly charged for).

Public management is necessary in most cases to provide a pick-up network plus adequate dumping capacity. But the whole design of capacity, service provision, and prices needs overhauling in many cities.[9] Few cases show so clearly how the efficiency of public enterprise depends on how it is designed and priced. Since other specialized private haulers operate alongside the regular service, the basic problem—and opportunity—is to optimize the basic system while also applying some degree of competition from alternative haulers for the high-cost, commercial loads. The inefficient treatment—presently only too common—is to make disposal free, with a service design which overloads large high-cost users into the basic system.

Lending Libraries and Museums

These exemplify the public enterprise with cultural effects. They also have permanent natural-monopoly conditions, and demand is probably elastic at any significant price level.

Libraries are funded directly, rather than by user charges. There are

---

[9] Also, equity is often at issue. Thus, high-income households may have four or more times as much garbage as poor households, thereby imposing more costs than they pay in taxes or fees. See S. J. Mushkin, *op. cit.,* p. 227, and Chapters 8 and 9.

occasional entrance fees to museums. Where they are only nominal, such entrance fees and library fines still leave the basic social function nearly intact: to make knowledge and culture available widely.[10] If charges are also adjusted to ability to pay, then virtually everyone is able to share at low or zero prices.

But even here there are intriguing issues of design and equity. First, design. Libraries are necessarily in few locations, not equally near to all. Moreover, their hours often penalize those not able to come in during standard working hours.[11] And recent cut-backs under budget pressure have borne most heavily on weekend and evening hours. In some areas, "bookmobiles" bring service out to neighborhoods during certain hours, but these are of slight total importance.

And so, second, the equity benefits of libraries and museums are relatively narrow. Use is mostly by middle and upper groups, according to income and education.[12] This is less broadly based than the city tax revenues which pay for them. Therefore, even in these exemplary units —and even assuming they are internally quite efficient and yield large total social benefits—there may be a negative net effect on equity.

Summary

We have accentuated the negative about urban enterprises, to show where the main problems of structure and pricing lie. If they were designed and priced as public enterprises, in line with basic policy analysis, they would be more efficient and equitable.

But these criticisms do not challenge their being *public* enterprises. In these cases, public enterprise is appropriate and, probably, necessary. It is mainly their pricing and coordination that need review and revision. Most of them would offer gains from better marginal-cost pricing. Many city governments are aggravating their own problems by running these units according to old rules of municipal finance rather than modern industrial organization and pricing.

SOCIAL ENTERPRISES

Social enterprises are familiar as government or public-agency functions, and some are very large (see Table 22–1). Their central operations and problems are often closely related to industrial organization. When they deviate from efficient and fair patterns, it is often from a neglect of these attributes and an isolation from market processes. These enter-

---

[10] In a major departure, U.K. museums were forced in 1973 to set significant entrance fees (on the order of 50 cents), in order to be more "business-like." Attendence dropped to less than half (in some cases below 30 percent) of previous levels, so the charges undercut the social purpose while harvesting little revenue. They were abolished in 1974.

[11] The Metropolitan Museum of Art in New York did not open in the evenings before 1968; and these hours are being removed again as an austerity measure.

[12] This is true also in Britain and presumably in the U.S. In 1973, some 70 percent of museum goers in London had university degrees, though only about 5 percent of the adult populace does. Only about 20 percent of visitors were working class (blue collar jobs, secretaries, and lesser skilled workers), though they are the great majority of the population. Study by Communication Research, Ltd., reported in *London Illustrated News,* April 1974, pp. 27–29.

TABLE 22-1
Several Sets of Social Enterprises in the U.S.

	1950	1960	1970
Public Education	(*million students enrolled*)		
Elementary schools	19.4	27.6	32.6
Secondary schools	5.7	8.5	13.0
Higher education	1.4	1.8	5.1
Correction	(*1,000 prisoners present*)		
Federal prisons	17.1	23.2	20.0
State prisons	149.0	189.7	176.4
Local jails	(n.a.)	(n.a.)	160.9
Federal Courts	(*1,000 cases disposed of*)		
Supreme Court	1.2	1.9	3.6
Appeals Court	2.4	2.7	6.1
District Courts	80.1	79.4	115.8
Public Housing	(*$ million*)		
Expenditure	15	177	697

Source: *U.S. Statistical Abstract.*

prises usually have a degree of competition and complex pricing and allocation choices. These are suited to a variety of market tests.

Here we briefly consider four of them: the education-correction system, the courts, public housing, and national parks. First, their common features are noted.

How do these activities differ from, say, selling cabbage or pencils?

1. They are subsidized to users, entirely or in part.
2. They are designed to provide comprehensive coverage, so that no group is excluded by inability to pay.
3. The user often is compelled to participate, as part of the social purpose of the operation.
4. Equity is a central objective, as well as social externalities.
5. Yet many of their functions can be, and are, provided by private units selling under market process.

Therefore, one needs to ask of all of them: Is an alternative structure more efficient? Should their capacity be at different levels and forms? Are their prices optimal? Is more competition appropriate? In this light, these agencies have different character and results than the old government-agency image implies. They are public enterprises with certain special purposes and conditions.

Education and Correction

The activities which we call "education" and "correction" are parts of the same basic process. Both involve trainees under supervisors of

584   Public Policies toward Business

varying kinds (the variety is suggested in Table 22–2). Together they do much to sort out and shape the futures of each new generation.[13] In doing this, they strongly affect (and reflect) the fairness of the society and its economic efficiency. They are both carried on mainly in public enterprises, with a high degree of public subsidy. Both can be run with varying degrees of commercial motivation and competition. In both of them, the content and design of service are important. And both can malfunction.

Their services are traditionally regarded as primarily public goods, to be analyzed and treated in terms of public finance. Yet market behavior can be decisive for their performance.

TABLE 22–2
Educational and Correction Operations, 1970

	Number of Units	Expenditure ($million)	Number of Students (million) or inmates (1,000)
Primary and Secondary Schools			
Public	95,274	46,800	45.6
Private	18,600	4.900	5.7
Higher Education			
Public	1,089	16,100	5.1
Private	1,467	4,300	2.0
Correction			
Federal		83	20
State		1,051	176
Local		572	161

Source: U.S. Statistical Abstract.

Special Features. For each member of a cohort, opportunity is determined by several factors.[14] One is family background, which includes wealth and status, parental attention and support, location, etc. Another is innate personal qualities and capacities. A third is the training acquired at successive levels of education, from whatever source.

The first two are outside one's control: the first is usually settled at birth and the second by age six.[15] The third is primarily a matter of effort (and some degree of luck), in a succession of personal choices about the levels and directions at which one will work. These choices are concentrated primarily in the learning years between 5 and 25, and particularly during 5 to 18. The effort factor can offset some degree of disadvantage

[13] Among the 1960s outpouring of research on the economics of education, see G. S. Becker, Human Capital (New York: Columbia University Press, 1964); and the reprint volumes by M. Blaug, The Economics of Education, Vols. 1 and 2 (London: Penguin Books, 1968–69).

[14] Among recent studies, see C. Jencks, et. al., Inequality: A Reassessment of the Effect of Family and Schooling in America (New York: Basic Books, 1972); and K. J. Arrow, "Higher Education as a Filter," Journal of Public Choice, July 1973, pp. 193–216.

[15] B. S. Bloom, Stability and Change in Human Characteristics (New York: Wiley, 1964).

In this context, the choice situation has three marked peculiarities:

1. Important choices are made at early, immature stages of life, under conditions of ignorance and short-sightedness.
2. These decisions are largely irreversible.
3. The higher ranges of career opportunity require, for those not advantaged by factor 1, a virtually complete avoidance of incorrect decisions.

Opportunity ranges from the highest career achievements down to routine jobs, to undesirable jobs, and on down to criminal activities, etc. Family and genes set the initial ranges. Then the person's successive decisions and actions determine at each point the remaining set of future possibilities. Youthful choices can keep upper opportunities open, or close them off.[16]

Therefore, the basic consumer of education and correction services—the student or inmate—is least competent to make decisions precisely during those early years when the choices are critical and largely irreversible. Schooling can tend to offset the advantages of birth—to "equalize" opportunity—or instead to reinforce them. In abstract ideal, equalizing is a function of universal free public education and of subsidized higher education. But it requires more than just training skills; indeed, technical skills are often the least part. In addition, an equalizing process must provide supportive counsel and also financial payments which are fully compensatory (equal to all schooling costs plus the foregone income from job alternatives).

Also, it needs to provide full choice among alternative interests and skills (intellectual, vocational, arts, industrial, financial, etc.) and among personality types (aggressive, selfless, artistic, miserly, etc.). And further, it needs to provide fresh chances for those who temporarily waver.

Large public resources are provided both for education and correction, and there is direct public control through extensive public school, university, correctional and prison systems. In addition, a large share of the political process is devoted to supervising these agencies (e.g., in many cities, schooling is the largest single item of public business).

Education. The basic structure of the system is familiar to most readers, so that only certain special features need to be reviewed.[17]

---

[16] Illegal activity especially reflects the way in which early choices set the field for later ones. Each deviant act in early years conditions the child's teachers and other authorities to expect—and therefore partly induce—similar future behavior in school and elsewhere. To acquire even a small record of offenses is virtually to rule out an entire range of upper opportunities. A series of wrong choices successively closes off upper levels of income, status, and job types. As the set of remaining alternatives evolves downward, a person's maximizing choices may shift to include illegal activities, whose discounted returns seem comparable or superior to the remaining available legal ones. (See G. S. Becker, "Crime and Punishment: An Economic Approach," *Journal of Political Economy*, 1968, pp. 169–217.) The choice of criminal activity is primarily rational, involving no more myopia than is true of advantaged children. The choice sequence is simply more irreversible. The real penalties are not usually the fine or detention, but rather the conviction itself (or even merely the arrest).

[17] It is also common to much of Canada, Britain, and other western European societies.

Monopoly is the prevailing condition of supply. Public schooling in grades 1 through 12 is provided by one system in each locale. Further, the "neighborhood school" basis is prevalent, leaving users no choice even among schools within the system. Access to private schools is directly related to family wealth and income, so that the poor face the highest degree of monopoly in educational supply. To some extent, moving one's residence can give one a choice among schools, but this element of choice is also directly related to economic (and racial) status.[18] Users of correctional agencies have, of course, virtually no choice among units.

Quality of supply is also related to income. Commonly, better neighborhoods have better schools; better in plant, teachers, equipment, location, amenity, etc. Despite frequent proposals for inverting the pattern, so that ghetto schools in deprived areas will be models, the pattern remains strong and deeply rooted.

Tracking within each school system begins early and takes hold with enough force to determine the future field of opportunity for most children. It commonly reflects the inequalities in family support which the child brings to school. There are exceptional teachers and children who offset this pressure or who get re-tracked at later stages. And the degree of tracking in U.S. schools probably is less than it is in many other western countries (but possibly more than in Scandinavian countries). Still, a degree of tracking is the normal effect of public school operations.

Correctional institutions, on their part, tend to breed further criminal activity rather than avert it. The picture is mixed, of course, for some state and local systems are well designed and funded. But their task is large: not only to instill law-abiding attitudes but also to equip their inmates with skills so that their income from future legal activities clearly exceeds their discounted gains from illegal occupations. In short, they must overcome inequalities which the schools themselves have reinforced. Instead, most correctional agencies attempt only to change attitudes, for they lack the schooling objectives, resources, and design needed for equalizing opportunity. This pattern is even more deeply set in prisons for older persons. The emphasis is on secure imprisonment rather than on learning and a productive use of time, so as to raise the prisoner's set of future opportunities clearly above illegal alternatives.

A high degree of public subsidy is the common basis for financing both education and correction. In grades 1–12 and in correctional facilities, the subsidy is virtually total. For higher education, the subsidies to public universities cover only part of the cost, but this share is large in many cases. The net incidence of such college tuition subsidies is regressive, because college students are drawn primarily from upper economic groups.[19]

Effects. The natural outcome is a loss of equity and efficiency. Opportunity is not equalized; rather, the schools and prisons tend on the whole

---

[18] Even where one may choose among schools in one's city (as is true in Britain), the practical degree of choice is limited by such other factors as income, transportation, and overcrowding in some schools.

[19] See W. L. Hanson and B. A. Weisbrod, *Benefits, Costs and Finance of Public Higher Education* (New York: Markham Publishing, 1969). Also, E. Dennison, "An Aspect of Inequality of Opportunity," *Journal of Political Economy,* 1970, pp. 1195–1202.

to reflect and, in part, to reinforce the original disparities. Monopoly and rigidity are particularly present in the early years (grades 1–12), where children's choices are the least informed and reversible.

Efficiency is lost in the failure of budding talents to develop. If innate talent is randomly distributed, this loss would be very large. Efficiency is also lost via the social and economic impact of crime which the system fails to avert.[20] And efficiency is also lost in the internal management of the agencies themselves, for there is a high degree of monopoly.

The absorption of public resources by the sector is also large. Therefore, the system may be regarded as departing seriously from optimum design and allocation, but not necessarily from the optimal level of total resource usage.

Possible Revisions. The most sensible revisions would tend to merge the educational and correctional systems, to reintroduce competition in certain directions, and to adjust public enterprise features in line with the more general lessons we have drawn. These methods are most visibly suitable for certain aspects of grade-school and prison operation.

Primary and Secondary Education. The recent voucher proposal would give each student a ticket which could be used at any public or private school. This would provide a degree of choice for users and of competition among schools.[21] But it does not obviate (though it mitigates) the need for reversing the relationship between neighborhood income and school quality. Also, travel to school would need to be provided at zero price, lest that continue to limit educational choice (and even so it imposes unequal burdens in loss of time and content). Nor does it remedy the problem of tracking. All this is clear from Britain, where a large degree of choice among schools *is* provided along lines sought by the voucher proposal, and yet the basic problems remain.

The voucher proposal does include private schools. This would induce valuable competition—on an equal footing—from outside the public system. And the location and variety of private schools could possibly tend toward optimal patterns, after a period of adjustment and growth. But the technology is sufficiently lumpy and slow-adjusting to guarantee that large deviations will remain. For example, few private schools comparable to those of the highest quality would soon locate in the many innercity areas or low-income suburbs.

Correction. The basic objective of correction is an increase in the "legitimate" productivity of inmates (including the probability that they will avoid illegal activity after they are released) per unit of prison resources. The direct resources include buildings, food, staff, space, and the time of the inmates. This function is just a corner of society's whole effort to raise productivity, in industry and schools. The efficient correctional unit therefore operates as a training school, with incentives for inmates to learn and accumulate *and* for supervisors to generate an economic surplus (or minimize the deficit) via the rise in inmate productivity.

---

[20] For one set of estimates, see the President's Commission on Law Enforcement and Administration of Justice, *Crime and Its Impact: An Assessment* (Washington, D.C.: U.S. Government Printing Office, 1967).

[21] Its best-known proponent is Milton Friedman. A version of the idea has been tested in several communities, with various positive, but not radically favorable, results.

Prisons are public enterprises, which could be operated far more efficiently than most of them presently are.

By contrast, many prisons presently are highly subsidized systems lacking sensitive public controls to avert damaging effects on inmates: a classic case of high cost, low controls (recall Chapter 19). Their content is often pathological, and by fostering criminality they create large external costs. Presence in them, however brief, usually excludes the inmate from a wide range of the better jobs in the future.

Inmate productivity could be developed and, concurrently, used to generate revenues to reduce the subsidies. This does occur in many of the better prisons. Under such a quasi-educational system, working conditions need not be exploitative. They would come under standard occupational protections, and inmates could have a degree of choice about their jobs and workloads. The products could compete in normal markets as well as supply internal needs. If the inputs are properly compensated and outputs correctly priced, the result would be fair and beneficial all around, including the markets where their products add new competition. Indeed, much work could be subcontracted from private firms. A primary need is to replace guards with efficiency-motivated managers, who regard inmates primarily as trainees. Prisons should mingle with the market place, as do many healthy public and private enterprises.

Revised correctional units are not sufficient, by themselves. Prisons are only part of the whole correctional sector, which includes police, judicial, and after-prison programs. They also need to be integrated with educational choices and provisions.

The Courts

The courts are a set of devices, or arenas, for social decision and compromise. They are merely the visible tip of the whole process. Parallel to them is the mass of private negotiations, which settle conflicts and reach specific decisions about individual rights and property.[22] Cases that reach the courts are often the toughest ones, which have resisted any other means of resolution (or in which one party is able to pursue its interests without limit). This is the "justice" system, which decides right and wrong, or at least resolves issues short of violence. (Important cliches: The courts are to temper justice with mercy. The punishment is to fit the crime, or is it the criminal? Justice to the winner often still seems injustice to the loser. And justice delayed is justice denied.)

The system has many separate parts and layers (see Figure 22–3). It is complex, and to the ordinary person it is unknown and hostile terrain, to be avoided if possible. It is run by lawyers: both those appearing in cases and those presiding (judges are all former lawyers). In the adversary process, the conflict of presentations can clarify the issues for decision either by a jury of common folk or by trained jurists. But underlying the daily clash of individual interests is the larger incidence of the sys-

---

[22] For example, less than 5 percent of automobile injury cases reach a court hearing. See Posner, *Economic Analysis of Law, op. cit.,* p. 337.

tem's effects. It may provide justice. It may also be regarded as a system, or perhaps *the* system, by which those with advantages perpetuate them.[23] Therefore the functioning of the courts—as simply another, but important, public enterprise system—needs a skeptical appraisal.

Courts are a series of related public enterprises in which inputs are used to generate outputs.[24] The output is the decision reached, at least in some cases. Thus a murder acquittal or conviction (and sentence) is the end point of the exercise (unless there is appeal). But in many cases the trial activity simply speeds or crystallizes—or is used by one side to drag out—the settlement among disputing private interests. Where the solution was largely preordained, the court's service as an arena is of

FIGURE 22–3

Parts of the Court System

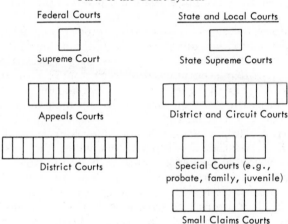

Federal Courts

Supreme Court

Appeals Courts

District Courts

State and Local Courts

State Supreme Courts

District and Circuit Courts

Special Courts (e.g., probate, family, juvenile)

Small Claims Courts

little value. It can even be of negative value, when resort to the courts in a litigious strategy is used to prevent a "fair" outcome. The court system in fact is often used or abused as a free good, in order to gain advantage in private strife.

The inputs of the enterprise are several: the court resources themselves (judges, recorder, clerks and personnel, space, utilities, archives, etc.), lawyers, witnesses, other sources of information to be used in the case, and of course the laws themselves which are written by legislatures and modified by court decisions. These inputs are combined within a formal procedure and structure, which affect the speed and often the content of the outcome. This structure includes burdens of proof in civil

---

[23] The working of individual claims in the system starts from the inequality of the status quo. Any justice system which protects private property rights as they are distributed will therefore largely preserve the status quo. Also, wealth itself can purchase superior and larger legal resources, which often affect the outcome. The silent stress underlying the whole judicial system is between the preexisting inequality of distribution and the principle of *equal legal rights;* the outcome is not determinate. For a more roseate view, see Posner, *op. cit.;* see also the various sources he cites.

[24] Posner, *ibid.,* discusses these concepts perceptively.

and criminal cases, advantages of time for one side against the other, rules of evidence, standards of precedent, rules of pretrial discovery and conduct at trial, and other features which were noted in Chapters 3 to 5.

The social aim is to minimize the costs of both (1) operating the system, and (2) erroneous decisions. Cases actually reach trial—rather than get settled privately—for four sets of reasons.[25] (1) The two sides may differ in expectations, risk preferences, or access to legal resources. (2) One side may be so desperate that trial offers at least a hope (or valuable delay). (3) Court services are provided at zero price, which increases the level of usage.[26] (4) The larger the stakes, the more likely trial is to be used.

A basic fact is that access to legal counsel and information about the use of court resources are not equal but, rather, highly correlated with wealth (see below).

As enterprises, the courts raise the two standard economic questions, about their efficiency and equity. The first is about the funding and supply of resources to the court system, and how its services are priced. This also includes optimizing the total size of court resources and the selection of matters which take up court time. The second concerns how closely its results fit either the status quo or even greater inequality, on one hand, or the strict equality of legal rights.

Efficiency. A primary fact is the increasing congestion of court dockets. This is most acute at the upper levels, where the most important decisions are reached. Delays of years in beginning trial—much less reaching a final resolution—are common. These intervals cause uncertainty and, in most cases, losses for one side or both. Some degree of delay is optimal, to allow pretrial preparations and possible settlement. But present delays clearly exceed the optimum for large categories of suits.

Some, perhaps much, of the congestion occurs because the courts are provided free. Pricing at most includes an *ex post* levying of court costs on the loser in some cases, along with possible fines. But in most cases, both sides can treat the courts as a strictly free good, even though the direct social costs of them are high and the indirect costs from delaying other cases may be a multiple of that.[27] The wonder is that these delays

---

[25] Posner, *op. cit.,* discusses part of this, in Chap. 24.

[26] The exception to this is when the loser is assessed court costs. But this is not known in advance; and the formal costs levied usually greatly understate the true direct costs—and more so the full opportunity costs (see footnote 27, below).

[27] Direct social costs of a typical federal district court can be estimated as follows. Personnel include judge, clerk, transcriber, bailiff, secretary, jury selection officers, etc. These total at least $100,000 per year. Each trial day involves at least another day of meetings in chamber, preparation of opinion, etc. At 130 trial days per year, this is $760 per trial day. The premises costs include space rental for the courtroom, offices, jury rooms, jury selection offices, library, etc.; fittings, equipment, references; upkeep; air conditioning, other building services, etc. These would easily be $3000/month, or $300 per trial day. A jury adds perhaps $1,350/day (18 juror equivalents, allowing also for nonselected jurors, at an average value of $75 per day). Estimated trial cost is at least $1000 per day; with jury, about $2500 per day. See also W. M. Landes, "An Economic Analysis of the Courts," *Journal of Law and Economics,* Vol. 13 (1971); and D. L. Martin, "The Economics of Jury Conscription," *Journal of Political Economy,* Vol., No. (1972). This does not include private costs, with lawyers and expert witnesses commonly at $300–500 each per day, and often much higher.

have come to be accepted. The delays often generate large losses and inequities. Some citizens, for example, are routinely imprisoned while awaiting trial for periods which are regarded as intolerable for people of means and "good" social standing. One solution is to enlarge the resources; but as with highway expansion at zero user charges, this tends only to stimulate more demand so that congestion continues. (The lags and congestion in the courts suggest that the system tends towards protecting the status quo. They give the advantage of time to those who can best afford to tolerate delay or use it tactically.)

An efficient solution includes several parts. *One* is to price court services at costs, including external costs of delay and congestion.[28] This would raise the cost of bringing suit and serve as a normal indicator of true scarcity. (But it might violate the objective of equal access, favoring richer litigants.) *Another* is to improve the internal management of courts. Especially in handling jury sources, there is much room for using resources more efficiently. But the major scope for change is, *third,* in removing or excluding from courtroom handling whole ranges of cases which presently congest the courts: these include the wide variety of private compromises which could as well be handled by professional private mediators and arbitrators.[29] By contrast, we now have many courts, with high opportunity costs, mired in trival private-party tactics.[30] The social benefits are so low, compared to the true costs, as to reflect gross waste and inequity.

Equity. By common agreement, the system favors those who can afford the best counsel and who are most aware of their legal rights and strategies (recall Chapters 3 and 4). There are several levels to this problem. First, most citizens are unaware of their full legal rights and/or too awed by the court system to seek them out. Second, among those who are aware, most are unable to afford counsel to represent their interest fully. Third, there are vast differences among lawyers in their quality and standing, with the best talent being priced so high that the mass of citizens are left only with the lower levels of legal talent. (Some of this emerged in the discussion of antitrust, in Part II.) Consequently, the legal scales are often tipped by the quality—or even the presence—of superior advocates.

A partial solution is to make legal aid universally available at zero costs.[31] Yet even if such free legal aid were supplied (as small programs

---

[28] This is complex, for pricing must avoid excluding poorer claimants. Some degree of price discrimination, with a sliding scale based on income, might be optimal.

[29] This sector of activity is already well developed, in handling labor disputes and settling claims. In fact, a wide range of disputes are resolved among lawyers, acting in quasi-judicial fashion. But there is much room for expanding it. Probably half or two-thirds of courtroom activity could thus be excised, leaving the remaining cases for brisker treatment.

[30] This is accentuated by the judicial custom of exhaustive procedures. See M. Fleming, *The Price of Perfect Justice* (New York: Basic Books, 1973).

[31] This would run the risk of wasting legal resources, since they would be used up to their level of zero marginal productivity rather than up to the level at which their true cost was in line with their marginal productivity. Yet the gain in equality by underpricing in this way might justify the marginal misallocation, at least for some categories. For many wealthy or powerful corporate interests, legal talent is virtually used as a free good, up to the point where the marginal benefit from litigation is reached.

have recently been made for certain categories), it will presumably be of inferior quality. Moreover, it will not overcome the inhibitions which most citizens feel about asserting their legal rights. At present, federal legal aid programs are adopting the form of a public enterprise. But their size, management, and incidence will need marked changes in order to approach, even remotely, the social optimum.

The efficiency and equity of the judicial system as a whole are shaped by forces outside it, which limit its resources, procedures and pricing. The courts are also a complex of public enterprises which are managed by officials untrained to optimize their operations. The larger effects are predictable and well known. Efficient revisions in pricing and procedures are not easy to specify precisely. Yet changes are in order, and the directions for improvement are fairly clear. They should fit the nature of courts as specialized public enterprises.

Public Housing

The U.S., like virtually all societies, provides some publicly owned housing at subsidized rents. The stock of public housing is extensive, though it is less than 2 percent of all urban dwellings. These programs generate problems and performance characteristics which are matters of dispute. *Private* home ownership is also subsidized publicly, via the insuring agencies which we noted in Chapter 20. The direct public housing programs are an important part of the whole public subsidy of housing.

The federal government began, in 1933, to finance the construction of houses as a means of increasing employment. At first, it confined itself to making loans to private, limited-dividend housing corporations. But progress, through these agencies, was slow. Then the government itself bought large tracts of land in cities, often involving the clearance of slums, and built large-scale housing developments, renting apartments to families in the lower-income groups. The 50 projects constructed in some 30 cities during this period were later transferred to municipal governments. Construction of public housing as a permanent policy dates from the Housing Act of 1937. Here, the purpose was to provide low-rent housing for the poor.

The law calls for the creation of municipal housing authorities whose function it is to assemble the land required for new housing developments, design the structures, let contracts for their construction, and own and operate the finished dwellings. Such authorities have been created in more than 1,500 communities. The federal government approves the sites selected, sets and enforces standards governing the quality and cost of construction, and makes loans and grants to the local authorities.

Local governments are required by the law to contribute 10 percent of the captial invested in each project. They raise this money by selling bonds whose interest is exempt from the federal income tax. Their contribution thus includes a federal subsidy. In effect, the federal government contributes virtually all of the capital required for a project. The local government is supposed to break even on the operating costs.

In absolute numbers, public housing is impressive. There were 801,-000 dwellings under public management in 1970. The annual number of public housing starts, depending on congressional appropriations, has run between 30,000 and 90,000, standing at 35,000 in recent years. Relatively, public housing is of small significance, accounting for only 1.5 percent of the stock of urban dwellings and sheltering little more than 1 percent of the families in the country as a whole.

The supply of public housing falls far short of the demand. It could be rationed by raising the rents, but this would defeat the purpose of providing low-rent housing for the poor. The rationing is therefore done administratively. Entry is limited to families whose incomes are less than five times the rents, preference being given to applicants of good character in accordance with the urgency of their needs. Continued occupancy is limited to families whose incomes, following entry, do not increase by more than 25 percent. The median income of public housing tenants is less than $2,500 a year. Many are broken families. A quarter are over 65 years of age. A quarter are on relief. The average cost of operating a unit of public housing in the mid-sixties was $70 per month. The average rent was $44. The housing obviously was provided, not on a commercial basis, but as a form of public charity.

Housing actually is on the margin of "social" activities. The great mass of housing choices are strictly private matters, properly decided in private markets. Public housing is a residuary passive public enterprise, to which is relegated the least lucrative parts of the market. By definition, public housing absorbs those who cannot meet market tests either for housing prices or for maintaining housing quality. There are long waiting lists for public housing at the subsidized rent levels. This may indicate large social benefits from public housing. Or it may be that rents are set too low and that social benefits are small.

In any event, public housing tends to be funded, designed, and operated differently and separately from private housing markets.[32] Many economists suggest that public housing should be merged with the private housing sector by simply subsidizing rents of deserving citizens, rather than directly providing housing units. This might dissolve the conventional isolation of public housing in self-created ghettos.

The actual performance of public housing units can be evaluated in terms of public enterprise. There are familiar conditions of old-style public firms: public ownership is complete, it is directly subsidized by public funds and guarantees, it is assigned customers which private markets do not supply, and it is insulated from various market tests of efficiency. In addition, it must operate through the local political process, which often tends to minimize the political power of the poor. Therefore, it is likely to exhibit the classic symptoms of costly public enterprises. In addition, U.S. programs have developed corruption and abuses which have actually destroyed significant amounts of the housing stock.

---

[32] On U.S patterns, see Henry J. Aaron, *Shelter and Subsidies: Who Benefits from Federal Housing Policies?* (Washington, D.C.: Brookings Institution, 1972) and references cited there. On British and other national patterns, see David V. Donnison, *The Government of Housing* (London: Penguin Books, 1967).

As operating entities, public housing groups are required to meet performance targets which go beyond their resources and political standing. They are required to locate and consolidate their housing stock differently from what they know to be the social optimum. The result usually is a series of large and poorly designed public housing projects, which are shunted into the least appropriate areas of the cities, and therefore often become expensive instant ghettos. The inevitable emphasis on minimum cost per unit results in defective design, despite decades of experience. Thus in the U.S., large public housing projects permeated with disfunctional design features and a lack of minimum amenities continue to be built.

The preferences of users for specific housing attributes are virtually ignored. What is needed, broadly, is a conversion to some degree of direct competition with private housing markets, so that user preferences are considered in designing structures and locating them, and so that operations are set economic targets which correspond to those of competing entities. Some shifts in this direction are already occurring, but their extent is small. Rent subsidies and scattered-site housing using existing buildings have been tried, but on a limited basis in many cities.

In short, much—possibly most—public housing shows an excess of public cost over probable benefits. This arises both in the total level of activities and in the way the programs are designed and priced. These programs appear to be part of a stable equilibrium, which persists because it nicely suboptimizes among a special set of private interests. But certain wastes and inequities do derive predictably from some of its departures from good public enterprise design.

National Parks

The National Park Service manages 298 areas with more than 30 million acres in total, including 31 National Parks and 170 monuments and other sites of national or historical interest. This domain is large and varied (though it is a small share of all public land: see Chapter 26). Some parks are congested with visitors, while others are virtually untouched. The Park Service's activities include primarily (1) deciding the degree and form of tourist capacity, and (2) maintaining the basic land, monuments, access roads, and facilities. The Service also makes commercial decisions in commissioning private enterprises to operate tourist facili-

TABLE 22–3
National Park Service Activities, 1972

	Number of Areas	Acres (million)	Personnel	Total Visits (million)	Revenues ($ million)
Total	298	30.4	7,839	215.5	162.6
Natural sites	72			64.2	
Historical sites	151			81.3	
Recreational sites	30			58.7	
National capital	1			11.0	

ties at some parks. Although the main content of many such decisions is commercial, it also touches on deep social and cultural questions of preservation and use. Tables 22–3 and 22–4 contain more details about Park Service activities.

A main element of performance—the location and accessibility of parks to the full range of the populace—is mostly beyond Park Service control. Thus most parks are remote from the main population; only 7 of the largest 50 cities have a major Park Service site within 100 miles. The parks are used more heavily by upper income and educational groups, as Table 22–5 indicates.[33]

TABLE 22–4

Recreational Visits to the Main NPS Sites, 1972

	Million Visits
3lue Ridge	11.1
National Capital Parks (D.C.)	10.1
Great Smoky Mtns.	8.0
Williamsburg, Va.	6.2
Cape Cod	5.1
Lake Mead	4.8
Gettysburg Battlefield	2.7
Rocky Mountain NP	2.6
Olympia Park, Wash.	2.5
Grand Canyon	2.3
Yellowstone	2.3
Everglades	2.2
Shenandoah	2.2
Mt. Rushmore	2.0
Lincoln Memorial, D.C.	2.0

FIGURE 22–4

Economic Choices for Parks

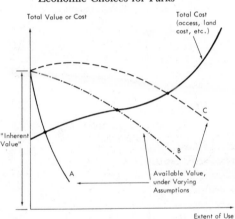

The basic economic choice is illustrated in Figure 22–4. The inherent value of the parks depends on preservation, while the use of that value rises with the number of visitors permitted and the extent to which they can stay, travel, explore, and play in the parks. The main factual issue is the slope of the available value curve. To a wilderness buff, the steep slope of curve A applies: as soon as any significant use occurs, the park is at least partly spoiled. By contrast, a trailer-toting vacationing family looking to make friends at the campground may be reflected by line C; to them the presence of other people subtracts little from nature and does add social interest. In this situation, the optimum solution may not be clearly determinate. It depends on many things: on the preferences and incomes of the users, the degree to which crowding will technically degrade the site's beauty, the various multiple uses of the site, the costs of "developing" the site, etc. Moreover, the pricing of park access and

---

[33] See *National Parks for the Future* (Washington, D.C.: Conservation Foundation, 1972), pp. 180–90.

facilities will also influence the outcome. Its levels and structure can be complex.

Actual Park Service pricing policy is inefficient in certain standard ways. The obvious efficient condition is for rates to reflect peak and off-peak costs. Instead, park service fees primarily are flat or—in the case of season tickets—set the unit price of park access at zero, even though season tickets are likely to be used at high season when marginal costs are very high. With exceptions, this is the general pattern. Therefore, predictably, many parks are congested with large backlogs of would-be camp users during the summer season, but virtually empty the rest of the time. Moreover, the rationing of demand generally is not solved efficiently by the Park Service, but instead by various queing and physical rationing tactics. Optimal policy would require fitting the long-run investment in access routes and facilities to the long-run pricing strategy.

TABLE 22–5
Park Service Users

	Total Population (18 and over)	National Parks Users (18 and over)
White-collar occupations	30.5%	44.2%
Over $7,000 income	46.8	58.1
Nonwhite..............................	13.2	4.4
Less than high school education...........	44.0	26.6

For the many crowded parks, this has not been done precisely or even by guesswork.[34]

In handling private concessions, policies are more efficient. From private concessionaires the Park Service does draw substantial fees, often bid on a competitive basis. Also they do limit profits and discrimination. But once the concession is set, the Park Service's leverage is low. The operator then maximizes among several directions: service quality, prices, and capacity. The results may roughly fit efficient criteria, though no studies exist to evaluate |this.

The Park Service, like other social enterprises, has a range of possible optimal outcomes, depending on the nature of its services and the design of their pricing. Within this range, the Park Service does set actual patterns, but with little close evaluation of the alternatives. Some of its economic policies probably need revision, with a clear understanding of their equity effects (among rich and poor, as well as present and future generations). Still, the broad variety of Park Service operations are acknowledged widely to be handled with reasonable efficiency. Therefore, the Park Service is a public enterprise with relatively good performance.

---

[34] During 1973–4, certain pricing and reservations schemes were tried for some campsites, and then dropped. But they were not well handled, and so they prove little.

SUMMARY

We have surveyed a number of urban and social enterprises, in order to show their common performance characteristics. They operate as public enterprises, which are improvable in various respects. Certain forms of competition are excluded or poorly understood. Some efficiency criteria are scarcely considered. And there are several structural and pricing possibilities which derive from industrial organization but are often ignored. Some of these possibilities are being applied increasingly, and this may develop further. Marginal-cost pricing, in particular, may spread, even to social enterprises. The possible economic and social gains might be very large. These urban and social enterprises may be the richest frontier for study and revisions in industrial organization, offering even more than antitrust and regulation in conventional sectors.

CHAPTER TWENTY THREE

Public Enterprise Appraised

Public enterprise needs a sophisticated evaluation, which recognizes its variety and complexity. It is evolving and assuming new forms, well beyond its old-fashioned roles. Its experience is growing rapidly, but it has been little researched.

Still, certain basic attributes do recur. We will summarize them and then consider the further evolution of public enterprise.[1]

BASIC PROPERTIES

1. Public enterprise can be suitable for a wide range of markets and social sectors, not just for utilities.

2. It is not a substitute for regulation or antitrust. Rather it needs to be combined with them (and with other policy devices) in balanced policy packages.

3. Public enterprise can assume a variety of forms, market positions, financial constraints, and economic criteria. These include varying degrees of public ownership and public operation: they range from government departments to public corporations and to partial public holdings and investment banks. A public enterprise can be largely private in secondary features, but be quite public in essentials. Moreover, this variety is at least matched in the range of pricing and investment policies which public enterprises can follow.

4. A broad shift is occurring from older totally public forms toward the more mixed and flexible varieties of public enterprise.

5. The publicness by itself does not transform the enterprise. But it does alter some basic relationships and make large changes in behavior and performance possible.

---

[1] The public and private industrialists at page 519 in Chapter 19 are: (1) Clifton C. Garvin, Jr., Exxon Corporation (private). (2) A. E. Hawkins, U.K. Central Electricity Generating Board (public). (3) F. H. Jones, General Electric Corporation (private). (4) Derek J. Ezra, U.K. National Coal Board (public). (5) Monty Finniston, U.K. British Steel Corporation (public). (6) John H. Gerstenmaier, Goodyear Tire & Rubber Company (private). (Photos are courtesy of the various companies.)

6. The forms, market position, and criteria of public enterprises will govern their performance more closely than the mere fact that they are publicly owned.

7. Public enterprise is not generally inferior to private enterprise by any of the main criteria of economic and social performance. It can be, and is, inferior in some cases, but in others it is superior.

A Digression on Comparisons

Comparisons are difficult, for the two kinds of enterprise often differ sharply in their *opportunities:* that is, their positions, cost factors, and outside constraints. Yet the overall lesson is quite clear. Also, several common opinions about public enterprise need revision. These notions concern:

Efficiency. Public enterprises are not routinely bureaucratic, rigid, and wasteful of resources. Some of them are, especially where public accountability involves detailed supervision and adherence to standard rules. In fact, *efficiency* and *public accountability* may often be at odds: an independent, flexible public enterprise may avoid public scrutiny and deviate from optimum results; while close supervision may stifle efficiency.

These tendencies are stronger in government bureaus which hold monopoly power and are free of market tests. Generally, the efficiency-accountability conflict is least severe where a degree of market competition and criteria are applied.

The newer types of public enterprise therefore minimize both rigidity and the accountability problem. Yet even in the older firms, bureaucracy has not been great and independence has not fostered gross neglect of performance criteria.

Profitability. Financial losses are less frequent than commonly believed, and they usually reflect special external burdens or deliberate policies imposed by the government on the public enterprise. These social burdens and controls are hard to quantify. But if they were filtered out, many (perhaps most) public firms in industrial countries would show net profitability at least as great as private criteria would require. Financial losses, where they do occur, are often in line with optimal criteria. Where they are not, it is often (not always) because of external decisions.

Centralization. The matter is quite complex. A number of utility public corporations in Britain may have been overcentralized for a period after 1945–50. But this is debatable, and some shifts toward decentralizing have more recently been carefully reversed. There is little substance to the overcentralization notion, in the whole range of sectors and countries, apart possibly from certain problems in public housing.

Use of Capital. The investment programs of public firms are often said to be extravagant, on several asserted grounds. Projects are not screened for commercial returns, and benefits are exaggerated. Funds are supplied below true costs. Investment is allocated to hopelessly unprofitable units.

Some of this does occur, especially in U.S. river projects. But much of the opinion is erroneous, arising from the necessarily high capital-intensity of many utility public firms. Often the investment is part of an efficient, but extensive, once-for-all reorganization. The screening process is often as meaningful as the average evaluation in private firms. Often, investment choices are influenced by decisions imposed on the firms by the government.

Therefore, there are only slight grounds for regarding public firm investment as tending to be too large. If anything, regulated *private* firms may be more likely to overuse capital (recall Part IV).

Innovativeness. Public firms are not inherently slow to innovate. Some of them are unusually quick and fertile in developing new processes and products. Those under tight financial constraints are especially likely to be active in trying major cost-reducing innovations (e.g., in United Kingdom telephone switching technology).

Other Basic Properties

8. Some categories of public enterprise give predictable negative net benefits. These tend to be *passive* enterprises: high degrees of subsidy and low degrees of public control, combined with monopoly and overcentralization. How these factors interact to give defective results can be seen fairly clearly, and so those negative cases can be identified. The costly results are primarily matters of form and criteria, not simply of publicness itself.

9. Conversely, certain types of *active* public enterprise, under certain definite conditions and policies, tend to yield high net benefits. These too can be identified with some clarity. The fitness of the treatment depends partly, too, on the sector involved and the specific social objectives at stake.

10. The main benefits come from (1) making large changes which have social impacts, (2) improving the inner content of the enterprises (e.g., sharing of power within the firm, labor relations), and (3) avoiding windfall capital gains from monopoly positions or other special advantages. These gains are, however, rarely achieved fully in practice.

11. The general rule that public enterprises tend to grow more regressive over time does hold, although of course with exceptions. The speed and depth with which the shift occurs depends in part on how rigid and extreme the public enterprise's structure, ownership, and policies are. In some cases, public enterprises are shifted and adapted over time so that their effects do not grow more regressive. But this requires foresight, effort, and a measure of good luck. It also requires a sympathetic policy environment. More generally, avoidance of the regressive shift often requires a finite life for the public enterprise in its original sector and purpose. Optimally, the whole group of public enterprises would usually shift as decades pass, some units being phased out, others being added.

12. Public enterprises are usually overloaded with economic and social targets, compared to their resources. This is the normal policy condition, in which the device is created, designed, and funded on a basis

which is inadequate to its formal social task. That emerged in Parts II–IV as being largely true of antitrust and regulation as well.

13. Usually the financial status of the enterprise is set by conditions and decisions outside its own control. These may cripple the enterprise from the outset. In any event, the enterprise usually has much control over its own inner economic structure and the configuration of its prices and investment flows. Usually, a degree of guidance from outside—by invited and uninvited criticism, and by official pressures—is beneficial. On peak-load pricing especially, and on pricing devices to generate sharply progressive effects, there is usually a need both for clear analysis and pressure from outside, and also for political support. Without clear analytical criteria, a public enterprise is often prey to outside pressures for special favors and pork-barrel decisions. At the least, the correct economic guidance for pricing and investment decisions can help public enterprises to fend off extraneous and regressive pressures.

14. Generally, public enterprises need a continuing skeptical evaluation. There usually is a need to consider increasing competition, to constrain the use of public resources, and to improve the efficiency and equity impacts. The distributional effects, in particular, need to be analyzed critically, because of their regressive tendency. More broadly, the need to *experiment* with new forms and sectors for public enterprise is a continuing one. There is no final form or sectoral pattern for public enterprises to reach. On the contrary, public enterprises—singly and collectively—normally need to evolve and to cope with new changes so that forms and resources do not become frozen.

FURTHER CHANGES

Several lines of future evolution of public firms can be predicted from recent trends. Abroad, there will be more experimenting with public firms and holding companies in industry and finance. There will be fewer sharp changes, even though socialist parties in each country have evolved long, familiar lists of industries "to be nationalized."

The actual gradual spread will enrich our knowledge about the performance of public enterprise, and their treatment will continue to become more sophisticated. This will come especially from financial public firms, operating both as competitors to private units and as supervisors of public and quasi-public firms in other sectors. Yet these changes will probably be slow and have large exceptions. One should not expect any dramatic new forms or lessons. Nor is there likely to be any large shift of public firms toward private status.

In the United States, discussion and action will probably continue to be biased against objective uses of public enterprises—though perhaps this will diminish. In *practice,* public enterprise will still be used freely where powerful interests can gain from it. The ideological bias will not only help to limit the evolution of public enterprises but will also make more favorable the private terms upon which any new experiments in public enterprise will be started.

There will probably be further instances of the more negative, passive types of public enterprises (recall Chapter 19). These will rightly warrant criticism, though they will be primarily the outcome of their setting.

Across the range of sectors in the U.S. economy, one may expect some improvements and adjustments toward more efficient forms and criteria, especially in urban and social enterprises. There will be less than an efficient degree of experimenting with public enterprise in industry, finance, and especially utility sectors. Of these, the greater loss will be from the financial sector, where unrealized social gains now appear to be appreciable. It is precisely because effective public enterprises in finance would impinge on deeply set private interests that the prospects for them now seem limited. Only if some private interests can be engaged to promote and operate effective financial public enterprises will this impasse be eased. In any event, such enterprises will fail—or be converted to other negative uses—if they are imposed upon a united and hostile financial sector.

Therefore, to anticipate the evolution of public enterprise in U.S. and elsewhere, one must understand both (1) the inner forms and criteria, and (2) the surrounding political economy. Public enterprises and their determinants continue to operate in the context of a private system where ingenuity and flexibility are great. Actual benefits are often absorbed by nondeserving groups. Defects—real or imagined—are exaggerated. And objective analysis is not encouraged.

Ultimately, the prospects for public enterprise are comparable to those of antitrust and regulation. There is potential for inefficiency and abuse, but also for excellent performance. Many of the hazards are predictable, and most of the essential issues can be cast in a sensible cost-benefit form. *No rational analyst will be either for or against public enterprise on the whole, except for purely personal or ideological reasons.* The economic task is to identify what is happening in the existing public enterprises, to define the directions for at least the most obvious corrections, and then to derive the optimum conditions under which new enterprises might be tried.

Part VI

SPECIAL CASES

CHAPTER TWENTY FOUR

Departures from Standard
Policy Treatment

The main policy treatments cover over half of the economy (recall Tables 1-1 and 1-2), but exempt and special cases are a large and diverse lot. This chapter covers a variety of exemptions and special controls.[1] Promotion and subsidies are surveyed in Chapter 25. Then four important special sectors are given a chapter each: natural resources, health care, arts and sports, and weapons.

This chapter covers, broadly, (1) exemptions from antitrust and other constraints, and (2) various price-raising barriers and restrictions. After reviewing them, we look more closely at price controls and labor markets.

EXEMPTIONS

The main exempted sectors were noted in Table 5-2. Exemption can be formal, or by usage; and complete or partial; or any combination of these. Labor is formally exempt from antitrust, while weapons supply is exempt by usage, though both are touched by other policies.

Farmers' and fishers' cooperatives are mostly exempt. They are extensive and varied, some with great market power, some with little. Since 1922, under the Capper-Volstead Act, farmers can use cooperatives as common agencies in sorting, grading, and packaging their crops; in producing such foodstuffs as butter, cheese, and canned goods; in marketing their output; and in fixing prices and terms of sale. Under various other side limits, such cooperatives are permitted to operate even where they might violate the antitrust laws.[2] In the most basic agricultural goods,

---

[1] Some have already been discussed above (e.g., patents, airline rate cartels, and stock-exchange fee-fixing).

[2] This privilege is confined to associations operated for mutual benefit, each of whose members has a single vote or whose dividends are limited to 8 percent per year, and whose supplies are drawn predominantly from within their membership. One other safeguard is provided: "If the Secretary of Agriculture shall have reason to believe that any such associa-

605

they usually have little market power. But where producers are geographically concentrated as they are in the cases of fruits, vegetables, nuts, and milk, a cooperative may possess much market power. In some cases, cooperatives equalize the bargaining powers of sellers and buyers. But in others, they are simply a license to monopolize. A similar exemption resides in the Fisheries Cooperative Marketing Act of 1934. Under it, fisheries can form cooperatives, some of which are able to affect the prices and terms of sale.

In 1918, the Webb-Pomerene Act exempted "associations entered into for the sole purpose of engaging in export trade." Such associations are not exempt as they may affect domestic trade, but the foreign trade exemption is not trivial. The FTC is given jurisdiction over them, but the supervision has been nominal. There have been only about 30 such associations, which have handled less than 5 percent of the goods exported from the U.S. The exemption offers possible public gains; the associations may offset foreign cartels, or achieve economies in the handling of foreign sales. But these and other possible benefits are likely to be relatively small.

Newspapers are another major exemption from antitrust. In recent decades their numbers have been dwindling, partly because the economies of scale in production and distribution have risen. (Also the profit gains from increasing the share of local advertising have also risen.) In 1970, after a series of adverse court decisions against newspaper mergers, the newspapers succeeded in getting Congress to pass an act exempting joint arrangements between pairs of papers for mutual printing and business organization of newspaper production. This is, in effect, a large special application of the failing-firm criterion (recall Chapter 8). The contention is that, if joint operations were not permitted, one or the other of the participants would fail and so a true monopoly would result. It is possible that genuine economies of scale (plus the gains from monopolizing advertising) might lead to a virtually complete situation of one-paper cities throughout the country. Therefore the exemption may marginally promote variety and competition. Yet it does acquiesce in an extraordinary degree of monopoly in most newspaper markets.

Chapter 16 noted that many transport price-fixing groups are permitted. These affect ocean shipping rates, international airline fares, truck-

---

tion monopolizes or restrains trade . . . to such an extent that the price of any agricultural product is unduly enhanced," he may issue a complaint, hold a hearing, and issue an order to cease and desist which, upon noncompliance, he may request the Attorney General to enforce.

This exemption has not been held to permit cooperatives to conspire with other distributors, to fix resale prices, or to discriminate unlawfully among their customers. But it is nonetheless a sweeping one, enabling cooperatives to make exclusive contracts with hundreds of farmers and to combine in the establishment of common marketing agencies. It encompasses not only farming operations but also manufacturing establishments engaged in processing agricultural commodities. The safeguard embodied in the law affords but scant protection against abuse. No criterion is established by which to judge whether prices have been unduly enhanced. The Secretary of Agriculture, moreover, may be expected to view the activities of agricultural cooperatives with a not unsympathetic eye. It should be noted, too, that such associations were authorized by the Cooperative Marketing Act of 1926 to collect, disseminate, and interpret trade statistics, an activity that has brought many a trade association into conflict with antitrust.

ing, and railroad rates, and—in effect—domestic airline fares. Still other exemptions—banks, insurance, health, sports, etc.—are discussed elsewhere.

OFFICIALLY SUPPORTED RESTRICTIONS

We will consider barriers to global and interstate trade, the milk and sugar cartels, and the NRA saga of 1933–35.

Trade Restrictions

The most extensive and ancient restraints—since the mercantilist days and earlier—are those on foreign trade. For the U.S., leading features of these tariffs and physical limits are shown in Table 24–1 and Figure 24–1. Some approach a total exclusion of import competition. The degree of actual protection is often difficult to assess, for it reflects both output tariffs and tariffs on imported inputs. In part, many tariffs can be regarded merely as equalizers against corresponding tariffs set by for-

TABLE 24–1
Selected Trade Restrictions, 1974

Tariffs, on	*Rate of Tariff as Percent of Value*
Distilled liquors	18
Wool fabrics	47
Clothing	20–30
Furniture	11
Organic dyes, etc.	37
Shoes	15
Flat glass	17
Glassware	17
Steel products	5–15
Machinery	5–15
Motors	12
Appliances	10–12
Automobiles	6
Cycles	13
Sporting goods	19
Musical instruments	21

Other Restrictions, on	
Steel	"Voluntary" restrictions on steel sales to the U.S.
Ships	Foreign-made ships cannot (1) ply U.S. coastal routes nor (2) get shipping subsidies
Oil products	Restricted
Cotton	Restrictions are negotiated by governments. Japanese sales have dropped 60 percent
Sugar, wheat, cotton	Restricted
"Buy American"	Excludes foreign suppliers in a wide range of major industrial products
Nuclear fuel cores	Banned, unless enriched in AEC plants
Books	U.S. authored books cannot be imported

Source: Commission on International Trade and Investment Policy, *U.S. International Economic Policy in an Interdependent World,* papers, Vol. I (Washington, D.C.: U.S. Government Printing Office, 1971), and other sources.

eign countries in the same international markets. This makes extremely complex the effort to reduce tariffs as a means of fostering competition for domestic producers holding market power. Still, the net effect of a good tight tariff is to exclude competition, and the benefits are reaped by producers at the expense of consumers. In this sense, it is a classical monopoly tactic.

Supplementing or substituting for tariffs often are quotas or other physical limitations on imports. These have been most prominent in the oil and steel industries, especially since the middle 1950s. The oil import quotas lasted for about 14 years during a period when there were surplus

FIGURE 24–1
Tariffs Have Declined but Are Still Significant

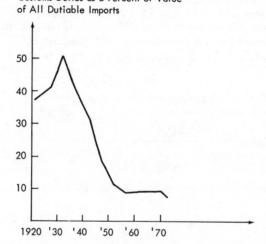

Customs Duties as a Percent of Value
of All Dutiable Imports

oil supplies both internationally and domestically. Since 1973, such quotas have been superfluous as oil supplies have tightened up, and so the import quotas were suspended (see also Chapter 26). In periods of boom, restraints on steel imports have also had little force. Nonetheless, there has existed since 1968 an effective international cartel limiting imports of steel from Japan and Europe to the United States (recall Chapter 6).

Interstate Limits

The federal constitution forbids the imposition of duties on trade between the states. In the case of alcoholic beverages, however, the 21st Amendment (abolishing national prohibition) permits state governments to restrict imports as a means of regulating the liquor business. Many states have used this power not so much to check the consumption of intoxicants as to prevent producers outside their borders from competing with local maltsters, brewers, vintners, distillers, and growers of hops, grapes, and grains.

Many states have protected local nurseries by employing their horticultural laws to curtail the importation of nursery stock. At one time, the federal government was imposing quarantines against 11 plant diseases and insect pests, the states against 239. Some states, through grading and labeling requirements, have restricted imports of chicken and eggs. Florida has defined "fresh dressed poultry" as poultry slaughtered in Florida; and Flordia, Georgia, and Arizona have each defined "fresh eggs" as eggs laid within the state. A number of states maintain rigorous standards in grading fruits and vegetables and exclude those falling in the lower grades. Georgia has empowered its agricultural authorities to embargo out-of-state fruits and vegetables when they believe the domestic supply to be sufficient for the markets of the state. State laws have handicapped out-of-state truckers. Some states have discriminated against trucks that come in loaded, prepared to sell, in favor of those that come in empty, prepared to buy. The Buy American Act has its counterpart in state law. Nearly every state requires that some sort of preference be shown to residents in making public purchases. State agencies and institutions have thus been forced to hire local labor, award contracts to local bidders, and purchase supplies from local firms. City councils have taken similar action. Urban markets for fluid milk have been closed to all producers but those whose dairies have been inspected and approved by local health authorities, a measure that limits competition when applications for inspection are refused. Building ordinances, likewise, though ostensibly designed to eliminate hazards to health and safety, have contained provisions which operate to exclude from local markets materials produced by outsiders and to compel builders to use materials produced by local firms.

These measures have the same defects as do the barriers to international trade. In fact, they may be more harmful, since the area they leave open to freedom of competiton is a smaller one. As we move from "Buy American" through "Buy Indianan" and "Buy Middletown" to "Buy Main Street," the consequences differ, not in kind, but in degree.

Milk and sugar are the two leading U.S. examples of official cartels, now that some oil controls have been superceded by events. They are typical of the way government departments go about controlling agricultural and other resource production.

Milk

Since 1937 the Secretary of Agriculture can enter into marketing *agreements* and issue marketing *orders.* These cover the processing and distributing of farm products. An agreement binds all handlers who agree; an order binds all handlers, period.[3] Among small crops that have

---

[3] The issuance of agreements and orders proceeds through the following steps: (1) Producers, acting through their cooperatives, agree upon a program and present it to the Secretary of Agriculture. (2) The Secretary holds public hearings, considers the evidence presented pro and con, and prepares an agreement. (3) If the agreement is to be accepted voluntarily, he submits it to the handlers for signature. If compulsion is required, he puts it to a vote. (4) If two-thirds of the producers and half of the handlers involved accept it (or three-fourths and four-fifths, respectively, for California citrus fruits), he issues an order. And with producer approval, he may also issue an order even though the handlers disapprove.

been covered, the one big product covered—always by orders—is milk. At any time there may be 75 orders in effect for milk and around 40 agreements for all other products.

Milk is inelastic both in supply and demand, and it is sold in tight local markets. Dairying is the most important single source of agricultural income. Milk is produced commercially on more than a million farms, most of them in states near urban centers in the East and Middle West. Its supply remains about the same from year to year, depending upon the number of cows and the output per cow. A higher price does not quickly increase the number of cows: three years elapse from the time a cow is bred until her heifer begins to give milk. A lower price does not reduce the number; cows could be slaughtered, but the price of meat is also likely to be low. Changes in price, moreover, have little effect on bovine physiology. The supply of milk fluctuates with the seasons, rising as much as a third above the yearly average in the spring when calves are born and cows are put out on green pasture, and falling as much as a fourth below it in the fall.

Demand. The demand for milk has a high degree of income elasticity. But it has a low price elasticity, sales falling less than proportionately when prices are increased and rising less than proportionately when prices are reduced. Consumption is fairly steady throughout the year, falling but 5 percent below and rising but 5 percent above the annual average.

Half of all milk is consumed in fluid form. Half is sold to manufacturers who turn it into butter, cheese, and concentrated and powdered products. These two markets differ in their susceptibility to control. Because milk is heavy and bulky in relation to its value, the cost of transport is high. Because it is easily contaminated and affords a medium favorable to the growth of bacteria, city governments require that dairies be inspected and that milk sold in its original form be pasteurized. The region from which a city draws its milk, known as its milkshed, is, therefore, limited in size both by the economic factor of transport cost and by the political factor of inspection requirements. Entry into the business of distributing milk is also limited by the cost of pasteurization facilities. In recent years, with changes in technology, milk has come to move in bulk tank trucks to large bottling and distributing plants, serving wider market areas. But the urban market for fluid milk is still a sheltered one, lending itself to the application of private and public controls. In its manufactured forms, however, milk can be shipped more cheaply, lasts longer, and is little related to public health.

Most of the milk sold in a typical city is distributed by two or three large concerns. As sellers, the distributors behave as oligopolists. They complete in the duplication of delivery services, in brand names, advertising, and salesmanship. They seldom compete in price. Despite the fact that supply varies widely from season to season, the price of milk remains the same throughout the year. And every company delivering milk to the doorstep charges the same amount. Where prices competition has entered the market, it has come from delivery through stores.

In buying milk the large distributors appear as oligopsonists. The sellers are thousands of dairy farms. Unorganized, the farmer would be at a disadvantage in making his sale; organized, he can bargain collectively for better terms. Milk producers have, therefore, established cooperative associations and, through these associations, have entered into negotiations with distributors for the purpose of determining the farmer's price. Such associations now control two-thirds of the milk that is offered for sale in all the major markets in the United States (recall section above).

Fixing Prices. For the purpose of fixing prices to be paid producers, milk is classified according to use. Class I, which brings the highest price, contains milk that is sold fresh for consumption in fluid form. The other classes, which bring less, contain milk that goes through various manufacturing processes before it is consumed. Class I milk would normally bring more than other milk because the transport charges restrict its supply and sanitary precautions add to its cost. But the price difference also reflects discrimination. Distributors can do this because demand in the urban market is inelastic, because supply is under their control, and because inspection and pasteurization requirements protect them from the entry of competitors. *The structure of milk prices is thus deliberately discriminatory,* with markets separated and prices adjusted to variations in the conditions of demand and supply.[4] It is further bound by pooling and equalization, plus still other complications. The result is a complex, frozen structure of price discrimination in local milk markets, enforced by public agencies.

Producers of milk fared little better than other farmers in the decade that followed World War I. But they were able to get help in the early 1930s. More than half of the states enacted temporary or permanent milk control laws, beginning in 1933. These laws typically established a milk control board, composed of representatives of producers and distributors, and gave it regulatory powers.[5]

Action was also taken by the federal government. Marketing agreements were established, under the first AAA, for 15 markets in 1933. Then, in 1937, rules governing the federal regulation of milk markets were spelled out in the Agricultural Marketing Agreements Act.[6] These standards are so vague as to leave the Secretary free to adopt any price

---

[4] In theory the farmer receives different prices for different gallons of identical milk, depending upon where they are ultimately sold. In practice he gets a single price, known as a blended price, which is an average of the prices for the different classes weighted by the quantities sold in each class.

[5] It was the purpose of these measures, in general, to increase the incomes of producers by underwriting the prices negotiated between producer associations and distributors, by regulating output, and by obstructing entry, and to maintain the margins of distributors, by fixing resale prices and by preventing the development of competing methods of sale. The power of a state government to fix prices for milk was upheld by the Supreme Court of the United States in the Nebbia case in 1934 (*Nebbia* v. *New York,* 291 U.S. 502).

[6] The federal government can regulate markets when interstate commerce is involved. It can act only by order, when two-thirds of the producers consent. It cannot limit the size of a milkshed (although local health authorities still may do so). Its order must classify milk according to use and prescribe the method of fixing the price of each class. They may provide either for an individual-handler pool or for a marketwide pool, but in the latter case, they must also provide for the equalization of returns. The prices set in an order must also provide for the equalization of returns. The prices set in an order must equal parity or, at the discretion of the Secretary of Agriculture, an amount which he deems adequate to insure "a sufficient quantity of pure and wholesome milk." They must also reflect the price of feeds and other economic conditions which affect supply and demand. And they must be in the public interest.

upon which producers and distributors agree. Enforcement of such prices through federal orders was upheld by the Supreme Court in the Rock Royal case in 1939.[7]

Milk markets are usually under federal orders where cities are located near state borders and where milk is drawn from more than one state. Nearly all of the great urban markets for milk are under federal orders: the 61 areas include 142 million people. Each of the orders delineates the market area it covers, defines the classes of milk, sets forth the price of each class or the formula to be used in computing it, describes the manner of pooling, requires the presentation of reports on the quantities of milk that were sold for different uses, prescribes the method of payment, and provides for the auditing of distributor records and accounts. Each of the orders provides, further, for the appointment of a market administrator and for the imposition of assessments to cover the costs of administration.

Prices.   Under such orders, prices have been fixed in two principal ways: by administrative determinations following public hearings, and by adjustment in accordance with the provisions of a formula. The first method is slow, costly, and cumbersome. The second method seems quick and clear, but it is commonly ignored when emergency conditions arise. About a third of orders have been negotiated at higher levels in recent years.

The price of Class I milk—the milk you drink—in all the major markets is now fixed by formula. In two-thirds of the market orders, under the formula that has had the longest and widest use, this price is determined by taking as a base the average price currently paid for milk by manufacturers of dairy products in Minnesota and Wisconsin and adding a differential to cover something more than the extra costs of sanitation, transport, and handling involved in supplying milk for Class I use (see Table 24–2). In Chicago, recently, the price paid for manufacturing milk was $5.65 per cwt; the price paid under this formula for identical milk for fluid consumption was $6.26. But the price of manufacturing milk does not itself reflect the play of free market forces. For the government supports the price by purchasing, in the form of butter, cheese, and dry milk powder, 3 to 9 percent of the milk produced in the United States, at prices that yield the farmer 75 to 90 percent of parity. It supports the price, too, by imposing quotas on imports of dairy products. The whole structure of fluid milk prices is thus erected on a foundation that is held up by artificial props.

In 20 states, prices paid to milk producers are fixed by public agencies. Covering intrastate markets, they are generally similar to federal controls but tighter. Resale prices are fixed for milk under the laws of 15 states. Sales below cost are forbidden by the laws of ten other states. They too restrict sales and raise prices.[8] Distributors' margins are also protected by regulations that restrain competition. Such regulations have

---

[7] *U.S.* v. *Rock Royal Cooperative, Inc.,* 307 U.S. 553.

[8] U.S. Department of Agriculture, Economic Research Service, Agricultural Economic Report No. 152, *Government's Role in Pricing Fluid Milk in the United States* (Washington, D.C.: Government Printing Office, 1968).

made prices as high for sales across the counter as for home delivery, or limited the difference between the two.[9]

Summary. In short, milk is marketed under a thick network of overlapping controls which assure continuity and stability in markets and a higher price of milk. It fixes market structure and permits high-cost operators to continue. Milk markets are managed in the interests of sellers; the effects on efficiency are not small. A modest public gain from a stable supply of safe milk is overlain with excessive market controls and

TABLE 24-2
Leading Milk Markets under Federal Orders, 1972

	Producer Deliveries (billion pounds)	Average Minimum Prices per 100 Pounds Payable to Producers: Class I Price
New York–New Jersey	10.1	$7.64
Chicago Regional	8.3	6.26
Middle Atlantic	4.5	7.79
Southern Michigan	4.0	6.61
Boston Regional	3.5	7.99
Ohio Valley	3.1	6.70
Minneapolis–St. Paul	2.3	6.07
Indiana	1.9	6.47
Puget Sound, Wash.	1.5	6.86
Connecticut	1.4	7.99
Georgia	1.3	7.31

Source: U.S. Department of Agriculture, *Agricultural Statistics,* 1973.

predictable losses of efficiency and equity.[10] Optimal policy would withdraw most federal controls and all state controls.

The Sugar Quota System

The United States has always consumed more sugar than it has produced, importing a major part of its supply, some of it from Hawaii, Puerto Rico, the Virgin Islands, and the Philippines; more of it, until 1960, from Cuba. Sugar is produced at low cost from cane grown in tropical and semitropical regions; at high cost from beets grown in the western states. In the absence of artificial arrangements, the beet sugar industry would disappear. Sugar beets and cane are grown by less than 3 percent of the farmers on the mainland and account for less than 1

---

[9] In Minnesota, a law enacted in 1957 requires wholesale distributors to file their prices and to adhere to the prices they file. It prohibits 17 specific methods by which the distributors might engage in nonprice competition when selling to retailers. And state officials, acting under its privisions, bring distributors and retailers together to obtain agreements eliminating competition from the field. The law has operated to check the trend toward lower costs in distribution. It has kept high-cost operators in business. It has harmed consumers without observable benefits to producers. Ronald D. Knutson, "The Economic Consequences of the Minnesota Dairy Industry Unfair Trade Practices Act," *Journal of Law and Economics,* XII (2) (1969), pp. 377–89.

[10] Reuben A. Kessel, "Economic Effects of Federal Regulation of Milk Markets," *Journal of Law and Economics,* X (1967), pp. 51–78.

percent of farm income. But these farmers are located in 19 states and influence the votes of 38 Senators. For many years, they have been sheltered from foreign competition by barriers to imports.

Before World War II, tariffs on sugar were high. But now quotas are the main limit, with net costs of about $200 million per year.

History. The sugar quota system, as it has evolved in laws enacted since 1934, is forbiddingly complex. It includes six major elements: (1) The Secretary of Agriculture makes an annual estimate of the total quantity of sugar demanded for consumption in the United States. (2) The law divides this quantity between domestic and foreign sources. (3) The domestic share is divided into market quotas on the basis of past sales, being distributed among producing areas, the area quotas between cane and beet producers, the beet quotas among factory districts, and cane and beet quotas, converted into acreage allotments, among individual growers. (4) Cash subsidies are paid to farmers who keep within their allotments. These payments have run around $50 million a year. To be eligible for a subsidy, a farmer must employ no child labor—once common in the beet fields—and observe such minimum wages as the Secretary may require. (5) An excise tax is levied on imports and domestic output to finance the payment of subsidies. (6) Quotas are imposed on refined, as well as raw, sugar, and on that coming not only from foreign countries but also from islands under the American flag.

The marketing quotas, under this system, depend upon the Secretary's annual estimates of total demand. The law directs him, in making these estimates, to take into account (1) the amount of sugar consumed during the previous year, (2) deficits or surpluses in sugar inventories, (3) changes in population, (4) the level and trend of consumer purchasing power, and (5) the relation between changes, since 1947, in the price of refined sugar and in the general cost of living, with a view to maintaining "prices which will not be excessive to consumers and which will fairly and equitably maintain and protect the domestic sugar industry." These standards are vague enough to leave the Secretary considerable latitude.

Under the law as it was first enacted in 1934, the Secretary of Agriculture divided the market between foreign and domestic producers at 30 and 70 percent respectively. In 1937, the division of the market between foreign and domestic producers was written into the statute. The former were given 29 percent of the market, the Philippines 15 percent, and other insular and domestic producers 56 percent.

During World War II, the quota system was suspended. The Act of 1948 again divided the market, now giving domestic areas and the Philippines absolute quotas totaling 5,418,000 tons and providing that requirements in excess of this amount should be divided between Cuba and other countries in the ratio of 96 percent to 4 percent. In 1956, the basis of allocation was changed again.[11]

---

[11] The basic need for sugar was set at 8,350,000 tons; the fixed quota of domestic producers at 5,424,000 tons. Cuba was given 96 percent of the difference, a fixed quota of 2,806,960 tons. Above the figure of 8,350,000 tons, the domestic areas were allotted 55 percent, Cuba 29.6 percent, and other foreign countries 15.4 percent. Under this formula, Cuba's share of the American market in 1960 was set at 3,119,665 tons, one-third of the total national requirement of 9,400,000 tons.

The system worked in many ways to Cuba's advantage. In supplying a third of the American market, she received prices that ran from 2 to $2^1/2$ cents a pound above those prevailing elsewhere. This gave her an added income of about $125 million a year. In addition, she retained her tariff advantage of 20 percent, which was worth another $8 million. In sum, she collected $133 million more than she would have received for her sugar on the world market.

In 1960, following the Cuban revolution and the deterioration of Cuban-American relations, imports of sugar from Cuba were barred by President Eisenhower and the Cuban quota divided among other suppliers. In 1962, Congress again revised the method of dividing the market. The new formula governing allocation, as it was applied in 1964, gave 58 percent of the market to areas producing under the American flag and 42 percent to foreigners.

In 1964, Congress failed to extend the law. The Secretary of Agriculture, acting under his administrative powers, imposed the quotas. In 1965, however, Congress enacted a new law, allotting shares in the American market for the years through 1971. This measure gave two-thirds of the market, then set at a total of 9.7 million tons, to American producers (nearly a third of it to producers of sugar beets) and a third to producers abroad. The law discontinued the reservation made for Cuba and fixed absolute quotas for more than 30 countries. In 1974 an effort was made to abolish the system, but the outcome is in doubt at this writing.

Effects. Apart from its bad diplomatic effects, the system has large economic costs. It establishes a rigid cartel. It imposes market quotas and acreage allotments on the farmers without asking their consent. It penalizes production in greater quantities than the allotments may allow. It subsidizes a tiny minority of American farmers, rewarding them for wasting the nation's resources by expanding an uneconomic industry. Since 1934, it has increased the acreage devoted to sugar beets by more than 40 percent and the output of beet sugar by more than 130 percent. The program's benefit to American growers of sugar cane and beets amounts to $200 million a year. Its cost to American taxpayers and consumers each year runs around $800 million, more than $80 million of this to pay for its administration and to finance the subsidies; more than $700 million in higher prices.

The NRA

It is difficult now to convey fully the trauma of the Great Depression of the 1930s, but it does explain the oddity of some policy treatments tried then. One was the National Industrial Recovery Act, rushed through in June, 1933, as an early Rooseveltian effort to stabilize prices and promote industrial production. The episode was quickly recognized as a bizarre economic failure. But it graphically illustrates the effects of suspending antitrust, and it immunized at least a generation of Americans against such self-regulation by industry.

The new program had its origin in a deal between organized labor and organized business. Labor had long sought maximum hour and minimum wage limits, union recognition, and collective bargaining. Business was seeking the right of "self-government," meaning freedom to make and enforce rules restricting competition, to be obtained by suspending the prohibitions of antitrust. Gerard Swope, President of the General Electric Company, had published a widely discussed plan for a nationwide "coordination of production and consumption" through legalized cooperation in controlling prices and methods of competition. The United States Chamber of Commerce had issued a report proposing revision of the antitrust laws to permit similar programs of economic planning.

The law specified that all the codes must provide for maximum hours, minimum wages, and collective bargaining.[12] Beyond that, it left initiative in formulating their provisions to trade associations, requiring only that such groups truly represent their trades, do not restrict admission, and do not eliminate or oppress small competitors. Violation of the codes was an unfair method of competition, punishable as a misdemeanor by a fine of $500 for each offense. All practices permitted were exempted from antitrust.

The National Industrial Recovery Act.   This was administered by the National Recovery Administration. At its head, during the first year, was General Hugh S. Johnson, a former cavalry officer. Beneath him were 55 deputy administrators, most of them businessmen, each of them responsible for a different segment of industry. Advising these officials were a research division, a legal division, and three advisory boards, representing the interests of industry, labor, and the consumer. This organization, set up almost over night, proceeded at high speed to codify labor standards and trade practices throughout American industry.

The program was launched with a great fanfare. Pending the completion of the codes, a President's Reemployment Agreement, containing minimum labor standards, was signed by more than two million employers. These firms were permitted to display the emblem of the Blue Eagle at their places of business and to affix it to their goods. The public was invited, in effect, to boycott those who failed to do so. In the meantime, the work of drafting the codes got under way.

The first drafts were drawn up by the industry trade associations. They were a product of negotiation between these associations and organized labor, each conceding terms to the other in return for agreement to the terms that it sought for itself. Later drafts were given public hearings. If the Industry and Labor Advisory Boards had found them acceptable, they were approved. If the Consumers' Advisory Board had objected, its protest was ignored. The industry and labor boards had organized backing; the consumers' board did not. When the codes were approved by the deputies, they were rubber-stamped by the administrator and the President and given the effect of law.

Codes.   The codes were administered by bodies known as code authorities. These bodies were largely composed of, or selected by, trade

---

[12] As quoted in L. S. Lyon and others, *The National Recovery Administration* (Washington, D.C.: Brookings Institution, 1935), p. 758.

associations. The personnel and the policy of the authorities were controlled by trade associations. In three cases out of four, the code authority secretary and the trade association secretary bore the same name and did business at the same address.

The NRA approved 557 basic codes, 189 supplementary codes, 109 divisional codes, and 19 codes entered into jointly with the Agricultural Adjustment Administration—a grand total of 874. The codes spelled out more than a thousand different kinds of provisions for the regulation of 150 different types of competitive practices. They controlled terms of sale, prices, markets, production, capacity, and the channels of distribution. In the name of fair competition, they required adherence to practices that the Federal Trade Commission and the courts had held to be unfair. Industry by industry, they were designed by a majority to curb the competitive propensities of an obstreperous minority. Item by item, they copied the pattern of the standard European cartel.

More than 85 percent of the codes contained some provision for the direct or indirect control of price. A dozen of them permitted the code authorities to establish minimum prices without regard to costs of production and without approval by the NRA. In iron and steel, and in a few other industries, the codes legalized basing-point systems of delivered pricing, specifying each of the elements of the pricing formulas and prescribing their use.

Price Fixing. The fixing of prices was usually less overt. Some 200 codes permitted code authorities to establish minimum prices only to prevent "destructive price cutting" and to do so only in the event of an "emergency." These limitations, however, had little significance. The concepts were never clearly defined. "An emergency," it was said, "is something that is declared by a code authority." As the coal dealers put it, "We have always had an emergency in retail solid fuel."

In the codes for the wholesale and retail trades, price fixing took the form of provisions for "loss limitation." In some cases, these provisions forbade the distributor to sell goods for less than they cost him. In others, they required him to add a markup based upon some estimate of distribution costs. In still others, they compelled him to charge a price set by the producer or by the wholesaler from whom he bought. It is likely that provisions of the second type and it is certain that those of the third type involved something more than the mere limitation of loss.

The type of price-fixing provision which was most widely adopted, under NRA, was that which provided for "cost protection." Three-fifths of the codes prohibited sales below "cost." The effect of such a provision would depend, of course, upon the standard of cost that was employed. Depending on the choice of cost criterion, the prices set by this provision would be high or low.

More than half of the codes provided for the establishment of a standard costing system. More than 50 of them forbade sales below some average of cost, the rest forbade sales below the seller's individual cost. In many cases the procedure followed in the determination of an average cost led to the establishment of an arbitrary minimum price. Two-thirds of the codes provided for the establishment of open price-reporting systems. Most of these systems would probably have been outlawed under the earlier decisions of the courts.

Other Restrictions. Ninety-one codes provided for the restriction of output and the sharing out of available business. Sixty codes, most of them in the textile industry, imposed limitations on the number of hours or shifts per day, or the number of hours or days per week, during which machines or plants might be operated, thus curtailing production and allocating the resulting volume of business on the basis of capacity. A half dozen codes, including those for the petroleum, lumber, copper, and glass container industries, provided for the limitation of production in accordance with estimates of total demand, and for the assignment of production quotas on the basis of present capacity or past production or sales.

Some 50 codes imposed limitations upon the construction, conversion, or relocation of productive capacity, or made some provision for the imposition of such limitations. In some cases, the provision of new facilities and the inauguration of new services were forbidden.

Adherence to code requirements was enforced not only by penalties provided in the law but also by sanctions established in the codes. The requirements imposed on manufacturers by distributors and on wholesalers by retailers were enforced by organized boycotts. Twenty-six industries bound their members to pay "liquidated damages" into the treasury of the code authority in the event of a violation. Actually the liquidated damages were fines imposed on violators of the code rather than payments made to injured parties to reimburse them for losses actually sustained.

Decline and Fall. This saturnalia of cartelization soon drew criticism and doubt. In the spring of 1934, the President appointed a committee, under the eminent lawyer, Clarence Darrow, to investigate. The committee's report condemned the whole undertaking, denouncing it as "monopoly sustained by government" and as "a regimented organization for exploitation." The Supreme Court settled the matter in 1935, by its decision on the Schechter case.[13] The Court was unanimous. The law involved an unconstitutional invasion of intrastate commerce and an unconstitutional delegation of legislative power. The NRA was put to death on May 27, 1935.

The trade practice provisions of the codes were administered most effectively in industries that had not been vigorously competitive: those that were disciplined by powerful trade associations or dominated by a few large firms. Here, the legal sanction was not needed; suspension of the antitrust laws was all that was required. In more competitive industries, however, where firms were small and numerous and trade associations weak, enforcement of the codes was difficult if not impossible. And here they tended to break down.

The National Industrial Recovery Act contributed little, if anything, to recovery. But it did serve one useful purpose. It provided the country with a demonstration of the character and the consequences of carteliza-

---

[13] *Schechter* v. *U.S.*, 295 U.S. 495 (1935).

tion. It showed that industry, when given the power of self-government, could not be trusted to exercise it in the public interest; that enterprise would be handicapped and vested interests protected, progress obstructed, and stagnation assured.

It is probable that the NRA was like a vaccination, giving the United States a mild case of the cartel disease and immunizing it against the disease itself. It is certain that—as long as this experience remains in memory—there are few who would welcome its return. If American industry, in general, is again to be cartelized, the movement will have to take a different form.

PRICE CONTROLS

Formal price controls have been tried in the U.S. mainly during World War II, the Korean War, and 1971–74. Many U.S. economists have been part of the effort, and most regard it as frustrating and only partially successful. Since 1955 there have been many informal "jaw-boning" attempts—and quasi-formal "wage-price guidelines"—to abate price rises.[14] Expert opinion divides on the issue. Some economists regard controls as worth trying, at least during crisis periods. Others liken them to bandages applied to cure a fever. Price-wage controls during peacetime seemed necessary for the first time in many North Atlantic economies in 1971–73. Yet they now seem to have had slight effects and have once again gone out of style.

Lessons.   Four basic lessons hold: (1) Controls work best during a crisis, especially in war. Loyalty is high, and the situation seems to be temporary. (2) Price-wage controls fail when any important groups (especially upper groups: top executives, capital-gains receivers, speculators) are exempted from controls, while ordinary citizens are made to sacrifice. (3) Controls are most effective on major concentrated industries. (4) Price-wage controls are cumbersome, costly, and unfair to some groups. Inspired leaders can minimize these flaws.

In short, controls are best used selectively for selected situations. The reasons for focusing upon major tight oligopolies are strong. Fewness makes for ease of measurement and control. It also lends a certain theatrical drama to the event, by holding up for public attention those largest firms which might have a large impact. By contrast, attempts to control the scrappy, decentralized, competitive markets in clothing, furniture, or similar secondary products are likely to be futile. This was learned first in World War II, where price controls on major firms in large industries were the most successful.[15] The Korean War effort—on a smaller scale—confirmed this tendency.

---

[14] John Sheahan, *The Wage-Price Guidelines* (Washington, D.C.: Brookings Institution, 1968).

[15] World War II price controls (1943–46) paralleled the experience during 1951–53 and 1971–74. For most goods and services, prices were frozen at existing levels, being set at the highest figures charged in March, 1943. Where new goods were introduced and where new sellers entered the market, their ceilings were related in various ways to those of goods and firms already there.

Price ceilings, once set, had to be adjusted. The general freeze reduced the margins of

FIGURE 24–2
Did Price Controls Alter the Rate of Inflation?

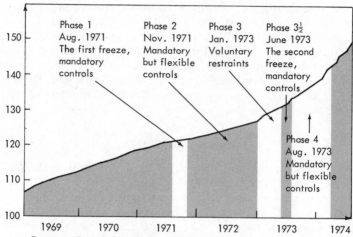

Consumer Price Index. All Items 1967 = 100. Not Seasonally Adjusted.
Source: Bureau of Labor Statistics.

The 1971–74 "Experiment."   Therefore, when the Nixon control effort began in 1971, controls were focused on precisely those industries which we have identified as major near-monopolies and tight oligopolies (Chapters 2 and 7).[16] This effort was echoed in Britain within two years by virtually a mirror image of the U.S. price controls. The U.S. effort was widely believed to be successful, although price statistics indicate only

distributors who were selling in March on the basis of prices they had paid for goods in earlier months. It perpetuated differences due to chance, catching some sellers with prices that were abnormally low. It created shortages in some localities. As costs rose, moreover, the ceilings left high-price firms in business, but threatened to eliminate their low-price competitors. They cut out needed segments of supply. Ceilings were, therefore, adjusted by administrative action, and higher prices were charged when permission was obtained.

Price controls were effective in some fields, ineffective in others. It was possible to enforce dollars-and-cents ceilings, difficult to enforce freezes, and virtually impossible to enforce ceilings that were to be computed by sellers through the use of formulas. Controls were effective where production was concentrated in the hands of a few large firms and where prices had been fixed through open or tacit agreement before the war. They were ineffective where producers were small and numerous and where industries had been actively competitive. Ceilings were evaded by reducing the quality of goods sold at the ceiling price, by moving goods, such as dresses, from a lower into a higher price class, by reducing discounts, and by worsening other terms of sale. In some trades and in some regions, ceilings were simply ignored.

With labor scarce and wages free, the cost of labor rose. With prices frozen, profits declined. If ceilings on prices were to be preserved, wages had to be controlled. This, too, was done by imposing a base-date freeze. And here, again, adjustments had to be made, raising substandard wages, permitting increases for merit and for length of service, and removing differentials between plants, industries, and communities. Adjustments were always upward. The principal contribution of wage control to the stabilization of prices was bureaucratic delay.

These controls were cumbersome. They were evaded in various ways. They brought the allocators and the price controllers into frequent conflict. But they worked, after a fashion, for a time. The wartime control measures were supported by patriotism. They were tolerated as temporary. But, even so, they encountered serious obstacles.

[16] J. K. Galbraith, *The Economics of Price Control* (Boston: Houghton Mifflin, 1952).

a gentle effect, if any, on price changes. Perhaps no controls could arrest the long-term upward movement of such prices. Still, the will to believe that an extensive apparatus must be accomplishing something has led many observers to conclude that the effort did have at least some effect (judge for yourself from Figure 24-2).

Yet the controls were not a proper experiment but only a hasty and skinny half-effort. There were a variety of major technical gaps and flaws. Profits, capital gains, dividends, and top executives' pay were effectively exempt. It took much time simply to assemble the staff and set rules. Decisions were often hasty and crude—and easily avoided.[17] Under Phase II, which lasted from late 1971 through to January 1973, major firms were to be permitted to pass on cost increases and raise prices as long as their rate of return did not exceed the average of two best out of the preceding years (Table 24-3 presents the control rules.) This stabilized the profit rates previously being earned. High ones were to be kept high but no higher; low ones were not to rise. This made some sense on an interindustry basis, but not among competitive firms within industries. And it exerted little more than atmospheric pressure.[18]

Note that this missed a unique chance to constrain precisely those firms whose market position and performance were contributing to the need for price controls in the first place. Moreover, the effort at price control, with such a trivial effect, had the larger effect of giving official approval to profit rates of 20 or 25 percent. Having been scrutinized, these high profit rates could be taken as officially acceptable, more so than if price controls had been absent. To this extent, price controls not only failed to impose optimal limits, but also tended to legitimize the conditions which were part of the problem itself.

The formal end of controls in 1974 brought a reversion to "jaw-boning." Price-wage controls no longer seemed a necessary treatment for industrial economics in peacetime. Yet, a variety of more selective limits on a relatively few large industries were likely to be tried.

LABOR MARKETS

There are two related policy issues. *One* is the exemption of unions from antitrust: this affects a wide range of *industrial* labor markets for unskilled and skilled blue-collar labor. The *other* issue is self-regulation and restrictions in *professional* trades (doctors, lawyers, embalmers, accountants, beauticians, barbers, and the like). The two are opposite ends of the same process: the effort of workers to use bargaining power to better their income and working conditions.

---

[17] See the revealing analysis of these defects by C. Jackson Grayson, the head of the Price Commission, and the excellent analysis by R. F. Lanzillotti, Mary Hamilton, and Blaine Roberts, *Phase II in Review: The Price Commission* (Washington, D.C.: Brookings Institution, 1975). There were, for example, only 6 economists in the Commission's staff.

[18] Thus in the automobile industry, General Motors and Ford were permitted to maintain profit rates of 20 percent and 15 percent, even though that involved substantial price rises. But by contrast, American Motors was not permitted to raise its prices even though its profit rate was only about 3 percent. The inequity of this did not appear to trouble the Price Commission.

TABLE 24-3

Regulations of the Controls Program, Phases II, III, and IV

Program	Phase II *Nov. 14, 1971 to* *Jan. 11, 1973*	Phase III *Jan. 11, 1973 to* *June 13, 1973*	Phase IV *Aug. 12, 1973 to* *April 30, 1974*
General Standards:			
Price increase limitations........	Percentage pass-through of allowable cost increases since last price increase, or Jan. 1, 1971, adjusted for productivity and volume offsets. Term limit pricing option available.	Self-administered standards of Phase II.	In most manufacturing and service industries dollar for dollar pass-through of allowable cost increase since last fiscal quarter ending prior to Jan. 11, 1973.
Profit margin limitations........	Not to exceed margins of the best 2 of 3 fiscal years before Aug. 15, 1971. Not applicable if prices were not increased above base level, or if firms "purified" themselves.	Not to exceed margins of the best 2 fiscal years completed after Aug. 15, 1968. No limitation if average price increase does not exceed 1.5 percent.	Same years as Phase III, except that a firm that has not charged a price for any item above its base price, or adjusted freeze price, whichever is higher, is not subject to the limitation.
Wage increase limitations........	General standard of 5.5 percent. Exceptions made to correct gross inequities, and for workers whose pay had increased less than 7 percent a year for the last 3 years. Workers earning less than $2.75 per hour were exempt. Increases in qualified fringe benefits permitted raising standard to 6.2 percent.	General Phase II standard, self-administered. Some special limitations. More flexibility with respect to specific cases. Workers earning less than $3.50 per hour were exempted after May 1.	Self-administered standards of Phase III. Executive compensation limited.

Prenotification:			
Prices	Prenotification required for all firms with annual sales above $100 million, 30 days before implementation, approval required.	After May 2, 1973, prenotification required for all firms with sales above $250 million whose price increase has exceeded a weighted average of 1.5 percent.	Same as Phase II except that pre-notified price increases may be implemented in 30 days unless Cost of Living Council requires otherwise.
Wages	For all increases of wages for units of 5,000 or more; for all increases above the standard regardless of the number of workers involved.	None.	None.
Reporting:			
Prices	Quarterly for firms with sales over $50 million.	Quarterly for firms with sales over $250 million.	Quarterly for firms with sales over $50 million.
Wages	Pay adjustments below standard for units greater than 1,000 persons.	Pay adjustments for units greater than 5,000 persons.	As Phase III.
Special areas	Health, insurance, rent, construction, public utilities.	Health, food, public utilities, construction, petroleum.	Health, food, petroleum, construction, insurance, executive and variable compensation.
Exemptions to price standards	Raw agricultural commodities, import prices, export prices, firms with 60 or fewer employees.	Same as Phase II plus rents.	Same as Phase III plus manufactured feeds, cement, public utilities, lumber, copper scrap, long-term coal contracts, automobiles, fertilizers, non-ferrous metals except aluminum and copper, mobile homes, and semi-conductors.

Source: *Economic Report of the President*, February, 1974, p. 91.

Market power held by labor groups may be large and appreciably affect national economic performance. It may help cause a wage-price spiral; it may rigidify labor practices and impede productivity. These would shift the Phillips curve (the unemployment-inflation border) outward. Strikes may reduce output sharply. At the upper end, professional labor services may be misallocated and restricted. These are only possibilities, and there are counterarguments.[19] Yet they stir frequent proposals to restore free competition in labor markets. Since 1955, as the union movement has reached middle age and "stagflation" problems have deepened, the calls to "curb union power" have increased.

Labor monopoly varies greatly in its incidence, forms, and effects. To understand its effects and optimal policy treatment, we need first to analyze how it works.

Labor Markets Differ

Labor, being human, is mortal. This distinguishes it from other forms of market power, since corporations are perpetual and their shareholders' interests are unlimited. By comparison, certain labor interests are temporary and changeable. They are also more specialized, since the personal talents and skills are so disparate.

Labor services also are closely involved with the character of work and of the working of the firm. Much of the effect of labor organization is on the nature, security, and sense of progression in the job, rather than on pay levels. It also touches on the worker's sense of identity and his sharing (if only slightly) in authority. Some labor organizations in fact seek only to change content, rather than wages, salaries, or fees. Therefore labor groups may have large social effects even if they do not affect the price of labor services.

Labor markets differ in no less than six important directions, which together define their structure and importance.

1. *Type of industry.* The range stretches from basic industry over to trade and commerce, finance, utilities, public agencies, and civil service sectors.

2. *Range of skills.* These go upward from raw manual labor to skilled, white-collar, managerial, and professional qualifications.

3. *Geographic scope.* The range is from local hiring points, on up to regional, national, and international scope.

4. *Potential for innovation.* This attribute arises partly from industry type, but it is an important trait on its own. The range is from a high potential for innovation and change in workers' activities, down to zero change in static industries.

5. *Range of buyer types.* The buyers of labor services are of many types. At one extreme is the informed monopsonist (utility, civil service). Intermediate is the partially competitive employer, on roughly equal

---

[19] Instead, it may induce greater effort and willingness to cooperate by workers. It may provide a means for negotiating and speeding change. Or, at the least, it may simply have few effects of any kind on efficiency.

terms with the employee. At the other extreme are customers who are—or can be made to be—inexpert and passive (such as some of those buying medical, legal, and educational services).

6. *Leverage.* Above all, markets differ in the degree of damage which labor sellers can inflict on their customers and others by *striking.* This depends partly on the other five conditions. The range is great: from small specialized groups with virtual life-and-death power over many others, down to large groups with no capability of inflicting damage on anyone but themselves. We will speak of this as leverage. Such leverage is the ratio between (1) the damage which this group can inflict on others and (2) the cost it suffers from taking such actions. Leverage is one element of market power in labor markets.

These conditions determine how much labor market power can be created and how it may affect performance. Unions or other formal bargaining groups are superimposed on these basic conditions, but it is the conditions which largely determine the outcome. There will be large labor sectors where market power in labor services simply cannot be established or—if it does arise formally—will still be inconsequential. And if there are effects, the conditions influence whether they will be socially positive or negative.

Effects

The problem markets are vectors of these conditions, where market power can be formed by combining workers and exerting bargaining power to improve its terms of work. The power and benefits inhere to those who settle the terms of work. The outcome will also depend on the interests advanced by other parties, including employers, customers, third parties who may bring pressure, and, on occasion, various governmental agencies will influence the result.

The economic effects of such power are likely to be:

1. higher payments for labor, and more favorable working conditions,
2. exclusion of nonmembers from at least part of the market,
3. retardation of labor-saving innovation (both autonomous innovation and innovation induced by the increase in labor payments),
4. occasional withdrawal of services from this and other markets (i.e., strikes),
5. ultimately, an increase in the macroeconomic problems of inflation and unemployment,
6. *and,* possibly, deep changes in the content of enterprise activity.

Process. The process is basically simple. A labor group first establishes itself as the exclusive provider of the labor services, by legal or other devices. This involves (1) excluding alternative providers (e.g., doctors excluding osteopaths), and (2) setting controls on entry into its own ranks. The resulting market power is then exerted in a general or specific threat situation. The union seeks changes in the job content and supply-wage terms so as to optimize the total job-related welfare (including income) of its members. The degree of restriction depends on the power to exclude and the relative monopsony power of the customers. Threats to strike or otherwise impede commercial activities may operate implicitly but still have real effect over long periods. An actual strike (or similar punitive action) may be infrequent, no more than is necessary to reaffirm that the threats mean business. Frequency of strikes is an ambiguous signal: it can reflect the application of great power, or it can indicate that implicit threats have not been effective. The strike, after all, is costly to members as well as to others.

Therefore, the costs of labor monopoly divide into two broad classes: (1) restrictions on supply and technical change, and (2) strike-related costs (both the direct damages and the extra costs—e.g., stockpiling, training—which are incurred in order to anticipate and offset strike damages). The range of possible net benefits or costs is wide. Equity and efficiency may both be increased, if members are at below-average income and if membership reduces alienation and increases effort. But they may both be reduced, if members are already at high income levels and if their combined activities cause obstruction and disruption for this and other industries.

This leads one to identify the acutely negative union cases as, primarily those in which (1) members are above-average in initial incomes and opportunity, so that their further gains have a regressive effect, (2) work conditions are made rigid, (3) potential growth and innovation in the industry are high, and so the retardation or distortion of innovation may be large, and/or (4) the leverage or damage inflicted on others by strikes is high. These tend to be certain professional "unions," or specialized workers at upper levels, who can cause whole industries to close down; key unions which can endanger the leading sectors; and major unions which face highly concentrated employers.

Treatment.   The optimal treatment focuses on the problem cases, not on all labor organizations or even just formal ones. Optimal policy is no more to ban all unions than it is to ban all corporations. The union problem arises in upper-level associations, as well as in certain industrial unions. Unions of *lower*-level workers are likely to cause net *benefits* of job content, equity, and—though the answers are still obscure—at least not large efficiency losses. On balance a small loss in efficiency (if any) may be offset by the probable gain in job content and equity. But in the *upper*-level labor groups, the effects are more likely to be negative.[20]

The contrast between actual and imagined costs is especially sharp for declining industries, which often are afflicted by obstructive union behavior. Railroad firemen are regarded as a classic example of this. But their actual market power—and the costs which compensating them outright for job loss would require—are often small and dwindling in comparison to the economy's capacity to compensate them. Their difficult episodes and seeming importance are commonly exaggerated, compared to the quiet functioning of other labor groups.

---

[20] This has long been pointed out by such classical liberal economists as Henry C. Simons, George J. Stigler, Milton Friedman, and Reuben Kessel.

The criteria are too complex to permit a precise listing of the problem cases, but one could in principle identify the more probable cases. In some of these cases, the monopoly is formal and structural; in others, it arises from informal rules and conduct. All of these groups—formal and informal—tend to impair opportunity, by discriminating on racial, sex, and ethnic lines. This one aspect weighs heavily against their possible benefits in other directions of content.

In a larger perspective, the problem may be of limited scope. The older industrial unions may have little real effect on wages (see below). Most cases with tight effects are in utility and public enterprise areas, where there already is a more direct basis for public intervention in case of a crisis. Many of the problem cases are located in the professions and in certain local trades. In most of them, the customers tend to be passive, and there are usually high entrance requirements.

Barriers to Certain Occupations: The Gilds of Today

We can now turn to actual policies. First, we will consider various restrictions on "professional" trades. There are entry barriers, formal rules against competitive practices, and informal limits or behavior. Often this self-regulation is enforced by public power.

Entry into professions affecting public health and safety—medicine, nursing, pharmacy, and the like—has long been regulated by the states. Qualifications have been established, examinations given, and licenses required. Over the years, this form of control has gradually been extended until, today, there are as many as 75 trades where entry is restricted by law. All of the states require licenses of accountants, architects, attorneys, chiropodists, dentists, embalmers, engineers, nurses, optometrists, osteopaths, pharmacists, physicians, teachers, and veterinarians, and most of them license barbers, beauticians, chiropractors, funeral directors, surveyors, and salesmen of insurance and real estate. A number of states also license such tradesmen as plumbers, dry cleaners, horseshoers, tree surgeons, automobile salesmen, and photographers. Altogether, there are more than 1,200 occupational license laws, averaging 25 per state. Every state has at least 10 licensing boards for such trades; some have as many as 45.

Most of these laws have been enacted, not in response to popular demand, but at the behest of organized producer groups. The boards that administer the laws are usually composed predominantly of members of the trades concerned. In some cases, the governor must appoint licensed practitioners; in others, a trade association picks the board. The powers of these bodies differ. Some are advisory: qualifications are established, examinations given, and licenses issued and revoked, in name, at least, by public officials. Others have complete authority. In general, the states exercise little or no control.

Some of these laws are doubtless needed to protect public safety, health, and morals. But many of them are obviously designed to limit competition. And all of them can be diverted to this end. The standards established for admission to a trade may be unnecessarily severe. Extensive educational requirements have been set up for barbers, and ten years of experience or a college degree asked for plumbers. Licensing may be employed as a means of defining the jurisdiction of competing trades. Some states have refused to license drug stores to freeze ice cream or to serve meals. Others have confined the sale of such products as bicarbonate of soda, witch hazel, iodine, and Epsom salts to licensed pharmacists. These statutes, finally, may be used to enforce agreements with respect to price. In Nebraska, under a law enacted in 1937, automobile dealers were licensed, and "willfully or habitually making excessive trade-in allowances" was declared to be a sufficient ground for denying or revoking licenses. In Oklahoma, minimum prices are set for dry cleaners and those who charge less are subject to license revocation, a fine of $500, and imprisonment for 30 days.

Like their predecessors, the medieval gilds, these groups try to close their trades, improve their lot, and perhaps benefit the public. The effects on price are often sharp, as a visit to a barber, a doctor or a lawyer will usually affirm. The public cost often exceeds any possible public gain. The problem is endemic—perhaps epidemic—and it shades over into the restrictive practices of unions for skilled trades.

Labor Unions

Policy toward industrial labor has evolved slowly, but with a shift during the 1930s toward permitting unions. The main events are listed in Table 24–4. Work conditions have been improved and abuses abated, since the 1830s. Government resistance to unions shifted in the 1930s to promotion of unions, under the Wagner Act. This was modified by Taft-

TABLE 24–4
Milestones of Labor Policy

1. Maximum and minimum standards

1842 . . . . Massachusetts child labor law	Maximum 10 hour day for children under 1² years old. Followed by many other states.
1847 . . . . New Hampshire women's labor law	Eventually 43 states.
1877 . . . . Massachusetts safety law	Conditions and inspection.
1938 . . . . Fair Labor Standards Act	Minimum wages (scarcely enforced). Covers about 80 percent of workers.
1945–73 . . . . Fair employment practice laws	Prohibits discrimination. Given strong powers only in 1973.

2. Unions

1842 . . . . Massachusetts decision	Unions not illegal *per se;* but generally restrained by government actions.
1914 . . . . Clayton Act	Strikes are permitted if "peaceable" and "lawful." Nullified by court actions. Does exempt unions from antitrust.
1932 . . . . Norris-LaGuardia Act	Legalized unions.
1935 . . . . National Labor Relations Act (Wagner Act)	Promotes unions; defines their rights and bases.
1940, 1941 . Apex and Hutcheson decisions	Affirm antitrust exemption of unions.
1947 . . . . Taft-Hartley Act	Restricts union controls.
1959 . . . . Landrum-Griffin	Protects against abuses by union officials.

Hartley in 1949 and Landrum-Griffin in 1959. Membership boomed and then, since about 1955, has stabilized. The AFL-CIO has been left by the two largest unions (Teamsters and United Auto Workers). But industry-wide bargaining in certain major industries is a fact of life.

Antitrust Exemption. Legal exemption from antitrust came slowly. The Sherman Act was originally directed toward restraints by industry. But unions were not exempted, and in the Danbury Hatters' case in 1908, the Court awarded damages to an employer who had been injured by a secondary boycott.[21] This led to the inclusion in the Clayton Act of a section providing that unions, as such, shall not "be held or construed to be illegal combinations or conspiracies in restraint of trade."

In subsequent decisions, however, the Court continued to apply the law to union activities, permitting labor organization, strikes, and picketing, but forbidding secondary boycotts,[22] intentional interference with the movement of nonunion goods,[23] and agreement with other groups to control the supplies and the prices of goods and services.[24] But activities not including other groups, following decisions handed down in the Apex case of 1940 and the Hutcheson case in 1941, would now appear to be outside the law. In the Apex case, the Court held that a sitdown strike, involving the seizure of a hosiery plant, destruction of property, and interference with shipments, did not violate the Sherman Act because it did not monopolize the supply or control the price of hosiery.[25] And in the Hutcheson case, where a carpenters' union had gone on strike and conducted a boycott against Anheuser-Busch because the brewing company had employed the members of a machinists' union to install machinery, the Court found that the law did not apply "so long as a union acts in its self-interest and does not combine with non-labor groups."[26]

This position was reaffirmed in the Allen Bradley case in 1945.[27] Here, though the Court upheld the government in condemning a conspiracy involving an electrical workers' union, equipment manufacturers, and contractors, it went on to say that "the same labor union activities may or may not be in violation of the Sherman Act, dependent upon whether the union acts alone or in combination with business groups." The immunity now granted to labor by the law extends beyond the market for labor to the markets for other goods and services. This privilege, denied to business, is not essential to unionization or to collective bargaining.

Where identical terms governing labor costs are written into the contracts that a union signs with competing employers the line between legality and illegality is the same as that in the cases discussed above. If a union, acting independently, undertakes to obtain identical terms in its contracts with each of the firms in an industry, its behavior is legal,

---

[21] *Loewe* v. *Lawlor,* 208 U.S. 274.

[22] *Duplex Printing Press Co.* v. *Deering,* 254 U.S. 443 (1921).

[23] *United Mine Workers* v. *Coronado Coal Co.,* 259 U.S. 344 (1922).

[24] *U.S.* v. *Brims,* 272 U.S. 549 (1926); *Local 167* v. *U.S.,* 291 U.S. 293 (1934); *U.S.* v. *Borden Co.,* 308 U.S. 188 (1939).

[25] *Apex Hosiery Co.* v. *Leader,* 310 U.S. 469.

[26] *U.S.* v. *Hutcheson,* 312 U.S. 219.

[27] *Allen Bradley Co.* v. *Local Union No. 3,* 325 U.S. 797.

whatever the consequences may be. But if it conspires with some firms to impose on others conditions that will make it difficult for them to compete, it will be found to violate the Sherman Act.[28]

Unions in various industries have attempted to make work for their members by adopting practices that have operated to reduce the productivity of labor and thus to increase its cost. First, they have resisted technological innovation, obstructing the adoption of new methods and refusing to work with new tools. Second, unions have limited the amount of work that a man is permitted to do. Third, unions have required the employment of unneeded labor. Fourth, unions have required the performance of unnecessary work. The practices described are confined, in the main, to fields where traditional skills are vulnerable to technical change. They are particularly notorious in railway transport, in building construction, and in printing.[29]

In contrast to these practices, there are ways in which unions make for greater productivity. By giving assurance of security, unions may reduce the need for restrictive practices. By providing machinery for the settlement of grievances, they may improve the worker's morale. By exerting pressure for higher wages, they may stimulate the employer to find new means of increasing efficiency and cutting costs. The net effect of these influences cannot be ascertained. It may be noted, however, that the growth of labor organization has coincided with growth and continuing productivity gains.

Effects. Unions may raise the prices the consumer pays for certain goods and services by restricting competition in product markets and by reducing labor's productivity. They may exert a wider influence by monopolizing labor markets, raising wages, and increasing production costs. What is the probable effect of labor monopoly? In answering this question, a distinction must be made between the cases in which a union bargains with a single firm and those in which it bargains with all of the firms that sell in a common market.

It is generally conceded that the workers employed by a *single* firm should be permitted to organize and to bargain collectively. To the

---

[28] A case involving such a conspiracy came before the Supreme Court in 1965. The United Mine Workers had entered into a contract with the Bituminous Coal Operators Association under which it had accepted mechanization of the mines in return for higher wages and contributions to its welfare fund. It had then insisted, in bargaining with weaker operators, on acceptance of contracts containing identical terms, thus threatening to drive them out of business. One of these operators brought suit for triple damages under the Sherman Act and was awarded $270,000 by a lower court. The Supreme Court, finding that the union and the operators' association had conspired to restrain trade, affirmed the decision. *United Mine Workers* v. *Pennington,* 381 U.S. 657.

[29] Labor practices impairing productivity have been approved, in a number of cases, by the courts. Some of these practices, known as featherbedding, were outlawed by a provision of the Taft-Hartley Act that made it an unfair labor practice to exact payment for services that are not performed. But in a case involving the requirement of a printers' bogus, the Supreme Court held, in 1943, that this provision does not apply to rules requiring work, however unnecessary, as long as the work is actually done. And in cases where union contracts in the construction trades contained clauses prohibiting the use of prefabricated materials, the court held, in 1967, that it was not a violation of the law for the union to go on strike to prevent employers from using such materials or from subcontracting their manufacture to other firms. *American Newspaper Publishers Assn.* v. *NLRB,* 345 U.S. 100. *National Woodwork Manufacturers Assn.* v. *NLRB,* 386 U.S. 612; *Houston Contractors Assn.* v. *NLRB,* 386 U.S. 664.

worker, the job is vital; to the employer, though labor is needed, the individual laborer is not. Without reserves to support him during prolonged negotiations, the worker must shortly come to terms; the employer can better afford to wait. The worker lacks market information and negotiating skill; the employer possesses both. In such a situation, a fair bargain is not to be obtained. It has thus appeared that bargaining power must be equalized.

But a union need not confine itself to bargaining with a single employer; it may bargain with *all* of the companies in an industry. These often criticized as existing where union power, which enhances inflation. But aside from industries that are geographically concentrated or those that are serving purely local markets, multifirm bargaining is not widespread. On a national scale, it is confined to a few such industries as steel and automobiles. Even here, its prohibition would have little effect. The wages set in one union's bargain with Bethlehem would still be the same as those set in another's bargain with U.S. Steel. The wages fixed for General Motors would correspond to those agreed upon by Ford. Indeed, that has occurred. The unions have moved toward selective bargaining with firms, one by one. Yet the final terms are similar. The nationwide pattern of wage rates, in such industries, results less from the form that is taken by bargaining than from the economic forces that underlie it.

Unions, by definition, are monopolies. One would expect this monopoly power of unions to be reflected in the level of wages, but empirical studies of the influence of unions on wages have yielded inconclusive results. Wages in union industries are higher than those in nonunion industries, but the significance of this comparison is obscured by the fact that unions are found in dynamic industries in the North; unorganized workers in traditional industries in the South. When union wages are compared with nonunion wages for workers in the same occupation, industry, and region, it is found that union wages generally are higher, but they are not invariably so, and the difference is slight. When the size of wage increases in union and nonunion industries is compared, it appears that increases received by union members are not much larger than those received by nonunionists. Some unions, in particular fields, have made extraordinary gains. This is true in building construction and in trucking, where the unions are large and powerful and the employers, by comparison, small and weak. It is true in such large-scale manufacturing industries as steel and automobiles, where the unions are strong enough to exact a share in the profits of oligopoly. But for unions in general, the measurable gains are small.[30]

The process of collective bargaining may well create the impression that union gains are greater than is actually the case. In the very nature of the process, the extent of disagreement between the union and the employer is exaggerated. The final bargain may set a wage no higher

---

[30] See H. Gregg Lewis, *Unionism and Relative Wages in the United States* (Chicago: University of Chicago Press, 1963), chaps. III and IV; and Frank C. Pierson, *Unions in Postwar America* (New York: Random House, 1967), chaps. III, IV, and V.

than would be obtained if the market were competitive. But it exceeds the employer's offer and enables the union to claim a victory.

There are limits, in the market, to union power. If union wages are raised too far above nonunion wages, nonunion firms may appear and grow. If wages in general are pushed too high, employers may substitute machinery. If wages and prices are raised too far, sales may fall off. If profits are cut too much, investment may decline. The consequence of higher wages may be lower employment.

Some critics of unions charge them with a major part of the blame for continued inflation. Wages, they point out, have risen more rapidly than the productivity of labor. Labor costs per unit of output have thus been increased, and the prices of products have had to be raised to cover their higher costs. In a business recession, it is said, employers resist the efforts of unions to increase wages. But during prosperity, they do not. To maintain profits, they must maintain production. To maintain production, they must accede to labor's demands. Higher wages are the cause; higher prices are the effect.

But labor does not always get higher wages simply because it wants them. It also gets them because demand is strong. In some fields, where unions are powerful, wages have risen even though demand is weak. But in others, where demand is strong, wages have risen even though labor is unorganized. In the first case, the cause of inflation is the push of cost. In the second, it is the pull of demand. For business in general, both factors are likely to be present, exerting their pressure in the same direction at the same time.

Unions, by demanding higher wages, do make some contribution to inflation. But this is not its only or its major cause. Of greater importance are the factors that sustain demand. Foremost among them are the nation's commitment to maintain full employment and the direction of monetary and fiscal policies toward that end. In the political struggles that led to the adoption of this commitment labor played a leading role. But the more direct role of unions in stagflation is probably limited.

CHAPTER TWENTY-FIVE

Promotion and Subsidies

A subsidy is the opposite of a policy constraint. Rather than limit a firm's profit opportunities, subsidies increase them (recall Figure 1–2). Subsidies and promotion take many forms, under four main categories: direct payments, tax forgiveness, risk-absorption, and various promotional devices. We will look mainly at subsidies to firms. They often relate closely to the structure and performance of industries. Some yield high benefits, while others are pathologically costly. They sprout, grow, and persist in all manner of markets, often independently of their social value.

The subsidies—and the terms upon which they are provided— reflect endless ingenuity and political effort. They touch nearly every market, and in some cases they sustain whole sectors. The total is large and deeply woven into the industrial fabric.

We first summarize their scope and properties, and next consider their economic merits. Then separate sections are devoted to agriculture, consumer protection, maritime subsidies, and multinational firms.

SCOPE AND VARIETY

The nation has subsidized a variety of private enterprises throughout its history, and the totals continue to grow.[1] The flow of federal subsidies is now deep and diverse (see Table 25–1). A large share goes to specific firms and industries. The precise extent cannot be defined, because many consumption subsidies are indirect subsidies to the suppliers of the service. Also Table 25–1 omits many subsidies given when public agencies pay extra-high prices or provide items at prices below costs.

Some subsidies are direct and visible; others are indirect and hidden. In the former cases, government has made outright gifts: grants of public lands or payments from the treasury. More often, it has given aid in less

---

[1] A superb source on the nature and scope of subsidies is U.S. Joint Economic Committee, *The Economists of Federal Subsidy Programs,* 92d Cong., 1st sess. (Washington, D.C.: U.S. Government Printing Office, 1972).

TABLE 25-1

Gross Budgetary Costs of Selected Major U.S. Federal Subsidies, 1971 ($ millions)

Category	Cash Payments	Tax Subsidies	Credit Subsidies	Benefits in Kind	Total
Total, all major subsidies..............	11,801	38,480	4,183	9,245	63,70
Agriculture........................	3,879	880	443	1,109	6,31
Medical care.......................	973	3,150	52	4,617	8,79
Medicare.......................	0	0	0	1,979	
Medicaid.......................	0	0	0	2,638	
Education.........................	1,976	785	434	409	3,60
Loans...........................	0	0	301	0	
International trade.................	106	420	623	34	1,18
Export financing.................	106	0	394	0	
Housing..........................	195	5,680	2,550	0	8,42
Commerce and development	2,041	15,635	59	1,518	19,25
Postal...........................	0	0	0	1,510	
Transport	300	10	0	362	67
Maritime.......................	262	10	0	0	
Air transport	38	0	0	229	

Source: Adapted from Joint Economic Committee, *The Economics of Federal Subsidy Programs,* 92d Congress, session (Washington, D.C.: U.S. Government Printing Office, 1972) as are Tables 25–2 to 25–5 also.

open ways: by rendering services for which it makes no charge, by selling goods and services for less than they are worth, by buying goods and services for more than they are worth, and by exempting some enterprises from taxes that others must pay. In all of these cases, the cost of the subsidy has been born, in the end, by the taxpayer. Acting indirectly, government has subsidized enterprise by sheltering it from the full force of competition and by granting it the privilege of uncontrolled monopoly.

TABLE 25-2

Selected Federal Cash Payment Subsidies, 1971

Program	1971 (estimated) ($ million)
Agriculture:	
Direct payments for commodity purchases	316
Feed grain production production stabilization	1,510
Sugar production stabilization...............................	84
Wheat production stabilization	891
Wool and mohair payments.................................	72
Cotton production stabilization..............................	918
Medical care:	
Health manpower training.....................	299
Health facilities construction grants...........................	170
Health professions facilities construction	144
International trade:	
Export payments...	166
Transportation:	
Air carrier payments	57
Operating differential subsidies..............................	224
Construction differential subsidies	238

TABLE 25–3
Selected Federal Tax Subsidies

Program	1971 ($ million)
Agriculture:	
Expensing and capital gains for farming.	820
International Trade:	
Western Hemisphere trade corporations	50
Exclusion of gross-up on dividends of less-developed-.	
country corporations	55
Deferral of foreign subsidiary income.	165
Natural resources:	
Capital gains treatment for cutting timber	130
Expensing of mineral exploration and development costs.	325
Excess of percentage over cost depletion.	980
Transportation:	
Deferral of tax on shipping companies.	10
Rail freight car amortization	105
Commerce and economic development:	
Excess bad debt reserves of financial institutions.	380
Expensing of research and development expenditures.	540
Corporate surtax exemption.	2,000
Exclusion of interest on life insurance savings	1,050

And here, the cost of the subsidy has been borne by the consumer in higher prices.

Direct payments occur in cash and in kind. The recipients often prefer indirect payments, which are less visible, harder to evaluate, and less liable to be stopped. Both kinds are shown in Table 25–2.

Tax subsidies occur for special exceptions from general tax burdens. They are for a variety of stated purposes, those for oil being perhaps the steepest. Table 25–3 shows some of them.

Tax subsidies also have a marked incidence among corporations. The standard corporation tax rate was about 50 percent in 1970–72. Yet many large industrial firms (especially in oil and steel) have effective tax rates well below that, with some at zero. Much of this arises from special minerals industry tax laws, and from the treatment of profits from operations abroad.[2] At any rate, the effects of tax forgiveness on corporate profits, on resource allocation, and on the market positions of leading firms, are not small.

Risk absorption is another indirect form of subsidy. It is focused in housing, agriculture, and foreign trade (see Table 25–4).

---

[2] The favorite of the tax law is the mining industry. Not only may mining companies deduct the costs of exploration and development—successful and unsuccessful, tangible and intangible—as current expenses in computing taxable income. They are also given the option of making arbitrary deductions, up to half of net income, for depletion of wasting assets (at rates that have run from 5 percent of gross income for coal, sand, gravel, stone, and oyster shells through 15 percent for the metals and 23 percent for sulfur and bauxite to $27^{1}/2$ percent—now 22 percent—for oil and gas) instead of deducting the depletion that actually occurs. The depletion allowance, moreover, may be deducted year after year even though every dollar invested in the property has long since been written off. The arrangement has reduced federal tax revenue by $1.5 billion per year. Yet many low-tax firms are not minerals based; of the largest 40 firms, 11 nonminerals firms had tax rates below 30 percent in 1970–71.

TABLE 25–4
Selected Federal Credit Subsidies, Fiscal 1971 ($ million)

Program	Gross Outlays	Subsidy Costs
Agriculture:		
Soil and water loans...........................	65	17
Rural electrification loans.......................	362	179
Rural telephone loans..........................	135	67
Price support loans............................	2,338	87
Farm ownership loans..........................	256	68
International trade:		
Development loans, revolving fund...............	560	320
Foreign military credit sales.....................	93	6
Public Law 480................................	494	226
Export financing—direct loans and participation		
financing....................................	1,569	65
Housing:		
Interest subsidy for home-ownership assistance.......		426
Interest subsidy for rental assistance...............		790
Below-market-interest-rate loans on multifamily		
dwellings....................................		69
Rural housing insurance.........................		118
Housing for elderly and handicapped people.........	106	53
Low-rent public housing.........................		1,064
Commerce and economic development:		
Disaster loan fund..............................	91	19
Development company loans......................	47	6
Small business loans............................	84	6
Small business investment company loans...........	56	1
Economic opportunity loans......................	35	1

Other *promotional devices* are numerous. Some (official cartels, mail, and nuclear-power subsidies) have been analyzed in earlier chapters. Others involve direct programs by agencies promoting growth, employment and the like (see Table 25–5).

We now consider a variety of actual subsidies, to give more concrete detail.

Free Services. Governments gives out vast amounts of free data. They are the principle source of the statistical reports that are used by businessmen in their daily operations. The *Statistical Abstract of the United States,* its annual issue running to nearly a thousand pages of fine type, serves as little more than an index to the vast quantities of statistics that are prepared, analyzed, and published by scores of agencies.[3] Many of these are of use only to specific trades and firms.

Sales at low prices. Such sales are common. During the 19th century, valuable mining and timberlands were sold for a song. Merchant ships built by the government during the two world wars were subsequently

---

[3] Special studies, covering many phases of business activity, are listed in each number of the *Monthly Catalogue of Government Documents.* Maps, charts, and other aids to navigation are published by the Coast and Geodetic Survey. Estimates of prospective crops are released by the Crop Reporting Service. And weather forecasts—of great importance not only to

TABLE 25–5
Selected Federal Benefit-in-kind Subsidies

Program	1971 ($ million)
Food:	
School lunch	581
Food stamps	1,369
School milk program	103
Commodity distribution	513
Medical care:	
Health insurance for the aged (Medicare)	2,070
Medical assistance program (Medicaid)	3,110
Education:	
Surplus property utilization	426
International trade:	
International trade and development policy	23
Foreign market development and promotion	17
Natural resources:	
State and private forestry cooperation	28
Watershed works of improvement	78
Rural water and waste disposal systems	40
Basic water and sewer facility grants	150
Construction grants for wastewater treatment works	1,200
Transportation:	
Airport development aid program	170
The Federal airways system	174
Urban mass transportation grants	270
National rail passenger corporation	40
Commerce and economic development:	
Postal service	900
Government-owned property	2,400
Sales to domestic ship scrappers	100

sold to private operators at a fraction of their cost. After World War II, other property that had cost the government $15 billion was sold by the War Assets Administration for $4 billion. In the case of iron and steel, 116 units costing $750 million went for $260 million, or about 35 cents on the dollar. In disposing of surplus materials, the emphasis was on speed, not price. Airplanes were sold for less than the value of the gasoline left in their tanks, and brand-new machinery, never uncrated, was sold for scrap. Great amounts of surplus military material are routinely disposed of at extremely low prices, under conditions that invite corruption.

So, too, with the sale of public services. When government engages in lending, guaranteeing, and insuring operations, the fees it charges fre-

agriculture but also to shipping, aviation, and other businesses—are issued daily by the Weather Bureau.

Government also carries on research and releases its findings for commercial use. The Geological Survey and the Bureau of Mines, the Forest Service, and the Fish and Wildlife Service, together with similar agencies in many states, function in effect as laboratories for the mining, lumbering, and fishing industries. The Tennessee Valley Authority has developed new chemical fertilizers and given its formulas to the fertilizer industry. The National Bureau of Standards engages in physical research, conducts tests, and establishes industrial standards when requested to do so by two-thirds of the members of a trade.

quently fail to cover its total costs, the administration of such programs being financed by the taxpayers.[4]

High Prices. Purchases at high prices are endemic in military procurement (see Chapter 29). Stock-piling of strategic materials also involves a degree of subsidy. For example, in 1965, these stockpiles consisted of 76 commodities, ranging from asbestos to zirconium and including goose feathers and castor oil, many of them bought in quantities well in excess of probable needs. Holdings acquired at a cost of $8.5 billion were then valued at $7.8 billion, representing a paper loss of $700 million.

Transportation. This has been perhaps the most heavily subsidized of all sectors. American railroads, during the 19th century, were the recipients of grants amounting to 183 million acres of public lands, some of them valuable mining and timber properties. They were also aided by cash contributions, by tax exemptions, and by governmental subscriptions to their securities. Altogether, the aid extended to railroads by federal, state, and local governments is said to have amounted to $1,282 million. As a result, the railroad network was extended and the West opened to development more rapidly than it would have been by private enterprise alone. Though government traffic was later carried at lower rates, this offsetting subsidy was much smaller than the original subsidies (with their accrued value over time.).

Since 1950, programs to rescue passenger service have been subsidized. And since 1970, Amtrak has been subsidized at over $100 million per year ($200 million in 1974–75). From 1940 to 1974, the federal government spent more than $100 billion on highways, waterways, and airways, more than half of it on highways. For 1971, the federal expenditure on highways, matched in part by the states, reached $4.5 billion. In the beginning, all motor traffic was subsidized. But for many years the taxes imposed on highway users have sufficed to cover highway costs. The burden, however, has been distributed unequally. Passenger cars were long required to pay more and trucks less than their proper share of these costs. As a result, the trucking industry was subsidized.

Commercial aviation is also subsidized in a number of ways (recall Chapter 17). Also, the ill-fated supersonic plane project cost over $1 billion before it was stopped in 1972. The British-French Concorde project has swollen to a severe subsidy burden, with no end in sight. The U.S. version would inexorably have piled operating and purchase subsidies upon development subsidies, towards $10 billion and more.

Maritime subsidies are of two kinds: (1) shipbuilding and (2) shipping

---

[4] Government has subsidized private forestry, not only by supporting research and education, but also by providing it with fire protection, with planting stock, and with technical assistance for less than cost. Government has subsidized the livestock industries by permitting sheep and cattle to graze in national forests and on other public lands for fees below those charged on private ranges. It has subsidized advertisers and the publishers of newspapers and magazines by delivering their products at a loss. In 1970, for instance, the subsidy involved was more than $545 million. In the postman's bag are pounds of periodicals that denounce the government for paying subsidies, but not (it may be assumed) for subsidizing publishers.

(see the special section below). *Atomic power* has been deeply subsidized (recall Chapter 21). Government has put over $3 billion into research. In a few cases, it contributed to the cost of building the reactors. In every case, it supplied atomic fuel at a rental charge so low as to involve a subsidy. A further subsidy may have been hidden in the price it paid for

Courtesy: Rolls Royce

R.B. 211 engines being made at the Rolls-Royce factory in Derby, England, for use in Lockheed TriStar airliners. Despite British government subsidies, the engine's cost over-runs put Rolls-Royce in bankruptcy and under public ownership in 1971 (the car operations remain private). Lockheed was forced to seek a $250 million loan guarantee from the U.S. Government to stave off bankruptcy. The engines, and planes, were still being produced in 1975. (Try to pin down who has paid the subsidies and who gets the benefits. Is this fair? Is it efficient?)

by-product plutonium. The cost of insurance against catastrophic accidents, finally, was largely borne by the government.

Oil. The oil industry has vied with agriculture as the most heavily subsidized industry in recent years (see also Chapter 26). During 1959–73 the subsidies were over $6 billion yearly, and the industry also has been partially exempt from antitrust. Only the onset of the energy crisis, with sharp rises in oil prices and profits, during 1973–74 has superseded some of these subsidies.

Housing. Housing is subsidized by a brace of credit-insuring agencies (recall Chapter 19). This has appreciably raised the level of home-owning and of housing construction.

Subsidies are a way of life for many private firms and consumers. (Try to identify five subsidies which you receive, directly or indirectly. And Try to find a firm among the largest 25 that does not receive some appreciable subsidy.)

ECONOMIC ISSUES

Which of them are optimal? They all arise from the real political process (recall Chapter 4), and so one may expect many of them to be inefficient, or inequitable, or both. They may also have side effects, depending on their forms and conditions. Often their purposes bear little relation to their reality and effects.

The political efforts to gain subsidies go on continually. They usually involve focused interest groups which have large individual stakes. They are limited by the claims of other groups and by the general scarcity of public resources. The outcome reflects the underlying pattern of interests and power. Rarely are full, explicit data on costs and benefits used in settling subsidies. Continuity and inertia are also important. Once begun, subsidies become part of the structure of values and expectations; to stop them usually requires an affirmative act. Investments, workers' lives, locales, managers' ambitions and other interests all come to rely on the subsidy.

Performance. The economic performance of a subsidy obviously turns on the allocative value of its effects, and on the fairness of its incidence (recall Chapter 3). These often hinge in turn on several technical features, especially openness, permanence, financing, specific duties, incidence, and incentives. *Open subsidies* are more likely to be known and screened adequately. Hidden subsidies (which the recipients naturally prefer) are likely to grow and persist without a fair appraisal.

Temporary subsidies are preferable to open-ended or permanent ones. The social need is usually temporary, and so the burden of proof properly goes against continuance. Renewal procedures should involve a genuine reappraisal: this requires independence and staff resources. *Financing* by taxes rather than higher consumer prices is preferable. Price-raising usually has a regressive incidence. Taxes can be arranged to fit ability to pay. *Specific duties* are often required of the recipients. These limit the net giveaway and provide a basis for monitoring the value of the subsidy. Simple grants to categories of recipients tend to lack constraints on the amounts taken and the ease of abuse.

Incidence among firms also can be important. Subsidies can favor firms against their competitors and potential competitors. Where dominant firms gain subsidies, the entrenching effect can deeply affect structure and performance. This effect needs to be anticipated carefully in designing subsidies, for the tendency to favor the established firms is a general one.

Finally, *incentives* are often critical. Since they come, not from the market, but from the public purse, they may divert the attention of managements from the cultivation of customers to the cultivation of Congressmen. Being paid, in general, when losses are incurred and not when profits are shown, they reward incompetence and penalize efficiency. Instead of encouraging the producer to stand on his own feet, they invite him to lean upon the state. Rather than progress, they make for lethargy.

Subsidies commonly chill incentives, by rewarding recipients for staying in the subsidized condition. Incentives for efficiency can be built in, by hinging payments on specific actions, on performance criteria, or on a sharing of cost reductions. The problem has analogies in regulation (recall Chapters 13 and 14) and other policies (especially weapons buying, Chapter 29). Every subsidy does apply a set of incentives: the question is whether they will be optimal or distorted.

Ideally, the subsidy's purpose will be clearly identified, and the likely direct and indirect effects of the subsidy will be known. Next, an optimal incentive structure is derived, to fit the criteria. Then the best level and design of the subsidy can be set, in open/and full discussion. The optimal incentives will often be complex, to induce specific actions, to avoid fostering inefficiency, and to phase out the subsidy in good time unless the burden of proof for continuance is fully met.

These attributes can be compared with actual subsidies, in this chapter and elsewhere in the book. The endless effort to minimize inefficient subsidies deals both in technical features and in the realities of political life.

AGRICULTURE

Government, in the United States, has aided agriculture for a century and more. Since the 1930s, its assistance has taken the form, in part, of cash payments from the Treasury: payments to producers of particular crops such as sugar and wool, and payments to farmers in general for retiring acreage, restricting output, and using soil-conserving practices. It has also taken the form, in larger part, of measures designed to raise the prices of the things the farmer sells. This has been done, as we have seen, by making loans and purchases, by restricting imports and by subsidizing exports, by curtailing the quantities produced, and by imposing controls on marketing. Public expenditures on such programs have run to more than $5 billion a year. But this is not all: government has also extended aid in other ways. It has supplied free land and services, financed educational research and education, provided water for irrigation, increased the supply of credit, promoted rural electrification, insured crops, and ameliorated rural poverty. Expenditures on these activities have approached another $1 billion a year.

The quantum rise in agricultural prices during 1972–74 suggested that some restrictive policies and subsidies might now end. But the basic pattern is more likely to continue. And even if price-raising policies were abolished, other large subsidies would continue or grow. Therefore we will look in detail at the whole set of farm policies.[5]

---

[5] For a basic review, see Geoffrey S. Shepherd, *Farm Policy: New Directions* (Ames, Iowa: Iowa State University Press, 1964).

Migration. The larger setting is the long-term migration from farms to town, as farm efficiency rose and the economy became industrialized (see Figure 25–1). This shrinkage continues, but it has a complex pattern among regions, age groups, and racial types. The political structure also favors subsidies, since the rural districts have been over-represented. There are also the old-time values and images of rural life as wholesome and upright.

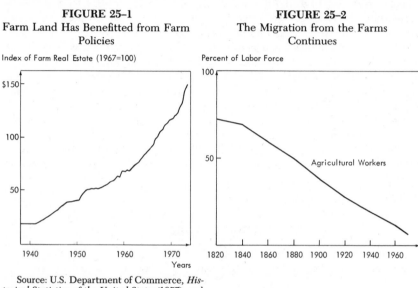

FIGURE 25–1

Farm Land Has Benefitted from Farm Policies

FIGURE 25–2

The Migration from the Farms Continues

Index of Farm Real Estate (1967=100)

Percent of Labor Force

Source: U.S. Department of Commerce, *Historical Statistics of the United States* (1957), and *Statistical Abstract* (1973).

The main present programs were set during 1920–40, when fluctuations bankrupted farmers by the millions and crop failures caused desperate farm poverty.[6] Yet farming includes many radically differing parts, by crops, regions, size, riskiness, etc. Moreover, it is increasingly integrated with world markets and their instabilities. The byzantine complexity of farm programs reflects all of these background factors.

Supply and Demand. The basic economic fact is that short-run demand and supply are *inelastic* for many farm products. Therefore, small

---

[6] The two decades before World War I were a golden era for American agriculture. Markets grew as industry expanded. On the farms, prices and incomes rose. Prosperity was sustained, uninterrupted, for the longest period the farmer had ever known. With the outbreak of war, production of foodstuffs in Western Europe suffered, and supplies from the Argentine and Australia were cut off by a shortage of shipping. The United States was called upon to feed her allies. Farm prices rose sharply, farm output was expanded, and farm debt grew, as new acres were bought on credit and the prices of crops were capitalized in the price of land. When the war ended, the farms of Europe came back into production and shipments from Argentina and Australia were resumed. Markets disappeared and prices dropped.

American agriculture did not participate in the prosperity that followed the war. And when the Great Depression struck, agriculture went from bad to worse. Demand at home collapsed, and prices continued to fall. The cash income of farmers dropped from $11 billion in 1929 to $5 billion in 1933. Farm wages sank to 10 cents per hour or a dollar a day, if one could find work at all.

shifts cause big price jumps, sharper than most other economic groups have to face. There is a strong case for insulating farmers from severe jolts, but their income depends on farm prices *and* other factors:

$$\text{Net Farm Income} = \text{Revenues} - \text{Costs}$$
$$= \Sigma \, P_i \cdot Q_i - \Sigma \, P_n \cdot Q_n$$
$$\underset{\text{Outputs}}{} \qquad \underset{\text{Inputs}}{}$$

and the rate of return for farming is

$$\text{Rate of Return} = \frac{\underset{\text{Outputs}}{P_i \cdot Q_i} - \underset{\text{Inputs}}{P_n \cdot Q_n}}{\text{Capital Invested}}$$

Farmers have to make complex speculative decisions, involving production techniques, future prices, costs of capital, weather risks, and public policies. A high order of skill is needed in several fields, plus a large chunk of capital (on the order of $500,000 in average grain-belt farms).

The long-trend rise of productivity for agriculture has been remarkable rapid and sustained. This reflects the creation of massive agricultural investment down the decades, plus a genuinely high technological opportunity in the sector. With newer hybrid strains, breeds of livestock, methods of crop rotation, fertilizers, insecticides, and equipment types, the potential for rising farm productivity has been very great indeed. Yields per acre and per worker have doubled and redoubled. In 1940 a farmer fed 10 people; now he feeds over 40.

This has operated to raise the capital invested in farming, to reduce the labor inputs required, and constrain the long-term rise of farm prices. In this context, the trends and configurations of farm incomes —on a per-farmer basis—have been the vector of several powerful forces working through the basic economic equations. The level of farm output prices is only one determinant of farm income. Yet farm policy has focused on it.

Farmers have always seen themselves as victims. Their incomes are below average. They buy from industrial suppliers (of equipment, construction, gasoline, mortgage credit, etc.) who can add in a margin of monopoly profit. But they must sell on purely competitive markets, where no such profit arises. This injustice is aggravated by the demands of new technology, which require ever larger scale and investment (and debt). And his income fluctuates from year to year as weather, the economy, and other factors shift.

Yet this view oversimplifies. Many markets they buy in are reasonably competitive. Where they are not, it would be better to make them so rather than monopolize farming. The key point is that incomes differ sharply among farmers.

Scope. Farming includes those who raise feed grains and livestock in the Corn Belt, wheat on the Great Plains, cotton and tobacco in the South, and range livestock in the Southwest. It covers the dairy farms of New England, the Middle Atlantic, and the Lake States; the citrus groves of Florida and California; and the apple orchards of Virginia and Washington. It includes the producers of ducks on Long Island, sugar cane in

Louisiana, and tree nuts on the Pacific Coast. With 200 different products, grown under widely differing conditions, there is no such thing, in actuality, as a typical farmer or an average farm.

Two-thirds of all farms, or about 2 million, are operated by their owners, three-fifths of them debt-free, two-fifths encumbered with mortgages. One-fifth, or more than 500,000, are operated by tenants, rents being paid by some of them in cash, by others in shares of agricultural products. This group is divided, in turn, into those who have their own equipment and plan their own operations and others, called sharecroppers, numbering 250,000, who contribute nothing but their labor and are paid not in wages but in shares of the crop.

A few thousand farms are operated by salaried managers. The great majority are family farms. A family farm is usually defined as an enterprise of such size that it can be financed, managed, and operated, with little or no hired help, by a farmer and the members of his family. Here, the farmer is owner, manager, and worker, his residence is both a home and an office, his wife and children are partners and fellow laborers. His income from farming and other sources may go into a common pool; his operating costs and his living expenses may be met from the same account. The family farm thus differs in character from other businesses. It combines a productive enterprise with a mode of life.

As farms are defined by the Census, they include suburban homes whose occupants have industrial employment and do a little farming on the side and farms occupied by aged owners who are in semiretirement. More than a third of the 3 million farms in the country fall into this category, their operations being part-time or nominal. When these are subtracted, there remain 2 million full-time farms. In this group, however, there are more than 500,000 farms that afford little more than subsistence to the farmer and his family. This leaves around 1,500,000 commercial farms. And of these, three-fifths account for nine-tenths of agricultural output. This is commercial agriculture. And it is to serve the interests of commercial agriculture that price and production legislation has been deviseed.

There are pockets of rural poverty, especially among the smaller, part-time, and subsistence farmers. But among normal-sized and larger farms, farmers' real incomes are equal or much higher than the averages elsewhere. Also, farmers make capital gains as the value of their holdings rises (farm land prices have tripled in the last 20 years). But these are not included in farm income statistics.

In short, rural poverty is a genuine problem, scattered in a number of states and lines of farming. But it is quite distinct from the mainstream of commercial farming, where the only legitimate social issue is short-run instability.

In this perspective, farm programs have had three directions: (1) stabilizing farm prices in the short-run, (2) raising farm prices in the long-run, and (3) directly subsidizing specific parts of farming. They have been highly complex and, in many ways, drastically inefficient and inequitable. They are the classic instance of competitive markets being controlled along monopoly lines, for purposes which could be met by direct policies at a tiny fraction of the present costs.

Stabilizing Prices. As Table 25–6 shows, the stabilizing effort really began in 1933–38. At that point, stabilizing was integral with raising farm prices. By 1938, prices were being supported as well as smoothed, and that has continued down to the present (see below). Stabilizing is provided both by (1) price supports, which set a guaranteed price for the coming year, and (2) various insurance and lending programs. The CCC has provided storage space and services on a large scale, so as to smooth fluctuations as well as to maintain price levels.

TABLE 25–6
Milestones of Farm Policy

1921–22..........	Tariffs on agricultural imports; ineffective.
1929–31..........	Federal Farm Board, with $500 to stabilize prices; swamped by the collapse of farm prices.
1933–36..........	Agriculture Adjustment Act, to restore farm price parity on seven "basic" products (wheat, cotton, corn, hogs, rice, tobacco, milk). Commodity Credit Corporation created to channel loans; acreage is restricted.
1938.............	Second AAA makes controls and price supports permanent.
1940–45..........	World War II restores farm prosperity.
1945–72..........	Prices supported near parity. Surplus grows, despite various acreage restrictions. Calls for abolition of controls have little effect.
1972–............	Worldwide food and commodity scarcities elevate prices, render most controls superfluous. Payments shift toward a direct basis, but basic control apparatus remains.

Price Supports. By 1938, the price support program was firmly in place. World War II restored farm prosperity, but parity and price supports had taken root. Coverage included scores of crops and livestock. Parity was the criterion for settling price floors. The formula has evolved, but the basic idea is the same; that farm output prices should not decline relative to farm input prices. It is managed by the Department of Agriculture, in ways which naturally benefit farmers.[7]

---

[7] The process involved in computing a parity price may be illustrated by showing how such a price was determined for hogs, per 100 pounds, in January, 1958:

a.	Determine the average price received by farmers for the commodity during the preceding 10 years. For hogs, this was...................	$18.90
b.	Compute an index of the average prices received by farmers for all agricultural commodities during the same 10 years, using the prices received in 1909–14 as 100. In January, 1958, this index stood at	262
c.	Divide (*a*) by (*b*). This gives an "adjusted base price" for hogs of	$7.21
d.	Compute an index of prices paid by farmers, taking those paid in 1909–14 as 100. In January, 1958, this index stood at........................	301
e.	Multiply (*c*) by (*d*) and divide by 100. The parity price for hogs is	$21.70

Parity, or $21.70, was the price to which the farmer was held to be justly entitled. Support prices, however, were set at less than parity. If fixed, in this case, at 80 percent, the price would be $17.36.

Parity price is said to be a "just" price. But, at best, the figure rests on fallible human judgment. And, at worst, it is subject to deliberate manipulation. Parity can be raised by shifting the base date from 1909–14 to some other period when price relationships were more favorable, and this has been done in the case of certain commodities. It can be raised by boosting the index of prices paid, and this was done when Congress required, at one time or another, that interest, taxes, freight rates, and wages be added. Before 1950, this index included 170 commodities used in farm production and in farm family living. Since then, it has included some 340. Each of these commodities is given a weight in making the computation. The index of prices received has included 52 agricultural commodities, each of which is given its own weight. The height of a parity price is influenced by the items chosen for inclusion in these indexes and by the weights assigned them. These decisions are made by the statisticians of the Department of Agriculture.

Since World War II, prices have usually been pegged at 75 to 90 percent of parity. Some 200 different commodities are produced on American farms. Of these, only six—wheat, corn, cotton, tobacco, rice, and peanuts—are designated as "basic" and these, together with certain nonbasic products, receive supports. The supported commodities accounted for 42 percent of farm market sales in 1967; the nonsupported commodities for 58 percent.

With prices supported, surpluses resulted. These have been stored, in amounts which had grown mountainous by the 1960s, costing $3 billion yearly.[8] Surplus disposal became a major problem. Large amounts have been dumped abroad, as part of foreign aid. This harms foreign farmers, of course, and invites retaliation, and so ingenious ways to present it as disaster relief and soft-currency sales have been used.

Surpluses are also dumped at home. School lunch programs subsidize 20 million school children, mainly from poor families. Various welfare distributions occur, through institutions and a food stamp plan. Much of this simply replaces food that would have been bought commercially. Therefore it has reduced the surpluses only marginally, while costing nearly $4 billion yearly.

Production controls therefore became critical. First, farmers were limited by average. But farmers naturally used their best acres and cultivated them more intensively. Output was scarcely reduced.[9] Output controls would be technically more effective for each crop, but they would also be costly.[10]

---

[8] The CCC has had its own storage bins. It has rented commercial warehouse space. It permits the farmer to store commodities on the farm, sending its inspectors to seal his bins and cribs. With other facilities exhausted, it has stored millions of bushels of wheat in unused airplane hangars, in abandoned movie theaters, and in the holds of hundreds of merchant ships riding at anchor on Puget Sound and on the Columbia River, the Hudson, and the James. Its storage costs alone have run to a million dollars a day.

[9] From 1953 to 1963, a cut of 33 percent in acres planted caused a drop of only 3 percent in the output of wheat; a cut of 45 percent in acres caused a drop of only 6 percent in the output of cotton; a cut of 40 percent in acres failed to change the output of tobacco; a cut of 14 percent in acres was followed by an increase of 42 percent in the output of corn.

[10] Tight controls, effectively enforced, would reduce the costs involved in acquiring, transporting, storing, and selling surplus commodities. They would lessen the international prob-

"The guvament paid me $132,000 fo' mah non-cotton crop. How'd you make out with youah non-soybeans?"

Copyright © 1969 courtesy of Wil-Jo Associates, Inc. and Bill Mauldin.

There have also been programs to retire land entirely. During the 30s, the government purchased and retired 12 million acres of marginal farm lands. The effect of this operation on agricultural output was imperceptible. A second land retirement effort was made under the Soil Bank Act of 1956. Under this law, the government offered to make rental payments to farmers who would enter into contracts to take land out of production. These payments covered the farmer's normal profit on the acres under contract, an incentive bonus, and the cost of conservation practices. The law set up two programs: an acreage reserve and a conservation reserve.

The acreage reserve was an emergency program designed to reduce surpluses of basic crops by making one-year contracts to retire the land on which they were produced. More than 21 million acres were placed

---

lems that are created by dumping surpluses abroad. They would reduce the burden that price supports impose upon the taxpayer. But they would not lessen the consumer's load. They would make for rigidity in the allocation of resources, obstructing adjustment to changes in demand and cost. If the output of one crop were successfully curtailed, the farmer would use his land and labor to produce another. New surpluses would appear, and these, in turn, would have to be controlled. The process could logically end, in the phrase of Henry A. Wallace, only when every plowed field had its permit sticking to its post.

in this reserve in 1957. But reduction in acres was offset, in large measure, by increases in yields. Save for corn, however, the program succeeded in effecting a moderate reduction in the output of basic crops. It did so at great expense. Payments amounted to more than $600 million in 1957 and nearly $700 million in 1958. In a few cases, the rents paid to farmers were very large. There were 67 who collected more than $50,000 each, two of them more than $270,000 each. In 1957, Congress put a limit of $30,000 on individual payments. As a result, in 1958, many of the larger farmers failed to renew their contracts. The acreage reserve was discontinued.

The conservation reserve was a long-run program designed to retire land from crop production under 3- to 15-year contracts, putting it into grass, trees, and water storage. Here, the contracts covered retirement of whole farms as well as parts of farms. By 1960, nearly 29 million acres, about 6 percent of the country's plowland, had been placed in this reserve. Retirement of whole farms under the program evoked the opposition of merchants and townspeople in rural communities, who saw in it a threat to the basis of their livelihood. Their fears were shared by their Congressmen. The government's authority to write new land retirement contracts was terminated. The effect of the conservation reserve on agricultural output is not known.

Land retirement is popular with farmers; it is easier to administer than production controls; it costs less than price supports. But the undertaking has serious disadvantages. Like the other indirect methods of reducing farm productivity, it is costly, inefficient, and inequitable.[11]

The price-support program has been riddled with inconsistencies and costly effects. It has been based on statistical deceptions about low farm incomes. The aim of fixing farmers' income at a prior level has little sense. Parity itself verges on a nonsense concept. Equity among farmers is not served, for benefits vary strictly with farm size, which is *inversely* related to need. The one million larger farmers, already better off, get 80 percent of the subsidy. The two million smaller farmers get the rest. The price of farm land has capitalized these benefits (see Figure 25–2), again enriching mainly the large owners.

The efficiency effects have been serious. Prices and crop patterns have

---

[11] Retirement of parts of farms, as we have seen, has little effect on output, since the poorer acres are retired and yields on the better acres are increased. Retirement of whole farms presents a dilemma. If the more productive farms are retired and marginal farms left in operation, output will be curtailed, but agricultural efficiency will be impaired. If marginal farms are retired, the effect on output will be small. But these are the farms that the government is more likely to get. Land that is poor and land that is owned by elderly farmers and by part-time farmers will be offered for rent; land that is highly productive will not. The cost of retirement, moreover, will be high. If the government continues to support the prices of agricultural commodities, it will be bidding against itself. Its rentals will have to be high enough to compete with the profits that can be made by remaining in production and selling at supported prices. Rents will have to be raised as the government seeks to acquire increasing quantities of land. Rental, over the years, will cost as much as purchase, and will leave the farmer with title to his farm. The principal beneficiary of land retirement will be the landowner.

In 1974, when 13 million acres were freed to return to production, only 7 million acres actually came back into use. The other 6 million acres had been phantom acres, falsely claimed as reserves by the farmers.

been distorted.[12] Substitute goods have been encouraged; for cotton, wool, and butter, the effects have been sharp. Some crops have been increased, others cut and misallocation within farming has been substantial. The programs have been costly, towards $100 billion from 1932 to 1974 and $4.5 billion per year in recent years. Productivity may have risen faster because farmers were given incentives and security. But much of the gain has come autonomously from technical opportunity.

Direct payments. These are a parallel form of farm subsidy. They make up the gap between the market price and some target price; evidently they too go mainly to larger farmers.[13] During the 1960s, payments increasingly replaced price supports, and in 1973 they became the central basis.

The Food and Agriculture Act of 1965 governed farm programs from the beginning of 1966 to the end of 1970. The law afforded different treatment to the producers of different commodities. It provided no price supports or direct payments to producers of livestock, fruit, and vegetables. It continued price supports for producers of certain basic commodities: rice, tobacco, and peanuts. It continued the subsidies paid to the producers of sugar and wool. It incorporated, in modified form, the dual systems of price supports and direct payments established in 1962 for feed grains and for wheat. It introduced a similar system for cotton.[14]

Supports for such major crops as feed grains, wheat, and cotton thus moved closer to the prices fixed by forces operating in the market. The farmer's income was supplemented by direct payments. And these pay-

---

[12] With tobacco, for instance, where an acre yields a gross income 20 times that yielded by an acre of wheat or corn, farmers have crowded in to share in the profits; allotments are now given to nearly 600,000 farms. As a consequence the size of the individual allotment has declined, the average for Burley tobacco dropping from 1.58 acres in 1948 to 1.16 in 1963. Where an advantage remains, it is capitalized in determining the prices charged for land. Without a quota, tobacco land may sell for $50 an acre; with a quota it will bring $2,500 or more. Here, the capital value of the added income resulting from the quota is appropriated by the man who owned the land at the time when the quota was imposed. The farmer who subsequently buys the land pays for the value of the quota as he would for any other form of property. Thereafter, though price is inflated by monopolistic restriction of output, he receives but a competitive return.

[13] Such payments have been made since 1934 to producers of sugar beets and cane under a production quota system described in Chapter 24. They have been made since 1936 under the Soil Conservation Act to farmers who agree to adopt soil-building practices. They have been made since 1954 to producers of wool. Direct payments were made under the soil bank program adopted in 1956 to farmers who contracted to take land out of production. They have come to assume increasing importance, during the sixties, in programs designed to enhance the incomes of growers of feed grains, wheat, and cotton.

Wool is also covered. The wool program is designed to encourage domestic production of wool. Under this program, the Secretary of Agriculture fixes an incentive price for wool at a figure that may be as high as 110 percent of parity. The domestic producer sells his clip on the market at the going price, a figure that exceeds the world price by the amount of the tariff. He receives the difference in a check from the Treasury. The tariff on wool has cost the consumer some $25 million a year. The visible subsidy has cost the taxpayer another $35 million. By thus spending $60 million, the American people have made it possible for a small number of sheepmen to remain in an occupation where their efficiency is low and their costs high.

[14] Under the cotton program, price supports were cut, in 1966, from 30 cents per pound to 21 cents, making it possible for American cotton to compete in world markets. Direct payments were made to growers who retired an eighth of their acres, at the rate of $9^{1}/_{2}$ cents a pound on the part of the crop that was sold at home, with further payments to those who made still further cuts in acreage.

ments were conditioned on the diversion of farmland, in accordance with government acreage allotments, from the production of crops to other purposes.

A new agricultural law, enacted in 1970, continued for another three years the existing program of price supports plus direct payments for basic crops. Under a new provision, known as a "set-aside," it required farmers to keep some acreage idle in order to qualify for these benefits. But it permitted them to use their remaining acres for any crops they may choose to grow and sell without a subsidy. It thus took another step toward free markets.

There is much to be said for direct payments as an alternative to price supports. The cost to the community may be lower. The expenses incurred in storing commodities are avoided; the whole supply moves into consumption; none of it spoils in storage; none of it is destroyed. The method can be used with commodities that are perishable as well as with those that are durable. Prices on the domestic market are lower; the consumer's burden is reduced. Commodities are sold on world markets on the same price basis as at home; the appearance of export dumping is avoided. The subsidy is made visible; it must be debated and voted each year.

But there are also disadvantages. A system that makes it easy to subsidize perishables may make for larger costs. A subsidy paid directly will be fully as powerful as one paid indirectly in stimulating increased output. The consumer's burden may go down; the taxpayer's burden will go up. There will still be surpluses to export; they will still cause international friction; they will still be attributable to artificial stimulation of production by the government.

In 1969, direct payments to three million farmers amounted to $3.5 billion. There were 353 farmers each of whom received $100,000 or more. There was one cotton grower who received checks from the Treasury amounting to $3.3 million; another who received $4.4 million. There were moves in Congress in 1968 and 1969 to limit direct payments to $20,000 per farmer per crop, but they failed to pass. In 1970, Congress finally established a limit of $55,000. Such a ceiling may invite evasion or avoidance. Farmers may split their farms or diversify their crops in order to qualify for multiple payments. They may drop out of the program and expand their output. Direct payments thus present the government with a dilemma. If they are large enough to be effective in controlling output, they invite political attack. If they are small enough to be tolerated, they are likely to be ineffective.

Other Subsidies.   Now we consider several of the older subsidies to farming. They have tended to increase output (clashing therefore with the price-support and direct-payment programs).

Government stimulated agricultural settlement, for more than a century, by selling land to farmers at low prices and by giving it away. Until 1819, land was sold at $2 an acre, first in tracts of 640 acres, then 320, and finally 160. In 1819, the price was cut to $1.25 and the acreage to 80. Under laws enacted in 1830 and 1841, squatters were given preemptive rights. And under the Homestead Act of 1862, farm families were given title to

160 acres each if they settled on the land and cultivated it for a period of five years. In 1902, the size of homesteads was increased to 320 acres where settlers undertook to irrigate arid land; in 1916, it was raised to 640 acres in the case of grazing lands. In 1902, also, government began to make more land available by building irrigation works. In the next 50 years, more than 4 million acres were reclaimed and opened to settlement. At the same time, land was made more accessible by the construction of farm to market roads.

Government also provides the farmer with a number of free services. It delivers the mail to his home, however remote, with no extra charge. It supplies him with current market information through its crop and livestock reporting service. It facilitates the distribution of his products by establishing standards and grades of quantity and quality. It protects him against loss from insect pests and plant and animal diseases. It finances agricultural research and education. These are large programs.[15]

Irrigation has conveyed extensive subsidies. At the present time, half of the cropland in the West is irrigated and, of this, a fourth is irrigated by water from federal projects. This irrigation is 80 percent of all water use in the entire nation. Owners do not pay interest on the irrigation investment, and they repay only during the 10th to 50th year after the work is done. The subsidy to the farmers of irrigated lands is about 90 percent of the costs.[16]

A complex of lending agencies was created during 1916–33, supervised by a Farm Credit Administration. It now is largely self-financing and stands as an internally efficient program. The Rural Electrification Administration provided loans at 2 percent, plus all other technical support, to bring electricity to farms. From 10 percent in 1934, farms with electricity are now 98 percent of the total. There are over 1,000 REA cooperatives, with 6 million customers in 46 states. Telephones, too, have been extended by the REA, from one-third of farms in 1949 to four-fifths. The interest subsidy has been attacked by private utility interests (recall Chapters 15 and 21), partly because REA coverage threatens expansion into new suburbs.

There has been federal crop insurance for some farmers since 1939, on a modest scale. There were losses and revisions during 1940–47, and coverage has shrunk to 24 crops in 1,363 counties. The subsidy is small, and the poorer risks tend to be over-represented.

---

[15] The Department of Agriculture, with over 100,000 employees, now functions as a gigantic agricultural service agency. Research in soil chemistry and plant and animal biology, in the improvement of fertilizers and feeds, in the control of pests and diseases, and in other aspects of agricultural technology is conducted by the Department and by the state experiment stations. Education in agricultural methods is provided to students by the land-grant colleges and is carried to the farmer through farmers' institutes, through demonstration projects, and through instruction on the farm, by thousands of country agents employed jointly by the Department and the colleges.

[16] See Otto Eckstein, *Water Resource Development* (Cambridge, Mass.: Harvard University Press, 1958), chap. viii; and National Water Commission, *Fiscal Report* (Washington, D.C.: U.S. Government, Printing Office, 1973). Thus the Manson unit being constructed in Washington will cost $414 per acre *per year* (compared to annual charges at present rates of $32.50 per acre). The annual *gross* crop receipts per acre are likely to be about $200, less than half of the true cost of the irrigation. Such projects are wildly uneconomic (recall also Chapter 21).

Only the Farmers Home Administration has, since 1946, specifically given help to small, poor farmers. It provides loans plus careful supervision for nearly all operations which will improve small farmers' prospects. Remarkably, only 1 percent of the loans are not repaid. For $70 million in administrative costs per year, the FHA provides at least some help to needy farmers. This is, of course, only a trifle compared to the subsidies for the well-to-do commercial farmers.

In a larger perspective, farm programs have eased the rural impact of the long-term migration from farms to cities. The rate of migration was increased, especially the small farmers and sharecroppers in the southeastern region. Farm programs have therefore intensified the urban problems of ghettos and decay.

The 1970s may bring large changes in these programs, for most of the structural changes now appear to have occurred. A limited program of stabilizing and crop insurance plus expanded FHA operations would probably be about optimal. But the older programs are part of a deep political equilibrium and are likely to persist.

PROMOTING CONSUMER INTERESTS

Consumer choices have a social aspect mainly when they lack good information, when consumers can be fooled or put under duress, and when products impose severe risks. The second problem is endemic in many markets; it can best be dealt with by general laws facilitating private suits for redress. The other two problems—(1) information and (2) safety—invite more specific treatments, which we will discuss here. There are agencies treating both of these, but only incompletely and with various dubious side effects. The main lines are given in Table 25–7. The older view is that protection can be assured by passing a law and creating an agency. But the net effects may be zero or actually harmful (recall Chapter 4).

Since 1965 there has been a boomlet of "consumerism," directed mainly at automobiles, advertising, and certain chemically doubtful products. It now appears to have been an interesting but thin and narrow movement, which has added only marginally to the small set of consumer-protection policies. *Caveat emptor* (let the buyer beware) still holds.

Information

Most consumer items are simple and repetitive (e.g., most foods, clothing, utility services), and so consumers' choices among them can be informed and flexible. But some goods are not, especially consumer durables (appliances, automobiles, houses) and medical care. Also, the larger items often involve credit, on complex terms. Large numbers of consumers may be routinely deceived in these consumption choices and suffer lasting hardship because of contrived ignorance. The losses are likely to be severely regressive in incidence, focusing on lower income and educational groups. Better information would therefore provide social benefits.

Optimal policy will promote this, and possibly intervene to stop certain action, up to the usual efficient margin (recall Chapter 3).

The main efforts have been toward "truth" in labelling, lending and advertising. They have amounted to a slow, scattered guerilla war against a variety of deceptive practices. Each foray takes time, and though a victory is often won—e.g., for truth in lending, or for standard pricing in supermarkets—it is usually only a partial treatment. And it

TABLE 25–7
Consumer-protection Agencies, 1973

Federal Trade Commission	
Consumer protection activities	
Funds	$14.5 million
Staff	700
Investigations initiated	1,100
Complaints issued.	406
Cease and desist orders issued	387
Compliance actions completed	2,450
Food and Drug Administration	
Total funds	$144.0 million
Food	57.5 million
Drugs.	45.2 million
Product safety	32.2 million
Staff	5,881
National Highway Traffic Safety Administration	
Total funds	$89.1 million
Motor vehicle	9.2 million
Traffic safety	27.4 million
Research and analysis	28.0 million
Staff	825
Department of Agriculture: Packers and	
Stockyards Administration	
Total funds	$3.9 million
Staff	204
Investigations and audits	7,250

Source: *Budget of the U.S. Government, 1973.*

evokes new ways to do the same practice. New rules are often empty and inspection only nominal. This is acutely true of misrepresentation. Lies and half-truths about products can often be nailed and penalized only by arduous efforts, and after the damage has been done. And then the deceptions can be repeated, requiring new correctives each time.

The FTC has been the main agency enforcing consumer interests, which absorb over half its resources (recall Chapter 5). Its conventional actions have concerned false labelling of textiles and furs, "hazardous substances," and a variety of claims about foods. Consumers can also complain to the FTC about any fraud or deception, and gain at least an official inquiry. Most of them are strictly small-change matters, where public resources have a low yield in each case. The social cost may be justified only by the general benefit of knowing a sympathetic agency is ready to pursue even the smallest consumer complaint.

During 1970–73 the FTC also mounted a campaign against deceptive advertising. This was part of the effort to "revitalize" the FTC (recall Chapter 5), but it only expanded the traditional FTC work on the problem.[17] Agency staff members monitored advertising claims both on television and in newspapers, and in doubtful cases then demanded proof for the claims. During the 1970–73 campaign, a large variety of contested cases was quickly built up, evoking a perfect shower of denunciations by advertising and producing interests. In the majority of cases, the FTC did establish that the contested claims had been deceptive. The net result may have been a modest rise in the standards of honesty in nationally advertised brands. But the whole economic effect was an order of magnitude below the super-heated controversy which it generated. The FTC was able to project a strict image and to win battles over matters which the ordinary consumer could readily understand. But the whole economic gain was modest, and the FTC advertising impact remains slight.[18]

This mainstream of consumer-interest activity by public agencies does serve a valuable safety-valve function, in assuring consumers that there is a group which will inquire about possible mistreatment. But it is a costly device, especially where it competes for FTC funds with other more basic activities. The optimum device for advancing consumers' interests is the *class action suit,* in which one or several parties sue a culpable seller on behalf of all customers. Each buyer may have suffered only several dollars' loss; together their losses may be in the millions. This builds up the possible gain to the claimant high enough to justify the legal costs involved.[19] Without class action, no individual consumer would ordinarily have an interest or the expertise to press the case. Class

---

[17] In the course of a year, the FTC receives thousands of complaints concerning deceptive advertising and, among these, investigates a few hundred. It examines hundreds of thousands of printed advertisements and radio and TV commercials, and questions one in 15 or 20. From all this, less than 500 items may lead to action.

[18] The usual case is closed by an assurance of discontinuance, which is nothing more than a slap on the wrist. An order carries no penalty for past deceptions and does nothing to prevent future ones. In one notorious case, the FTC, beginning in 1959, investigated claims by the manufacturer of Geritol that his product cured tiredness, loss of strength, run-down feeling, nervousness, and irritability by providing iron to "tired blood." In 1962, the Commission issued a formal complaint. In 1965, it issued an order to cease and desist. In 1967, this order was upheld by a circuit court, making it final and binding. In 1968, the Commission ruled that the manufacturer had violated the order. In 1969, it asked the Department of Justice to bring suit to compel compliance. In 1970, the Department sued, asking that the manufacturer be fined $500,000 and his advertising agency another $500,000 for violations of the Commission's order. In all this time the company continued to advertise the iron in Geritol as a remedy for bad blood.

The FTC has an uphill fight. The Commission, rather than the advertiser, bears the burden of proof. It must draw a difficult line between harmless exaggeration and harmful deception. It must base its orders on evidence that the advertiser's claims are false and on testimony that they are, in fact, deceptive. When orders are issued, cases won, and sanctions imposed, moreover, they apply only to the company that makes the advertised product, not to the advertising agency that prepares the misleading copy, to the publisher who prints it, or to the station that broadcasts it. And then the advertiser need only drop the old campaign and embark upon a new one as deceptive as the last. The Commission cannot require the publication of retractions. It cannot censor copy in advance. And it can scarcely be expected to keep pace with the inventive copywriters in the advertising agencies. The control that it exerts may moderate some of the more serious abuses of advertising. But it is not to be described as rigorous.

[19] This is well analyzed in R. A. Posner, *Economic Analysis of Law, op. cit.,* pp. 349–51.

action suits mobilize the true economic interests involved, translating their experience and drives directly into action. They also induce sellers, by anticipation, to avoid the deceptive practices.

By contrast, an FTC bureaucracy attempting to perform the monitoring, evaluating, and enforcing functions is both roundabout and ineffective.[20] Fines are nominal, compared to the damages which class-action suits could properly trigger. By any economic analysis, the FTC should seek to have much of its consumer interest activities transferred to the courts under effective class action rules. This would foster the growth of an active, probing, and aggressive set of private specialists in consumer action, directly promoting private interests.

Product Safety

Certain products are unsafe *and* involve a public interest in exclusion, because (1) they are too complex or hazardous to be evaluated properly by the consumer and/or (2) their failure would harm not only the owner of the product but also other people.[21] In practice, it is in pharmaceutical products and automobiles that the most direct public controls have been established, to exclude "unfit" products. The main agencies are the Federal Food and Drug Administration (FDA) and the National Highway Safety Bureau. In addition, in a wide range of products and services the power to exclude "inferior" offerings—however defined—has been delegated to private groups. This is true of the professions generally, such as doctors, lawyers, accountants, morticians, and all the rest. (Many of the results are dubious; recall Chapter 24 and see Chapter 27 below). In any case, the main public agencies for product safety are only the visible tip of the iceberg.

The FDA is a large agency with a wide range of tasks.[22] It has grown

---

[20] This holds even though the Supreme Court has recently discouraged the class action method, especially in the *Eisen* decision in May, 1974.

[21] For example, safety belts on cars may be a matter for public action, both because people do not properly evaluate their private risks and the technology involved, and because Smith's failure to buckle up may end up by harming Jones.

[22] The work load of the FDA is large and varied. Within a year, it examines hundreds of applications to certify new drugs and new food additives and tests thousands of batches of antibiotics and color additives, rejecting a minor fraction and clearing the rest for sale. In the same period, it inspects half of the 14,000 drug establishments in the United States and more than a third of the 88,000 food establishments. It examines thousands of lots of raw agricultural products, checking on residues of pesticides. It prepares standards by which to judge adulteration of foods, holds hearings on them, modifies them where necessary, and adopts them for use. It investigates tens of thousands of reports of poisonings attributed to drugs, chemical additives, cosmetics, pesticides, and hazardous household substances. It maintains surveillance over drugs after they have been cleared for use, recalling hundreds of them from the market and sending warning letters to physicians where it finds them to be unsafe. It undertakes to prevent illegal sales of prescription drugs by pharmacists and by dope peddlers.

The FDA is understaffed and underfinanced, its personnel for 1969 standing at 4,250, its appropriation at $73 million. Its leadership, since 1966, has been strong but constantly changing, with three different commissioners in four years. It has been repeatedly reorganized but has never had the active interest and support of the head of its Department. In 1969 a study panel appointed by the Commissioner reported that the agency was unable to develop the kind of concerted and coordinated efforts needed to deal adequately and simultaneously with its myriad problems. "We are currently not equipped," it said, "to cope with the challenge."

and added powers mainly when a scandal proves the need for new powers and staff.[23] It covers such diverse industries as drugs, foods, agricultural production, pesticides, cosmetics, and other household substances. It inspects thousands of premises, and tests other thousands of goods. It has gone through ups and downs of militancy and strictness, and it is under severe pressure, especially from those industries which it is intended to regulate. It is most successful where it is able to set the burden of proof against risky products, so that producers have to prove them safe (recall Chapter 3). It keeps some products off the market until their safety is clearly established, but the standards it should apply are controversial. Often its exclusions and penalties are repeatedly violated by the same offenders, and often its controls appear ineffective.[24] It is able to apply relatively mild penalties. Its criteria for approving drugs have been raised in recent years, requiring not only safety but also proof of effectiveness. But this applies only to new drugs.

The Highway Safety Bureau has set a series of requirements for automobile safety equipment, dealing with bumpers, seat belts, structure, and the like. These have improved safety *and* had the predictable side effect of putting the smaller and less conventional automobile sellers at a disadvantage. Thus, setting a standard bumper size at a high level suited to large U.S. cars caused difficulty for the smaller imported cars. The additional costs of mandatory safety equipment have been proportionally higher for smaller car manufacturers, again tending to benefit the larger producers relatively. As in setting high standards for medicine, setting costly safety standards for cars has tended to exclude whole ranges of lower-cost supply from the market. Against the benefits for public safety which this gives, must be laid the reduction in consumer choice. This reduction bears most heavily on the poorer part of the population, many of whom would prefer to make do with cheaper automobiles.

This aspect not only belongs in a fair evaluation of the safety effort and its costs, but it also helps explain why the main automobile producers have been so willing to go along with it. It has relatively helped their market position.

MARITIME SUBSIDIES

There are five main aids given to the U.S. maritime industries. They are summarized in Table 25–8.

---

[23] These scandals included foods in 1890–1906, Elixir Sulfanilamide in 1937 (which killed 93), and Thalidomide in 1962.

[24] Goods produced in violation of the law can be seized and persons guilty of violation fined and imprisoned. Each year FDA inspectors make hundreds of seizures of filthy and decomposed foods, of hazardous substances lacking adequate warnings, of harmful drugs and fraudulent cancer cures, scores of seizures of foods containing excessive pesticide residues, of foods containing illegal additives, of poisonous cosmetics, and fraudulent devices for the treatment of disease. Violators are turned over to the Department of Justice for prosecution. The record indicates that many offenders are found to be in violation again and again, that criminal penalties are sought only in the most flagrant cases, and that the sentences imposed by the courts are so light as to have little effect as a deterrent.

On the abuses of the drug industry and the performance of FDA, see Morton Mintz, *The Therapeutic Nightmare* (Boston, Mass.: Houghton Mifflin Co., 1965).

TABLE 25-8
Maritime Subsidies

	Since	*Total, to* *1973*	*Yearly Amount,* *Recent Years*
Operating differential..........	1936	$3 billion	$250
Construction differential........	1936	1.4 billion	300
U.S. flag shipping rules......... (cabotage laws)	1950	3 billion	150
Tax subsidies.................	1936	.35 billion	50
Cargo preference..............	1950	5 billion	200

Source: Joint Economic Committee, *The Economics of Federal Subsidies, loc. cit.*

Subsidies to Shipbuilders

Under the Merchant Marine Act of 1936, shipping companies receiving operating subsidies were required to have their ships built in American yards. This put them at a competitive disadvantage, since the cost of building ships in the United States was twice as great as that of building them abroad. The law therefore authorized the government to contribute, as a "construction differential subsidy," the difference between American and foreign costs. Until 1960, the government's contribution normally could not exceed half of the cost. In 1960, its share was raised to 55 percent; in 1962 to 60 percent. The largest ship to be subsidized under this law was the liner "United States," built at a cost of $76.8 million. Of this, $32.9 million was put up by the United States Lines, $43.9 million by the taxpayers.

From 1937, when the program began, to 1968, the government paid out nearly $1 billion in construction subsidies; in 1968, more than $100 million. At that time, the Johnson Administration proposed that the American construction requirement be dropped, permitting shipping companies to purchase ships built in foreign yards. The Nixon Administration rejected this proposal. Under a new law, enacted in 1970, cargo liners are to be built in American yards at the rate of 30 ships a year for the next 10 years, with the government's contribution to their cost dropping from 55 percent at the beginning to 35 percent in the mid-seventies. The law was expected to cost the taxpayer $2.7 billion for construction subsidies during the next decade.[25]

Subsidies to Shipping

Coastwise and intercoastal shipping has been reserved, since the early days of the republic, to vessels flying the American flag. Such protection has also been afforded, since the turn of the century, to trade with noncontiguous possessions of the United States. Exclusion of competitors thus operates, indirectly, to subsidize American concerns.

---

[25] On subsidies to shipping and shipbuilding, see Samuel A. Lawrence, *United States Merchant Shipping: Policies and Politics* (Washington, D.C.: Brookings Institution, 1966); and *The Economics of Federal Subsidy Programs, op. cit.,* Part 6.

Transoceanic shipping has been subsidized in many different ways. First, it has been granted cargo preferences. In 1904, Congress required that goods purchased for the Army or Navy be carried in American vessels. In 1934, it expressed its desire that exports financed by government loans be carried in such vessels. And in 1954, it required that at least half of the tonnage of all goods procured by the government or supplied by it, through loans or grants, to other governments be transported under the American flag. American shipping companies, protected from foreign competition, have thus obtained a subsidy in the form of higher freights, paid from funds that were nominally appropriated for other purposes, such as the provision of foreign aid. This subsidy has amounted to $100 million a year.

Second, the transoceanic lines have been enabled to acquire ships on terms that have cut their capital costs. Ships that were built for the government have been sold to private operators at a few cents on the dollar. After World War II, 843 ships that had cost $4,400 million were sold for $1,776 million, representing two-fifths of their original cost and a fourth to a fifth of their replacement cost. Not only have ships been provided at bargain prices; the government gives generous trade-in allowances on old vessels and offers easy-payment plans. Three-fourths of the price a company must pay may be loaned to it by the government, these loans being made on terms that themselves involve a subsidy.

Third, the shipping companies are given a tax subsidy, being permitted to put part or all of their earnings and capital gains into reserve funds on which they can draw to purchase new ships. The income thus sequestered is exempted from the corporate income tax.

Fourth, the operating costs of passenger and cargo liners providing scheduled service on established routes are also subsidized. For many years, a subsidy was hidden in excessive payments made for carrying the mails. Under the Merchant Marine Act of 1936, it was brought into the open, An "operating differential subsidy" has since been paid to cover the difference in cost in operating under the American rather than a foreign flag. In 1969, this subsidy was being paid to 15 companies operating 13 passenger liners and some 300 cargo ships. It met a fourth of their operating costs. From 1954 to 1969, the subsidy paid to keep these ships afloat rose from $100 million a year to $200 million. Under legislation enacted in 1970, the operating differential subsidy is expected to amount to $6 billion during the next decade.

These subsidies are widely agreed to have been costly and deadening to efficiency. Shipping, under more progressive management, might have been able to pay its own way. Ship design, port facilities, and cargo-handling devices all could be improved. More freight could be prepacked for loading in containers. Ships could be loaded to a higher fraction of capacity, sailing full and down. Time in port, standing idle, could be reduced and time at sea, earning money, increased. Subsidization has not sufficed to keep American merchant ships afloat. The number of ships flying the American flag has steadily declined. Since World War II, the share of American trade carried by such vessels has fallen from 60 percent to less than 10 percent. What has been needed is less an infusion of funds from the Treasury than a revolution in management. The subsidies are also siphoned in exotic ways into pockets far outside the officially eligible groups.[26]

On the whole, maritime subsidies exhibit the worst features of subsidies. They are too large. They yield small, narrow and inequitable benefits. And they have set a dead hand upon efficiency in the sector for nearly 40 years.

MULTINATIONAL FIRMS

U.S. businesses hold a variety of strong and profitable positions in foreign markets, both in Western Europe and various LDC's (recall Chapter 2). There are mixed effects; some inject fresh competition and

TABLE 25–9
U.S. Subsidies to Research and Development in Leading Trade-related Industries

	Federal Funds as a Percent of Total R D Funds, 1970
Aircraft and missiles.	79%
Electrical equipment and communications	55
Optical, surgical, photographic and other instruments	27
Motor vehicles and other transportation equipment.	17
Rubber products	17
Machinery.	16
Chemicals and allied products.	10

Source: National Science Foundation.

technology, while others seek just to extend dominant U.S. positions into foreign markets.

This may be influenced by U.S. subsidies, especially those giving R&D support and tax privileges (see Table 25–9). R&D subsidies can be particularly strong in major high-technology industries (e.g., aerospace, nuclear power, computers, satellites). The effects of the subsidies are mainly:

---

[26] Consider this current example, arranged by Elias J. Kulukundis of Burmah Oil (a foreign company), and described by *Fortune* magazine. "In Which a Greek Who Runs a Bermuda-Based Subsidiary of a British Oil Company Winds up with All Those U.S. Shipping Subsidies," (March 1973), p. 38. His maneuvers (similar to those by others) include the following: "To carry oil from the Mideast to the U.S., Burmah will charter six 380,000-ton supertankers built by Todd Shipyards with a subsidy of $234 million. The deal is intricately structured to place the ships' ownership in American hands, as the law requires if they are to receive the subsidy. Actual orders were placed by six U.S. corporations created for the purpose (one for each ship), with U.S. lawyers serving as officers. To meet requirements that each ship's operator be a U.S. citizen, the tankers will first be charted to Burmah Oil Inc., a wholly owned subsidiary incorporated in Delaware; then they will be time-chartered to Burmah Oil Tankers, Ltd., which is based in Burmuda for legal convenience."
The 1974–1975 tanker glut later killed this one scheme, but the methods are quite typical.

1. U.S. investment and exports are increased, as the private costs of investing and selling are reduced and so the marginally profitable level rises.
2. This results in higher market shares and profitability for U.S. firms abroad, on the average.
3. This may be partly offset by countersubsidies from foreign countries to their firms, or by other controls.
4. But generally, the U.S. subsidies do increase the market power of U.S. multinational firms.

The subject is new and little-researched, but the effects on international competition may be appreciable.

OPEC Resources and Control.   Meanwhile the rise of the OPEC oil cartel has cut across the old pattern of multinational firm's power. By

TABLE 25–10
The Scope of OPEC Revenues

At a rate of $60 billion per year (achieved during 1974–75), the following periods would be required to equal (at December 1974, market values):

Category	Period
All companies on all major stock markets...........	15.6 years
All firms listed on the New York Stock Exchange ...	9.2 years
All of Britain's industrial assets	6.0 years
All U.S. direct foreign investments.................	1.8 years
51 percent of the common stock of	
AT&T..	74 days
IBM..	73 days
Exxon..	40 days
Imperial Chemicals (U.K.)......................	6 days
Bank of America..............................	6 days
British Leyland Motor Corp.	18 hours

raising oil prices from about $2 to $11 per barrel in 1973–74, OPEC members—particularly the Arab oil states—have begun amassing wealth at a rate which may reach $60 to $100 billion per year (for analysis of the prospects, see Chapter 26, below). The sheer volume of this flow is suggested by Table 25–10. Apart from its impact on world monetary balance, the rise of OPEC wealth has changed corporate reality in three ways.

(1) *Oil companies* have been quickly bought out by the OPEC members, in a sizable shift toward state ownership. This asserts national sovereignty (recall Chapter 19). It has also cut the power of the companies' old cartel. That power had been strong but, recently, waning. These firms had also held a large share of U.S. corporate investment abroad.

(2) *Western corporate control has been put under challenge in a variety of world markets.* The thirteen oil countries are now able to neutralize multinational firms in their home markets. This will spread to other countries, too, as OPEC wealth brings increasing control of a range of

companies on the global scene. Many Western firms will encounter new competitors; others will have to accommodate to their new OPEC creditors and owners. U.S. multinational firms' supremacy is eroding. Indeed, (3) *Arab control may be extended to major firms and banks in the U.S. and Europe.* This could alter the very content of corporate control and behavior. Table 25–10 shows that this change might go very far. In 1975, its future scope was unsure. Its effects could be like those which new U.S. capital abroad caused during the 1950's and 1960's: less regard for local market traditions, a closer focus on sheer profitability, a changed setting for managers, etc. Some U.S. sectors are closed to foreign investment by laws already on the books. Defense-related industries are one. Others include airlines, shipping, broadcasting and, in part, banking and minerals. "Arab takeovers" could—and no doubt will—be resisted in many ways, including new legislation and diplomacy. No frontal challenge to corporate control in the U.S. seems likely. Yet some shifts are likely, perhaps involving firms whose stock prices are well below book value. The ultimate effects would include some social benefits, not just costs.

After decades during which U.S. firms came to dominate certain world markets, the OPEC rise may shift the balance in many sectors and countries. There will be policy responses, some of them perhaps ill-formed. The optimal policy treatment remains to be seen, as events mature.

SUMMARY

Subsidies come in many forms: direct payments, tax reduction, risk absorption and still others. Promotion of firms and activities also occurs in a variety of ways. Some of these transfers give great social benefits, but others are costly and distorting.

The conditions of "optimal" subsidies can be defined in some detail. Actual programs promoting agriculture, consumer interests, maritime activities and multinational firms depart from these conditions in many ways.

CHAPTER TWENTY-SIX

Conserving Natural Resources

Each generation inherits a finite set of resources. It exploits and/or conserves them, in varying degree, using its own time discounts and technology. To *conserve* resources is to use them economically, in line with the whole future set of probable needs. The extreme degree is *preservation;* nonuse, hoarding. Economic criteria usually suggest using resources, at carefully set rates which optimize their total value over present and future time. But unfettered private markets often use them faster than this. Also the degree of monopoly often affects the rate and pattern of usage. Meanwhile, social interests—in abundant resources, amenity, maintaining traditional patterns, or fairness—often require an even slower usage than the efficient economic rate.[1]

Therefore, holding the rate and pattern of use to the optimum for each resource can be a complex and uncertain task. And the stakes are big. Resources include (1) minerals (oil, ores, coal, . . .), (2) soil, terrain, and sea to support life, (3) fresh water, air, and tranquility, and (4) natural wilderness and beauty (see Table 26–1).[2] They affect all corners of our lives—what we eat, breathe, smell, see and touch—and will continue doing so for our descendants.

We will treat several groups of these problems. First, background and basic issues: what are the resources? What are the right rates of usage? How do monopoly and policy affect shortages, energy crisis, and the eventual limits to economic growth on this planet? Next, the evolution

---

[1] Good basic sources include S. V. Ciriacy-Wantrup, *Resource Conservation: Economics and Policies,* 3rd ed. (Berkeley: University of California Press, 1968); J. H. Dales, *Pollution, Property and Prices* (Toronto: University of Toronto Press, 1968); E. J. Mishan, *The Costs of Economic Growth* (New York: Praeger, 1967). Gerald Garvey, *Energy, Ecology, Economy* (New York: Norton, 1972), gives a lucid introduction to environmental problems. See also the excellent review of external effects in E. J. Mishan, "The Postwar Literature on Externalities: An Interpretative Essay," *Journal of Economic Literature,* Vol. 9, No. 1 (March 1971), pp. 1–28, and the sources cited there.

[2] Appraisals of actual resources are given in H. H. Landsberg, *Natural Resources for U.S. Growth* (Baltimore: Johns Hopkins Press, 1964); R. G. Ridker, *Economic Costs of Air Pollution* (New York: Praeger, 1967); and D. H. Meadows *et. al., The Limits to Growth* (New York: Praeger, 1972).

TABLE 26-1

The Main Natural Resources

Nonrenewable
   Fuels (coal, oil, gas), land, ores, chemical deposits; natural beauty sites
Replaceable at great cost
   Soil, wilderness, certain rivers and lakes, clean shoreline
Renewable
   Other rivers and lakes; urban fresh air
Self-renewing
   Forests, fisheries, other "crops"
Virtually inexhaustible
   Rural fresh air, solar energy

---

of conservation policies will be reviewed. Third, the energry crisis: its nature and treatment. Fourth, pollution: Does market structure affect it, and what devices to cure pollution work best? Fifth, we will look briefly at the fishing industry, as an important case of a renewable and fugacious resource.

BASIC ISSUES

First, one recognizes that the problem is important and that conservation criteria have been widely violated.

The Need for Conservation

In the exploitation of natural resources, competition cannot be relied upon to protect the public interest. Competing producers may cut the trees off hillsides, permitting the rains to wash the topsoil from farm lands, to shoal streams and clog reservoirs, and to flood the cities in the valleys below. They may scramble for petroleum, blowing natural gas into the air, flooding the pools with water, and leaving much of the oil underground. They may draw heavily upon supplies of water for use in agriculture or industry, lowering the water table for a whole community. They may pour wastes into the streams and lakes, destroying fisheries; release them into the air, endangering human life. In cases such as these the general welfare is endangered, and public action to conserve resources is appropriate.

When the first white men came to this continent, resources were so abundant in relation to needs that no thought had to be given to economy in their use. What man desired was his for the taking, and whatever was taken, there was more to take. And, so, for more than two centuries, natural wealth was wasted recklessly. It was converted into private fortunes. It was destroyed for the pleasure of destroying it. In time, as population expanded and as levels of living rose, requirements increased and resources grew scarce. It came to be realized that profligacy was no longer possible. And out of this realization came the popular demand that waste be prevented and natural wealth conserved. The conservation movement had its origin in the abuses of the past.

Three centuries ago half of the land that now comprises the United States was in timber—unbroken tracts of virgin forest stretching for hundreds of miles, dense stands of white pine to the north, yellow pine to the south, and softwoods in the far west, with giant trees centuries old, measuring from 5 to 10 feet through and towering 200 and even 300 feet into the air. Between the forests lay the grasslands of the Great Plains with deep layers of fertile soil built up over the ages as grasses rotted where they died. Everywhere, save in the deserts, water was plentiful, its surface flow controlled, its underground sources replenished by mois- ture-holding roots and leaves. The streams ran clear; rivers, lakes, and oceans teemed with fish. Plains and forests abounded with wildlife; great herds of buffalo, elk, and antelope roamed the prairies; countless flocks of wild fowl crossed the skies. Beneath the surface lay rich deposits of minerals: metals readily accessible, coal in quantity, oil and gas held in vast reservoirs waiting only to be tapped.

Upon this natural paradise the white man fell with weapons of de- struction, chopping, plowing, and shooting his way from east to west. The forests he regarded as a nuisance, felling giant trees to clear the land for planting, stripping them to get bark for tanning, burning them to get lye for soap. For generations he cut the forests clean, leaving dry slash to burn and scorch the soil, sparing no trees to scatter seeds and start new growth. By 1850 the center of logging had moved from Maine to New York, by 1860 to Pennsylvania, by 1870 to the region of the Great Lakes, by 1900 to the pineries of the South, by 1930 to the Pacific Coast. What axe and fire did to the forests, the plow, cattle, and sheep did to the hillsides and the plains. Plowing and overgrazing destroyed the grasses, removing the soil's protective cover, exposing it to wind and water, and leaving it to blow and wash away. The rain, instead of renewing stores of water underground, increasingly ran off the surface. Rivers were yel- lowed with silt, poisoned with industrial wastes, turned into open sewers. Fish were destroyed by pollution of the inland streams, by overfishing of the lakes and seas. The giant sturgeon of the Chesapeake Bay were slaughtered for their roe, their bodies thrown to rot along the shore. The numbers of birds and animals were reduced by the destruction of their natural habitat—the cutting of forests, the plowing of grasslands, and the drainage of swamps. Wildlife was eliminated, too, by trap and gun, to provide food and clothing, to protect crops and livestock, and merely for the pleasure of the sport. The egret was killed for its plumes, thousands of buffalo for their tongues, and elk to get two teeth to dangle from a chain. Methods of mining were equally destructive: the more accessible deposits were taken, the richer veins exploited, the poorer ones allowed to go to waste; gas was blown away and oil left underground.

Our resources, as a consequence, have been depleted. Nine-tenths of our virgin timber has been cut. Great stands have been turned into in- ferior second growth, or into worthless brush, stumps, and bare rock. Nearly a third of our topsoil has washed or blown away. Erosion is said to have destroyed or seriously impoverished some 280 million acres of crop and range land, an area equal to that of six midwestern states. The water table has been lowered; in the arid West and the industrial East, particularly, populations have approached the limits of supply. Important fisheries have been exhausted; catches have declined; species once plentiful have all but disappeared. Many forms of wildlife have been extinguished, among them the passenger pigeon, the great auk, the heath hen, and the Labrador duck; others would be extinct if not protected by the law. Minerals, too, have been moving toward exhaustion at a rapidly quickening pace. For many of them consumption in the United States since World War II has been greater than that in all the world in all the years before. From 1900 to 1950 the annual use of all materials increased 5 times, the use of crude oil 30 times. In that half century more copper, lead, and zinc was taken than was left in known reserves. Once self-sufficient in the basic metals, we must now import to satisfy our needs. The cream has been skimmed from our resources; the day when they could be taken for granted has long been past.

Not only has man reduced the quantity of natural resources; he has impaired the quality of what remains. He has polluted the waters with industrial wastes; with pesticides, detergents, and sewage. He has polluted the air with noxious fumes; with soot, dust, and chemicals. He has disfigured the landscape; raised the level of noise, in urban areas, close to the limits of human tolerance.

In coming decades, the growth of population and production will encounter increasing scarcity of resources. Past technological progress has relieved some of the Malthusian pressures. But in fuels, ores, space, and ecology, the next 50 years appear to pose newly severe scarcities. The natural economic solution is simply a rising trend in resource prices, and the drastic 1971–74 jumps in food, oil and minerals prices (recall Chapter 2) may only presage sharper future rises. But some analysts predict stresses and pollution so great as to cause worldwide social collapse.[3] Whether these Doomwatchers or the technological optimists are correct is too early to say. But severe individual problems will continue to arise and provoke conservationist efforts, as in 1890–1910 and since 1967. Resources and clean environment will, at the least, require hard choices about large costs (e.g., nearly $300 billion during 1972–81 for abating pollution; see page 683 below).

Economic Issues

To evaluate these issues, we apply the basic economics of conservation. The objective is to use efficiently—and equitably; within each generation and among generations—a physically limited, depletable resource. Some resources are renewable, such as forests, fish, and clean rivers. Others are nonrenewable—once used, gone forever—such as oil, ores and coal. Still others are in between: renewable only at great cost (topsoil, wilderness). For all of them, the basic aim is identical: to use the resource

---

[3] See especially Meadows *et al, op. cit.* The book's predictions include a collapse of civilization and production, as growing scarcities and pollution interact. In rebuttal, many experts argue that technology and public policies will abate the problems short of severe effects: scarcity? Yes, crisis? No.

at the rate which maximizes the total social value of its use, over the whole span of time.

Each resource is an asset, a stock (possibly renewable). It can be held in its present form or used—at some rate—either for consumption or investment purposes. Decisions affecting the use of resources are basically speculations on their future worth, either in its natural state or in some converted form. Physical *preservation* is only one alternative among the ways to *conserve* a resource. To avoid economic waste often requires physical *usage* of a resource.

One popular fallacy is to regard our resource base as a fixed inventory which, when used up, will leave society with no means of survival. A related fallacy is that physical waste equals economic waste: the feeling that it is wasteful to use materials in ways that make them disappear. This attitude can lead to devoting a dollar's worth of work to "saving" a few cents worth of waste paper and old string. These fallacies together lead to a hairshirt concept of conservation which makes it synonymous with hoarding.

Conservation is something very different from simply leaving oil in the ground or trees in the forests on the theory that by sacrificing lower value uses today we will leave something for the higher value uses of tomorrow when supplies will be scarcer. Using resources today is an essential part of making our economy grow; materials which become embodied in today's capital goods, for example, are put to work and help make tomorrow's production higher. Hoarding resources in the expectation of more important uses later involves a sacrifice that may never be recouped; technological changes and new resource discoveries may alter a situation completely. It may not be wise to refrain from using zinc today if our grandchildren will not know what to do with it tomorrow.[4]

For each asset, and for the whole bundle of natural resources, the optimum rate of use is not precisely determinate. It depends on the current rate of interest, on the length of time horizon which society and/or the owner of the asset applies, and on the ethical weights used in comparing the value of use between present or future generations. Costs of finding, using and renewing resources also affect the optimum. Also, the expected rate and direction of technological change may be decisive, for it may require increasingly more—or less—of the natural resource in question, as time passes.[5]

These and lesser factors are matters of social preference and of simple economic scarcity. The longer the time length of a horizon and the lower the social rate of time preference and interests rates, the slower will be the optimum rate of using natural resources. By contrast, if interests rates are high, the time horizon is short, and the interests of current citizens are considered urgent, then a society may choose to use up its resources here and now. The solution turns closely on predictions about

---

[4] President's Materials Policy Commission, *Resources for Freedom* (Washington, D.C.: Government Printing Office, 1952), Vol. I, p. 21.

[5] For example, there might be a fixed and small stock of natural gas available, so that scarcity and rising gas prices are imminent. But if nuclear power replaces gas entirely within twenty years, then the value of the gas will tend toward zero.

many technical factors, and on judgments about the social rate of time preference.

There is one additional wrinkle for renewable resources (such as fish). The rate by which they are cropped depends on the same basic factors, but there is a range of choice in establishing the steady-state harvesting levels. There is usually a yield curve given technically, as is shown roughly in Figure 26–1. The optimum yield is illustrated at point *A*. The

FIGURE 26–1
Optimizing the Use of a Renewable Resource

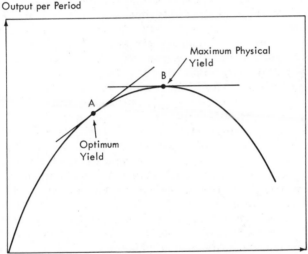

Output per Period

Maximum Physical Yield

B

A

Optimum Yield

Effort Expended on Harvesting per Period

resource will sustain a physically more intensive harvesting than this (at *B*), but the total yield is smaller than at *A*. The optimum rate as shown depends, again, on several factors. Of course, optimal conservation may require the resource to be gradually exhausted over time, even if it is cropped efficiently during that decline.

A further peculiarity is that resource values are partly economic rents, set by factors other than cost of production. These rents rise with scarcity, but they often are strictly residual and contain windfall elements. Being capitalized values of future benefits, they are influenced by expectations, by psychology. Any significant policies will affect these values.

Private Markets Optimize, Except . . .

These hornbook points about conservation are of long standing among experts, though not in common debate. Two main policy issues will be germane here. (1) The time discounts applied by private owners may diverge from the "true" social time preference, and (2) the degree of monopoly in resource markets may affect the outcome.

The Conventional Economic Lesson. This is quite clear and optimistic: *private markets operating with relatively perfect conditions of mobility, knowledge, and rationality will tend to fit the social criteria for conservation or resources over time.*[6] The owners will be guided both by their profit-maximizing motivation and by the objective conditions prevailing in financial and industrial markets. These will usually tend to reflect precisely those social valuations of time preference, productivity, and expected innovation which determine the optimum rate. Moreover, it is in the interests of the resource owners to seek out accurate information on these magnitudes and apply them in their own decisions. Therefore, the powerful premise is that private-market disposal of natural resources will normally optimize their use.

This holds for competitive markets under perfect assumptions. Monopolists will usually hold the rate of resource use lower, by restricting output and raising price in the present. Yet monopolists too will wish to maximize the value of resource use in the long run, and so the restrictive effect may distort their choices only slightly.

In well-functioning markets, with rational choices, the prices of natural resources will tend to anticipate future scarcities, so that the users of resources will act in accord with the genuine social costs of their use of resources. Further, as unexpected changes occur in these predicted future scarcities, the prices of resources will adjust quickly and automatically. Therefore both the present and future scarcities—even if they are changing and uncertain at each point—will be fully reflected in the prevailing prices and the rates of usage. This will occur spontaneously, without conscious or detailed social planning. In short, the "invisible hand" extends to conservation.

Limits and Biases. But this optimality is limited (as are the more general efficiency results: recall Chapter 1) and there may be specific biases. Six of these possible limits and biases follow.

1. *Shared ownership.* Where resources can be tapped by several separate owners, the shared access will invariably lead them to be depleted too fast. The classic instances include the many now-extinct species and other verging on extinction, oil fields, fisheries, and other oceanic resources, which have been open to multiple extractors. As with several people with straws in one milkshake, each owner's private interest is in taking it out as fast as possible, and so the private choices may depart radically from the social optimum. The corrective is to unitize the control of each such resource, so that the optimum technical pattern and rate of usage can be designed and applied. Though this is obvious, it took decades to begin "unitizing" U.S. oil fields, and international fishing and resource use is still far from organized.

2. *Time preferences and myopia.* The private rate of time preference (influenced by specific opportunities, time horizons, and personal atti-

---

[6] Dales, *op. cit.,* and Ciriacy-Wantrup, *op. cit.* But Ciriacy-Wantrup, and Mishan (*op. cit.*), among others, point out the limits to this optimum.

tudes) may be too high. Firms often have short time horizons, under the stress of commercial competition. This may under-represent the legitimate interests of future generations. Ultimately, a negative rate of time preference should perhaps be applied to some intergeneration choices. If population and income levels continue growing, the pressure on resources—especially certain key ones—may far exceed anything now imagined. Therefore, in a long perspective, it might be optimal for us now to set the value of future use higher than that of present use. At any rate, the social rate of time preference may be lower—perhaps much lower—than the rate established by private choices.

3. *Inadequate forecasting.* Present users may simply fail to foresee future developments. This may reflect a lack of sufficient research interest and capability to discern future changes. There may be close interactions among the uses of resources which are not presently apparent to the individual users of each (that is the crux of the Doomwatch projections). And some users may simply be careless or superficial in their judgments.

4. *Special influences.* Specific taxes and other incentive devices may encourage overly rapid use of resources. In fact, the use of almost every resource *is* affected by one or several artificial incentives. There are special tax provisions for almost all natural resource uses, such as oil, ores, and the like. The use of land surrounding cities has been intensified by special tax provisions which favor creating suburban developments as investment tax shelters. Farm policies affect the extent and intensity of cultivation. National policies affect the exhaustion of oceanic fish resources. These incentives almost invariably induce a more rapid use of resources, often drastically higher and perhaps extinguishing the resources in the end.

5. *External effects.* There are important externalities in the uses of many resources, so that private users ignore major degrees of pollution and other external costs.[7] This effects both the rate of withdrawal of earth resources and the degree to which the common environment of air, water, and habitat are degraded. Almost always, a recognition of such externalities will cause a slower and altered use of natural resources. Note that this problem is only one of six, though it has been the main focus of the "envoronmental movement" since 1967.

6. *Distribution.* Finally, private market decisions are based on the existing distribution of wealth and income. As resource users vote with their dollars, market demand will more strongly reflect the interests and preferences of the wealthy. This may conflict with broader social criteria, especially where amenity is differently affected among neighborhoods or locales. Thus, the best land may be held by the rich and used exclusively, even though it would be socially preferable to open it to all as parkland. Some impacts—such as congestion and pollution—affect the poor more acutely. And the poor have a greater need for common recreational space and facilities.

---

[7] This was stressed in the great work of A. C. Pigou at Cambridge; see *The Economics of Welfare,* 4th ed. (London: Macmillan, 1946).

Directions. In all, private maximizing may fail to yield true conservation of natural resources, in several ways. The real world confirms this amply. Explicit social choices and controls may need to be applied in many situations, perhaps sharply altering the rate and directions in which natural resources are used. Several directions are worth noting here. *First,* a lower rate of time preference may be imposed, using any of several tactics. Physical limits may be set on uses or pollution levels. Special interest loans may be provided. Tax subsidies or stockpiling may be tried. Resources may be put under public ownership—entirely or in part—for direct treatments. In short, many devices which have appeared earlier in this book might be strictly appropriate for optimizing natural resource use (or, conversely, they may be misapplied and cause waste).

Second, external effects may be offset by a range of incentives or penalties. Since these will operate on private decision-makers (as well as some public managers), their design may intimately relate to market structure and profit-maximizing behavior. The externalities may arise either in production or in use. Therefore, they may be involved with other choices of industrial policy.

Third, resource-managing industries may need to be restructured so as to avoid biases. This may include unifying control over shared-access resources, such as oil fields. Or it may involve creating greater degrees of competition; or, in other cases, changing the degree of monopsony power. Or it may involve establishing public enterprises for all or part of the market.

Public policies may also distort resource use. Resource owners are usually a focal group with strong economic interests, since they hold title to part or all of a specific scarce resource. If properly combined, they can obtain large windfall gains from their ownership. They can be expected to seek these gains, both by market controls and in political efforts. "Conservation" campaigns can cloak *anti*-conservation and selfish strategies. In practical terms, this often means the creation of a government agency which manages and controls the use of the resource. This department will often be effectively controlled by the resource owners and will set restrictions and direct subsidies (recall also Chapters 24 and 25). Conceivably, these choices will turn out to fit the social optimum. But that is unlikely, and capital gains will also normally accrue. Therefore, one should not assume that the creation of a public agency to manage a resource sector will promote conservation. Natural resource policies and agencies need the closest possible scrutiny. The solutions are usually debatable, and so the possibility for abuse and confusion is great. By the same token, there will often be large gains from correcting previous policies.

EVOLVING POLICIES

On this cautious note, we briefly review some past conservation efforts, before turning to the energy sector, pollution, and fisheries in some detail. Conservation activities have come in two waves—1890–1910 and since 1967—and have spread to many sectors, using a profusion of devices.[8] Meanwhile a steady series of other actions have set actual resource usage, often in wasteful and inequitable ways. Changes are slow and often reversed. Controls turn out to have loopholes and surprising beneficiaries. Huge pieces of public land and resources have been given away, often under seamy conditions, and such events have continued up to the present. A large domain of public lands and forests has been retained, but parts of it have been opened to private exploitation under dubious conditions.

The Public Domain. This was originally very large. How has it been treated? The areas comprising the public domain of the United States were acquired, first, by cession to the federal government of lands extending to the Mississippi claimed by the 13 original states, and then, in 1802, by purchase of claims to lands beyond the Mississippi from France. They were subsequently extended by the purchase of Florida from Spain in 1819, the occupation of the Northwest Territory in 1846, and the cession of vast southwestern regions by Mexico in 1848, supplemented by purchase from Mexico in 1853. Title to many of these lands was confirmed through conquest and through treaties with the Indian tribes. In this way, a century ago, the federal government came to own 1,442 million acres, or three-fourths of the area then within the boundaries of the United States. These holdings were further augmented by the purchase of Alaska, involving another 378 million acres, from Russia in 1867.

Of the 1.8 billion acres that once constituted the public domain, a billion acres have been transferred from federal ownership, while 761 million acres, a third of the nation's area, remain in federal hands.[9]

Disposal. Disposal has taken several routes. Large tracts were given to states and to railroad companies. Before 1862, private disposal was a revenue-raiser. Then homesteading became the main objective. This was widely abused, in forming large commercial tracts with rich forest stands and mineral beds.

After 1891, this was reversed and public lands were increasingly reserved and expanded. But 96 percent of public land lies within just 11 states, where it is more than half of their area. Strong sectional and industry interests have therefore borne on the uses of these lands. The continental shelf also has involved intense stresses between local and national interests.

Accumulation of recreational and scenic lands has been slow and complex. Most are far away from population centers, and many are still encumbered by private rights and limits. Adding lands closer to the cities is arduous, expensive and slow.[10]

---

[8] See S. P. Hays, *Conservation and the Gospel of Efficiency* (Cambridge: Harvard University Press, 1959), and the many sources cited there.

[9] Of this total, only 186 million acres are in National forests, and only 24 million acres in National parks. Most of it is in Alaska.

[10] Under the Land and Water Conservation Fund Act of 1965, money received by the federal government from several sources (receipts from the sale of surplus lands, entrance fees at national recreational areas, charges for the use of camp sites, and a tax on fuel used by motor boats) is kept in a separate fund. Two-fifths of this fund is to be used by the government to purchase outdoor recreational facilities near urban areas. Three-fifths of it is to be

Access to the public domain has been under a great variety of rules and incentives, some of them intensely controversial. Forest cropping is permitted under diverse conditions, on a sustained-yield basis. After decades of modest harvest, the cut was sharply increased and now brings about $400 million per year. The terms do not maximize the public revenue and often are not openly let, but the basic management is along efficient lines.

Grazing on public lands and forests occurs on a large scale under permits and at modest prices. For decades, ranching groups set policies for grazing lands. Fees were nominal; permits were capitalized and sold. Supervision was cut to derisory levels in 1945–48.[11] In 1953–54 a bill supported by President Eisenhower would have made the permit permanent and transferable and permitted their holders to construct improvements, excluding newcomers and creating private property rights on forest lands. This was eventually stopped, and more recently the fees have been raised toward economic levels (from 33 cents to $1.23 per animal per month).

Mining on public lands is under the Mining Act of 1872, except for oil, gas, coal and certain others which are under the Mineral Leasing Act of 1920. The most important of the current issues of minerals policy has to do with the conditions that are to govern the exploitation of oil shale in Wyoming, Colorado, and Utah. The technology of exploitation is still to be developed. But the oil in these shales may be five times the size of the world's known reserves, its value exceeding $300 billion. Four-fifths of the deposits lie under federal lands. The oil industry seeks leases to exploit them, observing government rules and paying royalties. Conservationists contend that their exploitation should be managed by a public agency (or possibly by a semipublic agency such as Comsat) with the oil companies doing the work under contract and the profits going to the government. The issue is still in dispute.

THE ENERGY SECTOR

Among the recent new scarcities, an "energy crisis" has come to the fore during 1971–74. It has had certain dramatic practical effects, familiar to all readers of this book. Many experts doubted that a crisis really existed, perceiving instead a degree of contrivance by special interests. Actually, the 1971–74 episode was a convergence of three specific problems, in oil, natural gas, and electricity. Moreover, it was only a brief episode within the larger trends of increasing energy scarcity.

We begin by considering oil and gas, which are partly related technically.

granted to the states, on a matching basis, for the same purpose. But the amounts involved under this and later provisions remain small.

[11] During the 40s, Senator McCarran of Nevada launched an investigation of Grazing Service "bureaucracy" that ran for seven years. As a result, the agency's appropriation was cut from more than $1 million in 1945–46 to around $500,000 in 1947–48 and its staff from 250 to 86, leaving but 50 men to supervise 158 million acres of grazing lands. In effect, the senator's campaign repealed the Taylor Grazing Act, delivering the grazing districts into the hands of the local boards of stockmen and leaving the Washington office too weak to exercise control.

Oil and Gas

The *oil* side is involved with international supplies, import controls, new Alaskan oil supplies, and power plays between the large oil firms and the Middle Eastern oil countries. The *natural gas* side, by partial contrast, is related mainly to FPC price regulation (recall Chapter 15). In both cases, shortages may arise from market control by the basic suppliers.

World Oil Markets.[12]   There are two cardinal facts: (1) the lop-sided patterns of world oil supply and consumption (see Figure 26–2), and (2) the remarkable 1973–74 rise of the OPEC cartel. The posted price of Middle East crude oil had long been just below $2 per barrel. The large oil companies dominated the market, acting as a noncompetitive cartel in setting prices and planning production and exploration. The oil countries chafed under oligopsony limits which kept the countries' royalties low, at about 25¢ per barrel. Also, the world oil price was held down by new discoveries and improved shipping methods (pipelines, "super-tankers," etc.).

OPEC was formed in 1960, but a 1960s oil glut limited its bargaining power. Small gains were made by OPEC after 1965, but it was the 1973 war with Israel that triggered OPEC's assertion of monopoly power. Oil prices were pushed up to $11 per barrel and seemed likely to stay at least that high until 1980 or later. Meanwhile the major U.S. oil firms had fitted oligopoly behavior by restricting their refinery capacity in the U.S. This accented the crisis further, helped cause gasoline prices to rise from about 38 cents to 60 cents per gallon, caused long lines at service stations, put many thousands of independent stations out of business, and swelled oil-company profits by many billions.

The cartel's prospects depend on complex supply and demand conditions, and on the policy steps that may be taken. The main parts of this interaction are as follows.

Supply.   Oil occurs under special conditions (see the next section), in all sorts of odd places. The locations vary (Figure 26–2). Costs also differ, from about 12¢ per barrel in Saudi Arabia to 60¢ in Venezuela and $2.50 and higher in the U.S. and other locations (U.S. costs are enhanced by the U.S.'s own policies, as we will shortly see). Currently the Arab oil states dominate the holdings of low-cost proven reserves. They also consume little.

Therefore these OPEC countries (1) hold monopoly power in selling to consuming nations (such as Europe, Japan and the U.S.), and (2) earn large economic rents. Their rents are so large, indeed, that some OPEC members can easily cut production and forego current revenues. (The private oil firms now only get about 20¢ to 50¢ per barrel, down sharply from the $2 or so before 1970.)

Potential reserves are much larger, lying in widely disparate sites. They will greatly augment present *proven* reserves, perhaps reducing

---

[12] See especially, Morris A. Adelman, *The World Petroleum Market* (Baltimore: Johns Hopkins Press, 1972) and R. B. Mancke, *The Economics of Energy Policy* (New York, Columbia University Press, 1974) for reviews of basic conditions.

FIGURE 26-2

Where the Oil Is—and Goes

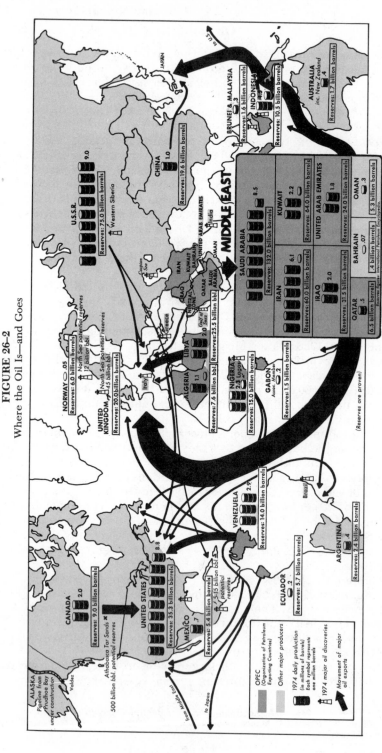

Adapted from "Where the Oil Is—and Goes," *Time*, January 6, 1975, pp. 10–11.

the relative importance of OPEC supply. Yet discovery—especially by deep-water rigs—is difficult and full of surprises. New reserves may have high production costs; current estimates are at $8 per barrel and up. Other substitutes (shale oil, tar sands, nuclear breeder reactors, etc.) are also costly and speculative.

Accordingly, the long-run supply of oil is only partially elastic. For the next decade at least, OPEC oil is likely to gain high rents and to bulk large in world oil sales.

Demand. Two large oil users—the U.S. and the U.S.S.R.—also have large reserves. By contrast, continental Europe and Japan require large imports (see Figure 26–2). Yet all industrial economies face rises in oil demand so great that imports are likely to grow more critical. Demand is generally income-elastic (motoring, home heating, plastic products, etc.), but only moderately price-elastic. The growth of consumption has been rapid and seems likely to continue so.

Since 1973, industrial countries have groped for methods of abating this growth, including taxes, quotas, allocation schemes, closure of gas stations on Sundays, simple pleas for voluntary restraint, and others. These efforts will continue, for growing demand will tend to keep OPEC cartel prices firm. The margin of reduction need not be large, especially for the U.S. A reduction to about 2 percent per year—*plus* the onset of new North Sea, Alaskan, and other oil—could sharply cut their reliance on the 30 million barrels per day that OPEC countries now sell.

The importing countries differ widely, in oil reserves, growth rates, balance of payments stresses, etc. Therefore, a buyers' cartel among them is difficult to form (see Figure 26–2 and Table 26–2). Beyond a minimal level, concerted action to offset the OPEC cartel is likely to be unstable. The Israel-Arab issue adds further complications, tending to crystallize Arab unity and divide the consuming countries.

Cartel Prospects. At this writing, the most careful estimates are that OPEC will maintain the $11 price until at least 1980. (Try to forecast it yourself. Make the elements in your forecast explicit.) Table 26–1 suggests the stresses for consumers and wealth for producers which such a continuing flow might create.

Within OPEC, there are two groups. Group One includes the seven populous, poor and developing countries: Iran, Venezuela, Indonesia, Iraq, Nigeria, Algeria and Ecuador. They need the funds and will be loath to restrict production significantly. The other six, in Group Two— Saudi Arabia, Libya, Kuwait, Abu Dhabi, Dabai and Qatar—are lightly populated and are collecting far more money than they can possibly spend. They are also most deeply involved in the Israel-Arab conflict, by proximity and religious conviction. Future restrictions will evolve mainly upon Group Two, while Group One is more likely to "chisel" or leave the cartel ranks. Iran, Venezuela and Nigeria are the critical swing sellers, who may eventually weaken OPEC's price front. The consuming nations will try to widen this divergence of interests by diplomatic, commercial and other means. A range of threats and incentives will be used.

The outcome will reflect a complex but classic bilateral oligopoly process, operating under uncertain and changing conditions. Policies to

TABLE 26–2

The Incidence of Yearly Oil Spending and Revenues

Spending for Oil Imports	1972	1974 (and possibly 1975 to 1980?)
		(*$ billion*)
United States	3.9	24.0
Japan	3.9	18.0
West Germany	2.9	11.3
France	2.5	9.5
United Kingdom	2.4	8.5
Italy	1.8	7.5
Brazil	.5	3.0

Revenues from Oil Exports	1972	1974 (and possibly 1975 to 1980?)
		(*$ billion*)
Saudi Arabia	2.8	28.9
Iran*	7.4	20.9
Venezuela*	2.0	10.0
Nigeria*	1.2	9.2
Libya	1.6	8.9
Kuwait	1.5	8.5
Iraq	.6	7.6

* Group two members (see text).

abate OPEC's power will need to fit the standard lessons of industrial organization, as seen elsewhere in this book.

Drilling and Unitization. OPEC's effects have superseded a complex system of official controls in the U.S., which had operated as an internal cartel with government support. This was a pathological form of "regulation." Since it may recur, it will be summarized here shortly.

But first we need to understand the problem of shared access.[13] Deposits of crude petroleum are found, at depths varying from a few hundred to several thousand feet, in reservoirs of irregular shape lying between successive folds of rock. In these deposits, oil occurs with gas and water, the three being separated in accordance with their specific gravities: the gas above, the water below, and the oil between. When the rock that seals a reservoir is punctured by drilling, the oil is forced to the surface by the pressure of expanding gas. If wells are so placed, in relation to the conformation of the underlying strata, as to make full use of this pressure, a maximum of oil and gas will be recovered at a minimum of cost. But if they are not, the gas may be permitted to escape, its pressure will be wasted, and the oil will have to be brought up, at higher cost, by pumps. A pool of oil, moreover, is a geologic unit. If wells are properly spaced, and rates of flow adjusted, gas pressure can be so distributed as to economize its use. But if wells are close together and operated independently, gas and its pressure may both be thrown away.

For economy in exploitation, a pool should be under common management. For the pool illustrated in Figure 26–3, drilling would proceed slowly, wells being placed in accordance with the conformation of the reservoir, spaced to take full advantage of gas pressure, and carefully cased to prevent water from flooding the pool. There would be no well on the land of C. The gas trapped at this point would be used to drive the oil up through the wells of B and D. Assume, however, that property lines are drawn as indicated by the markers on the surface and the dotted lines below. Now C, sinking a well, strikes gas. He finds no market for it in his vicinity. He cannot store it. And if he leaves it underground, it will go to work producing oil, not for him, but for B and D. So he blows it off, in order to reach the oil.

All of the owners move so swiftly that they cannot drill with care. Most of them case their wells effectively to seal off water. But D does not. So water from above now floods the pool. Water also advances from below. It could be held back, and more oil pumped out, if A and E would pump in air. But they have no incentive to do so, since the costs would be charged to them and the profits collected by B, C, and D. So gas is thrown away, and oil mixed with water and left underground. The situation has been even worse than that depicted here. For wells have been drilled, not at the center of each man's property, but to offset one another at its outer limits, the feet of derricks all but touching along the boundaries.

Despite this compelling technical need, unitization, in general, is not

---

[13] Erich W. Zimmerman, *Conservation in the Production of Petroleum* (New Haven, Conn.: Yale University Press, 1957); Wallace F. Lovejoy and Paul T. Homan, *Economic Aspects of Oil Conservation Regulation* (Baltimore: Johns Hopkins Press, 1967), chap. 4.

compulsory. In some states, as has been noted, pooling of interests in a drilling unit may be required. But this principle is not usually extended to an entire field. In some states, too, voluntary unitization agreements have been exempted from the antitrust laws. But agreement here must be unanimous: if one landowner holds out, the project fails.

In Oklahoma, a unitization order can be proposed if owners of more than half of a pool request it, but will not become effective if owners of

FIGURE 26–3
Cross-Section Sketch Showing the Occurrence and Mining of
Oil and Gas

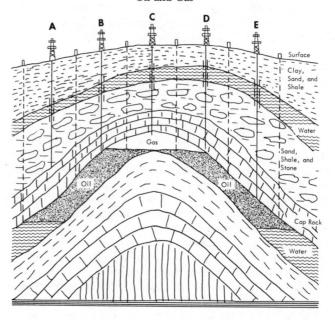

more than 37 percent object. In Louisiana, an order cannot be issued if owners of more than 25 percent object. In Texas, where production is greatest, unitization cannot be required.

In short, the simple unitizing of oil fields has not been achieved. Policy tolerates inefficiency and waste.

Controls, Quotas and Taxes. Now we turn to the restrictions on oil markets. Domestic oil supply was bound hand and foot by cartel controls during 1935–73. Texas led the way by having its Railroad Commission control the rates of production of most wells. Under "prorationing," production at each well was set at a percentage of capacity: during 1936–69 (apart from World War II) the rate was usually well under 50 percent, and often 20 percent. The system spread to all other oil states and was supported by the Bureau of Mines, which made the demand estimates upon which the whole system pivoted.

The procedure followed by the regulatory agency in such a state is this: (1) It determines total output for the state by forecasting total demand at the prevailing price, using the estimates made by the Bureau of Mines and such other data as it may choose. (2) It subtracts from this total the probable output of wells that are exempted from control: wells producing small quantities, those producing on artificial lift, those in secondary recovery, etc. (3) It divides the remainder of the state's allowable output, in accordance with the provisions of an allocation formula, among the remaining wells, determining the output allowed each pool by multiplying that allowed per well by the number of wells in the pool. (4) At the middle of each month, it issues an order, fixing the allowable output for the coming month. Formerly, Texas set its quotas in terms of the number of days per month in which wells were permitted to produce. This proved, however, to be a clumsy method of control and, in 1963, Texas joined the other states in fixing its quotas as a percentage of the wells' total capacity. Following this procedure, in June, 1966, prorated wells were producing at 34 percent of capacity in Texas, at 35 percent in Louisiana, and at 38 percent in Oklahoma.

Control by the states is aided by the federal government. The Bureau of Mines makes its monthly forecasts of consumer demands for gasoline, fuel oil, and other petroleum products, translates these forecasts into an estimate of the demand for crude, and divides this total into separate estimates for the producing states. It then transmits its estimates to the regulatory agencies of the states. The Bureau's forecast of total demand is an estimate of the quantity that will be bought at the prevailing price. It does not show how much less would be bought if the price were raised or how much more would be bought if it were reduced. It assumes the legitimacy of price fixing, accepting without question the proposition that price should be taken as given and supply adjusted to demand.

The economic effects were predictable.[14] Drilling has been excessive, in order to get quota rights. This extra cost has been as much as $1 billion a year. The thousands of extra wells reduce recovery by leaking pressure from the oil field. And the conventional monopoly effects on oil consumers occurred. Some marginal conservation benefits also occurred, from keeping oil in the ground. But these could be obtained in other ways, which would not cause such waste and inequity.

Though the official rate rose to 100 percent in 1973—lifting the controls for the time being—the control system remains intact and can be easily reactivated.

Import quotas were imposed during 1959–73, for the most part limiting imports of oil to 12.2 percent of domestic output. This preserved a price gap, so that the lucky firms holding quota rights imported oil at $2 a barrel and sold it at $3.30 or more. The sheer windfall gain was enormous: American consumers paid $6 billion more per year and oil firms gained $4 billion per year. The quotas were abolished during the oil crisis

---

[14] Wallace F. Lovejoy and Paul T. Homan, *op. cit.,* Chap. 6; see also James W. McKie and S. L. McDonald, "Petroleum Conservation in Theory and Practice," *Quarterly Journal of Economics,* Vol. LXXVI (1962), pp. 98–121.

in 1973 after resisting all previous efforts to modify or remove them.[15]

The third policy set affecting oil conservation involved two kinds of special tax treatment. Under the corporate income tax law, the industry may write off most of the intangible costs of drilling oil wells in a single year instead of spreading them—as other industries must do—over the life of the assets, this privilege resulting in a tax saving of some $300 million per year. And from 1925 until 1969, the industry could deduct from income, under the percentage depletion provision described above, 27.5 percent of the value of its properties, up to half of its income, each year. Other industries pay the government half of their profits; the oil industry has paid only 6 or 7 percent.[16] This favor has provided a subsidy of $1.5 billion per year. An attack was made on the depletion allowance when Congress debated the so-called tax reform bill of 1969, but its opponents succeeded only in reducing it from $27^1/_2$ percent to 22 percent. The 1973–74 surge in oil profits evoked more calls to reduce the tax concessions, but the outcome is doubtful. This is because reductions are asserted to discourage exploration for new supplies.

In short, the oil industry has joined with public agencies in setting restrictive, costly and conservationally dubious controls. Most of the basic ones continue.

Natural Gas. As for this sector, the possible role of the FPC in inducing a shortage has been considered earlier, in Chapter 15. The lessons are mixed. The shortage may have been aggravated by FPC price limits, but it also could be explained by mere expectations, or even in part by a degree of effective joint behavior by the major suppliers. To a large extent, price controls on gas could be effective if they break the suppliers' expectations of higher future prices. And in any case, the large windfall capital gains for the small group of owners could have been treated so as to avoid a large disequalizing effect.

Electricity

Next we turn to shortages in electricity supply.[17] We have seen (Chapter 15) that these shortages are largely artificial. They have been aggravated by promotional pricing, which increases the total rate of usage, as well as the load level at peak times. For several decades this has increased the necessary peak-load capacity above the optimum level. In recent years, this induced waste has made the capacity problem more acute. The rush to nuclear power—which has been subsidized and presents more hazards than have been properly researched—has also come up against difficulties which sharpen the recent stresses.

---

[15] They and other controls may have provided certain national defense benefits, but they were small, doubtful, and highly costly; see Richard B. Mancke, *The Economics of Energy Policy* (New York: Columbia University Press, 1974), and A. E. Kahn, "The Depletion Allowance in the Context of Cartelization," *American Economic Review* (June 1964), pp. 286–314.

[16] Recall from Chapter 25 that many leading oil firms have paid little or no profits tax at all in recent years, even though those profits doubled during 1972–73. The average tax rate for the 10 largest oil firms has been under 10 percent.

[17] Electricity is extremely inefficient in converting primary to retail energy: only about 17 percent of the original energy reaches the consumer. It is automatically an inferior mode of supply on conservationist grounds, whatever its convenience may be.

Restructing energy prices has become an important conservation task, even though it can be expected to require many years to occur. Indeed, the 1971–74 energy crisis may well have eased by the time electricity prices are genuinely shifting towards more rational marginal-cost criteria. But even though it is delayed further, such a revision of electricity prices will offer significant gains for the conservation of resources.

THE PROBLEM OF POLLUTION

Conservation of the environment touches on living conditions which, for many people, are degraded by air, water and noise pollution and by other forms of blight. There are two broad subtopics. One is the dispersal of pollutants—such as smoke, chemicals in streams, and also noise —especially in urban areas. The other is the maintenance and use of natural wildlife and terrain, much of it away from cities. The first question relates most closely to the industries which produce the pollution and the urban policies dealing with them; while the second set of issues is primarily in a meta-urban and federal context.

Urban Pollution and Congestion. These arise primarily from the operation of factories and vehicles which emit fumes and particles. The problem resides mainly in the design of the factories and vehicles. It also relates to the urban balance between pollution-intensive devices, particularly the private automobile—compared to pollution-minimizing systems such as public transit. These further relate to the pricing of urban transport services and of other public-enterprise activities (water, housing, etc.: recall Chapters 21 and 22). Here we will look primarily at the industrial side of these issues.

By 1968, pollution had become an intense problem, surfacing at last for national attention. Many of the nation's streams are polluted with wastes discharged by steel and paper mills, oil refineries, packing plants, canneries, and the like, with pesticides and herbicides washed off the farmer's fields, with detergents discharged by households, and with sewage dumped by local governments. There were 1,582 communities in 1969 that provided no treatment for human wastes; 2,117 that provided only primary treatment. Cities have treated and used the waters that have been polluted by those that lie along the streams above them and, in turn, discharged their sewers into the waters used by those below. Normally, the streams would have cleansed themselves of such pollutants. But now their quantity is so great that this cannot occur. The consequences are serious. The organic pollutants provide food for the growth of algae which rob the waters of their oxygen. Inert materials— dirt, oil films, and other industrial wastes—cut off the light of the sun, inhibiting other growth. The fish, deprived of oxygen and food, die out. The fisheries of Lake Erie, it is said, are gone beyond recovery. Ponds and lakeshores are coated in green slime. The beds of rivers lie deep in oily muck.

Even more serious is pollution of the air. Dense clouds of smoke and soot, noxious fumes and deadly chemicals are discharged into the air by factories and power plants, by incinerators and burning dumps, by commercial and residential buildings, by automobiles, trucks, and airplanes.

So *that's* where it goes. Well, I'd like to thank you fellows for bringing this to my attention.

Credit: Drawing by Stevenson; © *1970 The New Yorker Magazine, Inc.*

Under favorable conditions, these pollutants are dispersed, in part, by the winds. But when there is a temperature inversion, with a warmer layer of upper air preventing cooler air on the ground from rising, the concentration of pollutants becomes dangerously high. Short of this, contaminants in the air attack property, darkening paint, corroding metal, embrittling rubber, and disintegrating stone. They damage crops and injure livestock. And what is worse, they do harm to human lungs, increasing the incidence of respiratory diseases and shortening the span of life.

FIGURE 26-4
Predicted Distribution of Total Environmental
Expenditures 1972-1981*

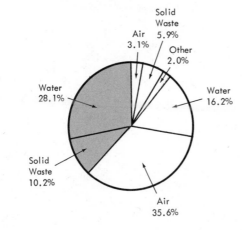

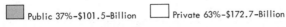
Public 37%-$101.5-Billion   Private 63%-$172.7-Billion

Total—$274.2-Billion

* Figures do not total due to rounding.
Source: Council on Environmental Quality. The New York Times, Sept. 18, 1973.

Nor is this all. There is the destruction of natural beauty: loggers denuding the hillsides, mines building up slag heaps, stripmines cutting great gashes through the landscape. There is the assault on the wilderness: superhighways driven through the forests, jet ports built in wildlife refuges. There is the creation of ugliness: the mountains of industrial and household wastes, the junk yards, billboards, and hideous commercial enterprises that line our roadsides. And there is noise—unceasing and increasing noise.

The costs of abating pollution during 1972-81 were estimated in 1973 at $274 billion (see Figure 26-4) under current policies. Major improvements had occurred by 1975, but most of the problem remained.[18]

---

[18] The Hudson River had been made clean enough for fish to live again along much of its length, for example. Air pollution was marginally less. But acute problems remained, and noise had scarcely been treated at all.

Efficient abatement of pollution often requires applying direct limits, or incentives and penalties. The objective is not zero pollution, but rather the optimum degree consistent with other economic costs and benefits. Determining that optimum level is itself a major problem, and the practical effectiveness of alternative incentives and compulsions are not thoroughly known.

In practice, a rough process of negotiation and learning has occurred, involving a variety of inducements. There are flat prohibitions; quantitative standards; fines and other incentives; tax remissions (e.g., pollution control bonds, etc.); and others (see Table 26–3). The normal regulatory

TABLE 26–3
Some Recent Actions to Abate Pollution

1948	Water Pollution Control Act	Loans for local sewage works. Trivial until 1956; $800 million yearly by 1970.
1959–64		Orders against industrial pollution begin; still minimal effect.
1965	Water Quality Act	State standards required by 1967; tightened in 25 cases. Expanded after 1970.
1965	Clean Air Act	Sets air quality standards, especially on auto emissions.
1967	Air Quality Act	Set up National Center for Air Pollution Control
1970	National Air Quality Act	Requires cutting auto emissions by 90%. The goal is now set for 1977.
1975		Many pollution goals are postponed, on grounds of cost.

bargaining process has occurred in scores of industries, with frequent overstatements looking toward a compromise. Any appraisal of this complex process is beyond this book, but there is one strong industrial aspect: the controls and penalties almost always bear harder on small and marginal producers than on the major firms. With their survival threatened, these lesser firms have special incentives to resist pollution controls. When applied, the controls will tend to increase concentration, unless they are carefully designed to avoid it. (Recall that this asymmetric effect is true of certain other antitrust and regulatory policies.) In the long run, conservation may justify even a degree of unfair and concentration-inducing effects. But these effects do exist and may be significant.

Industrial structure may also play a causative role: Does the degree of monopoly affect the degree of polluting? The problem subdivides again into two parts. First, there are externalities among firms which are still *internal* to the industry. These will tend, of course, be greater under competition than monopoly. Unitizing the industry under single control will apply incentives to eliminate such external effects, though anything less than pure monopoly will not suffice.

Second, the greater mass of externalities are *external* to the entire industry. These will be affected primarily by the level of output in the industry. This will be greater under competition than under monopoly, as we have seen since Chapter 1, and so competition gives more pollution than monopoly. But monopolizing will only slightly abate the effect. And oligopoly may tend to maximize pollution, when the design of the product itself is concerned. Innovations to reduce the emission of pollution are usually optional to the manufacturer, and shared-monopoly outcome may minimize such innovations.

A leading example of this is the automobile industry's efforts to develop antismog devices for automobiles during 1955–70.[19] The social need for cleaner cars become apparent in the 1950s, but little was done by the auto firms until the late 1960s, and then only under direct rulings by a public agency. In the 1950s, the automobile makers agreed not to compete in antismog technology. Instead they formally agreed on a joint-venture approach, covering both the development and application of new technology.

By 1962, Chrysler had developed a new control system, but it was discouraged from applying it by pressure from other firms under the joint approach. Yet the competitive situation would strongly induce the smaller firms to make extraordinary efforts to be the first with antismog devices, especially if they would be made mandatory for all cars by a public ruling. In fact, such rulings have occurred, under the automobile emission-control program since 1965.

The smaller auto firms have indeed had intense incentives to develop the device first, so as to become the monopoly supplier to all of the rest of the entire industry. Chrysler's behavior precisely fitted this incentive structure, as also did the lack of innovation by the larger firms.

A strong antitrust case against this pattern was developed, but in 1969 it was dropped amid persuasive charges of political influence. The joint controls have been eased, but a degree of inhibition remains. In any event, the situation illustrates a general condition: that shared-monopoly incentives abate the development of technology that would reduce external costs.

Parks and Scenic Resources. This poses issues of public ownership. Inherently, private market processes will always adjust and equalize the degree of use and amenity, so that no substantial tract of land or natural scenic beauty will remain untouched. The best parts will be picked out and the character of the whole will be eroded; the greater the value, the greater the incentive.[20] Furthermore, if private owners do maintain a natural landmark, they will still rationally restrict and sell access to it so as to maximize their private gain.

---

[19] See R. F. Lanzillotti and R. D. Blair, "Automobile Pollution, Externalities and Public Policy," *Antitrust Bulletin,* Vol. 18, No. 3 (Fall 1973), pp. 431–47.

[20] A good recent example is the 307-foot private sight-seeing mast opened in July 1974 at Gettysburg battlefield. Erected despite intense public opposition (including the Governor of Pennsylvania, two Secretaries of the Interior, scores of historians, experts and preservationists, and the U.S. Park Service), the structure now dominates the historic skyline. At an initial ticket price of $1.35, it is a "business bonanza." Its owner said, "I'm dedicating this to the American enterprise system. I had to beat the whole establishment—local, state, Federal, intellectual, you name it—to get this done, and this country let me do it" (*New York Times,* July 28, 1974). Such incentives operate universally to erode other sites and resources.

Therefore, public ownership and management is usually necessary in order to maintain the minimum stock of natural terrain and landmarks and to make them fairly available. The lesson is universal: in Europe the outstanding parks and wilderness areas, both in cities and in the countryside, have survived only because commercial interests were abridged or excluded. Thus Kensington Gardens, Hampstead Heath, and St. James and Regents Park in London were all preserved by aristocrats insulated from commercial incentives. This holds also for most of the large rural estates and tracts which have become national parks and monuments, in Britain, the U.S., and elsewhere. If the older aristocratic, religious or other shields against commercial exploitation will not suffice, public action is the only recourse.

Yet public ownership of cultural and national assets should not be immune from all economic considerations. Maintenance is often costly and should be set at the right level and format. Timber and other resources often can be harvested without destroying or even altering the significant features. And those who visit such landmarks can be—and often are—charged some form of price related to their usage and costs. In the U.S. this fosters endlessly debatable policies on granting mineral and forest rights to private interests on public lands (recall above). There is also the hidden but important converse problem that portions of many public lands and parks are in fact still held by private owners.[21]

The problems of setting the capacity, format, and charges for park use are intricate (recall Chapter 22). The basic principle is that even the publicly owned lands and monuments will tend to be overused if treated strictly on economic grounds. The development and use of natural and cultural landmarks almost always erodes their inherent character. The evaluations which determine capacity and prices for using them should usually lean towards less use. This is heightened by the insufficiency of budgets for most public conservationist agencies dealing with natural and urban landmarks. Like other public agencies serving broad social purposes, they are nearly always well below their optimum budget levels and lacking adequate powers.

There is one added proviso: the criterion of fairness is often neglected in these evaluations. Yet it can be important, because the location and charges for such access often favor the middle and upper classes (recall Chapter 22). Therefore efficient prices reflecting true social cost may have a regressive incidence. As in so many other policy treatments, special adjustments in format and pricing may be necessary to serve equity.

FISH

The taking of fish is an increasingly important activity using oceanic resources. It fits within the analysis of optimum yield (recall the first section). These optimum harvesting conditions are complicated by the mobility of the fish themselves, and so there are deep problems in management and pricing, as well as in international diplomacy. Though

---

[21] Thus, significant parts of Yosemite Park, among others, are still in private hands.

unified management is usually necessary (though not sufficient) for optimal harvesting, this is often impossible in international waters.

The Optimum Harvest. This can often be determined precisely, in technical terms. One estimates the initial stock of fish, the technical costs involved in cropping the fish, and the conditions for maintaining the fish population. The optimum rate of take can be derived, and the efficient set of fishing technology can be applied so as to reach the optimum. Conditions may vary from year to year as unexpected changes occur, but these can be readily accommodated in the analysis. The manager of the

FIGURE 26–5
International Fishing Poses the Unification Problem Acutely

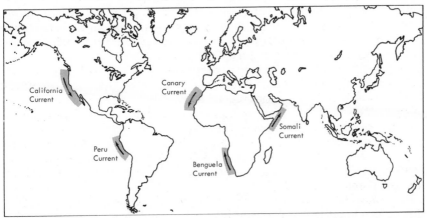

Along the current paths shown in the map, prevailing winds and the earth's rotation cause surface water to move away from the coast. It is replaced by nutrient-rich water rising from the ocean depths. The upwellings make these waters especially fertile areas for concentrations of fish. But these can be—and have been—depleted by intensive, competitive fishing. Unless they can be organized and managed efficiently, global food scarcities may be aggravated.

unified fishery would, of course, need to be placed under appropriate constraints, if his position involved a high degree of monopoly. This can be done along conventional lines.

International fishing poses the unification problem in acute form (see Figure 26–5). The efficient answer is a joint agency with powers to compel cooperation. However, this has anciently been a difficult task. There are the classic cartel incentives for each claimant to stay outside or to break ranks. This often is enough in itself to avert any joint controls. It is sharpened by the differences in economic status and interests among the countries. One claimant country is often much poorer and militarily less powerful than others. Thus, Iceland can well believe that her interests in controlling fishing within a hundred miles of her coast are more pressing than those of Britain, Russia, and other more affluent economies. Such discord of motives further undermines fishing agreements, to the point of armed conflicts around Iceland and off South America in recent years. Such conflicts have occurred throughout human history. The modern instances confirm the continuing power of the incentives and the difficulty of reaching solutions.

Several Actual Cases Illustrate the Problems. For fisheries within countries, prime examples are oyster fishing off the East Coast and salmon fishing on the Northwest Coast. In both cases, unified management is needed and feasible. But competitive fishing is permitted and runs to excess. The technology of boats and tackle is increasingly powerful, so that the race for catch has quickened. The public interest requires reducing the rate of take. Yet as long as entry is permitted, this can only be done by limiting the size of nets, the power of motors, the size of boats, the time period permitted, and so forth. This has been done, but the limits induce further adaptation and innovation and so the controls must be continually tightened. The result is an increasingly wasteful technology, which nonetheless results in a continuing depletion of the fish population (even past point *B* in Figure 26–1).

Salmon harvesting in the U.S. northwest is the classic case where unification yields efficiency. Each year, salmon go upstream in clearwater rivers to breed. In some rivers they pass over salmon ladders which by-pass dams and other obstructions. In others there are precise points where netting could be managed. There can be complete control over the cropping of salmon, by replacing salmon fishing with unified harvesting. Instead, state regulations ban this, and so private fishing engenders extra fishing equipment and costs, distorted innovation, and the depletion of the fish population itself.

Quotas were imposed in 1966 on the major yellowfin tuna ground in the eastern Pacific. These encourage the fastest rate of catch; by 1973 the rate was so high that the season lasted only 69 days. Controls on fishing equipment often approach the bizarre.[22] Federal efforts to reform the rules have been stalled because they threaten the large number of inefficient operators which state regulation has protected.

The U.S. Fishing Industry. Fishing has declined sharply in recent decades, owing to misguided policies as well as innate inefficiency.[23] The U.S. catch has stayed about constant during 1948–74, while world production rose from 18 to 76 million tons. Foreign ships handle about 10 times as much fish per man-day as do U.S. ships. The U.S. haddock catch has dropped from 40 to 5 million pounds between 1965 and 1972 (see Figure 26–6). Almost all economy fish (frozen fillets, fish sticks, etc.) are now imported. Foreign technology stresses large factory ships on long tours with advanced freezing and processing capability. The Soviets and Japanese have led this progress. Except for tuna, U.S. fishing technology involves old, small, and specialized ships, on short trips and bound by wage agreements which often discourage effort. There is little innova-

---

[22] Virginia oystermen must employ cumbersome twenty-foot tongs to raise oysters laboriously from public waters, instead of using efficient dredges towed by boats. In Maryland, dredges can be used, *if* they are towed by *sailboats; except* that motorized push-boats can be used—on Mondays and Tuesdays only. T. Alexander, "American Fishermen are Missing the Boat," *Fortune* (September, 1973), pp. 192 ff.

[23] T. Alexander, *Fortune, op. cit.*

tion or effort to develop markets for new, cheaper kinds of fish (e.g., croaker, sablefish, blowfish tails, and *squid*).

Two U.S. policies have deepened the decline. One has required all U.S. fishing ships to be built in U.S. shipyards. This doubles the cost. The second policy permits only U.S.-built ships to land fresh seafood in this country. This has induced U.S. fishers to specialize in high-cost fresh fish, and to neglect the more efficient and fast-growing frozen fish markets.

FIGURE 26-6
Declines in the U.S. Catch of Certain Fish since 1960

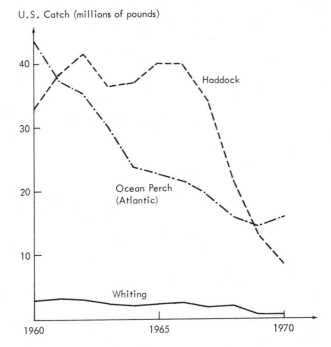

Two large, efficient, federally subsidized ships were launched in 1968, at a public cost of $12 million. But experienced crew were lacking, and poor management and wage incentives had killed their prospects by 1970.

Open-Seas Fishing. This involves large degrees of overfishing, which threaten the whole supply. At present practices, the potential sustainable yield of major species is about 110 million tons; present growth rates would reach that by 1980.[24] Better management might triple this yield, and the use of less familiar species could further double or triple the yield. Most of the species and fishing grounds are now overfished. Unified and efficient management is therefore a critical task. There is now a race

---

[24] J. A. Gulland, ed., *The Fish Resources of the Oceans* (Rome: U.N. Food and Agricultural Organization, 1971).

between decentralized economic interests and the effort to organize this complex industry, so as to restore incentives for conservation. The world stakes are very high.

SUMMARY

Conservation relates both to cost-benefit analysis and to industrial structure. The solutions draw on the same policy concepts that have applied throughout this book.

Many actual policies have strayed from the optimum, with a variety of clear costs. Some involve windfall gains; others are continuing wastes. Most of them have grown familiar over a long series of decades. Their scope and urgency are increasing, both in the U.S. and on a world basis.

CHAPTER TWENTY-SEVEN

Providing Health Care

H ealth care is intensely personal and important. It also touches on many problems and services, from doctors to blood banks to nursing homes. And it is increasingly costly, as Table 27–1 and Figure 27–1 show.

Medical services can be organized and paid for in a great variety of ways, some more efficient and equitable than others. A society's health system reflects its character, and yet the components of the system can also be changed. Health care in many other countries differs sharply from current U.S. patterns, and they too are evolving. Indeed, U.S. health care has recently been said to be in crisis, and it has come under deep research and rethinking. Like other sectors, it may develop major changes during the 1970s.

The sector's structure and policies are in the mainstream of this book.[1] What degree of competition and of public enterprise should there be for doctors, hospitals, and blood supply? What regulation may be appropriate? We look first at the special attributes of health care as a personal service. Then we summarize the main varieties of health-care systems in western countries. Next we discuss several parts of the sector: doctors, hospitals, blood supply, and nursing homes. The last section briefly summarizes certain alternatives for U.S. health care.

ATTRIBUTES OF MEDICAL CARE

Most readers of this book, being young and robust, will have to use their imaginations to appreciate how important health care generally is. As Figure 27–2 illustrates, most youths need little health care. But as Father Time moves on, the body matures, ages, withers, and eventually

---

[1] Excellent basic sources include H. E. Klarman, *The Economics of Health* (New York: Columbia University Press, 1965); H. M. Somers and A. R. Somers, *Doctors, Patients and Health Insurance* (Washington D. C.: Brookings Institution, 1961); U.S. Department of Health, Education and Welfare, *Medical Care Prices: A Report to the President* (Washington, D.C.: U.S. Government Printing Office, 1967) (the "Gorham Report"); M. J. Feldstein, *Economic Analysis for Health Service Efficiency* (New York: Markham, 1968); and *The Economics of Health and Medical Care* (Ann Arbor: University of Michigan, 1964).

TABLE 27-1

National Health Expenditures, by Type of Expenditure and Source of Funds, Fiscal Year 1972–73 (in millions)

| | | Source of Funds | | | | | |
| | | Private | | | Public | | |
Type of Expenditure	Total	Total	Consumers	Other	Total	Federal	State and Local
Total (1972–73)	$94,070	$56,516	$51,925	$4,591	$37,554	$24,620	$12,934
Health services and supplies	87,562	53,553	51,925	1,628	34,009	22,005	12,004
Hospital care	36,200	16,951	16,483	468	19,249	12,609	6,640
Physicians' services	18,040	13,999	13,986	13	4,041	2,992	1,049
Dentists' services	5,385	5,097	5,097	—	288	188	101
Other professional services	1,680	1,439	1,404	35	241	168	73
Drugs and drug sundries*	8,780	8,110	8,110	—	670	360	310
Eyeglasses and appliances	2,109	2,025	2,025	—	84	48	37
Nursing-home care	3,735	1,512	1,485	27	2,223	1,350	873
Expenses for prepayment and administration	4,198	3,335	3,335	—	863	685	178
Government public health activities	2,811	—	—	—	2,811	1,215	1,596
Other health services	4,624	1,085	—	1,085	3,539	2,392	1,147
Research and medical-facilities construction	6,508	2,963	—	2,963	3,545	2,615	930
Research*	2,277	220	—	220	2,057	1,977	80
Construction	4,231	2,743	—	2,743	1,488	638	850
Publicly owned facilities	971	—	—	—	971	136	835
Privately owned facilities	3,260	2,743	—	2,743	517	502	15

* Research expenditures of drug companies are included in drugs and drug sundries and excluded from research expenditures.
Source: Department of Health, Education and Welfare, Publication No. (SSA) 74–11701, Dec. 27, 1973.

FIGURE 27-1
Rising Health-care Costs

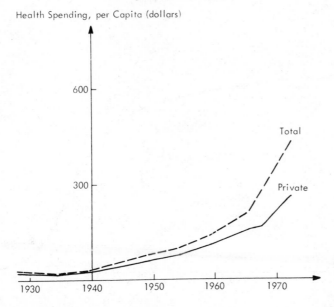

Health Spending, per Capita (dollars)

gives up the ghost. By age 50, many people have a serious health problem, by 60 the doctor may be seen often, and by age 70 most of the survivors greet each new month—or morn—gratefully. Along the way, too, there are sicknesses, accidents, and deaths. Health-care services are matters of life or death, and/or of easing pain, both for one's self and for family and friends. Some medical problems are chronic, others acute, still others partly optional (smoking, overeating, overworking). Some are predictable, while others strike out of the blue. As you, your relatives, and your friends go through this life, you will regard health services as increasingly important and, probably, increasingly costly and complicated. Health care is a crucial industry, with very strong social effects.

Medical Problems. Medical problems are of a remarkably wide variety, and so private choices might well optimize their treatments. But most of them share the following special features:

1. *Unpredictability.* Accidents and sickness are often highly unpredictable, and so they entail varying degrees of risk, from small to catastrophic.[2] This creates the need for pooling risks among individuals, on well-known insurance principles. However, the risk varies and is partly predictable, especially by age, prior medical condition, and occupation. Therefore, groups of people can be singled out fairly precisely by their degree of medical risk. Private insurors' incentives therefore may

---

[2] See Klarman, *op. cit.;* and K. J. Arrow, "Uncertainty and the Welfare Economics of Medical Care," *American Economic Review,* Vol. 53 (December 1963), pp. 941–73.

FIGURE 27–2
The Downhill Lifetime Health Curve

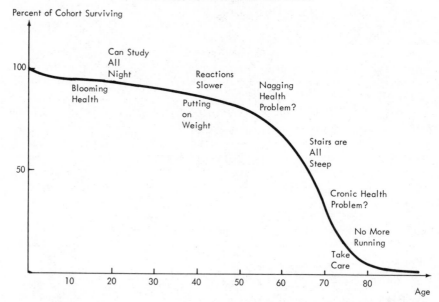

Percent of Cohort Surviving

Can Study All Night

Reactions Slower

Nagging Health Problem?

Blooming Health

Putting on Weight

Stairs are All Steep

Cronic Health Problem?

No More Running

Take Care

Age

clash with the social aim of equal and universal coverage. Still, much medical hazard is quite unforeseeable by each individual.

2. *External effects.* Some diseases are contagious, posing external costs. Prevention or cure is then in the public interest as well as a private matter, and so public measures are justified.

3. *Lack of knowledge: professional trust.* The medical client customarily does not know what is wrong with him, nor what the choices of treatment are; that indeed is why he goes to the doctor. Diagnosis is part of the mystery, and so is prognosis and prescription. The client is in the specialist's hands, and this automatically creates a conflict of interests for the expert. His monetary gain from the treatment is subject to his own choice, since the client is ordinarily passive.

From this arises the common condition of doctors as professionals, in whom there is—or can be—trust. The trust covers both (1) the expert opinion and answers, and (2) the avoidance of unprofessional exploitation of the client. One can seek additional medical opinions, and so this can limit or moderate any single doctor's position of power. But this is rarely done, because, again, the patient usually must assume a passive role.

4. *Quality differences.* There are wide differences in quality among doctors, among hospitals, and among other inputs for medical care. Allocating them optimally is a complex task. Who gets the attention of the world-famous heart surgeons and other specialists; or even of the best ones in the city? Who gains access to the best hospitals? Who is to be given the costly treatments for mortal diseases (e.g. a kidney machine, cobalt treatment, intensive care, pacemakers)? Is it to be decided by who can pay the most, or by random chance, or by personal preferences of the

doctors or administrators? The possibilities both for inequity and inefficiency are great. The arrangements of health care do resolve this; the social interest is in doing it optimally, whatever that may entail.

5. *Irreversibility.* Many of the medical problems have effects which are irreversible: in some cases invariably, in others if treatment is lacking. One only dies, or loses an arm, or is debilitated, once. This departs from the norm of repetitive market choices. Therefore, there is special importance in making correct decisions and allocating the resources fairly among those who need them.

6. *Personal service.* Most medical care includes a large component of personal service, by doctors, nurses, and others. This has assured that medical costs—like those of other labor-intensive services—will rise more rapidly than the average for all goods and services. It also—and particularly—creates large possibilities for price discrimination by the suppliers. The services are given directly, often by suppliers who treat a range of clients, and so setting prices in line with ability to pay is often a technically possible and common outcome.

7. *Nonprofit units.* In part because of these other special features, much medical care is provided by nonprofit units, rather than the ordinary profit-making enterprise. This can introduce special costs and incentives into the choices.

8. *Joint production.* Some medical services are provided by units which also are teaching or research facilities, such as a university hospital. Therefore, the value of the specific health care need not be financed privately so as to cover all costs, since the other results may also have high value. This is especially true of rare diseases and special conditions, which these leading hospitals usually specialize in. Therefore, this special feature is relatively limited. Still, it does effect many of the more sensitive and productive medical-care units in the country.

9. *Equity.* Health care touches deeply on equity, for it allocates relief from pain, disability and death. Who gets care is of acute personal concern, and the solutions inevitably have a social dimension.

Some medical services have none of these features; much cosmetic surgery is one example, among many others. But much medical service is ingrained with all of these attributes. The demand for health care has high income-elasticity. The demand for treatment of these core problems is price-inelastic. Yet even for core treatments, price elasticity varies in relation to some dimensions of service, such as speed, quality, and location. Also, service often has several technical dimensions of choice—for example, doctor-intensive, drug-intensive, hospital-intensive, or equipment-intensive—so that the demand for any individual form of treatment will be more elastic than the demand for treatment itself. Little is yet known about the true elasticities of demand for medical services. Some analysis of the factors affecting medical costs has been done, but there is not yet a firm research basis for defining the efficient allocation of medical resources.[3]

Some Medical Care Is Clearly a Public Good. The most obvious example is prevention of contagious diseases. But if basic health care is re-

---

[3] See Feldstein, *op. cit.;* and Klarman, *op. cit.*

garded as a "human right" which should be equally accessible to all, then the public interest is much broader. That has fostered comprehensive programs in most industrial economies and China, covering at least the major diseases and accidents which cannot be avoided or predicted. Until modern times, such an ethical right to medical care was often recognized by charitable treatment for indigent patients. At various times from 1900 to 1950, these were superseded by broader public systems in Europe. In the United States and some other countries, they have been supplemented by specialized programs for the elderly and for low-income groups. The charitable, nonprofit hospital persists as a major hybrid form of enterprise, with unusual attributes and problems.[4]

In this broader context, several special issues can be stated in conventional economic terms. The frequent fears of a doctor shortage convert into the question of allocation of doctors among the populace. There can be regional shortages of doctors—as indeed there are in the rural areas of most countries—while the overall supply is adequate. Also, the supply of doctors may be more than adequate to provide one standard of medical quality, but not adequate if the criteria are higher. Further, doctors are only one input for medical treatment, along with drugs, hospitals, equipment, and other paramedical personnel such as nurses, assistants, osteopaths, midwives, even acupuncture specialists. There may be a shortage of accredicted doctors to provide the full range of medical treatment, even though the larger supply of all medical treatment would be fully adequate if unnecessary restrictions are removed.

Hospitals.   Hospitals impose intriguing questions of special objectives and constraints. Most of them are on a nonprofit basis, and so their costs may tend to rise in line with their potential revenues.[5] The problem is analogous to cost-plus incentives in regulation (Part IV) and weapons supply (Ch. 29). If hospitals are financed by charges upon insurance programs which do not exert monopsony power to minimize prices and costs, then hospitals may behave so as to maximize equality regardless of costs. A growing literature analyzing hospital suggests that indeed this is the case.

At present, hospitals have inadequate incentive to be efficient. They are not under strong pressure from patients, because a substantial part of the patients' bills are paid by third parties. Third parties have usually reimbursed hospitals for cost incurred without pressing for greater efficiency. Hospital administrators often lack the training required for effective management. The medical staff of the hospital often presses the hospital administrator and board of trustees for acquisition of the latest medical equipment without regard to the cost implications involved. Trustees are often subject to pressures imposed on them by the community and medical staff. Even where the incentive does exist, initiation and application of cost-reducing innovation is often beyond the resources of an individual institution.[6]

---

[4] See S. Berki, *Hospital Economics* (Lexington, Mass.: D. C. Heath, 1972), and Karen Davis, *Economic Theories of Behavior in Nonprofit, Private Hospitals* (Washington, D.C.: Brookings Institution, 1971).

[5] See Berki *op. cit.;* Davis, *op. cit.;* and Anne R. Somers, *Hospital Regulation: The Dilemma of Public Policy* (Princeton: Industrial Relations Section, Princeton University, 1969).

[6] The "Gorham Report," *op. cit.* pp. 7–9.

Many hospitals, including some of the largest ones in major cities, exhibit high degrees of X-inefficiency, as well as being part of a system which provides an inequitable distribution of care among rich and poor. The analysis of costs has been absent or incomplete at best in most hospitals, so that the setting of prices in line with costs has usually been only primitive. Satisfactory cost-benefit analysis on the components of hospital operation are accordingly difficult or entirely lacking. This has permitted great looseness in the allocating and pricing of hospital resources. It has also added to the rapid rise in hospital cost levels (to over $100 per patient day in 1974).

Altogether the sector and its policies are heterogeneous. This reflects the difficult problems of efficiency and equity; the crucial position of the sector as a close personal matter; and the special role and power of medical specialists, able to extract high payments. The resulting arrangements reflect both the cultural values of the society and the current status of continuing struggles for control and advantage.

Moreover, there is almost endless variety among the different types of systems that can be used. A universal program can be priced, financed, and managed in many different ways. And conversely, a largely private system can be supplemented by public provisions at many or perhaps most specific points. Depending on the internal conditions of the system, a "national health service" can be less optimal than a private-public system: or vice versa.

VARIETIES OF SYSTEMS

National programs which provide universal coverage for at least basic medical care are normal in industrial countries. In most countries, doctors are an elite group, with extensive training and tight credentials for entry into the profession. In most systems, the program is financed mainly from tax revenues; usually there are also moderate payments by all participants and nominal charges for certain items (e.g., drugs). Therefore, most systems provide full or nearly universal coverage, although the degree of equality in the financing the systems varies somewhat.

One point of substantial variety is the basis upon which physicians are paid. A critical difference is whether the doctor is paid per capita for tending the health care needs of a given panel of patients (for example, in Britain each doctor has a panel of up to 2,000 persons), or is salaried, or is paid for doing specific services. The fee-for-service basis is the linchpin of U.S. medical pay, but it is relatively unusual elsewhere. In Sweden, the shift was recently made from fee-for-service to a salary basis. The role of specialists also varies among systems, in some cases being on a fee-for-service basis and elsewhere being more integrated with the routine operation of hospitals. All western countries permit private medical practice to continue, for those who wish additional care outside the publicly financed system. This permits the supplying of special treatment for those who can afford it, as a supplement to the basic universal coverage.

Therefore the U.S. is distinctive in still relying on fee for service, in lacking universal basic coverage, and in the unusually high economic status of doctors.[7] But the systems have been evolving, and major changes in the U.S. system are widely expected to occur by 1980. Also, the special advantages of doctors have arisen only in recent decades, as a vector of several factors, including their exclusionary practices. Another unusual feature of the U.S. arrangements is the role of Blue Cross-Blue Shield and other health insurers. They have dealt with hospitals largely on a passive basis, not questioning the charges or hospital efficiency. On the whole, they merely transmit the rises in hospital costs to the broad range of subscribers, rather than acting as monopsony purchasers who will force suppliers to minimize price. (Certain public programs—especially Medicare and Medicaid—have also adopted a passive role.) Elsewhere, the financing and supply of services are combined, so that the management of costs can be directly controlled.

U.S. ARRANGEMENTS

We will focus briefly on the special market position of doctors; on hospital management; on blood supply, and on facilities and services for the elderly.

Doctors

Doctors now dominate the management and pricing of health care services, making most of the basic decisions affecting efficiency and equity. Their supremacy and prosperity have arisen in recent decades, and the basic outlines can be traced back to the Flexner Report of 1907. That report established the high criteria for medical practice, medical education and hospital management, as a way of assuring that the special "trust" relationship would not be abused. By limiting medical schools and excluding other quasi-medical operators (osteopaths, chiropractors, acupuncturers, midwives, and others), and by restricting behavior, pricing and access to hospitals, doctors controlled competition and created a high degree of monopoly in the markets for its services.[8] Doctors must be qualified on the basis of lengthy and costly training, and they operate within tight prohibitions on competition among themselves. They cannot advertise or compete on a fee basis, and their access to hospital facilities is controlled by their local associations in ways which assure compliance.

Although the power of the American Medical Association, once leg-

---

[7] U.S. physicans' income—net of costs—now averages above $50,000; see annual analysis in *Medical Economics* periodical (reprinted in the *U.S. Statistical Abstract*). This is up from $22,100 in 1959.

[8] The classic criticisms of medical monopoly are in Milton Friedman and Simon Kuznets, *Income from Independent Professional Practice* (New York: National Bureau of Economic Research, 1945); and Reuben A. Kessel, "Price Discrimination in Medicine," *Journal of Law and Economics,* Vol. 1 October 1958), pp. 20–53. See also Elton Rayack, "The Physicians' Service Industry," Chapter 12 in W. Adams, ed., *The Structure of American Industry,* 4th ed. (New York: Macmillan, 1971).

endary, is receding, the main lines of monopoly in medical supply are still intact. They have been transferred—with some changes—from the family-doctor era into the large-scale provision of specialists' services. Doctors no longer engage in deep price discrimination among their rich and poor customers, because fees are now more standardized under insurance payments. Yet many of them did not discriminate much in favor of the poor in any event. As the degree of specialization has risen in recent decades, and the general physician has become scarcer, the practice of medicine has become more a high-pressure, high-income technical activity, in place of the old-fashioned basis of personal trust and long family relationships.[9] The "doctor-patient relationship" is often a mere shadow or completely empty (e.g., pathologists analyzing tissue slides).

So far, doctors have been able to maintain the fee-for-service basis even as part of new public programs—Medicare and Medicaid—which since 1965 have financed a large share of medical care for the aged and the poor. Their insistence on keeping this basis is absolute, since it is regarded as critical for maintaining their independence and control of the content and organization of medical care. We may expect, therefore, that further extensions of public financing of medical care will still preserve the high-income status of doctors and their ability to continue managing the system in accord with their interests.

The exclusions have borne most heavily upon (1) minorities, especially women and blacks, and (2) paramedical suppliers of many kinds, who perform functions virtually equal to those of doctors.[10] By controlling hospital access, doctors have excluded a wide range of medical services and choices, forcing us all to consume at high quality levels from them—or not at all. In fact, supplementary personnel (especially nurses) often provide the real substance of health care, but they are excluded from drawing fees. This is widely conceded among those who are familiar with hospital operations. As a whole, doctors have been drawn from the middle and upper classes, because of the great costs, severe educational discipline and specialized preparation required—under conditions set by the accredited medical profession—to succeed in medical training. Therefore, medical activity has tended to focus high rewards on a medical elite without guaranteeing an equitable provision of services among the population.

The geographical allocation of doctors is biased toward the larger cities. That inevitably reflects differential income opportunities, and so many large cities have an oversupply of doctors while rural areas tend to have shortages.

The market position of doctors remains monopolistic, and the result

---

[9] This is being reversed marginally by the campaigns for primary care in some medical schools, and by experiments with new forms of medical practice, such as health maintenance organizations (see below). But the mainstream of specialist care remains firm.

[10] See the discussion by Kessel, *op. cit.* Women and blacks have been tiny percentages of the total ranks of doctors.

On other defects of public programs, see Karen Davis, "Lessons of Medicare and Medicaid for National Health Insurance," House Subcommittee on Public Health and Environment, *National Health Insurance—Implications,* 93d Cong., 2d sess. (Washington, D. C.: U.S. Government Printing Office, 1974).

includes a known degree of inefficiency in their allocation and a marked inequality in the incidence of their origins and pricing. A degree of this is present in most western medical systems, but the conditions peculiar to American medical practice have made it sharper.

Hospitals

American hospitals are a diverse lot, including municipal, veterans, church-related, nonprofit, and recently a small but growing share of

TABLE 27–2
U.S. Hospitals

		1950	*1960*	*1970*
Hospitals		6,788	6,876	7,123
Beds	1,000	1,456	1,658	1,616
Rate*		9.6	9.2	7.9
Type of Service and Ownership				
Federal hospitals, all types		414	435	408
Beds	1,000	189	177	161
Nonfederal hospitals		6,374	6,441	6,715
Beds	1,000	1,266	1,481	1,455
Short-term general and special		5,031	5,407	5,859
Beds	1,000	505	639	848
Long-term general and special		412	308	236
Beds	1,000	70	67	69
Psychiatric		533	488	519
Beds	1,000	620	722	527
Tuberculosis		398	238	101
Beds	1,000	72	52	20
Nonfederal Ownership or Control				
State hospitals		(2)	556	577
Beds	1,000	(2)	752	558
Local government hospitals		1,654†	1,324	1,680
Beds	1,000	844†	201	219
Nongovernmental nonprofit hospitals		3,250	3,579	3,600
Beds	1,000	368	482	619
For-profit hospitals		1,470	982	858
Beds	1,000	55	46	59

* Beds per 1,000 population.
† State hospitals included with "Local."
Source: *U.S. Statistical Abstract.*

private profit-seeking hospitals (see Table 27–2). Their prices have been rising faster than all other medical prices (see Figure 27–3). Most of them lack precise cost analysis or controls. The optimum size of hospitals is not known conclusively, but recent trends suggest that medium-size hospitals fit the social optimum best.[11] Certain services are best performed on a neighborhood basis, while highly specialized activities are only efficient within very large hospital and regional drawing areas.

But the normal hospital in a normal urban setting is of medium size,

---

[11] See Berki, *op. cit.;* Feldstein, *op. cit.;* and Somers, *op. cit.*

when all dimensions of service and their costs are considered. Many actual hospitals lie well outside this range and so they may embody inefficiency. Also many hospitals are poorly sited and designed for their tasks (this has often been caused by large urban shifts). Moreover, the operation of many hospitals can best be optimized by coordination on a regional basis, with each hospital specializing to a degree. Actual hospital coordination of services tends to be incomplete or lacking. By contrast, collusion among hospitals in dealing with input suppliers and other

FIGURE 27-3
Hospital Costs Are Rising Especially Rapidly

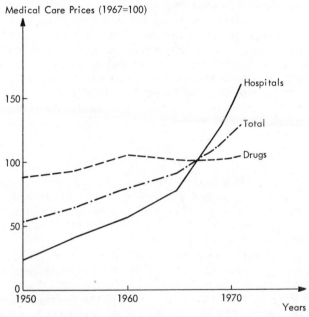

Source: *U.S. Statistical Abstract.*

groups is often high. This is apparent in wage negotiations with nurses and also in the setting of standard fees among hospitals within cities. Therefore hospitals exhibit many of the classic conditions of tight oligopolists with weak constraints on cost.

Some of the rise in hospital prices represents real rises in quality and in input prices, but some of it represents inefficiency which could be reduced by better coordination, costing, and pricing. To some observers, the problem has seemed to call for public regulation of hospitals, and indeed this could abate some of the economic problems.[12] But the biases of conventional regulation (recall Part IV), suggest that regulation of hospitals might simply cloak some problems and add others. If regulators were doctors, they would tend to ratify hospital results; if they were

[12] See Somers, *op. cit.;* and Berki, *op. cit.;* and sources they cite.

not doctors, they would be resisted for trying to interfere in professional matters. And in either event their cost-plus basis might foster still more inefficiency.

Instead, the solution may lie mainly in the monopsony power of private and public insurers or other groups, who would benefit from higher hospital efficiency and who can enforce it directly. At the least, a finer degree of cost analysis and pricing of hospital services is needed. The techniques for this are already reasonably well worked out, and so only the specific choices—probably reinforced by external pressure—need to be developed.

Certain major public city hospitals pose more serious and unattractive problems of mismanagement and inequity. Some of them serve as mere catchments for the castoffs of society. Some of them embody medieval conditions; classic cases of underfunded public units required to carry social problems and tasks which are quite beyond their capacity. But here again the main problems can be analyzed with our conventional concepts, and efficient and fair treatments can be defined in standard terms. Perhaps the political economy of medical care has engendered such deviant hospitals and will tend to perpetuate them. But the directions for improvement do derive from the analytical tools in this book.

Supply of Blood

The supply of blood is mainly from voluntary donors, in all countries. Blood is a highly specialized product; it must be pure and accurately known, it must match the blood type of the recipient, and it must be used quickly. This creates important and difficult problems of storage and transfer and of safety to the recipient.[13]

Private blood supply poses the safety problem directly, because many of those most in need of the money from selling their blood are highly likely to have unsafe blood. In the U.S., private blood sources regularly have rates of hepatitis ten times those of voluntary donors. Some of this risk could be removed by more stringent screening procedures, and indeed a variety of quasi-private supply can be developed. Since blood is something we all—or nearly all—can provide, letting people sell it can be highly equitable.

Yet the voluntary supply of blood may carry important social benefits, both for the giver and the taker. It may be that few opportunities for social contribution are so direct and important as that of giving blood. If one could, with a magic wand, wipe out the safety problem, then a mixed system of donated and paid supply would seem optimal. But the safety problem resists treatment, and so the risks remain high.[14] Moreover, management of the donated supply has also been of dubious efficiency, partly for lack of competitive and budgetary pressures.

---

[13] See especially Richard Titmuss, *The Gift Relationship* (London: Allen and Unwin, 1971).

[14] Thus, during 1973–74 the FDA closed one-quarter of the 265 private plasma-supply centers in the U.S. because of unsafe conditions.

The optimal solution is a complex exercise in competition, pricing, managements and social equity. The present arrangements are probably nonoptimal in several respects.

Nursing Homes

Facilities for treating the aged and infirm have evolved from earlier times, when older people commonly lived with their families. The modern micro family, in which older people do not live with their children or other relatives, presents a need for specialized facilities. Recently, population trends have increased this need.

There has been a rapid growth of retirement homes and communities, but the need for units with greater practical and medical help has also grown. The nursing home has become a conventional form for this. A great variety of them recently have developed in the United States, catering to a wide range of economic groups. Many are charitable or church-related, while others are strictly profit-seeking. In other countries, living facilities for old persons—on a residual basis—are more extensive than in the U.S. But everywhere, these public provisions are normally scanty. They and private nursing homes offer many abusive and inefficient instances.[15]

Therefore, society faces difficult choices in allocating resources for the maintenance of its older members, either on a public or private basis. A natural response to problems with private nursing homes has been the demand to regulate them. But once again, the urge to do something may breed regulation which distorts and adds problems, as well as limits certain defects.

If regulation controls entry and sets high standards of quality, it may exclude a whole range of intermediate-to-cheap services which are all that many citizens could afford. This would bear hardest on poorer citizens. Only if public facilities would then be funded liberally and operated well might a balanced outcome result. Regulation of quality would also limit innovation of new forms of care. The result—similar to other sectors—might be a rigid, narrow, and expensive range of services, with considerable inefficiency. A more flexible, mixed solution is needed.

In any case, this emerging sector poses problems whose character and solutions are still unclear. An optimal treatment will need to apply the common principles of industrial structure and behavior, as well as a delicate concern for social values.

EVOLVING PATTERNS

It is now widely expected that U.S. policies toward medical care will evolve—perhaps rapidly—toward the patterns common elsewhere. This would include universal coverage of basic care, a coordinated system in which public and nonprofit ownership of the main facilities—hospitals

---

[15] Defective U.S. conditions have been widely documented. See also Mary A. Mendelson, *Tender Loving Greed* (New York: Knopf, 1974) on private nursing homes.

and neighborhood clinics—is prevalent, and some relative abatement in the income of doctors. Yet some defects of present American medical arrangements could be resolved by different and lesser changes. The correct image of modern health care includes a great deal of change and experimentation. The main lines of optimal policy do seem to include universal coverage of a range of basic services, at the least, but the basis for financing the system and for compensating the providers of service offer wide choices.

A key choice will concern the barriers between accredited doctors and other operatives. In recent decades, doctors have assumed increasing power and control over the whole management of health care. This has imposed clear costs, including a large degree of over-specialization. Doctors are over-trained and over-specialized for many of the activities they do. Basic revision of credentials and requirements for health care practice could immediately broaden the supply and variety of services, and ease many of the inefficiencies and inequities in the system. It and other loosening of restrictions on medical behavior are indicated by the standard criteria of well-functioning markets, as well as by social criteria.

Another alternative is the "health maintenance organization," which contracts to provide all service to specific groups. It was rapidly expanded with public support during 1973–74, with 22 Blue-Cross plans and 20 insurance firms involved in 1974 with 59 HMOs.[16] They are essentially private units, with business participation, and they are described as a private alternative to public programs. They offer prepaid service, in place of fees for service. If their 5 percent share of U.S. health care rises as predicted to 25 percent by 1984, the effect on medical practice, on Blue Cross as the present major financer, and on individual choice, could be large.

There are limits. Past programs have not proved superior, by medical criteria of preventive care and mortality. Fees are not small (averaging $500 per year for families). And coverage misses precisely those high-risk, disadvantaged groups which are already omitted from coverage. Still, the method does offer an alternative which may be a valuable part of a balanced future system.

In short, the medical sector now offers an unusually wide variety of possible revisions. A direct move to a monolithic, publically financed, universal system—still under the control of doctors organized on their present basis—would neglect other important directions for improvement. It would violate some basic criteria for efficiency. It might improve on present arrangements; there is clear evidence that universal systems have worked well in Britain, Canada, Sweden, and elsewhere. Still, the benefits of flexibility, of completion among alternative methods, and of providing choice, can be great. They need attention in the continuing search for optimum medical arrangements.

---

[16] Yet by 1975 this "private enterprise" approach was stalled, as its costs and incentive problems became recognized.

CHAPTER TWENTY-EIGHT

The Performing Arts and Sports

People entertain and edify themselves in a remarkable variety of ways. Some hunt, others play bingo or the cello, others float in balloons, or train poodles, or doze at Wagnerian opera, or drag race, or climb severe rock, or vent their hearts and wallets at the racetrack, or—most of all—watch TV. We will look at two sections of this leisure life: the performing arts and professional sports. Both present shows for people to watch, in person or by broadcasts. Both share certain basic features common to industrial organization. But they also diverge in several ways. The most obvious difference is that professional sports have been booming, while the arts exhibit chronic problems of financial health.

Why this happens, and what an optimum public treatment of the problems would be, are analyzed here. First, we lay out the basic economics of these markets. Next we consider the performing arts: plays, opera, music, dance. Then we turn to pro sports, such as baseball, football, basketball, and hockey. We will see that public policy shapes market structure and profitability, in familiar ways. It also feeds in a variety of subsidies, which have dubious incidence.

BASIC ECONOMICS

One begins with basic facts. Our culture is two things: our heritage of works and cultural capacities from the past, plus what we use and create now. This culture embraces much variety, from common to refined interests, from mass spectacles to elite and esoteric arts. One need not regard it as a pyramid, with vulgarian pleasures at the broad bottom and a pinnacle of high culture at the top. Rather there is a kaleidoscope of many specialties: the finer points of, say, drag racing are at least as complex as listening to the *Messiah*—once more—in a crowded hall. What matters to the economics of it is only that some activities attract vastly more people and dollars than do others.

In the U.S. there is a common ethos of personal striving and change, within a relatively brief and narrow cultural context. Most people are of modest circumstances, wishing and trying to improve their lot. Most have distinctive hobbies, some pursuing them to astonishing lengths. But in their leisure moments, their spectator interests tend toward aggressive activity; in short to competitive sports. U.S. sports audiences may differ little in this from other and earlier societies: recall the Roman circuses

TABLE 28–1
Attendance at Arts and Sports, U.S.

Arts	Attendance, 1971 *(million)*
Theater	(16)
Concerts	(10)
Opera, ballet	(5)
Total	(31)
Sports	
Baseball: Major leagues	30
Other (minor, little, softball)	(25)
Football: Professional	11
College	31
High school	(20)
Basketball: Professional	8
College and high school	(30)
Hockey	(4)
Racing: Horse	74
Greyhound	14
Boxing	(5)
Other (auto-racing, tennis, track, golf, etc.)	(40)
Total	(292)

Parentheses indicate estimates.
Source: *U.S. Statistical Abstract;* Scitovsky (see note 2).

and gladitorial combats; Japanese sumo wrestling; bullfighting; and the world's greatest game of all, soccer (called "football" everywhere else).

In any event, sports are big time, as shown in Table 28–1 and discussed later. The live arts performances probably draw less than one-twentieth of paid sports performances.[1] For a variety of reasons, the fine arts have even a narrower basis in the U.S. than in many other modern societies. Most of us are philistines, even low-brows, unashamedly and with gusto. Demand for fine arts is focused among relatively well-to-do groups. Larger numbers of people are willing to pay equal or higher prices for sports tickets; but even these are a small fraction of those who follow sports on TV and radio and in the newspapers.[2] Supply also influences

---

[1] *All* arts draw less than one-half of horse-racing and just above baseball.

[2] W. J. Baumol and W. G. Bowen, *Performing Arts: The Economic Dilemma* (New York: Twentieth Century Fund, 1966); Tibor Scitovsky, "What's Wrong with the Arts Is What's Wrong with Society," *American Economic Review,* Vol. 62, No. 2 (May 1972), pp. 62–69; and T. G. Moore, *The Economics of the American Theater* (Durham: Duke University Press, 1968). Also see the excellent symposium, R. G. Noll, ed., *Government and the Sports Business* (Washington, D.C.: Brookings Institution, 1974).

the mix, by limiting the variety and capacity of shows of all kinds. The net effect is a sports and arts diet that closely fits our cultural interests.

Demand

Private demand for arts and sports tickets reflects both preferences and income. Preferences differ widely, of course. The arts are attended primarily by people with high levels of education and income, primarily in the larger cities. Sports interest lies more in the middle and lower classes, finding outlets both in attending, watching broadcasts, and in a wide variety of participation in a small-scale local level. Big league tickets sales are to a relatively narrow range of fans, within a relatively few major cities. Ticket demand is of course highest in large high-density cities; in smaller cities, fans must come from further away and the transport costs subtract from the amounts that will be paid for tickets.

The benefits from watching the arts or sports are primarily private, of course. But there are also externalities, especially in the arts. Putting on a symphony or ballet benefits those who attend, *and* it also may help induce the creation of new works of art. Society has a strong collective interest in the creation of arts, to refresh and enlarge the cultural heritage. Therefore, there are public benefits in sustaining the performing arts, though their extent in the various arts cannot be estimated with any precision. There is also some public benefit from maintaining the country's level of cultural activity. Though intangible, this does help define any society's image of itself, as being austere, or barren, or creative and culturally alive. Therefore, even if there were no fostering of new works, the performing arts might provide social benefits.

Sports also generate social benefits, especially by creating shared interests and experiences for much of the population. It is said, for example, that Detroit avoided summer riots in 1968 primarily because the Tigers were engaged in a successful pennant race that year. More generally, an active and wholesome sports culture may foster social cohesion and stability, and divert attention from deep-seated social strains and animosities. The ultimate effect of this is debatable: to the radical, sports are the opiate of the masses, while to loyalists, sports help keep society tranquil, wholesome, and cohesive. The effect may be limited by the narrowness of the clientele for actual attendance at professional games. But in any case, some sports have a degree of public benefits.

Therefore, there may be valid grounds for public support or constraints, both on the arts and on sports. And they will deal with activities which affect the very substance of cultural life.

Supply

Performance. A performance consists of (1) the content of the show; (2) the performers and supporting personnel; and (3) the place for the performance, including supporting facilities. These main inputs are common both to sports and arts, and they yield the usual U-shaped cost curve (which turns up as the capacity for effective viewing is reached).

In each city, the supply conditions for a play, a football game, or a symphony concert define the optimum scale for performance. This optimum scale ranges widely, of course, from the intimacy of a chamber music ensemble up to, say, the 100,000 roaring fans at Soldier Field in Chicago or Michigan Stadium.

There are also external transport costs from the congestion caused by major sports events. These costs, borne by the city's citizens, may rise to high levels. The facilities required to handle a major performance—sports or arts—are complex and costly, including subways, parking facilities, police cars, access roads, lighting, and so forth. Also, neighborhoods may be eliminated in building new stadiums. Altogether, external costs may be large.

The position of the cost curves will depend on city policies, which may subsidize the performances or, instead, impose charges for the external costs. The net profitability is then a vector of several main determinants. Generally, performances will be viable mainly in the largest, affluent cities. This may be offset by high economic rents and congestion costs. Yet social benefits may also be largest in large towns. Public policies may often be influential, if not decisive. Questions of monopoly as well as subsidy may be critical.

Performers. The performers in both arts and sports are drawn from each cohort, with varying degrees of *talent.* Their minimum required wages may be far below what their employers would, if necessary, pay. The outcome will reflect bilateral bargaining, with the outcome determined by bargaining power. Some performers—stars—have extremely high marginal revenue products; at the other extreme margin are the workaday athletes who just make the squad.[3] Stars can add millions to ticket receipts but rarely are able to extract most or all of that value.

One difference between arts and sports is that in many arts performances, the *substance of the show* has to be renewed more frequently. A play or opera may run two weeks or a month; pro sports run a whole year. There are exceptions: some shows run years, and other strictly reproduce old war horses. On the whole, the difference does make arts more expensive. But it also provides special collective benefits in fostering new creativity.

Both arts and sports can provide *external benefits* to aficionados not actually attending. The broadcasts, the publicity, and the critical reviews are part of the total flow of benefits. Ball teams and opera alike gain from the extensive free publicity which they get on the sports and culture pages. Also, recordings broaden the exposure of great artisits. This secondary exposure is often the more important, socially. It often cannot be internalized: this is especially true of recordings, which now can be easily copied.

A further major arts-sports difference is the *sports league.* In part, the home team is not a competitive firm, but only a plant or subdivision of a natural-monopoly sports enterprise: the league. The visible sporting

---

[3] Thus Kareem Jabbar changed the Milwaukee Bucks from large losses to large profits, more or less single-handedly. Star actors have done even more for a musical or play.

competition is merely part of the entertainment presented by the entire league firm, involving competition among the subsidiaries for the league championship. This season-long progression of sporting dramas constitutes the output of the league enterprise. If the league itself is a true natural monopoly, then a wide range of monopolistic behavior by the league (and/or team owners acting as a cartel) may be socially justified.[4] This is a focal issue of the section on sports (below). In the performing arts, by contrast, such multiple-unit operations—with mutual competition—simply does not exist.

In both sports and arts, there is a wide gulf between (1) those who own and manage, and (2) those who supply the personal inputs. There are virtually no owner-proprietors also in the performer's role. Also, those who put up the cash and own the special franchises and performing locations are the ones who hold the power of decision. There are no significant cooperatives, mutual societies, or player-controlled groups, in either arts or sports (this is true throughout Western economies).[5] There is thus a natural strain between owners and performers, and this defines many of the performance and structural characteristics of arts and sports. This division has special cultural overtones, because the sponsors—"angels" for Broadway plays, "sportsmen" owners of ball teams, etc.—are often drawn from upper-wealth groups with special cultural interests. This is remote from the normal industrial capital that is common elsewhere in the market economy. Abroad, too, sports owners and arts patrons are a special sample from the higher wealth and social strata. Tax questions are often foremost for these sponsors. All of this explains some of the limits and fallibilities of the management in these sectors; also, secretiveness, eccentricity, and, alas, a degree of greed.

PERFORMING ARTS

Clientele. The clientele for the fine arts is narrow (much the same as for museums: recall Chapter 22). As shown in Table 28–2, those going to plays, operas, concerts, and ballet are primarily of the upper middle and higher classes, by income, occupation and educational level. Only a small fraction of the typical audience is from the lower middle and lower income groups. This narrowness affects all public policies toward the arts.[6] It explains the financial difficulties of most fine arts groups: their expenses are high, but the demand is limited. Most Americans are, in fact, little interested in the arts, and so chronic deficit and decline may be the optimal condition.

---

[4] See W. C. Neale, "The Peculiar Economics of Professional Sport," *Quarterly Journal of Economics,* Vol. 78 (February 1964), pp. 1–14. Note that this view excludes the intrinsic value of sport (how you play the game) in favor of sheer victory (whether you win or lose). The shift to winning as the single goal is characteristic of the rise of pro sports. Generally, economic incentives ignore *quality of play* and stress winning. The cultural difference—between amateur and professional—has important social repercussions, which managers of the Olympics and tennis, for example, have contended with (not too successfully). See also Noll, *ed. cit.*

[5] The La Mama Troupe is a recent exception, but—during the 1960s—it was tiny, struggling and could only survive abroad. Its more recent prosperity has also brought more "businesslike" methods.

[6] See the lucid analysis of Scitovsky, *op. cit.;* and Baumol and Bowen, *op. cit.*

This holds even though performers are poorly paid, on average. Actors' wages are constrained by competitiveness and the monopoly power of many of their employers. Actors, by and large, subsidize play-goers.

Public support. This is summarized in Table 28–3. The total volume of direct subsidies in the U.S. is small, by international comparisons. There are certain subsidies—mainly by tax shelters—which would in-

TABLE 28-2
The U.S. Arts Audience Compared with the Population in
20 Cities

	Urban Population (1960)	Performing Arts Audience (1963–65)
*Occupation**		
Professional.................	13%	63%
Managerial	13	21
Clerical and sales............	17	13
Blue collar..................	58	3
Education†		
Graduate school.............	5	55
Completed college	6	23
Completed high school	22	7
Less	57	2
Income		
$25,000 and over............	2	17
15,000–24,999	4	22
10,000–14,999	12	24
10,000 and over.............	18	63
7,000–9,999.................	23	17
5,000–6,999.................	24	11
3,000–4,999.................	19	6
Under $3,000...............	17	3

* Males.
† Male, over 25.
Source: Baumol and Bowen, *op. cit.*, pp. 75–77.

crease the U.S. total, but it is still relatively slight. In fact, public support of the arts in the U.S. scarcely existed until 1965. It has been a preserve of private contributions, in a mixture of charitable, civic, and thoroughly selfish motivations. Throughout Western and Eastern Europe, the degree of public support is much higher. This relates further to the broader attendance at the arts in these and other countries (though it is still far from truly democratic).

That is the U.S. dilemma: the arts are limited, but so is their appeal. Much as expanded public support seems desirable to many observers, its efficiency and equity effects might be narrow and dubious. The weakest case for arts subsidies would be for enriching the present kinds of offerings to the present clientele. There are other directions. Equity and efficiency will be served by subsidies which (1) sponsor creative activity with general public benefits, (2) aim for a wider audience, and (3) flow mainly to performers rather than owners. This holds both for direct subsidies and for tax-exemption and other indirect assistance.

Strict economic factors reinforce this lesson, that widening the audience coverage should be a primary direction of subsidy effort. Economies of scale hinge strongly on the length of run of a show. Therefore subsidies that foster longer runs will automatically reduce the subsidy flow. One device for this is the touring group, which would reach wider audiences with mainstream presentations. This overcomes the natural bias toward large-city locations to maximize the clientele. A second technical factor is the diseconomies of size of audience for any given presentation.

TABLE 28–3

Public Subsidies to the Performing Arts (current operating expenditures only)

Country	Amount (in millions)	As % of GNP
United States (1969–70)	$30	.003%
United States (public subsidies plus private contributions from foundations, business and individuals) (1969–70)	$80	.008
United Kingdom (1970)	£ 6.6	.015
West Germany (1968) . . . . DM	505.5	.09
France (1968) . . . . Fr	83.5	.013
Sweden (1969–70, 1965–66) . . . . Kr	222.6	.15
Norway (1968, 1970) . . . . Kr	29.2	.04

Source: Scitovsky, *op. cit.*

The private incentive is to fill giant theaters, but these often dilute the quality of the artistic experience. The social interest lies mainly in proliferating smaller theaters and presentations rather than maximizing audiences in big halls.

The general objective is to increase offerings, rather than to make them bigger. So efficient and fair subsidies would mainly foster more groups, more touring companies, and other provisions for the arts in smaller cities. Also, the effort would be to increase showings in the less affluent areas of the larger cities. This effort would reach the middle or "mass" levels of audience interests, rather than enrich the offerings at the higher, "refined" cultural levels. It might not seem to raise the level of edification and cultural refinement. It would revise the traditional effects of public support for the arts, and move towards a more democratic level and coverage.

The upper groups could still afford and foster cultural interests. Creativity can be fostered directly by subsidies to the artists themselves. Also, a greater variety of theaters in being would provide outlets for authors and composers to try new works.

These problems are paralleled abroad. In Britain, support funnelled by the Arts Council has gone mainly to benefit elite interests. The collective benefits of maintaining high cultural activity have been appreciable. Still, the funds have gone primarily to a relatively few units in a few major cities, playing for a relatively few theater goers, mostly from upper economic levels.[7] Direct support for playwrights and composers is slight, and there is only a modest attempt to spread participation widely. Much the same holds in the continental countries.

Public policy toward the arts therefore faces complex issues. The core elements are economic and need fuller analysis than has yet occurred. But equity is of peculiar importance, and it may normally weigh more heavily than efficiency. Both of them suggest that any large increase in arts subsidies should aim to change existing patterns.

SPORTS

There are a vast array of sports, from soccer to baseball, hockey, golf, bowling, professional wrestling, fly casting, chess, and bridge. We focus here on the main American professional leagues because they are the core of commercial spectator sports. Table 28–4 and Figure 28–1 summarize their conditions. The pro sports craze since 1960 has raised the incentives and pay-offs to some owners, and also posed more acute policy questions. Though other countries have also had sports booms, the U.S. patterns are distinctive.

Conditions

The Basic Conditions Are These.   The league is the controlling unit. It is a cartel among the private owners of individual franchised teams. They are in business to maximize profit, as well as, perhaps, satisfy the owners' personal sports interests. The league controls franchises and other competitive conditions. Players are under restrictive rules which assign them among teams and give power to trade them to the teams. The league cartel sets the division of gate receipts between home and visiting teams, and it bargains for broadcasting revenues and divides them also. The three focused interest groups are owners, players, and broadcasters.

Where separate leagues exist—e.g. football leagues before 1967 and basketball leagues at present—the pressures to merge usually prevail. There are important public subsidies via tax laws, stadium rentals, and other services. Data on revenues, costs, and profits are secreted, and decisions are made privately. Public knowledge is slight, and public policies are passive. Neither antitrust nor regulatory policies are very significant.

These sports have been big business only since about 1960, and the sector is evolving. But the basic patterns fit the old baseball leagues of

---

[7] See the Arts Council, *Annual Report* (London: H.M.S.O., 1974) for detailed data on the support. Though 90 percent of the number of grants go to the regions, well half of the *amount* goes to London (especially to Convent Garden, which specializes in grand opera and ballet). See Karen King and Mark Blaug, "Does the Arts Council Know What It's Doing?", *Encounter,* 1973.

TABLE 28–4

Aspects of Professional Leagues

	Number of Teams, 1974	Number of Games, 1975 season	Attendance 1971 (thousands)	Visiting Team's Share of Receipts	Degree of Profit Disparity among Teams	National Broadcast Payments as Percent of Revenue	New League Founded Recently?
Baseball							
National League 12		972	17,324	10–20%	Large	~30%	No
American League 12		972	11,869				
Football							
National Football League 26		182	10,560	40	Moderate	~45	AFL, 1960; World Football League, 1974
Basketball							
National Basketball Assoc. 18		702	6,195	0	Sharp	~20	ABA, 1967
American Basketball Assoc. 10		390	2,230				
Hockey							
National Hockey League 18		720	~4,000	0	Sharp	~20	World Hockey League, 1971

Source: *U.S. Statistical Abstract;* and Noll, *ed. cit.*

another day. The profits, player policies, and subsidies raise intriguing
—even pressing—policy issues.

There are some noneconomic components. Like soccer teams elsewhere in the world, these teams are city-based, cultivating local identification. Their players are bred into a sports culture which reveres the star
and the team player. The business is Janus-faced, trading upon these
loyalties to increase the owners' profits and league controls.

Public Policies. Public policies have accepted the leagues as natural
monopolies, and so antitrust limits are minimal.[8] Owners set market

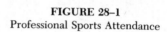

FIGURE 28–1
Professional Sports Attendance

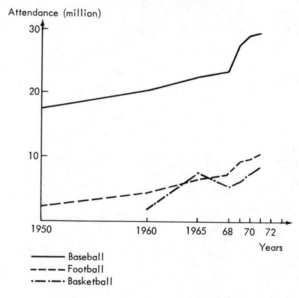

conditions in a formal cartel mode (recall Chapter 6). Franchises are
created and traded about under conditions tightly controlled by the
league itself. When new rival leagues emerge, they soon negotiate to get
legal exemptions to merge with the prior leagues.[9]

Defining the market is complex. If each sport is a relevant market,

---

[8] Baseball's antitrust exemption is explicit. The others enjoy *de facto* exemption which
is nearly as complete. See Noll, *op. cit.,* Chapter 11. Though the baseball exemption (*Federal
Baseball Club* v. *National League,* 259 U.S. 200 (1922)) is agreed to be doctrinally untenable,
its indulgent attitude has been extended to other sports. Note that baseball's cartel behavior
has been weaker and much less efficient than that of football. The number and capacity of
teams has been less restricted, and decisions about rules have been less efficient. See Lance
E. Davis, "Self-Regulation in Baseball, 1909-71," Chapter 10 in Noll, *ed. cit.*

[9] This occurred with the two football leagues in 1966–67 and has been attempted by the
basketball leagues since 1971. The new World Hockey League can be expected eventually to
pose this situation, as have other new leagues in the past. See "The Super Bowl and the
Sherman Act: Professional Team Sports and the Antitrust Laws," *Harvard Law Review,* Vol.
81 (December 1967).

FIGURE 28–2

The Sports Seasons Overlap, Increasingly

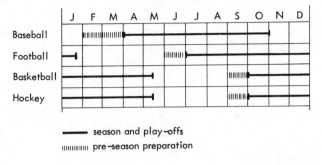

——— season and play-offs

ııııııııııı pre-season preparation

then its cartellization would cause the standard economic losses. But if each sport is merely one among many, then cartels may be an optimal mix of internal organization plus intersport competition. *Intra*sport market competition would be suppressed in order to foster sporting competition among the teams.[10] The aim is to keep the teams nearly equal, so that the drama is heightened and winning is evenly spread. That is the rationale for league cartels. Figures 28–2 and 28–3 do show how widely the main sports seasons have come to overlap, and Table 28–5 shows the allocation of teams among cities. But even if the leagues do optimize the sporting competition, they will still restrict output (franchises, number of games), raise ticket prices, draw monopoly profits, and tend to be inefficient and not innovative.

   Sports Revenues and Profits Are a Complex Matter. They stem from (1) ticket sales, (2) the sale of TV and radio broadcasting rights, (3) various direct and indirect city subsidies in the form of stadiums and sup-

FIGURE 28–3

High Sports Activity and Overlap, Week of October 14–20,
1974, New York City TV (apart from ABC and CBS Saturday
afternoon shows)

Monday	Football
Tuesday	Baseball
Wednesday	Baseball, Hockey
Thursday	Football, Baseball, Basketball
Friday	(High School Football Night)
Saturday	Football, Football, Baseball, Basketball, Racing
Sunday	Football, Football, Football, Football, Baseball

---

[10] See Chapter 2 in Noll, *ed. cit.;* and the diverting discussion by W. C. Neale, *op. cit.*

TABLE 28–5

Location of the Main Professional Teams (as of July, 1974)

	Population	Baseball	National Football League	World Football League	National Basketball Association	American Basketball Association	National Hockey League	World Hockey Association
New York	17,300,000	**	**	*	*	*	*	
Los Angeles	8,900,000	**	*	*	*		*	*
Chicago	7,700,000	**	*	*	*		*	*
Philadelphia	5,400,000	*	*	*	*		*	
Detroit	4,600,000	**	*	*	*		*	
S.F., Oak., San Jose	4,400,000	**	**		*			
Boston	3,800,000	*	*		*		*	*
Washington	3,200,000	*	*		*		*	
Montreal	2,800,000	*					*	
Toronto	2,700,000						*	*
Dallas	2,500,000	*	*					
Cleveland	2,400,000	*	*		*			*
St. Louis	2,300,000	*	*			*	*	
Miami–Ft. Lauderdale	2,300,000		*	*				
Pittsburgh	2,100,000	*	*				*	
Houston	2,100,000	*	*					
Minn.–St. Paul	2,000,000	*	*				*	**

City	Population						
Baltimore	1,900,000	*					*
Seattle	1,800,000						
Atlanta	1,700,000	*			*		*
Cincinnati	1,500,000	*					
Milwaukee	1,400,000	*	*†		*		
San Diego	1,400,000	*	*	*	*		*
Buffalo	1,300,000		*	*		*	*
Denver	1,300,000		*				
Kansas City	1,300,000	*	*			*	
Phoenix	1,100,000		*		*		
Vancouver	1,100,000			*		*	*
New Orleans	1,100,000		*	*			
Portland	1,100,000		*				
Hartford	1,100,000			*			*
Indianapolis	1,000,000		*				*

WFL—Honolulu, 600,000; Birmingham, 680,000; Jacksonville, 600,000; Memphis, 850,000; Orlando, 480,000.
ABA—Virginia (Norfolk–Richmond–Hampton), 1,550,000; Utah (Salt Lake City–Ogden), 555,000; San Antonio, 900,000; Louisville, 900,000; Memphis, 850,000.
WHA—Winnipeg, 540,000; Edmonton, 500,000; Quebec, 500,000.
† Green Bay Packers.
Source: *New York Times*, July 25, 1974.

porting facilities, and (4) special tax breaks. Tickets involve complex decisions about fans' demand elasticities, and the structure of actual prices is thoroughly discriminatory, so as to maximize profits within the other constraints. Season tickets, box seats, bleachers, all reflect pervasive—often sophisticated—discrimination.

Broadcasting revenues are mainly bargained on a unified league basis, under a special law.[11] This permits a bilateral oligopoly outcome in the interests of the owners and broadcasters (not necessarily fans, either as ticket buyers or TV watchers). The league divides these more less

TABLE 28–6
Ownership of Sports Facilities, 1970–71 Season

Ownership	Number of Facilities				
	Baseball	Football	Basketball	Hockey	Total
Public	16	20	32	4	53
Private	7	6	7	8	18
University	0	1	4	0	5
Total	23	27	43	12	76

Source: R. Noll, ed., *Government and the Sports Business* (Washington, D.C.: Brookings Institution, 1974), p. 326.

evenly among the teams. TV revenues are now substantial, and local broadcasting also generates significant payments.

City subsidies are large and growing. They arise mainly from low stadium rentals and free provision of services (roads, traffic control, policing, etc.) which the games necessitate. Teams can drive hard bargains for these subsidies by threatening to leave, as has commonly been done since the 1950s.[12] Most stadiums are public (see Table 28–6): indeed, "the ubiquitous monument of urban America in the Seventies is the sports stadium."[13] City subsidies for stadiums range from 10 cents to $6.80 per capita per year; and the Superdome subsidy in New Orleans will be even larger.[14] New stadiums absorb the biggest subsidies, partly because they usually are poorly planned and reflect civic delusions of grandeur.[15]

---

[11] Public Law 87–331, enacted in 1971, exempts "any joint agreement . . . in . . . the organized professional team sports of football, baseball, basketball, or hockey . . . which sells or otherwise transfers" rights in telecasting of games (75 Stat. 732). The law tries to shield high school and college football by excluding telecasts on Friday nights and Saturday afternoons.

[12] Thus the Yankees euchred a $50 million renovation of Yankee stadium from the New York City treasury during 1973–76 by threatening to move.

[13] Charles G. Burck, "It's Promoters vs. Taxpayers in the Superstadium Game," *Fortune*, (March 1973), pp. 104 ff. See the clear analysis in B. A. Okner, "Subsidies of Stadiums and Arenas," in Noll, *ed. cit.*, Chapter 9.

[14] "If you are going to build a major sports stadium today, you start out by digging a hole. That is where you are going to put the stadium. And that is where the stadium is probably going to put you." Charles Maher, "Major Sports Stadiums: They Keep Going Up," *Los Angeles Times*, November 14, 1971, quoted by Okner.

[15] The Superdome, originally promoted at $35 million, has soared toward $200 million, all from Louisiana public funds. The Seattle stadium now abuilding will cost home-owners $1.38 per year for 40 years, instead of the predicted $1.21 for 10 years. Both of these, and other stadiums, too, require large extra costs for roads and support.

Specific tax breaks have become a decisive factor in profit levels. The key provision lets owners allocate most of their costs (the average is about 85 percent) to their players' contracts and then depreciate the contracts over a short period (three to five years).[16] This creates large flows of tax-exempt depreciation costs, so that many teams record paper losses. But these are valuable tax havens for offsetting other income. Therefore, teams are more profitable than they seem. The selling of team franchises also can make use of tax loopholes.

Altogether the tax and other subsidies have powerful effects which have become apparent since 1965. They make many teams financially viable. The value of the franchises (now at $25 million in the NFL) is raised, and the number of franchises grows. Only wealthy persons and large firms can take advantage of the tax haven, and so the days of the individual owner mainly interested in the team and its profit (e.g., Bill Veeck, George Halas, and Calvin Griffith) are gone. Instead, wealthy sportsmen pick them up and treat them as a hobby, among their other business interests. They have little skill and often mishandle team policies. Their horizons are usually as long as their tax benefits: usually five to seven years. This encourages frequent sell-offs of franchises and mining of the teams' assets. High bidders are likely to be in cities without franchises, and so team location is more unstable.

Baseball has shown these symptoms of dilution, poor management, and instability most acutely. But they are now powerful in all major league sports.

Controls over players also influence team profitability by limiting the players' share. Though baseball's reserve clause has drawn the most controversy, the basic conditions are common to all the leagues. Though the controls have been challenged in court and by players' unions, they persist. They do tightly constrain player income levels and alter the structure of wages.[17] In baseball, average players receive salaries over their careers equal to about 10 percent of their gross and 20 percent of their net marginal revenue product. Stars do worse, at only 15 percent of net marginal revenue product. Only mediocre players get paid their economic worth. Much the same is true elsewhere. The 25 or so stars in a league add perhaps $200,000–$500,000 each to their teams' yearly revenues, but they get only a modest share of it.[18]

Owners defend the controls as necessary to preserve balance within the league. But little such effect occurs, and balance can also be assured in other ways.[19] Meanwhile the player controls persist as an anachronism and a disruptive cause of ill will. They affect only the division of spoils between players and owners. Their abolition would not alter the sports structure nor benefit sports fans appreciably.

---

[16] B. A. Okner, "Taxation and Sports Enterprises," Chapter 5 in Noll, *ed. cit.* Though these provisions are under challenge in 1974–75, they may continue in whole or part.

[17] See Noll, *ed. cit.*, Chapters 2 and 6.

[18] Noll, *ed. cit.*, Chapters 2, 3, 4, 6, 11, and 12. See also Gerald W. Scully, *The Economics of Professional Sports* (Cambridge, Mass.: Schenkman Publishers, 1974).

[19] Gate-sharing between home and visiting teams can be made more equal. Locations can be more fairly divided. And team budgets for player salaries could be limited. Noll, *ed. cit.*, pp. 416–17.

Within the Leagues. These are sharp differences in the profitability of teams. Some teams are bonanzas; other run genuine losses, at least for a period. These are usually the newer expansion teams. High profits reflect mainly: (1) the size and affluence of the team's city, (2) winning, (3) star players, (4) the absence of other teams in the city, and (5) newness of the stadium. Because most football and hockey teams are sold out, their profits are influenced closely by stadium capacity. Profit disparity is extreme in basketball and hockey, where home teams keep all the ticket receipts (see Table 28–4); in football and baseball, there is more equality.[20] The rich big-city franchises have exerted league power to keep their brethren out; but they have eventually drawn entry by teams in the new leagues.[21] Generally, the richer teams have drawn disproportionally more of the tax subsidies. And they have also had greater bargaining power to extract city subsidies.

Outcomes. All in all, the outcome has closely fitted the predictable effects of market power. Restricted output, differential monopoly among cities, excess profits, and instability of franchises persist, with little public restraint: indeed, policies tend to enhance them. There are too few teams, and the subsidies are highly inequitable.[22] The leagues and firms do differ in efficiency. Baseball has been weak and inept, compared to football under Pete Rozelle. And the older leagues have all failed to avert entry by new leagues.

These deviant conditions are, to some, natural or even part of the charm of the game. But they do involve policies which cause inefficiency and unfairness. Growing pressures may well bring changes during 1974–80. What revisions would be best, by sporting and general criteria?

Policy Alternatives

Antitrust exemptions would be removed. This would have several effects, none of which would weaken the spectator value of the sport. (1) The player controls would be reduced or abolished. With simple safeguards, this would more likely increase intraleague balance than reduce it. Players—especially the better ones—would simply get a fairer share. (2) Leagues could not merge. This would preserve their independence

---

[20] For an excellent statistical analysis, see R. Noll's Chapter 4 in Noll, *ed. cit.* Owners keep their actual profits secret, so these studies are still provisional, using indirect data.

The most lucrative teams probably are: (1) Basketball: the Knicks, Bucks, and Lakers; (2) Baseball: the Dodgers and Mets; (3) Football: the Giants, Bears, Rams and Packers; (4) Hockey: the Rangers, Bruins, Blackhawks, Maple Leafs, and Canadiens.

[21] One outsider (Gary Davidson) has founded the American Basketball Assn., the World Hockey Assn., and in 1974, the World Football League. He appeals frankly to tax motives, predicting losses at $1 million for at least three years. Yet WFL franchises fetched at least $600,000 from the start, and WHL franchises were all worth above $3 million by 1974. ("A Quarterback for Tax Shelters," *Business Week,* January 12, 1974, p. 63.) Though WFL problems ousted Davidson during 1974, the basic approach remains.

[22] The shortage of franchises is clearest in football and hockey; it also applies to baseball and basketball in the largest cities (New York, Chicago). As for equity, the owners are a mere handful, and even the ticket buyers are usually less than 3 percent of city population, drawn mainly from above average income groups. Therefore, the subsidies have a highly regressive incidence.

and rivalry, while permitting other satisfactory arrangements (e.g., play-offs) to be made. Undoing the 1966 football merger might be advisable and would technically be quite easy. (3) Monopoly bargaining for TV rights would be replaced by a mixed process, offering more variety and coverage. At present, PL 87–331 mainly yields restriction and excess prof-its: it also limits the growth of specialized TV sports broadcasting (e.g., by cable TV: recall Chapter 16).

Sharing of revenue (gate receipts and TV revenue) could be made more equal in all leagues. This would ensure more balance among teams and foster teams in many more middle-size cities than is now possible. It would also reduce reliance on tax subsidies by the weaker teams.

Subsidies could be eliminated without impairing any essential sport-ing attribute. Instead, the franchise instability, amateurishness, and greed that now are common would abate, and sports could once again be run by professionals dedicated to the game and their players. In fact the 1965–75 period may be looked back on as the strange tax-haven decade which nearly ruined the character of professional sports.

Regulation, on a federal basis, has been proposed. But it would not touch the basic problems; indeed (recall Chapter 13), it would tend more to ratify them. It would freeze the structure of interests, make ex-perimentation even slower, and reduce chances for entry and expansion. Since there is little real investment (other than city-owned stadiums and related facilities), rate-of-return criteria could scarcely apply.

Multiple-level league systems are a major direction for innovation. Presently the booming major leagues lack a substructure of healthy mi-nor leagues. Also, losing teams often lack drawing power for most of the season, once they fall behind. The British system of soccer leagues solves this by having five layers of leagues, from "1st division" down to "4th division" and then the country leagues. After each season, the top three teams in each league rise to the league above, and the three at the bottom are relegated down.

This creates great suspense over "relegation," and so nearly all teams have drama throughout the season. This also maintains a full scale of team qualities, and permits even small-city teams to aspire to the very top (and many do make it). Top-division ranks are in fact a mixture of small and large-city teams rather than being the exclusive preserve of the largest and richest cities.

A "relegation" system would abate much of the rigidity and boredom in American sports. It might well broaden its access and appeal more than any possible change within the present system.

City ownership. Many cities lacking teams would gain—socially and economically—by founding their own teams, but they are presently ex-cluded by the present private leagues. Thus, Washington, D.C., has suffi-cient social interest in having a baseball team to justify starting one; it might well earn a profit, even without tax advantages. A recent attempt to start a city team was blocked by the leagues. The same possibilities hold for smaller cities and for some large cities where there is large excess demand (especially hockey, football, and certain basketball teams). Especially if a several-layer system were to evolve, city-owned teams could be part of the optimal pattern. At the least, city ownership would modify the balance of bargaining power, which presently enables private owners to extract large, inequitable subsidies.

Altogether, sports combines special qualities with conventional industrial concepts. The deviations from optimal policy are increasingly clear. Correcting them would serve both the fans and the general interest. The choices are wide, if one sees beyond the odd conditions that have recently come to plague pro sports. A greater degree of market competition and choice will enhance sporting competition, fairness to all parties, and the sheer fun of the game.

CHAPTER TWENTY-NINE

Procuring Military Supplies

The supply of weapons is an ancient and universal problem, which can be solved in many ways, none of them satisfactory.[1] The issues include monopoly, profitability, public subsidy, the costs of innovation, and sheer world survival. The capacity for waste and damage is great, and so "correct" public policies offer high yields.

We will first define the sector and its distinctive features. Next we pose the key economic conditions, which make optimum procurement difficult. Then we review the alternative policies, including competition, incentive contracting, renegotiation, and public supply. There is a summary section.

THE SECTOR

The weapons trade is now a major sector, in both the U.S. and the world economy. Since 1940, a large armaments sector has become established, with several score major suppliers plus thousands of smaller subcontractors relying on military orders (see Figure 29–1). Previously, a small core of military facilities plus a few producers was supplemented—whenever major wars came—by a rapid build-up from private suppliers. Now the private producers are more permanent, and they provide a great variety of weapons and other supplies. Domestic sales are only part of the total, for the international trade in weapons is brisk and growing. These patterns and trends appear to be stable and continuing.

Military supplies embrace a remarkable variety, from pencils, tomatoes, and uniforms to complex electronic defense and attack sys-

---

[1] Good basic sources include M. J. Peck and F. M. Scherer, *The Weapons Acquisition Process* (Boston: Harvard University School of Business, 1962); C. J. Hitch and R. N. McKean, *The Economics of Defense in the Nuclear Age* (Cambridge: Harvard University Press, 1960); and F. M. Scherer, *The Weapons Acquisition Process: Economic Incentives* (Boston: Harvard University School of Business, 1963). See also J. K. Galbraith, *The New Industrial State* (Boston: Houghton Mifflin, 1968) on the mutual process of military and industrial planning. On World War II, see J. P. Miller, *The Pricing of Military Procurement* (Cambridge: Harvard University Press, 1949).

tems. During 1955–70, large advanced systems were a main focus (see Table 29–1). They seemed inevitably to involve: (1) rapid development; even at high extra costs, (2) high degrees of discovery, innovation, and risk, and (3) rapid obsolescence and replacement with new systems. This attitude bred a tolerance for waste and error, for speed and new technology appeared to be worth great costs. More recently, a reversion toward conventional weapons and careful purchasing policies has occurred. Less than half of current weapons buying concerns the high technology items, and there is more concern that weapons not turn out to be superfluous or involve large cost over-runs (see below).

FIGURE 29–1
Military Spending

Yet even in these more standard items, there are usually several or more dimensions to the product: these include reliability, speed, weight, cost, firepower, accuracy, costs of production and maintenance, risk to personnel, rate of obsolescence, and the like. Simply defining the weapons is to be bought is an important set of choices. This creates difficulties both in obtaining the correct mix among weapons types and also in making sure that suppliers fit their output to the desired specifications. The methods of ordering and paying for weapons may bias the outcome.

The flow of purchases is large, and its treatment has repercussions in many markets. Pentagon decisions set or eliminate competition, both in weapons and in adjacent markets. Some firms are dependent on weapons orders (see Table 29–2): altogether, perhaps 15 major companies are primarily weapons producers. Most of the very largest firms keep military contracts to a small fraction. There is much instability in the orders: (1) There are shifts in weapons types, and military crises come and go; and (2) Orders shift or rotate among firms. Much military production is

TABLE 29-1
Military, Aviation, and Space Procurement Obligations to Domestic Industrial
Contractors: Fiscal Year 1965

Category	$ Millions	Cumulative Percentage
A. *"Complex" Systems*		
1. Military aircraft development and production	5,781	20.1
2. Military missile and space systems	4,233	34.9
3. Military electronics and communications equipment	2,788	44.6
4. Military research and development in nonprofit institutions, other than educational institutions	263	45.5
5. NASA space systems development	4,166	59.9
6. AEC weapons development and fabrication	753	62.5
7. AEC military and space reactor development	332	63.7
8. AEC production of fissionable materials, less sales and leases to civilian reactor users	371	65.0
9 FAA research, development, and production of electronic control systems and navigation equipment	101	65.4
B. *Conventional Items*		
10. Military combat vehicles	262	66.3
11. Military ships	1,691	72.2
12. Conventional weapons (i.e., rifles, torpedoes)	299	73.2
13. Military ammunition	759	75.8
14. DOD miscellaneous hard goods	307	76.9
15. DOD: miscellaneous services (including some engineering services)	1,740	83.0
16. Military construction, including missile bases	767	85.7
17. DOD noncombat vehicles	588	87.7
18. AEC acquisition of raw materials (natural uranium, etc.)	267	88.6
19. Military textiles, clothing, and equipage	361	89.9
20. DOD orders of less than $10,000 each	3,395	94.8
21. DOD: fuels and lubricants	818	97.7
22. Military subsistence	647	100.0
Total	28,689	

Sources: Department or Defense and NASA procurement reports and federal budget documents. See Scherer's chapter in W. Adams, ed., *The Structure of American Industry,* 4th ed. (New York: Macmillan, 1971) p. 338.

rightly regarded as unstable, with a large gambling element. Defense firms generally are not among the core of established firms, and some of them have been part of the conglomerate, outsider group of the 1960s (recall Chapters 2 and 8).

Beneath the narrow focus of primary contracts in a few firms and regions, there is a much broader substructure of weapons production. Subcontracting of components is widely spread across industries, company sizes, and regions of the country. Much of this subcontracting can be provisionally assumed to be on a more normal market basis, free of special distortions. This substructure does ensure that the motivation for high weapons spending is much wider than the narrow focus of prime

Photo by Alecio De Andrade © Magnum Photos, Inc.

Armaments for sale in the international market. A small selection at the Paris Air Show in 1973.

contracts on a score of firms would suggest. Much the same has been true also of the programs for space flight and nuclear energy.

Most military contracts are sought by at least several firms. For firms reliant on defense orders, the key economic fact is that their short-run *marginal* cost for new orders is quite low when the order backlog is

TABLE 29–2
Leading U.S. Weapons Producers

Rank among All U.S. Industrial Firms, by Sales, 1972	Company	Total Defense Contracts, 1971–72 and 1972–73 ($ million)			Average Annual New Prime Contracts as a Perce of Average Annua Sales, 1971–73
		Procurement	R&D	Total	
38	Lockheed Aircraft	$3,363	$795	$4,158	85%
32	McDonnell-Douglas	2,843	936	3,779	69
4	General Electric	2,674	532	3,206	16
43	Boeing	2,399	699	3,098	66
202	Grumman	2,028	533	2,561	187
10*	AT&T-Western Electric	1,895	567	2,462	19*
87	General Dynamics	1,996	357	2,353	75
56	United Aircraft	1,736	553	2,289	57
44	Rockwell International	1,407	802	2,209	47
(2)	Hughes Aircraft	1,234	368	1,602	(†)

* Western Electric only.
(†) Not available; Hughes Aircraft is privately owned.
Source: Defense Department yearly lists and *Fortune Directory.*

small. Yet the revenue from contracts must eventually cover their average cost, if the firms are to survive. Each supplier therefore tends to bid aggressively when short of orders but only nominally when its order backlog is long. This affects both competition and performance in the sector, as we will see shortly.

It is reinforced by the pooling of overhead costs among contracts. The larger defense firms often hold many research, development, and production contracts at any time, in varying stages of completion. Often funds, staff, and facilities mingle among the projects, so that costs, deficits, and performance are meshed in an ongoing process. Such firms normally wish to maintain the process, to keep their resources applied and profits flowing.

Many markets for the larger weapons are tight oligopolies or virtual monopolies. This reflects several factors, including the willingness of military purchasers to deal with only a few firms. There are exceptions; some military suppliers are standard off-the-shelf items which are bought repetitively. But in the bulk of military markets, the industrial setting gives only a limited range of choice.

Basic Conditions of Decisions

These special attributes interact with the ways in which military contracts are designed and let. *The cardinal fact is that weapons purchases are essentially made at the grass-roots levels of the Pentagon,* by middle-level officers (colonels, majors, captains) who are long and intimately familiar with their suppliers. These people—working closely with company personnel—prepare the contracting information about need, capabilities, and costs. This information, when processed on up to higher levels, usually defines the areas for choice. Most of these officers have been trained as engineers, and so their decision criteria are usually narrow, mingling engineering standards with personal aversions to risk.

Cost Is Commonly a Secondary Criterion. The apparent value of—or need for—a weapons system arises from joint planning by these officers and officials of the supplying company themselves. Therefore, public policies to modify weapons procurement must reach down to these military levels. Setting new policies at the top-most military levels usually will not suffice and has not sufficed.

These officials have little conception of, or interest in, competition in the wider range of the economy. Indeed, broadening the field of suppliers mainly adds to their tasks and insecurities. If their decisions tend to foster monopoly, that is only of incidental importance to them. Also their training and incentives favor high quality and maximum reliability as criteria, rather than the minimum cost. They are often anxious to preserve all of their suppliers even if that requires generous contract terms and loans of physical capital.

Despite past experience with war profiteering, the degree of profits earned on defense contracting is often said to be small. Reported profits tend to average about three or four percent of the total costs of supply. Yet such small profit margins are often deceptive. It is profits on investment which matter. These have been much higher, in some cases astronomical. There are exceptions, for contracts can turn out poorly for any number of reasons. In rare cases, some contracts imperil the survival of major companies. Still, on the whole, the rate of return on defense contracts has been at least as high as in civilian activities.

The Competitive Status of Weapons Contracting. This is indicated in Table 29–3 (patterns since 1967 are similar). Approximately two-thirds of purchases occur under conditions with virtually no competition at all. The military mind prefers usually to pick out a preferred supplier and then work with it; or to consider only several familiar candidates. The uncertainty and fluidity of competitive conditions are generally regarded as unreliable and troublesome.

Partly as a result of these unusual conditions, military purchases frequently exceed their predicted and contracted cost levels; during the 1950s and 1960s, over-runs by a multiple of three were frequent. Several notorious cases occurred during the 1960s, in part because of the haste in which military purchases rose during the Vietnam War. A degree of over-run is often natural, as the specifications for projects are changed and raised during their preparation. And the rises in Table 29–4 partly reflect allowances for future inflation. (Try to predict how far the costs of these major weapons will rise further, as they are produced during the next ten years and more. Compare with actual results as the years pass.) But part represents waste of various kinds. Why this happens and how it may be corrected is a focus of discussion here.

Yet companies performing poorly on contracts often escape any penalty, either immediate or eventual. Among the major current military suppliers are some who have recorded severe errors and inefficiency in past contracts.

Regulation. Finally, the Antitrust Division and related agencies concerned with competition have had virtually no role in monitoring or influencing military procurement.[2] Yet the choices may affect or exclude competition in large markets. This *de facto* lack of antitrust jurisdiction is virtually complete. It occurs partly because effective decisions are made so early and so deep in the military hierarchy.

In short, much weapons supply occurs under highly monopolistic conditions on both sides of the market, partly because the agents making decisions are usually oblivious to competitive conditions and effects. The choices often involve complex trade-offs among quality, speed, innovation, uncertainty, and cost, with cost often at low priority. In this setting, the results are likely to involve a degree of inefficiency.

ECONOMIC ISSUES

The basic economic objectives are part of a broad optimizing: (1) to get the efficient balance among the performance criteria of *each* weapon

---

[2] During 1967–68, the junior author was one of the two Antitrust Division members assigned to initiate "liaison" with the Defense Department. Little was accomplished, because the task was so vast and the decision process was immune to outside review or influence. Since the 1950s there have been extensive yearly congressional hearings on procurement; in the late 1960s they were instrumental in airing large cost over-runs. But even they have had only modest effects on the basic conditions and practices.

TABLE 29–3

Competitive Status of Defense Contracts, 1967

	Competitive Bids (1)	Negotiated					Percent of Total	
		Price Competition (2)	Design and Technical Competition (3)	Extension of a (2) Contract (4)	Extension of a (3) Contract (5)	Single Source (6)	Type (6) Contracts	Type (4), (5), and (6) Contracts
Airframes	$ 65	$ 632	$ 330	$477	$2,394	$1,596	29%	81%
Aircraft engines	1	183	68	42	921	332	21	84
Missile systems	34	153	183	11	1,652	1,678	45	90
Ships	960	59	33	1	33	425	28	30
Combat vehicles	149	42	—	—	20	230	52	57
Noncombat vehicles	351	157	12	1	—	63	11	11
Weapons	21	55	3	—	4	243	75	76
Ammunitions	146	575	32	85	12	2,177	72	75
Electronic, communications	250	377	210	48	288	1,376	54	67
Total (these and other items)	3,465	4,713	1,451	747	5,647	9,632	38	62

Basis of Contracting ($ million)

Source: Defense Department compilations, given in W. G. Shepherd, *Market Power and Economic Welfare* (New York: Random House, 1970), pp. 260–61.

730   *Public Policies toward Business*

system, and (2) to evolve these into the optimal bundle of *all* weapons systems. This will yield the right degree of cost-minimizing versus weapon quality, and it will provide only the minimum equitable reward to the suppliers.

Main Difficulty. The main difficulty arises from the gap between marginal and average cost. This was noted earlier; firms hungry for new

TABLE 29–4
Selected Major U.S. Weapons Projects with Cost Revisions Made in 1974

Weapon	Main Contractor	Cost Estimates for the Entire Project (billion dollars)	
		Before October 1974	October 1974
Air Force			
B-1 long-range bomber	Rockwell International	$15.00	$18.63
F15 fighter (Army version)	McDonnell-Douglas	9.27	10.94
F14 fighter (Navy version)	Grumman	6.35	6.31
Army			
SAM-D anti-aircraft missile system	Raytheon	4.90	6.39
UTTAS transport helicopter	Boeing and United Aircraft	2.67	3.40
AAH attack helicopter	Textron, Hughes Aircraft and Hughes Helicopter	2.00	2.52
XM-1 tank	General Motors or Chrysler	3.40	4.27
Navy			
Trident missile and submarine	General Dynamics and Lockheed Aircraft	12.44	15.45
SSN-688 attack submarine	General Dynamics and Tenneco	7.02	7.86
DD-963 destroyers	Litton Industries	3.08	3.60
PF patrol frigates	Bath Industries and Todd Shipyards	3.48	5.27
PHM missile-armed hydrofoil	Boeing	.76	1.11
Total		$70.37	$85.75

Source: Defense Department Report (see *Wall Street Journal,* October 2, 1974).

orders have low marginal cost, and they are therefore willing to bid at prices which they know are below their eventual average costs. A certain degree of this is routine in many other markets, but in weapons supply it interacts with the purchasers' special conditions and motives. The net effect is to reduce competition and cause a tendency to the "buying-in" of contracts. Firms bid knowingly below average costs—but at or above marginal costs—expecting to be able to push up the effective price at later stages. This is possible because the outputs are complex, and they usually undergo design changes during the long period between contracting and completion. This simulacrum of competition creates illusions of low weapons costs at the time when contracts are prepared and let. It also prevents effective minimizing of costs. It encourages weapons markets to evolve a limited set of suppliers, each heavily reliant on weapons orders, which are essentially rotated among them and which exceed the optimal total levels of weapons production.

The focusing of R&D support—aside from actual purchases—is also very tight, with a high degree of interdependence between the military and a relatively few firms. At the grass-roots level, there is no systematic attention to competitive effects in either the R&D support or the purchases. Therefore, the purchasers tend to become locked-in with non-competitive or sole-source suppliers in the majority of cases (recall Table 29-3). The dynamic logic of marginal cost and bidding is reinforced by the dynamics of R&D funds, which often flow to the same firm for several projects. These mingle as overhead with each other and with other ongoing production costs. This pooling further reduces the level of assignable costs to any one project, and so identifiable marginal costs are reduced even further below average costs. Accordingly, the element of unrealistic and pseudocompetitive underbidding is enhanced.

A striking instance of this has been aircraft production.[3] Successive models of military aircraft have been timed and allotted as if they had been designed, with remarkable precision, to keep the eight main private aircraft assembly lines in operation. This has amounted to *de facto* rotation, despite appearances (and some genuine degree) of competition and cost controls. The unusually large cost over-runs in these programs have been a natural result.

Interaction. These special cost incentives interact with the basis on which suppliers are paid. This basis can be summed up in the following formula for the actual profit realized on a contract:

$$\text{Realized Profit} = \text{Target Profit} + \alpha \, (\text{Target Cost} - \text{Actual Cost})$$

The key element here is α.[4] When α is zero, the firm realizes the target profit regardless of the costs it incurs in supplying the weapons. At the other extreme, if α is 1, the firm keeps whatever cost-saving it manages below the cost target, but it has to pay out of its own pocket any excess of actual cost over target cost. Therefore α is the degree of incentive felt by the supplier in trying to minimize cost. Typically α has been in the range of zero to .25. The strongest possible incentive is when α is 1. This is called a "firm fixed-price" contract. At the other extreme the notorious "cost-plus" incentive basis tends to eliminate incentives for efficiency and may even induce a preference for higher costs.

Getting α right is therefore part of optimizing the trade-offs among the various performance criteria for each project. In fact, α has often not been right, and a large majority of contracting has been done—and continues to be—essentially on a cost-plus basis. On a larger basis, choices among all weapons types require valid cost-price signals from potential

---

[3] J. A. Kurth, "The Political Economy of Weapons Procurement: The Follow-on Imperative," *American Economic Review,* Vol. 62 (May 1972), pp. 304–11.

[4] This is lucidly explained in Scherer, *op. cit.* Compare with utility regulation, where α tends to be at zero during Stage 2 and much of Stage 3 (recall Chapter 14). See also J. G. Cross, "Incentive Pricing and Utility Regulation" *Quarterly Journal of Economics,* 1970, pp. 236–53.

suppliers. Yet the conditions of contracting encourage firms to make unrealistic estimates or—where there is bidding—to submit deceptive bids. These then distort the global choices made by military officials. Believing company estimates that a weapons system will only cost the company's asserted level, a military committee will often pick firm A to supply it, but on a cost-plus basis. The natural result includes cost over-runs, a degree of X-inefficiency, and an imbalance between that weapons system and all the rest. Weapons have always posed problems of efficiency and profiteering; the present specific technical conditions are merely one definite set of biases among many.

Yet it is not enough just to set α at a tight incentive level. For α is only one of the elements in the choices being made both by the buyers and the suppliers. If α is set higher—therefore putting stronger cost-incentives on the supplier—then company effort will be shifted to getting the cost target itself higher, perhaps inflating it so as to enable illusory cost-cutting. After the contract is let, the firm will then adjust among other elements of the contract, cutting corners on performance criteria which have not been made binding in the contract. These adjustments (also paralleled in utility behavior under regulation) may reduce or distort weapons performance.

A Summary.   In short, the whole contracting system operates with rubbery parameters, and α cannot just be maximized. Leaning heavily on one criterion tends to transfer the adjustments to others. Such adaptive responses can operate with a vengeance on weapons, where product characteristics are uncertain—indeed, the project often discovers these attributes.

Probable Costs

Altogether, the weapons sector is managed in ways likely to generate appreciable net costs. Inefficiency in production is substantial, probably on the order of 20 percent of costs for the more complex systems, and in some cases reaching much higher.[5] This reflects both cost over-runs and routine inefficiency.

Further, weapons quantities and quality both tend to exceed the optimum. There is excess ordering of many items, in part because of the cost illusions fostered by underbidding. And armaments often embody service qualities which exceed the levels of efficient design. These added costs are likely to be on the order of 10 percent of actual costs.

Loss from Inefficiency.   These forms of inefficiency probably are not far off 30 percent of costs, on average. And during the rapid expansions of programs in the 1960s they have been higher in many large instances. To this, one would add the capital loaned to suppliers in a variety of industries. This is on the order of $25 billion—though nobody knows accurately how much. How to determine the deadweight loss from this free capital is not clear, since much of it did have private yields.

---

[5] This is apparent in the voluminous yearly hearings on weapons procurement by the Joint Economic Committee of Congress. See also Scherer, *op. cit.;* and Peck and Scherer, *op. cit.*

Finally, there are equity effects from the profit flows. These too are hard to estimate, for the official profit figures are not complete or reliable. Moreover, capital gains during 1960–68 for shareholders of many weapons producers have been reversed by sharp drops in share prices more recently. Yet informed holders are likely to have realized their gains in good time.

Unlike other sectors, weapons supply may well have inefficiency and high profit rates in tandem. Indeed, that is precisely the effect of the various versions of cost-plus contracting. By contrast, market power in industry usually tends to cause either high profitability *or* inefficiency. This combination presents special problems of treatment.

The primary causes of malfunctioning are two: (1) the nature of grass-roots military decision-making, and (2) a high degree of commitment by some firms to weapons work. Reconstituting the lower-level decision process and criteria would probably be both necessary and sufficient to achieve a reasonable cure. It is extremely unlikely even to occur, even in moderate degree. By contrast, limiting weapons work to no more than, say, 30 percent of any supplier's total revenue would avert inefficiency in several ways. It would put the main body of the firm's activities under some degree of competitive discipline: that is, average costs would be under constraint. Marginal costs would not diverge sharply below average costs, because civilian production would absorb most of each firm's capacity. Incentives for underbidding—with all its effects—would be less.

Note that the private supply of weapons—imperfect though it is—does place at least a range of valuations on the goods supplied, in at least some relation to opportunity cost in the economy. If all production were instead on a self-supply basis within the government, the evaluation of true cost might go even more seriously astray.[6]

ALTERNATIVE TREATMENTS

Since the 1950s, experiments with new treatments have been directed to the criteria used in designing and allotting contracts. "Incentive contracting" in various forms has been seen as a way to induce greater

---

[6] International weapons markets have grown to major scale in recent decades, and they pose further wastes, risks, and policy issues. The global trade in aircraft, munitions, and equipment of all kinds is on the order of $10 billion yearly and is growing at about 6 percent annually. It imposes a degree of competitive constraint on some suppliers. But because the possession of weapons has external costs—in arms races, inducements to belligerence, and indiscriminate destruction when applied—this industry may constitute a clear exception to the traditional optimizing effect of free trade.

The competition is intense, and it occurs under special conditions: (1) low marginal costs on additional sales; (2) government assistance, both in R & D funding, in arms sales, and in applying related inducements (such as U.S. training of foreign officers, provision of technical support, etc.); (3) second-hand markets in which prices are often a tiny fraction of costs, and in which corruption is frequent. Even if the unsavory aspects were absent, this process of competition-in-proliferation would lead to outcomes which are wasteful and which may make world survival improbable. Suppliers and their governments have strong incentives to increase foreign sales, even at "cutthroat" prices. Public policies accentuate these pressures, by further reducing sellers' costs and by applying pressures which stimulate demand. Each sale to a client nation raises its neighbors' demand for matching purchases; but even without the ratchet effect of such micro arms races, proliferation and instability are increased.

efficiency. Other proposals have been: to use companies' past performance in deciding which ones will get future contracts; to inject broader objectives—competition, efficiency—into procurement decisions; and, most recently, to convert weapons suppliers into public enterprises. We will consider several possible methods for treatment.

More Competition

A long-standing proposal is to apply a greater degree of competition in contracting. Although at each juncture the contracting officials commonly believe that a more direct (i.e., bilateral monopoly) approach is essential, in the long run a reliance upon a more flexible and competitive range of suppliers would tend to correct much of the inefficiency.

This can be supplemented by two other shifts. One is toward resolving the larger primary contracts into their constituent parts for separate handling. The pyramiding of many layers of supply under one giant contract for one firm has created many of the more conspicuous wastes. A reduction in this pyramiding would be likely to improve performance.

A second method is for the public agencies to assume more of the development risk directly, probably by performing more of the planning and learning function themselves. This will reduce the mingling of development and production costs in major firms. Unless the specific performance of supply tasks can be more exactly determined, there will be no effective way in which the companies or the agencies can assign blame and penalize bad performance.

The corridors of the Pentagon are stony ground for cultivating more reliance on competition. Military officials profess uneasiness at having only one supplier, but they behave as if averse to having more than two or three. Past efforts have only brought competitive contracting up to minor levels (perhaps 15 to 25 percent of purchases). Further marginal increases will be difficult to get and are likely to remain on the fringe.

Incentive Contracting

Much can be done to improve contract design in order to reward efficient performance. But the practical gains will be the least precisely in those cases—complex systems which explore new technology, etc.—where performance is chronically worst. The two most promising tactics are (1) to adjust α to optimize incentives for cost-minimizing, and (2) performance contracting (in which good past performance gives a firm priority in getting future contracts).

In principle, α can be optimized and then applied so as to induce efficiency. In practice, it interacts with the other contract variables (profit rate, time deadlines, renewal prospects, etc.) and has little force where it is most needed. In fact, fixed-price contracts—with α at 1.0 for a maximum incentive effect—are workable mainly in the simpler, routine items. On those, such contracts are already common. But for complex systems, many parameters are uncertain. Raising α then causes firms to seek and get compensating adjustments in the other contract terms. And still later, when large losses nevertheless result, there ensues a semipolitical struggle in which the firm has good odds of winning a price adjustment after all.

Therefore, incentive contracting may offer new yields only for certain moderate-size contracts for intermediate weapons: those which are neither simple nor extremely complex. And the grass-roots contracting process will tend to erode even these yields, by permitting other compensatory adjustments. Incentive contracting (like incentive regulation: Chapter 14) is at most a supplement to other treatments.

Performance contracting also offers certain marginal new yields.[7] To some extent it is already implicitly used. Firms with notoriously bad past performance are often excluded from later contracts, because the one strength of lower Pentagon officials is that they (usually) do know their suppliers' capabilities. But to extend this treatment, a formal procedure of performance rating would be required. This would appraise performance objectively, circulate the ratings to contracting officials, and then see to it that the ratings do influence later decisions.

Unfortunately, there are close practical limits to this. Performance often cannot be reliably rated, especially in the middle range of cases where mitigating factors can always be turned up. The ratings will be difficult to enforce, for several reasons. Later contracts for firm X will differ from what firm X supplied before. Personnel come and go, both in the firms and the contracting offices, so that memories are short, forgiveness is long, and hope springs eternal. And in the most complex cases, the ratings would be just one among many considerations.

In practice, contracts keep going to poor performers, including some big ones in Table 29–2. Performance ratings are a valuable device, if only to apply an added discipline to suppliers' efficiency in the current contract. But they would remain as a supplementary treatment. And the lower-level contracting process may be largely untouched, so that rotation and reduced incentives for efficiency will continue despite the existence of performance ratings.

Renegotiation

Where excess profits are earned on defense contracts, they might be recaptured under a review process. Since World War II, the Renegotiation Board has had that task.[8] It reviews contracts and, in cases where it identifies excess profits, attempts to renegotiate them with the supplier. The actual recapture is minimal. The Board has scant funds and resources, weak legal powers, and little political standing. Its renegotiations affect mainly the smaller, simpler contracts. Even on those, the profit left after refunds has often still been excessive.[9] The Board also

---

[7] It is proposed by Scherer, *The Weapons Acquisition Process: Economic Incentives, op. cit.*

[8] See J. P. Miller, *op. cit.*

[9] During 1971–72, the Board required refunds from 131 firms, mostly in bombs, fuses, ammunition and other ordinance. Yet even after the refunds, returns on net worth for the contract—as a percent of net worth—still were: 4 firms over 500 percent, 22 over 200 percent, and 94 over 50 percent. None of the contracts was over $5 million: the Board touches only the fringes of the problem. (*New York Times*, May 16, 1973).

makes technical errors; thus, it uses return on sales as a criterion, rather than return on capital (recall Chapter 2). Yet perfecting the inner technique of such systems of recapture will be largely fruitless unless the Board is given sufficient powers, resources, and political backing.

In fact, the basic problem is virtually insoluble by this method. Excess profits are often converted into costs, in various forms of inefficiency. They also mingle with the other contracts and activities of the firm, often so much so that they are virtually impossible to trace. The more weight is put on renegotiating profits, the more adaptive response occurs to pool them in with the other operations of the firm. This process operates most strongly on the main stream of large contracts. Therefore, renegotiation offers only slight possible benefits. Once the profits arise, they can rarely be recaptured, even in part.

Revising Ownership

In certain cases, the public provides much of the capital and bears the main commercial risks of weapons supply. But it does not have ownership or the benefits (net revenues, capital gains, control) which ownership provides. This may be the worst of both worlds, and predictably it has yielded some of the highest social costs. A natural remedy is to arrange genuine public ownership, in order to align public controls with public costs (recall Chapter 19).[10] Such a nationalizing of the weapons industry could abate current anomalies in certain cases, but its net yields are uncertain. The alternative is to reduce the public subsidy.

As ever, the presence of public enterprise is not, by itself, a solution (recall Chapter 19). The basic problems are the gap between marginal cost and average cost, the cost-plus contract basis, and the overuse of public funds without compensating public benefits. Much of the marginal-cost problem would continue. It might even deepen, for the pressure to keep *public* arms factories going could be high. That, at least, has been true of arsenals and Navy shipyards in the past. A large public weapons sector might establish a floor under the level of weapons production.

The committal of public funds would also probably increase under any large-scale shift. And there would be no way to earn a high profit for the public, because the State is itself the customer. Therefore the only possible gains are mainly in efficiency and in averting excess arms levels; and these would not necessarily be achieved.

SUMMARY

In short, there are no easy methods to improve the process of weapons supply. The main problems and biases can be identified, but they are deeply ingrained. The interests of the military and the private firms are so densely interwoven at the grass-roots contracting level that little

---

[10] See Galbraith, *Economics and the Public Purpose, op. cit.* "The large weapons firms are already socialized, except in name; what is here proposed only affirms the reality." (pp. 284–5).

change can be expected. Conceivably, this avoids worse outcomes which public ownership of the main suppliers might yield. And the present losses are not catastrophic, though at about $5–10 billion per year they are not small.

Several directions for making procurement more efficient can be defined. Competition could be used more widely. The marginal-average cost gap could be abated by reducing the heavy reliance of some firms on military orders. Cost accounting could be made more thorough, to give better guidelines for efficiency and recouping excess profits. Haste in development can be avoided. Incentives for efficiency can be imbedded more carefully in contracts.

Yet each of these can offer only moderate gains, because the process itself and the surrounding political economy are not favorable. No single large reform—or nicely balanced package of reforms—is likely. Most reforms have been tried in the past, with indifferent success. The sector continues as a test of one's ability to perceive a complex set of industrial conditions, to evaluate their effects objectively, and to understand which economic deviations are likely to persist.

CHAPTER THIRTY

Balance among Policies

We end where we began, but wiser. There is a set of basic concepts which define policy choices and their probable effects. These can be used to define "optimal" choices—at least approximately—and to appraise actual policy treatments. The analysis rarely yields precise answers, but it does usually identify the problem areas. There is often a wide range of plausible policies to choose among, since the evidence about markets and the policy instruments is usually soft. But whatever policies one actually favors, the real task is to use the concepts rationally and fairly. Illusions and deceptions are thick around us, and so one needs to practice clear, analytical skepticism. Otherwise we trap ourselves in our own—or worse yet, other people's—biases.

This chapter first rehearses the main lessons which have recurred throughout the book. Then it reviews the problem of balance among the main policy treatments.

THEORY AND PRACTICE

Principle. In principle, reaching optimal policy choices is quite straightforward. One defines and estimates the costs and benefits of alternative treatments, using standard categories for the various elements in the comparison. If a policy's yields are positive and higher than those of all alternatives, then that treatment is optimal. The magnitudes included in the appraisal are reasonably well-known and agreed. They must be discounted and adjusted in various ways, but these are also matters for reasonable judgment. It is important to get the burden of proof set neutrally and to avoid biases in the advantages of time. Also, an incentive structure to induce optimal behavior will usually be more effective than enforced restorative actions which go against the interests and expertise of the main actors.

Policy evaluation therefore requires skill and good sense, and it can be baffled in some cases. Yet the main elements are relatively clear and logical, and they are basically the same for all industrial policy choices. This unity knits the whole subject together. Policies are not separate

738

boxes, each belonging in certain sectors. They are alternatives, supplements, and packages, which evolve and need adjusting. Their content and effects are often misunderstood, and deviant policies often persist even when their harms are manifest. Yet the logical core of optimal policy is quite clear and general for all sectors.

Policy choices often go astray for lack of good data. The most critical data are usually highly sensitive, and so there are strong interests in secreting or biasing them. Some key data may never be available in reliable forms, either for technical reasons or because the interests at stake are so powerful. But the larger mass of needed information—including much that is totally unavailable now—could be prepared with a modest degree of insistence and care. A further problem of information is that certain broader costs and benefits are hard to measure and easy to neglect—and so they are frequently excluded altogether. Data about them are often soft or absent. If these elements are indeed important, then narrow technical appraisals of costs and benefits may routinely be nonoptimal.

Still, on the whole, cost-benefit analysis can be a useful and consistent approach, to which all industrial policies should be subjected. It is, indeed, the soul of good sense. This book has offered practice in using it, both to illumine the character of sound policies (and to display the variety of deviant ones) and to show how difficult it can occasionally be to decide whether a policy is sound or deviant.

Even if the method were unequivocal and data were ample, the prospects for rational policy would face practical limits. The democratic process is encased in the larger tissue of past patterns. These include vested property rights, precedents, expectations and concrete social patterns. Revision comes slowly and often with a lag of decades. The political economy frequently blocks policy reform quite directly and predictably. Policy agencies themselves evolve biases in their own procedures and incentives. Often they come in due course to perpetuate deviant policies. *In light of this, the minimum hope is that policy choices can at least be understood, be revised in the right directions, and be kept from being merely deceptive or worse.*

This is a main reason why competition is a reasonable norm—a basis for avoiding or moderating the abuses that can arise under direct manipulation of public policies. Such competition is not the arcane, extreme version of perfect competition. Rather, it involves the intermediate degrees of reasonable and effective contending among genuine competitors, whose striving tends to neutralize each others' independent power. As in religion, politics and other social affairs, a system of neutral balances and checks may be the best single method for getting reasonably efficient and fair outcomes. The burden of proof correctly rests against excluding competition.

Practice. Now consider briefly how the main policies have worked out in practice. Antitrust has come to operate only weakly against dominant firms in major markets. It presses most tightly upon middle and lesser firms, which may attempt to collude or merge to do as the dominant firms do. Further down, among the truly small enterprises, antitrust is barely known. This is partly because of the intrastate exemptions from antitrust and the scantiness of antitrust resources. In fact, antitrust has a relatively narrow coverage, once the wide variety of formal and *de facto* exemptions are subtracted.

Therefore, antitrust is a checkered and limited set of tools. Some of them operate with precision, while others are genuinely empty. The net effect may be a basic twist, which hardens structure and benefits dominant firms. Or, conceivably, innovation and oligopoly rivalry may be fostered. Perhaps the main favorable sign since 1960 has been the extension of antitrust constraints into regulated sectors and others previously untouched.

Regulation of utilities is often shadow rather than substance. It tends to evolve perversely, rather than to shift toward competition as the utility evolves back toward normal conditions in Stages 3 and 4. The long-run optimizing of regulatory treatment therefore requires a forceful lifting of franchise barriers and of the regulatory constraints, so that most utilities can normally revert back to a competitive status. This difficult adjustment is often prolonged and obstructed by regulation, so that regulatory commissions routinely cause problems which transcend their powers and understanding.

As for the static tasks and effects of regulation, the direct effects of regulatory action are often weak, while the side effects—many of them quite negative, and socially costly—often are strong. These side effects are of several varieties, all of them tending to undermine the total efficiency of utilities in defining their output mix and producing it. So far, the true dimensions of these possible wastes have not been factored out, even though there are good indications that they are not small. By the most reasonable guesses, regulation probably induces substantial inefficiency, while yielding marginal gains in equity. Therefore, regulation often tends to avert the evolution toward competition while failing in certain directions to deliver the results of competition. These faults cannot be remedied just by reforming or strengthening regulation. The faults go deeper and often require removing regulation, or at least treating pricing and investment more thoroughly.

About public enterprise, even less is known. It is extensive and diverse, both in the U.S. and abroad, though it tends to be confined to the narrow conventional form of a fully owned, national, partly subsidized utility monopoly. The conventional fear that public enterprises will be bureaucratic and rigid has not been borne out in practice. Rather, their behavior seems to approximate those of other enterprises of their size. The old ideological bias against public enterprise in the U.S. is now increasingly seen to be empty, so that the chances for objective trials over a wider variety of cases are now reasonably good. Experience is growing on many facets, especially in western Europe where more flexible public enterprises have evolved in addition to the older utility firms. Therefore, on the whole, public enterprise offers a wide set of lessons and openings for future experimenting. It still needs regulating as much as comparable private firms do. But its deviances under regulatory constraints may be less serious.

Then there is the wide range of *special treatments* and *ad hoc* cases. These, regrettably, include many dark corners of policy choice, where the social results are quite negative. Inherently, such special cases tend to generate inequity and inefficiency, because each has its own rules and subsidies. In many of these cases, a focused and active set of special interests has cut the sector off from standard policy evaluations, so that it can be milked for special purposes. The general rehabilitation of these parts will require a return to the more general criteria; this will usually involve more competition and a more open and skeptical review of the results than now occurs. In these sectors, applying the concepts of industrial organization anew might yield remarkably high social benefits. How to arrange the shift is beyond this book; but the directions for change are reasonably clear.

BALANCE AND EXPERIMENT

For the future, the main lessons are: (1) use the concepts of industrial organization across the whole range of industry types, and (2) rely on a degree of competition, wherever it is at all possible. Loose oligopoly is the main standard of reference, even for sectors where entrenched groups claim that it is not "feasible." This includes financial markets, whose activity influences structure and performance in the rest of the economy. Even where little competition seems possible, it should usually be nurtured carefully.

This sort of unified approach to industrial economics in all sectors is an essential for understanding rational treatment and evaluating actual policies. Individual markets will differ, of course, in their own inner conditions of demand and technology. Therefore the unified treatment needs to be adjustable for actual cases. But all markets share the same underlying conditions, and they tend to evolve through the same basic conditions. Therefore, no sector should routinely be declared a natural monopoly—or exempt from competitive conditions for a variety of reasons—except under close conditions of proof. This is especially important for "utility" sectors, which actually share basic conditions with many industrial markets. Conversely, many near-monopolies in industry may be suited to some degree of regulation. Another attribute of optimal policy is that it will *anticipate* changes, so that current policy design can fit the evolving conditions of markets. In the utilities especially—but also in antitrust and other treatments—good policy must look ahead, anticipate unavoidable lags, and design solutions around what is *coming to be,* rather that what *is.*

The general principle is that unconstrained high market power is not tolerable in the modern economy, and that rational policy can deal effectively with it. We now have adequate analytical tools to define the main lines of good treatments reasonably well, even for the most complex cases. True, judicial and other procedural problems often twist or obstruct efficient policy treatments, and they can be expected to continue to make optimal policy difficult. Yet the lessons need to be pursued apart from—or rather, anticipating—the procedural problems, for without clear guidelines no procedural improvements will matter in any event.

The need is for new experiments and new policy types, as well as a better balancing among the old ones. Policies need to apply better incentives for firms to comply, and they need to engage company skills and interests rather than run squarely against them. There are high stakes; failing to solve these problems may leave us with heavy and increasing economic burdens as decades pass. The crust of the conventional policy treatments is thick and hard, but it needs to be loosened none the less. Once one sees the traditional policies for what they are—fallible treatments, mostly designed long ago, and shaped by the evolving political economy—one can then think clearly and skeptically about newer techniques.

None of them will solve all problems at a stroke. But with care and logic, they may be blended in with the evolving older treatments so as to reduce the costs and improve the benefits. The matter is strictly clinical, but the lines for making future policies more effective are yet to evolve. This book has tried to bring you to the point where you can perceive the new possibilities as well as anyone else can.

INDEXES

Index of Cases

745

Index of Names

Index of Subjects

Capital-attraction, under regulation, 362–64
Capital-intensity, under regulation, 385
Capital structure; *see* Leverage, in labor markets
Capital structure, airlines, 489–90
Capper-Volstead Act (1922), 605
Cartels: 89, 91, 120, 149–52, 155, 282–83, 285, 300, 306, 316, 317, 354, 389–90, 462, 487–92, 546–47, 606–7, 673–75, 709, 712–22; airlines, 565; conditions for success, 150; incentives, 687–88; milk, 609–13; oil industry, 678–80; steel, 608
Carterfone case, 434, 448
Castle & Cook Co., 214
Caterpillar Tractor Co., 198, 248
Cease and desist order, 143
Celler-Kefauver Act, 147, 192, 239–40, 243, 323
Cellophane, 188–90
Cement industry, 161, 165–68, 242 n
Census Bureau, 517
Central Electricity Board, U.K., 555
Central Electricity Generating Board, U.K., 598 n
Central Leather Co., 197
Central Pacific Railroad, 204
Centralization of government, 94–95
Cereals industry: 42–43, 51 n, 56, 130, 144, 169, 214, 217, 221 n; FTC action toward, 144
Cerro Copper Co., 248
Chamber of Commerce, 82
Channel Tunnel, 529
Charbonnage de France, 541
Chartering, 321
Charters, bank, 316, 536
Chemetron, 38 n
Chemicals industry: 43, 223 n, 231 n, 300 n, 525, 541, 659–60; public enterprise in, 541; subsidies to, 659–60
Chicago school, 76 n
China, 524, 696
Chrysler Corp., 685
Cigarette industry: 42, 51 n, 200, 205, 210, 221 n, 223 n; public enterprise in, 541
City power systems, 552–54, 563
Civil Aeronautics Board (CAB), 335, 471, 475, 487–92, 569 n
Civil investigative demand (CID), 147
Civil War, 97, 115
Class-action suits, 289–90, 654–55
Classical liberals, 16, 76, 287
Clayton Act, 112–13, 117–19, 127, 239, 245, 628–29
Clean Air Act (1965), 684
Clorox Co., 249
Coal industry, 156, 175, 524–28; public enterprise in, 541
Coca-Cola Co., 28, 37, 44 n, 47, 198
Columbia Basin, 395
Combustion Engineering, Inc., 417
Command economies, 14, 516, 521–22, 524
Commerce Department, 124
Commission on Money and Credit, 295 n, 296 n, 298 n
Committees, legislative, 78
Commodity Credit Corporation (CCC), 645–46
Common carriers, 338–39, 344, 433, 438, 441

Common law, 77, 85, 90–91, 114–15
Common Market, antitrust, 145–46, 159, 251
Commonwealth Edison Co., 157, 375, 394
Communications: 88, 429–60; public communications, 523–29; *see also* Telephone industry; Postal service; *and* Cable television
Communications Satellite Corp. (Comsat), 447
Comparable earnings, 362–64; *see also* Risk
Comparisons, public and private enterprise, 528–30, 535–74, 599–602
Competition: 6–7, 112–291, 461–97, 564–71, 634–35, 667–70, 684–85, 723–37, 739–41; as automatic conserver, 668; cost of, 9; and diversity, 454; early restrictions on, 90; in education and correction, 584–88; effects of, 8–9; electricity industry, 414–16; in finance, 313–14; gas industry, 419, 422–27; in politics, 74–76; under regulation, 388–90, 426–28, 509; in trucking, 492–94; *see also* Antitrust *categories*
Compromise in policies, 84
Comptroller of the Currency, 312–13, 316, 323, 535–36
Computer industry: 43, 48, 54–56, 130, 223, 238, 244 n, 300, 659–60; U.K., 146
Concentration: 42–48, 148–52, 285–86, 684–85; in banking, 323; errors in ratios, 43 n; ratios, 33, 200
Concorde program, 529
Conglomerate mergers: 38, 92 n, 130, 227–42, 291; policy rules toward, 285–86
Conglomerates, 30, 324, 725–26
Consent decrees: 128, 131–32, 134, 147, 242, 290–91; limits of, 132
Conservation: 662–90; definition, 665–70; economic criteria of, 665–70; and prices, 668–70; shared ownership problem, 668, 677–79, 686–90
Consolidated Edison Co., 157, 375, 394, 417, 465
Consolidated Foods Co., 195
Consolidated Rail Corp., 471, 483, 529
Conspiracy within a firm, 168–69
Constant costs, 31, 41
Constitution, U.S., 93–97, 106–7, 254, 281
Construction industry, 12–13, 88, 135
Consultants, 135; *see also* Witnesses, expert
Consumer goods industries, 282
Consumer groups, 81
Consumer protection, 633, 652–56
Consumers Power Co., 394
Container industry, 191
Continental Airlines, 485
Continental Can Co., 251, 268
Continental Illinois National Bank, 192
Contracts, 98, 101–2
Control Data Corp., 54, 215–16
Cooperation, among firms, 112
Cooperatives, 558, 605–6
Copper industry, 163, 191–92, 199–200, 214 n, 223
Copying equipment industry, 43, 130, 217, 223–24, 260, 278–79
Copyrights, 175, 282

Efficiency—*Cont.*
382, 387, 390, 414, 416–18, 436–38, 449, 459,
462–66, 468–71, 482–84, 487, 494, 495,
507–8, 510, 520, 530–34, 539, 542, 545–50,
563–66, 569–72, 581–82, 586–88, 590–91,
596, 613, 626–27, 630–32, 640–41, 648–50,
658–59, 662–90, 696–702, 704, 719, 727–37
Egypt, 522
Elasticity of demand, 31 n, 152, 307, 345–48,
377–83, 389, 410–12, 419–20, 442–43, 450,
486, 581, 610–11, 642–43, 675, 695
Elasticity of supply, 642–44, 674–76
Electric lamp industry, 214 n, 221 n, 273–75,
277
Electrical equipment industry: 43, 48, 56,
214 n, 221, 223, 238, 260, 300 n, 529; price
conspiracy, 131, 157–58; subsidies, 659–60
Electricite de France, 553
Electricity industry: 41, 43, 56, 99, 120, 240,
334–35, 338, 340, 347, 349–50, 354, 372–73,
391–418, 438–39, 523, 537, 680–81; attributes of, 392–413; competition in, 397–98,
415–16; cost structure, 408–12; history,
399–404; holding company abuses, 399–
403; management, 357, 403; marginal-
cost pricing, 410–14; pricing, 383–84,
404–13; public enterprise in, 395–97, 524,
532–33, 551–64; rate requests, 405; rates of
return, 372–75, 404–5; regulation of, 391–
418; reorganization after 1935, 401–3;
service areas, 395–97; technology, 392–99
Eli Lilly & Co., 55
Eminent domain, 96, 106, 333, 416
Enterprises, variety of, 15
Entry: 31, 228, 279, 350–52, 383, 388, 390, 447,
486, 488, 490, 495, 610, 720, 721; into banking, 314, 322–24; into "professions,"
627–28
Environmental problems, electricity industry, 403, 416–17
Equal protection, 102–3
Equity: 8–9, 19, 56, 284, 295–97, 310–11, 352,
384, 403, 427, 489, 508, 521, 530, 533, 537,
539–42, 546, 552, 576, 579–80, 582–83,
588–92, 619–21, 626–27, 640, 648–50,
652–55, 669–70, 680, 686, 695–704, 710–12,
720–21, 733, 740–42; effects of market
power on, 51–52; of opportunity, 584–88
Equity Funding scandal, 308 n, 321–22, 326
ESB Industries, 38
Establishment, 92 n
Estoppel, 65
European markets, 221
European policies: 89–92; antitrust, 251; per-
forming arts, 710–12; public enterprise,
522–31
Evolution of policies, 60, 89–92, 97, 114–18,
348–52, 509–11
Excess capacity, under regulation, 382–84
Exclusion, 148, 152, 172–76
Exclusive dealing, cases, 129
Executive branch, 77–78, 95–107, 356
Exemptions, 12–13, 119–21, 124, 128, 159, 285–
286, 288, 422, 605–7, 629–30, 714, 720–21,
740–41
Expectations, 27–29

Exploitation: 20–21, 53, 331, 376, 508, 618,
685–86, 694; under regulation, 508
Explosives industry, 214 n
Export-Import Bank, 527, 538, 540
External effects, 19, 67, 349, 377 n, 459, 461,
521, 531–33, 547–48, 564–65, 567, 569, 575,
580–82, 624–27, 655, 669–70, 684–85, 694,
702, 707–8
Exxon Corp. (Standard Oil of N.J.), 28, 38, 54,
598 n; *see also* Standard Oil *categories*

F

Failing firm, 228–31, 244–45, 606
Fair Labor Standards Act (1938), 99, 628
Fair Packaging and Labeling Act, 143 n
Fair rate of return, 87, 331, 378, 344–45, 477
Farm machinery industry, 117, 200, 300 n
Fascism, 221–22
Federal Aviation Administration, 484, 488,
517
Federal Bureau of Investigation, 124
Federal Communications Commission
(FCC): 54, 335–39, 356 n, 429–60, 509; ef-
fects of, 440–41, 449–50, 460; exclusion of
cable TV, 451–59; fully-allocated-cost
standard for prices, 444–45; license re-
newals, 459; Seven-way Cost study, 444;
study of Bell System, 438–44
Federal Deposit Insurance Corp. (FDIC),
312–14, 316, 322, 539–40
Federal Housing Administration (FHA), 321,
517, 540
Federal Intermediate Credit Banks, 540
Federal Land Banks, 540
Federal National Mortgage Assn. (FNMA),
529, 540
Federal Power Commission (FPC), 307 n,
335–37, 356 n, 392, 401, 404–5, 409, 413,
418–27, 509, 552–63, 680
Federal Reserve System, 118, 296, 300, 302 n,
312–14, 316–18, 322–24, 517, 535
Federal Savings and Loan Insurance Corp.,
540
Federal Trade Commission: 32, 87, 91, 111,
142–45, 161–62, 167, 169, 171, 173, 175,
179–85, 234, 242, 247, 279, 286, 288, 291,
316, 357 n, 400–401, 439, 606, 617; advertising controls, 653–55; Bureau of Economics, 144; effectiveness of, 142–45;
process of, 143; resources, 143 n
Federal Trade Commission Act, 114, 118,
143 n
Fees, in antitrust litigation, 125–26
Fertilizer industry, 221 n
Finance: 12–13, 30, 48, 88, 91, 163, 229–30, 295–
329, 741; public enterprise in, 516, 602
Fines, 289, 655–56
Firm, nature of, 23–32
First National City Bank, 298 n
Fisheries, 88, 663, 667, 687–90; controls on,
688–90; optimal harvesting, 687–90; tech-
nology, 687–90
Fixed costs, 307, 379–81, 467–71, 473–74, 486
Flexner Report, 698
Florida Power & Light, 375, 394
Food and Agriculture Act (1965), 649
Food and Drug Act, 101

*This book has been set in 9 and 8 point Primer,
leaded 2 points. Part numbers are 24 point Gael
italic and part titles are 16 point Gael. Chapter
numbers are 12 point Gael italic and chapter
titles are 16 point Gael italic. The size of the type
page is 27 by 46½ picas.*